THE 'MILITANT DEMOCRACY' PRINCIPLE IN MODERN DEMOCRACIES

In 1937 Karl Loewenstein under the impact of the Weimar Republic's demise developed a principle of militant democracy which was subsequently implemented by the German Grundgesetz. His controversial concept has been widely discussed in various national contexts but rarely from a comparative perspective. This unique collection of essays proves that the German example is no isolated precedent and that many democracies have developed means for defending themselves.

Wolfgang Durner, University of Bonn, Germany

With surprising regularity, all democracies turn 'militant' and proclaim the right to exclude from the political process those who would undermine democracy itself. How they do it, why they do it, and which groups are likely to feel the wrath of the state vary significantly. This edited volume is a major contribution to the emerging literature on how democracies maintain their integrity in the face of internal opposition, a topic of great contemporary relevance in the age of national security and the war on terror. Placing the national examples under a comparative light illuminates the risks and indispensable protections for democratic viability. Each chapter provides rich insights for the study of democratic politics.

Samuel Issacharoff, New York University, USA

Manifestations of the pre-emptive defence of democracy – whether termed 'militant' or simply 'muscular' – have become commonplace during this decade, with the terrorism of our neighbours becoming the prime contingency. This impressive survey of comparative constitutional settings and detailed responses provides the reader with knowledge and insight within a rich discourse.

Clive Walker, University of Leeds, UK

The 'Militant Democracy' Principle in Modern Democracies

Edited by

MARKUS THIEL
Heinrich-Heine-Universität Düsseldorf, Germany

ASHGATE

Published by
Ashgate Publishing Limited
Wey Court East
Union Road
Farnham
Surrey, GU9 7PT
England

Ashgate Publishing Company
Suite 420
101 Cherry Street
Burlington
VT 05401-4405
USA

www.ashgate.com

British Library Cataloguing in Publication Data
The 'militant democracy' principle in modern democracies.
1. Democracy. 2. Constituent power. 3. Constitutional law--
Cases. 4. Radicalism.
I. Thiel, Markus, 1973-
342'.02-dc22

Library of Congress Cataloging-in-Publication Data
The militant democracy principle in modern democracies / edited by Markus Thiel.
p. cm.
Includes index.
ISBN 978-0-7546-7183-1 (hardback) -- ISBN 978-0-7546-8847-1
(ebook) 1. Democracy. 2. Internal security. 3. Civil rights. 4. Rule of
law. I. Thiel, Markus, 1973-
JC423.M5994 2009
321.8--dc22

2009019240

ISBN 978 0 7546 7183 1 (hbk)
ISBN 978 0 7546 8847 1 (ebk)

Mixed Sources
Product group from well-managed forests and other controlled sources
www.fsc.org Cert no. SA-COC-1565
© 1996 Forest Stewardship Council
FSC

Printed and bound in Great Britain by
MPG Books Group, UK

Contents

Contributing Authors

Andreas Auprich, Administrative Judge at Unabhängiger Verwaltungssenat für die Steiermark, Graz, Austria, formerly Researcher at the Institute of International Law and International Relations at the Karl-Franzens-University Graz and Legal Advisor to the Austrian Federal Chancellery.

Claire-Lise Buis, Research Associate, Centre Marc Bloch, Berlin, Germany.

Stefano Ceccanti, Professor of Comparative and Italian Constitutional Law, Faculty of Political Science, 'La Sapienza' University of Rome. Currently Senator of the Italian Senate of the Republic, Italy.

Francesco Clementi, Associate Professor of Comparative Public Law, Faculty of Political Science, University of Perugia, Italy.

Helen Irving, Professor, Faculty of Law, The University of Sydney, Australia.

Eduardo Aldunate Lizana, Professor of Constitutional Law, School of Law, Pontifical Catholic University of Valparaíso, Chile.

Richard Mullender, Reader in Law and Legal Theory, Newcastle Law School, Newcastle University, United Kingdom.

Benyamin Neuberger, Professor of Political Science, The Open University of Israel, Raanana, Israel.

Bertil Emrah Oder, Associate Professor, Law Faculty, Koç University, Istanbul, Turkey.

Carlos Vidal Prado, Professor of Constitutional Law, National University of Distance Learning, Madrid, Spain.

Shojiro Sakaguchi, Professor of Public Law, School of Law, Hitotsubashi University, Tokyo, Japan.

Markus Thiel, Senior Lecturer/Assistant Professor, Faculty of Law, Heinrich-Heine-Universität Düsseldorf, Germany.

Mark V. Tushnet, William Nelson Cromwell Professor of Law, Harvard Law School, Harvard University, Cambridge, USA.

Renáta Uitz, Associate Professor of Comparative Constitutional Law, Legal Studies Department, Central European University, Budapest, Hungary.

Preface

It has been quite a long journey from an idea for a scholarly piece to a printed and bound book, especially because it is an anthology on a controversial matter, touching different sciences, for example, jurisprudence; constitutional and democratic theory; and political sciences. The idea for this book emerged in 2004, and now, the gentle reader holds it in their hand.

An editor on such a journey is in need of reliable companions – I count myself lucky to have them. I would like to thank Ashgate Publishing for including this book in their publishing programme, and the publisher's staff – especially Alison Kirk and Emily Jarvis – for their very friendly and helpful support, and for their thankworthy patience with an editor who – literally spoken – dawdled and strayed on his journey and significantly exceeded the agreed closing date.

I have to express my acknowledgements for the authors of the reports on the other countries. I am fortunate to have recruited international experts of such a high reputation to write chapters for this book. Although involved in the duties of their occupation in research, teaching and administration, they all participated in the project and contributed valuable and interesting articles, each with a slightly different, intriguing focus.

This book is dedicated to my beloved parents for their unconditional help and support.

Markus Thiel

Chapter 1
Introduction

Markus Thiel

A Weak Flank of Democracy – Vital Questions of Democratic Self-Defence

Democratic systems frequently come under fire. Their very existence is threatened by acts of terrorism committed by separatists; political extremists from the extreme right or left; 'enemies' of the democracy pulling the strings behind the scenes; agitating in the underground; partaking in the political process in disguise; or even openly fighting the present political system. In addition to these menaces 'from within',[1] democratic states (and the so-called 'Western' model of democracy in general) are endangered by terrorist attacks 'from the outside', for example, by fundamentalist followers of a radical persuasion of Islam.

Some democracies declare themselves under siege or at war,[2] taking steps to defend against such threats. Defensive measures promoting homeland security often have negative effects on the rights and freedoms of the people: immigration control; intensified security checks at airports; video surveillance of public places and public transport vehicles; automatic vehicle monitoring; biometric control devices; individual observation; or sneaking access to electronic data processing systems and personal computers. This list could be continued almost endlessly, and it is understandable that individuals feel controlled, hassled or threatened by such measures. Regarding internal security aspects (which cannot be separated accurately from questions of external security anymore), these issues culminate in the old question of the balancing of freedom and security. The traditional dilemma of a state who is expected to guarantee security, on the one hand, and who, on the other hand, may face legal action from individuals by trying to enforce security.

But, according to the most recent development in democratic theory, freedom and security cannot be understood as mere antipodes. The freedoms people have become so fond of require the perpetuation of the democratic system, including fundamental rights and freedoms and, for example, the endurance of the rule of law. 'Constitutional comfort' is dependent on a certain level of security. Many critics of

1 We will not deal with other 'endurance tests' and dangers to democratic systems, like a 'functional depletion', problems of social exclusion and marginalization or 'globalization', in this book. See Müller 2001 (on the German situation) and, with a wider scope, Faulkner and Shell 2009.

2 For example, the US; see the books of Bobbitt 2008; Stone 2005: 550 et seq.; Tushnet 2005.

security measures ignore the fact that the aim of, for example, Islamist terrorists[3] is not only to abolish states and their institutions, but to defeat the democratic legal order altogether and to replace it with a theocratic regime (including the *Sharia* law) contradictory to the free democratic order or at least characterized by a restrictive attitude towards certain fundamental rights and freedoms. Human rights and the rule of law are challenged by the *Sharia* law, although its legitimate status in Islam is highly controversial. Offences by fundamentalists are directed not only against the abstract democratic idea of the state, but against real democratic states with real legal systems and real guarantees of personal freedoms. As Karl Loewenstein has pointed out, the authoritarian enemies of the constitution try to substitute 'emotionalism' for the rule of law, which must lead to the decline of basic rights and liberties. On the other hand, security is not only a function of the state using its 'monopoly of coercion' and penal power, but is regarded – for example, in Germany – as a task and a duty the state cannot completely neglect, delegate, privatize or give up.[4]

Hence, a democratic state may have to defend at least its very existence on behalf of its citizen. The legitimacy and range of self-defence is, therefore, a vital question of every democratic system. It can be 'traced back to the very beginning of democratic theory itself' (Pfersmann 2004: 47).

As a matter of course, this applies to *any* state with *any* form of governance. However, only in a democracy the balancing of freedom and security, and the question of whether enemies of the democracy are allowed to use democratic structures and rights to destroy it (the 'weak flank' of every liberal democracy) culminate in the dilemma and debate around the idea of a 'militant democracy'. The essential problem here is the choice between the 'open democracy' or a democracy constituting (at least) a 'minimal stability' (Pfersmann 2004: 53 et seq.), which leads to the question as to whether the democracy should actively fight efforts using the 'democratic framework' to abolish the democratic system or not.[5] This democratic dilemma has not been satisfactorily solved yet (and it is to be feared that a generally accepted solution cannot be found in a pluralistic, liberal and 'majoritarian' democratic system at all).

The Birth of a Project – A Sort of 'Constitutional Curiosity'

In 2003, I edited and published a book about the 'militant democracy' principle in German constitutional and sub-constitutional law; a book entitled '*Wehrhafte Demokratie. Beiträge über die Regelungen zum Schutze der freiheitlichen*

3 In the context of this book, the term 'Islamist' is understood as an orthodox follower of Islam. The term 'Islamist terrorist' means a person who adheres to a fundamentalist persuasion and who violently aims for the spread of this faith.

4 See Möstl 2002 (in German).

5 See Klamt 2007: 134 et seq.

demokratischen Grundordnung'.[6] It contains several papers dealing with a wide range of topics closely connected to the protection of Germany's constitutional order from threats. Topics covered include, for example, the treatment of 'enemies' of the constitution in public services; the provisions for a 'state of emergency'; regulations to protect the constitutional order in criminal law; the administrative protective measures of the intelligence services; the deployment abroad of the *Bundeswehr* (military forces); irrevocable elements of the German *Grundgesetz* (Basic Law); the forfeiture of fundamental rights (Article 18 of the German Basic Law); and the banning of extremist political parties (Article 21 Section 2 of the Basic Law). What seemed to be a 'spotty', loose synopsis of heterogeneous legal requirements and provisions turned out to be manifestations of an overarching constitutional 'militant democracy' principle, derived from these regulations especially by the *Bundesverfassungsgericht* (Federal Constutional Court) in a number of eminent, yet controversial judgments.

From the insights of these studies dealing with the instruments and measures in which the 'militant democracy' principle becomes apparent, the question emerges as to whether Germany is an 'isolated case' or if other democracies could be qualified as 'militant' as well. Is there an affinity with or disapproval of such a principle in modern democracies' constitutions and legal systems? And, if a constitutional militancy principle is not acknowledged in a country, are there at least legal and political provisions to defend the democratic structure against attacks? Even if a democratic system does not agree with the general idea of a 'militant democracy' as an argument and criterion in weighing up legal positions (for example, in Germany – the fundamental rights of an extremist public servant against the interests of the state to maintain its function), they may have some kind of regulations to cope with dangers that threaten the fundamental democratic order 'from within'. Where such regulations do not exist, it would be interesting to learn about how and why alternative ways are expected to secure a sufficient level of prevention – for example, why a society trusts more in the self-regulative powers of election than in judicial proceedings to prohibit or dissolve right- or left-extremist political parties.

After analysing the status quo of 'militancy' in diverse countries, the final step is an examination of whether the idea of a 'militant democracy' is (or should be) a ubiquitous principle, valid in every democratic country, as a kind of 'constitutional common feature' or a consensus in democratic theory, or if at least some 'core elements' of militancy could be identified in the different legal systems. For this purpose, I initiated this project and invited scholars of constitutional law, democratic theory and political sciences from a number of countries around the world to contribute.

---

6 'Militant Democracy. Essays on the regulations aiming at the protection of the free democratic basic order'.

A Closer Look – The State of Research

'Militant democracy' has been dealt with in several monographs and articles.[7] But publications using a wider, comparative or international approach are rare.[8] Most essays and books cover the 'militancy' problem only in respect of a single country, considering 'transboundary' aspects in historical retrospection at best, and – in that case – predominantly by mentioning the scholarly activities of emigrants Karl Loewenstein and Karl Mannheim (as the originators of the term, if not the idea, of the 'militant democracy') or the Weimar experiences and spectres of the German Nazi past.

In recent years, the topic of militancy has become a broad-front matter of interest among scholars of jurisprudence and political science.[9] This interest was boosted by the fact that the democratic world became aware of the novel threats posed by religious fundamentalists of a new generation.[10] Issues of internal and external security, converging in a so-called new 'paradigm of security', were intensively debated. The question of democratic self-defence is only a sub-area of this overarching topic. As a scholarly opus containing a rich diversity of papers concerning the 'militant democracy', the book of the same title, edited by András Sajó in 2004, should be mentioned (Sajó 2004a). It is, according to the back cover, a 'collection of contributions by leading scholars on theoretical and contemporary problems of militant democracy', and provides – besides the essays by Karl Loewenstein that could be called the 'cradle' of the term – a bundle of articles illuminating various aspects (political parties, anti-terrorism, 'militancy' in 'transitional democracies'),[11] theoretical groundwork[12] and the question of 'militancy' in selected countries (for example, Israel and Spain).[13]

It can be concluded that several aspects of the 'militant democracy' have been examined thoroughly, but – as far as can be seen – a more comprehensive study, attempting to develop a rudimental basis for a theory of the 'militant

7 Especially in German literature; see, for example, Jaschke 1991; Jesse 1980; Lameyer 1978; Sattler 1982; Wu 1998; in general: Fox and Nolte 1995.

8 See Capoccia 2001: 435, the concept of militant democracy is 'largely understudied in a comparative perspective'; Klamt 2007: 135.

9 From the comprehensive literature, see from Germany: Boës and Schwegel 2005; Papier and Durner 2003; Thiel 2003; from Spain: Revenga Sánchez 2005; from the US: Crosston 2006; Viotti et al. 2008; Weinberg 2008; in general: Brysk and Shafir 2007; Issacharoff 2007; Macklem 2006. For further reading, see the references sections of the chapters in this book.

10 On the 'war on terror' and its facets, see, for example, Bobbitt 2008; Stone 2005.

11 See Ferreres Comella 2004; Roach 2004; Sajó 2004b; Tardi 2004.

12 For example, Dyzenhaus 2004, on the Schmittian way of identifying the 'enemy'; Pfersmann 2004, on the origin of the 'militant democracy' idea, especially p. 49 et seq.

13 See Ferreres Comella 2004; Kremnitzer 2004.

democracy' and with a comparative approach based on status reports of a selection of countries, is still missing.[14]

The Pitfall of Comparison – Methodical Remarks

Comparison is one of the legal scholar's few digging fields for new discoveries. In recent years, an increasing interest in comparative law, especially in the field of constitutional law, can be observed.[15] This is based to some extent on the need for more comprehensive inquiries regarding the advance of supranational and international institutions and regulations, which revert to the national systems (Möllers 2008: 116). In addition to that, a general discomfort with a 'nationalist' approach to constitutional law, history and theory is spreading.[16]

Although the term of 'comparative law' is not absolutely clear and understood uniformly,[17] it can be accepted as a basic principle that only such institutions, regulations and other legal phenomena can be compared that fulfill similar tasks and functions. From this principle, other cornerstones of comparative jurisprudence emanate: the selection of the legal systems to compare; the scope of the analysis; and the systematization (Zweigert and Kötz 1996: 33). As 'form follows function', a comparative study in constitutional law and democratic theory is based on the definition of a problem (or a complex of problems).

This may cause some difficulty here because comparative studies run the risk of being biased by the authors' perception, which is necessarily rooted in their national legal systems.[18] In particular, the term 'militant democracy', coined by a German émigré, can only be conceived against the background of the historical experiences with fascist movements. Therefore, the 'militant democracy' issue is intimately connected with the particular country's history, its coming to terms with a (totalitarian) past and the formation of constitutional law, legal and political theory. This fact complicates the comparative analysis.

In addition, comparative legal studies are often confronted with further methodological barriers. First of all, such an approach inevitably has to be highly selective. As Zweigert and Kötz have stated, the selection of countries to be compared must not be arbitrary (Zweigert and Kötz 1996: 40). This book contains country reports on a dozen democratic countries and leaves aside many more,

---

14 Anyhow, the article by Martin Klamt on militant democracy in different European countries (Klamt 2007) offers an insightful overview, and his forthcoming doctoral thesis (Klamt 2009), will close a gap here.

15 See, for example, von Bogdandy et al. 2007; Reimann and Zimmermann 2006. Namely in the field of civil law, the comparative method has a much more established tradition.

16 See, for example, Scheppele 2004: 391 et seq.

17 See, for example, Jaluzot 2005.

18 See Zweigert and Kötz 1996: 34 et seq.

unfortunately, even those where an analysis of the democratic systems would have been intriguing. But since it is impossible to include a contribution from every democratic country, there had to be a selection, and so this book focuses mainly on European and North American countries, with the addition of Chile, Israel and Japan.[19]

The countries chosen for this study are representative for various reasons. They have an assured democratic tradition, although many of them have encountered several threats to their very existence and their fundamental constitutional order over the last decades. Most of the countries have developed quite different ways of coping with these threats: the empowerment of measures against individuals and groups threatening the democratic system, the state as a whole or single institutions of the state. And every chosen country provides a stable legal order (including an elaborate constitutional jurisdiction) able to confine the said measures – by restricting legislative powers or 'dyking' the executive's competences – to prevent the state and its institutions from becoming too authoritarian and from neglecting or excessively curtailing individual rights and freedoms guaranteed by constitutional law.

Some may feel that the approach of this book is too 'eurocentric', and that African, Asian and Latin American countries should have been awarded more space and attention. It can be conceded that a focus on Europe shortens the quantum of possible insights, and that country reports especially from 'younger' democracies, democracies 'in transition' or emerging democracies would be of great interest. However, with all due respect, some of these countries may not provide a level of 'stabilized' constitutional theory necessary for a project like this. In addition, not all of those requested to contribute to this study were able to do so, which leaves a small number of gaps that unfortunately could not be filled.

Another objection may be that one compares – to say it with a proverb – apples and oranges. The initial enthusiasm may be dampened when the scholar undertaking comparative studies becomes aware that even such superficially clear terms as 'the state', 'fundamental rights' and 'society' dramatically differ in comprehension, depending on layers of preconceptions of, for example, historical; philosophical; political; jurisprudential; or sociological provenance. The idea of the 'state' is, for instance, recognized in a quite different way in Germany than in the United States because the federal tradition, connexions of the juridical terminology and the comprehension of 'democracy' and 'freedoms' are (somewhat) different (Möllers 2008: 9). As Christoph Möllers has remarked, it is not that the German term '*Staat*' is, for example, untranslatable in other languages, but the juristic conception behind (Möllers 2008: 90). The same applies to the perception of 'constitution' and 'constitutional law', and to the (presumably) equivalent terms in other languages. Therefore, a comparative study like this book must not cling to

19 Israel and Chile have been included because of the obvious influence of the German concept of a 'militant democracy', Japan because of its decided refusal of this idea. For a short summary on Greece and Portugal, see Klamt 2007: 147 et seq.

nomenclature and the exact meaning of terms, but has to examine (and compare) the different *practical* manifestations of militancy. This challenge is aggravated by the fact that scholars in comparative studies might tend to act on the assumption that the political and legal system and situation of their home country are the 'normal case', so that they become the 'pivotal point' of the comparison in a partial or even biased way – a problem especially for a German scholar because of the country's specific choice of a 'militant democracy'.

A last objection is that, by comparison of different legal cultures, one often arrives at the quite poor single conclusion that the (legal) world is 'colourful'. Of course, it is to be expected that a comparison between democratic states will result in the conclusion that there is a wide scope of different legal, political and sociological approaches to a single topic. Such a study may be confined to merely providing a descriptive overview, lacking a profound analysis of the substantive characteristics of the countries' response to the said topic. However, the promise to identify similarities in the various democratic systems justifies comparative efforts; basically, it would be a significant achievement to clarify terms and concepts, and trace mutual influences between several democratic systems, in a historic retrospective in particular.

Another circumstance that makes a comparative study on the 'militant democracy' difficult is that the topic is quite a 'touchy' one. Although most democratic states had or have to deal with enemies – extremist political parties and fundamental religious groups; violent secessionists; extreme left or right-wingers in public service; hate speech agitators; and many more, and although many countries have provided legal measures to defend the status quo, to the point that it seems now to be common opinion that a democracy has the vital right to defend itself against attacks and to prevent such attacks, these measures are broadly considered to be in friction with liberal democratic theory. *Benyamin Neuberger* (Israel) has called it a 'slippery slope' of democracy. The democracy fights against persons or groups who make use of their democratic rights, and thus the tolerant state form of democracy suddenly turns intolerant. But this 'democratic dilemma' and the quest for its solution make this study even more fascinating.

The Colourful World of Constitutions – A Spectrum of 'Militancy'

The book starts with a chapter by *Helen Irving* on *Australia*. As in other countries with a common law tradition, the concept of 'militant democracy' is unknown as a constitutional, legal or political overarching principle in Australia. The country has been untroubled to a large extent by political extremism and violence and by terrorist attacks on its territory. Nevertheless, as Helen Irving points out in a historical retrospect, there have been legislative measures to fight 'subversion, sedition and the erosion of democracy' (especially, as in many other countries, against communists) and currently there are several (controversial) laws governing, for example, threats by terrorists. These include allowing bans of organizations and the suppression of financing of terrorism. In particular, Helen Irving discusses the problems associated with freedom of speech and its legal restrictions, and the so-called 'Control Orders' imposed under the Commonwealth *Criminal Code*.

In his country report on *Austria*, *Andreas Auprich* first focuses on the 'perspective of international law'. He examines if the legal regulations of the United Nations and the European Union demand a 'minimum standard' of democratic legitimacy and, therefore, a certain degree of protection for the democratic system. Second, he qualifies Austria as a 'mixed constitutional order', combining neutrality against political movements in principle with a number of material policy prohibitions and legal protective measures. Austria, as Andreas Auprich emphasizes, is not a 'militant democracy' in the Karl Loewenstein sense, because its democratic system (apart from an emphatic anti-fascist character) lacks legal provisions to hinder its own abolition using legal and democratic means – on the contrary, it deliberately allows a complete constitutional revision.

Chile had, as *Eduardo Aldunate Lizana* points out, a strong 'militant democracy' tradition resulting of incorporating the German model into Section 8 of the constitution of 1980. This provision, and a number of complementary laws, explicitly allowed several measures to be used against the enemies of the democratic system, especially the banning of parties and organizations and the exclusion from eligibility for public duties and positions and from a number of occupational activities in eminent key positions (for example, in education, mass communication or trade unions). These measures were used on only a few occasions. Section 8 was replaced in 1988 by a less 'militant' regulation.

Claire-Lise Buis, in her country report on *France*, accentuates the 'extremely unstable constitutional history' of this country, namely the 'heritage of the French Revolution', and the numerous threats to its democratic system of different provenance. Although the concept of 'militant democracy' is not rooted in the French democratic tradition, a number of legal regulations and judicature guard the 'core principles' of the (modern) French democracy, especially the Republican principle. Claire-Lise Buis points out the 'mix of anticipatory and reactive tendencies in defensive strategies' and highlights some aspects, for example, the handling of political extremism from the left and the right (which follows an 'integrative' policy); the control of political organizations, dominated by administrative procedure; the dealing with 'political crisis'; and the restrictions to the freedom of expression.

Germany can be regarded as the 'cradle' of the 'militant democracy' idea without doubt. *Markus Thiel* describes the evolution of this idea to a principle of 'constitutional rank', conducted by the German Federal Constitutional Court in a number of eminent (and controversial) judgments and seconded by a broad majority of legal and political scholars. The German democracy does not rely on selective legal regulations that protect the democratic system only, but has developed an overarching 'militant democracy' principle, usable as an argument, criterion and reasoning in judicature, and provides constitutional and sub-constitutional measures, for example, the ban of political parties and other organizations; the forfeiture of fundamental rights; and the duty of allegiance for public servants. Although neither democratic theory nor constitutional law urges the acceptance of the 'militant democracy' as an independent constitutional value and principle, the German Constitutional Court unmistakably chose this interpretation.

The country report on *Hungary*, written by *Renáta Uitz*, presents a survey of the different threats and violent incidents the country had to face in the past decades, conducted particularly by right-wing extremists and nationalists, and a closer examination of the Hungarian 'political landscape'. Renáta Uitz provides the examples of the dismissal of political organizations; the measures available against racist hate speech; and the utility of regulations prohibiting the display of totalitarian symbols. She emphasizes Hungary's role as a democracy having an elaborate 'armoury' at its disposal to defend itself from anti-democratic forces (dating from the critical transitional period), but repeatedly failing to put them into practice effectively.

Israel has been facing threats and attacks by Arab nationalists, on the one hand, and by Jewish extremists, on the other hand. After depicting the theoretical idea of a 'militant democracy', *Benyamin Neuberger* deals with the country's answer to these threats. He stresses the influence of experiences in Germany at the collapse of the Weimar Republic; several constitutional justices in Israel have been refugees from Nazi Germany and introduced the German 'militant democracy' concept to the Israeli constitutional judicature. In the early years of the state of Israel, an approach to the problem of the defence of the democratic system similar to the United States had been preferred. Benyamin Neuberger traces this formation and provides an in-depth analysis of the proceedings against nationalist and extremist organizations, such as the *Kach* or the *El-Ard* movements, and a detailed discussion of the problems relating to hate speech.

In their country report on *Italy*, *Stefano Ceccanti* and *Francesco Clementi* outline the predominantly non-militant orientation and tradition of the Italian constitution. Apart from singular legal measures (taken especially against communists in the past), which have to be regarded as exceptions, Italy – deeply divided by a civil war – chiefly relied and still relies on a political, not a legal containment of the enemies of the constitution. The idea of the representative democracy was progressively promoted by the integration and implementation even of extremist parties in the political procedures and institutions, although, in practice, the communist parties were kept out of the government.

Shojiro Sakaguchi initially presents the theoretical background and the historical development of the 'militant democracy' idea, describes the paradox of tolerance and discusses current conceptions of militancy among legal and political scholars. He qualifies *Japan* as a country with a constitution remaining 'silent' regarding a 'militant democracy' and explains the unfavourable attitude of most post-war Japanese scholars towards the German concept. Shojiro Sakaguchi points out that Japan has, nevertheless, experienced a kind of 'militant democracy': not as a principle provided in the constitution, but as a *de facto* feature of the Occupation Forces' Government, promoting the democratization of Japan and using measures like the 'Red Purge'. In general, he advocates a 'constitutional patriotism' instead of the provisions and regulations of a 'militant democracy'.

In *Spain*, the historical experiences with the Franco regime and the rather short 'tradition' of the democratic constitution influence the perception towards the idea of a 'militant democracy'. After explaining a common classification of democracies as 'substantial' or 'procedural' with regard to the 'militant democracy' issue, *Carlos Vidal Prado* clarifies the country's democratic model and highlights the commitment of the Spanish Constitution to some outstanding values. Using the examples of the role of political parties, the regulations of the Parties Act concerning the banning of parties and the pertinent judicature, especially on organizations like the *Batasuna* Party (which is linked to ETA), he demonstrates the 'militant' elements of the legal system in Spain. The legislative reforms and judicial actions against extremist parties are held constitutional, and there are – although the constitution does not provide 'intangibility' clauses – limits on constitutional reforms. Carlos Vidal Prado finally expresses the assumption that there cannot be any absolutely 'non-militant' democracy.

In her country report on *Turkey*, *Bertil Emrah Oder* describes in great detail the 'constitutional boundaries for ideological pluralism' stipulated in the Turkish constitution of 1982 and its amendments, decisively influenced by Mustafa Kemal Atatürk's model of Turkey as a modern, laical republic. The constitution puts an emphasis on the nation, the national culture and values, and the state's integrity and unity. It contains irrevocable constitutional principles, such as the Republican state form, sets limits for the use of fundamental rights and freedoms (for example, in a state of emergency), and allows measures against political parties disregarding the general constitutional principles (ban, dissolution, warning orders or exclusion of state aid). Bertil Emrah Oder delineates the leading decisions of the Turkish Constitutional Court, banning or dissolving political parties, and the control (and affirmation) of these decisions by the European Court of Human Rights.

Richard Mullender vividly depicts the 'piecemeal' approach of the *United Kingdom* towards the implementation of a 'militant democracy' and of the legitimacy of legal measures to defend the democratic system. Having been forced to deal with threats and attacks by extremists and terrorists, in common with several other European countries, the United Kingdom enacted a number of legal provisions and measures to fight these menaces. The Common Law tradition and the absence of a written constitution offer a 'considerable scope for altering the law in the light of circumstances'. After a brief historical review on the British 'response' to the French Revolution, Richard Mullender focuses on several challenging issues, such as the conflicts in Ireland; the miners' strike in the 1980s; the development of defamation law; the 'gutter fascism' of Oswald Mosley and his 'British Union of Fascists'; and radical Islamism, including the British responses to the 9/11 terrorist attacks. He clarifies that – even if the United Kingdom preferred an 'empirical' approach to the question of defence – intimations of a 'principled approach' to the defence of constitutional fundamentals are to be found.

In the *United States of America*, the idea of and term 'militant democracy' is unfamiliar. Nevertheless, the country has stipulated a number of legal provisions and measures, mainly applied to extremists. *Mark V. Tushnet* names two areas of constitutional law where a 'resonance' of the idea of 'militant democracy' can be found: the efforts to combat terrorism and campaign finance rules. He examines some further issues, for example, the law of subversive advocacy; the handling of illegal political organizations; loyalty oaths and related regulations concerning employment opportunities; and the regulation of 'hate speech'. Against the background of constitutional protection of the freedom of expression, Mark V. Tushnet highlights the Supreme Court's relevant judicature (and its history) on these topics. He comes to the conclusion that, with few exceptions in the 1950s, many mechanisms used in other countries to protect democracy have not been and are not part of the US constitutional law, because the democracy is not seen as being under 'internal' threat.

In his final chapter on *Comparative Aspects*, *Markus Thiel* attempts to generate a general theory of the 'militant democracy' idea, treating *inter alia* the prevailing models of classification. Because most countries do not follow the German model of a constitutional principle, it is necessary to point out the diverse significance and functions the legal measures and regulations to defend the democratic system can have, and to develop a novel system of classification based on the arrangement of topical 'clusters' of regulations and measures. Markus Thiel examines if a 'minimum asset' of measures exists, or at least a consensus on the treatment of particular threats, or if the elements of the 'militant democracy' are merely 'ephemeral' phenomena, implemented in the constitutional reality (or the sub-constitutional legal order) as a reaction to historical experiences and subject to the regular process of constitutional amendment or legislation, more or less at the legislator's will.

References

Bobbitt, Philip (2008) *Terror and Consent: The Wars for the Twenty-First Century*. New York: Knopf.

Boës, Stefan Axel and Schwegel, Andreas (2005) 'Terrorismus und wehrhafte Demokratie – Impulse für eine Heimatschutz-Strategie der Zukunft', *Politische Studien* 56(399): 91–102.

von Bogdandy, Armin, Huber, Peter Michael and Cruz Villalón, Pedro (eds) (2007) *Ius Publicum Europaeum, vols. I and II*. Heidelberg: C.F. Müller.

Brysk, Alison and Shafir, Gershon (eds) (2007) *National Insecurity and Human Rights: Democracies Debate Counterterrorism*. Berkeley: University of California Press.

Capoccia, Giovanni (2001) 'Defending Democracy: Reactions to Political Extremism in Interwar Europe', *European Journal of Political Research* 39(4): 431–60.

Crosston, Matthew (2006) *Fostering Fundamentalism: Terrorism, Democracy and American Engagement in Central Asia*. Aldershot and Burlington: Ashgate.

Dyzenhaus, David (2004) 'Constituting the Enemy: A Response to Carl Schmitt', in András Sajó (ed.) *Militant Democracy*. Utrecht: Eleven International Publishing, 15–45.

Faulkner, Robert and Shell, Susan (eds) (2009) *America at Risk: Threats to Liberal Self-Government in an Age of Uncertainty*. Ann Arbor: University of Michigan Press.

Ferreres Comella, Victor (2004) 'The New Regulation of Political Parties in Spain, and the Decision to Outlaw Batasuna', in András Sajó (ed.) *Militant Democracy*. Utrecht: Eleven International Publishing, 133–56.

Fox, Gregory H. and Nolte, Georg (1995) 'Intolerant Democracies', *Harvard International Law Journal* 36(1): 1–70.

Issacharoff, Samuel (2007) 'Fragile Democracies', *Harvard Law Review* 120(6): 1405–67.

Jaluzot, Béatrice (2005) 'Méthodologie du droit comparé. Bilan et prospective', *Revue internationale de droit comparé* 57(1): 29–48.

Jaschke, Hans-Gerd (1991) *Streitbare Demokratie und Innere Sicherheit: Grundlagen, Praxis und Kritik*. Opladen: Westdeutscher Verlag.

Jesse, Eckhard (1981) *Streitbare Demokratie. Theorie, Praxis und Herausforderungen in der Bundesrepublik Deutschland*, 2nd edn. Berlin: Colloquium.

Klamt, Martin (2007) 'Militant Democracy and the Democratic Dilemma: Different Ways of Protecting Democratic Constitutions', in Fred Bruinsma and David Nelken (eds) *Explorations in Legal Cultures* (Recht der Werkelijkheid 28:3). Den Haag: Elsevier, 133–59.

Klamt, Martin (2009) *Die Europäische Union als Streitbare Demokratie. Grundgesetzliche, rechtsvergleichende und europarechtliche Dimensionen einer Idee*. Darmstadt: Wissenschaftliche Buchgesellschaft.

Kremnitzer, Mordechai (2004) 'Disqualification of Lists and Parties: The Israeli Case', in András Sajó (ed.) *Militant Democracy*. Utrecht: Eleven International Publishing, 157–70.

Lameyer, Johannes (1978) *Streitbare Demokratie. Eine verfassungshermeneutische Untersuchung*. Berlin: Duncker and Humblot.

Macklem, Patrick (2006) 'Militant Democracy, Legal Pluralism, and the Paradox of Self-Determination', *International Journal of Constitutional Law* 4(3): 488–516.

Möllers, Christoph (2008) *Der vermisste Leviathan. Staatstheorie in der Bundesrepublik Deutschland*. Frankfurt a.M.: Suhrkamp.

Möstl, Markus (2002) *Die Staatliche Garantie für die öffentliche Sicherheit und Ordnung. Sicherheitsgewährleistung im Verfassungsstaat, im Bundesstaat und in der Europäischen Union*. Tübingen: Mohr Siebeck.

Müller, Friedrich (2001) *Demokratie in der Defensive: funktionelle Abnutzung, soziale Exklusion, Globalisierung*. Berlin: Duncker and Humblot.

Papier, Hans-Jürgen and Durner, Wolfgang (2003) 'Streitbare Demokratie', *Archiv des öffentlichen Rechts* 128(3): 340–71.

Pfersmann, Otto (2004) 'Shaping Militant Democracy: Legal Limits to Democratic Stability', in András Sajó (ed.) *Militant Democracy*. Utrecht: Eleven International Publishing, 47–68.

Reimann, Mathias and Zimmermann, Reinhard (eds) (2006) *The Oxford Handbook of Comparative Law*. Oxford: Oxford University Press.

Revenga Sánchez, Miguel (2005) 'El tránsito hacia (y la lucha por) la democracia militante en España', *Revista de Derecho Político* 62: 11–31.

Roach, Kent (2004) 'Anti-Terrorism and Militant Democracy: Some Western and Eastern Responses', in András Sajó (ed.) *Militant Democracy*. Utrecht: Eleven International Publishing, 171–207.

Sajó, András (ed.) (2004a) *Militant Democracy*. Utrecht: Eleven International Publishing.

Sajó, András (2004b) 'Militant Democracy and Transition Towards Democracy', in András Sajó (ed.) *Militant Democracy*. Utrecht: Eleven International Publishing, 209–30.

Sattler, Andreas (1982) *Die rechtliche Bedeutung der Entscheidung für die streitbare Demokratie: untersucht unter besonderer Berücksichtigung der Rechtsprechung des Bundesverfassungsgerichts*. Baden-Baden: Nomos.

Scheppele, Kim Lane (2004) 'Constitutional Ethnography: An Introduction', *Law and Society Review* 38(3): 389–406.

Stone, Geoffrey (2005) *Perilous Time: Free Speech in Wartime from the Sedition Act of 1789 to The War on Terrorism*. New York: W.W. Norton and Co.

Tardi, Gregory (2004) 'Political Parties' Right to Engage in Politics: Variations on a Theme of Democracy', in András Sajó (ed.) *Militant Democracy*. Utrecht: Eleven International Publishing, 81–111.

Thiel, Markus (ed.) (2003) *Wehrhafte Demokratie. Beiträge über die Regelungen zum Schutze der freiheitlichen demokratischen Grundordnung*. Tübingen: Mohr Siebeck.

Tushnet, Mark (ed.) (2005) *The Constitution in Wartime. Beyond Alarmism and Complacency*. Durham and London: Duke University Press.

Viotti, Paul A., Opheim, Michael A. and Bowen, Nicholas (eds) (2008) *Terrorism and Homeland Security: Thinking Strategically About Policy*. Boca Raton: CRC Press/Taylor and Francis Group.

Weinberg, Leonard (ed.) (2008) *Democratic Responses to Terrorism*. New York: Routledge.

Wu, Chih-kuang (1998) *Streitbare Demokratie: Ihre Entwicklung in Deutschland und ihre Rezeption in Taiwan (Republik China)*. Frankfurt a.M.: Peter Lang.

Zweigert, Konrad and Kötz, Hein (1996) *Einführung in die Rechtsvergleichung auf dem Gebiete des Privatrechts*, 3rd edn. Tübingen: Mohr Siebeck.

Chapter 2
Australia

Helen Irving

Introduction

Australia is one of the oldest continuing democracies in the world today. It was founded under a written constitution, as a modern, federal nation (the *Commonwealth of Australia*) through the union of six self-governing British colonies in 1901. At the time, the Commonwealth was arguably the leading democracy in the world. It had male and female suffrage, broad, gender-neutral eligibility to run for Parliament, and a Parliament with both chambers directly elected. Property qualifications and plural voting were prohibited. The constitution itself, having been approved by popular referendum in all the colonies before its enactment, was only to be altered by referendum.

In both the nineteenth and twentieth centuries, Australia was also a world leader in experiments with electoral systems. Proportional representation was introduced in some of the colonies prior to 1900. Along with preferential voting (or STV: 'single transferable vote'), it was later adopted by the Commonwealth and the states. Compulsory voter enrolment was introduced in 1918 and (legally enforced) compulsory voting in 1924.

Some of these institutions and practices are entrenched in the Australian Constitution, others are statutory. Regardless of their form, all are treated effectively as 'constitutional' in the sense of foundational and continuous. Compulsory voting, for example, would be regarded in some countries as 'undemocratic', but it is strongly supported in Australia and considered to be a cornerstone of Australian democracy. Notably, however, Australia does not have a Bill of Rights, either constitutional or statutory. Whether this absence undermines a claim to full democracy, and whether it should be rectified, are controversial questions in Australia at present.

Having known only an uninterrupted history of advanced democracy, the Australian public remains relatively complacent about threats to its democratic institutions. The concept of 'militant democracy' is unknown to the Australian public and largely unfamiliar in intellectual and political circles.[1] Public

1 Paradoxically, a chapter by David Dyzenhaus, 'Constituting the Enemy: A Response to Carl Schmitt' in Sajó 2004 takes an Australian High Court case (on the attempted banning of the Communist Party of Australia) as the core exemplar of an argument on militant democracy. Dyzenhaus, however – while well known in Australian academic circles – is a Canadian academic.

fears about the use of democratic freedoms for non-democratic or democracy threatening ends have been relatively infrequent in most of Australia's history, although organizations considered a threat to Australia or its government have been proscribed during time of war.

However, as in the rest of the democratic world in recent times, Australians have become significantly concerned about the tensions inherent in pluralism, including expressions of racial hatred and the potential for inter-communal violence. Since 2001 in particular, the overwhelming security concern has focused on individuals and organizations that promote anti-democratic goals, in particular through Islamic fundamentalism. As in other 'Western' countries, new laws governing terrorism and related offences have been promulgated, along with new measures of surveillance, detention and control. In recent years, new regimes of proscription have been adopted and new targets identified. Laws of sedition, long disused, have been reactivated and 'modernized'.

And, as in other comparable countries, these actions have been controversial. Liberal lawyers and civil libertarians have raised concerns about the potential inherent in these measures to undermine the very democracy they are intended to protect. Without knowing it, Australians have, thus, been engaged in militant democracy and drawn into the dilemmas it creates.

The Australian Constitution

The Australian Constitution establishes a representative democracy within a federal system. It entrenches an unusual separation of powers – a hybrid of a Westminster-style 'responsible government' and a United States-style separation of the judiciary. Under this arrangement, members of the executive government are also elected members of the Parliament, but the judicial arm of government is strictly separated. Australia retains constitutional links – now very slight – with the United Kingdom. The British Queen, Elizabeth II, is also Australia's Queen and titular Head of State. Under the constitution, her representative in Australia is the Governor General, who acts as effective Head of State. By convention, since the 1930s, the Prime Minister of Australia nominates the Governor General, while the Queen issues his or her commission.

There is much debate in Australia today over the desirability of maintaining these constitutional links with the British Crown. While this debate is not directly relevant to the subject of militant democracy, it is worth noting the potential confusion in the constitution with respect to control of Australia's defence forces. The constitution states that the Governor General is vested with the command in chief of Australia's defence forces 'as the Queen's representative'. This provision, expressed in the traditional (albeit misleading) British language of regal and vice-regal government, is not intended to mean what it says. The Governor General has never been Australia's commander in chief. The constitution itself does not provide guidance about where the real command lies; namely, these days with the Australian executive government, specifically, the Commonwealth Minister for Defence. Legislative powers with respect to defence are conferred upon the Commonwealth Parliament by the constitution. The constitution, however, is silent with respect to related defence matters, including matters of current concern, such as how the government may exercise power in time of emergency.

As Australia is a federal system, its constitution divides powers between the federal and the state legislatures. Most of its powers can be exercised concurrently, but federal (Commonwealth) laws prevail where there is an inconsistency between state and federal laws on the same subject. The power to pass laws with respect to defence is concurrent. However, the constitution prohibits the states from raising or maintaining defence forces without Commonwealth consent. The 'external affairs' power is also concurrent, but state legislative power over external affairs is limited by the fact that international law only recognizes nation states as parties to treaties and conventions.

The power to make laws giving effect to international treaties is particularly important in Australia's constitutional scheme for dealing with certain threats to democracy. There are virtually no limitations on the laws that can give effect to treaty obligations, other than the requirement that the purpose of the law must be 'to implement the treaty'.[2] Several Australian laws regarding terrorism have been passed giving effect to international treaties: For example, the United Nations Convention for the Suppression of Unlawful Seizure of Aircraft has been incorporated into the *Crime Aviation Act* and the Convention on the Suppression of Terrorist Bombings into the *Extradition Act.* Commonwealth laws protecting the rights of minorities against identity motivated discrimination or violence have also been enacted to give effect to international obligations. Among other examples, the *Racial Discrimination Act* of 1975 incorporates the principles of the United Nations Convention on the Elimination of All Forms of Racial Discrimination into Australian domestic law.

Several other constitutional provisions are relevant to laws concerning militant democracy. In an unusual provision (s 51 (xxxvii)) the legislatures of the Australian states are empowered to confer (or, as it is known, 'refer') powers on the Commonwealth Parliament, in cases where federal laws are thought valuable or necessary, but Commonwealth powers are lacking. Criminal law is not, in itself, a federal power.[3] Recognizing this limitation, the Australian states referred their powers over the criminalization of terrorism to the Commonwealth in 2002, thus allowing for uniform national laws.

The executive power is broad, although the relevant constitutional section in which the 'executive power' is defined is imprecise. It is assumed to incorporate the traditional prerogative powers of the British Crown. These include the power to declare war and peace; to make treaties and to issue pardons; among others.

2 *Victoria v. Commonwealth* (1996) 187 CLR 416, at 488.

3 The federal legislature can create criminal offences only 'incidentally', to support laws made under existing federal heads of power.

The executive power, combined with the power to appropriate money and a more generalized power inherent in national sovereignty, are thought to create together an implied 'nationhood' power, permitting the Commonwealth, among other things, to take measures to protect itself or its constitution.

As noted, the Australian Constitution does not include a Bill of Rights. This is unusual these days, at least by comparison with other 'Western' constitutional democracies. It does, however, contain several provisions that have a rights conferring character. These include the requirement that 'just terms' must be offered in return for property compulsorily acquired by the Commonwealth; a prohibition against state laws that discriminate against persons on the grounds of residence; a guarantee of trial by jury for indictable federal offences; and a prohibition on federal laws establishing a religion, prohibiting or requiring religious worship, or requiring religious test for public office. There is also a guarantee of freedom of interstate trade, commerce and 'intercourse'. The latter is taken to refer to the movement of persons or ideas around Australia. It has had very little application, so far, but it stands as a potential source of protection against laws that restrict movement even in the name of democratic security.[4]

Of central importance to our subject, the constitution contains an implied freedom of political communication, grounded in its provisions for representative democracy. The constitution does not make provision for freedom of association or assembly, although the possibility remains that such freedoms may be identified in future, as incidents of the freedom of political communication. The history of Australia's constitution, however, does not lend much encouragement to this prospect.

History

Since its establishment in 1901, the Commonwealth of Australia has adopted a range of legislative measures against subversion, sedition and the erosion of democracy, including banning associations during time of war. Outside war, however, such powers have been restricted. This distinction between war and peace is not clear-cut nowadays, however, and we consider the current situation below. In the First World War, under the Commonwealth *Crimes Act* of 1914, 'Unlawful Associations' were prohibited.[5] In addition, under the *War Precautions Act* of 1914,

4 For example, in one of the few cases to invoke this particular provision, a wartime law requiring official permission to travel interstate by train was held constitutionally invalid by the High Court, as a restriction of the freedom of intercourse – a restriction that was impermissible even in time of war: *Gratwick v. Johnson* (1945) 70 CLR 1.

5 'Unlawful Associations' were defined as 'any body of persons … which encourages the overthrow of the Constitution of the Commonwealth by revolution or sabotage; overthrow by force of violence of the government of Australia or of any other civilized country, or the destruction or injury of Commonwealth property' etc.

German nationals, identified as enemy aliens, were interned. Individuals who were regarded as advocates of the German cause were prosecuted. Immigration from Germany was banned until 1925.

During the Second World War, under *The National Security (Subversive Associations) Regulations* (1941), the Commonwealth also proscribed certain associations or political parties, 'the existence of which the Governor-General … declare[d] to be in his opinion, prejudicial to the defence of the Commonwealth, or the efficient prosecution of the war'. The Communist Party of Australia was among the associations proscribed, although its ban was lifted after the Soviet Union joined the European allies following the German invasion of Russia. During the war, several thousand Japanese and German residents of Australia were interned. These included supporters or sympathizers of the German National Socialist Party, and also, unfortunately, a number of Jewish refugees who had fled from Germany.

The scope of the Commonwealth's defence power (under which these regulations were made) is treated as very wide during wartime. Under this power, many laws have been permitted during war that would have been held unconstitutional in time of peace, including those restricting civil liberties. It is not, however, unlimited. An attempt to ban and confiscate the property of the Jehovah's Witnesses as a 'subversive association' was held unconstitutional in 1943, and the regulations (as first drafted) were struck down by the High Court, on the grounds that they were excessive and not proportionate to the purpose of Australia's defence.[6]

In the period between the wars, Australia was relatively sheltered from the extreme right parties that emerged in Europe and the United Kingdom. A couple of quasi-fascist parties, the 'White Army' and the 'New Guard', were formed in the eastern states, with membership of several thousands, creating some concern for state governments. Their activities reached a peak in 1931, with mobilization of members, as well as protests, the most celebrated of which was the 'up-staging' of the opening of Sydney Harbour Bridge in 1932. In a gesture that was captured on film, a member of the New Guard cut the ceremonial ribbon with his sword, as a deliberate protest against the socialist Labor Premier of New South Wales. These parties never became mass organizations, however. They neither attempted to, nor had any prospect of overthrowing government and their support declined rapidly from around 1932 onward.

The Cold War posed the greatest challenge to Australia's capacity to use democratic means to control undemocratic associations without overstepping the boundaries or undermining the fabric of the democracy. When 1949 saw the election of a conservative national government (a coalition of the right-of-centre Liberal Party of Australia and the rural-based Country Party) deeply committed to the elimination of communism from Australia. This government was to remain in power for the next 23 years.

---

6 *Adelaide Company of Jehovah's Witnesses Inc. v. Commonwealth* (1943) 67 CLR 116.

Under the previous Labor Government, measures had already been taken to contain communism and to suppress sedition. Prior to its defeat, the government established the Australian Security Intelligence Organisation (ASIO). The purpose of this organization was to replace the defence forces in gathering intelligence and information about activities considered harmful to Australia. Such activities ranged from local political protests to foreign espionage and threats of sabotage or communal violence. Communists were closely monitored by ASIO.

The organization has continued and expanded since then, and it has been joined by other organizations, including the Australian Secret Intelligence Service (ASIS), the overseas intelligence agency. The post-2001 role of these organizations in collecting intelligence on terrorist threats has been significant. The government has conferred greatly expanded powers on ASIO under recent anti-terrorism laws. Until the late-twentieth century, however, Australian governments perceived communism to be the most significant internal threat to Australian democracy.

In the immediate post-war years, the government grew increasingly concerned about the presence and, in some cases, dominance of communists in certain trade unions, as well as the commitment of the Communist Party of Australia (CPA) to the goal of a single-party state (or 'dictatorship of the proletariat'). In reality, the degree of threat posed by Australian communists was low. The CPA did not promote violent revolution, but professed to support a democratic path to government. However, support for the CPA was never sufficiently high to achieve the election of a single communist member of federal Parliament, let alone a full government. Attaining communist leadership of key unions was not an unrealistic goal, but the likelihood of orchestrating a general strike was low and was diminished when the Labor Government showed itself willing to use the defence forces to break a protracted strike in the mining industry in 1949.[7]

Although economic conditions were poor during the years of the Great Depression, the level of public discontent was never sufficiently widespread for a mass anti-democratic movement to have been a possibility. By the 1950s, Australia's economy was strong and conservatism was ascendant. There was a high level of public support for government action against the CPA and its members. Elected on a promise to suppress communism, the conservative government of Prime Minister, Robert Menzies, set out immediately to ban the CPA. As noted above, the CPA had been banned in the early years of the Second World War, with the Australian Parliament employing the constitution's 'defence power' to support the relevant laws. The new government believed that the same power could be drawn on in the Cold War context.

In 1950, the government passed a bill for the *Communist Party Dissolution Act* through Parliament. The Act purported, among other things, to proscribe the CPA, seize its property and assets and place these in the hands of an appointed receiver, and prohibit the Commonwealth public sector or trades unions employment of persons 'declared' to be communists. It allowed the Governor General to make

7 Under the *National Emergency (Coal Strike) Act* 1949 (Cth).

such 'declarations' about groups and individuals, and reversed the onus of proof respecting such declarations. In its Preamble, the Act declared what it considered to be the nature of the threat. Among other things, that the CPA 'engages in activities or operations designed to bring about the overthrow or dislocation of the established system of government …'.

The year after the Act was passed, a defence alliance with the United States was formalized through the creation of the ANZUS Treaty and Australia became engaged militarily in the Korean War. The Prime Minister announced that Australia needed to prepare itself for war within three years. Even in such an atmosphere, with public opposition to communism running high, the CPA and several trades unions were successful in their constitutional challenge to the Act. The High Court of Australia, hearing the challenge, concluded that the scope of the constitution's defence power was not sufficiently wide to support such a measure in peacetime. Among its concerns were the Act's restrictions on civil liberties and common law rights. These included the reversal of the onus of proof: an individual who had been declared a communist was required to prove otherwise. The court also noted that the Act took the form of an Act of 'Attainder' (or Bill of Pains and Penalties), directed at a named group of persons. At the same time, it did not state the offence of which they were presumed guilty, other than the mere fact of their membership. The purported preventive character of the legislation also attracted judicial criticism. In the words of one of the judges, Justice Frank Walters Kitto, 'You cannot have punishment that is preventive. You can't remove [a man's] tongue to stop him speaking against you.'

With the defeat of this Act in the High Court, the Menzies Government sought alternative means to achieve the same goal. After several other unsuccessful steps, it sought popular approval for an amendment to the constitution by referendum, expressly giving it the power to ban the CPA. At the start of the referendum campaign, support for the proposal was as high as 70 per cent, and the majority of newspapers lent editorial support to the referendum campaign. Sensationalist press coverage was continuous. Communists were depicted as 'vermin' and 'cancer', traitors and enemies. A vote against the referendum, wrote one Sydney newspaper, 'will aid totalitarian saboteurs … whose clearly stated aim is to overthrow your democratic governments and democratic ways'. Another editorial expressed the view that the communists' right 'to the protection of the laws they are pledged to destroy cannot be logically defended'.

Opposition grew, however. An alliance was formed of leading individuals from churches, universities, cultural organizations and the non-Conservative Political Parties, led by the leader of the Opposition Labor Party, Herbert Vere Evatt. They campaigned against the suppression and punishment of opinions, and raised the prospect that the powers to ban communists might be applied to other groups. They asserted that the rule of law should apply, even to those whose views we oppose. Evatt exhorted Australians to uphold their traditions of civil liberty and of the presumption of innocence, as well as to be mindful of the greater dangers in driving political organizations underground.

The campaign encapsulated the dilemma at the core of militant democracy: whether democratic liberties can legitimately be restricted in the name of safeguarding democracy and how far such measures can be taken without themselves undermining the very thing they are designed to protect. By the end of the campaign, the balance had tilted. Despite predictions of success, the referendum was narrowly defeated. This exhausted the constitutional processes that the government could follow. What remained was only the test of time: whether the threat posed by the now lawful communists was indeed as high as the government believed. In the event, no peril to democracy and no erosion of democratic institutions followed and the CPA was peacefully wound up in 1991.

Parallels have been drawn in recent times between this Cold War example and constitutional questions post-2001. In 1951, the government had attempted to 'recite itself into power' by inserting claims (or 'recitals') of constitutional validity in the Act itself. With one exception (the Chief Justice, a former Attorney General), the High Court majority rejected legislative self-validation and subjected the Act to constitutional scrutiny. With the defence power in particular, much will depend upon the extent to which the court is prepared to be deferential to the legislature's own judgment about the need for defensive measures and the corresponding necessity for curtailment of democratic and civil liberties. The High Court in the early 2000s has been more deferential than in most of the post-war years. This has been significant, as we see below, for laws restricting liberties in the name of protecting democracy.

Banning Organizations Today

Under recent federal laws, organizations defined as 'terrorist' can be banned by the executive in Australia. Following the *Criminal Code Amendment (Terrorist Organisations) Act* 2004 (Cth), the Attorney General is empowered to proscribe such organizations by regulation and no longer depends on the United Nations Security Council to identify them. Under the Act, the minister must be satisfied 'on reasonable grounds' that the organization in question 'is directly or indirectly engaged in, preparing, planning, assisting in, or fostering the doing of a terrorist act (whether or not the terrorist act has occurred or will occur)'. The minister is also required to brief the leader of the Opposition on the individual organization. The parliamentary Joint Committee on Australia's security organizations may review the decision, reporting back to Parliament within a specified disallowance period. The term 'terrorist act' is defined to mean an action or threat of action

> made with the intention of advancing a political, religious or ideological cause; and … with the intention of: coercing, or influencing by intimidation, the government of the Commonwealth or a State, Territory or foreign country, or of part of a State, Territory or foreign country; or intimidating the public or a section of the public …

> The action causes serious harm to a person or serious damage to property, endangers another person's life, creates serious risk to public health or safety, or seriously interferes with or destroys an electronic system, including for communications or transport.

Exceptions are included in the Act for industrial action and lawful advocacy, protest or dissent, so long as such action is not intended to cause the type of harm defined in the Act. The definition ties opinions to a particular intention, and to action causing actual harm. It does not permit proscription of an organization merely on the grounds of opinion, values or point of view. In this respect, it meets the definition of 'militant democracy' by Karl Loewenstein in 1937: That is, adopting 'robust mechanisms to challenge … anti-democratic [associations] all the while operating … within the letter of the law of democratic constitutional norms' (Avineri 2004: 1). In the view of some legal commentators in Australia, this definition is 'one of the best in the common law world' (Golder and Williams 2004: 270; Lynch and Williams 2006).

Nevertheless, some concerns about the Act remain. An organization may be proscribed because of the actions of an individual member, acting on the organization's instructions. Persons who are 'informal' members or not yet members can be included under the definition of members. An organization can be proscribed if the minister is satisfied that it is connected with an individual who claims to act on its behalf, even if the individual is not defined as a member.

Some commentators have expressed concern that the inclusion of *indirect* incitement of terrorism under the definition of 'advocates' may have serious consequences: 'Individuals, be they either a member … or an associate … could be prosecuted merely because someone in their organisation praised terrorism – even if the organisation has no other involvement in terrorism; even if the praise did not result in a terrorist act; and even if the person praising terrorism did not intend to cause terrorism' (Lynch and Williams 2006: 4–5). In 2004, the Palestinian *Islamic Jihad* was the first to be banned under this legislation. Since then (at the time of writing), 18 further organizations have been banned, including *Al Qa'ida* and *Jemaah Islamiyah*.

This law is complemented by a range of other legislation, including the *Suppression of Financing of Terrorism Act* 2002 (Cth), and new laws allowing the military to quell civilian unrest, as well as new laws governing treason and sedition (we consider the latter below). The surveillance, detention and interrogation powers of ASIO have been expanded.

It is sometimes claimed that the absence of a Bill or Charter of Rights in Australia permits oppressive laws that otherwise would be *ultra vires*, or at least subject to a declaration of incompatibility with enumerated rights. However, there is little evidence that Australia's internal security regime is more restrictive than in other jurisdictions. To give one example, the period in which a terrorist suspect may be held without charge is significantly shorter in Australia than in the United Kingdom, which has recently extended its detention without charge period to

42 days, notwithstanding its 1998 Human Rights Act. Under Australian law, the comparable detention period is 12 days.

Where legitimate criticism may lie with respect to the protection of liberties under Australian law is in the processing of illegal immigrants and unauthorized persons seeking refugee status. Under laws in force since 1992, all such persons (with the recent exception of children) are held in detention centres, in conditions not dissimilar to a low-security prison. Some are held for years, while hearings of their claims and processes of review are conducted. The government has attempted to close off legal avenues on the part of unauthorized immigrants, first by inserting 'privative clauses' (or 'court stripping' provisions) in some legislation, ruling out any judicial review (except that constitutionally conferred upon the High Court) of decisions made by the Migration and Refugee Review Tribunals. Second, by relocating and outsourcing several detention centres on Pacific Islands outside Australian territory (a practice now discontinued) and third, by 'excising' from the 'migration zone' several thousands of islands in Australian territorial waters, with the effect that persons arriving by boat and landing on these islands have no right even to apply for refugee status.

At the same time, the law regarding naturalization of lawful immigrants as Australian citizens has been tightened, with an amendment to the *Citizenship Act* in 2007 extending the qualifying period of residence from two to four years, and introducing a test of knowledge about Australian democratic institutions, Australian history and culture for intending citizens.

Although none of the above measures relating to the status of non-citizens is expressed in terms of protecting Australia from threats to democracy, it was clear at the time of their introduction that the legislative intention included such a purpose. The context in which the changes to the *Citizenship Act* must be understood included controversies surrounding certain Australian citizens by naturalization. Among these, Sheikh Taj El-Din Hamid Al-Hilaly, a controversial Islamic Imam, caused a storm of media controversy in 2006 with comments in a sermon suggesting that sexual assault is a consequence of the inappropriate manner in which Australian women dress. Calls for the Sheikh's deportation were met with the recognition that he was a naturalized Australian citizen. The understanding that naturalization may confer rights on individuals who are believed by the public to be 'un-Australian' fed the government's desire to control the character of the immigrant population, and hence indirectly contributed to these legislative amendments.

'Militant democracy' laws and public responses have focused in recent years on organizations promoting Islamic fundamentalism or extremism. While there have been no terrorist attacks on Australian territory, the terrorist bombings of nightclubs in Bali in 2002 held an especial significance for Australians, since Bali was a popular destination for Australian tourists, and over a third of the persons killed in the bombings were Australian nationals. Inside Australia, some instances of inter-religious violence involving Muslim Australians (including violence targeted at Muslims or mosques) have occurred.

There have also been several arrests of individuals charged with planning terrorist attacks and the trial of a number of these persons is currently under way. In 2007 following the terrorist attacks on Glasgow Airport, a Pakistani national, Mohamed Haneef, who held a temporary visa while working as a doctor in a Queensland hospital, was held in detention without charge and interrogated by the Australian Federal Police for several days. Dr Haneef's arrest followed the discovery that, on a visit to the UK the previous year, he had given the SIM card from his mobile phone to his second cousin, one of the perpetrators of the attack. His detention, the subsequent cancellation of his visa by the Minister for Immigration and his expulsion from Australia caused intense controversy, with a deeply divided public response that ultimately shifted significantly towards support for Haneef, once the suspicions on which his arrest was based emerged as highly questionable. The new Commonwealth Government elected in November 2007 has established a Commission of Investigation into Haneef's case, which is currently conducting inquiries.

While Islamic extremist groups are the principal target in the current 'war on terror', a number of other organizations in Australia have attracted attention and raised concern over the same period. These include right-wing groups that oppose non-European immigration. The 'One Nation Party' has attracted probably the greatest attention. The party was formed in 1996 under the leadership of a Queensland woman, Pauline Hanson, with a platform that included opposition to Asian immigration and to government assistance to Aboriginal people. After some initial success in running candidates for state and federal legislatures, the party has declined, suffering loss of membership and experiencing disputes over leadership. Party leaders have been prosecuted for electoral registration fraud.[8] While it was popular, however, the One Nation Party caused great concern among many Australians who feared that it was the harbinger of an upsurge of racist and right-wing movements in Australia. Its effective demise has left Australia mercifully free of such a party. There was, however, never a suggestion that the One Nation Party intended to engage in anti-democratic politics, either before or after election. Although its level of Queensland support came close to 10 per cent at its height, there was also never a realistic chance of its gaining anything more than minority representation in the legislatures.

Freedom of Speech

If militant democracy is to be effective (neither over restrictive nor over permissive), much revolves around the balance between protecting freedom of speech and curtailing or controlling speech that incites the destruction of democratic institutions.

---

8 Hanson herself was imprisoned for a short period, before her conviction was overturned on appeal.

As already noted, Australia does not have a Bill of Rights. It does, however, have a limited, but relevant, constitutional protection of political speech. The Australian Constitution does not protect the freedom of speech or of the press generally, but is limited to protecting political speech or communication. The freedom of political communication arises by implication from the constitution's provisions (Sections 7 and 24) requiring members of Parliament to be 'directly chosen by the people'. These provisions, the High Court has held, entrench a system of representative democracy in Australia. Their wording 'incorporates an implication of freedom of communication of information and opinions about matters relating to the government …' including 'an implication of the freedom of the people of [Australia] to communicate information, opinions and ideas about all aspects of the government …'[9].

This freedom was identified in 1992, in two landmark constitutional cases concerning, first, a Commonwealth legislative attempt to criminalize speech that was intended to bring members of an industrial tribunal into disrepute,[10] and second (the more important case), a Commonwealth legislative attempt to restrict electoral advertizing on television and radio.[11] The laws in both cases were struck down.

Cases invoking the implied freedom of communication cases have come steadily before the Federal and High Courts since then. These have ranged across: defamation laws; laws governing advice about voting; laws governing the giving of immigration advice; indirectly restricting a form of protest; suppressing a non-political publication; and prohibiting offensive language in public. With the exception of one early case (subsequently overruled), in none of these cases has the freedom of political communication directly protected the individual applicant from prosecution, although in some cases the law in question was held to burden political communication. In at least one case, however, a proposal for new legislation (creating an offence of 'flag desecration') did not proceed because the government was advised that it was unlikely to survive a constitutional challenge. Surprisingly, however, the implied freedom has not been tested against laws governing sedition, the proscription of 'terrorist organizations' or racial vilification. Yet Australia has a good number of such laws.

Case law has established that the freedom of political communication extends beyond election periods and is not limited to speech about Australian matters or to verbal communication. It is, however, subject to limitations. Laws that are not directly intended to suppress political communication, that have a legitimate legislative purpose and are proportionate to that purpose, may survive constitutional challenge, even if they have the effect of restricting political speech or communication.

---

9 *Nationwide News Pty Ltd. v. Wills* (1992) 177 CLR 1, at 73, 74 (Deane and Toohey JJ).

10 *Nationwide News Pty Ltd. v. Wills* (1992) 177 CLR 1, at 73, 74 (Deane and Toohey JJ).

11 *Australian Capital Television Pty Ltd. v. Commonwealth* (1992) 177 CLR 199.

In 1997, in the leading case, *Lange v. Australian Broadcasting Corporation* (ABC), the High Court established that the implied freedom does not create a personal right, but merely imposed a limitation on legislation or government action. It settled the test for legitimate limitations on the implied freedom, in the form of two questions to ask of a law's validity:

> First, does the law effectively burden freedom of communication about government or political matters either in its terms, operation or effect? Second, if [it does], is the law reasonably appropriate and adapted to serve a legitimate end the fulfilment of which is compatible with the maintenance of the constitutionally prescribed system of representative and responsible government?[12]

If the first question is answered in the positive and the second in the negative, the law is invalid. A positive answer to both will likely render a law valid, notwithstanding the burden it places on political communication. This test creates substantial scope for laws that restrict speech or communication with the goal of protecting democracy from attack or erosion.

Restrictions on Speech: Sedition

Australia has long had a range of laws that restrict speech in the name, either expressly or impliedly, of protecting democratic institutions or democratic values. Some of these pre-date the identification of the implied freedom of political communication. Other, more recent laws, are controversial, yet have, so far, avoided a constitutional challenge.

From its early years, the Commonwealth took measures to restrict the circulation of anti-democratic ideas. The importation of revolutionary literature was prohibited under the *Customs Act* (1901). By the First World War, associations advocating violent revolution were proscribed. In 1920, the *Commonwealth Crimes Act* (1914) was amended to create a Commonwealth offence of uttering and publishing seditious words (previously, this had been a matter for the states, relying on the common law of sedition) (Douglas 2002). This law continued in force, albeit with very little enforcement. Several Communist Party members were tried for sedition between 1948 and 1953, but few prosecutions were successful. The last success was in 1950 when the publisher of the Communist Party newspaper, *Tribune*, was convicted for publishing criticism of the anti-communist campaigns in Korea and Malaya.

In 2005, the Commonwealth sought to 'modernize' the law of sedition (Bronitt and Stellios 2006: 923). Despite recommendations from the Australian Law Reform Commission that the word 'sedition' should be removed and replaced by

12 *Lange v. Australian Broadcasting Corporation* (1997) 189 CLR 520, at 567.

references to 'offences against political liberty and public order',[13] it was retained and redefined. The sedition provisions in the *Crimes Act* 1914 were, however, repealed and new sedition offences were inserted into the Commonwealth *Criminal Code*. Several of the new offences 'deal with behaviours closely aligned to treason, namely, urging others to overthrow the Australian Constitution, the Commonwealth or the government ... or urging others to assist the enemy or those engaged in armed hostilities' (Bronitt and Stellios 2006: 927).

The relevant provisions also create the offence of urging other people to interfere with parliamentary elections or urging violence between defined groups. 'While the new sedition offences cover diverse territory, they are linked by a common thread of advocacy (or "urging" ...) of violence or force in defined circumstances' (Bronitt and Stellios 2006: 927). Reckless conduct is also an element in the offences of sedition.

A defence of 'good faith' is provided. Acts done in good faith are defined as: Acts that attempt to point out errors or defects in the Sovereign, members of government (at any level, or overseas) or government advisers, and acts suggesting law reform of legislation, the constitution or the judiciary. The defence is also available where a person

> points out in good faith any matters that are producing, or have a tendency to produce, feelings of ill-will or hostility between different groups, in order to bring about the removal of those matters; or ... does anything in good faith in connection with an industrial dispute or an industrial matter; or ... publishes in good faith a report or commentary about a matter of public interest.[14]

Nevertheless, some suggest these defences are inadequate. In the words of Ben Saul, '[t]he range of human expression worthy of legal protection is much wider than these narrowly drawn exceptions, which appear more concerned about not falling foul of the implied constitutional freedom of political communication than about protecting speech as inherently valuable' (Saul 2005: 875).

Saul notes that there are no express exceptions for academic, artistic, scientific, religious and journalistic purposes (Saul 2005: 875). This is also noted by Simon Bronitt and James Stellios, who caution that there is little doubt these provisions would survive a constitutional challenge built around the implied freedom of political communication (Bronitt and Stellios 2006). They also note the new offence of urging violence in the community and the requirement in the *Criminal Code* that urging of violence between groups must threaten the 'peace, order and good government of the Commonwealth'. There are doubts, they write, about the scope of the Commonwealth's power under this provision: 'In terms of both scale and effect, this means that the prosecution would need to prove that the violence

13 Final ALRC Report: 'Fighting Words – A Review of Sedition Laws in Australia', Report no. 104 (2006).

14 Criminal Code, Section 80.3.

urged would impinge upon the security of the Commonwealth. This would arguably rule out its application to small-scale and localised intrastate violence' (Bronitt and Stellios 2006: 942). Saul agrees and also cautions that 'requiring that the incitement must also threaten the peace, order and good government of the Commonwealth leaves groups unprotected from incitements which do *not*' constitute such a threat (Saul 2005: 877). Such small-scale violence may be illustrated, he states, in the events of December 2005, when several hundred Lebanese-Australians and 'Anglo'-Australians fought each other in a 'race' riot at Cronulla Beach in Sydney.

Such violence, however, does not essentially threaten Australian democracy. From the perspective of militant democracy theory, it is desirable that it should not be covered by sedition provisions. The offence of sedition is a matter of extreme gravity, attracting a penalty of seven-years imprisonment. Both the theory of militant democracy and Australia's own history suggest that the liberal side of the democratic balance is the preferable path, unless the threat is genuinely extreme and it associated with mass mobilization.

Racial Vilification

Again, notwithstanding the constitutional protection of political communication and speech, anti-vilification laws are in force around Australia. The first law was introduced in New South Wales in 1989 (as an amendment to the New South Wales *Anti-Discrimination Act* of 1977). Under this law, prosecution of the offence of serious vilification requires consent of the Attorney General, and carries penalties of fines and imprisonment (up to a maximum of six months). There have been no prosecutions so far under these provisions. One other state, plus the Australian Capital Territory, have similar legislation. Other states rely on both civil and criminal laws. Western Australia has only criminal sanctions (up to two-years imprisonment) but confines its definition of vilification to written or pictorial material and does not include verbal comment. Again, there have been no prosecutions.

Thus, every Australian jurisdiction has adopted new legislation or amended existing laws to include racial or ethnic vilification. Some jurisdictions also include 'religious' vilification in their laws; the New South Wales *Anti-Discrimination Act* also refers to 'ethno-religious' discrimination (which is intended to extend to Jews, Sikhs and Muslims) (Gelber 2005: 863). The 1975 Commonwealth *Racial Discrimination Act* was amended in 1995, prohibiting conduct that is likely to 'offend, insult, humiliate' or 'intimidate because of' a person's race. Governments in all jurisdictions have also begun considering other forms of regulation of organized racism. In early 2008, State and Federal Attorneys General met to consider legal avenues for cutting Internet access to racist and anti-Semitic websites.

In 1995, the *Racial Discrimination Act* was extended to incorporate offences of racial hatred. Complaints under the Act may be lodged with the Human Rights and Equal Opportunity Commission (HREOC). HREOC undertakes arbitration or conciliation of disputes where these can be settled (to give one example, between complainants and a newspaper in which articles derogatory of English tourists were published). As a federal tribunal cannot exercise judicial power, prosecutions and enforcement are the domain of the Federal Courts.

HREOC describes the aim of the *Racial Hatred Act* as 'to strike a balance between two valued rights: the right to communicate freely; and the right to live free from vilification'.[15] This Act makes public acts unlawful if they are 'done, in whole or part, because of the race, colour or national, or ethnic origin of a person or group AND [are] reasonably likely in all the circumstances to offend, insult, humiliate or intimidate that person or group'.[16] It includes defences of reasonableness and good faith, including for artistic works or performance; academic and scientific publications; discussion or debate; fair and accurate reporting of a matter of public interest; and fair comment as an expression of a person's genuine belief. A public place is defined under the Act as 'any place to which the public have access as of right or by invitation, whether express or implied and whether or not a charge is made for admission'. 'Public' incorporates acts done in virtual public space, including the Internet and electronic media. Private acts or private conversations are not unlawful, and trivial impacts or 'mere slights' are not actionable. Only an aggrieved person may lodge a complaint; a third party, who is not from a targeted group that is offended, insulted, humiliated or intimidated because of race, cannot complain on another's behalf.

In introducing the bill into Parliament in 1994, the then Attorney General stated that the *Racial Discrimination Act* 'does not eliminate racist attitudes. It does not try to, for a law cannot change what people think. But it does target behaviour – behaviour that causes an individual to suffer discrimination … [and] which affects not only the individual but the community as a whole'. The Attorney General emphasized that the law was intended to apply only to 'extreme' racist behaviour and to fill a gap in state and territory laws that punish the perpetrators of violence, without adequately dealing with 'conduct that is a pre-condition of racial violence'.

The Attorney General also outlined the background to the introduction of this law, including a 1992 national inquiry into racist violence which documented a significant number of incidents and an 'upsurge' in the activities of extremist racist groups. These included violent disruption of ethnic community meetings, arson attacks on synagogues and gang violence directed at persons of Asian background. He underlined the need to employ both legislation and education as strategies to combat racist ideas and the importance of balancing freedom of speech against the right of Australians to live 'free of fear and racial harassment'.

15 See, http://www.hreoc.gov.au/racial_discrimination/racial_hatred_act/.

16 See, http://www.hreoc.gov.au/racial_discrimination/racial_hatred_act/.

Since the adoption of this law, several hundred complaints (mostly about the media, neighbourhood disputes, employment, personal conflict and public debate) have been lodged with HREOC,[17] and a number of cases have proceeded in the courts.[18] In several cases, the defences of artistic freedom or good faith have been successful. For example, the comments of leaders of the One Nation Party published in a book were held to be genuine contributions to public debate and therefore not unlawful. The HREOC Commissioner inquiring into these comments noted that 'the suppression of political expression would be justified on only extreme grounds'.

The most publicized cases have involved, first, the publication of material on the Internet denying the Holocaust and vilifying the Jewish people;[19] and second, public statements made by the leader of a Christian Church organization about the Koran and Muslims.[20]

The first is the only case to date dealing with publication on the Internet. It began with a successful complaint to HREOC in 2000, followed by an application to the Federal Court for enforcement of the Commission's determination by the complainant, the President of the Executive Council of Australian Jewry. The judge in this instance issued an injunction ordering the removal of the offending material from the website.[21] The respondent then appealed to the full Federal Court.

On appeal, Dr Fredrick Toben, representing the Adelaide Institute, challenged (among other things) the constitutional validity of the amended *Racial Discrimination Act* as an Act giving effect to the International Convention on the Elimination of all Forms of Racial Discrimination. The court acknowledged that the Act did not fully implement the relevant part of the Convention, but held that it was nevertheless consistent with the Convention, including in its intention that a State Party should 'nip in the bud' racially-motivated public acts before they 'can grow into incitement or promotion of racial hatred or discrimination'.[22] The defence of reasonableness and good faith were argued, but were unsuccessful:

> In the context of knowing that the Australian Jewish people would be offended by the challenge [to Holocaust history] which the appellant sought to make, a reasonable person acting in good faith would have made every effort to express

---

17 See, http://www.hreoc.gov.au/racial_discrimination/cyberracisim/vilification/.

18 For example, concerning an individual's shouting from his front veranda words racially disparaging of Aboriginal people: *McMahon v. Bowman, Federal Magistrates Court* (2000) FMC 3.

19 *Toben v. Jones* (2003) 129 FCR 515.

20 *Islamic Council of Victoria v. Catch the Fire Ministries Inc.* (2005) VCAT 1159 (first hearing).

21 The defendant, Dr Fredrick Toben, had already been imprisoned in Germany for publishing similar material.

22 *Toben v. Jones* (2003) 129 FCR 515 (Carr J).

> the challenge and his views with as much restraint as was consistent with the communication of those views.[23]

A judge of the court, Justice Susan Mary Kiefel, emphasized that the provision in the Act 'does not render unlawful insensitive statements or those made in poor taste' and recognized that in some cases 'in pursuing an historical or other discourse, offence cannot be avoided'.

The compatibility of the law with the implied freedom of political communication (surprisingly) was not raised. However, Justice Allsop adverted briefly to this freedom and to United States jurisprudence where, he stated, 'even in circumstances of the clearest constitutional guarantee of freedom of speech ... [the Supreme Court] recognises the powerful effect of deeply entrenched symbols and habits of intimidation'.[24]

The second case began with a complaint in the Victorian Equal Opportunity Commission, followed by a hearing in the Victorian Civil and Administrative Tribunal of Victoria. It was the first case under Victoria's *Racial and Religious Tolerance Act* of 2001. It concerned speeches made by two pastors of the 'Catch the Fire Ministries' at a seminar in 2002, which included derogatory statements about the Koran and Islamic practices (including *jihad*) that were the subject of complaint by the Islamic Council of Victoria. The Tribunal found that the men had incited religious hatred and ordered them to pay for newspaper advertisements explaining the reasoning behind the judgment. The decision was subsequently overturned on appeal in the Victoria Court of Appeal and the case was remitted to the Tribunal for a rehearing. A final decision was made not to reprosecute, but to conduct a mediation between the parties. Following the mediation, a joint public statement was issued by the pastors of Catch the Fire and the Islamic Council of Victoria, affirming: the dignity and worth of all human beings regardless of religious faith; the right of all persons and communities to express religious beliefs and conduct their lives consistently according to those beliefs; the right of all to debate and criticise religion 'in a free, open and democratic society'; the value of friendship, respect and cooperation between Christians, Muslims and all people of faiths; and the recognition that racial and religious tolerance forms part of the law of Victoria.

Terrorism and 'Control Orders'

The most recent Australian case to test the limits of the Commonwealth's power to take measures against persons identified as posing a threat to Australia concerned the validity of 'Control Orders' imposed under the Commonwealth *Criminal Code*. Under the relevant provisions, Orders may be made against a person who

23 *Toben v. Jones* (2003) 129 FCR 515 (Carr J).

24 Quoted in *Toben v. Jones* (2003) 129 FCR 515 (Carr J).

has acted or threatened to act in a manner coming under the Act's definition of terrorism; that is, an act intended to cause death or serious injury, directed at the government or the public (or section of the public) with the intention of advancing a political, religious or ideological cause.

The Commonwealth Attorney General's written consent is required for a Control Order to be imposed, and a court must be satisfied that the person in question has committed or intends to commit such an act. Mere advocacy of a political, religious or ideological cause is excluded from the Act, as is protest or dissent that is not intended to cause death or serious injury. On application, the Attorney General may issue Control Orders placing restrictions, prohibitions or obligations on an individual who is a member of, or trained by, a listed terrorist organization and likely to engage in conduct falling within the Act's definition of terrorism.

In 2007, Jack Thomas, an individual who had received training in paramilitary techniques, was placed under Control Orders restricting his conduct. He was not permitted to meet or associate with certain groups or individuals. He was required to report to the police several times per week and was subject to a curfew, restricting him to his home between certain hours at night. Thomas challenged these orders on several grounds. He argued that the *Criminal Code* provisions fell outside the Commonwealth's constitutional legislative powers and that they breached the separation of powers by purporting to confer judicial power on the political branches, contrary to the constitution's exclusive vesting of Commonwealth judicial power in the Federal Courts.

With two dissents, the majority on the High Court held the laws to be constitutionally valid. The Justices stated that the defence of the Commonwealth required wide, new powers and that the old idea of defence as being primarily directed at external enemies (with internal regulation only arising 'incidentally' in support of these measures) was now outdated.

While parallels were inevitably drawn by commentators (as well as by one of the dissenting judges, Justice Michael Donald Kirby) between these laws and the Act under which the government attempted to ban the Communist Party in 1950, there are important differences. The burden of proof in the *Criminal Code* provisions falls not on the suspect, but on the party making the application for a Control Order. Rules of evidence apply, and the subject's personal circumstances are to be taken into account in issuing the order. Although the test of proportionality to which the defence power is subject (laws relying on the defence power must be 'appropriate and adapted' to the purpose of defence) was not applied or even considered in any depth, the court's recognition of these safeguards amounted to an effective application of the test. Surrounded by procedural justice, and justified by the Parliament's view that the defence of the Commonwealth required such measures, the provisions were held to be constitutional.

Albeit in a minority, the two dissenting judges drew attention to one of the central challenges to measures designed to restrict liberty in the name of protecting democracy. These included the purported exercise of judicial powers by the legislature, rendering itself effectively legislator, prosecutor and judge at the same time. The separation of the judicial power from the other branches of government is understood to be a central means by which liberties are protected, and the constitution does not permit the legislative or executive branches to exercise judicial power. Neither the executive nor the legislature can order punitive detention; to punish is a function of the judiciary alone.[25]

Preventative or pre-emptive detention, however, creates jurisprudential dilemmas. Again, it raises the dilemma inherent in militant democracy: how to protect against threats to democracy without at the same time eroding the very thing one wants to protect. In recent years, the High Court has held that, so long as a law is not directed at a named individual, and the judiciary is not required to play a role that is incompatible with the exercise of the judicial power, then such measures are not unconstitutional.

The reach of Australia's defence power appears to have been considerably broadened with the *Thomas* case. Would the *Communist Party Dissolution Act* of 1950 have survived a challenge in 2007? The response, although tentative, might now be positive. The *Thomas* Court majority appeared to lean towards a test for the defence power that gave wide deference to legislative judgment and allowed the Commonwealth itself to judge the need for certain measures to serve the purpose of defence.

Might the attempt to restrict or ban an association or party, other than a terrorist organization, face different constitutional obstacles? It is highly likely that such a ban would be challenged under the implied freedom of political communication. An argument has yet to be made for an implied freedom of association or assembly, but this is likely to arise in the future. For militant democracy to work successfully in Australia – protecting democracy without undermining it – these freedoms must be tested, as soundly, and eventually as carefully as the implied freedom of political communication has been.

Conclusion

Australia is geographically sheltered from many of the great upheavals that have shaken Continental Europe and the UK in the twentieth century, or the United States more recently. It has a long history of successful democratic institution building and reform, straddling long periods of institutional and social stability, even stasis. Its military forces have taken part in the great world conflicts and in incursions into individual countries (Korea, Vietnam, and most recently, Afghanistan and Iraq), but it has suffered little direct territorial impact from these events. By world standards, it has also been relatively free of political extremism, populist discontent or political violence. The history of engagements in war has,

25 *Chu Kheng Lim v. Minister for Immigration, Local Government and Ethnic Affairs* (1992) 176 CLR 1.

however, been symbolically very important in Australian culture, hand in hand, until the 1960s, with a restrictive immigration policy that had the purpose of keeping the majority of the Australian population 'white' and relatively ethnically homogeneous.

These symbols and strategies have contributed to the relatively conservative character of Australian politics, at the same time as sitting side by side with a genuine commitment to the institutions of democracy. Pluralism, multiculturalism and globalization have caught up with Australia in recent decades and the threat of terrorism has, as elsewhere, severely tested the balance between democratic freedoms and their necessary restriction.

While the concept of militant democracy is largely unfamiliar, Australian governments have been taking the steps it requires and the Australian population has – to a degree – been engaged in the debates and controversies it necessarily engenders. Taken as a whole, the tendency of both Australian law and culture has been liberal rather than repressive. This may appear paradoxical, given the absence of an Australian Bill of Rights. Some proponents have suggested that recent events (such as the *Haneef* incident) illustrate the repressive potential in Australian law. Opponents, on the other hand, highlight the relative freedoms in existing Australian institutions and the flexibility of Australian law to respond to strains on democracy. It is critical to democracy – and the success of militant democracy – that these debates should be free to continue, indeed, as an illustration of the very values to be protected.

References

Avineri, Shlomo (2004) 'Introduction', in András Sajó (ed.) *Militant Democracy.* Utrecht: Eleven International Publishing, 1–14.

Bronitt, Simon and Stellios, James (2006) 'Sedition, Security and Human Rights: "Unbalanced" Law Reform in the "War on Terror"', *Melbourne University Law Review* 30(3): 923–60.

Douglas, Roger (2002) 'Saving Australia from Sedition: Customs, the Attorney-General's Department and the Administration of Peacetime Political Censorship', *Federal Law Review* 30(5): 135–75.

Dyzenhaus, David (2004) 'Constituting the Enemy: A Response to Carl Schmitt', in András Sajó (ed.) *Militant Democracy.* Utrecht: Eleven International Publishing, 15–45.

Gelber, Katherine (2005) 'Hate Speech in Australia: Emerging Questions', *University of New South Wales Law Journal* 28(3): 861–7.

Golder, Ben and Williams, George (2004) 'What is "Terrorism"? Problems of Legal Definition', *University of New South Wales Law Journal* 27(2): 270–95.

Lynch, Andrew and Williams, George (2006) Gilbert and Tobin Centre of Public Law, UNSW, *Submission to Security Legislation Review*, 1 February 2006.

Saul, Ben (2005) 'Speaking of Terror: Criminalizing Incitement to Violence', *University of New South Wales Law Journal* 28(3): 868–86.

Sajó, András (ed.) (2004) *Militant Democracy.* Utrecht: Eleven International Publishing.

Chapter 3
Austria

The Democratic Entitlement and the Militancy or Not of the Austrian Legal Order

Andreas Auprich

Introduction

Democratic pluralism is based on tolerance for different political opinions, on compromise in political discussion and on complying with the rules of democratic procedure. Democratic decisions have to be accepted, although they are not compatible with one's own interests. Nonetheless, democratic acceptance and tolerance are limited. The institutions of democracy may not be used to abolish democracy itself. Political opinions beyond the basic democratic consensus shall be hindered to neglect or misuse the values of democracy with its own democratic ways and means. Karl Loewenstein (1937a: 423, 1937b) had in mind the breakdown of the Weimar Republic when he pointed out the 'loopholes' of democracies unable to realize that their own democratic rules are a Trojan horse, allowing the enemy to conquer the city.

In explaining the paradox of tolerance, Karl Popper (1950: 293) wrote that, 'if we extend unlimited tolerance even to those who are intolerant, if we are not prepared to defend a tolerant society against the onslaught of the intolerant, then the tolerant will be destroyed, and tolerance with them'. The solution proposed by Karl Popper does not leave any doubts:

> We should therefore claim, in the name of tolerance, the right not to tolerate the intolerant. We should claim that any movement preaching intolerance places itself outside the law and we should consider incitement to intolerance and persecution as criminal, in the same way as we should consider incitement to murder or to kidnapping, or to the revival of the slave trade as criminal.

To protect democracy also means to protect something which is felt as worth and necessary to be protected. A democracy therefore has to be 'militant': it should provide protective mechanisms and counter measures even against those, who intend to abolish the democratic order in a democratic and therefore legal way.

The circumstances today are without doubt different from those after the downfall of the Weimar Republic. With the end of the Second World War, the international legal environment has profoundly changed. The United Nations have been founded with the aim to promote peace, security and development. In this regard, the strengthening of democracy became one of the key issues. The codification of human rights on global and regional level has decisively upgraded the position of the individual. Human rights were no longer a matter of internal affairs, but a common issue of the international community.

Arising north–south issues and the end of the east–west conflict have led to the resurgence of nationalism and to the rise of ethnic conflicts and civil wars in various parts of the world. Thus, the question emerged whether democracy, human rights and development are interdependent issues. The promoters of a 'democratic intervention' claimed the legality to support or establish a democratic system of government in another state against 'illegitimate' regimes (Franck 1992: 159; Lukashuk 1992: 143).[1]

The general provision of the democratic intervention theory is that there is a necessary structural link between democracy and the effective guarantee of human rights. Accordingly, a democratic system provides the framework for a valuable protection of human rights, and human rights themselves require a democratic political and governmental system. In fact, some authors consider democracy a human right itself, to be granted through basic rights of participation in the political process, freedom of opinion and expression, and the right to free and fair elections (Alexy 1998: 261).

Democratic states generally do provide more or less mechanisms to protect their own democratic system. Today, self-protection can be considered as a genuine and essential part of a modern democracy (Thiel 2003: 23). It is the *right* of sovereign states to safeguard democracy, with certain limits drawn by human rights law. But is it more than that, is there a *duty* for states to protect their democratic system?

This chapter will explore the question whether the pleadings for militant democracy have gained any international legal relevance for states as the subjects of international law in general, and for Austria in particular. The first part highlights the occurrence of democratic aspects in main documents of the international legal order and takes stock of what has been reached in terms of binding constituents of democracy. In the second part, a coarse overview will be given on the non-militant character of the Austrian democratic order. Finally, we will come back to the question whether a militant democracy is favoured or even demanded by the international legal environment Austria is embedded in.

The Democratic Entitlement

International law traditionally does not pay attention to the democratic legitimacy of states. The principle of non-intervention in internal affairs, as laid down in Article 2(7) of the United Nations Charter, is a significant cornerstone of the classic international legal order. From an international legal point of view, it is therefore no surprise that the claim for democracy is rather unclear. A definition of democracy in international law still does not exist. The Vienna Conference on Human Rights in 1993 avoided a definition and spoke of a 'full participation of

1 See the works of Gregory H. Fox and Brad R. Roth (2001).

people in all aspects of their lives' instead.[2] Besides that, it can be highly doubted that a universal definition of democracy could easily be found at all, as states do have quite different opinions of values, not to speak of the given sociocultural differences. It has thus been rightly pointed out that there is no universal democratic concept, as democracy depends on particular sociocultural, structural and ethical preconditions (Böckenförde 1998: 239). At the occasion of the 2005 World Summit, the United Nations General Assembly has confirmed in its Resolution 60/1 of 18 September 2005 that 'democracy is a universal value based on the freely expressed will of the people to determine their own political, economic, social and cultural system and their full participation in all aspects of their lives' as well as that 'while democracies share common features, there is no single model of democracy'. Nonetheless, particular democratic aspects can be found in binding international legal instruments on global as well as on regional level.

The Promotion of Democratic Governance on the Level of the United Nations

Within the United Nations, the democratic spirit dates back to the *Universal Declaration of Human Rights*, a Resolution of the General Assembly of 10 December 1948,[3] which states in its Article 21(3) that 'the will of the people shall be the basis of the authority of government'. This will shall be expressed in periodic universal elections by free voting procedures. Although not binding, the Universal Declaration is considered one of the most important human rights documents.

To secure compliance with the principles of the Universal Declaration, the *International Covenant on Civil and Political Rights* (ICCPR) of 1966 has been adopted. Together with the *International Covenant on Social, Economic and Cultural Rights* and the Universal Declaration, it forms the so-called 'Bill of Rights'. The Covenants of 1966 have been ratified on a large scale and took on the force of international law in 1976.

The ICCPR clearly states in its Article 25 the right of every citizen to take part in the conduct of public affairs, to vote and to be elected by universal and equal suffrage held by a secret ballot. Together with other civil and political rights, in particular freedom of expression (Article 19); freedom of assembly (Article 21); and association (Article 22); Article 25 ICCPR constitutes a basic pillar of a democratic government (Pippan 2007: 138). Although the 1966 Covenants are far from determining a particular model of democracy, they contain necessary and binding conditions for the participation of citizens in the conduct of public affairs, as an important and constituent part of the democratic understanding.

Since the end of the Cold War, the United Nations General Assembly annually pays attention to the democracy issue and emphasizes the importance of elections as the basis of democracy and a synthesis of all human rights. The General Assembly explicitly stated that

2 International Legal Materials 1993, 1661.

3 GA Res 217 A (III), UN Doc A/810 (1948).

> elections are a necessary and indispensable element of sustained efforts to protect the rights and interests of the governed … and that … the right of everyone to take part in the government of his or her country is a crucial factor in the effective enjoyment by all of a wide range of other human rights and fundamental freedoms, embracing political, economic, social and cultural rights.[4]

In 1993, the participating states of the World Conference on Human Rights asserted in the Vienna Declaration that 'democracy, development and respect for human rights and fundamental freedoms are interdependent and mutually reinforcing' and that 'democracy is based on the freely expressed will of the people to determine their own political, economic, social and cultural systems and their full participation in all aspects of their lives'.[5]

As a result of the debate on the key role of elections in democratic processes, the United Nations became extensively involved in election monitoring and gave the concept of democracy content and contour (Maogoto 2006: 16). The moving of the United Nations beyond a mere verification of the honesty of the vote count is, for example, shown in the Nicaragua case, where significant adds for electoral legitimacy have been formulated. The task embraced, *inter alia*, to verify that political parties are equitably represented in the Supreme Electoral Council and its subsidiary bodies, to verify that political parties enjoy complete freedom of organization and mobilization, without hindrance or intimidation by anyone, and to verify that all political parties have equitable access to state television and radio in terms of both the timing and the length of broadcast.[6]

At the same time, democracy became increasingly identified with the maintenance of peace and security. The Haitian coup of 29 September 1991 seemed to evidence that the norm of popular participation became an international index of governmental legitimacy.[7] The United Nations Security Council declared that the obstruction of the restoration of democracy in Haiti constituted a threat to peace.[8] By imposing sanctions and authorizing military intervention in order to restore democratic rule in Haiti, the Security Council further recognized democracy as an entitlement. The pro-democratic intervention in Haiti, sanctioned by the United Nations, was part of their move to assume and implement a bold new agenda – the promotion of democracy and the connection between a democratic form

4 UN GA Res. 45/150 of 18 December 1990.

5 Vienna Declaration and Program of Action, International Legal Materials 32 (1993), 1661, 1666.

6 The Situation in Central America: Threats to International Peace and Security and Peace Initiative, GA Res 44/10, UN GAOR, 44th session, Annex I, Agenda Item 34, Appendix at 3 UN Doc A/44/375, 1999.

7 The Situation in Central America: Threats to International Peace and Security and Peace Initiative, GA Res 44/10, UN GAOR, 44th session, Annex I, Agenda Item 34, Appendix at 3 UN Doc A/44/375, 1989.

8 SC Res 917, UN SCOR, 49th session, 337, 6th meeting, UN Doc S/RES/917, 1994.

of government and the protection of human rights. Demands for democratic participation encouraged international involvement, which in turn facilitated democratic elections, resulting in international legitimacy for election monitoring by the United States (Stoelting 1992: 372 et seq.).

The efforts in the field of election aid and monitoring illustrate the commitment of the United Nations to give democracy a shape beyond the programmatic obligation to hold elections. At the same time, it becomes clear that democratic rights require extensive measures in the fore court of legal obligations to finally be able to comply with them.[9]

Democratic Governance on Regional (European) Level

In Europe, the Organization for Security and Cooperation in Europe (OSCE) has pushed the progress in specifying key elements of democratic governance. In the Copenhagen Document resulting from the Copenhagen meeting in 1990, members of the then CSCE have spelled out the characteristics of democratic systems, including free elections and the need for representative government.[10] One year later, the Charter of Paris for a New Europe has been adopted. It commits the OSCE members to specific duties of democratic government. In particular, the Charter pledges to 'build, consolidate and strengthen democracy as the only system of government of our nations'.[11]

After the dissolution of the Union of Soviet Socialist Republics, the European Communities recognized the new states on the territory of the former Soviet Union under the condition that they comply with the UN Charter, the Final Acts of the CSCE and the Charter of Paris. A democratic constitution, therefore, became a precondition for the international acceptance of those newly independent states (Ipsen 1999: 378).

A democratic government system is, in addition to that, a precondition for the membership to the Council of Europe and the European Convention on Human Rights as the most developed system for the guarantee of civil and political rights. Though the role and importance of human rights and democracy are not mentioned in the founding treaties of the European Communities, the strengthening of a European identity has been a crucial issue for a long time. The Declaration on European Identity of the Council of 14 December 1973 corroborated the link between human rights, parliamentary democracy and the European identity. With the Single European Act of 1987, the importance of democratic principles and the protection of human rights was explicitly incorporated in the treaties, and the current Article 6 EUT contains the complete value catalogue hitherto written down in the Preamble only. In the case of violations of Article 6, a specific sanction procedure is provided for in Article 7 of the Treaty of the European Union.

9 SC Res 917, UN SCOR, 49th session, 337, 6th meeting, UN Doc S/RES/917, 1994.

10 International Legal Materials 29 (1990), 1305.

11 International Legal Materials 30 (1991), 190, 193.

According to Article 130u paragraph 2 of the Treaty of Maastricht, the promotion of democracy, the rule of law as well as the protection of human rights are key issues of the European foreign policy. The European Commission has also keenly emphasized the importance of human rights and democracy in development cooperation. Over 120 cooperation and association treaties of the European Union made with Third Parties since 1990 contain clauses for the protection of democratic principles and the respect for human rights with the consequence of suspending development cooperation in case of violation (Pippan 2002: 345 et seq.).

The dense institutional framework of European integration and human rights tradition obliges European states to base their government systems on common democratic values. For the question of militant democracy it seems less important to ask for a definition of democracy, but for what is to defend in a given democracy. In other words: which democratic constituents are implied by international law or which are forbidden to give up by international law?

Is There a Common Minimum Standard for a Democratic Order?

Thomas Franck (1994: 4) has pointed out that what public policy and law seek to define and protect through the democratic entitlement is not some unattainable, impractical absolute democracy, nor the highest possible degree of democracy, but rather a minimum standard for democratic validation. Such a minimum standard could be extracted from regional and universal human rights instruments which guarantee a spectrum of freedom from the state and political participation in the conduct of public affairs. Gregory H. Fox (1992) has listed periodic elections at reasonable intervals; a secret ballot; honesty in vote tabulation; universal suffrage; an absence of discrimination against voters and candidates; freedom to organize and join political parties which must be given equal access to the ballot and equal opportunity to campaign; the right of all parties to present their views through media; and supervision of the election by an independent council or commission as substantive criteria gathered from human rights instruments and United Nations practice in monitoring elections as the substance of an emerging right to democracy.

The General Assembly applied the formula that

> the essential elements of democracy include respect for human rights and fundamental freedoms, inter alia, freedom of association and peaceful assembly and of expression and opinion, and the right to take part in the conduct of public affairs, directly or through freely chosen representatives, to vote and to be elected at genuine periodic free elections by universal and equal suffrage and by secret ballot guaranteeing the free expression of the will of the people, as well as pluralistic system of political parties and organization, respect for the rule of law, the separation of powers, the independence of the judiciary, transparency and accountability in public administration, and free, independent and pluralistic media.[12]

12 GA Res 59/2001 of 20 December 2004, no. 1.

With this 'recipe', the General Assembly reiterates the basic civil and political rights as written down in the ICCPR. A common denominator of democracy on universal level, however, is only a very general one. Regional understandings of democratic rights are more precise due to common history and socio-political circumstances though still rather programmatic. This is particularly the case for Europe, where, for example, the European Court of Human Rights has extensively animated the Convention.

To summarize, there is no international legal definition of democracy as such, but there are essential constituents of democracy with binding character, such as the holding of free and fair elections and the granting of essential civil and political rights.

Militant Democracy from the Perspective of International Law

The existence of a general requirement of democratic legitimacy as customary international law is a contentious issue. Those who consider an obligation of states to guarantee democratic governance point out the rights to political participation of the individual in the most important human rights instruments and the state practice in the field of electoral assistance and promotion of democracy (Fox 1992; Ramcharan 1998). However, the lack of a legal definition of democracy is a barrier to consider democracy as a right (Ipsen 1999: 375), as it is not clear what specifically could be claimed (Cassese 1995). From this point of view, an international legal commitment to 'democracy' is to be doubted, at least on a global level. A broad consensus exists mainly among Western states which do acknowledge that democratic governance has become a subject of international concern, though Islamic and Asian states, and particular the developing world is wary of the democratic discourse, which is seen as promoting a conservative and protective form of liberal democracy 'as part of a subtle Western expansionist agenda' (Maogoto 2006: 31).

Besides that, European countries are embedded in a system of international legal commitments to democratic standards by their membership to the European Union; the European Convention on Human Rights; the Organization for Security and Cooperation in Europe; and the Council of Europe. A regional obligation under international customary law in Europe is therefore considered possible (Macklem 2006: 516; Pippan 2002: 346).

Although a general obligation to democratic governance of a regime is still not uncontested under international law, it can be said that there is a strong and continuous process of legal compression, which at least – to speak with the words of Gregory H. Fox – has given rise to a normative expectation (Fox 1999: 359). In this regard, the minimum standards, such as the right to free and fair elections, can be taken for points of orientation of a developing and more general notion of democracy in international law (Pippan 2007: 160).

There is, without doubt, a strong commitment of the international community to promote democratic standards. What remains from a positivistic point of view in terms of binding rules of international law, is the circle of civil and political human rights in binding legal instruments. From this point of view, there are no international obligations for democracy as such, but for constituents of democracy in diverse intensity and extent. If we, for example, compare the regional instruments European Convention, Charter of American States or the African Charter on Human Rights, the differences in legal mechanisms to enforce human rights are obvious. Where the European Convention provides for a court system with legal implication for states violating the Convention; a violation of the Africa Charter can at the most be considered by the African Commission, an institution consisting of state member representatives.

For the question of a legal duty for a democracy to be militant, it can be concluded that there is no sufficiently identifiable democratic obligation as such, but a set of binding civil and political rights as characteristic constituents or the 'minimum standard' of a democratic order. A non-compliance with these rules would constitute a breach of the respective international treaties and therefore a breach of international law. Moreover it is very likely that a non-compliance with minimum democratic standards would evoke the reproach of a violation of the democratic entitlement itself. The same is likely for an abolishment of what goes beyond the minimum standard, for example, the common principles mentioned in Article 6 EUT.

For the present question, it is important to emphasize that as long as states are committed by international law to democratic standards, they are obliged at the same time to transform the international legal obligation on national level. That includes necessarily that states are also *entitled* to provide for measures on national level in order to be able to comply with international legal obligations, in particular to defend the reached democratic standard.

The European Court of Human Rights apparently confirmed an entitlement to 'militant democracy' in the Case of *Refah Partisi v. Turkey* of 13 February 2003. The court has endorsed the ban of *Refah Partisi* (The Welfare Party) in Turkey and implicitly confirmed the duty of the member states to offer effective protection against anti-democratic parties. *Refah Partisi* had advocated a religious *jihad*, the introduction of *Sharia*, and the use of political violence to achieve its ends. In his judgment, the court relied on the positive obligations of Contracting States under Article 1 of the Convention to secure the rights and freedoms of persons within their jurisdiction. Thus a

> contracting State may be justified … in imposing on political parties … the duty to respect and safeguard the rights and freedoms guaranteed by the Convention and the obligation not to put forward a political programme in contradiction with the fundamental principles of democracy.

The Militancy – or Not – of the Austrian Democracy

After the First World War and the dissolution of the Austro–Hungarian monarchy, the provisional National Assembly proclaimed the Republic of Austria as a federal and democratic state. The constitution determines in its Article 1 that 'Austria is a democratic republic'. This norm of a programmatic character is filled by more detailed constitutional provisions, which establish Austria as a representative democracy with a two chamber parliamentary system. Most legislative power lies with the *Nationalrat* (National Council), which is elected by general federal elections every fourth year. On the other hand, the members of the second chamber, the *Bundesrat* (Federal Council), are nominated by the diets of the nine autonomous *Länder* (Provinces). The Federal Assembly represents the interests of the Federal Provinces. Austria's formal head of state is the *Bundespräsident* (Federal President), who is directly elected by the populace. The country's government is headed by the *Bundeskanzler* (Federal Chancellor), in whom most political power is vested. Federal legislation is first signed by the Federal President and then countersigned by the Federal Chancellor.

Civil and political rights of the citizens were first guaranteed in 1867. These rights were adopted and incorporated into the present constitution, along with the rights of the European Convention on the Protection of Human Rights and Fundamental Freedoms of 4 November 1950, ratified by Austria in 1958.

With the end of the Second World War, the constitution of 1920, as amended in 1929, was re-enacted on 1 May 1945. Nonetheless, it took ten more years until Austria's full sovereignty was re-established with the conclusion of the State Treaty for the Re-establishment of an Independent and Democratic Austria of 15 May 1955, between Austria and the allied powers France, UK, US and USSR.[13] The State Treaty of 1955 is one of the main founding documents of the Austrian Second Republic. In the same year, Austria declared its permanent neutrality by constitutional law.[14]

The Republican Principle and the Habsburg Act

The Austrian constitution in its original version of 1920, respectively 1929, does not contain any distinct militant features. The *Bundes-Verfassungsgesetz* (B-VG, 'Federal Constitutional Act') was rather a typical example of a 'neutral democracy' (Pernthaler 1996: 90), where also parties with anti-democratic programmes could participate in political rallies and only the voter decided on who was to gain

13 *Staatsvertrag betreffend die Wiederherstellung eines unabhängigen und demokratischen Österreich*, BGBl. 1955/152.

14 Bundesverfassungsgesetz vom 26. Oktober 1955 über die Neutralität Österreichs, BGBl 1955/211. For a selection of Austrian laws in English translation, see the Legal Information System (RIS) of the Austrian Federal Chancellery (at http://www.ris2bka.gv.at). The quotations of Austrian Laws in this article follow these translations.

political power. For Hans Kelsen, who notably drafted the Austrian Constitution, the freedom of the individual constituted the main goal of democracy. Democracy should deliver the formal frame in which political opinions could freely develop (Kelsen 1929: 91 et seq.).

The only aspect with a somehow militant character was the so-called *Habsburgergesetz* ('Habsburg Act'), a constitutional law of 3 April 1919, concerning the House of Habsburg-Lorraine, which abolished all rights of the family Habsburg-Lorraine in Austria. With the dissolution of the Austro–Hungarian monarchy, the National Assembly had decided to establish Austria as a Republic. In the interest of the Republic's security, all members of the family Habsburg-Lorraine were banned from Austria according to Article 2 of the Habsburg Act, if they did not explicitly renounce on any claims to participate in state affairs and declare themselves as loyal citizens of the Republic. With regard to Article 3(2) of the Additional Protocol no. 4 to the European Convention, a reservation was made in order not to violate the right of every citizen to enter the territory of the state of which he is a national. Today, Article 2 of the Habsburg Act can be regarded as out of application, as all living members of the family Habsburg-Lorraine have renounced on ruling claims and given corresponding declarations of loyalty to the Republic.[15]

With Article 10(2) of the State Treaty of 1955, Austria took the explicit obligation to maintain the Habsburg Act in force. Austria is therefore obliged under an international treaty to prevent a reinstallation of monarchy. In this regard, Article 60(3) of the constitution also provides that members of a former ruling house are excluded to run for the federal presidency.

Republican and democratic systems are not necessarily congruent, as there are monarchies with democratic governments, for example, the UK and republics with dictatorial regimes, similar to the USSR under Stalin. However, the common commitment of Article 1 B-VG expresses the close historical connection between the republican and the democratic principle in Austria (Funk 2006: 94).

The Prohibition of Nazi Organizations

The creation of the Second Austrian Republic is inseparably associated with the erasure of all remnants and structures of the Nazi regime and the prevention of any resurrection of the Nazi ideology in the future. Two weeks after the Declaration of Independence on 27 April 1945, the Provisional State Government adopted the *Verbotsgesetz* ('Prohibition Act'). The Prohibition Act was essential to the Federal Constitution and should eradicate all traces of the Nazi regime and eliminate the National Socialists' spirit and ideology from Austria (Müller 2005). The restrictions are not limited to the historical National Socialism. According to § 3 VerbotsG, it is prohibited for everybody to set any activities inspired by National Socialist ideas. This comprehends all forms of neo-Nazism, which in its diverse forms can

15 *Wiener Zeitung*, no. 92, 20 April 1996, 7.

be punished with up to 20 years of imprisonment. The strong commitment in this regard is, for example, shown by the fact that in 1992 the denial of the Holocaust was made a punishable offence with the newly introduced § 3h VerbotsG.

With Article 1 of the State Treaty of 1955, the Allied and Associated Powers recognized that Austria was re-established as a sovereign, independent and democratic state. Article 9(1) of the State Treaty of 1955 states that Austria shall complete the measures, already begun by the enactment of appropriate legislation approved by the Allied Commission for Austria, to destroy the National Socialist Party and its affiliated and supervised organizations, including political, economic and paramilitary organizations on Austrian territory. Austria shall also ensure that Nazi organizations are not revived in any form and prevent all Nazi and militarist activity, and propaganda in Austria.

According to Article 9(2) of the State Treaty of 1955, Austria undertakes to dissolve all fascist-type organizations existing on its territory, political, military and paramilitary, and likewise any other organizations carrying on activities hostile to the United Nations, or which intend to deprive the people of their democratic rights.

It is a controversial question whether the constitutional norm of Article 9(2) of the State Treaty constitutes a legal basis to prohibit political parties hostile to democratic values in general. On the one hand, it was argued that Article 9(2) comprises a prohibition of any other organization which intends to deprive people of their democratic rights (Wieser 2001a: 35). On the other hand, a systematic interpretation in view of the header of Article 9 – 'Dissolution of Nazi Organizations' – delivers the result that 'any other organization' comprises only fascist ones (Thienel 2005: 164). In fact, no other parties than the NSDAP have ever been forbidden in Austria. Not even the Communist Party (KPÖ) was prohibited after the attempted coups of 1947 and 1950, though it officially aimed at the transformation of Austria into a 'peoples democracy' (Zeleny 2004: 186 et seq.). It was therefore concluded that Article 1 of the Prohibition Act did not constitute a shift to a militant democracy (Zeleny 2004: 187).

The Formation of Political Parties

The formation of political parties is regulated by the Federal Act on the Functions, Financing and Election Campaigning of Political Parties (*Parteiengesetz* – 'Political Parties Act'). Besides the rules on financing and election campaigning, there is in fact only the provision of Article 1 to draw the constitutional frame for political parties.

Article 1(1) of the Political Parties Act, with reference to Section 1 of the constitution, states that the existence and the diversity of political parties are essential elements of the democratic system of the Republic of Austria. According to Article 1(2) of the Political Parties Act, one of the functions of the political parties is to participate in the formation of the political decisions. The formation of political parties is free to the extent that the Federal Constitution Act does not provide otherwise. The activities of political parties shall not be subject to any restriction by particular provisions of the law, Article 1(3). The political parties shall adopt by-laws to be published in a periodical product of printed matter which are to be deposited with the Federal Ministry of Interior. The by-laws shall in particular specify the organs of the parties and which of them are authorized to represent them vis-à-vis third parties, as well as the rights and duties of their members. According to Article 1(4) of the Political Parties Act, the legal structure of the political parties shall be legally effective as soon as the by-laws are deposited with the ministry.

It is remarkable that the Political Parties Act does not give a definition of a political party. Sections 1 to 4 of Article 1 constitute the one and final legal framework for the formation of a political party with amazingly few prerequisites. An association comes to exist as a political party with legal personality as soon as it has deposited its by-laws with the Ministry of Interior. The Constitutional Court has ruled in standing jurisdiction that the Ministry of Interior is not allowed to reject by-laws, no matter what ideas they contain. It lies within the exclusive competence of all administrative authorities and the courts to incidentally prove the by-laws of a political party on its compatibility with the legal order. The Constitutional Court argued that it was the historical intention of the legislator not to give the authorities any competence to encroach upon the freedom of the foundation of political parties.[16] The wording of Article 1(4) of the Political Parties Act ('to be deposited with') implies that the Ministry of Interior is reduced to a mere passive depositor of the by-laws with, for example, the possible consequence that an association which formally pretends to participate in the political process but *de facto* is just business oriented, cannot be dissolved by the authorities (Wieser 2001b: 253). As a consequence, a party with a programme not in conformity with law and order, gains legal existence as a political party at once. The party can be checked as soon as it starts any activities or becomes involved in administrative procedures, but its formation cannot be hindered from the beginning.

The only exception is the case of § 3 VerbotsG, which states the prohibition to set any activities inspired by Nazi ideas. The Constitutional Court has ruled that it stems from § 3 VerbotsG that any legal act violating the prohibition of Nazi ideology is null and void. In such a case, the depositing of a by-law would not lead to the legal existence as a political party.[17] Furthermore, the Political Parties Act does not demand of political parties to have any internal democratic structure (Raschauer 1988: 557). For example, there is no legal necessity that party leaders must have a democratic legitimacy by periodic elections with respective participatory rights of the ordinary party members.

Moreover, the Austrian regulations do not explicitly oblige political parties to choose a name or to state it in the by-laws. It is concluded only by interpretation of Article 1(4) sentence 4 that the political party has to choose a name as it is

16 VfSlg. 9648/1983.

17 VfSlg. 9648/1983.

necessary to identify the political party when it comes to existence as a subject of law (Kostelka 1983: 43). Yet there is no obligation to choose a specific name which cannot be mixed up with the name of other institutions or entities. In the case of a possible mistaking of the name, it stays with the civil law to dissolve a dispute with an action for injunction (Merli 1983: 4 et seq.). In addition to that, there is no obligation to name a seat of the party, to regulate the acquisition and loss of membership, to foresee an internal procedure for solving disputes or for the change of the party's by-laws.

The publishing of the parties by-laws in 'a periodical product of printed matter' before its deposition with the Ministry of Interior prescribed in Article 1(4) of the Political Parties Act offers a broad room for manoeuvre. The law neither demands a particular print run, nor a print medium with a certain service area, although there is a periodical with an official gazette ('*Amtsblatt zur Wiener Zeitung*') for the publication of official administrative matters (Wieser 2001b). And last, but not least, political parties are not obliged to offer their ideas and programmes in their by-laws, nor could anybody take insight in the deposited by-laws with the Ministry of Interior.

The lack of more detailed legal prerequisites for political parties has been heavily criticized by legal scholars (Wieser 2001b). In practice, there is no overflow of political parties, and it does not mean that a political party, though easily founded, necessarily gains any political weight. But it has been ironically pointed out as a 'miracle' that there are about 100,000 registered associations and more or less 700 political parties and not vice versa (Wieser 2001b).

Freedom of Assembly

The freedom of assembly and association is granted by Article 11 ECHR and Article 12 of the *Staatsgrundgesetz*, the Basic Law of 21 December 1867 on the General Rights of Citizens. Article 12 of the Basic Law states that Austrian nationals have the right of assembly and to constitute associations, whereby the exercise of these rights will be prescribed in special laws. The Assembly Act of 1953, which is not constitutional but (ordinary) federal law, regulates the exercise of the right to freedom of assembly and provides, *inter alia*, that any public assembly must be given notice of at least 24 hours in advance, indicating the purpose, place and time. The competent authority must prohibit any assembly which would contravene criminal law or endanger public order or security. Furthermore, the Prohibition Act of 1947 (*Verbotsgesetz*) in the rank of constitutional law forbids the NSDAP and other Nazi groups, as well as any acts in favour of the NSDAP.

The Austrian Constitutional Court has found recently[18] that the freedom of assembly is not violated if the national authority prohibits an assembly due to its appreciation that re-engagement into Nazi activities is to be expected in the course of an assembly (Fuchs 2007: 55 et seq.). It happened that the head of the

18 Judgment of 16 March 2007, B 1954/06.

'documentation centre of resistance' in Wels, a city in Upper Austria, had notified to the district administrative authority that he would be holding a demonstration on the subject, 'Bring an end to multiculturalism. For our home country!' The authorities prohibited the meeting, because on a prior meeting slogans closely related to Nazi watchwords have been used. The authorities therefore saw a risk that xenophobic statements mixed with Nazi slogans might be repeated and put the public good at risk. The application to the Constitutional Court argued that the authorities only may prohibit an assembly if this is inevitable with regard to the legitimate aims recognized in Article 11(2) ECHR, and the prognosis has to be predicated on a realistic and comprehensible valuation of the events to be expected.

The Constitutional Court stated that the freedom of assembly was not violated. In former judgments, the court has held that the Prohibition Act forbids anybody to act in favour of the NSDAP or its aims. Any forms of re-engagement into national–socialist activities ('*Wiederbetätigung*') are declared unlawful without exception. The authorities had correctly assumed that the assembly puts the public good at risk if the speeches planned are likely to reactivate Nazi aims and thinking. Because of the diction on the leaflets and the fact that a group of participants similar to a prior meeting was expected, the authorities were legally obliged to prohibit the notified assembly (Fuchs 2007: 55 et seq.).

Amendments of the Constitution

Constitutional law is given a higher status by virtue of the fact that it is harder to amend. An amendment to a constitutional provision requires a two-thirds majority in Parliament, with at least half of the members present and voting. By contrast, to pass a valid motion in Parliament relating to a law that is not constitutional in nature, a simple majority of votes is required, with one-third of parliamentary members present and voting.

The highest ranking laws in the Austrian legal hierarchy are outlined in the 'Fundamental Principles' of the constitution. 'Fundamental Principles' are the democratic principle; the principle of the separation of powers; the principle of the rule of law; the republican principle; and the liberal principle. These principles form the 'basic constitutional order'.

Particular constitutional weight is thus accorded to the fundamental principles, so that any 'total revision' or 'fundamental change' ('*Gesamtänderung*') of the national constitution can only take place if first agreed by the Austrian people in a referendum. A 'total revision' of the constitution takes place when the constitution is so radically amended that either one of the fundamental principles needs to be removed or the relationship of the principles to each other becomes essentially altered.

Any total revision of the Federal Constitution shall, according to Article 44(3) B-VG, before its authentication by the Federal President, be submitted to a referendum by the entire nation. On the other hand, a partial revision requires that procedure only if one-third of the members of the National Council or the Federal Council demands so. The wording of Article 44(3) B-VG therefore seems to allow even a complete abolishment of democracy (Berka 2005: 35) and the abolishment of Article 44(3) B-VG itself (Mayer 2002: 199).

The hitherto only total revision of the Austrian Constitution took place due to the accession of Austria to the European Union. The supranational character of the European Union required a modification of the democratic principle because law making power was transferred to the European Community (Cede et al. 2003: 81 et seq.). Accordingly, the Constitutional Act for the Accession to the European Union ('*Beitritts-BVG*') was agreed upon in a national referendum.

It is highly contentious an issue among Austrian legal scholars whether there is a kind of unalterable core of the constitution and whether the democratic principle is part of it. This is a crucial question without doubt, because if there is a kind of perennial constitutional democratic principle, it must be admissible to protect the democracy against attempts to abolish it in a constitutional way (Thienel 2005: 168). The overwhelming scholarly opinion denies the existence of perennial constitutional principles with reference to Article 44(3) B-VG (Adamovich et al. 1997: 12; Mayer 2006: 473).

The Constitutional Court has vaguely intimated the possible existence of unalterable constitutional principles insofar an answer to this question was not necessary for the judgment and thus left open.[19] Nonetheless it was argued that the democratic principle constitutes a perennial principle of the Austrian constitution which cannot legally and constitutionally be abolished (Janko 2004: 150 et seq.; Morscher 2005: 239). This opinion is deduced from Article 1 and Article 44(3) B-VG because the wording 'be submitted to a referendum by the entire nation' does not allow any other meaningful interpretation (Oberndorfer 2007: 9). The necessity of a referendum thus constitutes a clear borderline which allows though decisive modifications of the democratic principle, but cannot be interpreted at the same time as an authorization to self-destruction of democracy. The complete sacrifice of the people's constitutional power through the referendum would constitute 'a sin to the spirit of the Austrian democratic national identity', as revolutionary created by the people in 1918 and confirmed by the declaration of independence of 27 April 1945 (Oberndorfer 2007: 10). The abolition of the democratic principle would be a contradiction in itself and could therefore not be considered as constitutional.

However, given the wording of Article 44(3) B-VG, there are good reasons to doubt the existence of an unalterable core of the constitution, and the arguments in favour appear too fragile to deliver a solid basis to consider the democratic principle as a kind of perennial part of the constitution.

19 VfSlg. 16.327/2001.

The Role of the Federal Army

According to Article 9a of the constitution, Austria subscribes to universal national defence. The task of universal defence is to preserve the Federal territory's outside independence as well as its inviolability and its unity, especially as regards the maintenance and defence of permanent neutrality. In this connection, the constitutional establishments and their capacity to function, as well as the democratic freedoms of residents, require to be safeguarded and defended against acts of aimed attack from outside.

Besides that, the duty of the Federal Army goes beyond military defence. The tasks of the Federal Army according to Article 79(2) no. 1 lit. a and b of the constitution embrace the protection of the constitutionally established institutions as well as their capacity to operate, and the population's democratic freedoms, and the maintenance of order and security inside the country in general. It is important to emphasize that these tasks can be fulfilled by the Federal Army only on request of the civil authorities.

Protection of Democracy in Ordinary Laws

Means to protect the system against anti-democratic attacks can be found primarily in criminal law. The *Strafgesetzbuch* (StGB – 'Criminal Act') contains a number of offences to directly or indirectly protect the democratic order.

§ 242 StGB – high treason – punishes with imprisonment from 10 to 20 years who undertakes with the use of force or threat to alter the constitution or to separate a part of the territory. From six months up to five years in jail is to punish who founds an association, with the purpose to illegally endanger the independence, the form of government or one of its constitutionally formed institutions. Further offences are, for example, the use of force or dangerous threat against the Federal President (§ 249 StGB); the founding of a terroristic association (§ 281 StGB); or the public incitement to general disobedience against a law (§ 281 StGB).

The offences of the Criminal Act aim to punish individual wrongdoing. The *Vereinsgesetz* (VerG – '*Associations Act*') delivers a basis to proceed against organizations. The founding of an association can be prohibited (Article 12(1) VerG), or an association already existing could be closed down by the authorities given the conditions of Article 11(2) ECHR, that is, if the association violates criminal law or exceeds its statutory purpose or the legal conditions of its existence, Article 29(1) VerG.

The *Fremdenpolizeigesetz* (FPG – 'Foreigners Act') of 2005 provides the possibility to deny visas or to ban foreigners if the public good is at risk by membership to a criminal or terrorist association, incitement to public unrest, etc., Article 21(5) nos. 4, 5 and 7; Article 60 FPG.

After 9/11, a set of laws has been enacted, mainly with amendments of the Criminal Act and Criminal Procedure Act to adapt to the European Union law. New offences have been introduced to the Criminal Act concerning terrorism and financing of terrorism, such as bugging operations and computer search (Polli 2002: 30). The likewise moderate legal measures have been criticized to go partly beyond the aim of counter-terrorism in taking the chance to inappropriately extend anti-crime instruments to the disadvantage of liberal freedoms, such as policing Internet communication (Benedek 2002: 35).

International Legal Obligations of Austria to have a Democratic System

The Preamble of the State Treaty of 1995 makes clear that the Allied and Associated Powers and Austria desired to conclude a treaty to re-establish Austria as a free, independent and democratic state. According to Article 8 of the State Treaty of 1955, Austria shall have a democratic government based on elections by secret ballot and guarantee to all citizens free, equal and universal suffrage as well as the right to be elected to public office without discrimination as to race, sex, language, religion or political opinion. Article 8 therefore imposes a clear obligation under international law to have a democratic government based on elections by secret ballot.

The Protocol to the Convention for the Protection of Human Rights and Fundamental Freedoms, as amended by Protocol no. 11 of 20 March 1952 (European Treaty Series no. 9) was ratified by Austria in 1958. According to its Article 3, the High Contracting Parties undertake to hold free elections at reasonable intervals by secret ballot, under conditions which will ensure the free expression of the opinion of the people in the choice of the legislature.

On 1 January 1995, Austria became a member of the European Union. The then Article F(1) EUT stressed that the Union shall respect the national identities of its member states, whose systems of government are founded on the principles of democracy. At the time of the accession of Austria to the European Union, Article F EUT was already understood as an obligation of member states to have a democratic government system (Grabitz and Hilf 1995). The consolidated Treaty on European Union after the Amsterdam Treaty concretized in Article 6(1) that the Union is founded on the principles of liberty, democracy, respect for human rights and fundamental freedoms, and the rule of law, principles which are common to the member states. A sanction mechanism provided in Article 7 EUT whereby the council may determine that there is a clear risk of a serious breach of principles in Article 6(1) and decide to suspend some of the rights deriving from the application of this Treaty. Furthermore it is explicitly stated in Article 49(1) EUT that only such states may apply to become a member of the Union which respect the principles set out in Article 6(1).

In the light of these provisions, members of the European Union have a clear obligation to have a democratic governmental system. As long as Austria is a member of the European Union, it is inadmissible to renounce its democratic structures (Thienel 2005: 171).

Conclusions

The Austrian democratic system is inspired by the strong spirit of freedom and political neutrality. Hans Kelsen wrote in 1934 that a democracy which wants to stay loyal to itself has to tolerate political movements, even if they aim at the destruction of democratic structures, as long as no force is involved (Kelsen 1934: 98).

For example, the absolute freedom of the formation of political parties is a sign of liberalism and tolerance. Singular militant aspects to protect the democratic and republican system are, on the level of constitutional law, the prevention of a reinstallation of a monarchy and a pronounced prohibition of any resurgence inspired by Nazi ideologies. The prohibition of any Nazi ideology or organization is a punctual exception of the neutrality of the constitution and can hardly be generalized to the prohibition of other extremist groups or movements. Besides that, there are regulations to protect the democratic order in ordinary laws, primarily in the Criminal Act.

The Austrian system was therefore characterized as a 'mixed constitutional order', combining neutrality against political movements in principle with a number of material policy prohibitions (Pernthaler 1996: 90).

However, there are no rules to hinder political movements to abolish democracy with legal ways and means. A minority and contentious opinion states that a higher level of militancy of the Austrian democratic system than hitherto thought can be deduced by interpretation of regulations of the constitution. The wording of Article 44(4) of the constitution seems to allow the complete abolishment of the democratic principle with a referendum and a majority of two-thirds in Parliament. In general, it can be said that the Austrian democracy is not a militant one in the sense of Karl Loewenstein's pleadings because there are no legal provisions to hinder an abolishment of the democratic system with legal and democratic ways and means.

Quests for a militant democracy have been raised in the past. It has been argued that, from a democratic point of view, the preservation of democratic rights for future generations justifies to counteract undemocratic movements, even if they aim to abolish democracy with democratic ways and means (Koja 1966: 582). Thienel (2008: 66) criticized that it cannot be concluded from the neutrality of the constitution that militant acts against anti-democratic movements are *per se* inadmissible and endorsed that there is a duty of the state to defend democracy.

Apart from the question whether it is appropriate or not to take action against legal anti-democratic movements or to which extend action is allowed in the Austrian legal system, it is primarily to stress out that Austria is obliged to maintain its democratic system under several provisions of international law. First and foremost by the State Treaty of 1955, as a member of the European Union as well as a party to the European Convention, by the 1966 Covenants and as a member state of the OSCE.

A strengthening of the Austrian legal order against anti-democratic movements in respect to its lack of militancy is therefore strongly favoured by the international institutional and legal framework Austria is embedded in. In this regard, it cannot be argued in favour of a necessary ideological indifference to democracy any longer. On the contrary: if there are specific obligations under international law for democracy, an abolishment of constituent aspects of democracy would constitute a breach of the respective obligations taken by the state as subject of international law. If there is an international legal obligation to have a democratic system, there is, at the same time, an intrinsic entitlement to provide for preventive measures to defend the due democratic standard. Considering the international obligations for democracy, a justification for a theoretical abolishment of democracy could hardly be seen in the mere fact that the will of the people prevails in any case. It is a nearly paradox situation, that, given the fact that democracy could legally be abolished by a majority of the people, the state as the obliged subject of international law cannot guarantee the fulfilment of its international obligation to have a democratic system.

This should not be misunderstood as a quest for a stronger state – Sir Karl would turn in his grave – but as an argument for actions to secure the fulfilment of international legal obligations, for the erection of an advanced legal barrier against an abolishment of the democratic order, and last but not least, as an argument for the safeguarding of the programmatic constitutional confession to democracy.

References

Adamovich, Ludwig K., Funk, Bernd-Christian and Holzinger, Gerhart (eds) (1997) *Staatsrecht, vol. I: Grundlagen.* Wien: Springer.

Alexy, Robert (1998) 'Die Institutionalisierung der Menschenrechte im demokratischen Verfassungsstaat', in Stefan Gosepath and Georg Lohmann (eds) *Die Philosophie der Menschenrechte.* Frankfurt a.M.: Suhrkamp, 244–64.

Benedek, Wolfgang (2002) 'Die legislativen Maßnahmen nach dem. 11 September aus der Sicht der Bürgerrechte', in Bernhard Moser (ed.) *Sicherheit und Freiheit.* Wien: Politische Akademie, 31–9.

Berka, Walter (2005) *Lehrbuch Verfassungsrecht.* Wien, New York: Springer.

Böckenförde, Ernst Wilhelm (1998) 'Ist Demokratie eine notwendige Forderung der Menschenrechte?', in Stefan Gosepath and Georg Lohmann (eds) *Die Philosophie der Menschenrechte.* Frankfurt a.M.: Suhrkamp, 233–43.

Cassese, Antonio (1995) *Self-Determination of Peoples: A Legal Reappraisal.* Cambridge: Cambridge University Press.

Cede, Franz, Hafner, Gerhard and Thun-Hohenstein, Christoph (2003) *Europarecht*, 4th edn. Wien: Manz.

Fox, Gregory H. (1992) 'The Right to Political Participation in International Law', *Yale Journal of International Law* (17): 539–607.

Fox, Gregory H. (1997) 'Remarks: Implementing Democratization. What Role for International Organisations?', *ASIL Proceedings*, 357–63.

Fox, Gregory H. and Roth, Brad R. (2001) 'Democracy and International Law', *Review of International Studies* 27(2): 327–52.

Franck, Thomas M. (1992) 'Intervention against illegitimate regimes', in Lori Fisler Damrosch and David J. Scheffer (eds) *Law and Force in the New International Order.* Boulder, San Francisco, Oxford: Westview Press, 159–76.

Fuchs, Claudia (2007) 'Freedom of Assembly and National-Socialist Prohibition Act', *Vienna Online Journal on International Constitutional Law* 1(1): 55–8.

Funk, Bernd-Christian (2006) *Einführung in das österreichische Verfassungsrecht*, 12th edn. Graz: Leykam.

Grabitz, Eberhard and Hilf, Meinhard (eds) (1995) *Das Recht der Europäischen Union, Kommentar*, vol. I. München: C.H. Beck.

Ipsen, Knut (1999) *Völkerrecht*, 4th edn. München: C.H. Beck.

Janko, Andreas (2004) *Gesamtänderung der Bundesverfassung.* Wien: Verlag Österreich.

Kampits, Peter (2002) 'Sicherheit, Freiheit, wehrhafte Demokratie', in Andreas Khol, Günther Ofner, Günther Burkert-Dottolo and Stefan Karner (eds) *Österreichisches Jahrbuch für Politik 2001.* Wien and München: Verlag für Geschichte und Politik.

Kelsen, Hans (1929) *Vom Wesen und Wert der Demokratie*, 2nd edn. Tübingen: J.C.B. Mohr.

Kelsen, Hans (1934) 'Verteidigung der Demokratie', *Blätter der Staatspartei* (2): 90–98.

Koja, Friedrich (1966) 'Streitbare und neutrale Demokratie', *Neues Forum, Österreichische Monatsblätter für kulturelle Freiheit* XIII, 576 et seq.

Kostelka, Peter (1983) 'Politische Parteien in der österreichischen Rechtsordnung', in Oswin Martinek (ed.) *Arbeitsrecht und soziale Grundrechte, Festschrift für Hans Floretta.* Wien: Manz, 37 et seq.

Loewenstein, Karl (1937a) 'Militant Democracy and Fundamental Rights I', *American Political Science Review* 31(3): 417–32.

Loewenstein, Karl (1937b) 'Militant Democracy and Fundamental Rights II', *American Political Science Review* 31(4): 638–58.

Lukashuk, Igor I. (1992) 'The United Nations and Illegitimate Regimes: When to Intervene to Protect Human Rights?', in Lori Fisler Damrosch and David J. Scheffer (eds) *Law and Force in the New International Order.* Boulder, San Francisco, Oxford: Westview Press, 143–58.

Macklem, Patrick (2006) 'Militant Democracy, Legal Pluralism, and the Paradox of Self-Determination', *International Journal of Constitutional Law* 4(3): 488–516.

Maogoto, Jackson Nyamuya (2006) *Democratic Governance: An Emerging Customary Norm?* bepress Legal Series, Working Paper 1351 (available from: http://law.bepress.com/expresso/eps/1351).

Mayer, Heinz (2002) *Das österreichische Bundes-Verfassungsrecht*, 3rd edn. Wien: Manz.

Mayer, Heinz (2006) 'Gibt es unabänderliches Verfassungsrecht?', in Metin Akyürek, Gerhard Baumgartner, Dietmar Jahnel, Georg Lienbacher and Harald Stolzlechner (eds) *Staat und Recht in europäischer Perspektive, Festschrift für Heinz Schäffer.* Wien und München: Manz und C.H. Beck, 473–84.

Merli, Franz (1983) 'Zum Schutz des Namens politischer und wahlwerbender Parteien', *Öffentliche Sicherheit* (4): 4–6.

Morscher, Siegbert (2005) 'Über "unabänderliches" Verfassungsrecht', in Karl Weber and Norbert Wimmer (eds) *Vom Verfassungsstaat am Scheideweg, Festschrift für Peter Pernthaler.* Wien and New York: Springer, 239–54.

Müller, Felix (2005) *Das Verbotsgesetz im Spannungsverhältnis zur Meinungsfreiheit. Eine verfassungsrechtliche Untersuchung.* Wien: Verlag Österreich.

Oberndorfer, Peter (2007) 'Art. 1 B-VG', in Karl Korinek and Michael Holoubek (eds) *Österreichisches Bundesverfassungsrecht, Textsammlung und Kommentar, vol. II/1.* Wien and New York: Springer.

Pernthaler, Peter (1996) *Allgemeine Staatslehre und Verfassungslehre*, 2nd edn. Wien and New York: Springer.

Pippan, Christian (2002) *Die Förderung der Menschenrechte und der Demokratie als Aufgabe der Entwicklungszusammenarbeit der Europäischen Gemeinschaft.* Frankfurt a.M.: Peter Lang.

Pippan, Christian (2007) 'Gibt es ein Recht auf Demokratie im Völkerrecht?', in Erwin Riefler (ed.) *Popper und die Menschenrechte, Symposium anlässlich des 10-jährigen Jubiläums der Sir Karl Popper Society und des 10. Todestages von Sir Karl Popper.* Frankfurt a.M.: Peter Lang, 119–60.

Polli, Gert-René (2002) 'Die Konsequenzen aus dem 11. September 2001 aus der Sicht der Terrorismusbekämpfung', in: Bernhard Moser (ed.) *Sicherheit und Freiheit.* Wien: Politische Akademie, 21–30.

Popper, Karl (1950) *The Open Society and Its Enemies, vol. I: The Spell of Plato*, 2nd edn. Princeton: Princeton University Press.

Ramcharan, Bertrand G. (1998) 'The Evolving Doctrine of Democratic Legitimacy', *The Review, International Commission of Jurists, no. 60, Special Issue: The Evolving African Constitutionalism*, 179–98.

Raschauer, Bernhard (1988) 'Die Rechtsstellung der Politischen Parteien', in Anton Pelinka and Fritz Plasser (eds) *Das österreichische Parteiensystem.* Wien: Böhlau, 557 et seq.

Scheffer, David J. (1994) 'The Democratic Entitlement', *University of Richmond Law Review* 29(1): 1–39.

Stoelting, David (1992) 'The Challenge of UN-Monitored Elections In Independent Nations', *Stanford Journal of International Law* 28(1): 371–424.

Thiel, Markus (2003) 'Zur Einführung: Die "wehrhafte Demokratie" als verfassungsrechtliche Grundentscheidung', in Markus Thiel (ed.) *Wehrhafte Demokratie.* Tübingen: Mohr Siebeck, 1–24.

Thienel, Rudolf (2005) 'Wehrlose oder streitbare Demokratie?', *Journal für Rechtspolitik*, 163–78.

Thienel, Rudolf (2008) 'Militant Democracy – Can Democracy Defend Itself?', in Harald Eberhard, Konrad Lachmayer, Gregor Ribarov and Gerhard Thallinger (eds) *Perspectives and Limits of Democracy, Proceedings of the 3rd Vienna Workshop on International Constitutional Law.* Baden-Baden: Nomos, 63–9.

Wieser, Bernd (2001a) 'Art. 1 B-VG', in Heinz Peter Rill and Heinz Schäffer (eds) *Bundesverfassungsrecht.* Wien: Verlag Österreich, 2 et seq.

Wieser, Bernd (2001b) 'Defizite des österreichischen Parteienrechts in rechtsvergleichender Perspektive', *Journal für Rechtspolitik*, 251–8.

Zeleny, Klaus (2004) 'Enthält die österreichische Bundesverfassung ein antinationalsozialistisches Grundprinzip?, Teil I', *juridikum*, 182 et seq.

Chapter 4
Chile

Eduardo Aldunate Lizana

Introduction

'Militant democracy' is understood in Chile, in a broad sense, as a modification of the classic liberal democratic regime. The modification consists of the inclusion of mechanisms for its protection against the enemies of democracy, in particular those who attempt to destroy the democratic regime from within. This is: using actions enabled by the political structure of this form of government. According to Section 19(15) paragraph VI of the Chilean Constitution, political parties, movements and other organizational forms may be declared unconstitutional by the Constitutional Court if they threaten the foundations of the democratic and constitutional regime, or advocate violence as a means of political action or the instauration of a totalitarian regime. The effect of such a declaration is the prohibition of the participation of those parties in the electoral and institutional processes of the democratic regime. Besides the declaration of unconstitutionality of the political party, the Constitutional Court may declare responsibility of the individuals participating in the acts that served as a basis for the declaration, imposing temporary suspension of certain rights on them.

The precedent for the current article is the original Section 8 of the constitution of 1980, which is considered to have introduced militant or combative democracy in Chile. The Constitutional Reform of 1989 repealed Section 8 and introduced the current provision in Section 19. The objective of this paper is to analyse the political evolution that led to the inclusion of this institution in the Chilean constitutional regime, its legal and constitutional precedents, and its application under the 1980 Constitution, as well as to briefly analyse the current provisions.

Synthesis of the Political and Constitutional Evolution in Chile

Chilean independence was formally declared in 1817 and militarily consolidated in 1818. Following that year, a series of failed constitutional drafts were produced until the constitution of 1833 inaugurated a stable government regime. The 1833 Constitution allowed for different interpretations. Hence, due to the absence of political parties and even opposition in the Parliament, the regime initially took the form of a presidential regime allocating strong power to the President of the Republic, being both Chief of Government and Head of State and not politically responsible to the Parliament. During the 1850s, a few uprisings and liberal 'revolutions' aimed at confronting the presidential authoritarianism took place, but they were isolated movements without popular support. Towards the end of that decade, political parties were formed and started an opposition that gradually strengthened parliamentary practices, such as interpelling the ministers and, later on, denying approval to budget bills whenever the Cabinet did not enjoy the Parliament's confidence. In that period, the relevant political *clivage* was the so-called 'doctrinal issue', which aligned the political forces between those who wanted to maintain the union between state and Church as established in the 1833 Constitution, and those aspiring to their separation. This issue was solved through the so-called *leyes laicas* ('laic laws') in a peaceful and practical way during the 1880s, without altering political life.

A first political fracture occurred in 1890. The parliamentary practices had been consolidated since 1870, and the constitutional regime could be qualified, at that time, as parliamentarian: the Head of State appointed his ministers with the support of a Parliament majority, and a vote of no confidence forced the resignation of the Cabinet. The elected President for the 1886–1891 period, José Manuel Balmaceda, entered into conflict with the Parliament when he refused to change the Cabinet after a vote of no confidence. The Parliament responded by refusing to approve the budget and tax bills. In response, Balmaceda unconstitutionally deemed the previous year's budget as approved. The Parliament dismissed him, the President resisted, and thus a bloody civil war between the Parliament and the government forces began. The Parliament forces won. Between 1891 and 1924, the parliamentary practices continued, but without either a proper regulatory framework or party discipline. This led to ministerial shuffles and government instability. The continuity of the system in these circumstances can only be explained through the lack of civilian participation in politics,[1] the abundance of fiscal resources due the saltpetre exploitation, and the absence of major political conflicts.

In 1920, due to changes in the electoral legislation, for the first time a candidate won the Presidency appealing directly to the population: Arturo Alessandri Palma. His government programme addressed the labour issue, which rose in Chile in the last third of the nineteenth century, for the first time by considering major social reforms. However, that programme was blocked by parliamentary practices. In 1924, a bloodless military coup forced Alessandri to resign and the Congress was dissolved. At the beginning of 1925, at the request of the army, Alessandri accepted to resume the Presidency under the condition of the constitution being reformed. The result was not an amendment to the constitution, but the new

1 The 1833 Constitution, along with the electoral legislation, established a democratic regime with suffrage restricted to landowners that, although softened in time, excluded during most of its period of validity the majority of the population from having full voting rights.

constitution of 1925, establishing a presidential regime that drastically restricted the parliamentary control of the government.

A period of instability followed between 1925–1932, including a four-year dictatorship under Carlos Ibáñez del Campo (1927–1931), some ephemeral attempts to install a socialist republic, and the emergence of the first self-denominated national-socialist Chilean groups. Afterwards, Alessandri was elected for a second presidential period from 1932–1938, and finally the 1925 Constitution could be fully applied. During this period, an event occurred that would have major significance in the political evolution of the country. A group of young National Socialists squatted in the Labour Insurance building in Santiago. Instead of being expelled by the police forces, they were massacred. That event affected the next presidential election in favour of the radical party at the expense of the right-wing candidate, Gustavo Ross, who was widely considered to be the successor in Alessandri's political line. The National–Socialist Party, at the time representing 4 per cent of the electorate, supported the radical candidate Pedro Aguirre Cerda, which was significant since he defeated the right-wing candidate Ross by less than 5,000 votes (Urzúa Valenzuela 1992: 504 et seq.).

In the period following Alessandri's second government, the party system was structured around the left-centred Radical Party, which acted as a hinge between the left-wing, represented primarily by the Socialist Party of Chile and the Communist Party of Chile, and the right-wing parties, represented by the Liberal and the Conservative Parties and later on by the *Falange*. The Radical Party would ally with one or the other wing, according to the subject at hand. During the Presidency of Gabriel González Videla, elected with the support of the Communist Party, the first law aimed at banning a political party was enacted under the claim that it was an enemy of democracy, namely the Communist Party.

The existing party system in Chile, referred to as the 'three thirds' system because right, centre and left parties garnered each about 30 per cent in the elections, functioned until 1964 as a centripetal force. Both left and right-wing avoided extreme positions as to engage the less ideologized political centre. In 1964, Eduardo Frei Montalva was elected President. He represented the Christian Democracy, formerly the *Falange*, a party that split from the Conservative Party in the late 1930s. In this election, the Christian Democracy arose as a strong political force, dispensing with the political party support that prevailed during the radical governments between 1938 and 1958, and even during the government of the independent but right-oriented Jorge Alessandri Rodríguez (1958–1964). It has been observed that the victory of the Christian Democracy and its refusal to enter into electoral agreements with other political forces were decisive in the polarization of the country that preceded Salvador Allende's election in 1970, as well as the change of political party dynamics to a centrifugal and extreme one.

During this period, in 1965, the *Movimiento de Izquierda Revolucionaria* ('Movement of the Revolutionary Left', MIR) was founded. This was the first group expressly vindicating use of violence as a mean of political action. Although both the Communist Party and the Socialist Party shared this vision, at least from the ideologic-Marxist view of the state as part of the bourgeois superstructure for dominating the proletariat, they had been content with participating according the rules of the democratic and electoral regime. The MIR departed from this by actually undertaking violent actions to achieve their objectives.

For the 1970 election, the Radical Party allied with the left coalition named *Unidad Popular* ('Union of the People') that included the Communist and Socialist Parties. Together they supported Salvador Allende as Presidential candidate, while the Christian Democracy and the National Party supported their own candidates (Radomiro Tomic and Jorge Alessandri Rodríguez). It is worth mentioning that the Christian Democracy presented itself as a non-marxist left political force, therefore displacing the *Unidad Popular* away from the political centre. In 1970, Salvador Allende was elected President with a relative majority.[2] His ideological programme upheld the possibility of building a socialist regime out of the legal and constitutional order in force, on the basis that the 'bourgeois legality' could be transformed into a 'socialist legality' without destroying it. The Christian Democracy and the National Party feared that this could imply the establishment of a people's democracy of totalitarian type, as in the Cuban case. In order to prevent that risk, the Christian Democratic Parliamentarians demanded a constitutional amendment known as the 'Warrant Statute', as a condition to support Allende's election in the Congress. This constitutional reform is important because it bound the prevailing unrestrictive political pluralism regime to certain loyalty duties to the constitution and the democratic government regime. Thus, as a result of the Constitutional Reform by Law Nr. 17,298 of 9 January 1971, the constitution established that it 'ensures all the citizens the free exercise of the political rights, within the democratic and republican system' and added that Chilean citizens '... can freely group in political parties, which have legal personality according to public law and whose objectives are to concur, in a democratic manner, to determine the national policy'. With these dispositions, the democratic system was considered to be protected against the attempts to install a single party or a totalitarian regime.

Despite this, and in a context of immense concealed intervention of the American Government only exposed in the 1990s,[3] Allende's Government was accused of violating constitutional rights and attempting to transform the Chilean institutions to a popular democratic regime of totalitarian character. In addition to that, Allende was not able to unify two different trends within the Unidad Popular.

---

2 According to the 1925 Constitution, if no candidate obtained the absolute majority in the Presidential election, the Congress was entitled to appoint the President. Traditionally, the Congress had recognized the first majority and had appointed that candidate as the elected President.

3 A review of the US intervention prior and during Salvador Allende's Government, instigating and supporting the coup of 11 September 1973, supported by extensive documentation of American agencies, can be found in Verdugo 2003. A well-balanced analysis of the institutional crisis can be found in Valenzuela 1978.

The trend held by the Radical and Communist Parties, who favoured the idea of consolidating the social reforms and pursuing understandings with the opposition; and the trend held by the Socialist Party, within which important factions called the Head of the Executive Government to move forward and take the lead in a popular movement towards socialism, even facing the risk of armed confrontations. On the other hand, a right-winged paramilitary assault group known as *Patria y Libertad*, was operating in the country. *Patria y Libertad* was originally formed as a response group to MIR, but it was responsible for an important part of the street violence between 1971 and 1973. During 1972 and the months prior to September 1973, Allende sought an understanding with the Christian Democracy so as to appoint a Cabinet of national unity. However, due to the awkward environment created by various political attacks, the most conservative fraction of the Christian Democracy, whose leader was Patricio Aylwin Azókar, closed the door to this alternative and brought the discussions to an end. In an environment of generalized confrontation between the Executive Government, the judiciary and the Parliament, and of economic crisis worsened by the US intervention, a military coup violently deposed the President on 11 September 1973. The official reason for the coup was to impede the establishment of a totalitarian regime in Chile. In the words of one of the leaders of the coup, Gustavo Leigh, it pursued 'the extirpation of the Marxist cancer in Chile'. It is worth mentioning that, until the coup, the Congress worked normally, with an active opposition blocking most of Allende`s legislative and governmental programme. The press, as well, operated without restrictions, even the important radio, television and newspaper media owned by the opposition including the television channel *Universidad Católica* and the most important newspaper of the country, *El Mercurio*.

The coup dissolved the Congress; later on, activities of any political party were prohibited and the existing parties were dissolved. Between 1973 and 1978, the text of a new constitution was debated during a period of strong repression of any political activity (real or presumed), absolute lack of press freedom and a judicial power tolerant to violations of human rights and political freedoms by the Executive Government. The new constitution entered into force on 11 March 1981 and introduced militant democracy in Chile in its Section 8.

Legislative Precedents

From the time of independence and while the 1833 Constitution was in force, Chile did not have regulations restricting the political participation of any groups or parties. A broad freedom prevailed, and the attacks against the institutional order were sanctioned using general criminal forms, such as sedition, illicit association, etc. During the period of validity of the constitution of 1925, different special legal instruments (outlined below) were enacted to sanction those agents attacking the democratic regime. The impetus for these regulations should be understood in the context of emerging Marxist Parties (for example, the Communist and Socialist

Parties) and others that were deemed, rightly or just as propaganda means, by the incumbent government to destabilize the institutional system through violent acts or sabotage. Only in the extreme case of the so-called *Law for the Permanent Defense of Democracy*, a political party was totally and nominally excluded from political life. Government regulation D.L. Nr. 50 of 24 June 1932 established in its Section 1 that

> any person will be considered as an enemy of the Republic who propagates or foments, orally or in writing, doctrines that attempt to destroy the social order or political organization of the State using violence, whether attacking its fundamental institutions, or attempting to depose the government, or fomenting disrespect of authority and of the rights established under the Constitution and the laws.

This provision has been considered the most remote precedent of Section 8 of the constitution of 1980, in its original version. It is worth noticing that the sanctioned behaviour is the diffusion of doctrines. Therefore, it was a limitation of the freedom of speech.

Law no. 6,026, published in the Official Gazette on 12 February 1937 and known as the *Law of Interior Security of the State*, consolidates several provisions regarding state security. For the purposes of this paper, the relevant provision is contained in Section 1 Subsection 4 and sanctioned those who

> propagate or foment, orally or in writing or by any other means, doctrines that attempt to violently destroy the social order or the political and legal organization of the Nation.

Section 3 of the same Law prohibited the existence or organization in Chile, of any militarized or uniformed movement, faction or party that pursues the implementation of a regime opposed to democracy.

Law no. 8,987, published in the Official Gazette on 18 October 1948 and known as the *Law for the Permanent Defense of Democracy*, was enacted in Gabriel González Videla's Government. It has the distinctive characteristic of specifically addressing the Communist Party, expressly banishing its existence, action and propaganda. It also sanctioned those individuals who propagate its doctrine and those who become members of it. It also banned the exercise of civil and labour union rights for its members. According to the Presidential message to the Congress, the objective of the bill was to maintain the democratic and constitutional regime of the Republic. Besides this declared objective was, however, another significant objective: the need to impede the action of the Communist Party at the labour union level. Indeed, the action of the party had been responsible for significant strikes and productivity loss, in particular in the coal industry.

Interestingly, the law did not address other parties of the socialist family, which had the same ideological root and, in some cases, had shown less loyalty with the institutional system than the communists.

Law no. 12,297 of Interior State Security, published in the Official Gazette on 6 August 1958, repealed the previous law for the Permanent Defense of Democracy, and the proscription of the Communist Party. However, it maintained two offences related to doctrine propagation: Section 4f, sanctioning 'anyone who propagates or foments, orally or by writing or by any other means, doctrines aimed at destroying or altering by violent means the social order or the republican and democratic form of government', and Section 6d, sanctioning 'any individual making apology or propaganda of doctrines, systems or methods that promote crime or violence of any kind, as means of achieving political, economic or social changes or reforms'.

This is a brief summary of the legislative precedents of Section 8 of the original 1980 Constitution, through which the constituent power was considered to have introduced militant democracy in Chile. It should also be remembered that the Constitutional Reform of 9 January 1971, mentioned in the previous paragraph, implied a loyalty duty of the political actors to the constitutional and republican democratic system.

The Constitutional Reception of Militant Democracy in Chile. Section 8 of the Original 1980 Constitution

The military Junta that assumed the government after the coup entrusted the preparation of a new constitution to a special commission named *Comisión para el Estudio de una Nueva Constitución* ('Commission for the Study of a New Constitution'), composed of academics and politicians of centre and right-wing orientation. The Executive Government, headed by Augusto José Ramón Pinochet Ugarte, provided certain specific guidelines for the Commission's work. One of those guidelines was to incorporate mechanisms aimed at ensuring the politician's loyalty to the values of a democratic system. The memorandum from the Junta to the Commission, known as 'Fundamental goals and objectives for the new constitution of the Republic', states that

> the new constitutional structure … b) will contemplate a section establishing that the political parties must be organized and act according to the principles of democracy, and keep in their ideological definition and in the behaviour of their members an unrestricted and permanent adherence to the democratic and republican system of government and to the principles and values that constitute the essence of the rule of law. Consequently, parties that, according to their objectives or the political action of their members, undermine the democratic government system shall be considered contrary to the constitution. Furthermore, individuals who commit acts that undermine the democratic regime or who promote its alteration or destruction shall not be eligible for public duties or

> positions, whether or not of popular vote. The same shall be applicable to those individuals who advocate crime or political violence.[4]

For its work in relation to this specific subject, the Commission took into account the legislation mentioned in the previous section and the German model of militant or combatant democracy ('*streitbare*' or '*wehrhafte Demokratie*'), which was specifically mentioned in the working papers of the Commission. In their very first session, the Commission's President, Enrique Ortúzar, stated that in order to reinforce any democratic government system

> it was indispensable to take into account, among others, the following measures: 1. the establishment of a constitutional provision similar to one in the Federal Germany Charter, declaring contrary to the constitution the parties and movements that sustain Marxist ideas or doctrines; 2. the prohibition, for those who follow those ideologies, to serve public duties or positions obtained through popular vote, sanctioning the violators with dismissal from those positions.[5]

The preparation of the new constitution extended over a long period of time, between October 1973 and its approval in September 1980. On 11 September 1976, while the text was under discussion, the government enacted Constitutional Act no. 3. This Constitutional Act contains the most direct precedent of Section 8 of the original 1980 Constitution. Section 11 of that Act established:

> No one can invoke any legal or constitutional provision to undermine the rights and freedoms that this Constitutional Act recognizes, nor to undermine the integrity or the performance of the commonwealth under the rule of law or the established regime.
>
> Any action by an individual or group intended to propagate doctrines against family, or which advocate violence or a concept of society based on class warfare or contrary to the established regime or the integrity and performance of the commomwealth under the rule of law, is illegal and contrary to the institutional code of the Republic.

Taking this provision as a basis, the drafts of the Commission and, later on, the original 1980 Constitution, included the following Section 8:

---

4 Memorando sobre metas u objetivos para una nueva Constitución, de la Junta de Gobierno a la Comisión de Estudios para una Nueva Constitución, 26 November 1973, no. 14, in Ordenamiento Constitucional, Editorial Jurídica de Chile Colección de Textos legales no. 71, Santiago de Chile, Abril de 1980: 11 et seq., 28–9.

5 Actas de la Comisión de Estudios para una Nueva Constitución, first session, p. 5.

> Any action by an individual or group intended to propagate doctrines against family, or which advocate violence or a concept of society, the State or the legal order, of a totalitarian character or based on class warfare, is illegal and contrary to the institutional code of the Republic.
>
> Organizations and political movements which, according to their objectives or the actions of its adherents, pursue such objectives are unconstitutional.
>
> The Constitutional Court shall have jurisdiction to decide on the violations of the provisions set forth in the preceding paragraphs.
>
> Without prejudice to the other penalties established by the constitution or by the law, anyone who incurs or have incurred the aforementioned violations shall not, for a period of ten years from the date of the Court's decision, be eligible for public duties or positions, whether or not of popular vote. Likewise, they will not become rectors or directors of educational establishments or teach thereat or exploit any medium of mass communication, or become directors or administrators thereof, or hold positions therein, related to the broadcast or dissemination of opinions or information. During the aforementioned period, they will not be able either to act as leaders of political organizations or students associations, and in general, organizations related to education, or occupy positions in community, professional, entrepreneurial, labor or trade unions.
>
> If at the time of the Court's decision, those persons referred to above are holding a public office or position, whether or not as the result of a popular vote, they shall lose it ipso jure.
>
> Persons penalized in accordance with this precept shall not be eligible for reinstatement during the period indicated in the fourth paragraph.
>
> The duration of ineligibility as prescribed in this section shall be doubled in case of recurrence of the offense.

It can be noticed that this provision, like its immediate precedent, sanctioned the propagation of ideas or political propaganda. However, it included the unconstitutionality of parties that, due to their purposes or the nature of the activities of their members, pursue such objectives. It was not clear, however, if the reference to 'such objectives' referred to the propagation of ideas, to the destruction of the family, or to the establishment of a regime of totalitarian character or based on social warfare.

The organ with jurisdiction to declare the unconstitutionality was the Constitutional Court (*Tribunal Constitucional*), which in its original composition consisted of seven members: three were appointed by the Supreme Court among its members; one was appointed by the Senate; one by the President;

and two members were appointed by the National Security Council (*Consejo de Seguridad Nacional*). This council, in turn, was composed by civil and military representatives, the latter holding a majority. Its members were the heads of each of the three military branches and the chief of the military-trained police force (*Carabineros de Chile*), and only three civilian members – the President of the Senate, the President of the Supreme Court and the President of the Republic.

Section 82 of the original 1980 Constitution gave the Constitutional Court the following mandate:

> (8) To declare, in conformity with Section 8 of this constitution, the responsibility of persons who attack or have attacked the institutional order of the Republic. However, if the affected person were the President of the Republic or the President-elect, said declaration shall, in addition, require the agreement of the Senate, adopted by a majority of its members in office.

Its paragraphs XIII and XIV stated:

> Public action shall be available to petition the Court regarding the powers conferred thereupon by Subsections 7, 8 and 10 of this Section.
>
> However, in the case of Subsection 8, if the person affected were the President of the Republic or the President elect, the petition shall be filed by the House of Representatives or a fourth of its members in office.

Act no. 17,997 of 19 May 1981 regulated the procedure for the petition regarding the declaration of unconstitutionality of political parties. Its Sections 63 to 72 contained a form of trial with summons and default rules for the accused, a 15-days term for the presentation of evidence and a hearing before the case resolution.

The Application of Section 8 of the Original 1980 Constitution, While in Force

While in force, Section 8 of the original 1980 Constitution was invoked on four occasions, three of which were resolved by substantive sentences by the Constitutional Court.

In the first case, dated 16 May 1983, two members of the Journalist Professional Association took action against the, by then, Ministry of Interior, Enrique Montero Marx. The action was based on the following grounds: (1) the events of 1 May 1983 and 2 December 1982, when third parties attacked national and foreign journalists in the Chilean capital, abet by the guilty omission of the police forces; (2) Supreme Decree no. 593 of 13 May 1983, that prohibited the emission of news shows by certain radio channels, except for official communications; and (3) the fact that the Osorno-based radio station *La Voz de la Costa* was silenced through the intentional destruction of the emission antenna by government agents or third parties acting under government protection.

The action was dismissed by sentence of 2 June 1983 (File no. 16). The sentence made an interesting statement regarding the scope of application of the sanction, stating that:

> the behaviour sanctioned in Section 8 is neither the simple ideological discrepancy that is not expressed in one of the forms mentioned in the constitution, nor an attack against the institutional code that does not imply the propagation of one of the doctrines precisely and specifically mentioned by the constituent body.

Thus, the sentence diverged from the traditional mechanisms of control and sanction established in the regulation between 1925 and 1973, and considered Section 8 as a protection mechanism against the propagation of doctrines considered dangerous by the constitution, rather than a more general protection mechanism for the maintenance of public order.

In the second case of application of Section 8 of the original 1980 Constitution, a petition was filed to declare the unconstitutionality of various left-wing political movements: *Movimiento Democrático Popular* ('Popular Democratic Movement' MDP); *Partido Comunista de Chile* ('Communist Party'); *Movimiento de Izquierda Revolucionaria* (MIR); and *Partido Socialista de Chile* ('Socialist Party', whose leader was Clodomiro Almeyda Medina).

Even though the activities of political parties were banned early on by the Military Government, at the beginning of the 1980s the left-wing political groups were reactivated. These groups first worked underground and then openly within the underclass and university circles, undertaking propaganda against the government, and in favour of their political doctrines affiliated to Marxism. A group of 30 citizens, exercising the public action granted by the constitution, filed a petition against these groups on 3 August 1984. The case was sentenced on 31 January 1985. The sentence accepted the petition and declared the unconstitutionality of the MDP and the related movements, based primarily on the following grounds: (1) the aforementioned organizations advocate the Marxist-Leninist doctrine, which involves violent political action as a means of warfare; (2) Marxism-Leninism is a doctrine that upholds a totalitarian notion of society, the state and the judicial order, and the MDP and its member organizations and movements adhere to that specific concept of the doctrine; (3) the accused organizations not only adhere to the Marxist-Leninist doctrine, but also engage in proselyting propaganda; and (4) consequently, the accused organizations undermine the regime of democracy and freedom ensured by the constitution.

It is interesting to note that this sentence explicitly addressed the origins of the institution, by stating in paragraph no. 24:

> in this respect, the Constitutional Tribunal of the Federal Republic of Germany, while applying Section 21 Subsection 2 of their constitution, which is the

> immediate source of Section 8 Subsection 2 of our Fundamental Charter, has stated that the program or the party objectives, in the context of that section, should not only be examined in the programs, declaration, official principles, etc., but also in the light of the whole party's image, what they want to achieve as expressed in its secret programs and objectives, in speeches, writings, propaganda material, and the behaviour and composition of its organs and members; in summary, the political style adopted by the party.

Afterwards, the court was requested to decide about the imposition of sanctions to members of the MDP, a request that was dismissed since they had not been parties to the process.[6]

The third case where the Tribunal was requested to apply Section 8 involved a petition from the Ministry of the Interior against Clodomiro Almeyda Medina, former Minister of Foreign Affairs during Salvador Allende's Government. Almeyda was accused of propagating doctrines that advocated violence through different radio stations, with the objective of gaining members for its movement or party, awakening revolutionary sentiments against the government and encouraging violent acts. The sentence in File no. 46 of 21 December 1987 accepted the action by a narrow majority of four judges against three.

The sentence clarified the interpretation of Section 8 regarding retroactive sanctions, which was one of the critiques made to that section. The Tribunal applied the principle *nullum crimen et nulla poena sine lege*, even though it was not applying criminal sanctions. At the same time, the Tribunal established the compatibility between Sections 8 and 5 of the Constitution, which recognizes the respect for the fundamental rights of the human race as a limit of the sovereignty. This section had been mentioned by the defence as a provision that prevented the application of Section 8 to Clodomiro Almeyda Medina.

The minority vote is of particular interest. According to it, even if Clodomiro Almeyda Medina had actually called for participation in protests and demonstrations, they were aimed at the return to democracy. Thus, his behaviour did not imply a pleading for violence as a means of political action or the propagation of doctrines that support a totalitarian regime.

The repeal of Section 8 of the 1980 Constitution and its replacement by a provision with a similar purpose but a different text, gave grounds for another decision of the Constitutional Court. This is the only decision made after the repeal of Section 8 and the inclusion of militant democracy in the new Section 19 Subsection 15, paragraphs 6, 7 and 8. The sentence in File no. 113, of 14 August 1990, rehabilitated Almeyda in his rights, due to the elimination of the offence that motivated his sanctions.

6 File no. 32 of 1985, sentence on 31 January 1985.

Complementary Legislation

Seven years after the entry into force of the original 1980 Constitution on 11 March 1981, Law no. 18,662 was enacted to regulate the effects of the sentences of the Constitutional Court, and in particular those arising from Section 8. According to this law, any organization declared unconstitutional by a sentence of the court loses its legal personality, if applicable, and relinquishes its assets to the state. Its members, as well as any individual promoting it or trying to reorganize it after the unconstitutionality has been declared, are sanctioned with absolute ineligibility to serve public duties or positions, become rectors or directors of educational establishments or teach thereat, exploit any medium of mass communication, or become directors or administrators thereof, or hold positions therein, related to the broadcast or dissemination of opinions or information. They were also prohibited from acting as leaders of political organizations or organizations related to education, or occupying positions in community, professional, entrepreneurial, labour or trade unions. The law also sanctioned individuals who explicitly accept the support of organizations or movements declared unconstitutional, who defend or propagate their doctrines or accept their representation in mass communication media.

It is worth mentioning that the sanctions considered in this Act for the aforementioned individuals were similar to those considered in Section 8 of the original 1980 Constitution. However, Law no. 18,662 was not applied prior to the repeal of Section 8 and, as complementary legislation, must be considered consequently repealed by the Constitutional Reform of 1989.

The Current Constitutional Provision

In 1988, the possibility of Augusto Pinochet remaining in the Presidency of the Republic for another period of eight years was precluded through a plebiscite. Thus, a strengthened opposition was in a position to negotiate several constitutional amendments, including those provisions that were considered contrary to democracy. The constitutional amendment was approved by Law no. 18,825, on 17 August 1989. It included the repeal of Section 8, which was considered by democratic sectors as an instrument for the proscription of certain ideologies, rather than an instrument for the defence of democracy. Besides repealing Section 8, the reform included new dispositions in Section 19 Subsection 15, aimed at protecting democracy in a manner compatible with its libertarian values. The new provisions modified the sanctioned behaviour so as to exclude any interpretation that could lead to the sanction of propagation of ideas. In addition, this sanction was linked to the protection of political pluralism. Section 19 Subsection 15 paragraphs 6, 7 and 8 of the Chilean Constitution in force establish:

> The political constitution guarantees political pluralism. Parties, movements and other organizational forms whose objectives, acts or behaviours do not respect the basic principles of a democratic and constitutional regime, pursue the establishment of a totalitarian system, as well as those using, promoting or inciting violence as a means of political action, are unconstitutional. The Constitutional Court has jurisdiction to declare that unconstitutionality.
>
> Without prejudice to the other penalties established by the constitution or by the law, anyone who incurs or have incurred the aforementioned violations shall not, for a period of five years from the date of the Court's decision, participate in the organization of other political parties, movements or other forms of political organizations, nor run for public positions elected by popular vote, nor hold the positions mentioned in Section 57 Subsections 1–6. If at the time of the Court's decision, those persons referred to above are holding any of the aforementioned positions, they shall lose it ipso jure.
>
> Persons penalized in accordance with this precept shall not be eligible for reinstatement during the period indicated in the previous paragraph. The duration of ineligibility as prescribed in this section shall be doubled in case of recurrence of the offense.

Section 93 Subsection 1 No. 10 regulates the respective jurisdiction of the Constitutional Court, and its paragraphs 15 and 16 follow the paragraphs 13 and 14 of Section 82 of the original constitution closely.

After the entry into force of the reformed constitution in 1989, no political party or organization has been declared unconstitutional. Both the Communist Party and the Socialist Party have legal existence. Communist Party members have served in public positions at the municipal level, while the Socialist Party is a member of the political coalition *Concertación de Partidos por la Democracia*, ruling the government since 11 March 1990, and its members have served in positions at the governmental and parliamentary level. No petition according Section 19 Subsection 15 has been filed against the self-called national socialist or neo-Nazi groups. It is also worth mentioning that since 1990 there has not been political violence, besides some rare activities that could be classified as common crime more than terrorism, and no group has raised public debate in respect to their constitutionality.

The emergence of indigenous groups claiming ancestral rights since the late 1990s has been managed and perceived as a problem of public order but without invoking the aforementioned hypothesis of the constitution, even though since 2001 it is clear from the public opinion that these groups consider the systematic use of violence as a legitimate means of action.

References and Further Reading[7]

Literature about militant democracy is scarce in Chile. After an initial interest due to its novel incorporation in the constitutional order, and the commentaries of the Constitutional Reform of 1989, neither scientific works nor public discussion has addressed this subject.

The following works, produced while original Section 8 was in force, can be mentioned:

Cumplido, Francisco, Guzmán, Jaime and Dietze, Gottfried (1984) 'Pluralismo y Proscripción de Partidos Antidemocráticos', *Revista del Centro de Estudios Públicos* (13): 5–22.

Larraín Cruz, Rafael and Nuñez Tomé, Leopoldo (1984) *Protección de la democracia en Chile ¿Deben proscribirse los partidos marxistas? Historia fidedigna del artículo 8° de la Constitución Política de 1980.* Santiago: Jurídica de Chile.

Rojas Sánchez, Gonzalo (1981) 'La situación del partido comunista de Chile, de acuerdo al artículo 8° de la Constitución. Fundamentos históricos', *Revista de Derecho Público*, 29–30, 177–85.

After the 1989 Constitutional Reform, which repealed original Section 8 and introduced Section 19 Subsection 15, the following works can be mentioned:

Bruna Contreras, Guillermo (1989) 'Reforma sobre derechos políticos', *Revista Chilena de Derecho* 16(3): 591–8.

Cea Egaña, José Luis (1988) *Tratado de la Constitución de 1980.* Santiago: Jurídica de Chile.

Fermandois Vöhringer, Arturo (1991) 'Notas sobre el futuro de las normas constitucionales que protegen el sistema democrático', *Revista Chilena de Derecho* 18(1): 27–38.

Luksic Sandoval, Zarko (1990) 'Límites jurídicos de la democracia. Derogación del art. 8 e incorporación de los incisos 6 y sigs. del art. 19 núm. 15 de la Constitución de 1980', *Cuadernos de análisis jurídico* 13(1): 19–34.

Molina Guaita, Hernán (2006) *Derecho Constitucional.* Santiago: Lexis Nexis.

Pfeffer Urquiaga, Emilio (1985) *Manual de Derecho constitucional, vol. I.* Chile: Jurídica Ediar Conosur.

Urzúa Valenzuela, Germán (1992) *Historia Política de Chile y su Evolución Electoral.* Santiago: Jurídica de Chile.

Valenzuela, Arturo (1978) *The Breakdown of Democratic Regimes: Chile.* Baltimore: The John Hopkins University Press.

---

7 I am grateful to Walda Flores, student in the Faculty of Law at the *Pontificia Universidad Católica de Valparaíso*, for her assistance with the literature search for this work.

Verdugo, Patricia (2003) *Allende: cómo la Casa Blanca provocó su muerte.* Santiago: El Ateneo.

Verdugo Marinkovic, Mario, Pfeffer Urquiaga, Emilio and Nogueira Alcalá, Humberto (2005) *Derecho Constitucional, vol. I.* Santiago: Jurídica de Chile.

Zapata Larraín, Patricio (1990) '¿Protección a la democracia? El sentido del art. 8', *Jornadas de Derecho Público* 20(1): 89 et seq.

Chapter 5
France

Claire-Lise Buis

Introduction

'We should never confuse politics with war. For no Frenchman another fellow citizen should be an enemy except when he betrays France, when he denies its ideal and its values.' This sentence was pronounced by Nicolas Sarkozy in Montpellier, in May 2007, during the electoral campaign for the French presidency.[1] Apart from any strategic interest in political mobilization and leaving aside the question what 'ideal and values' could mean in this context, this assertion reveals a fundamental preoccupation in modern democracy: how to transform conflictual relationships into a regulated debate between opponents and how, at the same time, to define what degree of hostility becomes unacceptable, so that the designation of an enemy becomes unavoidable and legitimate.

The last part of the sentence could be also interpreted as an echo of the famous declaration of Antoine de Saint-Just concerning those 'enemies of liberty' who would not deserve liberty. Historical comparisons should be used with conceptual caution, but the identifying of an argumentative thread indicates that the presence of enemies of democracy has been a permanent, or at least recurrent, concern in the political history of France. The existence of enmity at the core of a political system raises a particular problem in a democratic context: how can democracy withstand the threat of anti-democratic forces without forfeiting the principles of tolerance and pluralism on which it is supposed to be founded? This 'democratic dilemma' is exactly what the notion of a 'militant democracy' intends to overcome. Karl Loewenstein (1937a, 1937b) and Karl Mannheim (1943), as first promoters of the concept, suggested that a democracy had no choice but to arm itself against extremism and to take all legislative and constitutional measures necessary to sustain itself.

Theoretically, France should represent an ideal field of experience in this matter, because of its extremely unstable constitutional history and its record of political crises since the French Revolution. The threats that democracy in France has been confronted with have been numerous and of variable kinds: Royalist, Bonapartist, anarchist, communist or nationalist, separatist, and so on.

---

1 My translation from: 'Nous ne devons jamais confondre la politique avec la guerre. Pour aucun Français, un autre Français ne devrait jamais être un ennemi sauf quand il trahit la France, quand il renie son idéal et ses valeurs'. Quoted at http://www.up.univ-mrs.fr/veronis/Discours2007/transcript.php?n=Sarkozy&p=2007-05-03&e=ennemi&e2=#n1.

But a French paradox can be identified: although French democracy often has been challenged and although those confrontations have frequently succeeded in overwhelming the Republic, the concept of 'militant democracy' – as a defence strategy – has largely been ignored by political actors, by the social sciences and in the juridical literature. During the time when Loewenstein developed the concept, the Third Republic faced strong anti-parliamentary centrifugal tendencies. After the outbreak of anti-republican leagues on 6 February 1934, the Government of Pierre Etienne Laval decided to forbid armed movements and militias.[2] But some of the extremist forces re-emerged by infiltrating new political parties. Charles Eisenmann, one of the first thinkers of the control of constitutionality in France, formulated the democratic dilemma described above in 1937 at an international conference of jurists and pointed out:

> It is indeed legitimate that the legislation of democratic states defends itself against anti-democratic parties, against parties which would establish their dictatorial regime if they came to power. Democracy cannot recognize the right of dictatorship without denying itself and even being inconsistent.[3]

These few traces of recognition of the problem of 'militant democracy' are nevertheless too informal and scarce to adequately constitute a distinct French reception of the concept. It is highly significant that the word has still not found any satisfying translation into French: the adjective *militante* refers to the basis of the structure of political parties. A *démocratie militante* would mean, then, a democracy ruled by activists.[4] The French language consequently needs a phrase ('*démocratie capable de se défendre*') to describe a democracy 'able to defend itself'. In contrast to its reception in the German language through the notion of '*streitbare*' or '*wehrhafte Demokratie*', the concept was neither translated nor introduced in any institutional or academic French discourse. Generally speaking, the protection of democracy in France has not been examined as such in the literature. The elements of a protective strategy are mostly considered separately. It may also be significant that the only single all-embracing study authored on the subject in the last ten years focuses on a comparison with the German case and has not been published in France.[5]

2 For a historical approach, see Berstein 1975; Chavardes 1966; Pellissier 2000.

3 My translation from: 'Il est [donc] tout à fait légitime que la législation des Etats démocratiques prenne des mesures de défense contre les partis anti-démocratiques, contre les partis qui, au pouvoir, établiront leur dictature … La démocratie ne peut pas reconnaître le droit de la dictature sans se nier et même se contredire', in Association Juridique Internationale 1938: 31.

4 That is the reason why Guy Haarscher, for example, employs the concept with quotation marks, see Haarscher 2007 (at http://www.philodroit.be).

5 Canu 1997.

Does this mean that the concept of 'militant democracy' does not fit the French experience or make sense within its political culture? To what extent is the lack of theorization a clue to detecting a fundamental confidence in the stability of the regime? Does confidence characterize the actual French Republic in a more compelling way than militancy?

To examine the French case, it is necessary to clarify definitions and identify criteria. According to Loewenstein, a militant democracy is a 'rational system' (Loewenstein 1937a: 428) that develops techniques to combat the 'emotional attacks' of its fascist enemies and avoid the trap of 'suicidal lethargy' (Loewenstein 1937a: 431). These techniques are mostly legislative ones, because the 'very nature' of democracy 'can appeal only to reason' (Loewenstein 1937a: 428). The exiled German political scientist listed a range of instruments, from the forestalling of the formation of military groups to the ensuring of loyalty in the administration. That list is a useful tool to circumscribe possible measures but insufficient to investigate the actual French way of coping with dangers. The banning of uniforms or the training of a political police were possibly effective in the interwar Europe but seem to be outdated or unsuitable in the context of the Fifth Republic. Eckhard Jesse selects more general criteria to test the militancy of a democracy (Jesse 2003). In a comparative analysis, he identifies three elements with which to appraise the ability to guarantee protection: the normative orientation of the political system (*Wertgebundenheit*); the will to protect superior norms (*Abwehrbereitschaft*) and, finally; the degree of anticipation of measures of protection (*Vorverlagerung*) (Jesse 2003: 459). These concepts are useful insofar as they add a certain degree of generality to Loewenstein's list. The problem with such an approach lies in some of the normative choices of the German '*Extremismusforschung*', which insists on the parallel between left and right-wing extremism and whose analysis of the party-system cannot be transferred straightforwardly to the French case. Furthermore, Jesse focuses his analysis on non-violent parties. It would seem that the conception of the 'enemy' presented above cannot overlook violent manifestations of danger and the way to deal with them. Giovanni Capoccia (2005) also focuses on what he calls, like Giovanni Sartori, 'anti-system' parties. According to him, militant democracy is characterized by a repressive (as opposed to 'accommodative') attitude toward those parties (Capoccia 2005: 47 et seq.). Both these subject – and object – variables seem too narrow to embrace the case of France.

Without ignoring the risk of stretching definitions to make the examined case fit into the chosen categories, it is more judicious to adopt a wider perspective. Loewenstein himself wanted to identify 'every possible effort' (Loewenstein 1937a: 432) of democracy to rescue itself. Aside from constitutional or legislative instruments, it can be useful to integrate historical events, political behaviours and discourses into the inventory of the protection system. It is anticipated that this wider perspective should allow us to consider the evolution of the French attitude to new dangers, such as Islamic terrorism. While it is important to keep the amount of criteria in reasonable number and to avoid a weakening of the relevance of our comparative analysis, an important restriction should nevertheless be spelt out clearly. A militant democracy entails an unambiguously protective attitude and short or middle-term strategies. More than the structures – similar to the social or economic context, which can also make a democracy unstable – actors and their calculations are at the core of militancy.

Following the clarification of the criteria, the question posed above concerning the identification of France as a militant democracy needs reformulating: more than to the 'if', the political scientist should pay attention to the 'how'. How has the French democracy protected itself? How militant has it been? Our aim is, in this sense, to present a critical panorama of the options chosen in France.

The first part of this chapter deals with contextual and theoretical backgrounds, each according to a historical, constitutional and political approach. The methods employed within the French context will then be listed, and their efficacy and legitimacy tested. Finally, I will try to show how the French case offers the opportunity to sharpen the concept of 'militant democracy' in order to understand recent challenges to democracy and to pay attention to new dimensions ignored by Loewenstein.

Context

The very possibility of conceiving the defence of democracy depends on different principles. First, a certain idea of liberty and sovereignty is at stake: that one should authorize a breach of the absolute power of the people. A militant democracy anticipates the ambition of a dangerous minority or overcomes the ruthlessness of the majority. A militant democracy is based on fundamental choices affecting institutions. Second, a democracy can be militant only if it elevates some of these fundamental choices to the status of non-negotiable basic principles. What ought to be protected needs clarification, at least in very general terms, and should be labelled an unchangeable norm. Third, the defence of democracy presupposes a dual partition of the political system, which separates friends (the 'centre' or 'moderates') from enemies (the 'extremists'). To what extent can these conditions be discerned in the French case?

The Ambiguous Heritage of the French Revolution

A historical perspective gives some indication of the way France dealt with the issue of defending democracy. The heritage of the Revolution, as the concrete origin of the democratic ambition, is in this sense highly ambivalent. Although the experience of 1789 gave birth to the first challenges for the supporters of democracy, it seems that options chosen – theoretically and practically – have not promoted any effective defensive strategy.

The end of the eighteenth century marked the first realistic chance to enforce democracy in France as a regime that both protected rights and transferred the sovereignty from the monarch to the people. But at exactly the same time as its birth, the revolutionary democratic ambition was endangered by the mobilization of resistance inside and outside the new political system. Facing that opposition, particularly of royalist movements supported by its European neighbours, the new holders of power invented some mechanisms of exclusion in order to protect the newly constructed edifice. The political context of the Revolution and its aftermath is in reality much more complex than the dual separation between democrats and anti-democrats. It would be necessary to separate the democrats from the Republicans and, of course the '*révolutionnaires*'. But the important step here is to take note of the introduction of inclusion–exclusion mechanisms in the early stage of democracy in France.[6]

Those mechanisms belong to those legitimating strategies which function 'by contrast' and which are also encompassed in a wider conception of militant democracy. At the level of discourse, the vocabulary of the 'enemies of the Revolution' illustrates a radical division, made by political actors, between the Self and the Other. Agnès Steuckardt has proven, on the basis of content analysis of the journal *L'ami du peuple* (Steuckardt 2002), that categories, such as 'enemy' or other negative terms, preceded self-designations in the revolutionary lexicon. At the level of institutions, some mechanisms, such as the robbing of the status of the citizen, also intended to protect the political system against its rivals.[7] Some classical instruments of the protection of democracy were also developed in the revolutionary or post-revolutionary decades: the penal code, the notion of *sûreté* ('safety' or 'security' of state) (Noyer 1966), and surveillance techniques, such as intelligence or listings (*fichage*, for example, in the army[8]). At the same time as the invention of democracy, the French Revolution tried to invent ways of safeguarding its achievements. The first French attempts to consolidate the Republican regime are so far 'militant': the actors are very conscious of the existence of opposition and broach the issue of enmity in various ways.

The heritage of the Revolution in the matter of militant democracy is nevertheless ambivalent. Some features of the French political or juridical culture emerge at the same time that seem to thwart the development of militancy. The Enlightenment had already queried the limitations of sovereignty and thus, indirectly, the possibility for the majority to decide to abolish democracy. For Jean-Jacques Rousseau, the answer is clear: democracy can survive only if the people, the sovereign, wish it. The only limitation to the power of the people that is acceptable comes from the

6 See, for a general presentation, Martin 2002.

7 See on that topic, Simonin 2007.

8 The development of modern intelligence methods is often attributed to Fouché, Minister of Napoléon Bonaparte. Later, the episode called *affaire des fiches*, around 1900, entered in the history of the Third Republic as one of its biggest scandal. The anticlerical Minister of War, the General André, ordered a secret surveillance of the officers who went to church. It is controversial if that action can be classified under the category 'defence of democracy'. At that time, the Government of Waldeck-Rousseau called itself 'government for the defence of the Republic'.

people itself, because 'a people is always in position to change its laws however good; for, if it chooses to do itself harm, who can have a right to stop it?' (Rousseau 1762 [1997], Book 2: 12). The social pact can be changed so long as the general will commands this evolution. To change the 'fundamental laws' with the same solemnity which has been used to create them, may be the only procedural self-limitation to the sovereignty of the people. The latter have the constitution at its disposal as regards content. Condorcet expressed a nearly identical position when he explained that no generation can appropriate the right to decide on a constitution in place of the following generation (Condorcet 1847: 148 et seq.). Before dealing with the institutional consequences of such a theory, it can be asserted that such political ideas are not compatible with the belief in a militant democracy: If there is no limit to sovereignty except a procedural one, democracy is not protected against what Loewenstein and others recognized as the main strategy of the anti-democrats, that is the penetration of democratic institutions via legal means. That is exactly how some jurists countered the arguments of the dominant legal positivism during the Weimar regime. This conception of unlimited sovereignty, coupled with the idea of 'nation', has been etched in the constitutional history of France after the Revolution. It resulted in some long-lasting principles, such as the superiority of the law and the role of the assembly, as the representative institution of the nation, in which sovereignty resides. The role of the law, as a central but possibly changeable norm, has been qualified as '*légicentrisme*' and interpreted as the reason why the principle of a control of constitutionality was long unthinkable in the French political culture.[9]

This conception of sovereignty aside, the idea of liberty expressed in the Declaration of the Rights of Man of 1789 seems to be improper to an affirmation of the militant democracy. Paul Boventer has tried to identify a 'French understanding of liberty' (Boventer 1984: 142 et seq.). According to him, the Declaration of the Rights of Man entails an 'individualistic' conception of liberty: the only limit to liberty is, as Article 4 confirms, the injuring of another person. That limitation is too weak to justify a protective attitude toward democracy as such. It could be argued, nevertheless, that Article 5 sets another limit, one that resides in the principle of equality of rights, which is supposed to guarantee the enjoyment of liberty by all. The anti-democrats who would destroy this equality principle could be sanctioned in the name of such a conception of liberty. Boventer sums up this uncertain balance: 'The political tradition in France is characterized by a permanent ambivalence between unlimited and limited liberty.' But it is important to note here, once again, the role of the legislator in the matter: he is the only one who can restrain liberty. The *légicentrisme* is, as it has been shown above, hardly compatible with the idea encompassed in the concept of militant democracy, that not everything which the law allows should be allowed or normatively approved.

The French Revolution is, finally, a moment of uncertainty insofar as the protection of democracy is concerned. The birth of democratic ambition is

9 For a comparison with Germany, see Grewe 1999.

matched by the first efforts to make the democracy militant in the sense of a general combative attitude. But other principles, whether political or philosophical, undermine all defensive strategies and probably render them ineffective. The constitutional instability that followed the Revolution could be interpreted as a result of that weakness in the implementing principles of militant democracy, or, in order to avoid anachronism, in achieving a balance between affirmation of the Self and tolerance of the Other. To explain that instability would go far beyond the scope of this study. It suffices here to take note of the ambivalence of the revolutionary heritage.

Normativism and Constitutional Change

The diagnosis of the French difficulty in establishing a stable constitutional order leads to one of the central issues of militant democracy: the possibility of eternal stability, which constrains any regime change in guaranteeing the preservation of democracy at the same time.[10] Expressed in terms of constitutional theory, the question is: to what extent can the power of amendment be circumscribed by substantive limitations? Let us turn to the specific case of the French Fifth Republic.[11]

The constitution of 1958 mentions two sorts of limits to the power of amendment. This should not be applied in the case of a threat to territorial integrity, in the case of application of Article 16 (extraordinary empowerment of the President), or during an interim period at the Head of the State. These limits are not insignificant with regard to the protection of democracy in exceptional circumstances, but they are only temporal and not substantive. What should demand our attention here is Article 89(5), which mentions that 'the republican form of government shall not be the object of an amendment'.

The same disposition was adopted by the new Republican majority of the Assembly in 1884: an amendment officially introduced that interdiction into the constitutional laws of the Third Republic. Apart from the fact that this guarantee was not strong enough to prevent the takeover of the Pétain regime in 1940, it had already provoked many controversial debates among French jurists. For Barthélèmy and Duez (1930 [1985]: 897), and Burdeau (1930: 3 et seq.), the significance of this amendment was more historical – as a final victory for the Republicans – than legal. Duguit developed the idea of the 'double amendment' (Duguit 1924: 538 et seq.): the amendment could be amended because the National Assembly, as the sovereign, retains the power of undoing what it has done. In the case of infringement, no sanction is provided in the constitutional text. According to Esmein (and later Carré de Malberg 1922 [1962]: 594, 603), the possibility of

10 That preservation can take the form of a list of principles that are made immutable, as in the German Fundamental Law (Articles 79, 39) or the form of a general guarantee with regards to the type regime, such as the actual French constitution.

11 For a comparison with the German case, see Wittekindt 2000.

amendment is not unlimited – an infringement would be illegal and revolutionary. But both also recognize that such a revolution would not have any negative legal consequence, and that the preservation of the Republic is finally a matter of political choice.

The debate on the 'eternity guarantee' and on Article 89(5) has been ongoing in the context of the Fifth Republic. The concrete application of Article 89(5) has been coupled, as a subject of dispute, with the idea of 'supra-constitutionality'. The question reminds us of the problem evoked above: Are there some principles that should be protected because they are situated above the positive norms and, among them, the constitution?

It is possible to sum up the French constitutional debate by distinguishing three main positions. The first position might be called the marginal one, because very few French theorists of law defend it. It claims that Article 89(5) testifies the existence of supra-constitutional norms. The 'republican form of the government' should be understood as being embodied in a group of higher principles, respect for which is mandatory for the constitutional power itself. Stéphane Rials, the most convinced supporter of this position (Rials 1984),[12] bases his argumentation on the decision of the Constitutional Council of 16 July 1971, that asserted for the first time the principle of liberty against the arbitrariness of the law. He develops a theory of hierarchy of norms, inspired by Hans Kelsen, where the Declaration of Human Rights plays the overarching role, and regrets that the Constitutional Council has failed to establish a list of imprescriptibly protected principles such as liberty, equality or safety (Rials 1984: 602). This interpretation seems to be inspired by German constitutional doctrine, which places some fundamental rights at the top of unchangeable principles (Wittekindt 2000: 116). The idea of militant democracy would find, in this possibility, the best concretization on a constitutional level because it would echo the normativity well known in the German system and as described by Eckhard Jesse. Gregor Paul Boventer (1984: 161) interprets Article 89 in this sense. The formulation would differ from the American constitutional rule, which only attaches formal conditions to the power of amendment. According to him, the 'republican form of government' has a wide significance, equivalent to that of democracy, and encompasses the content of Articles 1 to 4 of the French constitution, notably indivisibility and secularity.

But the theory of supra-constitutionality has been categorically rejected by the majority of French constitutional lawyers.[13] According to the French positivist tradition, supra-constitutionality would refer to norms that are situated outside the constitutional text; that is to say: not positive and therefore not litigable. Dimitri Lavroff has summarized that prevalent conception: 'It does not seem to us that there would be rules of supra-constitutional value, except if we want to refer, for

12 See as well Rials 1986. Another supporter of this position is Serge Arné (1993).

13 To name some of its most famous critics: Louis Favoreu; George Vedel; Michel Troper; or Bertrand Mathieu. For a general view, see the debate between Favoreu and Vedel in *Pouvoirs*, no. 67, 1993. For a more recent critical analysis, see Camby 2003.

philosophical reasons, to rules of natural law whose content is variable and whose existence is disputable.'[14]

Apart from this rejection, the dominant position consists in a suspicious attitude towards the idea of substantive limits to the power of amendment. Some professors claim that Section 5 of Article 89 would not have any significance. In the most influential part of the literature, Article 89(5) only indicates the superiority of the constitution in the hierarchy of norms; the latter is 'rigid' because its amendment is hindered through formal conditions. The differentiation between the constituent and the constituted power, first conceived by Sieyès,[15] is dissolved in a kind of identity that places the constituent power and the power of amendment at the same level, subsumed by the sovereignty of the people. The sovereign is, in this conception, the origin and the recipient of the norm; it is omnipotent. The limitation of the power of revision can only be formal – a substantive limitation would be equivalent to a self-limitation of the constituent power and would not make sense. One of the logical consequences is that the control of constitutionality applied to Article 89(5) can only bear on the amendment procedure.[16]

This dominant position has been questioned by other French jurists who have pointed out the paradoxical result of the confusion between the constituent and the constituted power. That confusion indeed transforms the revolution into a legal process because it supposes that any constitutional change is allowed. Olivier Beaud (1994) and Olivier Jouanjan (1996) represent a newly emerging tendency in constitutional law, which tries to overcome such paradox by recognizing the existence of substantive limits to the power of amendment. For these authors, the pre-existing constituent power can change the constitution as much as it wishes – that is to say: annihilate the form of the republican government – but if such an action may be legitimate, it cannot be enclosed by any argument of legality. The constituted power is, on the contrary, subject to conditions preset in the constitution by the constituent power. Consequently, not only the control of constitutionality should be restricted to the examination of formal measures, but also the constitutional council should check the content of the law, as a 'guardian' of the constitution.[17] Only the amendments adopted by referendum, as direct expressions of the sovereign, are not necessarily submitted to the control of the

14 My translation from: 'Il ne nous semble pas qu'il y ait des règles de valeur supra-constitutionnelle, sauf si l'on veut faire appel, pour des raisons philosophiques, à des règles du droit naturel dont le contenu est variable et l'existence contestable', see Lavroff 1997: 128.

15 Carl Schmitt referred to him, in Schmitt 1928.

16 The Constitutional Council confirmed it in its decision of 26 March 2003, by denying its competence for judging an amendment about decentralization. See CC 2003-469 DC – 26 March 2003.

17 In allusion to the '*Hüter der Verfassung*' by Carl Schmitt. In Schmitt 1928, the guardian is the President and not a Constitutional Court.

Constitutional Court.[18] According to this point of view, Article 89(5) limits the organs of the state (including the constituted power and the constitutional council itself), but not the sovereign.

Although the emerging conception of substantive limits has gained influence amongst French constitutional experts, the jurisprudence failed to bring the controversy to a close. The decision of the Constitutional Council of 2 September 1992 (the so-called *Maastricht II* – decision[19]) entails an ambivalence that has often been disputed. The decision states both that 'the constituent power is sovereign' and that the latter should take into account the conditions of Article 89(5). Some scholars read into this a confirmation or affirmation of the existence of supra-constitutional norms; others point out the influence of the judge, Georges Vedel, who wanted to disarm the naming of limitations but maintained the confusion by calling 'constituent power' what is actually the power of amendment (Lavroff 1997: 124 et seq.).

How are we to interpret this juridical analysis regarding the issue of militant democracy? The idea that constitutional principles have to be protected against the potential consequences of changing political majorities is no longer a strange anomaly in the French positivist tradition. The protection of 'the republican form of government' may not exactly correspond logically to the defence of democracy: a modern constitutional monarchy can indeed be democratic. But the stabilization of democracy was *de facto*, in French historical experience, parallel to the stabilization of the republican regime. That is the reason why the interpretation of Article 89(5) plays an important role here. More generally, the defence of core principles that constitute the modern French democracy seems to be more and more accepted as an important task in constitutional jurisprudence. The increasing role of the Constitutional Court as a controlling organ of the law, the affirmation of substantive elements of the constitution in particular in the jurisprudence related to the European unification, seem to bring the constitutional order in the direction of what Eckhard Jesse called '*Wertgebundenheit*'. Nevertheless, the content and exact range of the protected principles is still debated. The resistance of the positivist tradition seems to prevent a definitive clarification of ambiguities in that matter.

The juridical framework, such as the historical heritage, has thus not yet delivered a definitive conclusion to the question of militant democracy in France.

Extremism: The Integrative Republic

To take a closer look at the political reality and the evolution of the political system may complete our contextual analysis and help us yield more valuable answers.

A defence strategy can only emerge in a system where a clear distinction is made between the threatened and the threatening political forces. Concretely, there

18 Corresponding to the decision of the CC called 'Maastricht III' (CC 92-313 DC – 23 September 1992), which referred to an older decision from 1962.

19 See CC 92-312 DC – 2 September 2003.

must be an insurmountable separation between democrats and anti-democrats or between extremist parties and parties which show an unconditional fidelity to the democratic values. The pertinence of such a model, as a description of political reality, is controversial among political scientists.[20] But if we bear in mind the possible divergence between the language of actors and that of researchers,[21] it is possible to evaluate its appropriateness to the French case.

Jean Baudouin has analysed what he calls a 'republican dynamic' (Baudouin 2000) that tends to tame the differences more than deepen the cleavages between democrats and anti-democrats. The fact that the word 'extremism' appeared in France at the time of the stabilization of the Republic[22] underlines its ambivalent connotation. It indicates both a pathology of the regime and the ambition of the latter to civilize it, 'at least to integrate it to its own logics'. According to Baudouin, the birth of the Third Republic marks the beginning of an 'assimilationist' challenge that consists in domesticating both the monarchist and the proletarian oppositions. The explicit goal is to make the Republic endure. This ambition could equally be that of militant democracy. But the originality of the French Republic consists in the way of achieving it: not fighting enemies but seeking to persuade them. Education of the individual, confidence in the benefits of deliberation and in electoral procedures, all form the intellectual roots of the republican project. The laws concerning the liberty of the press and the liberty of association, voted into existence around 1900, testify to what Baudouin calls a 'republican concern to convert the enemy into an adversary, to push back as much as possible the boundary before which the legitimate contestation of the republican idea will not become an illegitimate rebellion against the republican form of government'.[23]

20 The problem is in particular the construction of a category, which would gather the characteristics of left and right extremism and level off the differences between them. The so-called '*Extremismusforschung*' (of Uwe Backes and Eckhard Jesse) has been vehemently criticized in Germany because of that confusion, assumed normatively as a scientific tool but sometimes inspired by a conservatism consisting in stigmatizing the left, supposed to be as much as dangerous than the extreme right. That discussion did not take place as such in France among political scientists. Nevertheless, the debate about the heritage of communism and totalitarianism among intellectuals dealt with similar issues. See in particular the controversy that followed the publication of Bartosek et al. 1998.

21 It is, in my opinion, what can be hold against the German *Extremismusforschung* (whose studies about militant democracy have been nevertheless outstanding). It adopts the same criteria of the analysis of the political system as the actors, without putting any critical distance between their own results and the discourse of the actors, and sometimes even legitimating the latter.

22 About the uses of the word extremism in the French political language, see Backes 1998; Gauchet 1992: 395 et seq.

23 My translation of 'souci républicain de convertir l'ennemi en adversaire, de reculer le plus loin possible le point où la contestation légitime de l'idée républicaine ne se transformera pas en une rébellion illégitime contre l'institution républicaine', Baudouin 2000: 346.

Republican tolerance is, according to that interpretation, not a sign of unconscious naivety, but the result of an optimistic integrative option.

Concretely, it is possible to show how, in the long term, the main radical sources of opposition to the Republic have been assimilated. The monarchist movement was gradually disintegrated by the extension of suffrage and above all the rallying strategy of the Church; by the end of the Third Republic, it no longer formed a political threat but an ideologically marginal splinter group that considered the defeat of 1940 as a 'divine surprise'.[24] '*Boulangisme*', a national-populism inspired by the Bonapartist tradition of plebiscite, recorded some remarkable electoral successes, but the phenomenon completely imploded after the Home Secretary, Constans, decided to make its leader appear before the High Court of Security (the Senate at that time) in 1889.[25] The socialist movement was also domesticated – at least that part that participated in the government of Waldeck-Rousseau around 1890. Also the end of the Third Republic seemed paradoxically a time of rallying and assimilation: the French Communist Party learnt to join to fidelity to Moscow the national priority of defending the Republic against fascism. The Popular Front constituted, according Baudouin, a 'decisive experience of national inclusion' (Baudouin 2000: 368).

In post-war France, the dynamic of de-radicalization seemed to be furthered. The *Parti Communiste Français* (PCF) was one of the only Western European Communist Parties that succeeded in joining together an intransigent Stalinism and huge national electoral anchorage – rooting therefore its legitimacy in the most significant instrument of representative liberal democracy. The strategic hesitations of the PCF, from the fidelity to revolutionary goals to the signing up to the '*programme commun*' and governmental participation, should not hide a progressive acceptance of democracy as a frame of action and basis of agreement. 'The word democratic socialism is in our eyes a statement of the obvious', George Marchais wrote in *Le défi démocratique* (Marchais 1973: 21). Democracy is here not understood in the Soviet way: the one party system is, by the mid-1970s, already outdated in the programme of the PCF. Generally speaking, the category 'extremism', understood as a radical opposition to democratic principles, does not seem to fit the history of French communism.

The integration process also affected the right-wing of the political space. The fortunes of the *Front National* (FN) since the beginning of the 1980s have been interpreted as a renewal of former anti-democratic ideologies (counter-revolutionary conservatism, racialist populism or anti-Semitic nationalism and state protectionism), or as an opportunistic political enterprise seeking to take advantage of electoral results. The examination of the origins of 'frontism' would take us beyond the scope of this chapter.[26] It is more relevant for our purposes to put

24 The expression is from Charles Maurras, leader of the monarchist *Action Française*.

25 About this episode, see Guarrigues 1992.

26 See, for example, Perrineau and Mayer 1996.

the stress on a tow-sided movement of integration: the assimilation of republican principles by the FN and, in return, the fact that its participation in the political system became an evidence also for the rest of its actors. The Party of Jean-Marie Le Pen abandoned, first, all revolutionary or counter-revolutionary ambition. No later than 1986, when it first entered the National Assembly, it did adopt fundamental rules and practices of parliamentary democracy – and demarcated itself from the attitude of the leagues in the 1930s. Second, the racist argumentation has been euphemized, in comparison with interwar France and in accordance with the most recent strategy of the party to reach wider parts of the electorate. The idea of national 'preference' is, moreover, no longer associated with biological difference, but it couples with a restrictive conception of citizenship, that is to say inside and not outside of the frame of the Republic (Baudouin 2000: 396). Finally, the FN permanently adopted the strategy of a 'march through institutions', for example, by competing in local elections and largely gave up every nostalgia about the fascist experience of paramilitary violence. Conversely, some elements of the traditional political centre completed this process of assimilation by permitting themselves to ally with the FN or to carry over some of its programmatic leitmotivs (Minkenberg 1998). Like the PCF, the FN has gradually formed an integral part of the French political system – and has not been maintained at its external margins.

This assimilation could be interpreted today as the first step towards extinction. Against the trend of 2002, when the results of the FN urged some millions of people to demonstrate, the last presidential election marked a very significant decrease in their attractiveness for both parties. The PCF is today nearly condemned to inexistence, and the FN lost ten points in popularity in comparison to 2002.

Does this mean that the integrative strategy previously discussed succeeded in mitigating the influence of extremism? Has the French case exactly met what Karl Loewenstein described as the aims of militant democracy? Michael Minkenberg has tried to establish a causal relation between repressive and assimilative strategies towards extreme right movements and their radicalisation (Minkenberg 2006: 26 et seq.). He certifies the insufficiency of state repression, but does not draw any definitive conclusion concerning the French case. Moreover, new types of radicalism have arisen in France in the last decades (for example, in the form of 'anti-globalization' movements) and the future of the FN after the Le Pen era still remains unclear. It is furthermore difficult to admit without caution that an institutionalized extreme right would be more tolerable than the existence of splintered and isolated skinhead groups.

To conclude, the political context of militant democracy in France is characterized by the republican challenge of assimilation, which seems to be the very opposite of the fighting strategy suggested by the concept of militant democracy.

In order to detail this divergence and to reinterpret the ambiguities of the historical heritage and the juridical context, it is now necessary to inspect further the instruments of a possible defensive strategy.

Instruments

Modern democracy in France is organized, institutionally, not only as a liberal regime in the sense that it protects the individuals against the state, but also as a system where the Republic is protected against potential dangers. What are, substantively, the constitutional and legislative tools suitable for the latter purpose?

They fall into three main groups, depending on their intermediary target: the organizing of political competition; the planning of an eventual crisis, and finally; the structuring of deliberation.[27] This range of measures will be evaluated with reference to specific criterion: their preventive and anticipatory character that reveals, according to Eckhard Jesse, the degree of militancy.

Organizing Political Competition

The first kind of constitutional and legislative measures existing in France are those that regulate political competition in order to prevent the undermining of republican institutions by anti-republican forces. Their objects are the electoral system and in particular, its actors, namely political parties and organizations.

The first mechanism of regulation is the majority voting system (the double-ballot, associated with the 'first past the post' principle) which puts an obstacle in the way of entrance to parliamentary institutions.[28] By creating a bonus for big parties – what is negatively called a 'plurality run-off' it prevents extremist parties that fail to reach a minimal size and legitimacy from entering the arena of political representation. Fisichella has pointed out the lack of transferability of the extremist vote to the second ballot to demonstrate this systemic prejudice (Fisichella 1984: 181 et seq.).[29] The *Front National* succeeded in entering the *Assemblée Nationale* only once in the history of the Fifth Republic, following the reform of the voting rules for the general elections of 1986, that introduced some elements of proportional representation. The leaders of the right extremist and other non-governmental parties regularly argue that a proportional system would be fairer. The integrationist project presented above seems to be qualified by the institutional rule.

Another important issue is the option of banning a party considered dangerous to democracy, either because of its programme or because of its actions. The

27 Capoccia also classifies the anti-extremist legislations on the basis of their goals, but in my opinion, the categories 'preserve public order' and 'deligitimizing the messages to the electorate' are not circumscribed enough; see Capoccia 2005: 58.

28 See the analysis about thresholds by proportional representation in Capoccia 2006: 62.

29 The influence of the ballot system on extremism is nevertheless not so univocal; see, for example, its consequences on the presidential elections presented by Lewis-Beck and Wittrock 2007: 106 et seq.

institutional regulation aspect of the problem in France is quite specific: it lies in a tradition of administrative enforcement, and not with respect to constitutional rules.

The 'founding fathers' of the constitution of 1958 certainly did not ignore the potentially destructive powers of political parties. Two senators proposed (during a meeting of the consultative committee) to introduce a condition on the liberty of parties into the constitution,[30] namely the absence of obedience to foreign powers. This proposal, implicitly rooted in suspicions concerning communist loyalties to Moscow, was not included in the final draft. Article 4 mentions that parties should respect 'the principles of national sovereignty and democracy'. As explained by Pierre Espuglas, an unambiguous interpretation of these limits is not possible (Espuglas 1998: 684 et seq.): Do they apply to the structure or the goals of the parties? How should democracy be understood here? A proposal for reform made by the committee of Georges Vedel, consisting in making allusion to the 'laws of the Republic', was, for mysterious reasons, ignored by the Parliament (Espuglas 1998: 692). But the most blatant failing of Article 4, regarding the banning issue, is the absence of any sanction and specific mechanism that could exercise real control.[31] Theoretically, a law that would specify banning procedures could be examined by the Constitutional Council. But the latter has already forbidden any *a priori* intervention by the legislator in the formation of a political organization,[32] and a solution along German lines is simply not entailed in the constitution. The absence of the possibility of banning through explicit constitutional provision and, on the other hand, the allusion to vague duties, may reveal the ambiguous attitude of the 'founding fathers' towards political parties: Charles de Gaulle's mistrust resulted in the neglecting of any juridical status and limiting conditions for it.

The control of political organizations is, in France, dominated by administrative procedure. The law of 1901 concerning the principle of association established the basis of a liberal conception according to which all associations (including political ones) can be constituted without authorization. Their dissolution can be commanded by the judge of common law if the association has an intention to attack 'the integrity of the territory or the republican form of government'. This condition reminds us of the constitutional limitations of amendment. It is still liberal in a sense that the power of decision limiting liberties is retained within the domain of the politically independent judicial authority ('*juge judiciaire*').[33] But

30 Comité national chargé de la publication des travaux préparatoires des institutions de la Vème République. *Documents pour servir à l'histoire de l'élaboration de la constitution du 4 octobre 1958*. 2, Le Comité consultatif constitutionnel: de l'avant-projet du 29 juillet 1958 au projet du 21 août 1958. Paris: La Documentation francaise 1988: 128–32.

31 About the birth of Article 4, see Avril 1992: 713.

32 See the decisions of June 1959 (CC 59-2 DC – 17/24 June 1959); and May 1971 (CC 71-42 DC – 18 May 1971).

33 It may be useful to recall the fundamental duality of the French judicial system, which differentiates the judicial courts and the administrative justice.

this law appeared insufficient to repress effectively the protest movements of the 1930s. The law of January 1936 still forms the juridical framework pertaining to the control of parties. Although it has been criticized, from the very beginning, as a 'circumstantial law' (M'Bongo 1998: 715 et seq.), it has nonetheless survived the historical context in which it was conceived. The power of dissolution is transferred to the administrative authority; its cancellation is possible following an appeal procedure of the Conseil d'Etat, but the President alone can declare a banning decree. The interdiction can affect organizations in a limited number of cases. These associations or '*de facto* groupings'[34] are similar to combatant groups or private militias because of their forms and their activities; furthermore, their intent is to attack the integrity of the territory or, 'by force', the republican form of government. Some remarks should be made about these conditions. The use of violence is the main operational criteria, but the other elements mentioned (that possibly justify dissolution) are far from precise. Some separatist movements have thus been forbidden, because the Conseil d'Etat has interpreted narrowly the idea of threat to territorial integrity and despite the fact that the movements in question had not begun to execute their plans.[35] The law of 1936 was amended in 1972, with the addition of the 'incitation to racial hate', and again in 1986, in the context of anti-terrorist laws. It is important to notice that the law of 1936 was loosely interpreted and widely applied by public authorities. Pascal M'Bongo has identified three waves of application of the law during the Fifth Republic (M'Bongo 1998: 721 et seq.): Between 1958 and 1967, when dissolution mostly affected extreme right movements related to the Algerian War; between 1968 and 1973, when left-wing protest movements became the principal target; and since 1975, when most dissolution procedures have concerned separatist or terrorist groups. In August 2002, President Jacques Chirac decided to ban the extreme right *Unité Radicale*; and this constitutes the most recent application of the law of 1936.

What kind of conclusion can be reached on the basis of the French record of dealing with parties understood as dangerous? Theoretically, the observance of the criteria of violence in judging their structure and actions guarantees strict respect for the *legality* principle. A measure is taken in case of a criminal offence, that is to say once it is performed and after an *a priori* confrontation between a rule and its damage. It does not conform exactly to the core of the concept of militant democracy, which tries to anticipate the danger and determines the *opportunity* to act *a priori*.

Therefore, the French system of control seems not to fit very well in the category of militancy. The French democracy shows confidence in making the executive and, possibly, the administrative judge responsible for a simple recording of violence. But critics of this system suggest that this surface impression should be tempered by a more precautionary observation. The violence criterion has not

34 The French notion is '*groupements de fait*'.

35 The affected associations were: Dame Tapua, Enbata and Battesti, see Espuglas 1998: 698.

prevented all anticipatory – and sometimes arbitrary – uses of the law of 1936. A constitutionalization of the control procedures on political parties is invoked as a desirable means of rectification here.[36] In 1972, George Burdeau expressed his concern regarding possible abuse of the law of 1936 against the political opposition (Burdeau 1972: 198). The fact that some members of forbidden associations hold electoral mandates has not embarrassed the Conseil d'Etat.[37] Furthermore, the famous *Andrieux* decision[38] showed the laxity of the violence criterion. Bertrand Pauvert demonstrated how political opportunity has often dictated the application of the law (Pauvert 1998: 247 et seq.). It leads to another kind of argument: the banning of the *Front National* would be, according to some authors, quite possible if the French political establishment really wished it.[39] On this view, the integration strategy mapped out above would no longer be a juridical problem but a genuine political choice, exactly like the reverse option of militancy through repressive strategies.

Planning the Political Crisis

Whereas the organization of political competition is oriented towards regulating the system during times of normality, democracy needs, in order to defend itself against its enemies, to develop crisis-overcoming strategies. Planning for an emergency situation, as the ultimate extreme of the danger, belongs (with the substantive limitation of constitutional reform) to the possibilities of controlling, as far as possible, uncertainty in order to make political time more predictable. The possibility of anticipating, which is at the core of the concept of militancy, seems to be an illusion in that particular case: how can democracy remain its own master in circumstances of upheaval? Carl Schmitt argued that the apparent contradiction, entailed in the idea of the possibility to rule exception, is a crucial problem, not only for democratic regimes but also as the exercise of sovereignty as such.[40] How does the French Republic deal with it? Like the organizing of political participation, planning for crisis is an object of a constitutional rule and of legislative and administrative measures.

Apart from Article 36, which outlines the declaration of the state of emergency (and fixes its maximum duration to 12 days), Article 16 of the constitution of 1958 contains the most precise reference to the conditions set to the exercise of power in the case of an acute crisis. It endows the President with an immense authority, often called 'exceptional power'. Article 16 allows him to take 'the measures

36 This is the position of Pierre Espuglas (1998).

37 See the decision about the *Mouvement corse pour l'autodétermination*: CE, 16 October 1992, Battesti.

38 CE, 4 April 1936, Pujo, de Lassus et Réal del Sarte.

39 That is, for example, the opinion of Emmanuel Dockes (2001).

40 See his famous sentence: 'Sovereign is he who decides on the exception', Schmitt 1979: 11–12.

required by the circumstances' according to two conditions: 'where the institutions of the Republic, the independence of the Nation, the integrity of its territory or the fulfilment of its international commitments are under serious and immediate threat' and 'where the proper functioning of the constitutional public authorities is interrupted' (Lavroff 1997: 793–9). The formal conditions are minimal: the Constitutional Council is to be held in a simple exercise in consultation and the President must inform the Nation through an official statement. The jurisdictional control is limited to the administrative acts,[41] and Parliament cannot be declared dissolved during the period of its application.[42] Article 16 has been one of the most criticized aspects of the text of 1958, the more so as Charles de Gaulle gave it a wide interpretation in applying it in the context of the Algerian War (Voisset 1969). Vague conditions, a lack of temporal limitation, unclear antecedents – the reasons to fear an abuse of power by the executive are numerous. Some French scholars have proposed the introduction of a short term to regulate the initial application of Article 16 (Lavroff 1997: 799). François Mitterrand suggested suppressing it. It appeared as a political strategy in the context of cohabitation, in 1993, and constitutional revision did not follow. Although the Conseil d'Etat insisted on the likelihood of a crisis, where the President would require exceptional powers, some experts have insisted that the constitutional framework is useless.[43] Guy Carcassonne argues, for example, that Article 16 is neither necessary (if the President is determined enough to protect the institutions) nor effective (if a broad democratic movement does not support the latter) (Carcassone 1996: 106–107).

Rather than pressing further the level of juridical argumentation, two remarks can be made that bear importantly upon the issue of militant democracy. First, Article 16 is ambiguous in what it anticipates and how it does it. The interruption in the normal functioning of institutions has in fact already begun once the President declares its entry into force. It means that the identification of the crisis precedes the empowerment of the President, and logically, according to the text, that the simple feeling that danger is coming – whatever a 'serious and immediate threat' supposes – is not sufficient to legitimate it. Article 16 is, theoretically, an instrument of action *a posteriori*: it should help to overcome an institutional crisis that already exists. In this sense, it should not be classified among those instruments of militant democracy that try to operate preventively. But this is exactly what was ignored

41 The Conseil d'Etat decided so in the decision 'Rubin de Servens' of 2 March 1962.

42 The role of the Parliament in those circumstances depends on the political praxis. Theoretically, the president of the Assembly can convoke an extraordinary session and pursue its work of control and legislation. But Charles de Gaulle refused to recognize the legitimacy of any legislative outcome when the Parliament assembled during the application of the Article 16 in 1961 (between 13 April and 30 September 1961). See Lavroff 1997: 796 et seq.

43 See *Etudes et documents du Conseil d'Etat*, no. 45. Paris: La Documentation française 1994: 140.

by Charles de Gaulle in 1961: public institutions functioned normally in Paris. The Constitutional Council did not reprehend de Gaulle, and the second condition set down in the text lost all significance. Article 16 became, in a certain way, a real instrument of militancy, organized around opportunity and anticipation, because the idea of an identified institutional crisis lost its determining character.

The second remark follows from this argument: it is the militant and anticipating character of Article 16 that makes it highly political and potentially dangerous or, on the contrary, salutary. François Saint-Bonnet calls it the 'alteration of the evidence' according to the definition of the threat (Saint-Bonnet 1998). This is, according to him, the reason why democratic conviction and political choice may be more important than constitutional reform, 'Those who today take seriously the democratic and liberal form of the exercise of power must fear the absence of profound faith for it, not the existence of such an article' (Saint-Bonnet 1998: 1718).[44] Like the organizing of political competition, political options seem to be the real driving force of militancy in the French case.

Apart from the constitutional empowerment of the President, the French way of coping with crisis has a legislative element: the authority to declare the state of emergency. The principal origins here are prior to the Fifth Republic, again in the context of the Algerian War. The law of April 1955 was voted in the particular context of a colonial war, where political powers refused to surrender all their prerogatives to the army.[45] Once the state of emergency is declared in a certain part of the territory, police powers are extended to the point where some fundamental liberties (circulation, privacy of the domicile, etc.) are called into question (Caille 2007). Although Parliament was first endowed with the authority of declaring a state of emergency, that power was transferred in 1960 to the government. It can declare it for a period of 12 days, 'either in the case of imminent peril resulting from grave damages to the public order, or in the case of events presenting by their nature and their gravity, the character of public calamity'. The law here is the ultimate instrument of the protection of public order; the executive and its administrative branch become the principal actors, not a political police, but at least a police with a political aim: the preservation of existing institutions. The National Assembly is charged with deciding, after 12 days, if the state of emergency ought to be pursued.

A state of emergency was declared at the very beginning of the Fifth Republic, after the crisis of May 1958, which reinstated Charles de Gaulle as the Head of the State. It has since been used between spring 1961 (by the military putsch in Algiers) and spring 1963 – two years where the prorogation had been made possible by the application of Article 16. The combination of the legislative emergency power and its constitutional provision made possible the extraordinary empowerment of

44 My translation from: 'ceux qui tiennent fermement aujourd'hui à la forme démocratique et libérale de l'exercice du pouvoir doivent craindre l'absence de foi profonde pour elle, non l'existence d'un tel article'.

45 The state of siege has been ruled in France since 1849.

the executive. The Conseil d'Etat reacted too late to limit it effectively.[46] A state of emergency was also declared in 1985, in relation to separatist disorders in New Caledonia, and at the end of 2005, during the riots in the French '*banlieues*'. Once again, controversy around the law of 1955 surfaced. The public law expert Frédéric Rolin sued the government for using an inappropriate – because exaggerated – method. The Conseil d'Etat decided that the circumstances justified the declaration of a state of emergency, but it then opened another procedure, enacted by a group of 74 other experts, arguing that the evolution of the circumstances would justify to putting an end to the state of emergency. The Conseil d'Etat anticipated the possibility of new disorders at New Year's Eve and authorized indirectly the prorogation until January. To avoid another juridical difficulty, the government then decided to bring it to a close on 4 January 2005. The declaration of a state of emergency seems to be non-anticipatory, because it is based on accomplished facts that are supposed to reveal the danger. But the law of 1955 has not only been a tool of simple police. Its political dimension was underlined in the '*exposé des motifs*'. The concept of '*hors-la-loi*', the roots of which can be found in the revolutionary times, is invoked to identify those who put themselves outside the framework of the Republican law. Sylvie Thénault argues that this implies respect to legality as well as political loyalty (Thenault 2007). We find here a reference to a democratic normativity: for some jurists, it is the way to arbitrariness, for others the way to a real militant democracy. To examine if the riots of the '*banlieues*' in 2005 constituted a real danger for French democracy would go beyond the scope of this study.

In general, it is possible to conclude that the Fifth Republic is, at least theoretically, well armed to confront an eventual emergency situation.

Structuring Deliberation

A third group of instruments can be identified as further tools available to modern democracy in France to defend itself against its enemies. Their specific aim is to structure deliberation by limiting the liberty of expression and, in a more indirect way because based on long-term considerations, by promoting civic education.

The limitation of the liberty of expression firstly has a very particular field of application, which concerns the state employees. Some comparative analyses on this subject, the motivation for which has been to bring in the German debate about '*Berufsverbote*', have dealt with the French case.[47] It is characterized by a general liberality that legally authorizes civil servants to have the same political engagements as other citizens. The employee status[48] guarantees that no consideration of religion or political conviction should appear in the personal files

46 CE, 22 June 1969, ministère de l'Intérieur contre les Editions parisiennes associées et le sieur Devay.

47 See Grewe-Leymarie and Umbach 1981; Hailbronner 1980.

48 The '*Statut de la fonction publique*' was created in 1946 and renewed in 1983.

and influence the employment in the public administration. The liberality of the French system must nevertheless be qualified. The jurisprudence of the Conseil d'Etat has been ambivalent. On the one hand, it decided in numerous cases that being a member of the Communist Party, for example, was not a legitimate reason to exclude any applicant from a public administrative office.[49] But on the other hand, it has not always behaved as such on the issue of personal files (Ayoub 1994: 236). Moreover, two principles can limit the liberty of expression in the public administration: the rule of neutrality, which compels the civil servants to consider firstly the general interest (positive duty); and the so-called '*obligation de reserve*', which entails a certain self-restraint in expressing opinions (negative duty) and is especially crucial in the highest positions of the state. Although loyalty to the Republic is not a restrictive condition in the French administration, the praxis seems to reveal more militancy in that matter than does the law.

But the most significant limitation of liberty of expression focuses, in France, more on what is said than on who says it. It was introduced by a law in 1972 ('Pleven Law') and concerns the inciting of race hatred; the law of 1881 on the liberty of the press was completed with Article 24 – renewed in 1990 ('Gayssot Law') to punish Holocaust denial. The limiting of liberty of expression was not, as such, a new element of the political and juridical culture of France. The Declaration of the Rights of Man refers to the maintaining of public order (Article 10), as a condition of liberty of expression and the law is empowered to define a repressive framework in which its abuses are punished (Article 11). Despite of this, the laws of 1972 and 1990 have been criticized because they suppose a causal relation between written or spoken opinions and concrete acts of race hatred (through the notion of incitation) (Troper 1999: 1254). Here we find, once again, the problematic question of anticipation that makes militancy possible because it tries to confront the danger presented as early as possible, but which at the same time makes it dangerous for the preservation of liberties and fundamental rights. For Michel Troper, this argument – that the 'presumptions' of the legislator are not necessarily verified – is inane (Troper 1999: 1254): Uncertain presumptions characterize every general rule. The specificity of the Holocaust may be controversial, but the specificity of its negation lies, according to Troper, in its rooting in anti-democratic movements and consequently justifies a defensive attitude on the part of the legislator and the simple implementation by the judge, with no consideration to the historical validity of the arguments. Anti-racist strategies in France have been also criticized by well-known academics (Taguieff 1995). The laws of 1972 and 1990 marked, in any case, legislatively decisive steps in the direction of abandoning of the John Stuart Mill's ideal of deliberation (Mill 1859 [1998]), in which the free competition of opinions leads to truth through the search for the best solution.

It should be noted, finally, that the structuring of deliberation has been, in the Republican political culture in France, associated with an educational ideal. The Republic arrived at a confidence in the expression of the universal suffrage only on

49 See the famous *Barel* case: CE, 28 May 1954, Barel.

the condition that citizens would be able to decide reasonably, that is to say, with an adequate educational background. The Third Republic gambled on the school ('laic, free and obligatory') to prevail over its clerical enemies (Ozouf 1963). Although civic education is today somewhat outdated in French schools and has not the dimension of *Politische Bildung* ('political education') as in Germany, the Fifth Republic still places faith in education to confront, for example, Islamic fundamentalism.

Let us sum up the conclusions from this listing of French instruments available to protect democracy. The constitutional determination of defence strategies appears, in general, insufficient, ambiguous or amendable. The '*légicentrisme*' evoked above has led to a focus on criminal and administrative law. The superior position of the legislator may arouse doubts concerning the existence of any serious militancy or, at least, militant intention. How can, indeed, the legislator maintain control of a process whose long-term aim is to bind the sovereignty of the people in order to prevent any anti-democratic eruption? An answer might be: either the former should surrender some authority or the latter is not to be taken seriously. Isabelle Canu has defended a similar position, but she based it on a quite different argumentation, rooted in the comparison with the German case. She argues that the prevalence of criminal and administrative law in the available protection strategies undermines every anticipatory dimension – the French democracy cannot, on this view, be called 'militant' (Canu 1997: 163). Whereas constitutional law could provide real *a priori* strategies, the very basic principle of criminal law is to punish accomplished offences. She insists, then, on the classical instruments of French legislation to punish damage to the integrity of the state and the nation. In my opinion, this argument overly simplifies the complex interplay, as revealed through the analysis of French instruments, between anticipation and punishment.

In order to understand fully the status of militancy in the French context, it is necessary to turn, finally, to new perspectives and challenges, especially those which current research needs to deal with.

Outlooks

The concept of militant democracy was born at a time of fascist threat that was acute in France, as in the rest of Europe. The Second World War discredited the fascist option for a long time, and subsequently the engagement of the French Communist Party in the fight against it brought it to the top positions of the state. Nevertheless, as discussed above, neither the dangers nor the arsenal to confront them disappeared in the context of the Fifth Republic. The question which follows is, then: how relevant is the concept of militancy to the French Republic today? To what extent should it be adapted? After questioning the idea of a new democratic dilemma, I will try to show, through the French case, how the notion of discourse can help to cut the Gordian knot.

A New Democratic Dilemma?

France today must cope, as well as many other Western democracies, with Islamic terrorism. The attacks on the World Trade Center of 11 September 2001 have inaugurated a time of permanent suspicion and obsession in matters, such as public security, freedom of movement and the exchange of secret information. France has not been, since 9/11, the direct target of a substantial attack, but was already familiar with the phenomena of violent terrorism. In the 1980s, the Libyan and Lebanese networks piloted many actions on French territory and in the 1990s, two large attacks were perpetrated on the Parisian metro and claimed by Algerian Islamic movements. This experience, combined with decades of fighting with nationalist terrorism in Corsica, led to the elaboration of extensive anti-terrorist legislation, which required only few adaptations after 9/11.[50]

The extent to which the Islamic terrorist threat is relevant to a study about militant democracy is controversial. According to Capoccia, non-violent extremism – and ways to deal with it – deserves a specific attention (Capoccia 2005: 232 et seq.). The challenge of national and international terrorism poses, according to him, specific problems related to the systematic use of political violence and which are, in any case, already well known. For Eckhard Jesse and other German upholders of the '*Extremismusforschung*', Islamic terrorism is, on the contrary, a threat on liberal democracy, along the same lines as non-violent extremism (Backes and Jesse 2006). It would oppose toleration and pluralism with a view of the political characterized by a totalitarian ideal of homogeneity. All extremist movements have in common the denial of democratic principles, such as freedom of speech and opinion, deliberation, procedural guarantees and so on. In my opinion, it is possible to retain a comprehensive view of what extremism is,[51] without giving up the ambition of identifying defence strategies that are appropriate to different kind of dangers. András Sajá, for example, adopts this research option by analysing different constitutional mechanisms for the state's self-defence, pointing out the strategic continuities between 'accommodation', 'militant democracy' and 'counter-terror-state' (Sajó 2006).[52] Although in the latter, preventive solutions are narrowly tailored so as to be applicable to terrorism only, militant democracy has a larger field of application.

If we adopt this theoretical option, it is legitimate to question the nature and evolution of French militancy in the light of its recent anti-terrorist policies. Alexis Debat describes a 'complex combination of centralization and flexibility, proactive and reactive policing, and the aggressive targeting of logistical networks' (Debat 2005/2006: 55). The second dimension is precisely the one I would like to

50 For an overview, see Cantegreil 2005: 12–22.

51 And avoiding thus the problematic confusion between the categories of Islamism and totalitarianism. See, for example, Del Valle 2002.

52 About the link between anti-terrorist law and militant democracy, see also Roach 2004.

emphasize: the mix of anticipatory and reactive tendencies in defensive strategies in France. Anti-terrorist policy in France is, first of all, based on a particular system of intelligence (Brodeur and Dupeyron 2002). One of its most important props is the *Direction générale des renseignements généraux*, whose responsibility has been, since its creation in 1893, the collection of information to prevent subversion. The lack of transparency in its works, the bureaucratic turf wars with other services, such as the *Direction de la Surveillance du territoire,* were detrimental to its reputation as 'political police' (Rougelet 1997). But more interesting for our purposes is the fact that their objects of inquiries are broadly defined: from the skinhead scene to the mosques in the '*banlieues*', anything that could represent a security danger according to the executive is a potential surveillance target. The criterion of violence is not, for such an institution, the decisive point that legitimates an intervention by the state; it is entrusted to act in advance, before violence even takes place. The increasing coordination with other intelligence services[53] has moreover blurred the line between 'high policing' (political policing) and 'low policing' (ordinary policing), on the one hand, and between intelligence and judicial activities, on the other. This confusion may be seen as a danger for democracy – or as the only solution through which to defend it, particularly by concentrating forces and by introducing preventive mechanisms. Preventive mechanisms, in the sense that the legislative power intends to prevent things before they happen, were also introduced quite early on in the French anti-terrorist legal regime.[54] The law of 9 September 1986 instituted the centralized prosecution of terrorist acts. In 1996, the legislator then decided to punish not only acts but also the intention to commit them. A new punishment was created, derogating to the common penal practice that is meant by 'criminal association in relation to a terrorist venture'. In the most recent version of the Penal Code, crimes are punished more harshly if they are committed with a terrorist intention or in relation to a terrorist organization. As Debat notes, it 'puts forward the belief that anything that happens before a terrorist act is already terrorism' (Debat 2005/2006: 60). This strategy of defence consists in facilitating the earliest possible treatment of the threat. After 9/11, while other countries discovered the principle of anticipation in matters of criminal law, the French legislators only needed to amend these mechanisms, in order to allow even wider investigations. What should be remarked upon here is the analogy between these preventive mechanisms and the anticipatory orientation of the concept of 'militant democracy'. In both cases, not only acts are supposed to be dangerous for the democracy, but so are preliminary indications of subversion or opposition

53 For example, in working units like the UCLAT (Unit for the Coordination of Anti-Terrorism) or the *Division Nationale Anti-Terroriste* (DNAT). The new President Nicolas Sarkozy plans to assemble all the services of the Ministry of Defence and Home Ministry in a big unique national security agency.

54 See Cantegreil 2005: 44–62; Cartier 1995; La documentation française, La France face au terrorisme. Livre Blanc du Gouvernement sur la sécurité intérieure face au terrorisme, 2006; Guimelanes and Tuaillon 2006; Loyer 2006; Mayaud 1997.

– violent or not. Opinions or simple support for offences can be incriminated. A danger is discovered as a potential threat before it even becomes concrete. The differentiation invoked above between constitutional preventive measures and administrative or penal measures, supposed to be more reactive, therefore collapses in the theory of militant democracy. If anticipation is an important element of a militant defensive strategy, and if anticipation can also take place in the regime of criminal law, militancy is not the exclusive property of democracies whose constitutions explicitly identify the defence of the regime as a priority. France may be an exemplary case in this.

Let us note, nevertheless, that reasserting criminal law as an instrument of militant democracy does not, as such, help to resolve the contradictions implicit in the concept. An anticipatory criminal law could become anti-democratic, and the defence of democracy against terrorists or other extremists could be, in that way, undermined by the choice of its own instruments. The debate about a possible '*Feindstrafrecht*' in Germany has dealt with this issue.[55] Günther Jakobs argues that a certain type of persons, the 'enemies' opposed to citizens deserve, because of their enduring hostility to juridical norms, a special legal regime. The latter is characterized by pushing forward the moment of punishment – the consequence of the anticipatory strategy evoked above – and consequently, the shift of the focus from offence to offender. This anticipation does not prompt any reduction of the penalty – in France, rather the contrary is the case – and may be associated with the shrinking of procedural guarantees. With this kind of 'enemy', criminal law appears to be dangerous in a normative sense because it is, indeed, non-democratic. Aside from the interpretation of Jakobs' own position, it can be argued here that the French solution to anti-terrorist legislation merely reproduces the democratic dilemma described in our introduction. The fight against enemies of democracy can lapse into an anti-democratic act. In terms of security policy, this dilemma is more often formulated as follows. Liberty is impossible without a minimal guarantee of security, but the struggle to achieve the latter can possibly lead to restrictions of liberty. How many of such restrictions can be tolerated in the framework of the democratic law and in which name exactly? It is here, in comparison with interwar Europe when confronted with the fascist threat, that the current dilemma of Western democracies reproduces questions posed by Karl Loewenstein.

Militancy and Democratic Identity

At the end of this analysis of the French case, it seems that the issue of militancy cannot be summed up in the terms of a simple alternative. The decision for or against a legal (and even constitutional) self-defence strategy that would end the apparently unanswerable question of liberty for the enemies of liberty. This question is, as in the French case, rearticulated in the current debate about security and terrorism.

55 See, for an embracing view of that debate, Saliger 2006. We did not find any theoretical reflection on that dimension about this issue in the French criminal law theory.

In my opinion, the problem of an indefinite reproduction of the same dilemma can be partly solved by enriching the concept of militancy with a dimension that goes beyond the strict legal aspect of it: the dimension of discourse. Without developing here the theoretical implications of the use of by now overcrowded category,[56] let us sum up the point at stake: The identification of the enemy and the discourse on it plays a decisive role in the self-defence strategy of democracy. Additionally, there is a link between militancy and self-identification because the stigmatization of the 'other' entails directly – by opposition – a definition of the 'self'. The democratic dilemma, mentioned above, poses an inextricable theoretical and practical problem only if the presence of enmity, in the sense of an existential threat, is considered an anomaly in a democratic system. The importance of this presence can be marginalized, for example, in a naïve liberal conception of pacification through deliberation: democracy is not in this case militant. Alternatively, this presence can be conceived as an inevitable problem – militancy is, as such, a concession that democracy makes to authoritarianism, abandoning its fundamental nature, positively in order to preserve itself or negatively in order to perpetuate the power of a pseudo-democratic elite. Militancy is, in this last case, a deception to justify security measures.[57] But an exit from this state of affairs is possible by formulating the following hypothesis: the existence of enmity and, more precisely, its regulation through a discourse on the threat, is not incongruent with, but on the contrary constitutive of democratic identity. Militancy, enlarged via a discursive element[58] is, from this point of view, a process through which a democratic regime defines itself in the very act of dealing with existential hostility. The defining of limits between acceptable and unacceptable differences sustains the construction of a collection of values and principles that form democratic identity. The concept of identity should not suggest an essentialist approach; procedural rules play a role here exactly like other norms, and that identity is everything but fixed. The logical connection between militancy and democratic norms may not only be the one described at the beginning of the chapter (whereby militancy supposes a norm to be protected), but may imply a reciprocal interaction, a discursive self-defence strategy produces, conversely, the construction of democratic norms. Moreover, the problem relating to a comprehensive definition of extremism is at the same time solved in this theoretical framework. The discursive reaction to a potential (and constructed) threat is the decisive element, not the nature of the threat and its manifestations in political reality.

56 For an overview of its utilization in social sciences, see Keller 2007.

57 The critical theories of exception developed after 9/11, for example, by Giorgio Agamben, or the ones inherited from the Frankfurt School may belong to that theoretical stream.

58 The notion of 'discursive elements' may express the fact that only parts of a more general discourse can be considered here. There is no ambition to catch hold of a discourse that would be 'saturated'.

Let us return specifically to the French case. How does it confirm the hypothesis formulated above of a link between militancy and democratic identity? A close analysis of parliamentary discourse reveals the pertinence of the imagined connection.[59] The identification of the enemy of democracy occurs mostly indirectly in French political discourse, in comparison to the German case.[60] This discursive self-control can be explained by the tradition of integration, as identified earlier as a fundamental background to the republican tradition. The French Republic does not stigmatize the enemy before it gives up any hope of assimilating it. Beyond this, the enemies of the democracy are much present in parliamentary discourse: they are designated as existential threats for the Republic. Some argumentative strategies testify to this: the use of the lexical field of war and aggressive rhetorical strategies; the metaphor of disease; the idea that past experiences should help anticipate future dangers;[61] etc. Political circumstances determine who is seen as an enemy: the separatist terrorist from Corsica or the Islamist *imam*. But what is important for us is the fact that the discourse on the enemy reveals more about the republican ideal and its various expressions than about extremism itself. A certain basic confidence in the future of the regime is notable. Unlike the German discourse, which is preoccupied with the possibility of a regime breakdown, French representatives do not explicitly envisage the end of the Fifth Republic. The threat is more often social than institutional. The cohesion of the system which is supposed to be endangered, goes far beyond its institutional dimension. The ideal of unity is often foregrounded. The constitutional principle of the 'indivisibility of the Republic' is a central element in the French self-defensive discourse and, once again, entails more than the centralist reallocation of administrative power. Violence still represents the decisive criteria, insofar as the enemies are denounced more vigorously in these parliamentary debates following attacks. But anticipation strategies, identified as characteristic of militancy, are also observable. In general, dealing with the enemy constitutes a good occasion for the representatives, to determine the meaning of concepts such as justice, liberty, normality and exception. Procedures are also at stake in such a discourse. Members of Parliament question their relations to the executive, concerning, for example, their ability to make quick decisions or the proper way of coping with consensus and dissensus when the existence of the Republic is called into question. French democratic discourse on the enemy is also characterized by the universalistic ambition of the French republican model, inherited from the Revolution. It is argued, in particular, that the existence of violent anti-democratic movements or the voting of strict security measures should not damage the image of France as the motherland of human rights.

59 I examined the plenary debates of the Assemblée nationale related to extremism, terrorism and security from the 1970s to the very recent anti-terrorist legislations.

60 For example, through the appellation of '*Verfassungsfeinde*'.

61 Murray Edelman called this phenomenon the 'narrative plot' implied by the naming of the enemy. See Edelman 1988: 75.

Democratic discourse on the enemies of democracy should be studied in all its dimensions – it may be possible to identify a juridical discourse. The point here is that militancy includes such dimensions that transcend the detailing of substantive limitations in the constitution; a certain way of dealing with threat implies a specific relation to principles, history and political culture. This relation is obviously two-way: political culture interacts with defensive strategies. Evoking human rights calls to mind the revolutionary heritage described at the beginning of the chapter, and thus completes the circle.

Conclusion

The examination of the strategies of self-defence of modern French democracy should be, to conclude, relocated in a more general theoretical and methodological framework.

Apart from ignorance of the problem, which is still widespread in the literature, the study of militant democracy can proceed from three different analytic designs. The first one can be called 'binary' because it poses a simple dichotomy between the existence and the non-existence of militancy. A democracy can either choose to defend itself or not to; there is no intermediate solution. This conception is one that is inherited from earlier theorizations of the concept by Karl Loewenstein and Karl Mannheim, as the seriousness of threat seemed to forbid any hesitation in the face of a choice between suicide and self-defence. This approach is also well established in German juridical literature, which has tried to find in the *Grundgesetz* ('Fundamental Law') or in constitutional jurisprudence clear grounds for the possibility of binding the sovereignty in order to guarantee the perpetuation of democracy. The implementation of this binary 'test of militancy' can only be erected through the listing of certain criteria, principles or concrete instruments at the level of the legal system. This approach is, in my opinion, too narrow to adequately capture the complexity of the French case. As concluded above, some juridical and political traditions bear witness to a republican integration ideal opposed to the logic of exclusion sometimes required by militancy. '*Légicentrisme*' seems incompatible with the prerequisite of fixing control upon the sovereign. But on the other hand, some long term tendencies reveal the steady affirmation of the rule of law and the protection of fundamental rights, which entails some concession to the original Rousseauist conception of sovereignty. If we consider the instruments of constitutional and criminal law, it is also impossible to find a univocal 'yes or no' answer to the militancy dual formula.

A second approach holds out the possibility of avoiding this difficulty: it consists in considering intermediate solutions and replaces the binary logic through a linear one. This would establish a gradual scale between 'less' and 'more' militant democracies. Otto Pfersmann takes up this solution:

> Militant democracy – as a legal structure – is on a scale of degree with other forms of democracy, in other words, that democracies are always more or less militant. At the same time, making democracy more militant increasingly modifies the structure from which it starts, so that a continuous extension of the domain of protection may amount to a decrease of the liberal heritage of constitutional democracy.[62]

The French Republic represents, in this approach, a half-way case between liberal '*laissez-faire*' and militant democracy in the German mode. This research design also elevates some criteria to the level of test variables and facilitates, once they are strictly clarified, large-scale international or historical comparisons. Apart from the selection of criteria here, these procedures raise two main difficulties. First, it supposes that the determination of positions on the scale is always possible because some factors weigh more than others. But how is that weight to be determined? Is the theoretical possibility of banning a party more militant than the selective prohibition of a public demonstration? The efficacy of instruments in a crisis period can constitute a good anchor for the researcher. But this would mean that only *a posteriori* analyses are possible. It would allow nothing but an historical approach and would therefore detract from the very possibility of drawing general conclusions on militancy. Second, the linear approach of Pfersmann refers explicitly to legal structure. The French case showed, however, that the legal regime is only one aspect of militancy, if we choose to take political culture and the dimension of discourse into account.

To establish the link between democratic militancy and democratic identity, it is, in my opinion, necessary to take a third way, turning toward a multidimensional approach to militancy. The integration of the dimension of discourse enables the articulation of the relation between norms, political culture and the identification of the 'enemies' of democracy. The latter is no longer considered an anomaly of the democratic system but, rather, the condition of its self-identification. Consequently, this approach helps to find a solution, which holds, at least temporarily, to the democratic dilemma that oppose rights and duties, tolerance and efficacy, liberty and security. One concept is no longer thinkable without the other. Moreover, the integration of the dimension of discourse allows us to consider the new challenges that the French Republic confronts, like other democracies, without supposing that all threats are equally dangerous or equivalent in nature. An appropriate approach to militancy should not make the error of confusing real threats and those which democratic public institutions argue over. Reality and discourse are sometimes disconnected. This is what a narrow legal approach may disregard.

The multidimensional approach may make comparisons more difficult. But it appears to be the most fruitful in a country report on France and can be seen as the first step towards wider investigations.

---

62 See Pfersmann 2004: 53.

References

Arné, Serge (1993) 'Les normes constitutionnelles', *Revue du droit public* 1993(2): 459–512.

Association Juridique Internationale (1938) *Régression des principes de liberté dans les réformes constitutionnelles de certains Etats démocratiques. Conférence réunie à la Sorbonne, 10–11 juillet 1937.* Paris: Rivière.

Avril, Pierre (1992) 'L'article 4: explication d'un paradoxe', in Didier Maus, Louis Favoreu and Jean-Luc Parodi (eds) *L'écriture de la constitution de 1958.* Paris: Economica.

Ayoub, Eliane (1994) *La fonction publique en vingt principles.* Paris: Frison-Roche.

Backes, Uwe (1998) 'Extrême, Extrémité, Extrémisme. Une esquisse de l'histoire de ces mots dans la langue politique française' *Mots* 55: 142–52.

Backes, Uwe and Jesse, Eckhard (eds) (2006) *Gefährdungen der Freiheit. Extremistische Ideologien im Vergleich.* Göttingen: Vandenhoeck und Ruprecht.

Barthélèmy, Joseph and Duez, Paul (1930 [1985]) *Traité de droit constitutionnel.* Paris: Economica.

Bartosek, Karel, Courtois, Stéphane, Werth, Nicolas, et al. (eds) (1998) *Le Livre noir du communisme: crimes, terreur, repression.* Paris: Robert Laffont.

Baudouin, Jean (2000) 'Dynamique démocratique et intégration républicaine', in Marc Sadoun (ed.) *La démocratie en France, vol. 1.* Paris: Gallimard, 332–412.

Beaud, Olivier (1994) *La puissance de l'Etat.* Paris: Presses Universitaires de France.

Berstein, Serge (1975) *Le 6 février 1934.* Paris: Julliard.

Boventer, Gregor Paul (1984) *Grenzen politischer Freiheit im demokratischen Staat. Das Konzept der streitbaren Demokratie in einem internationalen Vergleich.* Berlin: Duncker and Humblot.

Brodeur, Jean-Paul and Dupeyron, Nicolas (2002) 'Democracy and Secrecy: The French Intelligence Community', in Jean-Paul Brodeur, Peter Gill and Dennis Töllborg (eds) *Democracy, Law and Security. Internal Security Services in Contemporary Europe.* Burlington: Ashgate, 9–29.

Burdeau, George (1930) *Essai d'une théorie de la révision des lois constitutionnelles en droit positif français.* Mâcon: Buguet-Comptour.

Burdeau, George (1972) *Libertés publiques.* Paris: LGDJ.

Caille, Pascal (2007) 'L'Etat d'urgence. La loi du 3 avril 1955 entre maturation et dénaturation', *Revue du droit public* 123(2): 323–53.

Camby, Jean-Pierre (2003) 'Supra-constitutionalité: la fin d'un mythe', *Revue du droit public* 119(3): 671–88.

Cantegreil, Julien (2005) *Terrorisme et libertés. La voie française après le 11 septembre.* Suresnes: En temps réel.

Canu, Isabelle (1997) *Der Schutz der Demokratie in Deutschland und Frankreich.* Opladen: Leske and Budrich.

Capoccia, Giovanni (2005) *Defending Democracy. Reactions to Extremism in Interwar Europe.* Baltimore: The John Hopkins University Press.

Carcassonne, Guy (1996) *La constitution.* Paris: Seuil.

Carré de Malberg, Raymond (1922 [1962]) *Contribution à la théorie générale de l'etat, vol. 2.* Paris: CNRS.

Cartier, Marie-Elisabeth (1995) 'Le terrorisme dans le nouveau code pénal francais', *Revue des sciences criminelles* (2): 225–46.

Chavardes, Maurice (1966) *Le 6 février 1934: la République en danger.* Paris: Calmann-Lévy.

Comité national charge de la publication des travaux préparatoires des institutions de la Vème Republique (ed.) (1988) *Documents pour servir à l'histoire de l'élaboration de la constitution du 4 octobre 1958. 2, Le Comité consultatif constitutionnel: de l'avant-projet du 29 juillet 1958 au projet du 21 août 1958.* Paris: La documentation française.

Condorcet, Jean-Antoine Nicolas de Caritat, Marquis de (1847) 'Idées sur le despotisme, à l'usage de ceux qui prononcent ce mot sans l'entendre', in *Œuvres. vol. 9.* Paris: Firmin Didot Frères.

Debat, Alexis (2005/2006) 'Terror and the Fifth Republic', *The National Interest*, 51–5.

Del Valle, Alexandre (2002) *Le totalitarisme islamique: à l'assaut des démocraties.* Paris: Edition des Syrtes.

Dockes, Emmanuel (2001) 'Le droit et la dissolution des parties d'extrême-droite', in Bruno Villalba and Xavier Vandendriesche (eds) *Le Front National et le droit.* Villeneuve d'Asq: Presses universitaires du Septentrion, 143–52.

La documentation française (2006) *La France face au terrorisme. Livre Blanc du Gouvernement sur la sécurité intérieure face au terrorisme.* Paris: La documentation française.

Duguit, Léon (1924) *Traité de droit constitutionnel,* vol. 4. Paris: Edition de Boccard.

Edelman, Murray (1988) *Constructing the Political Spectacle.* Chicago: University of Chicago Press.

Espuglas, Pierre (1998) 'L'interdiction des partis politiques', *Revue française de droit constitutionnel* (36): 675–709.

Fisichella, Domenico (1984) 'The "double-ballot" electoral system as a weapon against anti-system parties', in Arend Lijpahrt and Bernard Grofman (eds) *Choosing an Electoral System: Issues and Alternatives.* New York: Praeger, 181–9.

Gauchet, Marcel (1992) 'La droite et la gauche', in Pierre Nora (ed.) *Les lieux de mémoire, vol. III – Les 'France'.* Paris: Gallimard, 395–497.

Grewe, Constance (1999) 'Das Verständnis des Rechtsstaates in Frankreich und in Deutschland', in Joseph Jurt, Gert Krumreich and Thomas Würtenberger (eds) *Wandel von Recht und Rechtsbewußtsein in Frankreich und Deutschland.* Berlin: Berlin Verlag, 157–67.

Grewe-Leymarie, Constance and Umbach, Dieter (1981) 'Der Zugang zum und die Entlassung aus dem Öffentlichen Dienst in Frankreich', in Ernst Wolfgang Böckenförde and Christian Tomuschat (eds) *Extremisten im öffentlichen Dienst.* Baden-Baden: Nomos, 117–91.

Guarrigues, Jean (1992) *Le boulangisme.* Paris: Presses Universitaires de France.

Guimelanes, Nicole and Tuaillon, Christophe (2006) *Droit pénal de la sécurité et de la defense.* Paris: L'Harmattan.

Haarscher, Guy (2007) *Liberté d'expression, blasphème, racisme: essai d'analyse philosophique et comparée.* Working papers du Centre Perelman de philosophie du droit, no. 2007/1 (available on http://www.philodroit.be).

Hailbronner, Kay (1980) 'Treuepflicht und die Grenzen politischer Betätigung im öffentlichen dienst Frankreichs', in Karl Doehring (ed.) *Verfassungstreue im öffentlichen Dienst europäischer Staaten.* Berlin: Duncker and Humblot, 93–158.

Jesse, Eckhard (2003) 'Demokratieschutz', in Eckhard Jesse and Roland Sturm (eds) *Demokratien des 21. Jahrhundert im Vergleich.* Opladen: Leske and Budrich, 449–74.

Jouanjan, Olivier (1996) 'La forme républicaine de gouvernement, norme supra-constitutionnelle?', in Bertrand Mathieu and Michel Verpeux (eds) *La République en droit français.* Paris: Economica, 267–87.

Keller, Reiner (2007) *Diskursforschung. Eine Einführung für Sozialwissenschaftler.* Wiesbaden: VS Verlag.

Lavroff, Dmitri Georges (1997) *Le droit constitutionnel de la Vème République.* Paris: Dalloz.

Lewis-Beck, Michael and Wittrock, Jill (2007) 'Experimenting with French Election Rules. Initial Results', *French Politics* (5): 106–17.

Loewenstein, Karl (1937a) 'Militant Democracy and Fundamental Rights I', *American Political Science Review* 31(3): 417–32.

Loewenstein, Karl (1937b) 'Militant Democracy and Fundamental Rights II', *American Political Science Review* 31(4): 638–58.

Loyer, Maxence (2006) 'La loi Sarkozy de lutte contre le terrorisme', *Regards sur l'actualité*, 321(5): 77–82.

Mannheim, Karl (1943) *Diagnoses of Our Time: Wartime Essays of a Sociologist.* London: K. Paul, Trench, Trubner and Co.

Marchais, Georges (1973) *Le défi démocratique.* Paris: Grasset.

Martin, Jean-Clément (2002) 'La Révolution française: aa généalogie de l'ennemi', *Raisons politiques* 2002(5): 69–79.

Mayaud, Yves (1997) *Le terrorisme.* Paris: Dalloz.

M'Bongo, Pascal (1998) 'Actualité et renouveau de la loi du 10 janvier 1936 sur les groupes de combat et les milices privées', *Revue du droit public*, (3): 715–44.

Mill, John Stuart (1859 [1998]) *On Liberty and Other Essays.* Oxford: Oxford University Press.

Minkenberg, Michael (1998) 'Context and Consequence: The Impact of the New Radical Right on the Political Process in France and Germany', *German Politics and Society* 16(3): 1–23.

Minkenberg, Michael (2006) 'Repression and Reaction: Militant Democracy and the Radical Right in Germany and France', *Patterns of Prejudice* (40): 25–44.

Noyer, Alain (1966) *La sûreté de l'etat: 1789–1959*. Paris: LGDJ.

Ozouf, Mona (1963) *L'école, l'église et la république. 1871–1914*. Paris: Colin.

Pauvert, Bertrand (1998) 'Considérations juridiques sur un impératif moral: réflexion sur les possibilités d'interdiction du Front National', *Le Banquet* (12): 247–62.

Pellissier, Pierre (2000) *6 février 1934: la République en flames*. Paris: Perrin.

Perrineau, Pascal and Mayer, Nona (eds) (1996) *Le Front National à découvert*. Paris: Presses de Sciences-po.

Pfersmann, Otto (2004) 'Shaping Militant Democracy', in András Sajó, (ed.) *Militant Democracy*. Utrecht: Eleven International Publishing, 47–68.

Rials, Stéphane (1984) 'Les incertitudes de la notion de constitution', *Revue du droit public*, 587–606.

Rials, Stéphane (1986) 'Supra-constitutionnalité et systématicité du droit', *Archives de philosophie du droit*, 57–76.

Roach, Kent (2004) 'Anti-terrorism and Militant Democracy: Some Western and Eastern Responses', in András Sajó (ed.) *Militant Democracy*. Utrecht: Eleven International Publishing, 170–207.

Rougelet, Patrick (1997) *RG: la machine à scandale*. Paris: Albin Michel.

Rousseau, Jean-Jacques (1762 [1997]) *The Social Contract and Other Later Political Writings*. Cambridge: Cambridge University Press.

Saint-Bonnet, François (1998) 'Réflexions sur l'article 16 et l'état d'exception', *Revue du droit public* (5–6): 1699–718.

Sajó, András (2006) 'From Militant Democracy to the Preventive State?', *Cardozo Law Review* 27, 2255–94.

Saliger, Frank (2006) 'Feindstrafrecht: Kritisches oder totalitäres Strafrechtskonzept?', *Juristenzeitung* (15–16): 756–62.

Schmitt, Carl (1928) *Verfassungslehre*. München and Leipzig: Duncker and Humblot.

Schmitt, Carl (1979) *Politische Theologie. Vier Kapitel zur Lehre von der Souveränität*. Berlin: Duncker and Humblot.

Simonin, Anne (2007) 'Etre non-citoyen sous la Révolution française. Comment un sujet de droit perd ses droits', in Raymonde Monnier (ed.) *Citoyens et citoyenneté sous la Révolution française Actes du colloque international de Vizille, 24–25 septembre 2004*. Paris: Société des études robespierristes, 289–304.

Steuckardt, Agnès (2002) 'Les ennemis selon L'Ami du peuple ou la catégorisation identitaire par contraste', *Mots* 69, 7–22.

Taguieff, Pierre-André (1995) *Les fins de l'antiracisme*. Paris: Michalon.

Thénault, Sylvie (2007) 'L'Etat d'urgence (1955–2005): De l'Algérie coloniale à la France contemporaine: destin d'une loi', *Le Mouvement social* (218): 63–78.

Troper, Michel (1999) 'La loi Gayssot et la constitution', *Annales* (6): 1239–55.

Voisset, Michèle (1969) *L'article 16 de la Constitution du 4 octobre 1958*. Paris: LGDJ.

Wittekindt, Christoph (2000) *Materiell-rechtliche Schranken von Verfassungsänderungen im deutschen und französischen Verfassungsrecht: Eine verfassungsvergleichende Untersuchung*. Frankfurt a.M.: Peter Lang.

Chapter 6
Germany

Markus Thiel

Introduction

The principle of a 'militant democracy' is a fundamental element of German Constitutional Law. At least in the contentious jurisdiction of the *Bundesverfassungsgericht* (the Federal Constitutional Court) militancy is acknowledged as a significant feature of the German Constitution, the *Grundgesetz* (Basic Law) and of the political system. Conscious of the Weimar Republic's failure to protect itself from destruction and thus against the backdrop of the 'bitter experience of the doomed Weimar Republic' (Klamt 2007: 138), the creators of the Basic Law installed, according to the prevailing opinion among constitutional law and political sciences scholars, the new democracy as a system 'bound to values' (*wertgebunden*, Tillmanns 2003); 'vigilant' (*wachsam*, Scheuner 1951: 140); 'ready to defend itself' (*abwehrbereit*, Schmitt Glaeser 1968: 31, 38); 'ready to fight', 'well-fortified', 'battlesome' (*wehrhaft*, Jahrreiß 1950: 88 et seq.); or even 'militant' (Dreier 1994: 751). Astonishingly, none of these attributes are to be found in the constitution's text. The means available for an interpretation of the constitution according to the textual canons for literal exegesis therefore are meagre. Furthermore, the scope of denominations, ranging from the passive-defensive 'vigilant' to the offensive 'battlesome' or 'militant', clarifies the problem of giving shape to the principle of a militant democracy and of incorporating it into the 'constitutional reality'. Nevertheless, Germany is 'known to have implemented a fairly explicit conception' of militant democracy 'in its constitution', and 'the German case is appropriate to exemplify the concept as a current constitutional crystallization' (Klamt 2007: 135). Therefore, the 'militant democracy' issue occasionally has been characterized as a 'German tradition' or even a 'German problem'.[1]

History

The term 'militant democracy' is said to have been introduced by Karl Loewenstein and Karl Mannheim. Loewenstein was a native German legal and political scientist of Jewish origin who had to emigrate to the United States in 1933. Having

1 See Boventer 1985: 24 et seq.; Klamt 2007: 154.

'introduced' the idea of a 'militant democracy' in 1935 (Loewenstein 1935a: 593), he published an essay on 'Militant Democracy and Fundamental Rights' which was printed in 1937 in the *Americal Political Science Review* (Loewenstein 1937a, 1937b). In this chapter, a 'lament on the inability of democracy to contain fascism' (Macklem 2006), Loewenstein – who may be regarded as an 'interdisciplinary vanguard' working at the intersection of political sciences, democratic theory and constitutional law[2] – pointed out that many European countries had already installed norms and regulations providing legal measures to fight against the threat posed to their political systems by totalitarian movements and forces. He highlighted that one of the core principles of democracy, tolerance of different political opinions and pluralism, had been misused for the democracy's own destruction, scarcely restrained by a kind of 'suicidal lethargy'. The democracy 'sharpened the dagger by which it was stabbed in the back' (Loewenstein 1935a: 580). Loewenstein referred to rational arguments and described the 'militant democracy' as a system that develops techniques and measures to combat the attacks of its fascist enemies. Taking the Weimar Republic as an example, he demanded that the democracy becomes 'militant'.

A couple of years later, in 1943, the Hungarian-born, Jewish sociologist Karl Mannheim – who fled to Britain in 1933 – wrote a 'diagnosis' of the wartime (Mannheim 1943 [1998]). He described 'militant democracy' as a 'third way' besides laissez-faire and exhaustive planning of society's architecture (aiming at a guarantee of freedom and variety, on the one hand, tending to dictatorship and conformity, on the other hand) (Mannheim 1943 [1998]: 8):

> Is there a possibility of planning which is based upon co-ordination and yet leaves scope for freedom? Can the new form of planning deliberately refrain from interfering except in cases where free adjustment has led not to harmony but to conflict and chaos? Is there a form of planning which moves in the direction of social justice, gradually eliminating the increasing disproportion in income and wealth in the various strata of the nation? Is there a possibility of transforming our neutral democracy into a militant one? Can we transform our attitudes to valuations so that democratic agreement on certain basic issues becomes possible, while the more complex issues are left to individual choice?

Loewenstein's contribution and Mannheim's book obviously were influenced by Europe's experiences with fascism, especially with German National Socialism. But it would be too short-sighted to assume that the idea of a 'militant democracy' was completely new. The problem of state self-defence does not only appear in democracies and can be retraced to the earliest emergence of states, but the specific protection issue as related to the 'militant democracy' idea did not arise until the creation of the first (written) constitutions.

---

2 See Lang 2007 (in German).

In post-war Germany, the question of constitutional defence arose quite early. The constitutional law scholar Hermann Jahrreiß saw the function of a 'militant democracy' as being an 'interim arrangement' until such time as the people have reached an 'inextinguishable awareness' of democracy. He noted (Jahrreiß 1950: 88 et seq.):

> To establish democracy, the state has to mobilize forces that could turn against itself in its current shape or against the state in general one day. To preserve democracy, does the state have to enchain or to abolish theses forces, as soon as they pursuit anti-democratic or even anarchistic objectives? Who answers 'yes' here, thinks the thought of the 'militant democracy'. He thinks a self-tormenting thought. Because: When does the use of the political freedom of discussion and of coalition … turn to misuse? … And who will decide … that the democracy has to act inconsequently to defend itself?[3]

Friedrich August von der Heydte, another constitutional law scholar, spoke of 'the Scylla of too much freedom' and 'the Charybdis of too few', with regard to political parties. In his opinion, both options – the murder and suicide of democratic thought – are to be avoided (von der Heydte 1954: 483).

The *Bundesverfassungsgericht*, the German Federal Constitutional Court, implemented the idea of a 'militant democracy' in constitutional theory in 1956. In its so-called 'KPD' decision,[4] it used the term in a mainly descriptive function, being aware of the problematic character of such a principle. In this leading decision, the court explicated:

> The Federal Constitutional Court has to answer the question, if the fundamental importance of the basic right to freedom of political expression for the free democratic basic order permits a regulation like Article 21 Section 2 of the Basic Law at all, if – in other words – a liberal-democratic constitution that exceedingly curtails one of its own fundamental values for the purpose of its own defence, the freedom of political expression, the constraining regulation has to be regarded as unconstitutional itself …[5]

The court solved this problem as follows:

> Article 21 Section 2 of the Basic Law … does not conflict with a fundamental principle of the constitution; it is an expression of the conscious constitutional-political will to solve a border problem of the free democratic form of state,

3 Translation from German by the author.

4 BVerfGE 5, 85.

5 BVerfGE 5, 85, 137. Translation from German by the author. Lameyer (1978a: 23, fn. 51) discusses the interesting question of whether the Federal Constitutional Court has appointed itself as a censor of the constitutional legislator, and the legal concept of 'unconstitutional constitutional law'.

> a reflection of the experiences of the constitutional legislator, who thought he could not realize the principle of neutrality of the state towards political parties in a pure form in a specific historical situation, a confession to a 'militant democracy'. This decision is binding the Federal Constitutional Court.[6]

In the aftermath, the court developed 'militant democracy' into an 'all-purpose' principle and uncompromisingly used it as an argument, criterion and reasoning in a couple of decisions.[7] Even though the 'KPD' judgment left the principle with 'blurred outlines', the constitution's decision in favour of a 'militant democracy' which influences all constitutional regulations, was refined by degrees and further 'operationalized' (Lameyer 1978a: 57 et seq.). For example, the court negated compensation for those victims of Nazi political persecution according to the *Bundesentschädigungsgesetz* (Federal Compensation Law) who had fought against the so-called 'free democratic basic order' after 23 May 1949.[8] In a few decisions, the court dealt with the question of the unconstitutionality of verdicts against former members of the KPD.[9]

The 'militant democracy' principle further legitimated disciplinary action against a staff sergeant who had questioned the free democratic basic order in a public political debate.[10] The Constitutional Court emphasized that the 'militant democracy' principle was in force even regarding internal affairs of the German *Bundeswehr* (the Federal Armed Forces):

> The Federal Republic of Germany is a democracy that expects of its citizen the defence of the free order and does not accept the misuse of fundamental rights to fight this order (Articles 9 Section 2, 20 Section 4, 18, 21 Section 2, 98 Sections 2 and 5 of the Basic Law). This principle of militant democracy applies to the internal order of the Federal Armed Forces, too. Therefore, it is a fundamental duty of the soldiers to advocate for the maintenance of the free order in their entire behaviour.[11]

The court added:

> A community based on the principle of militant democracy cannot tolerate if its free order is challenged, or even fought, in the course of political discussion in the ranks or by military superiors whilst on duty.[12]

6 BVerfGE 5, 85, 139.

7 For an insightful overview, see Becker 1992.

8 BVerfGE 13, 46, 49 et seq.

9 BVerfGE 25, 44; 25, 88.

10 BVerfGE 28, 36, 48 et seq.

11 BVerfGE 28, 36, 48 et seq. (translation from German by the author).

12 BVerfGE 28, 36, 49 (translation from German by the author); in addition, see BVerfGE 28, 51 – the Constitutional Court had to decide on the dismissal of a soldier in 1968 for fomenting his comrades and inviting them to insubordination.

Checking the compatibility of the new Article 10 Section 2 Subsection 2 of the Basic Law which allows statutory restrictions of the right to privacy of correspondence, post and telecommunication without prior notification of the person concerned if, *inter alia*, the free democratic basic order has to be protected, with constitutional law in the so-called (and very controversial) *'Abhör'-Entscheidung* ('wiretapping' decision), the court used the militancy principle as an additional reason for justification of the new provision.[13] In this prominent decision, the court explicates:

> When interpreting Article 10 Section 2 Sentence 2 of the Basic Law, the context of the constitution, especially fundamental decisions of the Basic Law and general constitutional principles must be taken into consideration. In the present case, it is of particular importance that the constitution of the Federal Republic of Germany has decided in favour of the 'militant democracy'.[14]

Concerning the interpretation of Article 33 Section 5 of the Basic Law and the element of the *hergebrachter Grundsatz des Berufsbeamtentums* (customary principle of public service), the court postulated a duty of allegiance for public servants with recourse to the militancy principle in the so-called *'Extremistenbeschluss'*.[15] The court ruled:

> The duty of allegiance demands to approve the state and its effective constitutional order, also insofar it is subject to constitutional transformation, not only verbally, but especially within the occupation by regarding and abiding by the constitution and by the laws and holding office in the spirit of this provisions. The duty of political allegiance asks for more than a formally correct, otherwise uninterested, cool, inwardly distant attitude towards state and constitution; it demands from the public servants to dissociate from organizations and activities that attack, fight, and defame this state, his constitutional institutions [and bodies], and the existing constitutional order. It is expected from the public servant that he perceives and recognizes this state and its constitution as a high positive value worth advocating for.[16]

These few examples show the 'ubiquitous' utilization the Federal Constitutional Court made of the 'militant democracy' principle as an 'insight of constitutional judicature'. The court adjudicated an autonomous legal character to this principle,

13 BVerfGE 30, 1, 19 et seq.; see the dissenting opinion of judges Geller, von Schlabrendorff, and Rupp (BVerfGE 45 et seq.), who point out the contradictoriness of restrictions to constitutional rights to protect the constitutional order; see in detail Lameyer 1978a: 56 et seq.; Sattler 1982: 13.

14 BVerfGE 30, 1, 19.

15 BVerfGE 39, 334, 349, 368 et seq.; see below.

16 BVerfGE 39, 334, head note 2 (translation from German by the author).

using it as a criterion for the interpretation of constitutional and sub-constitutional norms, the appreciation of conflicting constitutional values, and the justification of curtailments of (fundamental) rights (Sattler 1982: 16).[17] The court, on the one hand, deduced the existence of this principle from a look at the numerous manifestations in the constitution, and, on the other hand, declared it as an overarching constitutional idea that influences the norms of constitutional law.

It is important to note that some of the Federal Constitutional Court's decisions were not taken unanimously. Dissenting opinions were added to several judgments;[18] this shows an 'antipodal split' and a basically and essentially different comprehension of the constitution, especially in the Second Senate of the Court (Lameyer 1978: 42). Nevertheless, many courts followed the Federal Constitutional Court's concept, although they proved to be partly hesitant.[19] As we will see (below under 'Criticism'), also the opinions among constitutional scholars differed considerably.

In more recent decisions of the Federal Constitutional Court, the 'militant democracy' principle has become less important in comparison to the aforementioned early judgments. This is due to changes in the political situation in Germany; after the collapse of the Warsaw Pact and reunification with the former German Democratic Republic in 1990, the political climate changed – the menace of a revolution pursued by internal political enemies was regarded as having been averted. Today, the danger of the abolition of the 'free democratic basic order' by, for example, extremist parties is rather low; in over 60 years, the *Grundgesetz* has proven its value. Nevertheless, the measures and provisions of the 'militant democracy' have been sporadically activated in the past few years, especially in connection with the (failed) banning procedure against the right extremist *Nationaldemokratische Partei Deutschlands* (NPD, 'Nationalist Democratic Party').

The Function of Militant Democracy in German Constitutional Law

In democratic countries that have implemented fundamental rights in their constitutions, there must be and are limitations to these rights. At this point it is worth noting that a distinction has to be drawn between the terms 'human rights' and 'fundamental rights'. Human rights are rights that attach to any human being and are said to be possessed equally and by everyone. They are 'moral' rights. The fundamental rights, as written down, for example, in the German Basic Law and in many other written constitutions, are legal rights that in some cases may not apply to all human beings, but only to the citizens of that particular country. The (written) fundamental rights can be said to be 'mirrors' of the human rights.

17 For critics, see below.

18 See, for example, BVerfGE 30, 1, 33 et seq.; see Lameyer 1978a: 58 et seq.

19 For early decisions, see Lameyer 1978a: 68 et seq.

The use of any liberty ensured by fundamental laws regularly collides with the freedom and rights of other people. This may be illustrated by a short example from Germany. In 2007, the Federal Constitutional Court approved a sentence that was passed by the Federal Court of Justice and that prohibited the circulation of the novel '*Esra*' by the German author, Maxim Biller, because it contained a quite unfavourable depiction of the author's former girlfriend and her mother. The author's freedom of arts – secured in Article 5 Section 3 of the Basic Law – collided with the personal rights of the women, the rights were weighed up and the personal rights were held more important. To take another very basic example: even if freedom of religion allows you to live according to the religious regulations of your church or religious community, human sacrifices are still forbidden.

So even when the bearer of a fundamental right makes use of their liberties, this use may be subject to several limitations. In Germany, such limitations are not only drawn by the liberties of others, but by any value of 'constitutional status'. And the principle of a 'militant democracy' has been and is still considered such a value by the Federal Constitutional Court and by mainstream constitutional theory in Germany. So militancy does not only have a descriptive or emblematic character in Germany, comprising the measures the constitution and sub-constitutional laws offer to defend the free democratic basic order, but is a constitutional principle with a substantive content of its own: The Basic Law is more 'militant' than the sum of its militant elements (Lameyer 1978b: 50).

This view is due to the idea that apart from a legal, but limited use of fundamental rights that have to be weighed up with the rights of other individuals, there must be limitations to the so-called 'misusage' of fundamental rights, especially by the enemies of the democracy. There are enemies who attack from outside the borders of a democratic country, for example, by a military strike against one sovereign state by another in order to destroy the political system of the country under attack. Enemies may also try to defeat the democracy from inside, using the political structures or by attacks inside the borders as in the 9/11 terrorist attacks. The 'militant democracy' principle 'calls for limitations of political liberties to fight those who actively and aggressively fight democracy' (Baer 2000: 82).

Although the 'militant democracy' principle is regarded as a constitutional value, it does not directly impose a duty on the citizens. The Constitutional Court held that it could call upon citizens to act as democrats (and enables the state to fight against those who do not).[20] The democracy expects that every citizen will fight for the free democratic basic order (while at the same time granting them the right to resist everyone who aims at abolishing this order, as in Article 20 Section 4 of the Basic Law). But it does not go so far as to enforce a legal duty or responsibility on the citizen to protect democracy. This is because such a duty would in practice require an (inner) acceptance of the free democratic basic order which cannot be demanded: the 'militant democracy' principle reacts to an

20 See Baer 2000: 82.

attack against the democracy, not to simple disaffirmation.[21] Of course, a militant democracy needs 'militant democrats' that avow for a democracy that is open to discourse, but likewise defending its own basics. So it is, for example, desirable to teach the constitutional basic values in school[22] and to educate young people to a kind of 'constitutional patriotism'.[23]

Protected Values – The 'Free Democratic Basic Order'

The matter of protection of the militant democracy principle in Germany is the so-called 'free democratic basic order',[24] which appears several times in the text of the Basic Law (Articles 18 Sentence 1; Article 21 Section 2; and Article 91 Section 1). In 1952, the Federal Constitutional Court defined this basic order as follows:

> The free democratic basic order can be defined as an order which excludes any form of tyranny or arbitrariness and represents a governmental system under a rule of law, based upon self determination of the people as expressed by the will of the existing majority and upon freedom and equality. The fundamental principles of this order include at least: respect for the human rights given concrete form in the Basic Law, in particular for the right of a person to life and free development; separation of powers; responsibility of government; lawfulness of administration; independence of the judiciary; the multi-party principle; and equality of opportunities for all political parties.

The term 'free democratic basic order' therefore is congruent with the elements mentioned in Article 79 Section 3 of the Basic Law, the so-called 'Clause of Eternity' ('*Ewigkeitsklausel*'). Some authors add the principles of the Republic, of the Social State, and of the Federal State to the bundle of provisions building the basic order, but the prevailing opinion does not follow this dilatation; it is dispensable, because any violation of these principles will come along with an infringement against other elements explicitly mentioned by the Constitutional Court.

Most of the protective measures provided by the Basic Law directly affect fundamental rights. For example, Article 18 provides that whoever abuses the liberties mentioned in this article 'in order to combat the free democratic basic order, shall forfeit these basic rights'. The affection is justified by means of a balancing of the fundamental rights with the constancy of the 'free democratic basic order'.

21 For the special duty of allegiance of public servants, see below.
22 See, for example, Thiel 2000: 113 et seq.; Tillmanns 2003: 44 et seq.
23 See Müller 2007b, on 'constitutional patriotism'.
24 Or 'liberal democratic basis order' (Klamt 2007: 137).

Manifestations

The Basic Law provides several measures to defend the democratic system and the 'free democratic basic order' against its enemies. According to the 'militant democracy' concept developed by the *Bundesverfassungsgericht*, these measures are not the basis of the militancy principle, but its manifestations and, therefore, evidence of its existence. The following passages will deal with a selection of the most important and controversial regulations.

The Forfeiture of Fundamental Rights – Article 18 of the Basic Law

Article 18 of the Basic Law provides that whoever abuses the liberties mentioned in this article 'in order to combat the free democratic basic order, shall forfeit these basic rights'. It reads:

> Whoever abuses the freedom of expression, in particular the freedom of the press (paragraph (1) of Article 5), the freedom of teaching (paragraph (3) of Article 5), the freedom of assembly (Article 8), the freedom of association (Article 9), the privacy of correspondence, posts and telecommunications (Article 10), the rights of property (Article 14), or the right of asylum (Article 16a) in order to combat the free democratic basic order shall forfeit these basic rights. This forfeiture and its extent shall be declared by the Federal Constitutional Court.

The Basic Law assigns a special competence to the Federal Constitutional Court to interdict in the exercise of certain fundamental rights in cases where such rights are abused to fight against the free democratic basic order. Article 18 of the Basic Law is quite scant; §§ 36 et seq. of the *Gesetz über das Bundesverfassungsgericht* (*Bundesverfassungsgerichtsgesetz*, 'Law on the Federal Constitutional Court') contain further regulations. On a motion of the government (of the *Bund* or the *Länder*) or the *Bundestag* (the Federal Parliament), the court can decide whether a forfeiture of these rights is warranted or not. It is quite important to note that anyone who fights against the free democratic basic order by exercising their liberties loses the right to invoke these liberties when the state 'strikes back', for example, by criminal prosecution. But this loss, the forfeiture, has to be declared explicitly by the Federal Constitutional Court to become valid. The declaration is constitutive. The forfeiture will only be declared if someone 'fights' against the free democratic basic order, which requires an *active* and *aggressive modus operandi* (Thiel 2003b: 136 et seq.), although it is not necessary that the aggressor uses physical violence. The measures taken must aim at abolishing the free democratic basic order and they must be qualified as a 'misuse'. Regarding the 'militant democracy' principle, the 'misuse' criterion does not have a legal relevance of its own: everyone who *uses* his or her fundamental rights to fight against the constitutional order, *misuses* them (Thiel 2003b: 140).

§ 36 of the Law on the Federal Constitutional Court entitles the *Bundestag* (the Federal Parliament); the *Bundesregierung* (the Federal Government); and the *Landesregierungen* (the *Länder* governments) to file motions to declare the forfeiture of fundamental rights to the Constitutional Court. These institutions decide with free (political) discretionary power whether to file a motion or not (Gallwas 1967: 154; Thiel 2003c: 191 et seq.). To comment on the full particulars of the procedure would go beyond the scope of this analysis; some of the details are controversial, as are the legal consequences of the forfeiture. Some scholars hold that the fundamental law of the person misusing it to fight against the free democratic basic order is lost. Others claim that only the authority to make use of the right (or the entitlement to repel curtailments of the right by state institutions) is taken away. This problem is quite abstract (and hypothetical); in practice, the executive, the legislative and the judiciary would not have to respect the forfeited fundamental right (Thiel 2003b: 148 et seq.). For example, the courts would have to dismiss legal actions as inadmissible if a person alleged that his forfeited fundamental right had been curtailed.

In Germany, as yet, no legal action has led to a forfeiture, and only four motions to declare the forfeiture of fundamental rights have been filed with the Constitutional Court since 1949 (Klamt 2007: 139; Thiel 2003b: 130, 133 et seq.); some authors, therefore, regard Article 18 as obsolete. However, although it has been criticized as a 'comparatively unusual and symbolic "anomaly"' (Klamt 2007: 138), the provision does have an important 'appellative' character. With the practical insignificance of Article 18 of the Basic Law in mind, the forfeiture cannot be qualified as a 'repressive element to silence ideological opponents'.[25]

It is important to note that only some of the fundamental rights can be forfeited. Forfeiture is confined to the fundamental rights enumerated in Article 18 of the Basic Law (Gallwas 1967: 138 et seq.; Stern 1984: 202; Thiel 2003b: 154). In particular, human dignity, protected by Article 1 of the Basic Law and the constitution's central and supreme value, cannot be forfeited and must not be violated by any other treatment in the name of 'militant democracy'. Article 1 Section 1 provides that 'the dignity of man shall be inviolable', and Article 1 Section 2 reads 'the German people therefore acknowledge inviolable and inalienable human rights as the basis of every community, of peace and of justice in the world'. German constitutional law scholars hold by a vast majority that any infringement of human dignity is unconstitutional and hence forbidden. As a consequence, there must be no deliberation or attempt to balance opposing fundamental rights, interests or values of 'constitutional status'. A weighing up as in the Maxim Biller case will not take place in any circumstances where human dignity is affected.

The following are two examples of the pre-eminent role of Article 1: the human dignity. The first is the well-known case involving human rights and torture. In 2002, a young boy, a bank director's son, was abducted by a former law student and held captive for ransom. The police did not know the whereabouts of the

25 See Klamt 2007: 139; Papier and Durner 2003: 362.

victim, but captured the offender. Because he did not reveal the boy's location, the deputy chief of police at Frankfurt threatened him with torture. Under pressure, the kidnapper revealed the boy's whereabouts, but unfortunately it was too late to save him and the boy was found dead. In the aftermath, the threat of torture was regarded as an infringement of human dignity and the deputy chief was forced to resign. Of course there is absolutely no doubt that torture is a serious violation of human rights and therefore strictly forbidden by International Law, but the sacrosanct character of Article 1 of the Basic Law leaves some difficult questions. What if a criminal threatens to poison the water reservoir of a large city using a timer and there is no possibility of finding the poison, warning the inhabitants or evacuating them? Should the police catch the offender, if they are to remain within the law, and particularly constitutional law, they are not allowed to threaten torture. Hundreds of thousands of people may be sacrificed in order to protect the human dignity of a single person. This outcome becomes more absurd if we consider that the police would be legally justified in killing the offender if found with the poison near the reservoir.

A similar problem emerged from the German Aviation Security Act ('*Luftsicherheitsgesetz*') that was enacted in 2005. § 14 Section 3 of this act empowered the minister of defence to order the shooting down of a civilian passenger plane if 'in the circumstances, it can be assumed' that the aircraft was to be used 'against human life'. This rule was a response to the 9/11 terrorist plane attacks on the World Trade Center and the Pentagon. The Federal Constitutional Court ruled that the shooting down of a hijacked passenger plane would violate the human dignity of the passengers and crew members. As has been shown, this immediately leads to the unconstitutional nature of the legal norm.

The judgment, which also illustrates the substance of human dignity as it is perceived by the prevailing opinion in Germany, reads as follows:

> The hopelessness and inability to take evasive action which marks the situation of the passenger victims on the aircraft also extends to those who order and carry out the shooting down of the aircraft. The flight crew and passengers cannot evade this action by the state due to conditions outside their control, but are helplessly and defencelessly at its mercy, with the consequence that they and the aircraft will be deliberately shot down and they will almost certainly be killed. Such an action ignores the status of the persons affected as subjects endowed with dignity and inalienable rights. By virtue of their killing being used to save others, they are treated as objects and at the same time deprived of their rights. Given that their lives are disposed of unilaterally by the state, the persons onboard the aircraft who, as victims, are themselves in need of protection are denied the valuation which is due to a human being for his or her own sake.

The court rejected the claim that those who have been kidnapped with the aircraft have become 'part of a weapon'. In the court's view, this idea 'expresses in a virtually undisguised manner that the victims of such an incident are no longer perceived as human beings, but are seen as part of an object and are thus themselves objectified'. This is 'incompatible' with the 'conception that humans by their nature are disposed to freely determine things for themselves', and therefore may not be made 'the mere object of state actions'. The court did not decide how the ordering and implementation of a shoot down should be judged legally. The court's intention was obvious here: a shoot down should remain criminally unpunished as an action taken in a so-called 'supra legal emergency'. This impunity does not make the shoot down lawful; it still remains unconstitutional. The doctrine of sanctity of human dignity forbids any deliberation. Weighing the possible number of deaths in the shot down plane, on the one hand, against those in the attacked building, on the other, is interdicted, as is even considering giving preference to the life of persons who could be saved (perhaps in a building that is the target of a plane attack) over the life of those who are doomed in any case.

The doctrine of an untouchable human dignity evokes many problems that have not yet been solved. However, it is defended so vehemently that it seems unalterable. For example, a law professor, Horst Dreier, who was nominated for election to the Federal Constitutional Court as a new judge, has come under fierce criticism because he supported the concept of 'rescue torture' as a means of last resort to prevent imminent, large-scale terrorist attacks. His nomination was withdrawn.

As regards the concept of militant democracy, human dignity, which cannot be forfeited under any circumstances, imposes strong restrictions on measures to defend the democracy from its enemies. Even if we may speak of an explicit, elaborate and strong militancy in German democracy, human dignity poses an unbreakable limitation. Therefore, the forfeiture is not so extensive that the 'enemy of the constitution' would be 'deprived of all his rights for the rest of his life'; the use of a singular forfeited fundamental right is impossible only for a certain period (Klamt 2007: 139).

The Prohibition of Political Parties – Article 21 Section 2 of the Basic Law

Besides forfeiture, there are many other legal measures that may be taken against enemies of democracy in Germany. Article 21 of the Basic Law declares that political parties shall participate in the forming of the will of the people, but if the parties aim to impair or abolish the free democratic basic order, they will be deemed unconstitutional.

Article 21 Sections 1 and 2 read:

> (1) Political parties shall participate in the formation of the political will of the people. They may be freely established. Their internal organization must conform to democratic principles. They must publicly account for their assets and for the sources and use of their funds.

> (2) Parties that, by reason of their aims or the behaviour of their adherents, seek to undermine or abolish the free democratic basic order or to endanger the existence of the Federal Republic of Germany shall be unconstitutional. The Federal Constitutional Court shall rule on the question of unconstitutionality.

This article expresses the conviction of the drafters of the Basic Law, based on their historical experience that the state could no longer afford to maintain an attitude of neutrality toward political parties. An unconstitutional party can only be banned by the Federal Constitutional Court exclusively.

In Germany's history, parties have been banned only twice, once in 1952 and again in 1956 – one left, one right extremist. The right extremist *Sozialistische Reichspartei* (SRP, 'Socialist *Reich* Party') was founded in 1949 and obtained 11 per cent and 7.7 per cent in the elections to the Parliaments of Niedersachsen and Bremen in 1951. It was banned in 1952 by the Constitutional Court as a successor party to Hitler's *Nationalsozialistische Deutsche Arbeiterpartei* (NSDAP, 'National Socialist German Worker's Party').[26] The ban did not cause a sensation, because it was evident that Article 21 Section 2 had been introduced to the Basic Law to prevent neo-Nazi activities, so that the verdict against the SRP came as no surprise. In contrast, the launching of the ban action against the *Kommunistische Partei Deutschlands* (KPD, 'Communist Party of Germany') which had been much less successful in the *Länder* Parliaments elections in 1951 was highly controversial. The trial was accompanied not only by debates on the constitutional justification of party bans, but also by a discussion about their political effectiveness.[27] In 1954, the president of the Constitutional Court interpellated the Chancellor Konrad Adenauer if the Federal Government maintained its motion. This was widely regarded as an incitement to the waiver of the motion.[28] The banning procedure inflamed the political climate with the Constitutional Court failing to reach a decision until 1955 when the KPD was banned.

In 1993, the Hamburg Senate (as the government of the *Land* Hamburg) filed a petition to ban the *Nationale Liste* (NL, 'National List'), a very small right-wing group founded in 1989. In the same year, the *Bundesregierung* and the *Bundesrat* filed another petition to ban the *Freiheitliche Deutsche Arbeiterpartei* (FAP, 'Free German Worker's Party'). The latter was founded in 1979, but – like the NL – did not achieve noteworthy results in the elections to the *Länder* Parliaments and in local elections. The Constitutional Court dismissed both motions because, in the court's opinion, the NL and the FAP were not 'political parties' according to Article 21 of the Basic Law and § 2 Section 1 of the *Parteiengesetz* ('Party

26 BVerfGE 2, 1 et seq.

27 See Maurer 1971: 204, footnote 2 – especially the question of a 'readmission' of the KPD in case of its ban has been discussed; see Maurer 1971: 204, with further references in footnote 3.

28 See Morlok 2001: 2934.

Law').[29] They lacked the necessary organization and internal structure, had but few members, and did not show significant public awareness, which resulted in occasional participation in elections. With the classification as a 'political party' denied, the NL and the FAP could be prohibited by the Federal Minister of the Interior, respectively the Senator of the Interior in Hamburg, based on Article 9 Section 2 of the Basic Law:

> Associations whose aims or activities contravene the criminal laws, or that are directed against the constitutional order or the concept of international understanding, shall be prohibited.

§§ 3 et seq. of the *Gesetz zur Regelung des öffentlichen Vereinsrechts* (*Vereinsgesetz*, Law on Associations) regulate the competences and proceedings of a ban of associations.

In addition to the filed actions against (alleged) political parties, the initiation of further proceedings have been discussed, especially when the right extremist *Nationaldemokratische Partei Deutschlands* (NPD, 'Nationalist Democratic Party') was founded in 1964. This party served as a 'reservoir' for right-wing activists and was quite successful in several elections to the *Länder* Parliaments during the 1960s. When it failed to achieve a mandate in the 1969 *Bundestag* elections, the NPD's political importance dwindled rapidly to such an extent that the institutions authorized to file a banning motion refrained from doing so. The *Deutsche Kommunistische Partei* (DKP, 'German Communist Party'), founded in 1968 by former leaders and members of the banned KPD, was not considered as a threat either and the Federal Government decided instead to concentrate the fight against political extremists on a primarily political level (Morlok 2001: 2935; Thiel 2003a: 179).

In the late 1990s, the discussion about banning the NPD revived.[30] In 2001, the Federal Government, the *Deutsche Bundestag* and the *Bundesrat* attempted to ban the Nationalist Democratic Party. The Constitutional Court decided in October 2001 to hear the case. In July 2002, indications emerged that a large percentage of the NPD's inner circle were in fact undercover agents or informants of the German secret services and that those '*V-Leute*' had largely influenced the party's activities. The Constitutional Court demanded the disclosure of the names of all agents involved; the secret service authorities refused the disclosure and decided to uphold their own functionality and to protect their agents. This scene was accompanied by a vehement debate on the admissibility of so-called '*agents provocateurs*'. On 18 March 2003, the Second Senate of the Constitutional Court dismissed the motion; the two-thirds majority, necessary to reject a dismissal petition by the defendant according to § 15 Section 4 of the Law of the Federal Constitutional Court, was

29 BVerfGE 91, 262 et seq., 276 et seq.

30 Regarding the history of the NPD in the 1990s, see Pfahl-Traughber 2002: 30 et seq.

lacking. Three of the judges held that the absence of a clearly certifiable 'distance from the state' was an insurmountable hindrance to the proceedings. Thus, the court said that 'the party was, in part, responding to the government's dictates'. And it concluded that 'the presence of the state at the leadership level makes influence on its aims and activities unavoidable'. It is important to note that the Constitutional Court did not decide whether the NPD was 'unconstitutional' in the sense of Article 21 Section 2 of the Basic Law. This means that a new motion can be filed after the removal of the agents provocateurs.

Article 21 Section 2 of the Basic Law restricts the provisions in Section 1 which grants the right (and assigns the duty) to participate in the formation of the political will of the people, and to freely found new political parties (which have to comply with the requisites laid down in Section 1 Sentences 3 and 4). Independent of the question of whether Article 21 of the Basic Law contains a genuine fundamental right in favour of the political parties, a right similar only to the fundamental rights, or a simple 'subjective right', the norm clarifies that the parties are not 'original' entities of the state, but play a role at the intersection of government and society. It was argued that the traditional differentiation between 'state' and 'society' could not be maintained because both spheres could no longer be separated accurately. This is especially apparent with respect to the function of the political parties in Germany. They are institutions rooted in society, but extend into the sector of 'institutionalized statehood' (Maurer 1971: 219 et seq.). The 'constitutionalization' of political parties was and still is 'important to secure the political process' (Klamt 2007: 138). This societal tie-up implies that any curtailment of the rights of political parties provided in Article 21 of the Basic Law needs a (constitutional) justification.[31] In addition, the 'democracy principle' as one of the most important features of the constitution according to Article 20 Section 2 of the Basic Law, demands such justification because the political parties are an essential element of the democratic process. The banning of a party, as the most severe form of curtailment, consequentially requires a special regulation to be justified – Article 21 Section 2 of the Basic Law – which raises high hurdles and secures a '*forum privilegiatum* of political parties' (Klamt 2007: 139).

In view of this 'constitutional value' of a functional system of political parties, and concerns about possible abuse,[32] some authors object to the possibility of a party ban. But, in this author's view, this is an impact of 'liberal democratic optimism' regarding the self-regulating ability of political parties, on the one hand, and the 'democratic maturity' of the electorate, on the other hand. Hitler's NSDAP taught us another lesson. The ban is and has to be an *ultima ratio*, the 'last resort' of a democratic system under attack from the activities of a political party whose aim is the destruction of the free democratic basic order.

The Federal Constitutional Court accentuates the role of the party ban as a 'last resort':

---

31 See Stollberg 1976: 18 et seq.

32 See, for example, the references in Thiel 2003a: 182 et seq.

> Therefore, a party is not unconstitutional if it does not acknowledge the supreme principles of a free democratic basic order, refuses them, or sets against other [principles]. An actively combative, aggressive attitude against the existing order must be present; it has methodically to affect the functioning of the order, and aim for the abolition of this order over time. This means that the free democratic state does not proceed against hostile parties by itself, but acts in defense, repelling attacks against its fundamental order.[33]

If Article 21 Section 2 of the Basic Law was abolished, the democratically legitimate institutions would have no constitutional measure to defend against such activities. They would be forced to take action against the leaders and members of the party; in view of the fundamental rights, and the privileges of, for example, Members of Parliament (such as immunity and indemnity), this tends to be impractical, tedious, intricate and ineffective. Article 21 Section 2 of the Basic Law is not obsolete: it has a deterrence function. Moreover, the NPD incident does not show the ineffectiveness of the banning option, but is a lesson for the institutions authorized to file a banning motion.

Article 21 Section 2 of the Basic Law declares parties unconstitutional that 'seek to undermine or abolish the free democratic basic order or to endanger the existence of the Federal Republic of Germany'. This unconstitutionality has to be 'activated' by a Constitutional Court's decision (Section 2 Sentence 2), although the named parties are unconstitutional and illegal *ipso iure* (Maurer 1971: 209; Thiel 2003a: 188 et seq.). Therefore, no administrative and executive measures against the illegal parties are allowed until the Constitutional Court has ruled them to be unconstitutional. They may pursue their goals unhampered and submit their claims for party financing,[34] while no measures against their leaders and members are permitted.

It is disputed if a motion once filed can be withdrawn, so that the Constitutional Court must not decide on the ban (Ipsen 2002: 866 et seq.). The Law regarding the Constitutional Court is quite scant on this question; it only regulates a few basic aspects and leaves the details to the court itself.[35] The question of withdrawal is not regulated by the law. In comparison with the legal provisions for the civil and administrative courts, there are narrow confines for legal withdrawals after the lawsuit has reached a certain stage (Thiel 2003a: 195). The codes of procedure contain specific norms that inhibit an unlimited withdrawal. On the other hand, the party ban procedure cannot be compared to, for example, criminal proceedings: the applicant bodies of the ban motions act in a preventive manner, while criminal prosecution authorities pursue repressive goals. Neither are civil proceedings comparable because plaintiff and defendant try to push through their own interests. However, the possibility of a withdrawal can be deduced from the Law

33 See BVerfGE 5, 85, 141.

34 See, for example, BVerfGE 39, 334, 357.

35 See, for example, BVerfGE 1, 108, 110 et seq.

on the Constitutional Court's provisions concerning kinds of actions. For example, the impeachment action against the *Bundespräsident*. If the President willfully violates provisions of the Basic Law or another Federal Law, an impeachment can be filed according to Article 61 Section 1 of the Basic Law. The impeachment can be regarded as a further manifestation of the 'militant democracy' principle:

> (1) The Bundestag or the Bundesrat may impeach the Federal President before the Federal Constitutional Court for willful violation of this Basic Law or of any other federal law. The motion of impeachment must be supported by at least one quarter of the Members of the Bundestag or one quarter of the votes of the Bundesrat. The decision to impeach shall require a majority of two thirds of the Members of the Bundestag or of two thirds of the votes of the Bundesrat. The case for impeachment shall be presented before the Federal Constitutional Court by a person commissioned by the impeaching body.
>
> (2) If the Federal Constitutional Court finds the Federal President guilty of a willful violation of this Basic Law or of any other federal law, it may declare that he has forfeited his office. After the Federal President has been impeached, the Court may issue an interim order preventing him from exercising his functions.

§ 52 Section 1 Sentence 2 of the Law on the Constitutional Court allows the withdrawal with a majority of the members of the *Bundestag* or a majority in the *Bundesrat*. Although it could be assumed that the legislator would have – as he did in the impeachment provisions – explicitly regulated for the possibility of a withdrawal in the party ban procedure if he approved it, the Constitutional Court assumed that a withdrawal is admissible in most other actions nevertheless.[36] On the other hand, the party against which a party ban procedure has been initiated, may have an interest in a decision – for example, for reasons of rehabilitation. In conclusion, a withdrawal would be admissible, but only with the party's agreement. Before the completion of the *Vorverfahren*, the preliminary proceedings prescribed by § 45 of the Law on the Constitutional Court,[37] the motion can be withdrawn without any restriction.

The Right to Resist – Article 20 Section 4 of the Basic Law

Another measure of protection against threats to the political system and the free democratic basic order is the right of resistance in Article 20 Section 4 of the Basic Law. It reads:

---

36 See, for example, BVerfGE 1, 14, 31; BVerfGE 25, 308, 309; BVerfGE 68, 346, 351; BVerfGE 76, 99 et seq.; BVerfGE 79, 255.

37 The court has to give the party (more precisely: its representative) the opportunity to comment on the reproaches within a specified period of time. After that, the court decides if it rejects the motion or opens the ban proceeding.

> All Germans shall have the right to resist any person seeking to abolish this constitutional order, if no other remedy is available.

The 'right to resist' can be understood in two ways. On the one hand, it is the right of a person to refuse obedience to legal provisions and administrative acts – in the sense of the problems discussed as 'civil disobedience'. On the other hand, the 'right to resist' allows the possibility of fighting actively or passively against activities that try to destroy the constitutional order. Article 20 Section 4 of the Basic Law obviously refers to the latter; the right to resist, therefore, is tailored to exceptional political conditions. While 'civil disobedience' is, in many cases, a mere breach of law (wrongly) considered justified by the violator, the right to resist in the German constitution provides a 'real' justification in the legal sense. It is not intended to be used as a means of self-defence, guarding objects of legal protection, but to defend the 'constitutional order'.

The question of whether a right to resist is granted by natural or pre-legal law has long been discussed as a philosophical issue. The Basic Law grants it the status of a fundamental right (or at least a right similar to the fundamental rights; Heinemann 2003: 111 et seq.).[38] As in previous German constitutions, the right to resist was omitted in the initial Basic Law. The creators of the constitution feared that such a right could be used as a blockade of the state's institutions.

The Constitutional Court cautiously supported a supra-legal right to resist in its early decisions.[39] It was incorporated into the written constitution as Article 20 Section 4 of the Basic Law in 1968, when the constitutional provisions regarding the state of emergency were integrated in the constitution by the *Siebzehntes Gesetz zur Änderung des Grundgesetzes* ('17th Law amending the Basic Law') of 24 June 1968.[40] Article 20 Section 4 of the Basic Law served as a kind of 'antidote'; the right to resist should prevent the democratic system from a misuse of the state of emergency measures by the state and its institutions. On the other hand, the natural law based right to resist should be 'fenced in' by an explicitly written provision. Furthermore, it should raise the citizens' 'political vigilance'. It has been widely agreed that the right to resist merely had a declaratory function, because this right either exists as a natural law (Even 1951) or can be derived from other constitutional provisions (Klug 1984: 11, 22 et seq.).

The 'constitutional order', object of protection of Article 20 Section 4 of the Basic Law, is the 'free democratic basic order' already mentioned previously. However, no single element of this order is protected, rather it is the order as a whole. Therefore, this measure is different from the forfeiture of fundamental rights and from the banning of political parties because it cannot be applied by government bodies but by every citizen. Although the right to resist is numbered

38 A few constitutions of the *Länder* contain similar provisions, for example, Article 19 of the constitution of Bremen and Article 147 Section 1 of the Hessian constitution.

39 BVerfGE 5, 85, 367 et seq.; see Heinemann 2003: 102 et seq.

40 BGBl. I 709; see Böckenförde 1970: 168 et seq.

among the arsenal of militant democracy, it is a special case. In the so-called *Widerstandsfall* (case of resistance), the democracy does not defend itself by its own hands, but – speaking metaphorically – sends ahead its citizens as militia. Every single citizen has the right to resist; institutions of the state are no bearers of this right (Heinemann 2003: 124). The right can be exercised collectively, but not intermediately, for example, by representative groups. It is an 'immediate individual right'.

In the event that someone was trying to abolish the 'constitutional order', and there was no other remedy, the 'case of resistance' is applied, which activates the right to resist. An intention to 'abolish the constitutional order' has to become manifest in an action to provoke the case of resistance. Mere preparation is not enough; an actual attempt has to be made. We have to presume a 'reservation' for bagatelle cases, because not every attempt to abolish the constitutional order is feasible; single acts of injustice by the state do not cross the threshold of the case of resistance. On the other hand, it is not necessary for the attempts to be apparent.[41] The right to resist is subsidiary; if there are other options, especially judicial remedies, Article 20 Section 4 of the Basic Law is inapplicable.

In the 'case of resistance', every German (according to the constitutional regulations of citizenship) is allowed to take defensive measures. Article 20 Section 4 of the Basic Law remains silent regarding the question of which measures are constitutionally allowed, so that every German citizen is free in choosing any active or passive action that contributes to the perpetuation of the 'constitutional order'. For example, the spectrum ranges from simple disobedience, to the killing of the aggressor. A boundary is set by the principle of proportionality; the person resisting has to weigh up advantages and disadvantages of the chosen measure (Heinemann 2003: 125 et seq.).

A 'Clause of Eternity' – the 'Ewigkeitsklausel' in Article 79 Section 3 of the Basic Law

Article 79 Section 3 of the Basic Law reads:

> Amendments to this Basic Law affecting the division of the Federation into Länder, their participation on principle in the legislative process, or the principles laid down in Articles 1 and 20 shall be inadmissible.

This article is regarded as a coming to terms with the past (Dreier 1994: 747; Zacharias 2003: 57 et seq.). The creators of the constitution had in mind the National Socialist regime, especially the 'takeover' in 1933 (Dürig 1971: 46). The committees drafting the constitution made clear that the *Grundgesetz* must not enable anti-democratic forces to eliminate the constitutional order using

41 Some authors demand an apparentness of the activities aiming at abolishing the constitutional order, for example, Isensee 1969: 23 et seq.; Stern 1980: 1521.

democratic measures in a seemingly legitimate manner. Article 79 Section 3 of the Basic Law, the so-called *Ewigkeitsklausel* ('Clause of Eternity') should install a barrier to take the 'mask of legality' from revolutionary activities[42] and forces the agitators to act overtly. Therefore, the Clause of Eternity was included to prevent a 'legal revolution' (Huba 1991: 373; Klamt 2007: 137; Zacharias 2003: 58).

The article names some regulations that may not be 'affected' at all, not even by constitutional amendment. For example, the division of the German national territory in the so-called *Länder* (the federal states),[43] and – of course – Article 1 of the Basic Law which guarantees the *Menschenwürde* ('human dignity') as the primary fundamental right. Article 20 (except Section 4 on the right to resist[44]) of the Basic Law is also declared unalterable. It comprises some fundamental democratic principles, such as the republican form of government, which means that the Head of State is elected for a temporary period, the federal system and the rule of law.

The regulations and provisions mentioned in Article 79 Section 3 of the Basic Law seem to be exempt from any access by the (constitutional) legislator; they have been granted a constitutional right of continuance. Those who would like to change them will have to take the way of maximum upheaval, replacing the Basic Law with a new constitution (Dreier 1994: 749 et seq.). They would have to break the constitutional continuity; an 'amicable' and democratic change of the regulations enumerated in Article 79 Section 3 of the Basic Law is impossible (Bryde 1982: 235, 247; Zacharias 2003: 59). The Constitutional Court interprets the 'Clause of Eternity' restrictively: 'affecting' does not, according to the court, mean an interdiction of any change of the constitution having impact on the enumerated principles, but only changes that abandon them.[45] Therefore, they may be modified, but not dismissed. This judicature has rightly been criticized for weakening the function of Article 79 Section 3 of the Basic Law; a dissenting vote of three Constitutional Court judges complained about a 'minimalistic interpretation'[46] and several experts endorsed this objection.[47] Others conceded that Article 79 Section 3 of the Basic Law could just state general principles open to modifications (Schneider 1971: 349 et seq.).

---

42 See the sentence of Thomas Dehler, a Member of Parliament, cited from Füßlein 1951: 586.

43 Article 79 Section 3 prescribes that Germany has to be divided into *Länder*, but does not dictate how many *Länder*. With respect to the aim of this provision – to secure the *federal* state – there have to be at least two *Länder*; see Zacharias 2003: 70 et seq.

44 Section 4 was inserted into Article 20 in 1968, so that Article 79 Section 3 – which has been created as a part of the original *Grundgesetz* – does not involve this norm; see Heinemann 2003: 112 et seq.

45 BVerfGE 30, 1 et seq., especially 24.

46 BVerfGE 30, 33 et seq. (dissenting vote of judges Geller, von Schlabrendorff and Rupp).

47 Häberle 1971: 275 et seq.; Hall 1972: 135 et seq.; for further references, see Zacharias 2003: 64 fn. 43.

This was a significant alteration, compared with the Weimar Constitution, which – according to prevailing opinion among constitutional scholars (Anschütz 1933: Article 76 ann. 3; Ehmke 1953: 19 et seq.; Zacharias 2003: 58) – permitted the change of every article in the constitution, independent from its content and its political importance. Carl Schmitt depicted this openness as a neutrality that stays its course even if it ends up in suicide (Schmitt 1932 [1958]: 301). It is convincing when Schmitt points out elsewhere (Schmitt 1978 [2005]: 928) that the Weimar Constitution shied away from expressively excluding the possibility of a restoration of the monarchy, and thus strived not to block access to legal power completely. But, when Schmitt emphasizes that the Weimar Republic allowed *any* change, this idea – picked up by numerous followers and epigones – served to declare the *Ermächtigungsgesetz* of 23 March 1933 ('*Gesetz zur Behebung der Not von Volk und Reich*')[48] and the National Socialist seizure of power as an act of *legal* revolution. Schmitt himself held the Nazi takeover legal in later publications (Schmitt 1978 [2005]: 929 et seq.).

Nevertheless, it would be wrong to suppose that the Weimar Republic was completely defenceless, in the face of being confronted with totalitarian, anti-democratic or subversive activities. It has been stated by many generations of constitutional scholars that the Weimar Republic was helpless in the face of the National Socialist takeover.[49] On the contrary, the legal system of the Weimar Republic contained a bundle of statutory provisions protecting the state and the constitutional system. The legislator had several legislative powers regarding protective measures, and although the constitution itself did not safeguard the democratic republic, it did, at least partially, protect the democratic political process (Gusy 1991: 31). The thesis of the Weimar Constitution's 'relativism' therefore can be jettisoned.[50] In any event, it did not provide 'full protection' for the democratic constitutional system at the constitutional level as does the 'militant democracy' principle. In comparison with the Weimar constitution, the Basic Law's democratic system is considerably fortified and, literally speaking, 'armed to its teeth'. With the current exposure to internal threats in mind, the armoury of the 'militant democracy' is often regarded as exaggerated.

In addition to that, the 'Clause of Eternity' has been criticized for binding the subsequent generations in an inadmissible way and forcing a singular historical

---

48 Actually, the *Ermächtigungsgesetz* has been decreed with the necessary majorities in the *Reichstag* and the *Reichsrat* and thus was in accordance with Article 76 Section 1 of the Weimar Constitution; see, for example, Zacharias 2003: 58.

49 See, for example, the Constitutional Court's decision BVerfGE 5, 85, 138; Ule 1963.

50 Gusy has demonstrated this consistently and convincingly in his book '*Weimar – die wehrlose Republik?*' ('Weimar – the defenceless Republic?', Gusy 1991); for party bans in the Weimar Republic, see Mommsen 2002; Stein 1999; see also Klamt 2007: 136, who quotes the example of the prohibition by law of the Nazi NSDAP in Prussia (1922) and throughout the *Reich* (1923); the party has been re-established in February 1925.

decision on them.[51] This problem could be solved by a differentiation between the *pouvoir constitué*, the legislator changing and amending the constitution, and the *pouvoir constituant (originaire)*, the legislator having originally created the Basic Law. Only the *pouvoir constitué* is bound by Article 79 Section 3 of the Basic Law; the sovereign – in Germany the people, Article 20 of the Basic Law – as the legitimating subject of both the *pouvoir constitué* and the *pouvoir constituant* – may even change the inalterable regulations by using his constituent, supra-constitutional power.[52] The prevailing opinion, however, argues that even the *pouvoir constituant* is bound by the 'Clause of Eternity'.[53]

'Enemies' of the Constitution in Public Service

The Basic Law does not contain any provision explicitly dealing with the duty of allegiance of public servants ('*beamtenrechtliche Treuepflicht*').[54] Article 33 Section 5 of the Basic Law only demands the observance of the '*hergebrachte Grundsätze des Berufsbeamtentums*' (customary principles of public service). The duty of allegiance to the constitution is regulated in sub-constitutional law in the *Beamtengesetze* of the *Bund* and the *Länder* (Laws on Public Servants) and applies – in a lighter form – to employees and workers in the public sector (Rudolf 2003: 210).

The problem of the duty of allegiance has been discussed in the aftermath of the so-called '*Radikalenerlass*' (decree on radicals) or '*Extremistenbeschluss*' of 1972 (Rudolf 2003: 219 et seq.).[55] The Federal Chancellor and the Minister-Presidents of the *Länder* declared that the duty to advocate the free democratic basic order was an *active* one and that activities contrary to the constitution violated this duty. The membership of parties or other organizations that fight against the constitutional order was a breach of duty according to the *Radikalenerlass* and the employing corporate body had to decide on the disciplinary measures to be taken. This decree has to be considered as a reaction to the deep political uncertainty caused by the *Außerparlamentarische Opposion* (extraparlamentary opposition) and the student revolts of 1968. To contribute to the solution of several unresolved questions, the Constitutional Court made a landmark decision in 1975.[56] It classified the duty of allegiance as one of the customary principles of

51 See, for example, Preuß 1984: 11, 13; Tomuschat 1972: 147, 151.

52 See Zacharias 2003: 60 et seq., for further references.

53 See, for example, Even 1988: 101 et seq., and – especially against the background of the German reunification – Erichsen 1992: 55; Stern 1990: 293 et seq.; Weis 1991: 30.

54 The history of the public servant's duty of allegiance is elaborately described by Rudolf 2003: 212 et seq.

55 Gemeinsamer Beschluß des Bundeskanzlers und der Ministerpräsidenten der Länder, 28 January 1972, *Bulletin des Presse- und Informationsamtes der Bundesregierung* 1972, nos. 15, 142 (cited in BVerfGE 39, 334, 366).

56 BVerfGE 39, 334, 345.

public service, which were elevated to constitutional status by Article 33 Section 5 of the Basic Law (Rudolf 2003: 224 et seq.). It held that the duty should not only cover a 'formally correct', 'uninterested, cool, internally distant' attitude towards state and constitution, as well as an active dissociation from views and activities hostile to the constitution.[57] The public servant has to support the free democratic basic order.

This judicature led to a bundle of consequences. The duty of allegiance as understood by the Constitutional Court is a condition of employment; only a person who (prognostically) guarantees to advocate for the free democratic basic order can be appointed to the civil service (see, for example, § 7 Section 1 no. 2 of the Federal Law on Public Servants – *Bundesbeamtengesetz*; Rudolf 2003: 227). The concealment of relevant facts leads to the retraction of the appointment because of malicious fraud (Rudolf 2003: 211). The duty even outreaches the active period of service. Pensions can be curtailed should a former public servant be involved in activities that, for example, try to attack the free democratic basic order.

Like all manifestations of the 'militant democracy' and several decisions of the Constitutional Court, this has been criticized (Rudolf 2003: 231, for further references). The duty of allegiance as constructed by the court has been reproved for being imprecise and not giving any clear instructions, and the demand for an *active* acquittal has been animadverted for constituting a 'duty of resistance' inconsistent with the conception of Article 20 Section 4 of the Basic Law. It can be conceded that the idea of a duty of allegiance with constitutional status may cause some bizarre results: Bernhard Schlink has pointed out that an enemy of the constitution could become a Minister of Justice, but not a public prosecutor (Schlink 1976: 366).

Sub-Constitutional Provisions

The 'militant democracy' principle manifests in a multitude of sub-constitutional legal regulations that cannot be presented fully and in detail here. Two examples have been selected: the protection of the free constitutional basic order by the Criminal Law;[58] and the so-called '*administrativer Verfassungsschutz*' (protection of the constitution by Administrative Law).

The 'free democratic basic order' is mentioned only twice in the *Strafgesetzbuch* (StGB, Penal Code): § 86 Section 2 defines as measures of propaganda of organizations hostile to the constitution such instruments that turn against the free democratic basic order or the idea of international understanding (Deiters 2003: 291). § 92 Section 2 declares that facts violating the free democratic basic order are not protected as state secrets. But there are several norms that make actions a punishable offence that are directed against subjects of protection closely connected with the current constitutional order. Some offences have to

57 BVerfGE 39, 334, 348.

58 See Deiters 2003; Schroeder 1970.

be excluded here because they only protect the state, irrespective of its internal order – for example, the prohibition of a war of aggression (§ 80 of the Penal Code) – or government bodies and institutions, for example, § 196 (coercion of the *Bundespräsident*, Members of Parliament and other mandate holders) or § 107 a (election fraud) of the Penal Code.

§§ 81 Section 1 no. 2, 82 Section 1 no. 2, 83 of the Penal Code declares the *Verfassungshochverrat* (high treason against the constitution – the Basic Law or a constitution of a *Land* and its preparation)[59] a punishable offence, that is the attack against the constitutional order of the Basic Law or a constitution of a *Land*, conducted with force or the threat of force. §§ 84 et seq. deal with any danger or threat to the democratic state under the rule of law ('*demokratischer Rechtsstaat*'); they comprise, *inter alia*, non-violent activities against the free democratic basic order – for example, the distribution of the programme of a political party banned by the Constitutional Court (§ 86 Section 1 no. 1 of the Penal Code) or acts of anti-constitutional sabotage (§§ 87, 88 of the Penal Code).[60]

The protection of the constitution by administrative measures, especially those taken by the intelligence services, is too wide a subject to be discussed here in full. The *Bundesnachrichtendienst* (Federal Intelligence Service) is – as a superordinate federal authority – responsible for connaissance abroad (Schmalenbach 2003: 420 et seq.), while the *Militärischer Abschirmdienst* (Military Counter-Intelligence Service) and the *Ämter für Verfassungsschutz* of the *Bund* and the *Länder* (Offices for the Protection of the Constitution) conduct, for example, information procurement to guarantee internal security (Schmalenbach 2003: 421 et seq., 426 et seq.). The legal regulations that authorize the services are hotly debated in the minutest detail.

The distinction between the tasks of the Intelligence Services and those of the police is difficult and, especially so in recent years, has become even more blurred with the introduction of the *Terrorismusbekämpfungsgesetz* of 2002 (Law on the War against Terrorism),[61] (Schmalenbach 2003: 427 et seq.). In a nutshell, the police are in charge of protecting from danger and pursuing criminal prosecution, although this is mainly restricted to individual cases. The intelligence services engage in widespread observation of the behaviour of individuals and organizations (Schmalenbach 2003: 428). Both authorities collaborate, for example, in the fight against organized crime, and are at the forefront of preventing threats or dangers to the public or state. These intersections have been criticized for violating the *Trennungsgebot* (order of segregation), a principle with constitutional status[62] that

59 On the problem of whether preparatory activities are punishable, see Deiters 2003: 305 et seq.

60 For example, sabotage of infrastructural facilities for water supply with the intention of a fight against constitutional principles or against the existence or the security of the Federal Republic of Germany.

61 BGBl. I 2002, 1254.

62 See Schmalenbach 2003: 433 et seq., on the constitutional justification of this status.

forbids closer connections between police authorities and intelligence services, and that is rooted in a decree of the allied Military Governors to the President of the Parliamentary Council of 8/14 April 1949 ('*Polizeibrief*').[63] This laid down that a future Intelligence Service 'shall have no police authority' (Schmalenbach 2003: 432).

State of Emergency – Legal Provisions

The state of emergency is regulated in various articles of the Basic Law, not '*en bloc*'. These norms have been integrated into the constitution by the *Siebzehntes Gesetz zur Änderung des Grundgesetzes* ('17th Law amending the Basic Law') of 24 June 1968.[64] Article 81 of the Basic Law speaks of 'legislatory emergency'. On closer examination, the situation this norm relates to is not a case of emergency, but a simple 'disorder' of the constitutional proceedings (Windthorst 2003: 365, 368 et seq.). The 'emergency' is not defined in the Basic Law, but can be described as a situation with serious dangers for the existence of the state and public security and order (Stern 1980: 1295). In addition to that, this situation must become exceptional – the dangers cannot be eliminated using the measures provided for by the constitution (and the valid sub-constitutional legal order). Articles 35 Section 3, 80a, 87a Section 4, 91, and 115a of the Basic Law contain several provisions for states of emergency of a different kind and the authorization to take specific measures. The 'external state of emergency' occurs, for example, in a state of defence according to Article 115a of the Basic Law,[65] that is, if the Federal Republic of Germany is attacked by armed forces or if such an attack is impending. The 'internal state of emergency' is constituted by threats originating from inside the state or society, for example, a threat to the free democratic basic order (Article 91 of the Basic Law); a 'general internal state of emergency' (Article 35 Section 2 Sentence 1 of the Basic Law) caused by threats to or the violation of important subjects of legal protection; or the internal state of emergency in case of (regional or supra-regional) disaster (Article 35 Section 2 Sentence 2 and Section 3 Sentence 1 of the Basic Law). This differentiation depicts the classical dichotomy of war and rebellion (Windthorst 2003: 271 et seq.).

In emergency cases, several provisions of the constitution are significantly modified. The state of defence as an external state of emergency leads, for example, to an enhancement (and concentration) of the legislatory competences of the *Bund* and a 'shortened' law-making procedure (Article 115d of the Basic Law). The 'internal case of emergency' permits the threatened *Land* to request help from the *Bund* (requisition of federal police forces) or other *Länder* (police forces).[66]

63 See Huber 1951: 216.

64 BGBl. I 709; see Windthorst 2003: 374 et seq.

65 External states of emergency are regulated in Articles 80a Section 1 Sentence 1, 1st and 2nd Alternatives, and 80a Section 3 of the Basic Law.

66 See Windthorst 2003: 403 et seq.

Criticism

Although the common view seems to be that a democracy has the fundamental right to defend itself against attacks and to prevent such attacks, these measures are broadly considered to collide with liberal democratic theory. As John Stuart Mill expressed the 'credo' of classical liberalism in his work '*On Liberty*': 'We can never be sure that the opinion we are endeavoring to stifle is a false opinion. And if we were sure, stifling it would still be evil.' The democracy fights against persons or groups that make use of their democratic rights, the tolerant state form of democracy suddenly turns intolerant.

This is a common point of criticism of the 'militant democracy' principle in Germany. Many scholars insist that Article 21 Section 2 of the Basic Law that allows the ban of a political party should be repealed. They claim that forces of political self-regulation will eliminate any extremist party through the election process. In addition, Article 21 Section 2 of the Basic Law has proven to be something of a blunt sword or a 'paper tiger', since there have only been two successful legal procedures which led to a ban, yet the mere possibility of banning a party may prevent extremist political parties from overly zealous agitation. To put it simply, let us say this possibility is, like many of the other measures in Germany, something of a 'scarecrow'.

Mainstream opinion among constitutional law scholars in Germany accepts the 'admission' of the *Grundgesetz* of a 'militant democracy' as one of its core decisions. In the aftermath of the Federal Constitutional Court's first decisions, a number of books and articles were published which took a close look at the militancy principle from different points of view (Boventer 1985; Bulla 1973; Fromme 1981; Jesse 1981; Lameyer 1978a; Sattler 1982). Nevertheless, the idea of a 'militant democracy' and its 'elevation' to a constitutional principle useable in the balancing of legally protected interests and as a limitation for fundamental rights in the Constitutional Court's judicature has been vehemently criticized. As in matters of security in general, opinions are divided into two camps. While 'militant democracy' may have been outlined by the Constitutional Court and in legal doctrine, it has turned out to be difficult to embed the principle into modern democratic theory. Some scholars argue that militancy has slipped into crisis (for example, Jasper 1978: 725 et seq). In many cases, it appears that criticism of the 'militant democracy' principle is politically motivated and is aimed more at the conception of security behind the legal construction than at this construction itself. Nevertheless, we will have to take a detailed look at the common objections which can be grouped into several key arguments.

The first objection is of a methodical nature. The supporters of the militancy principle, the Federal Constitutional Court in particular, have been accused of forcing together single exceptional legal rules to an overarching principle that serves, in turn, as a 'well spring' for further legal measures of protection, or at least as a justification for such measures. This procedure may lead to a vicious circle where the state, or those institutions that are entitled to apply the legal protective measures, can choose provisions and sanctions to defend itself, which are almost exempt from any legal bonds. This argument raises the question of who will be authorized and able to supervise and control the 'militant democracy' from extensively taking measures to protect itself, thus ensuring the fundamental rights of the citizens against their annulment in the name of militancy. The 'militant democracy' is also criticized as a dangerous 'syncretistic row of addition' (Ridder 1957: 358). Several authors reject the possibility of accepting the 'militant democracy' as a 'constitutional decision' with a stand-alone *legal* importance (Bulla 1973: 346 et seq., 355 et seq.; Denninger 1979: 18 et seq.; Lameyer 1982: 151 et seq., Schlink 1976: 361 et seq., 160 et seq., 170 et seq.). Erhard Denninger, for example, points out that a far-reaching authority to take measures against the democracy's enemies cannot be deduced from a number of simple assignments of legal duties (Denninger 1979: 18 et seq.); the 'militant democracy' principle is, in his opinion, an unacceptable 'supra-legal' feature (Denninger 1979: 18 et seq.). This mirrors the distinction between task and authority (*Aufgabe* and *Befugnis*) in German legal doctrine. But if we understand the 'militant democracy' principle as outlined by the Constitutional Court, it does not extend the state's (or its institutions') authorities, for example, in curtailing fundamental rights directly, but is a criterion for interpretation, and the balancing of rights and values. It does not pave the way for a more 'etatistic' system; it avoids it. It does not try to level pluralistic points of view concerning the structure of a democracy and to denounce every opinion different from a hypothetical consensus. The close connection to the so-called 'free democratic basic order' links the militancy principle to the freedom guarantees of the fundamental rights provided in the Basic Law and thus averts the undesirable development of an all-purpose weapon of state protection.

The democratic dilemma between the principle of non-identification of the state and the decision for a system of values manifested in the free democratic basic order is solved by the provision of measures that only come into action if someone is actively 'fighting' against this order and not if someone is just having (or peacefully expressing) an opinion incongruent with the Basic Law's system of values. Such measures must not be taken in a 'legal vacuum'; the state has to respect legal boundaries.

It can be conceded that the legal rules that form the 'militant democracy' are quite heterogeneous. In German constitutional theory, the addition of different norms and regulations written down in the Basic Law to an overarching or supra-legal principle is common practice. This can be seen, for example, with regard to the principle of state neutrality arising from several provisions in the German constitution, to the legal complex of the so-called '*Kulturverfassungsrecht*' ('cultural constitutional law'), coined by Peter Häberle (Häberle 1980, 1982), or to the free democratic basic order itself. The Basic Law forms, according to the Federal Constitutional Court, a unit, so that single norms and provisions cannot be looked at or interpreted in isolation, separated from their constitutional context.[67] The concept of the '*Einheit der Verfassung*' (unity of the constitution) is a guideline for the interpretation of the constitution (Müller 2007b). From this, it appears that the protective measures the German Basic Law has erected as a wall around the core principles of the constitution as stipulated in Article 79 Section 3 of the Basic Law provide proof of an essential decision in favour of a 'militant democracy'. In turn, this decision influences the interpretation of the norms and provisions of the constitution.[68] Rejecting the possibility of extracting overarching constitutional principles from single regulations, we would relinquish an important instrument of juridical exegesis, and we would have to bid farewell to such well-established principles as the state's neutrality in religious and worldview matters. The aim of sustaining such principles would require practicing a variant of legal positivism left behind in jurisprudence long ago. The Federal Constitutional Court did not simply generalize some norms together, but referred to an underlying or overarching idea. Reflecting this origin accurately, the 'militant democracy' is not the result of deduction, but the recognition of a principle prior to written constitutional law, borne in mind by the creators of the German constitution, and 'exploited' by interpretation of the Basic Law's wording. The 'militant democracy' principle is not merely a 'Preamble' for the norms regulating protective measures; it would have no practical function if reduced to this task. It outreaches these norms and is in force even in 'unregulated fields'. Nevertheless, the principle of 'militant democracy' carries the venom of malpractice in itself. This is not to dismiss the argument against the existence of militancy as a constitutional principle; it only relates to the application of this principle and its limits.

The Basic Law has overcome the relativism of values that characterized the Weimar Republic (Thiel 2003c: 13). The declaration of Hans Kelsen, the famous exponent of legal positivism, that democracy has to tolerate even a movement aimed at the destruction of democracy to remain true to itself, and that one has to cleave to the flag even if the ship is sinking (Kelsen 1932 [1967]: 68), although a genuine and central quality of democracy according to a liberal democratic conception, has been rejected by the Federal Constitutional Court.

The 'militant democracy' principle in Germany has variously been criticized for solidifying a state of emergency or exception and as establishing a 'secondary constitution' (Ridder 1975: 134). To decry militancy as a feature of a somehow 'morganatic' constitution misconstrues its purpose. But the objective raised to the 'militant democracy' principle as understood and used by the Constitutional Court in referring to the abuse problem cannot be dismissed that easily. Some scholars assert that the principle leads the way for an 'authoritarian' conception of the state and overrates the 'sphere of the state' over the 'sphere of freedom'. Even authors who consider the militancy principle in a well-balanced manner evoke the danger

67 BVerfGE 1, 14, 32; 3, 225, 231 et seq.; see, for example, Sattler 1982: 31 et seq.; Stern 1984: 113 et seq.; and, more general, Wolff 1955: 33 et seq.

68 See, for example, Klein 1979: 67 et seq.

of an overemphasis on the state and its interests (Lameyer 1981: 178). The Basic Law guarantees not only measures of protection in favour of the state, but also and primarily rights and freedoms of the citizens and of all human beings. The Basic Law contains not only provisions to safeguard the democratic system against the citizens, but also the citizens against the state's institutions.

All these statements are correct, but they fall short if we consider the necessity of a militancy principle, at least of defensive measures. In constitutional law and political theory, the values of 'security' and 'freedom' often are regarded as antipodes – the more security the state provides, the more restrictions to freedom the people will have to bear. This point of view is one sided; security and freedom do not repulse magnetically, but are mutually dependent. A democratic system that guarantees rights and freedoms and is not able to defend itself against revolution could not sustain the 'level of freedom' held hitherto. So the perpetuation of the free democratic basic order as safeguarded by the militancy principle is a condition *sine qua non* for democratic rights and freedoms. The question is not if there have to be measures against the destruction of democracy, but the number and extent of such measures. It remains questionable if a specific level of security could only be guaranteed by 'upgrading' single defensive measures to a principle with ubiquitous validity and constitutional status. The Federal Constitutional Court has answered this question in the affirmative and, holding all serious criticism justifiable and worthy of further consideration, the court's opinion is crucial here, in view of its paramount importance for the interpretation and further development of German constitutional law. The court is the 'guardian of the constitution'; to invoke this may be a weak argument in favour of the substantial persuasiveness of the 'militant democracy' conception, but it is a fact that must be kept in mind by those who are applying the law.

A further argument against a 'militant democracy' principle in Germany is quite similar to the objection mentioned previously concerning the problem of malpractice. Even if it is unlikely that we need to fear a misuse aimed at the abolition of the democratic system itself, the militancy principle is sometimes criticized for absolving the Constitutional Court from diligently defining the range of acceptable measures in each individual case. The court could balance (and has, in practice), for example, fundamental rights with the decision of the Basic Law for a 'militant democracy' *in abstracto*, so that the latter tends to evolve into a 'knockout criterion'. But again, this objection disregards the constitutional boundaries of the 'militant democracy' principle itself. Although the rule of law, the human dignity as provided for in Article 1 of the Basic Law, and the sacrosanct essential content of fundamental rights ('*Wesensgehalt*') are all paramount constitutional principles and values, they cannot impact the 'whether' of the militancy principle, but they can definitely affect its 'how' (Lameyer 1978a: 156). They have to be included in any consideration conducted by the Constitutional Court; the concrete circumstances of the individual cases will not be neglected even if the 'militant democracy' principle is applied.

The creators of the constitution were aware of this problem; hence they installed procedural requirements in the Basic Law, for example, in Article 18 of the Basic Law on the forfeiture of fundamental rights and in Article 21 Section 2 of the Basic Law on the ban of political parties – measures which severely affect fundamental rights. Therefore, the 'militant democracy' principle is not unacceptable, although it restricts fundamental rights and liberties. This has to be stressed: it *restricts* these rights, but does not *undermine* them.[69] The 'militant democracy' does not fight the enemies of the free democratic basic order actively; it defends itself by reacting to concrete offences (Thiel 2003c: 24). By securing the free democratic basic order, it simultaneously secures these rights and liberties.

The last objection stresses the 'conservative', biased character of the 'militant democracy' principle and its liability to ideological manipulation (Bulla 1973: 355 et seq.; Häberle 1971: 146 et seq.; Schneider 1974: 308). A protective-conservative nature to the militancy principle is widely accepted without anything further; however, in the opinion of the author, this is neither a disadvantage we should be eager to discard nor a valid *legal* argument against the acceptance of this principle. As we have seen, it cannot be used to push through any ephemeral ideologies by misusing the measures provided in the Basic Law, but only to secure the free basic democratic order. The Basic Law defends itself against *any* kind of totalitarianism – even if the 'militant democracy' can be called 'conservative', it does not privilege, for example, right-wing activities and protagonists. This is apparent from the debate about the ban of right-extremist parties. The militancy, though, remains a legally decreed constitutional consensus.

Bearing this in mind, the concept of a 'militant democracy' as a constitutional principle can be seen to have some advantages. By describing its content, the German Federal Constitutional Court simultaneously erected constitutional boundaries for defensive measures. Democracies that regulate such measures without explicitly stated constitutional boundaries may 'overshoot'. This is an aspect the legal philosopher Giorgio Agamben pointed out in his book *State of Exception* (Agamben 2005). He describes the change of political structures and of the steps governments may take in times of crisis. Individual rights and the rule of law may be diminished or suspended, and the government may act without observance of the legal order. Agamben emphasizes the danger of a prolongation of this so-called 'state of exception', and criticizes the US Government, especially former President George W. Bush, for his military order of November 2001 and the status of the captured Taliban as 'enemy combatants' with drastically reduced rights. They were neither treated as prisoners of war as defined by the Geneva Conventions nor as people charged with a crime according to US laws.

Although Agamben's remarks have been criticized for being somewhat obscure and for producing dubious consequences, and although the state of exception in permanence he warns of is most likely fiction, they show that a 'militant democracy' principle cannot legitimate such extensive restrictions of fundamental rights.

69 A 'loss of freedom' is suspected by Hesse (Hesse 1975: 441; 1995: 694).

Alternatives[70]

The 'militant democracy' principle has been ridiculed as a 'fossile of democratic theory',[71] based on a historical and normative perception.[72] In the light of the 'shift of values', and regarding the time that has passed since the downfall of totalitarian systems on German territory – is militancy as a principle with a constitutional status and a substantive legal content on its own still necessary or would a 'softer' solution be conceivable? In my opinion, the militancy principle is not compelling and indispensible; but the threats posed on modern democratic systems are not completely abolished. They only have changed. The 'war' against international terrorism of any provenience who carries terror, menace and destruction into our home countries, should not only comprise military operations in far reaches[73] and the immediate protection of the citizens' rights (for example, life, health and property). Terrorists are (or will be soon) clever enough to use other 'channels' to pursue their sinister goals, and perhaps they will try to corrupt our democratic systems from within. A 'feeling of safety' against formerly threatening enemies of the free democratic basic order, such as political extremists in public service and extremist rabble-rousers, must not lull us, neglecting threats in new forms of appearance. We have to remain vigilant: that those enemies have not been successful at all must not lead us to provide an 'open flank' – their failure is, to some extent, due to the deterrent impact of the militant democracy's measures.

Every democracy needs provisions to protect itself – the German democracy does not rely on selective legal regulations only, but has developed an overarching 'militant democracy' principle including constitutional and sub-constitutional measures. According to the common classification developed by Fox and Nolte (1995), Germany can be qualified as a 'militant substantive democracy'. The 'constitutionalization' of the 'militant democracy' in the German Basic Law has therefore often been described as a 'reflex-action to history' (especially the experience of dictatorship and totalitarianism) and as a 'Copernican turn' in constitutional history.[74] Of course, this is not the only possible path – neither democratic theory nor constitutional law urges the acceptance of 'militant democracy' as an independent constitutional value and principle (Thiel 2003c: 23). The provisions in the Basic Law could just as easily be regarded as a 'piecemeal' system of single norms and regulations. It is the Federal Constitutional Court who chose an alternative way of interpretation.

70 This aspect is discussed in more detail in Chapter 15.

71 Fromme 1981: 215 et seq., speaks of an 'ageing process' and an 'erosion' of the militant democracy.

72 For criticism, see Jaschke 1990: 232 et seq.

73 The legal problems connected with such operations will not be discussed here; see, for example, Günther 2003: 329 et seq, with additional references.

74 See, for example, Klamt 2007: 140, with further references; Papier and Durner 2003: 343 et seq.

References

Agamben, Giorgio (2005) *State of Exception*. Chicago: University of Chicago Press.

Anschütz, Gerhard (1933) *Die Verfassung des Deutschen Reichs vom 11. August 1919. Ein Kommentar für Wissenschaft und Praxis*, 14th edn. Berlin: Stilke.

Baer, Susanne (2000) 'Violence: Dilemma of Democracy and Law', in David Kretzmer and Francine Kershman Hazan (eds) *Freedom of Speech and Incitement Against Democracy*. The Hague, London and Boston: Kluwer Law International, 63–98.

Becker, Jürgen (1992) 'Die wehrhafte Demokratie des Grundgesetzes', in Josef Isensee and Paul Kirchhof (eds) *Handbuch des Staatsrechts des Bundesrepublik Deutschland, vol. VII: Normativität und Schutz der Verfassung – Internationale Beziehungen*. Heidelberg: C.F. Müller, 309–59.

Böckenförde, Christoph (1970) 'Die Kodifizierung des Widerstandsrechts im Grundgesetz', *Juristenzeitung*: 168–72.

Boventer, Gregor Paul (1985) *Grenzen politischer Freiheit im demokratischen Staat: das Konzept der streitbaren Demokratie in einem internationalen Vergleich*. Berlin: Duncker and Humblot.

Bryde, Brun-Otto (1982) *Verfassungsentwicklung, Stabilität und Dynamik im Verfassungsrecht der Bundesrepublik Deutschland*. Baden-Baden: Nomos.

Bulla, Eckart (1973) 'Die Lehre von der streitbaren Demokratie – Versuch einer kritischen Analyse unter besonderer Berücksichtigung der Rechtsprechung des Bundesverfassungsgerichts', *Archiv des öffentlichen Rechts* 98(3): 340–60.

Deiters, Mark (2003) 'Der Schutz der freiheitlichen demokratischen grundordnung durch das Strafrecht', in Markus Thiel (ed.) *Wehrhafte Demokratie. Beiträge über die Regelungen zum Schutze der freiheitlichen demokratischen Grundordnung*. Tübingen: Mohr Siebeck, 291–328.

Denninger, Erhard (1979) 'Verfassungstreue und Schutz der Verfassung', *VVDStRL* (37): 7–51.

Dreier, Horst (1994) 'Grenzen demokratischer Freiheit im Verfassungsstaat', *Juristenzeitung*, 741–52.

Dürig, Günter (1971) 'Zur Bedeutung und Tragweite des Art. 79 III des Grundgesetzes (ein Plädoyer)', in Hans Spanner, Peter Lerche, Hans Zacher, Friedrich Badura, Peter von Campenhausen and Axel von Freiherr (eds) *Festgabe für Theodor Maunz zum 70. Geburtstag am 1. September 1971*. München: C.H. Beck, 41 et seq.

Ehmke, Horst (1953) *Grenzen der Verfassungsänderung*. Berlin: Duncker and Humblot.

Erichsen, Hans-Uwe (1992) 'Die Verfassungsänderung nach Art. 79 und der Verfassungsbeschluß nach Art. 146 GG', *Jura*: 52 et seq.

Even, Bert (1951) *Das Widerstandsrecht des Staatsbürgers*. Köln.

Even, Burkhard (1988) *Die Bedeutung der Unantastbarkeitsgarantie des Art. 79 Abs. 3 GG für die Grundrechte*. Frankfurt a.M. et al.: Peter Lang.

Fox, Gregory H. and Nolte, Georg (1995) 'Intolerant Democracies', *Harvard International Law Journal* 36(1): 1–70.

Fromme, Friedrich Karl (1981) 'Die Streitbare Demokratie im Bonner Grundgesetz. Ein Verfassungsbegriff im Wandel', in Innern des Bundesministerium (ed.) *Verfassungsschutz und Rechtsstaat, Beiträge aus Wissenschaft und Praxis.* Köln, Berlin, Bonn and München: Heymanns Verlag, 185 et seq.

Füßlein, Rudolf Werner (1951) in Klaus-Berto von Doemming, Rudolf Werner Füßlein and Werner Matz (eds) 'Entstehungsgeschichte der Artikel des Grundgesetzes', *Jahrbuch des öffentlichen Rechts der Gegenwart n.F.* (1): 573 et seq.

Gallwas, Hans-Ulrich (1967) *Der Mißbrauch von Grundrechten.* Berlin: Duncker and Humblot.

Günther, Thomas (2003) 'Zum Einsatz der Bundeswehr im Ausland', in Markus Thiel (ed.) *Wehrhafte Demokratie. Beiträge über die Regelungen zum Schutze der freiheitlichen demokratischen Grundordnung.* Tübingen: Mohr Siebeck, 329–64.

Gusy, Christoph (1991) *Weimar – die wehrlose Republik?* Tübingen: Mohr Siebeck.

Häberle, Peter (1971) 'Die Abhörentscheidung des Bundesverfassungsgerichts vom 15.12.1970', *Juristenzeitung* (26): 145–56.

Häberle, Peter (1980) *Kulturverfassungsrecht im Bundesstaat.* Wien: Braumüller.

Häberle, Peter (ed.) (1982) *Kulturstaatlichkeit und Kulturverfassungsrecht.* Darmstadt: Wissenschaftliche Buchgesellschaft.

Hall, Karl-Heinrich (1972) 'Abhörentscheidung und Grundgesetz – BVerfGE 30, 1', *Juristische Schulung*: 132–7.

Heinemann, Jan (2003) 'Das Widerstandsrecht nach Art. 20 Abs. 4 GG', in Markus Thiel (ed.) *Wehrhafte Demokratie. Beiträge über die Regelungen zum Schutze der freiheitlichen demokratischen Grundordnung.* Tübingen: Mohr Siebeck, 99–128.

Hesse, Konrad (1975) 'Bemerkungen zur heutigen Problematik und Tragweite der Unterscheidung von Staat und Gesellschaft', *Die Öffentliche Verwaltung*: 437–43.

Hesse, Konrad (1995) *Grundzüge des Verfassungsrechts der Bundesrepublik Deutschland*, 20th edn. Heidelberg: C.F. Müller Verlag.

von der Heydte, Friedrich August (1954) 'Freiheit der Parteien', in Franz L. Neumann, Hans Carl Nipperdey and Ulrich Scheuner (eds) *Handbuch der Theorie und Praxis der Grundrechte, vol. II.* Berlin, 457–506.

Huba, Hermann (1991) 'Das Grundgesetz als dauerhafte gesamtdeutsche verfassung. Erinnerung an seine Legitimität', *Der Staat* (30): 367–77.

Huber, Ernst Rudolf (1951) *Quellen zum Staatsrecht der Neuzeit, vol. II: Deutsche Verfassungsdokumente der Gegenwart (1919–1951).* Tübingen: M. Matthiesen.

Ipsen, Jörn (2002) 'Rechtsfragen des NPD-Verbots', *Neue Juristische Wochenschrift*: 866–8.

Isensee, Josef (1969) *Das legalisierte Widerstandsrecht. Eine staatsrechtliche Analyse des Art. 20 Abs. 4 Grundgesetz.* Bad Homburg v.d.H. – Berlin – Zürich: Gehlen.

Jahrreiß, Hermann (1950) 'Demokratie. Selbstbewußtsein – Selbstgefährdung – Selbstschutz', in *Festschrift für Richard Thoma zum 75. Geburtstag am 19. Dezember 1949.* Tübingen: Mohr Siebeck, 71–91.

Jaschke, Hans-Gerd (1990) 'Wertewandel in Politik und Gesellschaft. Ist die streitbare Demokratie noch zeitgemäß?', in Bundesamt für den Verfassungsschutz (ed.) *Verfassungsschutz in der Demokratie. Beiträge aus Wissenschaft und Praxis.* Köln, Berlin, Bonn and München: Heymanns Verlag.

Jasper, Gotthard (1978) 'Die Krise der streitbaren Demokratie', *Deutsche Verwaltungsblätter*: 725–33.

Jesse, Eckhard (1981) *Streitbare Demokratie. Theorie, Praxis und Herausforderungen in der Bundesrepublik Deutschland*, 2nd edn. Berlin: Colloquium.

Jesse, Eckhard (1993) 'Der Schutz demokratischer Verfassungsstaaten vor extremistischen Bestrebungen', in Bayerische Landeszentrale für politische Bildungsarbeit (ed.) *Politischer Extremismus in Deutschland und Europa* (München), 133–47.

Kelsen, Hans (1932 [1967]) 'Verteidigung der Demokratie', in Norbert Leser (ed.) *Hans Kelsen, Demokratie und Sozialismus. Ausgewählte Aufsätze.* Wien: Verlag der Wiener Volksbuchhandlung. Originally published in *Blätter der Staatspartei* (2): 90–8.

Klamt, Martin (2007) 'Militant Democracy and the Democratic Dilemma: Different Ways of Protecting Democratic Constitutions', in Fred Bruinsma and David Nelken (eds) *Explorations in Legal Cultures* (Recht der Werkelijkheid 28:3). Den Haag: Elsevier, 133–59.

Klein, Hans Hugo (1979) 'Verfassungstreue und Schutz der Verfassung', *VVDStRL* (37): 53–113.

Klug, Ulrich (1984) 'Das Widerstandsrecht als allgemeines Menschenrecht', in Werner Hill (ed.) *Widerstand und Staatsgewalt. Recht im Streit mit dem Gesetz.* Gütersloh: Gütersloher Verlagshaus, 11 et seq.

Lameyer, Johannes (1978a) *Streitbare Demokratie. Eine verfassungshermeneutische Untersuchung.* Berlin: Duncker and Humblot.

Lameyer, Johannes (1978b) 'Streitbare Demokratie contra Terrorismus', *Zeitschrift für Rechtspolitik*: 49–51.

Lameyer, Johannes (1981) 'Streitbare Demokratie', *Jahrbuch des öffentlichen Rechts der Gegenwart n.F.* (30): 147–96.

Lang, Markus (2007) *Karl Loewenstein. Transatlantischer Denker der Politik.* Stuttgart: Franz Steiner Verlag.

Loewenstein, Karl (1935a) 'Autocracy Versus Democracy in Contemporary Europe', part I, *American Political Science Review* (29): 571–93.

Loewenstein, Karl (1935b) 'Autocracy Versus Democracy in Contemporary Europe', part II, *American Political Science Review* (29): 755–84.

Loewenstein, Karl (1937a) 'Militant Democracy and Fundamental Rights', part I, *American Political Science Review* 31(3): 417–32.

Loewenstein, Karl (1937b) 'Militant Democracy and Fundamental Rights', part II, *American Political Science Review* 31(4): 638–58.

Macklem, Patrick (2006) 'Militant Democracy, Legal Pluralism, and the Paradox of Self-Determination', *International Journal of Constitutional Law* 4(3): 488–516.

Mannheim, Karl (1943 [1998]) *Diagnosis of Our Time: Wartime Essays of a Sociologist. Collected Works, vol. III.* London and New York: Routledge.

Maurer, Hartmut (1971) 'Das Verbot politischer Parteien. Zur Problematik des Art. 21 Abs. 2 GG', *Archiv des öffentlichen Rechts* (96): 203–36.

Mommsen, Hans (2002) 'Die stumpfe Waffe. Parteiverbote in der Weimarer Republik', in Carl Leggewie and Horst Meier (eds) *Verbot der NPD oder Mit Rechtsradikalen leben?* Frankfurt a.M.: Suhrkamp, 145–51.

Morlok, Martin (2001) 'Parteiverbot als Verfassungsschutz – Ein unauflösbarer Widerspruch?', *Neue Juristische Wochenschrift* 40(54): 2931–42.

Müller, Friedrich (2007a) *Die Einheit der Verfassung. Elemente einer Verfassungstheorie III*, 2nd edn. Berlin: Duncker and Humblot.

Müller, Jan-Werner (2007b) *Constitutional Patriotism.* Princeton and Oxford: Princeton University Press.

Papier, Hans-Jürgen and Durner, Wolfgang (2003) 'Streitbare Demokratie', *Archiv des öffentlichen Rechts* 128(3): 340–71.

Pfahl-Traughber, Armin (2002) 'Die NPD in der zweiten Hälfte der neunziger Jahre. Ideologie, Strategie und Organisation', in Carl Leggewie and Horst Meier (eds) *Verbot der NPD oder Mit Rechtsradikalen leben?* Frankfurt a.M.: Suhrkamp, 30–43.

Preuß, Ulrich K. (1984) *Politische Verantwortung und Bürgerloyalität. Von den Grenzen der Verfassung und dem Gehorsam in der Demokratie.* Frankfurt a.M.: S. Fischer.

Ridder, Helmut (1957) 'Streitbare Demokratie?' *Neue Politische Literatur*: 352–68.

Ridder, Helmut (1975) 'Die soziale Ordnung des Grundgesetzes', in Josef Mück (ed.) *Verfassungsrecht.* Opladen: Westdeutscher Verlag, 85–285.

Rudolf, Beate (2003) '"Verfassungsfeinde" im öffentlichen Dienst', in Markus Thiel (ed.) *Wehrhafte Demokratie. Beiträge über die Regelungen zum Schutze der freiheitlichen demokratischen Grundordnung.* Tübingen: Mohr Siebeck, 209–50.

Sattler, Andreas (1982) *Die rechtliche Bedeutung der Entscheidung für die streitbare Demokratie.* Baden-Baden: Nomos.

Scheuner, Ulrich (1951) 'Grundfragen des modernen Staates', in Hermann Wandersleb (ed.) *Recht – Staat – Wirtschaft. Schriftenreihe für staatswissenschaftliche Fortbildung*, vol. 3. Stuttgart – Köln: Kohlhammer, 126 et seq.

Schlink, Bernhard (1976) 'Zwischen Identifikation und Distanz. Zur Stellung des Beamten im Staat und zur Gestaltung des Beamtenrechts durch das Staatsrecht', *Der Staat* (15): 335–66.

Schmalenbach, Kirsten (2003) 'Administrativer Verfassungsschutz: Bürger unter Beobachtung', in Markus Thiel (ed.) *Wehrhafte Demokratie. Beiträge über die Regelungen zum Schutze der freiheitlichen demokratischen Grundordnung.* Tübingen: Mohr Siebeck, 415–45.

Schmitt, Carl (1932 [1958]) 'Legalität und Legitimität', in Carl Schmitt (ed.) *Verfassungsrechtliche Aufsätze aus den Jahren 1924–1954. Materialien zu einer Verfassungslehre.* Berlin: Duncker and Humblot, 263 et seq.

Schmitt, Carl (1978 [2005]) 'Die legale Weltrevolution. Politischer Mehrwert als Prämie auf juristische Legalität und Superlegalität', in Günter Maschke (ed.) *Carl Schmitt. Frieden oder Pazifismus? Arbeiten zum Völkerrecht und zur internationalen politik 1924–1978.* Berlin: Duncker and Humblot, 918–68.

Schmitt Glaeser, Walter Oskar (1968) *Mißbrauch und Verwirkung der Grundrechte im politischen Meinungskampf. Eine Untersuchung über die Verfassungsschutzbestimmung des Art. 18 GG und ihr Verhältnis zum einfachen Recht, insbesondere zum politischen Strafrecht.* Bad Homburg v.d.H. – Berlin – Zürich: Gehlen.

Schneider, Hans (1971) 'Die Einführung des offenen Sondervotums beim Bundesverfassungsgericht', in Hans Spanner, Peter Lerche, Hans Friedrich Zacher, Peter Badura and Axel Freiherr von Campenhausen (eds) *Festgabe für Theodor Maunz zum 70. Geburtstag am 1. September 1971.* München: C.H. Beck, 345 et seq.

Schneider, Hans-Peter (1974) *Die Parlamentarische Opposition im Verfassungsrecht der Bundesrepublik Deutschland, vol. I.* Frankfurt a.M.: Klostermann.

Schroeder, Friedrich-Christian (1970) *Der Schutz von Staat und Verfassung im Strafrecht. Eine systematische Darstellung, entwickelt aus Rechtsgeschichte und Rechtsvergleichung.* München: C.H. Beck'sche Verlagsbuchhandlung.

Stein, Katrin (1999) *Parteiverbote in der Weimarer Republik.* Berlin: Duncker and Humblot.

Stern, Klaus (1980) *Das Staatsrecht der Bundesrepublik Deutschland, vol. II.* München: C.H. Beck.

Stern, Klaus (1984) *Das Staatsrecht der Bundesrepublik Deutschland, vol. I*, 2nd edn. München: C.H. Beck.

Stern, Klaus (1990) 'Der verfassungsändernde Charakter des Einigungsvertrages', *Deutsch-Deutsche Rechts-Zeitschrift* (9): 289–94.

Stollberg, Frank (1976) *Die verfassungsrechtlichen Grundlagen des Parteiverbots.* Berlin: Duncker and Humblot.

Thiel, Markus (2000) *Der Erziehungsauftrag des Staates in der Schule. Grundlagen und Grenzen staatlicher Erziehungstätigkeit im öffentlichen Schulwesen.* Berlin: Duncker and Humblot.

Thiel, Markus (2003a) 'Das Verbot verfassungswidriger Parteien (Art. 21 Abs. 2 GG)', in Markus Thiel (ed.) *Wehrhafte Demokratie. Beiträge über die Regelungen zum Schutze der freiheitlichen demokratischen Grundordnung.* Tübingen: Mohr Siebeck, 173–207.

Thiel, Markus (2003b) 'Die Verwirkung von Grundrechten gemäß Art. 18 GG', in Markus Thiel (ed.) *Wehrhafte Demokratie. Beiträge über die Regelungen zum Schutze der freiheitlichen demokratischen Grundordnung.* Tübingen: Mohr Siebeck, 129–72.

Thiel, Markus (2003c) 'Zur Einführung: Die "Wehrhafte Demokratie" als verfassungsrechtliche grundentscheidung', in Markus Thiel (ed.) *Wehrhafte Demokratie. Beiträge über die Regelungen zum Schutze der freiheitlichen demokratischen Grundordnung.* Tübingen: Mohr Siebeck, 1–24.

Tillmanns, Reiner (2003) 'Wehrhaftigkeit durch Werthaftigkeit – der ethische Grundkonsens als Existenzvoraussetzung des freiheitlichen Staates', in Markus Thiel (ed.) *Wehrhafte Demokratie. Beiträge über die Regelungen zum Schutze der freiheitlichen demokratischen Grundordnung.* Tübingen: Mohr Siebeck, 25–55.

Tomuschat, Christian (1972, *Verfassungsgewohnheitsrecht? Eine Untersuchung zum Staatsrecht der Bundesrepublik Deutschland.* Heidelberg: Winter.

Ule, Carl Hermann (1963) 'Beamtenrecht im Wandel deutscher Staatlichkeit', *Deutsche Verwaltungsblätter*: 1–10.

Weis, Herbert (1991) 'Verfassungsrechtliche Fragen im Zusammenhang mit der Herstellung der staatlichen Einheit Deutschlands', *Archiv des Öffentlichen Rechts* 116: 1 et seq.

Windthorst, Kay (2003) 'Der Notstand', in Markus Thiel (ed.) *Wehrhafte Demokratie. Beiträge über die Regelungen zum Schutze der freiheitlichen demokratischen Grundordnung.* Tübingen: Mohr Siebeck, 365–414.

Wolff, Hans Julius (1955) 'Rechtsgrundlagen und verfassungsgestaltende Grundentscheidungen als Rechtsquellen', in Otto Bachof, Martin Drath, et al. (eds) *Forschungen und Berichte aus dem Öffentlichen Recht – Gedächtnisschrift für W. Jellinek.* München: Isar Verlag, 33 et seq.

Zacharias, Diana (2003) 'Die sog. Ewigkeitsgarantie des Art. 79 Abs. 3 GG', in Markus Thiel (ed.) *Wehrhafte Demokratie. Beiträge über die Regelungen zum Schutze der freiheitlichen demokratischen Grundordnung.* Tübingen: Mohr Siebeck, 57–97.

Chapter 7
Hungary

Renáta Uitz

Introduction

The Hungarian constitutional system is a moderate parliamentary regime, in which the opposition has a strong position. The Hungarian Party system is well known for its stability: all current parliamentary parties have been around since the time of the Round Table Talks in 1989. This party stability is accompanied by the stability of major constitutional institutions and a relatively low interest (and participation) in politics. Although stable, the political sphere is markedly polarized, the language of politics is often hostile, and consensus seeking is not a high priority.[1] The polarization of elite politics is also mirrored in social polarization with lack of trust in political institutions and political parties, while political participation is moderate at best.[2]

In Hungarian public discourse, it is not uncommon to encounter individuals and groups making nationalistic; racist; Hungarist;[3] anti-semitic;[4] anti-roma;

1 See Enyedi and Tóka 2006: 5, arguing that the bi-polarization of the Hungarian party system is the result of the two-thirds requirement in the constitution.

2 The stability of the Hungarian political system does not depend on the intensity of voter participation, see Körösényi et al. 2005: 51.

3 As a working definition for the present paper, Hungarists are people who believe in the supremacy of the Hungarian race and follow the teachings of the interwar Hungarist leader, Ferenc Szálasi, whose Arrow-Cross Party got into power after the exit of Governor Horthy on 16 October 1944 and ruled Hungary during the last months of the Second World War in a period known as the 'Arrow-Cross terror' until 1 May 1945. Outside Hungary, one may find a rather widespread and active Hungarist movement, with anointed leaders, meetings and publications (which are also available on the Internet).

4 See Merkl and Weinberg 2003: 298: 'In the countries of the former Soviet bloc the Jewish communities have shrunk to a minuscule size. This fact, however, has not meant that right-wing party leaders in Romania, Hungary, Slovakia and a few other countries have ignored "the Jews", even when there are few living ones on hand to attack … (T)he American Jewish philanthropist George Soros has proven to be a godsend for far right party leaders. His efforts to promote democratic institutions in Eastern Europe through, inter alia the European University in Budapest, have provided these leaders with an irresistible opportunity to denounce his work as an effort to destroy national cultures and replace them with American- and Zionist-inspired globally focused cosmopolitan societies'.

xenophobic;[5] or homophobic statements in tones that occasionally have been proven to be capable of triggering violence. Since the autumn of 2006, mob violence on and around symbolic days of remembrance of various sorts has become part of everyday reality.[6] Political analysts suggest that with the violent events of 2006 the organization and mobilization of radical right-wing forces has reached previously unseen proportions and intensity.[7] Lately, the international press carried images of a uniformed group calling itself the Hungarian Guard (*Magyar Gárda*) which has the appearance of a paramilitary group, committed 'to safeguard Hungarian culture and traditions'.[8] At present the militant group remains more of a nuisance than a considerable paramilitary force but, nonetheless, its emergence indicates the organizing and mobilizing potential of the extreme right in spite of concerned voices from international commentators and political forces.[9]

While legal solutions and procedures traditionally associated with militant democracy are well established in the Hungarian legal system, they appear rather toothless and ineffective even on those occasions when finally called upon. Prohibitions of political parties and other political movements are, nonetheless, relatively rare in Hungary. Also, prosecutions for hate speech are most often fruitless. Parliament's attempt to pass a hate speech bill recently failed for the fourth time

5 In Hungary, xenophobia is not triggered by mass immigration, but by a more deeply rooted intolerance towards minorities.

6 One of the canonized symbolic days is 15 March, the anniversary of the outbreak of the 1848 revolution, the other one is 23 October, the anniversary of the 1956 revolution. More recent commerative celebrations of mob violence events include the day the public television building came under attack on 17 September 2006. Another is the day of the 'taxi blockade'. This happened on 25–28 October 1990 when the first democratically elected government attempted to raise the price of fuel. Taxi drivers reacted with a major strike disabling traffic in Budapest until the government decided to find an alternative solution. Note that the last three dates all conveniently occurred during the autumn thus providing ample opportunity for continuous operations.

7 I do not attempt the difficult task of providing a definition of 'extreme/radical right'. For the purposes of this chapter I have opted to discuss those political formations which other analysts of the Hungarian scene commonly accept as such. See Fleck 2007: 1351 et seq.; Juhász and Somogyi 2008: 1321 et seq. For previous studies in English at large see, for example, Karsai 1999; Szőcs 1998. For a brief analysis from a similar perspective, see Sajó 2004a: 223–229.

8 'Hungarian Extremists Reflect Discontent, and Add to It', *The New York Times*, 24 October 2007 and 'The Changing of the Garda', *The Economist*, 20 September 2007.

9 Note that while extreme right radical groups have become abundant, extreme left groups are almost invisible; see the Yearbook of the National Security Services for 2007 at http://www.nbh.gov.hu/evk2007/07-0065.htm#4 (in Hungarian). According to the National Security Services, extreme left groups, such as the Left-wing Front–Communist Youth Association (*Baloldali Front-Kommunista Ifjúsági Szövetség*) managed to confine their activities within legally prescribed limits. The National Security Services are most worried about the international connections of the Hungarian radical left, which bring *Batasuna* activists to Hungarian events.

before the Constitutional Court at the end of June 2008.[10] The criminal prohibition of the display of totalitarian symbols is more or less pointless, as it simply cannot prevent the creative use of equally strong mutant emblems by radical groups. In practice, authorities have been most successful in preventing the operation of extremist groups via prosecutions for illegal possession of firearms, or for other violent crimes, and have resorted to means other than banning the organization. All in all, extremist groups with anti-democratic and anti-constitutional agendas did not only manage to find their cozy spot on the fringes of Hungarian politics, but appear to have been quite successful in mobilizing participants for their events via modern technology, thus also making themselves visible in the mainstream media. Sadly, at the same time the violent rhetoric of extreme right groups and the physical violence triggered by them seems out of control.

Thus, looking at party bans alone would tell little about the operation of militant democracy mechanisms in Hungary. Instead, a more comprehensive overview of the situation is expected to reveal a rich set of causes and effects which contribute to a better understanding of factors that might undermine the Hungarian democracy's capacities in encountering and confronting its visible enemies.

A broader focus is also necessary since political movements and formations devoted to intolerant or undemocratic agendas tend not to aspire to registration in the first place. As Diána Bácsfi of the Hungarist formation called the 'Hungarian Future Group' (*Magyar Jövő Csoport*) noted in 2004: 'The aims of our organization are anti-democratic, therefore we have never thought of registering'.[11]

In this chapter, I will not develop a genuine conception of militant democracy. Instead, I will draw on the minimum core of the concept as first expressed by Karl Loewenstein in 1937 and then developed by an impressive variety of authors including recently Fareed Zakharia, Georg Nolte and Gregory H. Fox. My main aim here is to see how legal mechanisms, generally understood to protect constitutional democracies from their enemies, deliver on the basic promises which brought them into existence. In exploring the causes and effects of the above phenomena, the chapter will first map the political scene in Hungary, in an attempt to sketch the broader context of the legal and constitutional analysis to come. The chapter will then turn to discussing the emergence and fate of political formations on the fringes of the constitutional playing field, reflecting on the dismissal of political organizations (political parties and other associations) and other legal means available against their behaviour endangering the foundations of peaceful coexistence in a constitutional democracy. Thereafter, we will explore the weaknesses of the means available against racist hate speech in Hungary, and we will also contemplate the utility of prohibiting the display of totalitarian symbols in Hungary.

10 See Decision 236/A/2008 AB, rendered on 30 June 2008.

11 See 'Útkeresések, Szélsőjobboldaliak bíróság előtt' (Pathfinders, Extreme right before courts), *HVG*, 8 December 2004.

Most empirical studies on militant democracy measures are devoted to exploring how, if at all, it is possible to apply these measures in practice without abusing the golden opportunities they present for suppressing the rights and opportunities of one's political opponents. The lessons of party prohibition jurisprudence from all around the world inform these discussions, which are also spiced by experiences on the limitations of freedom of speech in order to suppress criticism of the government.

The case study on Hungary, somewhat unexpectedly, presents a slightly different lesson. It is a story about a transitional democracy which has all the tools in its law-books to defend itself from anti-democratic forces, but, nonetheless, has repeatedly failed to put them into operation even in cases where the stakes are visibly high. This chapter will thus explore what inspires a constitutional democracy which is seemingly adequately equipped to restrain its enemies to let them roam freely even in the face of clearly worded legal provisions to the contrary. Indeed, as András Sajó noted in an essay on democratic transition and militant democracy in 2004, '(w)ere the constitutional order challenged today, these techniques could protect it only under the most fortunate circumstances' (Sajó 2004a: 217 et seq).

The conclusion is not that in Hungary the dominant political forces are less inclined or willing to extinguish their challengers when the opportunity arises than political elites in other constitutional democracies. The chapter argues that the meaningful application of militant democracy measures depends on the proper operation and cooperation of numerous governmental players, including – but not restricted to – the political branches, the Constitutional Court, the ordinary judiciary, the prosecutor's office, police and even the secret services, amid a robust public discourse wherein governmental actors and various layers of civil society interact in a meaningful fashion. This ideal state of affairs is extremely difficult to reach in the course of transition to democracy. Nonetheless, in a setting where these fundamental actors fail to understand their basic tasks or perform them to the best of their abilities, the misunderstood and half-hearted application of militant democracy measures is more likely to open constitutional institutions to the ridicule of a few extremist players than to safeguard and strengthen the institutions and reputation of constitutional democracy.

The Hungarian Political Landscape: A Review of Political Parties and Movements

Since becoming a constitutional democracy, Hungary has joined the Council of Europe (1990);[12] OECD (1995); NATO (1999);[13] and the European Union (2004).[14] Thus, Hungary managed to join rather rapidly the ranks of established democracies in international organizations wherein participation is conditioned upon respect for democracy, constitutionalism, the rule of law and the protection and promotion of human rights. At first glance, the political system appears fairly stable which is somewhat unusual in Central and Eastern Europe. The parliamentary system of government adopted in 1989 did not shift to 'semi-presidentialization', and the make-up of the current Parliament is determined by actors who were present at the negotiating table at the Round Table Talks in 1989. This calm surface, however, is glued together by the fears, tensions and unfulfilled expectations. It is important to look at these factors, albeit briefly, in order to better understand the context. This context is all the more important as – although the setting of parliamentary politics seems to change little – current developments outside parliamentary politics include not only a worrying loss of support for the current parliamentary majority, but also an increasing radicalization on the right of the political spectrum with considerable potential for mobilization and predictable instances of mob violence. Thus, a comprehensive review of the scene suggests that parliamentary democracy in Hungary was not properly equipped or was not able to defend itself from a series of unwelcome developments.

Transition in Hungary was largely the result of negotiations and came about in a relatively peaceful manner.[15] During the last years of the Communist regime, alternative voices began to appear in print (*samizdat*) and opposition became visible in the form of public demonstrations organized on symbolic days of commemoration.[16] While police action at these public assemblies was significant and at times bloody,

12 The official date of accession was 6 November 1990. See also Act no. 71 of 1991. According to Bennett Kovrig, a major reason of the outgoing Communist Government for filing an early application for Council of Europe membership was the fear for the rights of Hungarians living abroad, see Kovrig 1999: 255.

13 Official relations were established on 27 June 1990. Accession negotiations started on 8 July 1997 (with the Czech Republic and Poland). Hungary was granted membership on 12 March 1999.

14 Hungary applied for EU membership in 1994, in the same year as Poland. On this see OGY Decision 16/1994 (III. 31.). Hungary was invited for accession negotiations at the Luxemburg European Council in 1997, and accession negotiations began in 1998. Negotiations were concluded in 2002.

15 The Polish Round Table Talks were a clear inspiration. The interaction between Polish and Hungarian opposition intellectuals is well documented.

16 With the dissolution of the Communist regime on these symbolic days, smaller groups of dissenters would meet at symbolic public places of commemoration. Note that it was already a sign of a change of times that the commemoration events were moved from private apartments to the street.

by the end of 1988 the interaction between the protesters and the Communist police may be described as a tense (but not altogether brutal) encounter.[17] The growing number of participants at these illegal public demonstrations, however, was worrying for the Communist political elites. It was against this background that the Communist Parliament passed legislation on freedom of association (Act no. 2 of 1989) and freedom of assembly (Act no. 3 of 1989) in early January of 1989. With these short statutes, the Communist Parliament legalized dissenters' organizations and the operation of alternative political movements.[18] The assembly law adopted at the time (and still in force today) is conspicuously silent on spontaneous assemblies and only regulates peaceful demonstrations upon three days prior notice to the relevant police department.[19]

In this increasingly more vibrant public space, several historic parties announced their intent to reorganize themselves under the new association law. These included those such as the Independent Small-Holders' Party (*Független Kisgazdapárt* or FKGP); the Hungarian Social-Democratic Party (*Magyar Szociáldemokrata Párt*); and the Hungarian Peoples' Party (*Magyar Néppárt*). New parties in formation also included the Hungarian Democratic Forum (*Magyar Demokrata Fórum* or MDF); the Alliance of Free Democrats (*Szabad Demokraták Szövetsége* or SzDSz); or the Alliance of Young Democrats (*Fiatal Demokraták Szövetsége* or FiDESz).[20] These emerging parties and the meetings they organized have slowly become regular and are visible also in the still Communist-controlled press.

In the Hungarian transition canon, the commencement of transition to democracy is fixed at the Round Table Talks of 1989. The Talks brought together three sides: the Hungarian Communist Workers Party (MSzMP – or Communist Party),[21] the Opposition Round Table, and the so-called Third Side.[22] The Opposition

17 A useful source on these public demonstrations is the video journal of the Black Box Studio (*Fekete Doboz*) entitled *Magyar Változások* (Hungarian Changes), which is an edited documentary journal composed of footage recorded by concealed cameras at these events.

18 Note, however, that criminal provisions penalizing the expression of political dissent were removed from the Criminal Code only as a result of the Round Table Talks.

19 This shortcoming of the assembly law was successfully challenged before the European Court of Human Rights in *Bukta et al. v. Hungary*, 17 July 2007 (25691/04).

20 Political formations and parties which subsequently played a significant role in post-communist politics will be identified with their standard Hungarian abbreviation. MSZP is identified at times as the Socialist Party. In all other cases English translations of the names will be used to assist the reader in the maze of political formations.

21 MSzMP has never been formally outlawed in Hungary. The present day Hungarian Socialist Party (Magyar Szocialista Párt, commonly abbreviated as MSzP) referred to in the text is the offspring of the Communist Party, formed during the regime change. MSzP has been elected also to the first democratically elected Parliament in 1990. It subsequently became a governing party in 1994 and also in 2002 and in 2006 forming a coalition with a small liberal party, SzDSz. Their latest coalition government fell apart in the spring of 2008.

22 The minutes of the Round Table Talks were edited and annotated in a major, multi-volume publication: Bozóki et al. 2000.

Round Table (formed on 22 March 1989)[23] was comprised of all major political parties which have been influential in post-communist Hungarian politics, such as MDF, FiDESz,[24] SzDSz, FKGP, and KDNP (with the obvious exception of the Hungarian Socialist Party (*Magyar Szocialista Párt*, or MSzP). As a most important achievement, the Round Table Talks negotiated the terms of numerous statutory amendments, and the whole-scale amendment of the Communist constitution transforming it into a democratic instrument,[25] thus creating the foundations of constitutional democracy in Hungary.

Surviving parties of democratic transition dominate parliamentary politics today. The party system gravitates towards two large players: MSzP – the Hungarian Socialist Party (*Magyar Szocialista Párt*), which is a successful offspring of the reform wing of the Hungarian Socialist Workers' Party; and FiDESz-MPSz – the Alliance of Young Democrats – Hungarian Civic Alliance (*Fiatal Demokraták Szövetsége – Magyar Polgári Szövetség*), a Conservative Party on the right of the political spectrum.[26] In addition, two smaller parties are present in Parliament: on the liberal side SzDSz – the Alliance of Free Democrats (*Szabad Demokraták Szövetsége*) and on the moderate conservative side MDF – the Hungarian Democratic Forum (*Magyar Demokrata Fórum*). While the

23 The founding members include the Friends of Endre Bajcsy Zsilinszky (*Bajcsy-Zsilinszky Endre Baráti Társaság*); the Alliance of Young Democrats (*Fiatal Demokraták Szövetsége*, or FiDESz); the Independent Small-Holders' Party (*Független Kisgazdapárt*); the Democratic League of Independent Unions (*Független Szakszervezetek Demokratikus Ligája*); the Hungarian Democratic Forum (MDF); the Hungarian Peoples' Party; the Hungarian Social-Democratic Party; and the Alliance of Free Democrats (SzDSz). Subsequently, the Christian Democratic Peoples' Party (*Kereszténydemokrata Néppárt* or KDNP) joined the Opposition Round Table. Note also that the current Hungarian political system carries a deep-seated legitimacy problem: political parties which participated in the Opposition Round Table volunteered for this role and did not have democratic legitimacy.

24 FiDESz was elected into the first Parliament in 1990 as a strong liberal party. In 1998, it won in the parliamentary elections and was the senior member of a coalition government formed together with FKGP and MDF as junior members. Recast as FiDESZ – *Magyar Polgári Párt* (FiDESZ – Hungarian Civic Party), it has become the major conservative force in Hungarian politics, a true 'catch all' party on the right, serving in the 2002 and also in the current Parliament as the largest opposition force.

25 The official number of the constitution remains Act no. 20 of 1949. The most important amendment in the constitutional overhaul is Act no. 31 of 1989. The Hungarian Constiution has been amended many times ever since, but no amendment of such magnitude was put in place. An English translation of the Hungarian Constitution is available with the website of the Constitutional Court (at http://mkab.hu/en/enpage5.htm).

26 The name 'FiDESz-MPSz' was introduced in 2003. In 1995, FiDESz amended its name to FiDESz – MPP – the Alliance of Young Democrats – Hungarian Civic Party (*Fiatal Demokraták Szövetsége – Magyar Polgári Párt*), when giving up on its liberal orientation and seeking to establish a position on the right side of the political spectrum. On this development, see Körösényi et al. 2005: 172 et seq. An earlier edition of this book is available in English as Körösényi 2000.

smaller parties remain identifiable by some classic substantive agenda items, the difference between the two larger parties is primarily due to historical and cultural factors and has little to do with their social or economic policy aspirations.[27] The positioning of these parties over a left/right, conservative/liberal continuum and their comparative political weight unquestionably changed, and so did their voting base. Still, compared to other post-communist democracies, the Hungarian Party system is unusually stable.

Smaller political parties, on the fringe of the right, with strong populist inclinations were slowly eliminated from the Hungarian scene by the end of the 1990s. The true agrarian populist FKGP – the Independent Small-Holders' Party (*Független Kisgazda Párt*) led by József Torgyán – was the third largest political force in the mid-1990s. Yet, in the tussle for the strongest centre-right position the party dispersed during its adventure as a coalition partner in the 1998–2002 parliamentary term, in the FiDESz-led coalition government.[28] The right-wing radical populism of MIÉP – the Hungarian Truth and Life Party (*Magyar Igazság és Élet Pártja*), a party which broke away from MDF in 1993 under the leadership of István Csurka (the 'Hungarian Le Pen'), has never had voter support similar to FKGP, although the party made it to Parliament in 1998. In the 2002 elections, it was not returned to Parliament and has been on the margins of politics ever since.[29]

In 2006, after a very balanced election race, the first round of the election saw a 67.83 per cent turnout, while the second round brought 64.39 per cent of eligible voters to the polls. The Socialist Party has 186 seats in the current Parliament. Their original coalition partner, SzDSz, has 18 seats. The coalition used to control six more seats as a result of joint mandates. Since the break-up of the Socialist–Liberal coalition in the spring of 2008, the Socialists have run a minority government with relatively reliable outside support from their former coalition partner. The largest opposition party, FiDESz, retains 164 seats, and the

27 Angelusz and Tardos 2005: 84. Gábor Tóka notes that party preferences had less to do with ideological factors already in the first democratic elections, and depended on the role various parties played in the early days of transition. See Tóka 2005b: 252. Tóka also finds that the relationship between economic status and party preferences is weak in Hungary, see Tóka 2005a: 59.

28 FKGP was founded by Small-Holder veterans who participated in the old Small-Holders' Party before 1948. The modern FKGP was often described as a protest party: the right-wing opposition to the centre-right government. For a brief history of the FKGP, see Körösényi et al. 2005: 192–4.

29 For a brief history of MIÉP, see Körösényi et al. 2005: 196–7. MIÉP's voter base is closely linked with a narrow subculture. MIÉP claimed to represent low-income, marginalized elements, although the sociological make-up of its voters does not match this claim. On the relationship of MIÉP and the FiDESz-led governing coalition, see Bozóki and Kriza 2003: 506 et seq. They mention that polling outlets have not been able to obtain reliable data on MIÉP and its supporters ever since the party left Parliament, as MIÉP supporters are instructed not to trust pollsters and refuse to cooperate with them (Bozóki and Kriza 2003: 511).

second largest, MDF, holds 11 seats. The remaining seat went to the 'For Somogy' movement. The parliamentary scene thus remains rather polarized, gravitating towards the two large parties and burdening the two small parties in the house. It is discomforting that the two smaller parties had serious concerns as to whether they could meet the 5 per cent threshold.[30] In the event, SzDSz made 6.5 per cent, while MDF scraped 5.04 per cent.[31]

An interesting aspect of the 2006 parliamentary elections was the performance of an extreme right-wing election coalition, the Third Way (*Harmadik Út*). This alliance was formed specifically for this election by MiÉP (the extreme right party which had once found its way to Parliament in the 1998–2002 term) and a newcomer, *Jobbik*. *Jobbik*, or its full name *Jobbik Magyarországért Mozgalom*, literally 'Movement for a Better Hungary', emerged from a youth movement in the penumbra of FiDESz. From a movement it transformed itself into a political party in 2006 to form an electoral alliance with MIÉP. In the first round of the national election, they obtained about 120,000 votes, which translated to 2 per cent and thus did not pass the 5 per cent threshold. This figure is all the more interesting as between the 2002 and 2006 elections the number of votes cast for extreme right parties dropped by almost half (Juhász and Somogyi 2008: 1326 et seq.). Thus, this figure also suggests in the light of the events of the autumn of 2006 that this year was a real turning point in the contemporary history of extreme right movements in Hungary.

The stability of the political system cannot be explained by a rigid constitutional system. The Hungarian constitution is seemingly easy to amend,[32] which is not such a surprise as Hungary is a parliamentary democracy. The current constitution is actually the fruit of a series of amendments to the 1949 Communist constitution. There is but few evidence of an unalterable core of the constitution. Chief Justice László Sólyom's attempted to locate an 'invisible constitution' in his concurring opinion to the decision on the abolition of capital punishment in 1990 (23/1990 [X. 31.] AB decision). This much criticized metaphor[33] was meant to infuse constitutional adjudication with consistency to the point where components of constitutional jurisprudence would have been capable of surviving even the adoption of a new constitution. In the current highly hostile setting, there is no possibility of an overarching political consensus to pass a new constitution – technical amendments nonetheless take place regularly.

30 The chances of small parties (parties with weaker voter support) getting into Parliament are severely curbed by the 5 per cent threshold. It restricts mandates received from regional and national lists to those parties which received at least 5 per cent of all valid votes cast for regional lists. In Hungary, it is not only parliamentary parties who receive funding from the central budget.

31 The right-wing radical Hungarian Truth and Life Party (MIÉP) took 2 per cent of the votes.

32 It only takes the vote of two-thirds of all Members of Parliament, see Article 24(3) of the constitution.

33 For an early, yet still relevant account in Hungarian, see Sajó 1993, 1995.

Indeed, the stability of the party system inside Parliament and the scarcity of newcomers to the parliamentary scene have little to do with the constitutional framework, and are due mostly to the regulation of elections and party finance rules. Although the elections of 2006 did not result in a reduction of the Hungarian plural party space to a clear two-party model,[34] it is, with the dominance of the large parties, becoming increasingly difficult for the smaller parties – even those which have been around since the early days of transition – to retain their parliamentary positions. Indeed, it is due to the particularly complex election regulations which makes entry into parliamentary politics difficult and expensive, while those parties already in Parliament are in a significantly better position to finance lengthy and uncontrollably expensive election campaigns.

When talking about the behaviour of political players, it is important to point out that willingness to participate in 'anything political' is moderate in Hungary. The appeal of participation in the operation of constitutional institutions is relatively low. In the European Social Survey of 2002, on a scale of 1 to 10 respondents ranked the importance of politics at 3.8 and religion at 4.2, while work and friends received scores of 7.5 and family scored 9.8 (Laki and Szabó 2002: 48). According to the same survey when the qualities of a 'good citizen' were put on a 1 to 10 scale, observance of laws ranked at 9.1, casting votes at national elections was at 8.2, having an independent opinion scored 8, while active participation in politics was at a low 3.6 (Laki and Szabó 2002: 48). The European Social Survey of 2002 also revealed that the predominant form of political participation was shopping with a political consumer motivation, the second most frequent form of political activity was participation in a politically motivated boycott of goods, signing a political petition and participation in a lawful demonstration. Among the least frequent activities one finds participation in political movements, involvement in political parties and electoral campaigns.

It was against this backdrop that, after losing parliamentary elections by a small margin in 2002, the leader of the FiDESz, Viktor Orbán, refused to take the role as leader of the opposition in Parliament and continued to act as 'leader of the peoples', investing considerable energy in building a broad social movement around the party structure and, also, mobilizing visible popular support outside parliamentary and party structures. He explained his unwillingness to become a dutiful leader of the opposition in the following terms in his State of the Nation address in 2003:

> The opportunities available to the opposition in Parliament are few. It may form an opinion if it deems that the government is heading in the wrong direction, it may put forward alternative solutions, it may help its country on the international scene. Although the tools are scarce, the opposition, with the help of the people, has managed to score some results … First of all, let us forget

34 Some observers expected a continuation of the trend witnessed in previous elections to this effect, as mentioned in Karácsony 2006: 59.

> the idea that the exclusive terrain of public life is the Hungarian Parliament. In fact, public life is present everywhere in all communities. It is now our and your responsibility to save those values which we collectively represent in Hungarian public life: human dignity, family, work, learning, order, national solidarity. And these values are only present if we are also present everywhere. Centre-right forces cannot therefore aim lower than being present in every town, village and settlement throughout the country. Let us consider that ever since the civic circles have come into being, the values we cherish are ever more present, more and more people are talking about them, more and more people are standing by them in debates, which has contributed to a change in the country's spiritual make-up.

Extra-parliamentary politics of this kind seems to take multiple forms. The 'State of the Nation address' just mentioned is one example: it is a speech which Orbán delivers in a decidedly non-political space to an audience of his own party and movement even while in opposition. Many of these initiatives mimic what would be recognized as a genuine operation of civil society. Famous among these initiatives are the so-called 'civic circles' (*polgári körök*) which are local citizens' groups formed to discuss public affairs, to brainstorm for the party, and to allow Orbán to meet 'the people'. The organization of the civic circles and calls for signature and awareness campaigns are also among the means of perpetuating permanent presence and media attention without having to engage in parliamentary business. This strategy of taking politics to the people also heavily relies on populist moves which are considered to be antithetical to parliamentary decision-making, such as referenda, and more recently, on acts termed to amount to civil disobedience.[35]

This is not to suggest that supporting a referendum initiative and calling for mob violence against the government are one and the same, but it is merely intended to indicate that populistic techniques have been part of the arsenal of the largest right-wing political party (FiDESz) in Parliament for a while. Considering that this party picked up enough of the radical right-wing vote so that the smaller (and more) radical right-wing parties did not get into Parliament in the 2002 and 2006 parliamentary elections, one can see that the actions of FiDESz do have a complex indirect impact on the fate of the radical right formations in the Hungarian scene.

The by and large eventless scene to which Hungarians were used as far as parliamentary politics is concerned was severely shaken in the autumn of 2006 as a result of a series of events which sharply reordered the landscape of political organizations outside the walls of Parliament. First, the dynamics of support for major parliamentary parties did change significantly when a few months after the general elections in September 2006, a recording of a rather emotional speech

35 Police authorities 'forgot' the cordon around Kossuth square after the riots in the autumn of 2006, forgetfulness which in that very fashion was illegal. The cordon was removed only in the spring of 2007, when the parliamentary faction of FiDESz took it off in an action that they termed as an act of civil disobedience.

originally made by freshly elected Prime Minister, Ferenc Gyurcsány, in May 2006 was leaked to the press. In this infamous speech the Socialist Prime Minister said to his circle of confidants:

> We have screwed up. Not a little but a lot. No country in Europe has screwed up as much as we have. It can be explained. We have obviously lied throughout the past 18 to 24 months. It was perfectly clear that what we were saying was not true … I almost perished because I had to pretend for 18 months that we were governing. Instead, we lied morning, noon and night.[36]

In response to the leak, street violence erupted on 17 September 2006 and mob violence continued on the streets of Budapest for several days. The first reaction of the police was rather lame and unprofessional, this is how the group of protesters (a united front of ultras of otherwise hostile football clubs joined by extreme right-wing formations) managed to enter into the public television's building, set fires and caused much damage to surrounding property. The next evening, the police took harsher action resulting in rather unfortunate acts of police brutality. Within the coming days, the reactions of the police became tamer and more in accordance with the law.[37] Eventually the demonstrations were restricted to the square before the Parliament building, which was cordoned off by the police in order to prevent further violence at the upcoming commemorations of 23 October. In October 2007, one year after the street riots, a second wave of street violence erupted in order to commemorate the first anniversary of the Prime Minister's speech.

During these rather violent waves of demonstrations, and several other interlinked ones, radical right-wing protesters took centre stage. It added a special layer of interpretation to the events that the leaders of FiDESz, the senior opposition party, did not rush to distance themselves from the violent elements and were themselves willing to give speeches and organize mass rallies. Nonetheless, the key actors and organizers at the events resulting in mob violence were figures from the radical right who had never before entered the mainstream political scene. Many of these organizations are not even registered as parties or associations, their major form of political participation is limited to spreading hate propaganda via

36 As available in English translation at 'Excerpts: Hungarian "lies" speech', *BBC News*, 19 September 2006 (at http://news.bbc.co.uk/2/hi/europe/5359546.stm). The speech was made at a closed meeting of the coalition parties where they were negotiating the basic terms of restructuring the government at Balatonöszöd. It is still unknown who is responsible for the leak. Suspicion is nonetheless directed on the participants of the meeting as media presence was prohibited, and even cell phones and other communication devices were banned. For an English language press review of major Hungarian papers see, for example, 'Press split over Hungary turmoil', *BBC News*, 19 September 2006 (at http://news.bbc.co.uk/2/hi/europe/5359528.stm).

37 Two reports were prepared on the actions of the police. One by an inhouse commission of the Ministry of Justice and Law Enforcement headed by Katalin Gönczöl and an independent review chaired by Krisztina Morvai.

modern technology and organizing demonstrations – preferably involving open confrontation with the riot police at some point. What makes the autumn of 2006 especially notable for the present analysis is that it was in the course of these and the subsequent protests – most of them involving open confrontation with the riot police – wherein extreme right forces displayed their skills to mobilize relatively large crowds and engage them in open violence at rather short notice.

The extreme right groups were successful in carrying the legacy of mob violence into the following year. The yearbook of the Hungarian National Security Services (*Nemzetbizonsági Hivatal*), which gives account of a preventive intervention with the Hungarian '*Sinn Fein*' Movement (*Mi Magunk Mozgalom*), a group formed in 2006 which – on its Internet portal – was preparing for the commemoration of 15 March in 2007 with home-made Molotov cocktails to be used against police. The Security Services also reported on the '*Hunnia*' movement founded in April 2007 by a well-known radical right-wing figure – László Toroczkai. The aim of the movement was to form a shadow government supported by a paramilitary force. The group was determined to use force in its ordinary operations, yet, was not capable of cooperating with other right-wing radical groups, as noted by the National Security Services' 2007 yearbook.

In the area of parliamentary politics, Prime Minister Gyurcsány survived a confidence vote in Parliament in early October 2006,[38] but his popularity was at its lowest. FiDESz went ahead in all popularity polls, leaving the governing coalition behind with a considerable margin.[39] Despite peoples' demonstrated willingness to take to the streets, and FiDESz's clear lead in the polls with Viktor Orbán's popularity rising, pollsters were consistent in reporting fairly low levels of participation in instant elections. Median consistently suggested less than 60 per cent three weeks after the leak in October 2006 which dropped to around 52 per cent by April 2007; similarly, for the spring of 2007 TÁRKI forecasted 54 per cent participation. One important lesson, however, does emerge from these numbers: while the general overall level of projected voter participation at an upcoming election was low, FiDESz voters appeared much more willing to cast their votes than the MSzP camp, to the extent that according to a fair reading of poll data, in an instant parliamentary election in the spring of 2008, FiDESz would have received twice as many votes as MSzP. Although, by the middle of the summer

38 'Hungary PM wins confidence vote', *BBC News*, 6 October 2006 (at http://news.bbc.co.uk/2/hi/europe/5411022.stm).

39 According to TÁRKI's data, support for MSzP stood at 20 and 19 per cent in February and May 2007, while support for FiDESz increased from 26 to 31 per cent in the total population in the same period. Among those who would attend elections MSzP's support was at 37 and 34 per cent in this period, while FiDESz would have received 47, 52 and 51 per cent of the vote. See 'Változatlan erőviszonyok' (Unaltered power relations), 24 May 2007 (at http://www.tarki.hu/hu/news/2007/kitekint/20070524.html). In April 2007, Median showed 58 per cent of the vote for FiDESZ, and only 30 per cent for MSzP. See 'Állókép' (Frozen picture), 19 April 2007 (at http://www.median.hu/object.fcfc92c6-2277-4e9d-b369-889eb7e350af.ivy).

of 2008, the MSzP seems to have advanced somewhat in the polls, the lead of FiDESz is unquestionable.[40] Another important development in the polls is that the rather weak and insignificant third section of the party spectrum, represented by small extra parliamentary parties, seemed to retain its presence on the map of voter preferences, with *Jobbik* standing on 2 per cent and MIÉP receiving 1 per cent in the polls, and the current small parliamentary parties (MDF and SzDSz) staying under the parliamentary threshold. Due to the rather strong ties between FiDESz and its supporters, pollsters suggest that fringe parties received votes not from the FiDESz camp, but from the previously undecided voters.

To sum up, while the Hungarian parliamentary scene is relatively constant, since the autumn of 2006 there has been a sharp increase in the presence and violent activities of extreme right political formations. Although these groups are relatively small and volatile, they appear to present a major problem which militant democracy instruments at the disposal of the government failed to handle in a reassuring fashion. On the following pages, the chapter will reflect on these measures and their practical application.

The Legal Regulation of the Dissolution of Political Associations in Hungary: An Overview

The decision to establish a political association or a political party is a privileged one. It is closely associated with the freedom of association, a human right which has been accorded protection in a number of international human rights instruments. Nonetheless, those instruments often protect freedom of association without open reference to the right to form a political party. Consider, for instance, that while in its Article 22 the ICCPR provides that everyone 'shall have the right to freedom of association with others, including the right to form and join trade unions for the protection of his interests', it does not mention political parties explicitly. The European Convention on Human Rights echoes this language when providing in its Article 11(1) that everyone 'has the right … to freedom of association with others, including the right to form and to join trade unions for the protection of his interests'.

The Hungarian Constitution also protects freedom of association expressly in its Article 63(1): 'in the Republic of Hungary on the basis of freedom of association everyone has the right to establish associations for aims not prohibited by law and to join such associations'. In addition, the constitution proclaims the following in its Article 3:

40 Szonda Ipsos projected half a million votes lost by FiDESz by the end of June 2008. See 'Félmilliós FiDESz veszteség, A Szonda Ipsos júniusi felmérése a pártok népszerűségéről' (Half a million in loss for FiDESz, A Szonda Ipsos poll on the popularity of parties in June), *Népszabadság*, 26 June 2008 (in Hungarian) (at http://www.nol.hu/cikk/496925/).

> (1) In the Republic of Hungary political parties may be established and may function freely, provided they respect the constitution and laws established in accordance with the constitution. (2) Political parties shall participate in the development and expression of the popular will. (3) Political parties may not exercise public power directly. Accordingly, no single party may exercise exclusive control of a government body. In the interest of ensuring the separation of political parties and public power, the law shall determine those functions and public offices which may not be held by party members or officers.

Thus, while the Hungarian Constitution does protect freedom of association in explicit terms, it does not prescribe an expressed right to form political parties. Similar to other European constitutions, as the German *Grundgesetz* ('Basic Law'), the French Constitution of 1958 or the Spanish Constitution of 1978, the provision on political parties is not located in the Hungarian Constitution's chapter on fundamental rights. It is placed in the first chapter among the general provisions on various aspects of sovereignty.[41] The aim of the provision is not to define what a political party is, but to reinforce that political parties are 'constitutional institutions', and to define their role in the Hungarian constitutional democracy (Sólyom 2004: 10–11).

The text of the constitutional provision is in itself the result of numerous political compromises reached at the national Round Table Talks and then passed into legislation by the last Communist Parliament. The most important piece of law-making from this procedure is Act no. 31 of 1989; a whole-scale amendment to the Communist constitution (Act no. 20 of 1949); a statute which has served as the constitution of Hungary ever since.[42] Together with the transitional overhaul of the constitution, the act on the Constitutional Court, the last Communist Parliament also passed the Act on the operation and finances of political parties as part of this major constitutional package (hereinafter: 'party law').[43] The party law finished the project started with the association law in January 1989. It allowed for the registration of *de facto* existing political parties which had been more or less legalized by the new association law, among them the political parties which participated in the Round Table Talks.[44] In his early work on freedom of association, Gábor Halmai notes that postponing the adoption of the party law (instead of passing it together with the association law in January 1989) cannot be justified with conceptual reasons, and was solely a matter of political tactics (Halmai 1990: 106).

41 On the location of the provision, see also Sólyom 2004: 11.

42 Several major amendments were passed in the meantime, yet, a new constitution has not been passed.

43 Act no. 32 of 1989 brought the Constitutional Court into existence. Act no. 33 of 1989 on the operation and finances of political parties entered into force on 30 October 1989.

44 For a detailed account on the drafting history in Hungarian, see Sólyom 2004: 15–26. See also Halmai 1990: 97–107.

As a result of this complicated enactment history, the party law remains a subsidiary to the association law, meaning that parties operate under the association law in the light of the special rules applicable to parties. Also, it is relatively easy to turn associations into political parties, and *vice versa*. Indeed, parliamentary aspirations seem to set non-mainstream political formations apart. Those who intend to enter the race for Parliament need to form a political party, while those who merely wish to enter the race for a spot in the public exchange of ideas on public affairs may simply do so in the shape of registered political associations or (unregistered) movements and formations. This aspect of the regulation gains interesting practical significance once it is taken into account that political formations, especially radical formations, often seek registration not as parties but as associations. Indeed, for the purposes of an analysis on militant democracy it seems that the real difference is between registered and non-registered organizations – and not parties and associations. After all, reasons for disbanding a party or a cultural association which endangers the foundations of constitutional democracy do not seem to differ markedly in practice.

The language of Article 3(1) appears to use a strong reference to a militant democracy commitment when it reads that 'political parties may be established and may function freely, provided they respect the constitution and laws established in accordance with the constitution'. László Sólyom, however, explains in his commentary on the drafting history of this provision that the reference to 'respecting the constitution' was rather controversial at the time of the drafting as it was understood to refer to 'Socialist legality' and the 'Socialist character of the state', concepts with which a multi-party system is impossible to reconcile (Halmai 1990: 101–102; Sólyom 2004: 21–2). During the Round Table Talks, this qualification came to be understood as a minimum requirement, preventing the exclusive and aggressive exercise of state power, as also enshrined in Article 3(3) (Sólyom 2004: 23).

Under the Hungarian constitutional and legal regime it is relatively easy to form and register a political party.[45] Ten Hungarian citizens (private individuals) who agree to adhere to the legal rules on the operation and finances of political parties, organize a founding meeting where they draft a charter of operations and elect their leadership may form a political party. Parties have to have a registered membership (Article 1 of Party Law). The party law, however, does not establish any further substantive or material criteria to define a political party.

The registration process is administered by ordinary courts of law at the county court level and, in Budapest, by the Metropolitan Court (*Fővárosi Bíróság*). Registration cannot be denied if all conditions prescribed by the law have been met. As a result, requests for registration are very rarely denied. The dissolution of parties takes place (if at all) on the basis of their proven record of operation.

45 The generally applicable legal rules are in the association law, while party-specific provisions are in the party law (Article 1). Associations and parties are constituted by the gesture of registration. See association law, Article 4(1).

In 2007, the party register administered by the ordinary judiciary contained more than 170 registered parties.[46] Although this is a relatively high number, on the one hand, the register does not contain political organizations that define themselves in terms other than political parties (such as cultural associations registered under the associations law or similar unregistered formations). On the other hand, not all of these registered parties run for seats at national elections. In the 2006 national elections, 43 parties were certified by the National Election Commission (*Országos Választási Bizottság*) to name candidates. In sheer numerical terms, the four parliamentary parties were selected from among these 43 parties in 2006.

The legality of operations of associations and political parties is supervised by the public prosecutor (Article 14 of association act). The motion to dissolve a political party can also be filed by the public prosecutor and is carried out by the ordinary judiciary. Note that this solution is markedly different from the German model where the dissolution of an unconstitutional party is initiated by the government and the decision is taken by the Federal Constitutional Court. The original draft of the Hungarian Party Law was intended to introduce a solution based on the German model, but the procedure was then regulated in accordance with the association law already in force (Sólyom 2004: 100).

Like any other association, a political party may be dissolved if it is directed at the forcible acquisition or exercise of public power, or at the exclusive possession of such power (as provided in Article 2(3) of the constitution), if it commits a crime or calls for criminal activities, or if its activities result in the violation of rights or liberties of others (Article 2(2) of association law). In addition, armed organizations cannot be registered as associations or as parties.[47] The party law specifically prohibits the formation of parties in workplaces, bases of the armed forces, and in schools (Article 2(1) of Party Law).

Furthermore, the Paris Peace Treaty of 1947, concluded at the end of the Second World War, expressly prohibits the operation of fascist organizations in the following terms (Part II, Title 1, Article 4):

> Hungary, which in accordance with the Armistice Agreement has taken measures for dissolving all organisations of a Fascist type on Hungarian territory whether political, military or para-military, as well as other organisations conducting

46 'Pártalapítás: tíz magyar összehajol' (Establishing a party: Ten Hungarians join in), *Magyar Hírlap*, 2 February 2007 (in Hungarian) (at http://www.magyarhirlap.hu/cikk.php?cikk=120499). The data quoted in the text is based on the records of the National Judiciary Council.

47 Article 2(3) of association law. This provision mirrors Article 63(2) of the constitution. This prohibition carries with it a collection of bad memories from the Communist era regarding the armed guard of the Communist party, the so-called Workers' Guard (*Munkásőrség*). The Communist Parliament decided to disband the Workers' Guard on the session day when this provision was adopted to the association law. See Halmai 1990: 104.

> propaganda, including revisionist propaganda, hostile to the United Nations, shall not permit in future the existence and activities of organisations of that nature which have as their aim denial to the people of their democratic rights.

The association law and the party law, however, do not contain provisions referring to this Article of the Peace Treaty, which therefore slips relatively easily from the general sphere of attention.

Note that the Hungarian legal regulation suggests – on the face of it – that political parties are relatively easy to disband. In his early commentary on the association law, Gábor Halmai was rather skeptical of dissolving associations with criminal aspirations or groups which violate the rights of others. He argued that it would have been sufficient to allow legal action against such associations, without subjecting them to the threat of dissolution (Halmai 1990: 107). These words are undoubtedly inspired by the climate of the enactment of the above regulations, which are infused by distrust and fear from abuse by the relevant authorities.[48] Interestingly, or ironically, Halmai's early position resonates well with the words of the Venice Commission's guidelines on prohibition and dissolution of political parties adopted in 2000,[49] recommending (in paragraph 3) that:

> Prohibition or enforced dissolution of political parties may only be justified in the case of parties which advocate the use of violence or use violence as a political means to overthrow the democratic constitutional order, thereby undermining the rights and freedoms guaranteed by the constitution. The fact alone that a party advocates a peaceful change of the Constitution should not be sufficient for its prohibition or dissolution.

In addition, Halmai was also critical of the general supervisory role of the prosecutors (Halmai 1990: 107). This latter suspicion is at least in part explained by the fact that the Hungarian legal system has retained bitter memories of public prosecutors as almighty guardians of legality, who could file motions in non-criminal matters even against the will of the parties involved in judicial procedures.[50] At this point it is also worth noting that the prosecution has a curiously prominent constitutional status in Hungary which is not devoid of political undertones, despite the fact that prosecutors cannot be members of political parties (Article 53(2) of the

48 Further on this point see Sajó 2004a: 223 et seq.

49 Guidelines on prohibition and dissolution of political parties and analogous measures adopted by the Venice Commission at its 41st plenary session, Venice, 10–11 December 1999, CDL-INF(2000)001.

50 The democratic constitution retained the power of the prosecutor for general oversight to safeguard legality in Article 51(3) of the constitution. The Constitutional Court has noteable achievements in curbing this aspect of the prosecutors' powers which will not be discussed here.

constitution).[51] The political façade is ensured as the chief prosecutor is elected for six years by Parliament with a simple majority vote upon the nomination of the President of the republic (Article 52(1)). The chief prosecutor has to report to Parliament (Article 52(2)) and is subject to interpellation (Article 27). From this, it follows that the parliamentary majority can strongly disapprove of the activities and decisions of the chief prosecutor. In this model, the prosecutors' office functions as an agent of the government of the day.[52] Considering that the dissolution of political parties is usually considered to be a highly political matter, the initial fears of Gábor Halmai expressed in 1990 can be seen as generally justified. Past experience shows that initiating the dissolution of a particular political organization can be as political a decision as failing to do so. While in the former case the courts can still bar inappropriate outcomes, in the latter case – when the prosecution does not initiate proceedings – courts are divested from reviewing the operations of a problematic political formation. This is one of the reasons why András Sajó suggests that trusting the prosecutors alone with the initiative on the dissolution of unconstitutional political parties undermines the self-defence potentials of the Hungarian constitutional democracy (Sajó 2002).

Under the Hungarian legal regime, the operation of political parties can be prevented in two ways: either via an initial denial of registration, or after registration, when the dissolution of an already operating party is sought. As the former Chief Justice of the Constitutional Court, László Sólyom, points out in his commentary to the constitution's provisions on political parties. While denial of registration is based on assumptions and fears mostly triggered by a party's founding charter, the dissolution of already registered parties may be more properly based on their actual activities. According to his position, the proportionality of the limitation of the constitutional right of association can be meaningfully enforced in the latter scenario (Sólyom 2004: 96).

A rare instance of denial of registration *ab initio* occurred in 1994 when the Supreme Court sustained a denial of registration for a party which defined its aim as

> using consistent propaganda to turn the masses away from the current political parties, so as a result they ceased to exist. Pointlessly wasted material goods would thus be freed and used for the good of society, and thus the party would also be disbanded. It is the party's firm belief that a state shall not be governed through parties, but through intellectual and physical parties [inconsistencies and lack of proper grammar as in the original].

51 For an insightful analysis, see Hack 2005.

52 This is in line with the intent of the constitution's framers as explained in Hack 2005, also noting that the act regulating the operation of the prosecution service can be passed by simple majority (and does not require a qualified majority, such as the acts on the police or on the security services). The over politicized nature of the prosecution service is not addressed by the fact that the act on prosecutors defines the organization as independent.

On the basis of the founding charter alone, the Supreme Court was convinced that the operation of the party would violate the constitution as it clearly aims at extinguishing the multi-party system also enshrined in the Preamble of the Constitution.[53]

Note, however, that party dissolutions are rare, yet, when they happen, they take place after a party has been registered. In practice, this means that Hungarian Courts fairly regularly register extreme right parties, even in cases where the previous party established under the leadership of the same person had just been disbanded. A famous example of such series of action is Albert Szabó. His first party was among the few staple extreme right formations of the early 1990s: the World-nationalist and People's Rule Party (*Világnemzeti- és Népuralmista Párt*). The main aim of this duly registered party was the revival of the Hungarist movement and the spreading of Hungarist ideology. The party was openly racist, anti-semitic, and xenophobic, both in its closed meetings and at its public rallies. Members of the party openly wore banned emblems of the Hungarist Arrow Cross Party.

On 12 April 1994, together with the Hungarian National Front (*Magyar Nemzeti Arcvonal*), founded by István Györkös in 1990,[54] and the Association of the Persecutees of Communism (*Kommunizmus Üldözetteinek Szövetsége*), founded by György Ekrem Kemál,[55] they established the Hungarian Hungarist Movement (*Magyar Hungarista Mozgalom*) as a 'national political and cultural movement'.[56] In response to racist and xenophobic statements made at a subsequent press conference, prosecutions were initiated for incitement of racial hatred and also for the display of banned totalitarian symbols. However, the Supreme Court in 1997 ultimately agreed with the acquittal of the participants on the charges of incitement of hatred and with a light sentence (reprimand) for the display of totalitarian symbols.[57]

While the prosecution for incitement to hatred against Szabó was pending, his World-nationalist and People's Rule Party was banned on first instance in January 1995. Without waiting for the court's decision on the dissolution to become final, Szabó disbanded his own party and established a new, openly Hungarist

---

53 Reported as BH 1994.394. Note that such summaries of upper court decisions do not contain names or personal data. The events behind the cases were reconstructed on the basis of news reports.

54 In 1992, Hungarian National Front's Györkös was sentenced for the illegal possession of firearms, yet the organization was not banned and remains active even now. Their major activities since 1998 have involved organizing the public commemoration of Breakout Day (11 February 1945) when German and Hungarian forces attempted to breakout from the hold of the Soviet Army arriving to liberate Budapest from Nazi occupation.

55 The Association of the Persecutees of Communism (*Kommunizmus Üldözetteinek Szövetsége*) has never been registered, therefore, it cannot be dissolved.

56 Diána Bácsfi, who founded the Hungarian Future Group, is indeed rare for calling herself and her group openly Hungarist and a devout follower of Szálasi's Hungarist ideology.

57 BH 1997.165 and EBH 1999.5.

organization called Hungarian Welfare Association (*Magyar Népjóléti Szövetség*). The new formation was registered by the courts. The pending prosecution did not stop him either from making openly anti-Semitic comments at a public rally of about 150–200 people commemorating the 1956 revolution on 23 October. He called for Hungarian Jews 'to get out of our country' and demanded 'to kick them out from all offices'. When finding Szabó guilty of incitement to hatred, the Supreme Court noted during sentencing that it could not be counted an aggravating factor that he made these statements while another prosecution was pending against him for similar statements, as in that other case he was ultimately acquitted.[58] After his troubles with the law in Hungary, he was reported to have departed for Australia in 1999 and his organizations disappeared from the public scene.[59]

Note that these events were recorded in the mid to late 1990s, when radical right-wing movements were visible on the public scene but had relatively little appeal and a limited base of support. Nonetheless, public discourse was splintered with racist and often anti-Semitic statements which were more or less made without criminal consequences, by actors who were clearly standing outside the radical right. In 1998, a strong right-wing party MiÉP found its way to Parliament. While it was not formally part of the governing coalition led by FiDESz and joined by FKGP and MDF, in most agenda items MiÉP openly supported the coalition from the periphery. Its support was especially valuable in situations where parity-based committees were taking decisions. During its reign between 1998 and 2002, FiDESz slowly but surely transformed itself into the dominant party on the right, wiping FKGP off the political map and leaving MDF frail. It is generally agreed that MiÉP's falling out of Parliament in the 2002 election was by and large due to FiDESz's shift further to the right.

Another lesson from these developments is that, despite its electoral defeats, MIÉP had a relatively enduring presence on the Hungarian political map, while other radical right-wing fringe players were considerably more volatile. With some noted exceptions, radical right formations often did not seek official registration at all, or aspired to be registered as associations (*egyesület*) under the association law, and not as parties. Gaining status under the association law does not allow these organizations to contest elections or to receive funding as

58 EBH 1999.6.

59 In 2001, he was convicted for planning to abolish the constitutional system and illegal possession of firearms and given a two-year suspended sentence. In his case, the Supreme Court emphasized that his preparations presented no serious threat to national security. Ekrem Kemál remains the only person to this day to have been convicted for a crime against the constitutional system. (One of the organizers of the 2006 and 2007 riots, György Budaházy, was acquitted on similar charges by the first instance court in early 2008.) Like István Györkösi of the Hungarian National Front, György Ekrem Kemál also remains active and did establish another group called the Hungarian National Freedom Party (*Magyar Nemzeti Szabadságpárt*) which actively participated in the riots around the National Television building in 2006.

political parties. Nonetheless, they still receive legal recognition and thus can open a bank account or rent office space in the association's name. Under the association law, the prosecution service maintains control over the legality of their operations. Unregistered, more informal groups are more easily traced around famous personalities of the Hungarian right.

A formation which pursues registration as an association is the Hungarian filiale of the skinhead organization 'Blood and Honor'. The Hungarian Blood and Honor cultural association (*Vér és Becsület Kulturális Egyesület*) sought registration as an association in 2001, and received charitable status in 2002. The petition to dissolve the organization was filed in March 2003 by the prosecution upon the initiative of the National Security Services. The complaint was based on the association's record of activities that was fraught with undignifying statements at the meetings organized by the group. The second instance court added to the facts of the case that the group put special emphasis on their Hungarist and national socialist character. The red flag apparently was the rally on Breakout Day in February 2003, which attracted Jewish counter-demonstrators in great numbers. Furthermore, the prosecution successfully argued that the mere existence of the group violated the Paris Peace Treaty.[60]

After the Blood and Honor association's dissolution (which became effective by the final decision of the Metropolitan District Court – *Fővárosi Ítélőtábla* – as of 27 October 2005) was finally sustained by the Supreme Court in 2007, its founders decided to seek admittance to the registry of associations in an almost unaltered form as *Pax Hungarica* (literally: Hungarian Peace). When seeking re-registration, the founder, Endre János Domokos, argued that while the previously banned organization was a youth group specializing in the organization of public events and concerts, the newly planned *Pax Hungarica* intended to spread its ideology and the protection of the victims who suffered due to their Hungarist views and would also seek the review of people's courts' sentences rendered in 1945–1946. It is apparent even from this last remark how easy it is for a Hungarist group to emulate the vocabulary of victimhood and political persecution in a manner which is accepted by the mainstream of the political arena.

There is a further irony in the story, which highlights yet another shortcoming in the Hungarian approach to militant democracy (although it does not set this story apart from that of Albert Szabó, discussed previously). Note that throughout its existence, the Blood and Honor association was distinguished from other radical right-wing groups in one particular respect: unlike many others, it always insisted on registering its assemblies with the police, refrained from displaying totalitarian symbols at their public meetings and sought peaceful assemblies (to the extent that they stayed away from the street riots of 2006 to the surprise of many).[61] Indeed,

60 BH 2007.146.

61 On this, see 'Bejegyzik-e a Vér és Becsület utódszervezetét?: Jönnének' (Will the offspring of Blood and Honor be registered?), *Magyar Narancs*, 21 December 2006 (at http://www.magyarnarancs.hu/index.php?gcPage=/public/hirek/hir.php&id=14045).

while their appeal against the first instance decision of the Metropolitan Court in December 2004 was still pending, the Blood and Honor association celebrated Breakout Day in February 2005 in compliance with the notification requirement of the assembly law.

Then, by the time of the Breakout Day celebration of 2006, the Blood and Honor association had been dissolved by the final decision of the Metropolitan District Court. The rally of right-wing extremists on Heroes Square was thus convened by Endre Domokos in his private capacity. All this was perfectly legal as under the assembly law, in order to organize demonstrations or other peaceful public assemblies one does not have to obtain legal personality, registration as a party or an association. These events ensure continuing publicity for these groups in mainstream printed and electronic media. Note that these Breakout Day celebrations attract radical right-wing extremist speakers from abroad, indicating that Hungarian extremist organizations maintain lively international ties.

As was previously indicated, many of the radical right-wing formations have no intention of seeking registration in any form. With powerful and highly operational websites and communication networks,[62] they are perfectly capable of staging mass rallies and other events which attract a police presence, almost guaranteed violence and thus instant attention in the mainstream media. This was a rather predictable pattern of behaviour during the riots in the autumn of 2006 and 2007. The names of the formations speak for themselves, at least for the trained followers of Hungarian nationalist rhetoric. Among the more visible new formations which gained notice in the recent riots one finds the 64 Counties Youth Movement (*64 Vármegye Ifjúsági Mozgalom*)[63] headed by László Toroczkai.[64] The '64 counties' refers to the 64 counties which comprised Hungary before the Trianon peace treaty ending the First World War. (The website of the organization is quick to admit that at the time another six Croatian counties fell under the jurisdiction of the Hungarian Holy Crown.)

In October 2006, after the attack on the television building, the rioters settled on the square before the Parliament building. The makeshift stage was soon converted into a more permanent one, with professional technical equipment. Food and drinks vendors set up in the square. The format of the demonstrations was rather loose and allowed for improvisation. After the anti-government forces ran out of major speakers (like the dignitaries of FiDESz), self-appointed orators seized the stage. Speeches were followed by performances of Hungarian folk music and extreme right rock music. It was in this setting (cordoned off by the police) that the key figures of the demonstrations took hold of the microphone. It is unnecessary to detail the programmes of the speakers or to list the participating organizations. The most important lesson of these events is their mobilizing potential and the eruption

62 In addition to the organizations' own websites, there are several community and newsites targeting this audience. (The best known is http://kuruc.info.)

63 See their bilingual website (at http://www.hvim.hu/).

64 Toroczkai (formerly: Tóth) is the son of a MiÉP politician.

of extreme right nationalist and racist rhetoric which had been unseen before, and which seems to have had a lasting impact. As the networks of communication were operationalized, they seemed to have long-term potential. Their efficiency was clearly underscored by follow-up riots. It is noteworthy that the success of the organizers did not depend on registered organizations and was not prevented by foreseeable police intervention.

The radicalization of the rhetoric and the 'demand for more' is best illustrated by the popular success of the Hungarian Guard Cultural and Traditional Association (*Magyar Gárda Kulturális és Hagyományőrző Egyesület*), known by its shortened form as Hungarian Guard. This association was established by *Jobbik*, and was registered by the courts. Currently the Metropolitan Court is hearing the Metropolitan prosecutor's petition to dissolve the Hungarian Guard. The prosecutor's petition is based on accounts of incidents where the Hungarian Guard acted openly against Roma.[65] According to the petition, the Hungarian Guard's activities are not about preserving traditions, but result in such serious infringement of the rights of Roma that it would justify the dissolution of the organization.[66]

To summarize the most important lessons of this discussion: one can see that the Hungarian legal framework for the registration and judicial dissolution of political organizations – political parties and other political associations – does not appear to have much of an influence on the actors and actions in the political sphere, and, in particular, is not capable of providing even minimal safeguards against actors who regularly abuse the advantages of legal recognition. Without ensuing violence even the most radical speech is unlikely to result in judicial disapproval. It is worth noting that in the case of György Budaházy – a familiar extreme right figure who was organizing many of the major riots of 2006 and 2007 – the prosecution did not succeed in establishing that the defendant had been instrumental in organizing activities that were to bring down the constitutional regime. Although he was openly supporting the rioters in public rallies and shared ideas (on a website, in writing) on how an efficient blockade of the capital could be performed, his instructions were not specific enough to be carried into completion.[67] (The prosecution appealed the decision which is not final.)

On the one hand, it is clear that extreme right formations tend not to seek registration as political parties in large numbers and do not even attempt to run at national elections. MiÉP and *Jobbik*, the two parties which regularly make such attempts, are far the most moderate of this club. On the other hand, it is also clear that, once registered (in a highly formalistic proceeding), courts are relatively reluctant to take action against extreme right formations. Courts are willing to give

65 These incidents were widely covered in the mainstream media, but will not be recounted here in detail.

66 The prosecution's case was summarized on the basis of http://www.origo.hu/itthon/20080312-a-magyar-garda-feloszlatasarol-targyal-a-birosag.html.

67 'Felmentették Budaházyt' (Budaházy acquitted), *origo.hu*, 30 January 2008.

the benefit of the doubt even to repeat defendants. Finally, these cases demonstrate that dissolution procedures do not seem significantly to impair the capacity of extreme right actors to execute their projects. It only furthers the problem that currently there are no provisions in the Hungarian legal system prohibiting the abuse of freedom of association: Currently, there is no prohibition which would prevent the continuation of a disbanded party.[68]

The Limits to Freedom of Speech and the Enemies of Constitutional Democracy

As a complement to the analysis of the operation of extreme right political formations, this section explores jurisprudence on freedom of expression to the extent relevant for the above analysis. The first part of the section is devoted to a relatively well-known militant democracy measure: the criminal prohibition of the display of totalitarian symbols, while the second part provides a short overview of the relevant constitutional and criminal jurisprudence on hate speech in Hungary.

Legal rules on the display of totalitarian symbols seem to add flavour to the militant democracy exchange. Under Hungarian law it is a crime to distribute, use in public or publicly exhibit 'the *swastika*; the insignia of the SS; the arrow cross; the hammer and sickle; the five pointed red star or any other symbol representing one of those signs' (Criminal Code, 269/B § 1). An exception is created for act of display for the 'purpose of disseminating knowledge, education, science, art or information on historical or contemporary events' (Criminal Code, 269/B § 2).

The criminal prohibition was approved by the Constitutional Court in decision 14/2000 (V. 12.) AB, stating that:

> The constitutional limitations of restriction (on freedom of expression) are marked, on the one hand, by incitement to hatred and, on the other hand, by offending expressions or similar activities merely capable of disturbing public peace as conducts constituting the offence. Accordingly, a conduct endangering public peace by offending the dignity of communities may constitutionally be subject to restriction by criminal law, in a scope wider than the statutory definition of incitement to hatred but narrower than that of mudslinging. *Consequently, the limit of constitutionally acceptable restriction is where the prohibited conduct not only expresses a political opinion – deemed right or wrong – but it does more: it endangers public peace by offending the dignity of communities committed to the values of democracy* [emphasis added].[69]

68 On this, see Sajó 2004a: 225, explaining how the decision of the Constitutional Court where it struck down an overbroad criminal provision to this effect (decision 58/1997 [XI. 5.] AB) contributed to the above situation indirectly.

69 The decision is available in English translation on the website of the Constitutional Court (via http://mkab.hu/en/enpage3.htm).

Unfortunately, the manner in which the law is drafted allows ridiculous prosecutions, while the modalities of behaviour targeted by the prohibition (which undermine the dignity of communities) remain too easily outside the scope of the enforcement of the criminal prohibition. The fragility and limitations of the Hungarian criminal prohibition are displayed in a series of cases. A critically important decision of the Supreme Court concerning the display of a wide range of Hungarist symbols was rendered in one of the unsuccessful prosecutions against Albert Szabó. In one case, prosecutors charged him for displaying Hungarist symbols in his party quarters and on the covers of Hungarist publications distributed by the party. In the case, the Supreme Court reaffirmed that the education exception in the Criminal Code applied to a wide range of formats in which information is provided about the totalitarian regimes. The Supreme Court added that the quality of the teaching is irrelevant for the purposes of the exception.[70]

Emblematic suits in another genre concerned a piece of the decor in 'Marxim' – a pub and pizzeria: a somewhat distorted, yet five pointed red star which was the street face logo of the restaurant and which was also a part of an intentionally ironic design setting it alongside numerous other (not banned) Socialist symbols.[71] The first instance court was not willing to convict the establishment noting that when viewed in its context (as part of the general decor of the restaurant), the display of the red star did not amount to a danger to society and therefore did not constitute a crime. It seemed to have made a difference in this case that the red star was indeed distorted, this is, that the display did not include a 'proper' red star. In a similarly unlikely case the same provision of the Criminal Code was also invoked against the weekly (liberal left) *Magyar Narancs* by the *Jobbik* in 2004, on account of red stars used as a design component to separate blocks of text in its print version. The motion of *Jobbik* was also supported by the World Association of 56er Hungarians (*56'os Magyarok Világszövetsége*) as an attempt to protect the victims of communism and the memory of the 1956 revolution.[72]

These cases are not to suggest that prosecutions for the display of totalitarian symbols are led solely in pointless cases about the non-political display of Communist symbols. Under the above prohibition, Hungarian Courts convicted Attila Vajnai, the vice-president of the Hungarian Workers' Party, who wore a home-made cardboard red star on his clothing in a public rally in 2003.[73] Also,

---

70 BH 1997.165.

71 PKKB 5.B.21.918/1994/15. The first instance decision became final on 20 March 1998, while the Metropolitan Court sustained the acquittal for lack of a crime on 22 April 1999. The full text of the decision was published in *Fundamentum* 1999/1994: 115–18, also available online (at http://157.181.181.13/dokuk/99-4-11.pdf).

72 'A Jobbik feljelentette a Magyar Narancsot' (Jobbik complaint against Magyar Narancs), *Magyar Nemzet*, 24 March 2004 (at http://www.mno.hu/portal/210867).

73 Note that, according to decision 14/2000 (V. 12.) AB of the Constitutional Court, 'the penalization of using symbols of despotism is not in a direct constitutional relation with the freedom to establish and operate political parties and, therefore, it does not violate

when Diána Bácsfi of the Hungarian Future Group stood trial for the display of the arrow cross in 2004, the banned symbol of the Hungarian fascist (Hungarist) party from the Second World War period, Bácsfi said that, on one occasion, she did use the arrow cross properly, while on all other occasions, she wore an altered version and not the proper one.[74] Bácsfi was sentenced to a fine of 150,000 HUFs, and the court said that it was an unacceptable defence that someone used a symbol on purpose which was only reminiscent of the proper banned sign.

Nonetheless, most recently, in 2008, the Liberal Party, SzDSz, was suspected of displaying a red star on one of its referendum posters.[75] However, the police decided to drop the case, noting that the symbol on the problematic posters was 'an orange star covered up to ¾ (of its size)'.[76] While the decision of the police seems to contradict the lesson from the Bácsfi case, it is consistent with the decision of the Metropolitan Court concerning a poster used by the movement for a Free Hungary in the campaign on European Union accession in 2003. The poster against accession had the image of two hands locked in a handshake – one having a *swastika*, the other a red star on it, being approached by a third hand which carries the European Union logo on it. In 2007, the Supreme Court was of the view that the display of the totalitarian symbols did not constitute a danger to society. The symbols were not displayed in order to promote totalitarian regimes or ideologies, but were displayed in order to indicate that these ideologies were deplorable.

It is clear at the outset that the criminal prohibition on the display of totalitarian symbols, as phrased in the Hungarian Criminal Code, is rather difficult to apply consistently in practice. It has to be borne in mind that newly emerging totalitarian political movements are ready to use signs and symbols that are clearly reminiscent of the banned symbols, without actually displaying the select few symbols that are banned in the Criminal Code. A prime example is clearly Albert Szabó's Hungarist

---

Article 3(1) of the constitution'. After his conviction on first instance, the Metropolitan Court approached the European Court of Justice in Luxemburg for a preliminary ruling seeking 'the interpretation of the principle of non-discrimination as a fundamental principle of Community law'. The case was thrown out by the ECJ for lack of jurisdiction, noting at paragraph 14 that it 'is clear that Mr Vajnai's situation is not connected in any way with any of the situations contemplated by the provisions of the treaties and the Hungarian provisions applied in the main proceedings are outside the scope of Community law', see Case C-328/04, *Vajnai v. Hungary*.

74 See 'Útkeresések, Szélsőjobboldaliak bíróság előtt' (Pathfinders, Extreme right before courts), *HVG*, 8 December 2004.

75 The said poster mimicked in most of its graphic details the poster of FiDESz used in the same referendum campaign. The referendum was held on questions sponsored by FiDESz, the senior opposition party since 2006, as an attempt to undermine the Socialist-led government's economic stabilization pact. While FiDESz's original slogan reads as 'social referendum 2008', the slogan on the SzDSz poster says 'referendum on Socialism 2008'.

76 'Önkényuralmi döntés' (Totalitarian decision), *HVG*, 19 March 2008.

Party, one of the earliest visible extreme right movements in Hungary in the early 1990s, which used the image of a black cogwheel in the middle of a white circle on a red background as its emblem – thus creating a symbol clearly reminiscent of a *swastika*ed Nazi flag. Indeed, observers of the trial suggest that Diána Bácsfi's more recent conviction would have been more complicated has she not used the 'real' (this is, the banned) arrow cross at one of the party rallies. It is of little solace that in a more recent hate speech decision involving Szabó, the Supreme Court in an auxiliary argument said that the Hungarist emblem with the cogwheel as part of the Hungarian Welfare Party's system of symbols further reaffirmed the party's Hungarist inclinations.[77]

Furthermore, it is clear that the banned symbols might be used as complex references to a set of ideologies in a message which might not be dangerous to society. Nonetheless, the interpretation of ironic or critical messages is not the easiest to infuse in a criminal procedure. Also, as at least some of these examples indicate, opportunities for criminal prosecutions of this kind are relatively easy to use against one's political opponents. Since such criminal cases – if formal charges are brought – tend to run for a couple of years, these pending cases may present ample opportunity to discredit one's political opponent on a symbolic matter without raising any point of substance.

At the same time, despite the existence of a seemingly well-defined and solid criminal prohibition on the display of totalitarian symbols, neo-Nazi websites are easily identifiable to the trained Hungarian eye (as in 'Front14.hu' or 'nemzet88.uw.hu') via their references to '88' – standing for 'HH' (the 8th character of the English alphabet) as in '*Heil Hitler*', or '14' as a reference to the white supremacist slogan ('We must secure the existence of our people and a future for white children') consisting of 14 words. Such complex, indirect references do not simply show the globalization of Nazi symbolics, but also reflect the technical insufficiencies of the Hungarian criminal ban on totalitarian symbols.[78]

The spatial confines of this chapter do not allow for a detailed exposition of Hungarian constitutional and judicial jurisprudence on matters of hate speech. Suffice to say that ordinary courts, and also the Constitutional Court, tend to be reluctant to curb freedom of expression by imposing criminal sanctions.

The Criminal Code's group libel provision bans as a felony 'provocation of hatred before a large audience against the Hungarian nation or any national, ethnic, racial or religious group or other groups of society is punishable with up to three years of imprisonment'.[79] At face value, this provision seems to be

77 EBH 1999.6.

78 On this, see 'Cselezés kiskapura', *HVG*, 9 April 2008 (at http://hvg.hu/hvgfriss/2008.15/200815_Cselezes_kiskapura.aspx).

79 Article 269 of the Criminal Code, as amended by Article 5 of Act no. 17 of 1996 and revised by decision 12/1999 (V. 21.) AB. The title of Article 269 (the name of the crime) itself stayed as 'incitement to hatred', yet the activity prohibited was defined as 'provocation to hatred'. Since the Constitutional Court's decision centred around contrasting

capable of screening racial slurs and anti-Semitic insults which find their way into Hungarian public discourse. Important lessons follow, however, from a recent hate speech case which prompted considerable public attention. The case arose from a statement by a then Member of Parliament of MiÉP, Lóránt Hegedűs Jr. (who is also a Protestant Minister), who called for the 'exclusion of Galician vagrants' in a right-wing newspaper and later in a radio broadcast. Overturning the lower court's assessment, the appellate court found that the defendant's statement urging to 'exclude them, or they will exclude you' did not reflect a clear intent to call for violence.[80] In support of its position on the requirement of instant violence, the appellate court relied on the Supreme Court's decision of 1997 establishing the 'active violence' criterion. The acquittal received highly critical responses in the mainstream press. As a reaction, the Chief Justice of the Supreme Court issued a statement calling for the President, the Cabinet and Parliament to protect the independence of the judiciary from statements infringing the constitutional rights of the judiciary.[81]

This decision by ordinary courts is best explained in the light of the Hungarian Constitutional Court's longstanding jurisprudence concerning the unconstitutionality of criminal prohibition of hate speech. Since 1992, it has been the Constitutional Court's firm position to limit the criminal prohibition of hate speech to those utterances that present a 'clear and present danger' of disrupting public peace.[82] The most recent round of Hungarian developments is marked by a unanimous Constitutional Court decision[83] invalidating the government's latest attempt to expand the prohibition of hate speech in the Criminal Code.[84] The Constitutional Court reaffirmed the premises of its previous decisions on hate speech and group libel[85] and also referred to the European Court of Justice's position in the *Handyside*,[86] *Jersild*[87] and *Zana*[88] cases. At the same time, the Constitutional Court acknowledged that international obligations clearly call for limitations of freedom of expression. The Constitutional Court emphasized that limitations

'provocation' (*uszitas*) and 'incitement' (*izgatas*), these terms were preserved throughout the discussion of the case.

80 BH 2005.46.

81 For a comprehensive summary of views and the full text of the Chief Justice's statement, see 'Gyuloletbeszed: torveny es mozgalom' (Hate Speech: A Statute and a Movement), *Magyar Hirlap*, 12 November 2003.

82 Decision 30/1992 (V. 26.) AB. The judgment does contain the phrase 'clear and present danger', in English at ABH 1992, 167, 178–9.

83 Decision 18/2004 (V. 25.) AB. Justice Kukorelli wrote for a unanimous Constitutional Court.

84 Act no. 4 of 1978 on the Criminal Code.

85 See decisions 30/1992 (V. 26.) AB; 36/1994 (VI. 24.) AB; 18/2000 (VI. 6.) AB.

86 *Handyside v. United Kingdom*, Judgment of 7 December 1976, Series A no. 103, para. 41.

87 *Jersild v. Denmark*, Judgment of 23 September 1994, Series A no. 298, para. 37.

88 *Zana v. Turkey*, Judgment of 25 November 1997, Reports 1997-VII, 2549, para. 51.

imposed on freedom of speech in compliance with international obligations shall live up to the Hungarian Constitution's standard of speech protection and shall comply with the requirements of the necessity/proportionality test applied by the Constitutional Court to test the constitutionality of rights limitations.

The Constitutional Court emphasized that the criminal prohibition of hate speech is considered constitutional only if the utterance is of such intensity that it presents a 'clear and present danger' of disturbing public peace. The Constitutional Court said that the criminal prohibition of hate speech shall not be motivated by outlawing unjust, disturbing or shocking opinions.[89] While in the case of 'provocation of hatred' such danger of violence was sensed by the court, constitutional justices were of the view that the newly adopted criminal prohibition of 'incitement to hatred' would make the criminal prohibition over inclusive, thus decreasing the level of constitutional protection afforded to free speech. In reaching this conclusion, the Constitutional Court did not contest the justice minister's submission on the inconsistency detectable in the hate speech jurisprudence of ordinary courts. The Constitutional Court also found that the second phrase, which was introduced to prohibit 'incitement to violence', criminalizes such behaviour, which does not disrupt public peace or restrict rights of others, thus, this crime amounts to an unconstitutional limitation of freedom of expression.

In its hate speech decisions, the Hungarian Constitutional Court repeatedly refers to a rather unique reading of the 'clear and present danger' standard familiar from US constitutional jurisprudence. As defined in *Brandenburg*,[90] this standard distinguishes the constitutionally protected exercise of free speech from incitement to violence undeserving constitutional protection. As the majority said:

> the constitutional guarantees of free speech and free press do not permit a State to forbid or proscribe advocacy of the use of force or of law violation except where such advocacy is directed to inciting or producing imminent lawless action and is likely to incite or produce such action.[91]

Note, however, that in the United States the clear and present danger standard applies only to such utterances that are otherwise worthy of constitutional protection, but not to such expressions that fall short of First Amendment protection, such as hate

89 Cf. the words of the European Court of Human Rights finding in *Handyside v. United Kingdom*, at para. 49 that freedom of expression 'is applicable not only to "information" or "ideas" that are favourably received or regarded as inoffensive or as a matter of indifference, but also to those that offend, shock or disturb the State or any sector of the population. Such are the demands of that pluralism, tolerance and broadmindedness without which there is no "democratic society"'.

90 *Brandenburg v. Ohio*, 395 U.S. 444 [1969].

91 *Brandenburg v. Ohio*, 395 U.S. 444, 447 [1969]. In the case, concurring justices Black and Douglas rejected the application of the 'clear and present danger' standard.

speech amounting to 'fighting words'.[92] The plurality opinion in *Virginia v. Black*, the recent Virginia cross burning case, neatly fits within this paradigm. As Justice O'Connor put it for the plurality:

> while a burning cross does not inevitably convey a message of intimidation, often the cross burner intends that the recipients of the message fear for their lives. And when a cross burning is used to intimidate, few if any messages are more powerful.[93]

The Virginia prohibition of cross burning was found to be constitutional as the constitutional protection of freedom of speech does not extend to intimidation of the kind proscribed by the statute.[94]

As this account suggests, in Hungary principles of free speech jurisprudence were derived from lessons of foreign and international jurisprudence, premised on (somewhat idealistic) judicial visions of a robust public discourse. In over a decade, this public discourse became truly functional, yet it does not match completely the ideal picture detailed by the Constitutional Court. Discrepancies between vision and reality are signalled not only by the frequent acts of hate speech which trigger acquittals in ordinary courts, but also by Parliament's returning to the Constitutional Court with variations on essentially the same hate speech provision.

While sticking to its position developed in 1992, the Hungarian Constitutional Court has at no point seriously considered the fear and intimidation openly anti-Semitic utterances might trigger in certain circles of the Hungarian polity. One may argue that religious sentiments or subjective fears of violence should not become the guide of a secular Constitutional Court in deciding about the constitutionality of the criminal prohibition of hate speech. Nonetheless, it is worth considering the lack of such a reference in the Constitutional Court's hate speech jurisprudence in the light of the Supreme Court's refusal to consider the claim of the prosecutor in the extraordinary review proceedings in Albert Szabó's incitement case, discussed above.

In this case, the Chief Prosecutor argued that the inciting (igniting) potential of an utterance depends on its temporal and social context, therefore the courts

---

92 *Beauharnais v. Illinois*, 343 U.S. 250 [1952]; see Rosenfeld 2001:1536. See also *Chaplinsky v. New Hampshire*, 315 U.S. 568, 571–572 [1942]; *Cohen v. California*, 403 U.S. 15 [1971]; *R.A.V. v. City of St. Paul*, 505 U.S. 377 [1992]; *Virginia v. Black*, 538 U.S. 343 [2003].

93 *Virginia v. Black*, 538 U.S. 343 [2003].

94 *Virginia v. Black*: 'The First Amendment permits Virginia to outlaw cross burnings done with the intent to intimidate because burning a cross is a particularly virulent form of intimidation … Virginia may choose to regulate this subset of intimidating messages in light of cross burning's long and pernicious history as a signal of impending violence'. In *Virginia v. Black*, the justices disagreed about the constitutionality of the second part of the Virginia criminal provision, which reads: 'Any such burning of a cross shall be prima facie evidence of an intent to intimidate a person or group of persons'.

should take into account the still evolving public discourse space of the Hungarian transitional democracy; and also, the way the experience during the Second World War shaped the sensitivities of the Hungarian polity.[95] In response, the Supreme Court said that the proper application of the incitement provision required a consistent application of the language of the criminal provision as known since the time of the Royal High Court.[96] The lack of judicial sensitivity both in the Constitutional Court and in the Supreme Court towards the complex societal impact of anti-Semitic speech is striking. Nothing in the decisions of the Supreme Court or the Constitutional Court is meant to suggest that this effect is the outcome of a conscious judicial strategy. Yet, this observation might lead one to conclude that the high Hungarian judicial fora easily become intellectual prisoners of their own understanding of societal dynamic and proper judicial behaviour.

Also, there is a deep structural problem in Hungarian law which is relevant for the present analysis. The scope of free speech protection is significantly broader than foreseen by the criminal prohibition of totalitarian symbols, which makes the hate speech jurisprudence even more out of touch with reality. While the symbol ban at least in its justification provided by the Constitutional Court is supposed to be sensitive to the feelings and dignity of others, the language, justification and application of the hate speech prohibition do not seem to account for such considerations,[97] although this discrepancy has been pointed out by commentators many times.[98]

It is of little reassurance that, while the sensitivities and dignity of members of the audience does not seem to make a difference in hate speech jurisprudence, the Supreme Court seems to have found a way to translate at least one dimension of it: the potential for violence. In the relatively recent case concerning the disbanding of the Blood and Honor association, the fact that a Jewish organization (MAZSIHISZ) put up a counter-protest against the Breakout Day rally was taken as proof of the harm the Blood and Honor association caused to others.[99] Although it is a welcome development that the ordinary courts are finally willing to take into account the mysterious, faceless others in the hate speech cases, it remains a problem that they do this in a rather mechanical fashion. To say the least, it imposes an enormous burden on communities of 'others' (may they be

95 This argument in part was directed against the standard practice of the Supreme Court to accept the interwar jurisprudence of the Royal High Court in applying the incitement to hatred provision.

96 EBH 1999.5.

97 The consequences of this tension are explored and explained in detail in Sajó 2004b: 26 et seq. – Then Chief Justice László Sólyom – the author of the speech protectionist 1992 Constitutional Court decision – drafted a decision to abolish the criminal prohibition of the display of totalitarian symbols in its current form, but never took it before the full Constitutional Court, fearing that it might be too liberal. On this, see 'Cselezés kiskapura', *HVG*, 9 April 2008.

98 See, for example, Halmai 2001.

99 BH 2007.146.

Jewish, Roma or homosexual) to put up a counter-protest every single time they are denigrated by right-wing extremists. Also, it is clear that courts preferring to see such immediate counteraction did not consider the potential costs of policing such events, which are taking place more regularly with the increased visibility of extremist actors.

Conclusion

The Hungarian legal system has a series of militant democracy mechanisms in place. Most of these were adopted – or at least defined conceptually – in the very beginning of the transition to democracy, at a time of fear, distrust and uncertainty. Unlike in many other jurisdictions where similar measures are overused to suppress political opponents and dissenting voices, the Hungarian story is about the failure of constitutional actors to protect themselves and each other from radical political elements. This disappointing record may be attributed to the insufficiency of these legal mechanisms in some part. Yet, for the most part what we have witnessed in these pages is the story of a lack of cooperation between constitutional actors to perform their own constitutional obligations properly in their own best interest.

This incapacity would probably not have been exposed so crudely had extremist political forces not succeeded in an unexpected turn of history. Yet, in the current state of affairs, every instance of intervention which constitutional actors miss or misconceive starts to operate against them. Unfortunately, it was precisely stark reality which responsible constitutional actors did not manage to take properly into account.

Extremist political formations have proved that they are capable of mobilizing a segment of the polity which is literate in new technologies, and is capable of reacting rapidly. The techniques employed by these groups often evade legal responses in legal systems which respond much better to daily developments. In the Hungarian setting, ordinary courts are only learning to define the limits of freedom of association and freedom of expression by trial and error, without even attempting to use an extraordinary justification invoking militant democracy rationales. Indeed, in the Hungarian discourse space such attempts seem to remain the specialty of commentators and scholars. In recent decisions, prosecutors and ordinary courts displayed at least a sense and some interest of what is expected of them when facing the outcome of the activities of radical political formations. Nonetheless, the standard learning cycle of constitutional institutions might unfortunately be intolerably long this time around, taking into account the *modus operandi* of the invaders.

References

Angelusz, Róbert and Tardos, Róbert (2005) 'A választói tömbök rejtett hálózata' (The hidden network of electoral clusters), in Róbert Angelusz and Róbert Tardos (eds) *Törések, hálók, hidak, Választói magatartás és politikai tagolódás Magyarországon* (Cleavages, Nets, Bridges, Voter Behaviour and Political Process in Hungary). Budapest: DKMKA, 65–160.

Bozóki, András and Kriza, Borbála (2003) in András Bozóki (ed.) *Politikai pluralizmus Magyarországon 1987–2002* (Political pluralism in Hungary 1987–2002). Budapest: Századvég, 506 et seq.

Bozóki, András, et al. (eds) (2000) *A rendszerváltás Forgatókönyve. Kerekasztal-tárgyalások 1989-ben* (The script of transition, Roundtable Talks in 1989). Budapest: Új Mandátum Könyvkiadó.

Enyedi, Zsolt and Tóka, Gábor (2006) 'The Only Game in Town: Party Politics in Hungary', draft chapter for Stephen White, David Stanfield, and Paul Webb (eds) *Political Parties in Transitional Democracies.* Oxford: Oxford University Press. Final version of August 2006 (available at http://www.personal.ceu.hu/departs/personal/Gabor_Toka/Papers/EnyediToka06.pdf).

Fleck, Zoltán (2007) 'A szélsőjobboldali populizmus radikalizálódása' (The radicalization of extreme right populism), *Magyarország politikai évkönyve*, 1351–62.

Hack, Péter (2005) 'Ügyészség, A velünk elő múlt' (Prosecution, The past living with us), *Beszélő* (10): 12 (available at http://beszelo.c3.hu/cikkek/az-ugyeszseg-a-velunk-elo-mult).

Halmai, Gábor (1990) *Az egyesülés szabadsága, Az egyesülési jog története.* Budapest: Atlantisz–Medvetánc.

Halmai, Gábor (2001) 'Gyűlöletbeszéd és személyiségi jogok' (Hate speech and personality rights), *Fundamentum* (4): 105–18.

Juhász, Attila and Somogyi, Zoltán (2008) 'A magyar szélsőjobboldal újraszerveződési kísérlete 2006-ban' (The Hungarian radical right's attempt to reorganize in 2006), in Péter Sándor, Ágnes Tolnai and László Vass (eds) *Magyarország politikai évkönyve 2007 (Yearbook of Hungarian Politics 2007), vols. 1–2.* Budapest: Kossuth Kiadó, 1321–33.

Karácsony, Gergely (2006) 'Árkok és légvárak, A választói viselkedés stabilizálódása Magyarországon' (Ditches and cloud-castles, stabilization of voting behaviour in Hungary), *Karácsony, Parlamenti választások*, 59–103.

Karsai, László (1999) 'The Radical Right in Hungary', in Sabrina P. Ramet (ed.) *The Radical. Right in Central and Eastern Europe Since 1989.* University Park: Penn State University Press.

Körösényi, András (2000) *Government and Politics in Hungary* (translated by Alan Renwick), Budapest: CEU Press.

Körösényi, András, Tóth, Csaba and Török, Gábor (eds) (2005) *A magyar politikai rendszer* (The Hungarian Political System), Budapest: Osiris.

Kovrig, Bennett (1999) 'European Integration', in Aurel Braun and Zoltan Barany (eds) *Dilemma of Transition: The Hungarian Experience*. Lanham: Rowman and Littlefield, 253–71.

Laki, László and Szabó, Andrea (2002) 'Részvétel a társadalom "önkéntes" szervezetei életében', in László Füstös and László Guba (eds) *Társadalmi regiszter 2002, A magyar társadalom demográfiai összetétele, etnikai, kulturális, politikai tagolódása, értékorientációi* (Social register 2002, the democraphic composition of Hungarian society, its ethnic, cultural, political layers, (and) value orientations), 35–56.

Merkl, Peter H. and Weinberg, Leonard (2003) *Right-wing Extremism in the Twenty-First Century*. London: Frank Cass.

Rosenfeld, Michel (2001) 'Hate Speech in Constitutional Jurisprudence: A Comparative Analysis', *Cardozo Law Review* (24): 1523–36.

Sajó, András (1993) 'A "láthatatlan. Alkotmány" apróbetűi: A magyar Alkotmánybíróság első ezerkétszáz napja', *Állam- és Jogtudomány* (1–2): 37–96.

Sajó, András (1995) 'Reading the Invisible Constitution: Judicial Review in Hungary', *Oxford Journal of Legal Studies* 15(2): 253–67.

Sajó, András (2002) 'Önvédő Jogállam' (Self-protecting rule of law), *Fundamentum* (3–4): 55–68.

Sajó, András (2004a) 'Militant Democracy and Transition towards Democracy', in András Sajó (ed.) *Militant Democracy*. Utrecht: Eleven International Publishing, 209–30.

Sajó, András (2004b) '... a faji gyűlölet igazolása büntetendő' (... the justification of racial hatred shall be criminalized), *Fundamentum* (4): 21–34.

Sólyom, László (2004) *Pártok és érdekszervezetek az Alkotmányban* (Parties and representative organizations in the constitution). Budapest: Rejtjel.

Szőcs, László (1998) 'A Tale of the Unexpected: The Extreme Right Vis-à-vis Democracy in Post-Communist Hungary', *Ethnic and Racial Studies* 21(6): 1096–115.

Tóka, Gábor (2005a) 'A magyarországi politikai tagoltság nemzetközi összehasonlításban' (Hungarian electoral alignments in international comparison), in Róbert Angelusz and Róbert Tardos (eds) *Törések, hálók, hidak, Választói magatartás és politikai tagolódás Magyarországon* (Cleavages, nets, bridges, voter behaviour and political process in Hungary). Budapest: DKMKA, 17–64.

Tóka, Gábor (2005b) 'A törésvonalak, a pártok és az intézményrendszer' (Cleavages, parties and institutional arrangements), in Róbert Angelusz and Róbert Tardos (eds) *Törések, hálók, hidak, Választói magatartás és politikai tagolódás Magyarországon* (Cleavages, nets, bridges, voter behaviour and political process in Hungary). Budapest: DKMKA, 243–322.

Chapter 8
Israel

Benyamin Neuberger

Introduction

The Israeli sociologists Dan Horowitz and Moshe Lissak defined self-defending democracy 'as a democracy which excludes groups from the democratic game which aim to, or act in a way that may endanger the state, its political regime, or its basic national consensus' (quoted in Pedhazur 2000: 3). The question of self-defending democracy is not identical with the often made, but problematic connection between national security and democracy that has dominated the public debate in the Western world since the 9/11 attack on the United States of America. Most issues dealing with national security are related to external threats to the state – to its very existence, its integrity and security, and to other vital interests, such as the importation of oil. The focal point of a self-defending democracy relates to the protection of a democratic regime against internal threats by anti-democratic, revolutionary and violent parties, movements, groups or individuals. Democracy may be safeguarded by means of administrative acts, governmental decisions and activities, legislation, adjudication, changes in the political system (such as the electoral system), co-opting dangerous forces into the government in order to mitigate and constrain them, or boycotting them so as to isolate them and put them beyond the pale – as was done in France and Belgium, where the *Front National* and the *Vlaams Belang* are excluded from any coalitions with democratic parties. In Germany, a similar boycott was imposed on the *Nationaldemokratische Partei Deutschlands* (NPD) and the *Deutsche Volksunion* (DVU). Parliamentary sanctions, such as excluding anti-democratic parties from important committees, and boycotts by the public or private media, were also imposed. Democratic education in schools is another long-range strategy for defending democracy. In this context, one could also differentiate between actions 'from above', by the government, Parliament and courts, and actions 'from below', such as social boycotts, demonstrations and actions by civil society groups and organizations (Pedhazur 2004: 7).

In this article, we will not deal with all approaches to the defence of democracy, but will concentrate on the means employed 'from above' against anti-democratic forces intent on wrecking or destroying the essence and quality of democracy. These means must by necessity put limitations on democracy in order to defend and uphold it.

We must stress that – unlike parliamentary and presidential democracy, republican democracy and constitutional monarchy, and federal or unitary democracy – a self-defending democracy is not a regime type. It defines a policy any type of democratic regime may uphold or choose not to uphold, when it faces unbearable actions and threats against the democratic regime. A key variable in the strategy chosen will certainly be related to the question as to if and in what sense the threat to democracy is perceived as real and far-reaching.

'Self-defending democracy' is not the only term used in political science literature. Some scholars use the terms 'fighting democracy' and 'militant democracy' – terms coined in the United States in the 1930s by Karl Loewenstein and Karl Mannheim, German Jewish refugees who had both seen the collapse of the Weimar Republic and the rise to power of National Socialism (Leggewie and Meier 1995: 310; Loewenstein 1937). Sometimes the terms 'defensive democracy' or 'defending democracy' are also used. In German, common terms are '*wehrhafte*', '*abwehrbereite*' or '*streitbare Demokratie*'.

Ami Pedhazur differentiates between three ideal types of self-defending democracies, which he describes in medical terms, when the disease is the anti-democratic danger and the medication is what must be done about it (Pedhazur 2000: 10):

> The militant route might be compared to an aggressive treatment to a disease that was discovered while in a very advanced condition. In such case, the attempt to save the very ill patient may lead the physicians to use heroic measures that under different circumstances would not even be considered. Treatment is so aggressive that this affects healthy vital organs as well. However, according to the doctors, it is worthwhile saving the body even at the cost of leaving it weak and crippled. The defending route applies to a milder treatment. In this case, the eruption of the disease was less dramatic since the patient had undergone preventive treatment for years. Hence, there was no need to use the most aggressive medications; yet, even this milder treatment may weaken the body to a large extent. The third route, the immunized one, relates to a very healthy body with powerful antidotes. When a disease attacks such a body, the initial struggle takes place within the blood circulation prior to the appearance of the first symptoms. In many cases, the body itself may defeat the disease before its outbreak. However, even in cases when the patient starts to suffer from the symptoms, they are not too severe and thus require only light treatment. Such treatment does not leave scars on the patient's body, and he may return to normal function quickly.

The basic dilemma is whether it is appropriate to grant all the democratic freedoms to the enemies of democracy, and thus enable them to destroy democracy, for example, through the misuse of freedom of expression; freedom to publish; freedom of assembly; and freedom of demonstration, through the abuse of the rule of law and the principle of tolerance, and, finally, through the participation in free elections. Karl Popper defined this dilemma as the 'paradox of tolerance'; Raphael Cohen-Almagor called it the 'democratic trap' (Cohen-Almagor 1994a: 18). On the other hand, however, there is the 'paradox of the self-defending democracy' or the 'slippery slope syndrome' – indeed, just as purist-maximalist democracy can bring about its demise, the scope of oppressive measures for the sake of a totalist defence of democracy can result in the gradual disintegration or even collapse of the democratic regime. The slide down the slippery slope of anti-democratic measures may result in a plummeting into the abyss of dictatorship. The conflict arises from the fact that every liberal democrat feels a strong commitment to freedom of expression and political organization, to free elections, as well as to human dignity, individual liberties and the principle of equality – all of which may be endangered by their misuse by the totalitarian enemies of freedom.

As with any dilemma which lacks a clear solution, there are different schools of thought on how to respond to anti-democratic activities that pose a threat on and endanger democratic government. One school of thought stresses the threats to the democratic system and the need for a self-defending democracy, while another school of thought is perturbed by the danger that self-defending democracy itself might erode democracy. While John Rawls stresses that 'justice does not require that men must stand idly by while others destroy the basis of their existence … the only question, then, is whether the tolerant have the right to curb the intolerant when they are of no immediate danger to the equal liberties of others' (Rawls 1971: 218), Hans Kelsen, though an American Jewish-Austrian refugee from Nazi Europe, fiercely defends the freedom of expression of the enemies of democracy as long as they refrain from any violence. The major disagreements between the two schools of thought relate to the freedom of expression, publication and the press, to the freedom of assembly and demonstration, and to the right to participate in free elections. There is no disagreement regarding the need for governmental and legal intervention against violent and criminal acts by the enemies of democracy.

Kelsen's position had been clearly presented as early as 1935 (Kelsen, as quoted in Leggewie and Meier 1995: 262):

> Aber kann Demokratie tolerant bleiben, wenn sie sich gegen anti-demokratische Umtriebe verteidigen muß? Sie kann es! In dem Maße, als sie friedliche Äußerungen anti-demokratischer Anschauungen nicht unterdrückt. Gerade durch solche Toleranz unterscheidet sich Demokratie von Autokratie. Wir sind berechtigt, Autokratie abzulehnen und auf unsere demokratische Staatsform stolz zu sein, nur so lange wir diesen Unterschied aufrecht erhalten. Demokratie kann sich nicht dadurch verteidigen, daß sie sich selbst aufgibt. Aber es ist das Recht jeder, auch einer demokratischen Regierung, Versuche, sie mit Gewalt zu beseitigen, mit Gewalt zu unterdrücken und durch geeignete Mittel zu verhindern. Die Ausübung dieses Rechts ist weder mit dem Prinzip der Demokratie noch mit dem der Toleranz in Widerspruch. Es mag mitunter schwierig sein, eine klare Grenzlinie zu ziehen zwischen der Verbreitung gewisser Ideen und der Vorbereitung eines revolutionären Umsturzes. Aber von der Möglichkeit, eine

> solche Grenzlinie zu finden, hängt die Möglichkeit ab, Demokratie aufrecht zu erhalten. Es mag auch sein, daß solche Grenzziehung eine gewisse Gefahr in sich schließt. Aber es ist das Wesen und die Ehre der Demokratie, diese Gefahr auf sich zu nehmen; und wenn Demokratie diese Gefahr nicht bestehen kann, dann ist sie nicht wert, verteidigt zu werden.[1]

Kelsen rejects the concept of a self-defending democracy which acts against anti-democratic forces in order to prevent them from coming to power, even if they operate non-violently. The dangers of the slippery slope, he says, are too great. Claus Leggewie and Horst Meier share his view. They also reject the notion that in a democracy there is one 'correct' *Weltanschauung*, even not a correct 'democratic' *Weltanschauung*. According to Kelsen, any thoughts and expressed views should be defended, including anti-democratic thoughts and expressions (but not anti-democratic acts). This kind of absolutist concept of freedom of expression means freedom of expression also for false, dangerous, racist and totalitarian thought. Like Kelsen, Leggewie and Meier contend that there is 'no democracy without risks' (Leggewie and Meier 1995: 20). Kelsen and his supporters insist that the harm to democracy stemming from prohibition against the expression of anti-democratic views is greater than any benefits that might accrue from the freedom to express such thoughts. Free competition in the free market of ideas is therefore always preferable to suppressing the anti-democratic voice. The Kelsen–Leggewie/Meier school of thought further argues that it is better to let anti-democratic frustrations come to the open rather than push the enemies of democracy to covert revolutionary and violent acts.

Basic to the Kelsen approach is a clear distinction between freedom of expression, which has to be defended in all cases and freedom of action, which will not be defended if the act is criminal, revolutionary and violent. Self-defending democracy denies the basic distinction between words and deeds. Its supporters hold that anti-democratic words, publications and incitement may increase the power of anti-democratic parties and movements, even to the extent that it may become impossible to contain them or act against them. Basic to the concept of a

---

1 Translation: 'But can a democracy be tolerant in its defence against anti-democratic tendencies? It can – to the extent that it must not suppress the peaceful expression of anti-democratic ideas. It is just by such tolerance that democracy distinguishes itself from autocracy. We have a right to reject autocracy and to be proud of our democratic form of government only as long as we maintain this difference. Democracy cannot defend itself by giving itself up. But to suppress and prevent any attempt to overthrow the government by force is the right of any, even a democratic government. This right does not collide with the principles of democracy and tolerance. Sometimes it may be difficult to draw a clear boundary line between the mere expression of ideas and the preparation of the revolutionary use of force. But on the possibility of finding such a boundary line depends the possibility of maintaining democracy. It may be that any such boundary line involves a certain risk. But it is the essence and the honour of democracy to run such risk; and if democracy could not stand such risk, it would not be worthy of being defended.'

self-defending democracy is a more skeptical approach towards human nature and the 'free market of ideas', which is supposed to bring about policies that are always rational, liberal and democratic. The guardians of self-defending democracy are aware of the danger that a self-defending democracy may glide along the slippery slope toward dictatorship, but they agree that the dangers of an absolutist 'purist' democracy granting its gravediggers all the rights and tools is often much greater.

Those who favour a self-defending democracy will demonstrate the connection between words and deeds. They argue that direct incitement (the call for a violent revolution or for the assassination of an elected leader) or indirect incitement (words of praise and support for acts of violence and murder) clearly establish the link between words and deeds – not only expressions that call for violent and unconstitutional acts ('occupy the government compound', 'break into Parliament and paralyze it'), but also expressions that increase the danger that violent crimes may be committed. Calling people elected to serve in government or opposition 'murderers' or 'traitors' blurs the distinction between speech and action. The fateful connection between anti-democratic propaganda and crimes led Jean Amery to ask 'whether this or that opinion is still an opinion or complicity in a crime' (Amery, as quoted in Leggewie and Meier 1995: 314).

The supporters of self-defending democracy will argue that there must be 'no freedoms for the enemies of freedom', a Jacobin slogan during the French Revolution. The Kelsenites insist that the change from *liberté, égalité, fraternité* to Jacobin *terreur* is a prime example of how the suppression of the enemies of liberty – in the name of liberty – slid down the slippery slope, finally suppressing the freedom of anyone who disagreed with the government and creating the Jacobin terror machine (Leggewie and Meier 1995: 210).

However, should self-defending democracy be adopted, then many more questions will have to be asked. At what point should democracy defend itself against authoritarian incitement or totalitarian movements – when there is 'clear and present danger' to democracy, and only then? May it not be too late at that point? Is it legitimate to outlaw anti-democratic expressions, even when there is no certainty that these expressions pose a concrete danger? What is an anti-democratic expression, and is bad intention sufficient to outlaw it, even if there is no immediate danger? How does one determine which expression ought to be outlawed – is it public speech; a movie; a play; pictures and advertisements; symbols (for example, the *swastika*); or demonstrations? Does it include private talk or shouts in the soccer stadium? Should the content of anti-democratic expression (for example: 'the government is illegitimate'; 'government of traitors'; 'the Prime Minister should be killed'; 'a dictatorship must be established') or the way it is expressed (newspaper articles; public speeches downtown before thousands of demonstrators; an exchange with a neighbour) be relevant to the ways and means employed by a self-defending democracy? Is it important to know the objectives of the speaker? When he talks about 'traitors', does he mean that they should be treated as traitors? Is it his intention to sanction murder? Are there specific conditions (the growth of a totalitarian movement, war, terror or grave economic crisis) that call for intervention against authoritarian and totalitarian expressions and movements? Are there conditions which demand restraint and non-interference by the state? There will never be full agreement about what constitutes an anti-democratic party and about the exact meaning of extremism, incitement and rebellion that may call for intervention by a self-defending democracy (Cohen-Almagor 1994a; Leggewie and Meier 1995: 13–20; Pedhazur 2004: 167).

Self-Defending Democracy in Israel

In Israel, the theme of self-defending democracy has come up again and again in two different contexts: threats by Arab nationalists and right-wing Jewish nationalist extremists. There is, nevertheless, a basic difference between the two threats. While the Arab nationalist threat is perceived as a threat to the very existence of the state or to its existence as a Jewish state, and only indirectly as a threat to democracy, the threats of the Jewish extreme right are perceived as a direct threat against the democratic regime and not in any way a threat against the state or its Jewish character (though some people on the liberal left may argue that a non-democratic Israel might not survive).

The first threats to Israeli democracy came from the remnants of the pre-state Jewish terrorist organizations – the *Irgun Zvai'i Leumi* (National Military Organization, NMO) and *Lohamey Cherut Yisrael* (Fighters for the Freedom of Israel, FFI). The most spectacular incidents involving the NMO and the FFI after Israel's Declaration of Independence on 14 May 1948 were the *Altalena* Affair[2] and the murder of the United Nations Security Council's mediator, Count Folke Bernadotte.[3]

There is no disagreement among democrats that any violent and terrorist act should be punished according to regular criminal law or specific emergency regulations. Nevertheless, after the murder of Count Bernadotte, the Prevention of Terrorism Ordinance (1948) was enacted. It went beyond the idea of punishing terrorists and could be seen as the first instance when the new state applied the principle of self-defending democracy. The ordinance called for the prosecution not only of people who committed terrorist acts, but also of people who assisted or encouraged (for instance, through financial support or propaganda) terrorist organizations. Clause 4(a) of the ordinance stated that 'any person who spreads, in

2 *Altalena* was the name of a ship brought to the shores of Tel Aviv loaded with weapons designed for NMO. On 22 June 1948, Prime Minister, David Ben-Gurion, who suspected a putsch by the NMO after their refusal to hand over the weapons to the Israeli Defence Forces, ordered the ship to be bombed.

3 Count Folke Bernadotte was murdered on 17 September 1948 by members of the FFI, who accused him of being pro-Arab, and of drawing up peace proposals that would endanger Israel's hold on Western Jerusalem and other territories conquered in the War of Independence.

writing or orally, words of praise, sympathy, or encourages violent acts that may result in death, physical injury or threats of violence' will be punished with up to three years imprisonment. Clause 4(b) went even further by making it punishable 'to publicize in writing or orally any words of praise and calls for assistance and support for a terrorist organization' – even if they are not directly or indirectly connected to violent acts.

The ordinance which is in force to this day has raised many questions. Does it relate to the support of violence only when it is connected to a terrorist organization? Is praise of a terrorist act not connected to an organization – for instance, praise for Yitzhak Rabin's assassination or general support of the *intifadeh* (see, for example, Criminal Appeal 4147/1995) – punishable under the ordinance? In what way exactly is a terrorist act different from other acts of violence? Another issue concerns the question whether speech is punishable for its content only, or only when there is a probability that it might lead to violence.

In the years 1964–1965, the 'Weimar effect', the traumatic experience of the first German democratic republic, which was destroyed by the Nazis using all the democratic means available to them, was cited for the first time by Israeli Courts. In 1964, the Haifa District Commissioner in the Ministry of the Interior refused to register *El-Ard* ('The Land') as an association because its goals included 'a just solution to the Palestinian problem through its consideration as an indivisible unit according to the will of the Palestinian people' as well as 'national self-determination for the Arab people in the whole of Palestine'. This was interpreted as a denial of the legitimacy of the existence of the state of Israel. In addition to the refusal of the Ministry of the Interior to register the group, a decree on its dissolution was issued, based on the Defence (Emergency) Regulations that date back to the period of the British Mandate (1945). Sabri Jeryis, one of the leaders of *El-Ard*, applied to the High Court of Justice (High Court 253/64, *Sabri Jeryis v. Haifa District Commissioner*), but the High Court upheld the outlawing of the association. High Court Justice Alfred Witkon based his verdict on the Weimar experience (see Cohen-Almagor 1994b: 182; High Court 253/64):

> History has shown that fascist and totalitarian movements have taken advantage of the freedoms of expression, press and association granted to them by democratic regimes with the aim of destroying these regimes … Those who have witnessed this in the days of the Weimar Republic will never forget the lesson.

High Court Justice Moshe Landau concurred:

> It is the elementary right of every state to maintain its very existence and freedom, both against external enemies and those who follow from within … One cannot ask any government for the sake of freedom of association to accept the formation of a Fifth Column within the state's borders.

One year after the High Court 253/64 ruling, another *El-Ard* affair flared up. The leaders of the outlawed association formed a party, the Socialist List, in order to run in the 6th Knesset elections in 1965. High Court Justice Moshe Landau – this time as chairperson of the Central Elections Commission (CEC) – and the CEC disqualified the new list, grounding the decision on the fact that the Socialist List is an illegal organization since its initiatives deny 'the integrity and the very existence of the state of Israel' (Cohen-Almagor 1994a: 181). The court again argued that no democratic tools should be granted to the enemies of democracy. It argued that the Socialist List was a new version of *El-Ard*, which had been dissolved by the Defence (Emergency) Regulations 1945 and whose dissolution had been upheld by the courts. In a High Court verdict on the appeal filed by the List, the majority ruling (3:1) decided to reject the appeal against the CEC decision, and to accept the self-defending democracy principle. In this case, the majority explicitly said that they support disqualification although there is no specific law that enables disqualification. The High Court based its verdict on a supra-constitutional principle, which is above any positive law. Justice Yoel Sussman wrote (see Cohen-Almagor 1994b: 184; Electoral Appeal 1/1965, *Yeredor v. Chairperson of the Central Committee for the Elections to the 6th Knesset*, 390 Shachar 20/2/2001; Shachar 20/2/2001):

> Maybe it is no coincidence that the first court to establish the principle that a judge also has to rule on the basis of principles that are not written into the law, and stand above the law and even above the constitution, was the West German Constitutional Court … Just as a man does not have to agree to be killed, so a state too does not have to agree to be destroyed and erased from the map. Its judges are not allowed to sit back idly and to despair from the absence of a positive rule of law when a plaintiff asks them for assistance in order to bring an end to the state. Likewise no other state authority should serve as an instrument in the hands of those whose, perhaps sole, aim is the annihilation of the state.

One could once more see a reflection of the German experience in his words (Cohen-Almagor 1994b: 184; Electoral Appeal 1/1965, 390):

> The German Constitutional Court, in discussing the question of the legality of a political party, spoke of a 'militant democracy' which does not open its doors to acts of subversion under the cover of legitimate parliamentary activity. As far as I am concerned, regarding Israel, I am satisfied with a 'self-defending democracy', and we have the tools to protect the existence of the state even though we do not find them expressly specified in the Elections Law.

In Electoral Appeal 1/1965, Justice Sussman went one step further than the High Court in his decision 253/64, in the sense that he supported the disqualification of a party not only if it does not recognize the state or rejects democratic government, but also if it denies the Jewish character of the state. Some would argue that this is a good example of being trapped by the slippery slope, because it goes beyond any justifiable defence of democracy (Cohen-Almagor 1994b: 185).

Twenty years after the 253/64 decision, Justice Alfred Witkon again referred to the Weimar effect, this time in an article published in an academic journal (quoted in Salzberger and Oz-Salzberger 2006: 51):

> Those who see the example of the Weimar Republic cannot ignore the danger that a strict adherence to the hallowed values of freedom of expression and freedom of the press will pave the way for a totalitarian regime … The test of 'present danger' may fail democracy, because it overlooks the fact that the disintegration of democracy is not a sudden one-shot affair, but the result of a continuous process of subversion.

The Kahanist Threat

From the early 1980s onwards, the ultranationalist Jewish Kahanist movements have been perceived as a major threat to democracy (Issacharoff 2007: 1447–1450). The government, the Knesset, and the courts have dealt with this threat with decrees, laws and legal verdicts. The process started in the early 1970s with the immigration to Israel of Rabbi Meir Kahane, the founder and leader of the Jewish Defense League (JDL), an American-Jewish vigilante group, whose aim was to defend Jews in Brooklyn, the Bronx and other locations in New York, as well as in other parts of the United States. In Israel, Kahane founded the *Kach* movement, which participated in Knesset elections for the first time in 1973.[4] *Kach* propagated the idea of expelling the Arabs, of 'terror against terror' (that is Jewish against Arab terror, called 'T.N.T.' – *Terror Neged Terror* – in the Hebrew abbreviation), the 'removal' of the mosques from the Temple Mount in Jerusalem; the establishment of a (so-called national) censorship of the media; the prohibition to employ Arabs, compulsory dress codes; the criminalisation of Jewish–Arab marriages and sexual relations, physical separation between Jews and Arabs in public places; and the establishment of a nationalist Halachic-Orthodox state.[5] *Kach*'s goal was to found the 'State of Judea' as a theocratic 'total' state. Democracy was regarded as a foreign, non-Jewish idea (the term used was *demokratya goyit*, a pejorative name for 'gentile democracy') and the democratic majority bluntly declared a 'criminal majority'. *Kach* indulged not only in words but also in deeds. Some of its members were caught planning to blow up the mosques on Temple Mount, while others committed acts of violence there (1979). In 1982, *Kach* members – as part of the movement against withdrawal from the Sinai – violently opposed the evacuation

4 The name *Kach* ('This Way') taken from the slogan *Rak Kach* ('Only This Way') of the National Military Organization of the pre-state period and headed by Begin, who argued that British rule in Palestine can only be fought by armed means.

5 *Halacha* means orthodox religious law.

of the Yamit area in northern Sinai. Furthermore, armed Kahanites entered Arab villages to 'convince' the inhabitants to leave the country 'voluntarily'. *Kach*'s racism was harsh and brutal (in his speeches, Kahane called the Arabs 'dogs'). It failed to pass the electoral threshold of 1 per cent in the Knesset election of 1973 (0.81 per cent), 1977 (0.25 per cent), and 1981 (0.26 per cent), but entered Parliament in 1984 (1.2 per cent) (Cohen-Almagor 1994b: 154–73).

In 1981, High Court Justice, Moshe Etzioni, Chairman of the Central Elections Commission, asked the CEC to disqualify *Kach*. He argued that *Kach*'s goals contradict the Declaration of Independence and the basic values of a democratic government, and that the laws it propagates are similar to the Nazi Nuremberg Laws of 1935. The majority of the CEC rejected his request. This led the well-known legal expert Moshe Negbi to appeal to the High Court of Justice and to ask for its intervention against *Kach*. The High Court rejected his appeal because it found no legal support for disqualification by the CEC.

Before the Knesset elections of 1984, another attempt was made to disqualify *Kach*. This time, not only CEC Chairman, Justice Gabriel Bach, did support disqualification, but so did the CEC majority. The CEC decision was based, among others, on Meir Kahane's declaration (in April 1984) that he was willing to bomb the mosques on Temple Mount. It also cited the International Convention on the Elimination of All Forms of Racial Discrimination (which Israel ratified in 1979) and the Association Law, which denies registration to any association that opposes the democratic character of the state. *Kach* approached the High Court of Justice, which accepted its appeal against disqualification by a 5:0 verdict. The court argued once more that there is no law for disqualifying an anti-democratic party. The Association Law was not applied, because *Kach* was regarded as a party, not as an 'association'. It further argued that the precedent of the Socialist List of 1965 (Electoral Appeal 1/1965), when the High Court based its verdict on a 'higher law', applies only to parties that deny the state's right to exist. The arguments of Meir Shamgar, President of the High Court of Justice, for cancelling the decision of the CEC were as follows (Cohen-Almagor 1994b: 201; see also Parliament 12/01, 8; Electoral Appeal 2/1984, 3/1984, *Neiman and Avnery v. Chairperson of the Central Committee for the Elections of the 11th Knesset*, 279):

> There must always be a logical connection between the degree of danger and the means taken; and not any advocacy, even if it raises a justified indignation, may cause the denial of the entire scope of liberty. A democracy that activates restrictions without existential necessity … loses its spirit and force.

Kahane's election to the Knesset accelerated legislation in the spirit of self-defending democracy. Amendment no. 9 (1985) to the Basic Law: the Knesset, Section 7(a) stated the following (see Cohen-Almagor 2001: 51):

> A list of candidates shall not participate in Knesset elections if any of the following is expressed or implied in its purposes or deeds:

1. Denial of the existence of the State of Israel as the State of the Jewish people;
2. Denial of the democratic character of the state;
3. Incitement to racism.

Quite similarly, Section 5 of the Parties Law (1992) provides that:

> A party will not be registered if any of its purposes or deeds explicitly or implicitly contains:
>
> 1. Negation of the existence of Israel as a Jewish Democratic State;
> 2. Incitement to racism;
> 3. Reasonable ground to deduce that the party will serve as a cover for illegal actions.

The Basic Law: the Knesset was again amended in 2002:

> A list of candidates shall not participate in Knesset elections, and nobody will be a candidate in Knesset elections if any of their purposes or deeds explicitly or implicitly contains:
>
> 1. Denial of the State of Israel as a Jewish Democratic State;
> 2. Incitement to Racism;
> 3. Support of an armed struggle of an enemy state or a terrorist organization against the State of Israel.

There are several problems with the 1985 and 2002 amendments to the Basic Law: the Knesset. From a self-defending democracy point of view, one could dispute the disqualification of a party that only rejects the Jewish character of the state ('a State of the Jewish People' or a 'Jewish Democratic State'), while it accepts its democratic system. It could be argued (as did Ruth Gavison, for instance) that in any democracy it should be allowed to strive to change the character of the state, as long as it is done in a democratic way, and as long as the purpose is not to abolish democracy. Other problems relate to the exact meaning of words like 'implicitly' or 'terrorist organization'. (For example: is it only an organization that performs terrorist acts or also one that supports them?)

Following the harsh racist incitements of Rabbi Kahane and his heirs in the 1970s and 1980s, the Penal Law was amended in 1986 and a section on 'incitement to racism' was included (Penal Law [1977] Section 144A-E). Section 144A defined racism as follows (see Cohen-Almagor 2000a: 81):

> persecution, humiliation, degradation, manifestation of enmity, hostility or violence or causing strife toward a group of people or segments of the population – because of colour or affiliation with race or national-ethnic origin.

Section 144B defines any publication (including on radio and television) with the intent of inciting racism as an offence which may carry five years in prison. One should note that 'incitement to racism' disregards incitement on religious grounds. Section 144C of the Penal Law explicitly says that 'any publication of a quotation from religious sources and prayer books and any observance of a religious ritual will not constitute an offence under Section 144B [of the 'incitement to racism' legislation] providing that it is not carried out with the purpose of bringing about racism' (Cohen-Almagor 1994b: 238; Merushak-Clarman 1997: 37). Furthermore, the law applies only if the incitement is directed against a group and not against individuals.

Another 1988 amendment to the Penal Law relates to the prohibition of 'incitement to rebellion' (*hamrada*). Section 136 of the Penal Law defines sedition to rebellion as follows (Merushak-Clarman 1997: 38):

> a) To bring about hatred, disgust or disloyalty to the state or to its institutions of government, or to its courts, which were established lawfully;
> b) To incite the inhabitants of the country to try to achieve, by illegal means, a change of something constituted lawfully;
> c) To stimulate bad will and discontent among the inhabitants of the country;
> d) To create hostility and enmity among different sections of the population.

The Incitement to Rebellion Law was widely criticized because it does indeed open the way for the prosecution of any legitimate opposition. The slippery slope is clearly recognizable in this law, though the courts have prevented any slide down the slope over the last 20 years.

Beyond the 1985 amendment to the Basic Law: the Knesset – following Kahane's election in 1984 – further measures in the spirit of self-defending democracy were taken. The Knesset, which included Rabbi Kahane in the years 1984–1988, limited his parliamentary immunity with the intention, among others, of limiting his freedom of movement and preventing him from entering Arab villages and cause turmoil and violence. This initiative was a direct result of his attempt to enter the Arab town of Umm El-Fahm with his armed thugs on 30 August 1984 in order to 'convince' them to leave the country. In the Knesset, Rabbi Kahane tabled proposals of laws in the spirit of *Kach* ideology – laws prohibiting common beaches for Jews and Arabs; marriage and sexual relations between Jews and Arabs; and a law which would strip the Arabs of their citizenship and make them 'resident aliens'; deny them participation in elections; the right of employment in the public service; and the right to live in Jerusalem. Many, not only on the left, but also on the right (for example, *Likud*) compared these laws to the Nazi Nuremberg Laws. Knesset Chairman, Shlomo Hillel, and the Knesset Praesidium refused to handle Kahane's law proposals. Hillel said, 'we will not lend our signatures to the contempt of the Knesset through Nuremberg laws' (Cohen-Almagor 1993: 462). Kahane successfully appealed against this measure to the High Court of Justice, which argued that it was illegal, as it was not covered by the Knesset Rules of

Procedure. Thereafter, the Knesset Rules of Procedure were amended to enable the Knesset Praesidium to refuse to handle any proposed legislation that denies the existence of Israel as the State of the Jewish people or which is racist.

The media decided on measures in the spirit of a self-defending democracy, too. The newspapers did not publish any articles on *Kach* and Kahane. Kahane's news conferences were boycotted. The Broadcasting Authority (radio and television) boycotted the Kahanites, with the sole exception of reporting of a 'clear news-like character' (Cohen-Almagor 1993: 455). Further acts of boycott followed. State President, Haim Herzog, refused to invite Kahane for consultations after the 1984 elections, thus breaking a tradition that had existed since the foundation of the state in 1948, namely the tradition that *all* parties are invited by the president for consultations about the constitution of a new government. The Ministry of Education issued a decree prohibiting school principals and teachers from inviting Kahane to visit and speak in public schools.

In the 1988 and 1992 Knesset elections, the prohibition of the Kahanist list Kach in 1988 and of the lists '*Kach*' and 'Kahane is Alive' in 1992 became an issue once more.[6] This time the CEC disqualified the lists on the basis of the 1985 amendment to the Basic Law: the Knesset. The High Court, under the chairmanship of Meir Shamgar, ruled that the 'probability test' (that is: 'clear and present danger') is not necessary for disqualification, inasmuch as 'the saliency of the negative aspects in the identity of the list' suffices ('evidence test'). In 1995, *Komemiyut Yisrael* (the Independence of Israel), a local list running for municipal elections in Kiryat Arba, was also disqualified as a successor organization of the Kahanist lists. In 2003, however, the CEC majority rejected the recommendation of the attorney general and its chairman, Chief Justice Mishal Heshin, to disqualify Baruch Marzel, one of the former *Kach* leaders who ran for elections on the extreme right-wing *Herut* Party list. In 2004, ten years after it had been outlawed as a terrorist organization, Heshin said about *Kach* that it was 'the most racist of organizations … The material caught in its offices led me to the clear conclusion that the movement continues its operations in the spirit of Rabbi Kahane. Kach is such an extremist movement that you have to dip into the river seven times, and do so 70 times in order to cleanse yourself of its racism' (Alon and Shragai 30/12/2002). He did not doubt that Marzel would continue (and he indeed still does) to function as one of *Kach*'s leaders.

Talia Sasson of the State Attorney's Office warned, 'if this man [Marzel] will be elected to the Knesset, racism will gain legitimacy'. She, therefore, called for the application of the 'evidence test' and not the 'probability test' (Gorali 9/1/2003).

The High Court, nevertheless, rejected disqualification, thus upholding the CEC majority decision. It seems that this verdict was political, in the sense that it

6 Meir Kahane was assassinated in New York in November 1990. Following his death, *Kach* split into two parties. Kahane is Alive was led by Kahane's son Benjamin Ze'ev Kahane.

was intended to balance the qualification of all Arab parties in the eyes of a large right-wing segment of the wider public.

In 1994, after the massacre perpetrated by *Kach* member Baruch Goldstein among Muslim worshippers in the Cave of the Patriarchs (or Cave of *Machpelah, mearat hamachpela*), in Hebron, *Kach* and Kahane is Alive were outlawed as terrorist organizations – this time under the Prevention of Terrorism Ordinance of 1948.[7] Outlawing an organization as a terrorist organization under the Prevention of Terrorism Ordinance is a much more far-reaching measure than disqualification from participation in elections according to the Basic Law: the Knesset. It means that the very existence of the organization and all its activities, including registering members, maintaining party branches and holding demonstrations, are strictly prohibited.

Although declared terrorist organizations, the Kahanist movements continued to operate as extra parliamentary organizations. Their members were not imprisoned for displaying Kahanist symbols, nor for shouting Kahanist slogans (Negbi 6/1/2001). They did not hesitate to publish a pamphlet named 'Baruch the Man' (*Baruch Hagever*) in memory of Dr Goldstein. They continued to organize 'youth camps' for their gangs (Negbi 15/11/1996). In the year 2000, the police closed down the 'Institute for Jewish Thought' the fictitious name of a *Kach* branch, headed by Benjamin Ze'ev Kahane, the Rabbi's son (Peles 22/11/2000).[8]

Hate Speech

The question as to whether, and when, a self-defending democracy should intervene in cases of hate speech came up in Israel, especially after the 1993 Oslo Accords, when a vicious hate campaign was waged by the Israeli Right against Prime Minister Yitzhak Rabin (who was ultimately assassinated by an extreme rightist student on 5 November 1995), and later on against Prime Ministers Ehud Barak (1999–2001) and Ariel Sharon (2001–2005). Hate speech against Israeli leaders who were ready to make concessions and compromise with the Palestinians and who basically argued for the 'land for peace' formula, contained anti-democratic, religious and historical motifs, slogans and analogies. The traditional formulas of *din rodef*, *din moser* and *pulsa dinura* were proclaimed by right-wing rabbis and zealots against Rabin. *Din rodef* ('the law of the pursuer') means that it is permitted to kill a person who pursues another person with intent to kill. In essence, it is a traditional law of self-defence, but it was applied to Rabin, who stood accused of endangering Jewish life. Similarly, in medieval times and during the Spanish Inquisition, *din moser* ('the informer's law') was designed to allow the killing

7 The Cave of the Patriarchs or Cave of *Machpelah* is holy both to Jews and to Muslims; it is said to be the burial place of the Patriarchs and their wives.

8 Benjamin Ze'ev Kahane headed the Kahanist movement after his father's assassination. He was murdered by terrorists in the West Bank in December 2000 himself.

of informers who betrayed fellow Jews to the Christian authorities. Again, this rabbinical ruling was perverted in the 1990s by declaring Rabin (and to a lesser extent Barak and Sharon) an informer, so that killing him becomes legitimate. *Pulsa dinura* ('lashes of fire') is a kabbalistic ritual in which God is asked to curse, or even kill, a person. Avigdor Eskin, a member of *Gush Emunim* ('Bloc of the Faithful') recited the following maledictions of the *pulsa dinura* on the night of 6 October 1995:

> Angels of destruction will hit him. He is damned wherever he goes. His soul will instantly leave his body ... and he will not survive a month. Dark will be his path, and God's angel will chase him. A disaster he has never experienced will beget him, and all curses known in the Torah will apply to him. I deliver to you, the angels of wrath and ire, Yitzhak, the son of Rosa Rabin, that you may smother him and the specter of him, and cast him into bed, and dry up his wealth, and plague his thoughts, and scatter his mind that he may be steadily diminished until he reaches his death. Put to death the cursed Yitzhak. May he be damned, damned, damned!

Rabin was assassinated within the month. Rabin was also vilified as an Ahab and Jezebel, both of them negative biblical figures who deserved death, and his government was dubbed the Kingdom of Evil.

The anti-democratic, extremist hawks likened the dovish leaders to the long ago enemies of the Jewish people. Rabin was compared to Pharao, who enslaved the Jews; to Nebuchadnezzar of Babylon, who conquered ancient Israel; to the Roman emperor Titus, who crushed the Jewish rebellion in AD 70 and to Ferdinand (II of Aragon) and Isabella (of Castile), who persecuted the Jews during the Inquisition. Worse was the comparison drawn between Rabin and Adolf Hitler, Benito Mussolini, and their collaborators (such as Philippe Pétain, Pierre Laval and Vidkun Quisling) or to appeasers like Neville Chamberlain. They also likened Rabin's government to Nazi rule, accusing him of wanting the occupied territories to be *judenrein*, an allusion to the planned withdrawal of Jewish settlers from the West Bank and Gaza as part of a peace deal. He was also compared to a *Kapo*, and his government to the *Judenrat*. At times, other parallels were drawn – with Nikolae Ceauşescu and the Bolsheviks. Time and again, Rabin and his ministers were called 'traitors' who had committed 'treason' and the elected government was called 'illegitimate' and 'illegal', so as to deny its democratic credentials.

The hate campaign against Rabin was conducted not only by religious, orthodox rabbis – for example, former Chief Rabbi, Mordechai Elyahu, and the head of the Council of Judea and Samaria Rabbis, Rabbi Zalman Melamed – and leaders of the settler movement, but also by major political figures, namely *Likud* leaders Benjamin Netanyahu and Ariel Sharon (who, ironically, became a victim of a similar smear campaign in 2001–2005) or right-wing Knesset members, Rafael Eytan, Rehavam Ze'evi and Avigdor Lieberman.

Before Rabin's assassination in November 1995, both the police and the prosecution tended to disregard instances of hate speech. In some cases files were closed, while in others people charged with incitement to racism or rebellion received ludicrously low penalties. In one case, someone was given a three-month prison sentence for distributing stickers reading 'Rabin should be killed' (Cohen-Almagor 2000b: 3–4). Israel's self-defending democracy was clearly not effective. Free speech was merely an excuse for not acting, hiding the government's fear of rocking the boat and stirring up a major confrontation with the extreme right.

This policy of 'appeasement' toward right-wing radicals changed abruptly after Rabin's murder. A few examples will suffice to illustrate this:

Rabbi Edo Elba, who published 'An Examination of Religious Directives (*halakhot*) Concerning the Killing of Gentiles', in which he argued that the Commandment 'Thou shalt not murder'[9] applies only to Jews, and that it is a duty to kill even women and children in war, was put on trial for incitement to violence (according to the 1948 Ordinance for the Prevention of Terrorism), racism and rebellion (according to the 1986 and 1988 amendments to the Penal Law) only after the assassination of Yitzhak Rabin. He was sentenced to two years in Prison (see Criminal Appeal 2831/95).

Rabbi Yitzhak Ginsberg, who published 'Baruch the Man – Five General Commandments (*mizvot*) that are Intrinsic Perspectives in the Act of Saint Baruch Goldstein' in September 1994, and who justified the massacre in the Cave of the Patriarchs (February 1994), was not prosecuted. Only in 1996, when he told his students that it is a commandment to kill Arabs in retaliation for acts of terror, he was put in administrative detention (Cohen-Almagor 2000b: 7–12).

Avigdor Eskin, who called for a *pulsa dinura* curse against Rabin so that Rabin would die for his evil policy, was only put on trial after he repeated the curse against Rabin's successor, Shimon Peres. He received a four-month prison sentence.

Demonstrators who dressed as Rabin in SS uniform during a large anti-government demonstration on 30 October 1995 were detained by the police only after Rabin's assassination a week later. It turned out that the same people had put up signs after the assassination, saying 'Rabin the Victim of Peace [as was often claimed by the dovish liberal Left], Peres is Next' (Cohen-Almagor 2000b: 4–5).

The leaders of the 'This is Our Land' Movement, who conducted a campaign of civil disobedience against the Rabin Government, blockading roads and organizing unauthorized demonstrations, were put on trial for rebellion only after November 1995.

The policy toward hate speech has indeed changed dramatically after the Rabin murder. The Prosecutor General decided to enforce existing laws relating to incitement to violence and identification with terrorist organizations (the 1948 Ordinance for the Prevention of Terrorism), instigation to rebellion and seditious behaviour, and incitement to racism (the 1986 and 1988 amendments to the Penal Law). The government also established a special 'unit against incitement (*hassata*)

9 'Thou shalt not kill' is a mistranslation of the original Hebrew Biblical text.

and instigation to rebellion (*hamrada*)' in the Ministry of Justice. Attorney Talia Sasson, the head of the unit, said that 'we thought that we had to deal with criminals who wanted to undermine the very essence of democracy in the state'. The Prosecutor General also instructed that anyone who praised the Rabin murder in speech or writing be put on trial, and even asked the mass media not to report or quote hate speech.

Employment in the Public Service

In addition to the suppression of anti-democratic speech (or hate speech), self-defending democracy sometimes limits the employment of anti-democrats in the public service. A good example is the so-called *Radikalenerlaß*, which was implemented in West Germany in the 1960s and 1970s against left-wing and right-wing 'radicals'.

In Israel, there had been an attempt during the early state period to limit the employment of right-wing radicals. A celebrated case was the refusal of a high school to employ the former FFI leader Israel Sheib (Eldad) as a teacher. The rationale behind the decision was that the Ministry of Defence opposed his employment. When Sheib approached Defence Minister, David Ben-Gurion, (at that time also Prime Minister), he received the following reply (HCJ 144/50, *Sheib v. the Minister of Defence and others* – High Court Verdicts, vol. 5, 1951, 1156):

> The Ministry of Defence opposed your employment as a teacher because in your book and newspaper you call for the use of arms against the Israeli Defence Forces and the Government of Israel in situations you specify.

Following Ben-Gurion's reply, Sheib approached the High Court of Justice, arguing that the denial of employment constituted 'political persecution'. The High Court accepted his appeal on the following basis (High Court Verdicts, vol. 5, 1951, 1154–9):

> a) The Ministry of Defence has no say in the workings of the Ministry of Education;
> b) There is no law that authorizes the school to infringe on the basic human right for equal employment;
> c) The military censor has not censored Dr Sheib's publications calling for rebellion, and the Minister of Defence's argument that Dr Sheib is 'dangerous to the security of the public and the state' is thus not plausible;
> d) Any dismissal of a teacher for incitement or disloyalty against the state is legal only after a formal legal investigation.

Although the High Court's verdict is based on legal niceties and formalities, it did establish a precedent according to which the state cannot deny employment in public service for political reasons. This does not mean that there has not been any screening for sensitive jobs for security reasons (for example, in the defence establishment, military industries and foreign service), though the distinction between security and political reasons is quite often blurred. It is also common knowledge that for many years Arab teachers with a nationalist or communist orientation were not employed. However, the real reason for their disqualification was never acknowledged. In this case, there was clearly *de facto* discrimination of the Arab sector, doubtlessly based on an abuse of the self-defending democracy principle.

We may conclude that, with regard to professional disqualification, the self-defending democracy principle has not been applied since the Sheib case. This is not the case with 'administrative detention'. Basically, administrative detention is a non-democratic act by which people are imprisoned for shorter or longer periods of time without being formally prosecuted or put on trial. It is used to prevent criminal and violent acts rather than to punish for acts that have been committed. Since the state's foundation, this legal tool was used sparingly against Israeli Arabs for security reasons, but massively against Palestinian Arabs of the Occupied Territories during the first (1987–1993) and second (2000–2005) *intifadeh*.

As a tool of self-defending democracy, we may certainly regard the administrative detention of extreme and violent-prone Jewish right-wingers. Four events will illustrate this (see Cohen-Almagor 2000b: 7–12; Gavison 12/11/1006; Lahav 15/4/1996; Negbi 15/11/1996):

1. In 1994, after the massacre in the Cave of the Patriarchs, Kahanists, who had a past record of violence and incitement, were immediately detained in order to prevent a conflagration between Jews and Arabs that could lead to a bloodbath;
2. In 1995, after Rabin's murder, some extremists were rounded up and put under administrative detention;
3. In 1996, when the Israeli government under the leadership of Prime Minister Benjamin Netanyahu agreed to withdraw from most of Hebron, a violent reaction against the withdrawal was expected from the Israeli extreme right. Administrative detention of the extremist leaders made the withdrawal possible. In a way, it is quite ironic that Netanyahu, a major figure in the anti-Rabin hate campaign from 1993 to 1995, was withdrawing from a town holy to Jews and employing administrative detention against extreme right-wingers;
4. In 2005, before the disengagement from Gaza, some right-wingers, who were determined to employ any means at their disposal (including, perhaps, violence) to prevent withdrawal and undo the government's decisions, were put under administrative detention.

Arab Parties in a Jewish State

After 1984, repeated attempts were made to disqualify Arab lists and parties. In 1984 and 1988, the High Court of Justice rejected requests to disqualify the Progressive List for Peace (PLP) because it did not recognize Israel as a 'State of the Jewish People'. In 1984, before the amendment to the Basic Law: the Knesset, the High Court saw no basis in law to disqualify a list because it does not recognize the Jewish character of the state. Unlike the High Court of 1965 with relation to the Socialist List, the High Court did not see any evidence that the PLP wanted to destroy the State of Israel altogether. In 1988, the High Court could have disqualified the PLP according to the 1985 amendment of the Basic Law: the Knesset ('Denial of the existence of the State of Israel as a State of the Jewish People'), but it refrained from doing so because it could not unequivocally prove that 'the real, principal and operative goal of the PLP is to bring about the destruction of Israel as the State of the Jewish People' (Segal 13/5/2002). While in 1984 the High Court decided against the CEC, in 1988 it went along with the decision not to disqualify the PLP. In 1996, the High Court was asked to disqualify Ahmed Tibi's Arab Movement for Change (AMC) for registering as a political party that does not recognize Israel as a Jewish state. The court rejected the plea, arguing that the AMC platform ('Israel as a state of all its citizens') does not exclude acceptance of Israel as a Jewish State (Segal 13/5/2002).

In 1999, a citizen appealed to the High Court of Justice in order to disqualify the National Democratic Alliance (NDA) and its leader, Azmi Bishara. He based his case on the following quote from one of Bishara's speeches: 'Judaism is a religion, not a nation, and the Jews have no national status anywhere in the world … Historically, I regard the idea of a state for the Jews as illegitimate. If you ask me – no, I am not willing to grant Israel any historical legitimacy' (Gorali 9/1/2003). The High Court rejected disqualification, though acknowledging that Bishara had come very close to an 'acceptable limit not to be overstepped'.

In 2001, there were no Knesset elections, only direct elections of the Prime Minister. Nevertheless, following a terrorist attack by a member of the Islamic Movement, the *Likud* attempted to outlaw the Islamic Movement. The law it proposed took a stand against anyone who supports terrorism and acts of violence against the state. It targeted Arab Knesset members, specifically Azmi Bishara, who had visited Syria (an enemy state), presented himself as a representative of 'Occupied Palestine' (not the Occupied Territories in the West Bank, but Israel within the Green Line borders), and praised the heroic struggle of the *Hezbullah* (Alon 10/9/2001; Arens 13/11/2001). The initiative failed because the acts were committed before the law was enacted.

Before the elections for the 16th Knesset in 2003, an all out effort was made to disqualify all the major Arab lists – the Democratic Front for Peace and Equality/ The Arab Movement for Change (DFPE/AMC); the United Arab List (UAL); and the National Democratic Alliance (NDA). In addition to the request to disqualify the lists, requests were filed to personally disqualify members of the Knesset

'Abd al-Malik Dahamsha (Islamic Movement/UAL); Muhammad Barake (Israeli Communist Party/DFPE); Ahmed Tibi (AMC); and Azmi Bishara (NDA). All these requests were based on the 2002 amendment to the Basic Law: the Knesset, making it possible to disqualify a list if it does not recognize Israel as a Jewish Democratic State or supports an armed struggle or a terrorist organization against Israel. The requests for disqualification were as follows (Alon, 27/12/2002; Gorali, 9/1/2003, 8/6/2003):

Table 8.1 Disqualification attempts before the 16th Knesset election in 2003

Object of disqualification	Who requested disqualification	Argument for disqualification
The United Arab List and Knesset member 'Abd al-Malik Dahamshe	The National Union Faction	Denial of Israel's right to exist as a Jewish Democratic State and support of armed struggle against the state
The Democratic Front for Peace and Equality/ The Arab Movement for Change List and Knesset members Mohammed Baraka and Ahmed Tibi	Knesset member Michael Kleiner (*Herut*)	The denial of the Jewish character of the state and support of terror against it
Knesset member Ahmed Tibi	The *Likud* Faction	Tibi, a public relations agent of Yasir Arafat, mobilizes support for the intifadeh among Israeli Arabs and misuses his status as a Knesset member to promote the interests of Arafat and the Palestinians
The National Democratic Alliance List and Knesset member Azmi Bishara	The National Union Faction; Knesset members Michael Kleiner (*Herut*) amd Yisrael Katz (*Likud*); State Attorney Ariel Rubinstein	Based on a General Security Service Report which argues that the NDA denies the existence of Israel as a Jewish Democratic State, supports armed struggle by terrorist organizations and aims to replace Israel by a Palestinian state

The CEC decided by majority vote (21 votes of the *Likud*, SHAS, NRP, Tora Judaism, *Gesher*, National Union and Centre Party as against 18 votes of Labour, *Meretz*, *Shinui* and the Arab parties) to disqualify Knesset member Ahmed Tibi. Knesset member Azmi Bishara was disqualified by a vote of 22 to 19, and the NDA list by a similar vote of 21 to 20. Requests for disqualifying the UAL and

DFPE/AMC lists and Knesset member 'Abd al-Malik Dahamsha were defeated in the CEC. Appeals to the High Court of Justice were successful in overturning all disqualifications by the CEC of the Arab lists and candidates (and also of *Herut* candidate Baruch Marzel) (Alon 31/12/2002, 1/1/2003).

In the elections to the 17th Knesset (2006), the disqualification of the Arab lists was again on the agenda. The right-wing parties in the CEC tried to disqualify the UAL/AMC list, quoting Ibrahim Sarsur, who headed the list, as supporting the transformation of Israel into an Islamic State. Knesset member Gideon Saar (*Likud*) said in the CEC: 'we are facing a very significant development. The Islamic Movement is extremely dangerous because its goal is to establish an Islamic State on the ruins of Israel. I am convinced that if we do not disqualify the UAL/AMC list, history will not forgive us because such an omission would enable the enemies of the state to enter the Knesset and subvert the state from within' (Alon 1/3/2006). Ibrahim Sarsur, who headed the southern, pragmatic wing of the Islamic movement, denied the charges, insisting that he 'did not speak about the establishment of an Islamic State in Israel'. The request to disqualify the UAL/AMC list fell through by a narrow margin. Sixteen Knesset members of the *Likud*, National Union, NRP, SHAS, *Yisrael Beytenu* and Tora Judaism voted for it, while 18 Knesset members of Labour, *Shinui*, *Meretz*, DFPE, NDA and UAL voted against it.

Conclusion

In Israel, as in the wider democratic world, we may distinguish between a 'diminishing approach' (diminishing the violation of democratic values and standards in order to defend democracy) and an 'expanding approach' (expanding the violation of democratic values and standards in order to defend democracy). The diminishing, 'American' approach (best represented during the formative years of the High Court by the former president of the High Court of Justice, Shimon Agranat, who is of American origin,[10] and later by the presidents of the High Court Meir Shamgar and Aharon Barak) brought about the verdicts that enabled *Kach* to participate in the 1981 and 1984 elections, and the verdict that declared the anti-Kahane boycott by the Broadcasting Authority illegal (Salzberger and Oz-Salzberger 2006: 28). On the other hand, the 'incitement to racism' legislation, the 1985 and 2002 amendments to the Basic Law: the Knesset, and the disqualification of the Kahanist lists in 1988 and 1992 represent the expanding approach. This 'European' approach came to the fore as early as the 1960s in the verdicts against *El-Ard* and the Socialist list. It is no coincidence that these verdicts were led by justices of German–Jewish origin who had doubtlessly been influenced by the 'Weimar effect'. Leading the expanding 'German' approach was

10 Justice Agranat was born in Louisville, Kentucky, and was a graduate of the University of Chicago Law School.

High Court Justice, Alfred Witkon,[11] who sat on the bench from 1954 to 1980 and was the leading proponent of the verdicts against *El-Ard* and the Socialist List. Other well-known High Court judges of Jewish–German–Austrian origin during the formative years of the High Court were Moshe Smoira, Moshe Landau, Benjamin Halevi and Joel Sussmann.[12]

The division of the High Court into two schools of thought with regard to self-defending democracy is also reflected in academia. For example, in 2001, the Professor of Political Science, Shlomo Avineri, demanded that right-wing racists who shout 'death to the Arabs' in demonstrations, be put on trial (Avineri 5/2/2001). He was rebutted by Professor of International Law, Eyal Benvenisti, who argued that 'the law enforcement system should not be used to enforce morality', and that as long as there is no clear and present danger that someone may be harmed, there is no reason for the state to intervene (Benvenisti 7/2/2001). He was supported by Professor Alon Harel, who opposed Avineri in the name of free speech (Harel 7/2/2001).

Other law professors who supported the American approach are Professors André Marmor and Mordechai Kremnitzer. Marmor redefined a 'militant democracy' not as a self-defending democracy, but as 'a democracy which fights for the realization of liberal values and is not prepared to push these values aside in order to fight something else' (Marmor 1990: 29). Marmor thus disputes that a struggle against anti-democrats, which employs non-democratic means, is a struggle for democracy. Kremnitzer rejected the legal prosecution of those who call public figures 'murderers' and 'traitors' as long as there is no clear and present danger that a crime is going to be committed. On the other hand, however, Kremnitzer supported the prosecution of racist speech, not because it poses a danger to democracy, but because it violates the victims' basic rights to equality and dignity (Kremnitzer 1996). It is most probably not a coincidence that law professors tend to stress the legal dangers of self-defending democracy, while historians and political scientists – with Weimar always on their minds – insist on the dangers of adopting a lenient approach towards the enemies of democracy.

---

11 High Court Justice Witkon was born in Berlin in 1916 and studied law in Freiburg, Bonn, Berlin and London.

12 Moshe Smoira served as the Supreme Court President (1948–1953). He was born in Königsberg in 1888 and studied law in Königsberg, Frankfurt am Main, Berlin and Heidelberg. Moshe Landau served on the High Court between 1953 and 1982; he was Supreme Court President in 1980–1982. He was born in Danzig in 1912 and studied law in England. Benjamin Halevi was born in 1910 in Weißenfels and studied law in Freiburg, Göttingen and Berlin. He served on the court from 1963 to 1969. Yoel Sussman was born in Krakow (Austro–Hungary) in 1910 and studied law in Frankfurt, Berlin, Heidelberg and Cambridge. He served on the court from 1953 to 1980 and was its president from 1976 to 1980. Other High Court judges of German–Austrian origin were Menachem Dunkelblum, Haim (Hermann) Cohn, Gabriel Bach, Meir Shamgar, Shlomo Asher, Menachem Alon and Ben-Zion Schereshevski (see Salzberger and Oz-Salzberger 1998).

This division among judges and academics reflects the real dilemma involved in the self-defending democracy approach. Democracy may be in jeopardy because of 'underprotection', because the enemies of democracy are treated leniently, and because state intervention, conditioned on there being clear and present danger, may come too late to be effective. On the other hand, an activist self-defending democracy may pose dangers of democratic 'overprotection', of encroachment on free speech, and of also applying this policy against democratic opponents of a regime. This is precisely the slippery slope syndrome mentioned earlier in this chapter.

Ironically, Israel has had to face both dangers simultaneously. Its policy with regard to the enemies of democracy has hence been confused and inconsistent. Some may call it a prudent 'middle of the road' approach. The survival of Israel's fragile democracy is perhaps proof that this mixed policy has not been all that wrong. Given the strength of the anti-democratic forces in Israel, this writer would have supported a more determined and consistent self-defending democracy.

References[13]

Alon, Gideon (10/9/2001) 'Calls on Right to outlaw Islamic movement', *Ha'aretz*. [H]

Alon, Gideon (27/12/2002) 'Requests to disqualify Arab parties', *Ha'aretz*. [H]

Alon, Gideon (31/12/2002)'Tibi disqualified against Heshin's opinion', *Ha'aretz*. [H]

Alon, Gideon (1/1/2003) 'Electoral Commission disqualified Bishara despite Heshin's opposition', *Ha'aretz*. [H]

Alon, Gideon (1/3/2006) 'With a narrow majority: UAL will run for the Knesset', *Ha'aretz*. [H]

Alon, Gideon and Nadav, Shragai (30/12/2002) 'SHAS Representative: I don't care about Justice Heshin', *Ha'aretz*. [H]

Arens, Moshe (13/11/2001) 'Democracy – damaged through misuse', *Ha'aretz*. [H]

Avineri, Shlomo (5/2/2001) 'It is a matter of life and death', *Ha'aretz*. [H]

Benvenisti, Eyal (7/2/2001) 'Pertinent Response to Racism', *Ha'aretz*. [H]

Birnhack, Michael D. (ed.) (2006) *Be Quiet, Someone is Speaking*. Tel-Aviv: Ramot – Tel-Aviv University. [H]

Cohen-Almagor, Raphael (1993) 'Fighting Kahanism in Israel: Retrospect and Appraisal', *Anglo-American Law Review* 22(4): 447–74.

Cohen-Almagor, Raphael (1994a) *The Boundaries of Liberty and Tolerance: Liberal Theory and the Struggle against Kahanism*. Jerusalem: Nevo. [H]

13 References marked [H] are in Hebrew, article titles have been translated by the author.

Cohen-Almagor, Raphael (1994b) *The Boundaries of Liberty and Tolerance: The Struggle Against Kahanism in Israel.* Gainesville: University Press of Florida.

Cohen-Almagor, Raphael (2000a) *Liberal Democracy and the Limits of Tolerance.* Ann Arbor: University of Michigan Press.

Cohen-Almagor, Raphael (2000b) 'Limits to Freedom of Speech: The Case of Incitement', in Ejan Mackaay (ed.) *Les certitudes du droit/Certainties of the Law.* Montréal: Éditions Thémis, 3–15.

Cohen-Almagor, Raphael (2001) *Speech Media and Ethics: The Limits of Free Expression.* Basingstoke: Palgrave.

Galnoor, Itzhak and Hoffnung, Menahem (eds) (1993) *The Government of Israel: A Sourcebook.* Jerusalem: Nevo, 1154–62. [H]

Gavison, Ruth (12/11/1996) 'The Legitimacy Test of Detention', *Ma'ariv*. [H]

Gorali, Moshe (9/1/2003) 'Did Bishara cross the red line? Did Tibi exit the grey area?' *Ha'aretz*. [H]

Gorali, Moshe (8/6/2003) 'Bishara nears red line; Barak shifts it', *Ha'aretz*. [H]

Harel, Alon (7/2/2001) 'Within the law, but not legitimate', *Ha'aretz*. [H]

Issacharoff, Samuel (2007) 'Fragile Democracies', *Harvard Law Review*, 120(6): 1406–67.

Kremnitzer, Mordechai (1996) 'The limits of freedom of speech', *Ha'ayin Hashvi'it* 1–2, 26–27. [H]

Kremnitzer, Mordechai (2004) 'Disqualification of Lists and Parties. The Israeli Case', in András Sajó (ed.) *Militant Democracy.* Utrecht: Eleven International Publishing, 157–70.

Lahav, Hagar (15/4/1996) 'Law Proposal for the total abrogation of administrative detention', *Ha'aretz*. [H]

Leggewie, Claus and Meier, Horst (1995) *Republikschutz.* Hamburg: Rowohlt.

Loewenstein, Karl (1937) 'Militant Democracy and Fundamental Rights', *American Political Science Review* XXXI, 417–32, 638–58.

Mallah, Shosh (19/12/1997) 'The Unit [of the Ministry of Justice] for rooting out rampant weeds', *Seven Days – Yedioth Ahronot*. [H]

Marmor, André (1999) 'On the Limits of Democracy: Political Theory after Rabin's Assassination', in Ariel Rosen-Zvi (ed.) *The Yearbook of Law in Israel – 1999.* Tel-Aviv: Tel-Aviv University, Papyrus Publishers, 1–29. [H]

Merushak-Clarman, Ukki (1997) *Freedom of Speech and Incitement.* Jerusalem: Adam Institute. [H]

Negbi, Moshe (15/11/1996) 'Chop off the criminal hand', *Ma'ariv – Shabbat Supplement*. [H]

Negbi, Moshe (6/1/2001) 'Can the fuse of incitement be smothered?' *Ma'ariv*. [H]

Pedhazur, Ami (2000) 'Struggling Challenges of Right-wing Extremism and Terrorism within Democratic Boundaries: A Comparative Analysis'. Paper read at Conference on Terrorism and Beyond: The 21st Century, Oklahoma, USA.

Pedhazur, Ami (2004) *The Israeli Defending Democracy.* Jerusalem: Carmel. [H]

Peles, Dorit (22/11/2000) 'The police close the Kach branch', *Ha'aretz*. [H]

Rawls, John (1971) *A Theory of Justice.* Oxford: Oxford University Press.

Salzberger, Ali and Oz-Salzberger, Fania (1998) 'The German Tradition of the Israeli High Court', *Iyuney Mishpat* 21(2): 259–99. [H]

Salzberger, Ali and Oz-Salzberger, Fania (2006) 'The Tradition of Free Speech in Israel', in Michael D. Birnhack (ed.) *Be Quiet, Someone is Speaking! The Judicial Culture of Freedom of Speech in Israel.* Tel Aviv: Tel Aviv University Press, 27–70. [H]

Segal, Ze'ev (13/5/2002) 'Barriers to the Knesset', *Ha'aretz*. [H]

Shachar, Ilan (20/2/2001) 'Doomsday Weapon of High Court of Justice', *Ha'aretz*. [H]

Chapter 9
Italy

Militant Democracy in Italy. A Path between Rules and Politics

Stefano Ceccanti and Francesco Clementi[1]

Introduction

As in other democracies, the term 'militant democracy' is totally absent from the Italian constitutional system, and there is no 'auto-qualification' or related concept in the Italian constitutional text.

Nevertheless, during the period of constitutional transition – the time period between the fall of the fascist regime on 25 July 1943 and the establishment of the Italian Republic with the coming into force of the Republican Constitution on 1 January 1948 – many intellectuals reflected on a well-known democratic dilemma: how can one balance freedom and security in a measure that allows complete, open and democratic development of a society and its institutions after a totalitarian regime?[2]

During the drafting period (Assemblea Costituente, 1946–1947), the Italian creators of the constitution – including some of the aforementioned intellectuals – avoided the paradoxical 'slippery slope' towards a securitarian 'obsession',[3] through an idea of democracy established around three general political pillars:

a. The new Republican Constitution must not provide for a protected or militant democracy but, rather, politics and its mechanisms should be used to preserve the fundamental values;
b. All legal action against 'fascism and the fascists' must be concluded before the enforcement of the new constitution;[4]

---

1 This article reflects a common vision of the two authors but the conclusion was written by Stefano Ceccanti and the rest by Francesco Clementi. We want to thank to Augusto Barbera, Salvatore Curreri and Massimo Rubechi for their valuable comments on draft versions of the article.

2 To understand the different aspects of the dilemma in the opinion of Italian scholars, see Croce 1973: 159–73; Einaudi 2004: 85–110. See also Capoccia 2005.

3 See Hook 1970, especially p. 47. See also Joerges and Ghaleigh 2003; Murphy 2007.

4 Enacted by the Badoglio Provisional Government and, after that, by the Alcide De Gasperi Government, they were the following Acts: 28 December 1943; 27 July 1944; of 14 November 1945 (as 'Nenni Law') and, finally, the famous Act of Amnesty of 22 June 1946. For further details on this period, in English, see: Domenico 1991; Woller 1998.

c. The new regime's system of justice must not be used as a general instrument to heal the socio-political schisms, especially as a means of punishing those who were believed to have colluded with the fascist regime.[5]

On this basis, and especially following the Act of Amnesty of 22 June 1946, promoted by the Minister of Justice and Communist Party Leader, Palmiro Togliatti, during the first De Gasperi Government, Italy was the first country to conclude the process of reconciliation even though it was coming out of a transitional justice period. Conclusive evidence of this is that the only written provision within the constitution to 'protect' the Italian democracy from its past, the XII Transitory and Final Provision, was placed at the end of the Italian Constitution in the Transitory and Final Provisions. It states that:

> It shall be forbidden to reorganise, under any form whatsoever, the dissolved Fascist party. Notwithstanding Article 48, the law has established, for not more than five years from the implementation of the Constitution, temporary limitations to the right to vote and eligibility for the leaders responsible for the Fascist regime.[6]

A Militant Democracy *by* Politics: 'Constitutional Non-Fulfillment' and the Construction of the *Conventio ad Excludendum* Doctrine

In chosing a completely political path, the Italian Republic elected to conduct and to govern against any futures risks of authoritarianism or absolutism, or the possibility that they could take root in the new political-institutional democratic system.

There are several reasons to explain this choice: first, Italy was a country deeply divided by a civil war between fascists, anti-fascists and those who supported Mussolini, even after his fall in 1943, due to the creation of the illegitimate Salò Republic in Northern Italy; second, the geopolitical position of Italy during the Cold War, especially after 1948; and finally, the brevity of the Italian experience of democratic tradition and culture given the relatively recent origin and establishment of the unitary state under the monarchy (17 March 1861).

During the First Legislative Period (1948–1953), the Italian Government was led by Prime Minister, Alcide De Gasperi, (who had provided unifying leadership and a steady premiership for five years. He was also the (lifetime) leader of the *Democrazia Cristiana*, which was the biggest party in the Italian Parliament until 1991). It was in this context that the government joined with all political parties in

5 For more on the role of the 'transitional justice', see Elster 2004.

6 See the English version of the Italian Constitution on the Camera dei Deputati (Chamber of Deputies) website at http://legxven.camera.it/cost_reg_funz/345/346/listaarticoli.asp.

deciding to pursue a democratic goal: to govern Italian society as if it was a militant democracy but without using its well known legal instruments and mechanisms.

The idea behind this was to promote the growth of the principles of (representative) democracy by a social and political integration in the new political institutions, primarily the Parliament. This process was led *by* the parties and *in* the parties according to Article 49 of the constitution, which states:

> All citizens have the right to freely associate in parties to contribute to determining national policies through democratic processes.

The Parliament was enabled to absorb all issues, values and, foremost, ideologies which overwhelmed the political parties and the general political system in those periods.

Some mechanisms of the constitution and several institutions came into force slowly in order to realize this idea: a 'desired delay' that represents the special feature of this first constitutional period.[7] To the leaders of that time it was crucial that Italian citizens were introduced to democracy progressively, without infringements and ruptures, internalizing the democratic procedures and mechanisms, and learning the democratic 'rites and myths'.

Against this doctrine of 'desired delay', the famous jurist, Piero Calamandrei, wrote several articles and essays promoting a public debate. He qualified this doctrine as a 'constitutional non-fulfillment',[8] a complete deception of the citizen. In his opinion, several articles of the constitution were substantially unrealized because they existed only in constitutional law and not in reality. In fact, the laws of establishing and of the actual enforcement of the institutions provided for in the constitution were initially unfulfilled (for example, the Constitutional Court came into force only in 1956 and the self-governing body of the jurisdiction, the *Consiglio Superiore della Magistratura*, came into force only in 1958). Unfortunately, Calamandrei's protest remained substantially unheeded.

In the end, the focal political point of this doctrine of delay – especially for the Christian Democracy Party (*Democrazia Cristiana*) and its leaders – was to govern the country keeping the Italian Communist Party (*Partita Communista Italiana*) – and, until the 1960s, also the Socialist Party (*Partita Socialista Italiania*) – out of the government but not outside the constitutional and democratic system. That is the main difference between the Italian case and, for instance, the German one. As the famous former President of the Italian Constitutional Court, the late Leopoldo Elia, wrote in a very famous essay on the forms of government (Elia 1965): the Italian political and constitutional system has lived on a general and well-known '*conventio ad excludendum*' against the Communist Party (the biggest Communist

7 See Barbera et al. 1999.

8 See Calamandrei 1955: 226.

Party in Western Europe).[9] The goal was to keep this party not merely out of the government, but also short of a hypothetical governmental majority.

While this doctrine laid out the 'rules' of the political game, the Christian Democracy leaders considered enlarging the area of democratization in order to promote a better understanding of representative democracy principles to the Italian citizens. For them, every citizen – even those who may have voted for the Italian Communist Party – should slowly become accustomed to representative democracy, practicing the mechanisms and procedures of elections and the mechanisms, procedures, and rulings of the Parliament. Therefore, all parties were supposed to respect the same constitution and the same republican laws and rules. All parties, being subject to the same legal system, should ultimately aim at respecting the rule of law: no one would stay outside of the democracy; no one would fight in order to create a different political regime.

Apart from the question of the MSI (Movimento Sociale Italiano – Italian Social Movement), it can be concluded that only one sort of militant democracy existed in Italy: at first, against the left-wing parties, and later only against the Communist Party. The latter was realized politically but not in the legal system. Related to this doctrine, an important political attempt to effect a militant democracy was the Electoral Law (the so-called '*Legge truffa*'). This was enacted in 1953 to give a real majority of seats to the majoritarian party, but the *Democrazia Cristiana* – the pivotal party in Italy from 1948 to 1991 – did not obtain the necessary amount of votes to make use of the majoritarian clause.[10]

However, in the meantime, the Italian Parliament enacted the 'Scelba Law' (Law of 20 June 1952, no. 645) against the resurgence of and insurgence by the fascists' ideas, thus providing complete protection for the XII Constitutional Transitory and Final Provision. This law provided for the definition and punishment of associations that wanted to recreate the Fascist Party, fighting the democratic, anti-fascist and anti-racist values and, in general, abolishing the constitutional freedoms,[11] keeping them out of the legal system. In 1956, the Constitutional Court declared in a famous sentence on the basis of the Scelba Law that it is *contra legem* to defend and promote fascism because this would be an offence against the legal and constitutional order.[12]

9 On the contrary, progressively, there existed in the Italian political system also a sort of *conventio ad consociandum* at the parliamentary level between the *Democrazia Cristiana* Party and the Italian Communist Party on fundamental decisions, especially during the 7th Legislature (1976–1979).

10 See the chapters in Ceccanti and Vassallo 2004, especially Chapters 2 (by Quagliarello) and 3 (by Calderisi).

11 It is important to emphasize that the Scelba Law, repeating the second line of the XII Transitory and Final Provision, provided that any associates of the dissolved Fascist Party would be removed from the active and passive electorate for five years and would probably also be deposed from their parliamentary office. The Scelba Law was especially applied to the right-wing political group '*Ordine nuovo*' who had no parliamentary representatives. See Curreri 2004: 158–60.

12 Constitutional Court, 16 January 1957, no. 1.

This sentence represents the landmark of this topic, and has been used several times by the Constitutional Court and other courts to accentuate the pluralistic and anti-fascist theory underpinning the Italian democratic constitutional legal system.

Therefore, in the reality of the political system there existed a second, stronger *conventio ad excludendum* applied to the *Movimento Sociale Italiano* Party (MSI), a neo-fascist and, later, national-conservative political party formed in 1946 by supporters of the former dictator Benito Mussolini.[13] This party, in fact, did not participate in the constitution-making process in 1946–1948 to create the democratic Republic, and thus was relegated to a state of paralegality because it refused to acknowledge the legitimacy of the new republic. And when, during the governmental crisis of 1960, the MSI offered its votes to sustain the government, society and the parties of the so-called 'constitutional arch' responded accordingly in refusing to accept their votes to create a new government.[14]

A Militant Democracy *in* the Politics

In the 1970s, after the murder of Aldo Moro – one of the most important leaders of Christian Democracy Party, kidnapped on 16 March 1978 by the 'Red Brigades' and killed after 55 days of captivity, as a consequence of his so-called project *Compromesso Storico* (historic compromise) between the Christian Democracy and the Communist Party – the delayed democratization process was concluded, and Italy, after a form of government of 'national solidarity', became a complete and definitive democratic party-system, progressively erasing the *conventio ad excludendum*.

The only problems in those years were caused by attacks of terrorism from the extreme left (and extreme right) to destabilize the state and its institutions (and probably sometimes using deviated components of civil or military Italian Secret Services), but against this strategy (the so-called '*strategia della tensione*') all political parties, especially the left-wing parties, operated at full capacity to isolate the extremists.[15] Those political waves of violent dissent against the constitutional and social order were strongly repressed by the state, and also by virtue of special laws dedicated to these phenomena. Once the Red Brigades were suppressed, these laws were repealed.

---

13 The name *Destra Nazionale* (National Right) was added in 1972, when some moderate-conservative groups entered it. The party was dissolved in January 1995 by Gianfranco Fini, who founded *Alleanza Nazionale* (National Alliance).

14 Conversely, the votes of the MSI. probably were decisive in 1971 for the election of the President of Italy when Giovanni Leone was elected with votes from a right-centre majority of the Parliament (518 out of 996 votes) and succeeded Giuseppe Saragat.

15 To confirm this will, it is important to underline that the General Secretary of the Communist Italian Party, Enrico Berlinguer, said in a famous interview of 1976 that he was more comfortable 'under NATO's umbrella'.

In the meantime, the constitution was implemented in full. For example, the law on the referendum procedures came into force in 1970 and the regional institutional system was established in 1970.[16] Italy entered the period of a 'realized constitution' and a phase of open democratic participation of all political parties and political forces in the democratic institutions.

The fall of the Berlin Wall in 1989 allowed for a complete change, especially in political society, and the success of a small group of reformers in 1991 and 1993, using the referenda to modify the political electoral law and, subsequently, the political party system, ushered in a new era. The results of the referenda showed that Italy, like other democracies, was trying to become a 'non-consociative' 'Westminster Democracy'. As a result, Italy did not need to create a defence against some parts of society. No legal or political instruments of 'militant democracy' had to be used because Italian political society had already been pacified and had accepted the principles of democracy. The main idea, the vision of the democratic leaders of the 1950s was realized; they had built up a real democracy using only the strength of political discourse and acceptance of the democratic rules by any (probably) anti-system party of any provenance.

Subsequently, the plan to protect Italian democracy from the risks of destabilization was represented by a will of change in the cultural nature and political-social main stream, strengthening the *liason* between candidates and the electorate and introducing new electoral laws to select all monocratic institutional figures. This strengthening was realized[17] and would protect the democracy from the resurgence of problematical political ideas, especially in some emerging political parties. One such was the *Lega Nord per l'indipendenza della Padania* (Northern League for Independence of Padania), a political party which aimed at the political and territorial secession of the north of Italy, combined with complete autonomous sovereignty. During this time, to talk about 'militant democracy' was to talk about the possibility of containing and inserting the issues and the values of the *Lega Nord* into democratic procedures: tolerating its ridiculous folklore regarding the traditions and Celtic roots of the North, but firmly governing and controlling every fact and political situation opposed to the fundamental values and institutions of Italian democracy.

This 'second vision' of militant democracy in Italy was established to protect political discourse and political society in a special historical period of institutional change (1991–1996), the so-called passage from the 'First Republic' to the 'Second Republic'. This vision was realized by a new law, the so-called 'Mancino Law' (Law of 25 June 1993, no. 205), enacted to combat any fact or situation which promotes, sustains, and realizes racial, ethnic or religious discrimination. The Mancino Law, modified several times, has up to the present represented the landmark of militant democracy in Italy.

16 See, in general, Amato et al. 1979, especially Amato 1979: 79 et seq.

17 See, on that period, in general Fabbrini 2001.

In particular, this law preserves the fundamental values of social cohesion and freedom of expression throughout measures to defend institutions and individuals. In fact, the leader of *Lega Nord*, Umberto Bossi, often described African immigrants as *Bingo-bongos*, and in an interview suggested opening fire on the boats of illegal immigrants who wanted to disembark in Italy.[18] Another local leader from the Province of Trento, Erminio Boso, proposed to segregate immigrants in different train cars from native Italians. The former Mayor of Treviso, Giancarlo Gentilini, spoke – while in office – about those he called 'immigrant slackers', saying, 'We should dress them up like hares and bang-bang-bang.'[19] Sometimes used, especially against some violent activists in the *Lega Nord*,[20] the Scelba Law and the Mancino Law are now much less used against this party. The reason for this *modus operandi* is simple and founded on two pillars: the strategy of inclusion of the *Lega Nord* in the democratic system has functioned very well; and, second, the entry of Italy into the Euro currency zone has ruled out any possibility of and any appeal to secession.

The *Lega Nord* party, as a matter of fact, participated three times in a coalition government, and this coalition, led by Silvio Berlusconi, won in three general elections (1994, 2001 and 2008). The *Lega Nord* was appointed, as a part of the winning coalition, to important roles in the government.[21] Therefore, it is probably quite difficult now to think of an active 'militant democracy' against the activists of the *Lega Nord*, because it is a governmental party and 'inside the political game'. Furthermore, the *Lega Nord* uses populist arguments (like 'we are against that "big thief" Rome') as a political instrument to sustain its political basis only.

18 See *Il Manifesto*, 17 June 2003.

19 See *La Repubblica*, 3 Decembre 2002.

20 Who does not remember the *Lega Nord* activists who conquered Saint Mark's Basilica and its tower in 1998 to demonstrate the necessity of 'Free Padania' and the rights of the North against the South. They were put on trial, and the final judgement sentenced all eight activists to six years in prison. See, in general, Cassazione Penale, Sez. 1, sent. no. 7812 of 16 June 1999; Sez. I, sent. no. 556 of 16 March 1994; Cassazione Penale, Sez. 3, sent. no. 13234 of 13 December 2007. See also C. Cass., VI, 17 April 1996, no. 973 (Ferdjani Mouland et al., in Cassazione Penale, 1997: 51 et seq.); C. Cass., VI, 30 January 1996: 561 (Bendebka, in Giustizia Penale 1997, II, p. 158 et seq.); C. Cass., VI, 1 June 1999 (Abdaoui Youssef et al., in Diritto Penale e Processo, 2000: 485 et seq.).

21 The *Lega Nord*, as a matter of fact, has controlled important ministries: Five in 1994 (Roberto Maroni, Interior; Giancarlo Pagliarini, Finance; Vito Gnutti, Industry; Domenico Comino, European Affairs; and Francesco Speroni, Institutional Reforms); three in 2001 (Roberto Castelli, Justice; Roberto Maroni, Labour and Social Affairs; and Umberto Bossi, Institutional Reforms and Devolution, replaced by Roberto Calderoli in June 2004); four in 2008 (Roberto Maroni, Interior; Luca Zaia, Agriculture; Umberto Bossi, Reforms and Federalism; and Roberto Calderoli, Legislative Simplification) and five Under-Secretaries (Roberto Castelli, Infrastructures; Michelino Davico, Interior; Daniele Molgora, Economy and Finances; Francesca Martini, Health; and Maurizio Balocchi, Legislative Simplification).

In the period of the Italy's entrance to the Euro zone, a more important problem with the *Lega Nord* party arose. The *Lega Nord* wanted to give a 'special and particular' name as a 'title' to the parliamentary group in May 1996, a specific name linked to the idea of secession (at the Italian Senate parliamentary group, 'Parliament of Padania'; at the Italian Chamber of Deputies, 'Independent Padania'), but the President of the Senate of the Republic, Nicola Mancino – the same the 'Mancino Law' has been named after – and the President of the Chamber of Deputies, Luciano Violante, stopped this debate on titles, considering them contrary to Article 5 of the Italian Constitution, which protects – first of all – the unity of the nation.[22] It was a relevant topic in that period because the North *uti singuli* fulfilled the requisites for entry into the 'Euro zone Club', while Italy, as a whole, ran the risk of staying outside it. Nevertheless, with Italy's accession to the Euro zone in 1999 (by virtue of the first Prodi Government), the prospect of secession has substantially melted away.[23]

Currently, the doctrine of a sort of 'militant democracy' *in* politics continues to exist in Italy, but in reality is not really active.

Conclusion: 'Militant Democracy' in Italy post 9/11

Ultimately, the authors agree with the view of Augusto Barbera who holds that Italian constitutional history is a history of total political integration of extreme parties. This has been achieved because the political system chose a path of progressive integration, based on the gradual elimination of constitutional conventions of exclusion. The parties of the left accept the keynote of democratic decision-making, which came from the results of the election of 18 April 1948, in favour of Western-style democracy and rejection of the prospect of an Eastern popular democracy. The parties of the right accept the main principles of 25 April 1945 and the conclusion that anti-fascism was the only and necessary way to develop a real democracy.

Against this background, the rules and dispositions of the law and its mechanisms to protect democracy were the exceptions to the conventional and general symbolic political vision of 'militant democracy' as a typical political topic.[24] Therefore, the Italian choice not to use judicial means against the anti-system parties – as, for example, in Spain – seems to have been the 'winning strategy' for the better consolidation of democratic institutions in Italy. The only real and clear 'cost' was the impossibility of having any real change of government, as, for example, happens in German democracy.

---

22 'The Republic, one and indivisible, recognizes and promotes local autonomies, and implements the fullest measure of administrative decentralization in those services which depend on the State. The Republic accords the principles and methods of its legislation to the requirements of autonomy and decentralisation'.

23 See Ceccanti 2004: 136 et seq.

24 See Barbera 2007.

It may be that in the post 9/11 climate, a new form of militant democracy will come about in Italy but, for the moment, it remains the case that the democracy has not suffered any real threat from extremism or terrorists. This notwithstanding, the importance of the role played by the Abu Omar case in strengthening a defence plan for the democracy in 2007 (the most recent and significant case of extraordinary rendition in Italy) needs to be noted. In this case the recent State Secrets Law[25] was applied for the first time. This law reformed the structures of the Italian Secret Service and provided for more detailed regulation of the analysis of all types of information and the classification of any kind of criminal facts. In addition, the Parliament enacted a law against the financing of terrorism in 2001 (Law of 14 December 2001, no. 431), which has since been modified several times.

Italy has probably seen different aspects of 'militant democracy', but its tradition, up to the present, has been based on a model that has not differed significantly from that of the representative democracy minus the objective of having to protect other sections of democratic society. Historically, this is in contrast to the tendencies and experiences of other countries. However, for the moment it survives, even if we know that it could be reversed with 'a scratch of the pen' following an attack on or a threat to our institutions and fundamental values.

References

Amato, Giuliano (1979) 'Il Governo', in Giuliano Amato et al. (eds) *Attualità e attuazione della Costituzione.* Rome and Bari: Laterza, 79–90.

Amato, Giuliano et al. (eds) (1979) *Attualità e attuazione della Costituzione.* Rome and Bari: Laterza.

Barbera, Augusto (2007) 'Introduzione', in Augusto Barbera, *Una e indivisibile.* Milano: Giuffré.

Barbera, Augusto, Cammelli, Marco and Pombeni, Paolo (1999) *L'apprendimento della Costituzione (1947–1957).* Milan: Franco Angeli.

Benazzo, Antonella (2004) *L'emergenza nel conflitto fra libertà e sicurezza.* Turin: Giappichelli.

Bonetti, Paolo (2006) *Terrorismo, emergenza e Costituzioni democratiche.* Bologna: Il Mulino.

Calamandrei, Piero (1955) 'La Costituzione e le leggi per attuarla', in Achille Battaglia, Piero Calamandrei, Epicarmo Corbino, Luigi De Rosa, Emilio Lussu, Mario Sansone and Leo Valiani (eds) *Dieci anni dopo: 1945–1955. Saggi sulla vita democratica italiana.* Rome and Bari: Laterza.

Capoccia, Giovanni (2005) *Defending Democracy: Reactions to Extremism in Interwar Europe*. Baltimore: The John Hopkins University Press.

25 See Law of 3 August 2007, no. 124, '*Sistema di informazione per la sicurezza della Repubblica e nuova disciplina del segreto*' (at http://www.parlamento.it/leggi/07124l.htm).

Ceccanti, Stefano (2004) *Le democrazie protette e semi-protette da eccezione a regola. Prima e dopo le Twin Towers.* Turin: Giappichelli.

Ceccanti, Stefano and Vassallo, Salvatore (eds) (2004) *Come chiudere la transizione.* Bologna: Il Mulino.

Croce, Benedetto (1973) 'Libertà e forza', in Benedetto Croce, *Scritti e discorsi politici (1943–1973) vol. 2.* Rome and Bari: Laterza, 159–73.

Curreri, Salvatore (2004) *Democrazia e rappresentanza politica. Dal divieto di mandato al mandato di partito.* Florence: Florence University Press.

Domenico, Roy Palmer (1991) *Italian Fascists on Trial, 1943–1948.* Chapel Hill: University of North Carolina Press.

Einaudi, Luigi (2004) 'Major et sanior pars', in Luigi Einaudi, *Il buongoverno. Saggi di economia e politica (1897–1954).* Rome and Bari: Laterza, 85–110.

Elia, Leopoldo (1965) 'Governo (forme di)', in *Enciclopedia del Diritto, vol. XIX.* Milan: Giuffrè, 634–75.

Elster, Jon (2004) *Closing the Books: Transitional Justice in Historical Perspective.* Cambridge: Cambridge University Press.

Fabbrini, Sergio (2001) 'Features and Implications of Semi-Parliamentarism: The Direct Election of Italian Mayors', *South European Society and Politics* 6(2): 47–70.

Di Giovine, Alfonso (ed.) (2005) *Democrazie protette e protezione della democrazia.* Turin: Giappichelli.

de Guttry, Andrea (ed.) (2003) *Oltre la reazione: Complessità e limiti nella guerra al terrorismo internazionale dopo l'11 settembre.* Pisa: ETS.

Hook, Sidney (1970) *The Paradoxes of Freedom.* Berkeley: University of California Press.

Joerges, Christian and Ghaleigh, Navraj Singh (eds) (2003) *Darker Legacies of Law in Europe. The Shadow of National Socialism and Fascism over Europe and its Legal Tradition.* Oxford: Hart Publishing.

Murphy, Walter Francis (2007) *Constitutional Democracy: Creating and Maintaining a Just Political Order.* Baltimore: John Hopkins University Press.

Woller, Hans (1998) 'The Political Purge in Italy', in Stein Ugelvik Larsen (ed.) *Modern Europe After Fascism.* New York: Columbia University Press, 526–45.

Chapter 10
Japan

Shojiro Sakaguchi

Introduction: Liberal Democracy and the Paradox of Tolerance

With the conclusion of the Cold War, we saw the sudden rise of constitutionalism on a global scale. Many former communist countries rushed to enact written constitutions. Constitutionalism is now so popular that Bruce Ackerman claims that it stands 'on the brink of worldwide hegemony' (Ackerman 1997: 772). Yet if 'constitutionalism' merely meant having a written constitution, then virtually every country that has a written constitution could claim to embrace constitutionalism. Therefore, defining 'constitutionalism' to mean simply 'having a written constitution' is vacuous and fails to provide any meaningful insight into the legitimacy of a constitutional government.

The historical origin of modern constitutionalism lies in the religious wars in the sixteenth and seventeenth centuries following the Reformation. With the end of these bloody religious wars, many people recognized the existence of diverse, even mutually conflicting religious doctrines, each purporting to teach the 'true meaning' of the world. Exhaustion from these wars 'eventually led to the formulation and often reluctant acceptance of some form of the principle of toleration' (Rawls 2001: 1). The acceptance of tolerance was reluctant because all sides believed that their faith represented the truth whereas their neighbour's one was erroneous. Nevertheless, the principle of tolerance brought to the citizenry a peace that religious intolerance had not provided (Griffin 2003: 1631–32).

Religion, however typical, is just one example of sources of conflict. Liberal society is generally comprised of individuals who have diverse, even mutually irreconcilable, conceptions of what is good. For example, people tend to disagree with one another as to the 'true meaning' of life. For some people, a life worth living is one strictly within the confines of their religious beliefs. For others, it is a life spent living together with their loved ones. This plurality of incompatible conceptions of good should not be 'seen as disaster but rather as the natural outcome of the activities of human reason under enduring free institution' (Rawls 1993: xxiv), and be accepted as 'modern experience' (Larmore 1996: 12). Incommensurability means there is no scale of measure by which we gauge the value of each life.

Therefore, the scope of tolerance should be extended beyond religious beliefs and practices to the broader principle of restraint from governmental coercion with respect to a range of decisions and conduct implicating comprehensive moral doctrines or ways of life. This realization leads to the guiding principle of liberal neutrality which applies 'the principle of tolerance to philosophy itself' (Rawls 1993: 10). A liberal political order aims to be neutral with respect to comprehensive conceptions of good. This requirement of neutrality should be applied only to political questions involving 'constitutional essentials' and 'basic justice' (Rawls 1993: 214, 227–30), that is, the fundamental principles of political association which fix the basic rights and liberties of citizens and specify the general structure of government (Larmore 1996: 126). The terms and conditions of political association must be ones that could be endorsed by individuals with diverse, even irreconcilable, conceptions of the common good. As political principles are ones where force may be used to ensure compliance, we can say that the government treats each individual with 'equal concern and respect' (Dworkin 1977: 180) only if this requirement of liberal neutrality is met.

Constitutionalism embracing the principle of liberal neutrality is one of the powerful responses to the problem of irreconcilable pluralism inherent in a liberal society. How is it possible that a just and peaceful order under which people can live as free and equal citizens may exist despite a plurality of values among them? In order to achieve this delicate and difficult task, liberal constitutionalism aims to separate artificially people's lives into the public and private spheres. In the private sphere, each person can live his or her life in accordance with his or her comprehensive conceptions of good. A constitution makes this possible by strongly entrenching fundamental human rights which every individual should enjoy in order to live an 'autonomous' life. On the other hand, in the public sphere, people must abstain from invoking their comprehensive conceptions of good to justify the decisions they make in the name of society as a whole. A lack of such abstinence in the public sphere will destroy the fragile foundation of social cooperation in a liberal society.

These appear to be core concerns of liberal constitutionalism. Realizing and establishing constitutionalism is, however, far from easy, and still remains an unfinished business even in liberal democracies. The difficulty with constitutionalism is that it appears at once to be both necessary and difficult. It is necessary if we take 'the fact of reasonable pluralism' (Rawls 1993: 36) in liberal society seriously and still wish to construct and maintain a just and peaceful order. Yet it may well seem difficult because constitutionalism requires us to tolerate the intolerable and intolerant. Such a tolerant society is artificial and therefore inherently unstable.

Toleration is distinct from mere indifference. When we do not have any strong moral opposition to the practices of others, it is easy for us to permit such practices. The indifference involves no self-restraint. On the other hand, toleration is a matter of putting up with that which we disapprove. Reasonable pluralism is an essential precondition to toleration, but it is difficult to see why we should tolerate things which we find abhorrent. Toleration is a controversial value and an 'elusive virtue' (Heyd 1996).

Within liberal democracies, the principle of toleration is already well enshrined in constitutions. Political dissent is protected as a fundamental right and sometimes welcomed as a check on the function of governmental power. Toleration may, however, become suicidal in certain political situations. Some groups in liberal democracies hold doctrines committing them to suppress constitutional liberties and destroy liberal democracy whenever they have the power to do so. Fascist groups committed to the abolition of democracy, Marxist and Communist parties committed to the same aim, although for different reasons and, today, some religious fundamentalists who aim to abolish liberal democracy in favour of some kind of theocracy. These illiberal groups often choose the strategy of avoiding violent revolution in favour of an indirect strategy of undermining liberal democracy through the exercise of liberal democratic rights. It seems suicidal to extend constitutional liberties to these groups and permit them to take advantage of these freedoms to undermine liberal democracy. It may be argued that where the survival of liberal democracy itself is threatened, a constitution is not a 'suicide pact' and should not become a Trojan horse for the enemy and survival should take precedence over toleration.

On the other hand, toleration is the core principle of liberal democracy. It may be argued that it is also suicidal for a liberal democracy to deprive the intolerant of their constitutional rights. Thus, intolerant and illiberal groups create a paradox for liberal democracies. How can a liberal democracy be intolerant towards illiberal and anti-democratic groups without compromising and relinquishing its claim to liberal democratic legitimacy? Gregory H. Fox and Georg Nolte characterize the problem as 'the central paradox of democratic regimes' (Fox and Nolte 1995: 14).

This is the fundamental paradox to which all liberal democracies must respond. The terrorist attacks of 11 September 2001 brought this question to the forefront of constitutional discourse. Crisis illuminates the nature and scope of constitutionalism by raising critical questions regarding the underlying assumptions and principles of constitutionalism. We have been in such a period of crisis since 9/11 and will continue to be for the unforeseeable future. So now is a particularly appropriate time to examine the problem of how liberal democracy can protect itself against its enemies and still remain liberal and democratic.

Fox and Nolte describe two different approaches liberal democracies take to resolve this dilemma: one they call the 'procedural' model, the other one 'substantive' (Fox and Nolte 1995: 14–17).

The procedural democracy model views democracy as a framework for decision-making which does not prescribe the content of the decisions made. Rooted in the Enlightenment opposition to traditional authority, the procedural model rests on the faith that rational discourse ensures liberty. Because procedural democracies rely on free speech to counter anti-democratic faith, there is little need for governments to protect citizens from its influence.

In contrast to a procedural democracy, a substantive democracy does not view democracy as the process of ascertaining the preferences of political majorities, but rather as a state of society in which majority rule is made meaningful. According to this view, democratic procedure is not an end in itself, but rather a means of creating a society in which citizens enjoy certain essential rights. A substantive democrat rejects the procedural democrat's claim that a democracy must allow itself to become undemocratic if the majority desires so. Substantive democrats find it contradictory to say tolerance is the fundamental organizing principle of government, even to the degree that it preserves the possibility of intolerant government. Thus, substantive democrats prioritize the long-term survival of the democratic form over the political rights of anti-democratic actors.

Fox and Nolte classify the German democracy as a 'militant' substantive democracy, the US democracy as a 'militant' procedural democracy and Japanese democracy as a 'tolerant' procedural democracy (Fox and Nolte 1995: 24–6, 32–4). András Sajó points out that while Germany has been taking a risk aversive stance towards the enemies of democracy and toleration, the United States has been taking a risk taking one (Sajó 2004: 209, 214).

In this chapter, after briefly reviewing militant democracy in Germany, I examine how post-war Japanese constitutional scholars reacted to the idea of militant democracy. This reaction was and is overwhelmingly unfavourable. I investigate why they have militantly opposed the adoption of the idea of militant democracy. After investigating the reaction in terms of the peculiar development of constitutionalism in post-war Japan, I conclude that 'constitutional patriotism' may take the form of opposing the idea of 'militant democracy' in Japan.

Militant Democracy in Post-War Germany

One powerful response to the paradox of liberal regimes is that liberal democracies should be allowed to 'act not only to resist having their state authority conscripted to the cause of intolerance, but also, under certain circumstances, to ensure that their state apparatus not be captured wholesale for that purpose' (Issacharoff 2007: 1408). This is the response of 'militant democracy'.

The term 'militant democracy' was coined and popularized in an article by Karl Loewenstein in 1937. In 1933, Adolf Hitler and his National Socialist Party assumed control of the German Government. Over the next decade, persecution orchestrated by the Nazi regime forced hundreds of academics to seek refuge from Germany, and many of them found academic posts in the United States. Karl Loewenstein took up a post at Yale University in 1933. In an article he published in 1936 examining the transformation of German private law under Nazi rule (Loewenstein 1936: 780), he pointed out that

> By antithesis, National Socialism is anti-liberal and anti-individualistic; by implication it is irrational, mystical, and romantic; by its result it is totalitarian to the point of religious obsession.

Still, he could talk of the possibility of an eventual return to normalcy even at that time. Loewenstein wrote at the end of the article (Loewenstein 1936: 815):

> With due reserve, therefore, we may say that National Socialist legal concepts are only an incident in German legal history. Perhaps a necessary and justified incident, since excessive formalism and technicality needs at times a tonic in the form of a dynamic and even 'unjust' law. In due course, Germany's legal structure is likely to return to a more congenial substance and shape, incorporating – as is usual in revolutions – such elements of the National Socialist experiment which correspond to the national disposition. In spite of or because of its rationalism, National Socialist legal philosophy is nothing more than an unspirited relapse into romanticism, not the first one and probably not the last one in a nation whose unbalanced nature vacillates between the extremes.

However, the tone of his argument was clearly changed when Loewenstein contributed a series of two articles to the *American Political Science Review* the following year (Loewenstein 1937a, 1937b). Describing the essential nature of fascism as 'a supersession of constitutional government by emotional government', he stated that 'in brief, to arouse, to guide, to use emotionalism in its crudest and its most refined form was the essence of the fascist technique' (Loewenstein 1937a: 418, 423). The perception that fascist government rested upon the emotional manipulation inherent in a period of mass democracy[1] led him to recognize the inadequacy of legal measures as a panacea and the necessity of cultivating a reasonable citizenry. The Weimar democracy, which was considered one of the most advanced democracies of its time, was neutral, and the Nazis, enemies of the constitution, took advantage of the protection of constitutional rights to break it. Loewenstein recognized the weakness of the Weimar Constitution, describing it as follows (Loewenstein 1937a: 423–24):

> Its [fascist] success is based on its perfect adjustment to democracy. Democracy and democratic tolerance have been used for their own destruction. Under cover of fundamental rights and the rule of law, the anti-democratic machine could be built up and set in motion legally. Calculating adroitly that democracy could not, without self-abnegation, deny to any body of public opinion the full use of the free institutions of speech, press, assembly, and parliamentary participation, fascist exponents systematically discredit the democratic order and make it unworkable by paralyzing its functions until chaos reigns. They exploit the tolerant confidence of democratic ideology that in the long run truth is stronger than falsehood, that the spirit asserts itself against force. Democracy was unable to forbid the enemies of its very existence the use of democratic instrumentalities. Until very recently, democratic fundamentalism and legalistic

1 According to Loewenstein, 'fascism is the true child of the age of technical wonders and of the emotional masses' (Loewenstein 1937a: 418, 423).

> blindness were unwilling to realize that mechanism of democracy is the Trojan horse by which the enemy enters the city.

Consequently, democracy should fight against the enemies of democracy by banning political parties and restricting the rights of such enemies to assembly and free speech. In conclusion, he declared that 'democracy must become militant' (Loewenstein 1937a: 423).

The drafters of the Basic Law were haunted by the failure of the Weimar Republic. The Weimar Republic, Germany's first republic, had been based on what many saw as the world's most progressive constitution of its time, but Weimar had been made vulnerable by the most democratic mechanism the constitution set out, and was destroyed by enemies of democracy who abused that mechanism. Conscious of Germany's fascist past, the *Grundgesetz* – the German Constitution, drafted in the aftermath of the Holocaust and the Second World War, and generally known as the 'Basic Law' – accepted this proposal and established a militant democracy in order to defend itself against its enemies. Two factors influenced the drafting and contents of the Basic Law: fresh memories of the Nazi regime and the rise of communism in the East. These experiences led Germany to establish a militant democracy.

The fundamental principles of the Basic Law are embodied in the phrase 'free democratic basic order', which appears six times in the constitution's text.[2] In 1952, the *Bundesverfassungsgericht* (Federal Constitutional Court) defined the free democratic basic order as follows:

> The free democratic basic order can be defined as an order which excludes any form of tyranny or arbitrariness and represents a governmental system under a rule of law, based upon self determination of the people as expressed by the will of the existing majority and upon freedom and equality. The fundamental principles of this order include at least: respect for the human rights given concrete form in the Basic Law, in particular for the right of a person to life and free development; separation of powers; responsibility of government; lawfulness of administration; independence of the judiciary; the multi-party principle; and equality of opportunities for all political parties.[3]

As this definition indicates, the Basic Law is not a value neutral constitution. Human dignity is the central value of the Basic Law. Article 1(1) provides that 'the dignity of man shall be inviolable', and Article 1(2) provides that 'the German people therefore acknowledge inviolable and inalienable human rights as the basis of every community, of peace and of justice in the world'. Human dignity ranks

2 See Articles 10(2), 11(2), 18, 21(2), 87a, and 91(1). For more details on the concept of 'a free democratic basic order', see Doehring 1988: 25.

3 Judgment of the Federal Constitutional Court, 23 October 1952, BVerfGE 2, 1, 12–13, translated in Murphy and Tanenhaus 1977: 603.

highest in the Federal Constitutional Court's hierarchy of basic fundamental rights (Jacobs 1993: 565). In the famous *Lüth* case, the Federal Constitutional Court held that the value system established by the Basic Law 'centres upon the dignity of the human personality developing freely within the social community'.[4] The value of human dignity pronounced in Article 1 is so fundamental to the Basic Law that Article 79 (3) protects it even against constitutional amendment. The fact that the Basic Law consciously places human dignity at the top of the provision reflects the German will to distance itself from the horrors of Nazism and make a clear break with the immediate past.[5]

The most remarkable feature of the Basic Law is found in its imposition – not only on governmental power, but also on private citizens – of the obligation to defend the free democratic basic order against the enemies of democracy and constitution.

Although the Basic Law, as a constitution of liberal democracy, vigorously protects civil liberties, such as freedom of expression, Article 18 provides that whoever abuses these freedoms 'in order to combat the free democratic basic order, shall forfeit these basic rights'. The Basic Law gives special competence to the Federal Constitutional Court to interdict in the exercise of certain fundamental rights of the individual in cases where such rights are abused to fight against the free democratic basic order. On a motion of the government or Parliament, the Federal Constitutional Court can decide whether a forfeiture of these rights is warranted.

In particular, while Article 5(3) protects the freedom to teach, it declares that such freedom shall not absolve the person who exercises it from loyalty to the constitution. A professor at an university is free to criticize the constitution or to propose amendment, but he is not free to proclaim the abolition of the principles underlying the free democratic basic order. With respect to associations, Article 9(2) provides that an association, the purposes and activities of which conflict with criminal laws or which are directed against the constitutional order or the concept of international understanding, are prohibited.

Finally, and perhaps most significantly, Article 21 declares that political parties shall participate in the forming of the will of the people, but if the parties aim to impair or abolish the free democratic basic order, they will be deemed unconstitutional. This article 'expresses the conviction of the drafters, based on their concrete historical experience, that the state could no longer afford to maintain an attitude of neutrality toward political parties' (Wise 1998: 308). In fact, the Federal Constitutional Court declared, in the Cold War era, the Nazi-like *Sozialistische Reichspartei* ('Socialist Reich Party', SRP)[6] and the German

4 Judgment of the Federal Constitutional Court, 15 January 1958, BVerfGE 7, 198, translated in Kommers 1997: 363.

5 See Currie 1994: 11; Eberle 1997: 967.

6 BVerfGE 2, 1, translated in Kommers 1997: 218.

Communist Party to be unconstitutional.[7] The rationale behind these provisions is militant democracy: the enemies of freedom and democracy are not entitled to enjoy the benefits of freedom and democracy.

Recently, Kim Lane Scheppele has classified 'aspirational constitutionalism' and 'aversive constitutionalism' as two models of constitution building (Scheppele 2003). According to Scheppele, aspirational constitutionalism refers to a process of constitution building (a process that includes both drafting and interpretation by multiple actors) in which constitutional decision-makers understand what they are doing in terms of the goals they wish to achieve and the aspirations they wish to live up to. Other countries' constitutions and constitutional practices may be positively imported to express and realize these aspirations. Aspirational constitutionalism is fundamentally forward-looking and defines a country or nation in terms of its future, its goals and its dreams. Aversive constitutionalism, on the other hand, calls attention to the negative models that are prominent in the constitution builders' minds. Although constitution builders may have only the vaguest sense of where they are going and how they should get there, they have a clearer sense of what it is that they wish to avoid. Certain other countries' constitutions and constitutional practices may loom large in the constitution builders' minds because they provide examples of what not to do, of what to refuse in the strongest terms. Such a cross-constitutional example is not necessarily a foreign one, but rather a country's own past is oftentimes an example. Aversive constitutionalism, then, is backward-looking, proceeding from a critique of where past (or other) institutions and principles went badly wrong, and taking such critiques as the negative building blocks of a new constitutional order. While aspirational constitutionalism attempts to identify itself by knowing what it wishes to achieve, aversive constitutionalism identifies a deeper sense of knowing what it is by knowing what it is not (Scheppele 2003: 299–300).

As Scheppele notes, seen from this distinction, post-war Germany's choice of militant democracy in constitution building is a typical example of aversive constitutionalism. Militant democracy is a result of the failure of the Weimar Constitution. From the beginning, the drafters of the Basic Law were determined not to repeat the mistakes of the Weimar Republic.

Silence and Denial – The Case of Japan

Although both constitutions were products of defeat in the Second World War and drafted under allied occupation, the text of the Japanese Constitution, promulgated in 1946, is, unlike the Basic Law, silent as to militant democracy. It has no articles expressly adopting a militant democracy or equivalent to Article 18 of the Basic Law. While the Japanese Constitution does have a detailed Bill of Rights, with

7 BVerfGE 5, 85. Regarding this case, see Currie 1994: 218–21; Kommers 1997: 22–4.

Article 12 providing that, 'the freedoms and rights guaranteed to the people by this constitution shall be maintained by the constant endeavor of the people, who shall refrain from any abuse of these freedoms and rights and shall always be responsible for utilizing them for the public welfare', it does not stipulate a forfeiture of rights in cases of abuse.

Major academic texts usually interpret Article 12 as not imposing any concrete obligations or sanctions upon a citizen who abuses his or her constitutional rights and freedoms (Higuchi 1998: 290; Ito 1995: 408–409; Nonaka et al. 2006: 534; Tsujimura 2004: 180). While Article 21(1) of the Constitution provides that 'freedom of assembly and association as well as speech, press and all other forms of expression are guaranteed', Article 23 provides that 'academic freedom is guaranteed', as there are no particular limits except for natural limitations on individual rights in cases where there is conflict with the exercise of another person's rights or with vital public interests.

Hideo Otake, a professor of political science, has suggested that the difference between the Japanese Constitution and the German Basic Law could be attributed to the two and a half year gap between the dates of completion of the two documents. As the Japanese Constitution was enacted before the Cold War broke out, its dominant features were New Deal-type social democratic ideals, whereas the Basic Law, enacted during the Cold War, was characterized by a militant and anti-communist liberalism (Otake 2001).

Though Otake's argument is very interesting, it would be misleading to draw any conclusions only from a simplistic textual argument. The silence of the text does not necessarily compel the conclusion that the Japanese Constitution does not adopt the concept of militant democracy. If such silence does not imply the deliberate omission of the idea of militant democracy, one could still draw such a conclusion through textual interpretation. Clever theorists are quite capable of doing so. Even if a democratic country does not embrace the concept of militant democracy at the constitutional level, it can still introduce militant democracy at the legislative level. In fact, the legislations of many European democracies adopt the concept of militant democracy. It would grossly underestimate academic efforts to suggest that constitutional text alone explains the difference in attitudes towards militant democracy between German and Japanese scholars.

The reaction of Japanese constitutional scholars to the concept of militant democracy is, however, overwhelmingly unfavourable. Despite the silence in the text, Japanese scholars usually draw the conclusion that the Japanese Constitution does not adopt the concept of militant democracy. When any major textbook on constitutional law refers to the idea of militant democracy, such reference is made to show that the Japanese Constitution does not adopt the concept.

Article 99 provides that the Emperor or the Regent as well as Ministers of the State, members of the Diet, judges and all other public officials have the obligation to respect and uphold the constitution. It does not mention an obligation of private persons to do so. From this omission, some scholars draw not only the weak conclusion that the Japanese Constitution commits to modern constitutionalism on the ground that constitutional constraints are imposed upon political power by the people in order to prevent the abuse of political power by those who rule, but also the strong conclusion that the idea of militant democracy is quite alien to the Japanese Constitution, and that the constitution prohibits the imposition of the obligation to respect constitutional values upon private persons even through legislation (Higuchi 1998: 398–402).

Many leading constitutional scholars take a critical or skeptical position regarding the concept of militant democracy (Nonaka et al. 2006: 286; Tsujimura 2004: 217). Let me give you a couple of examples. After introducing and examining the idea of militant democracy, Shigenori Matsui arrives at the conclusion that the Japanese Constitution takes a completely different position from that of the German Constitution (Matsui 2002: 78). Koji Sato explains that since the Japanese Constitution stands on a completely relativistic and liberal position and is wary of the danger of invading constitutional freedoms on the pretense of defending the constitution from an enemy, the German way of prohibiting associations and political parties, the purpose and activities of which are contrary to the constitutional order, is not a suitable model for interpreting the Japanese Constitution (Sato 1995: 47).

Militant Democracy by the Occupation Forces?

As compared to Germany, the government has not always been eager to overcome the wrongs of the past, namely the past fascism of pre-war Japan. Although there were two notable occasions in which the protection of constitutional freedom to an 'enemy of freedom' was denied in post-war Japan, these being the 'purge from public office' and the so-called 'Red Purge', both were carried out based on the instructions of the General Headquarters of the Supreme Commander (GHQ). It might well be said that Japanese society experienced militant democracy, but that was not the product of a decision of the Japanese Government itself, but rather of the Occupation Forces.

Purge From Public Office

The constitution of the Empire of Japan in 1889 (the *Meiji* Constitution), which was modelled on the monarchical Prussian Constitution, had a Bill of Rights. The second chapter of the *Meiji* Constitution sets out the 'Rights and Duties of Subjects'. As the term 'subject' reveals, however, the *Meiji* Constitution did not embrace either the concept of 'human rights' or 'natural rights'. The rights of individual subjects 'were generally conceived as the gifts of a sovereign who was by definition sacred, kindly and paternal' (Beer 1990: 230). Western natural law and natural rights theory had been introduced to Japan late in the *Tokugawa* era, but 'did not take deep enough root to influence significantly the Meiji Era' (Ford 1996: 13).

The *Meiji* Constitution declared that sovereignty resided in the divine Emperor as head of state, and the Emperor gave the constitution as a gift to his subjects. Sovereignty resided in the Emperor not because the people desired it, but because the Emperor had a divine nature. Article 3 of the *Meiji* Constitution stipulates that 'the Emperor is sacred and inviolable', and this means that he stands above the law (Takami 2001: 9).

The protection of rights under the *Meiji* Constitution was very weak. First of all, nearly all rights were only protected 'within the limits of law' (Article 29). Rights were not protected against the majority will. There were many laws which severely restricted rights.

Perhaps the most notorious one is the Peace Preservation Law of 1925. Article 1 provided for punishment of those who 'organize or knowingly participate in an association which has as its purpose changing the *kokutai* (national polity) or repudiating the private property system'. According to Lawrence W. Beer (1984: 65):[8]

> *Kokutai* had become Japan's central shibboleth decades earlier and would remain so until after World War II. The term refers to the legal and constitutional structure of the state but also encompasses the closed national familial system of human relationships among Japanese, in their families and in general, under the emperor's paternal benevolence and the attendant emotional aura.

The principal target of the Peace Preservation Law was the Japan Communist Party, whose activity was severely repressed under the law.

Second, there was no judicial review and courts were deprived of jurisdiction over lawsuits relating 'to rights alleged to have been infringed upon by the illegal measures of the administrative authorities which shall come within the competency the Court of Administrative Litigation specially established by law' (Article 61). Based on the German idea of the dualism of state and society, courts were used only for solving legal disputes among citizens, and for dealing with criminal punishment. Courts could not try cases involving disputes between private citizens and administrative power. Litigation involving administrative law could only be handled by a special tribunal within the administrative branch (Luney 1993: 124–7).

Third, the rights of subjects under the *Meiji* Constitution could be regulated by the Emperor's prerogatives. For example, Article 8 permitted the issuance of Imperial Ordinances in cases of emergency 'to maintain public safety or to avert calamities'. Article 31 made clear that these provisions regarding the rights of subjects 'shall not affect the exercise of the powers appertaining to the Emperor, in times of war or in cases of a national emergency'.

The Potsdam Declaration, which defined the terms of surrender, was formally accepted by Japan on 14 August 1945 and signed on 2 September of the same year.

8 See also Ford 1996: 7–13.

Paragraph 10 of the Potsdam Declaration called for the removal of obstacles to democracy as follows:

> The Japanese Government shall remove all obstacles to the revival and strengthening of democratic tendencies among the Japanese People. Freedom of speech, of religion, and of thought, as well as respect for the fundamental rights shall be established.

After the war, the Japanese Government was placed under the authority of General Douglas MacArthur, the Supreme Commander for the Allied Powers (SCAP). In 1946, as a part of the policy of the democratization of post-war Japanese society, the initial occupation policy called for guarantees of freedom of speech; association; religion; assembly; and press; as well as demilitarization; the democratization of politics and economics; and establishment of liberal democracy. In 1945–1946, the GHQ ordered the Japanese Government to dissolve militaristic and ultra-nationalistic organizations, and remove and exclude from public office certain individuals who had suspicious war records. In 1946, the target of the purge was extended to the business community. As a result, some 210,000 people were purged from public and private positions.

Many of the purged, however, returned to powerful government positions as soon as the occupation was over. This is one of the reasons why the Japanese Government has not been keen to admit its past wrongs.

'Red Purge'

Although the *Meiji* Constitution did not specifically list labour and workers' rights among its catalogue of rights, such rights were interpreted as being included under the 'freedom of association' which was explicitly protected in Article 29. As stated above, however, the scope and degree of the protection of the rights were subject to the proviso 'within the limits of law'. Labour movements were harshly oppressed prior to the Second World War.

Against this historical background, it appears that the initial occupation policy carried out by the GHQ succeeded in promoting the democratization of Japan. The GHQ took many measures to protect workers' rights prior to the promulgation of the Japanese Constitution. For example, the Initial Post-Surrender Policy for Japan of 22 September 1945 noted that: 'Encouragement shall be given and favour shown to the development of organizations in labour organized on a democratic principle'. The United States directed the GHQ to 'remove all legal hindrances to the formation of organizations of employees along democratic lines'.[9] Article 28 of the Japanese Constitution protected the right of workers 'to organize and to bargain act collectively' without any restrictions. Consequently, labour movements mushroomed and frequent demonstrations became routine due to the policy of legal deregulation.

9 Cited in Mori 2001: 174.

However, with the change in both the international and domestic political climates in 1948–1950, the priority of the occupation policy clearly changed from democratizing Japan to making Japan a fortress against communism. In 1948, a Communist Government was established in the northern part of Korea, and the Chinese Civil War ended in 1949 with the Communist Party of China in control of the mainland. Since relations between the United States and the Soviet Union had deteriorated from cooperation to full-fledged cold war between 1948 and 1950, the GHQ gave top priority to preventing the spread of communism in Japan.

Hideo Otake pointed out (Otake 2001: 64):

> This shift of stance by Occupation Forces, from a position of social democracy to one essentially of 'liberalism', was quite evident in the case of Japan. The turning point came in June 1947, with Ordinance 201, which revoked the fundamental labor rights of workers in the public sector, and culminated in the Red Purge of 1950.

The political and labour movements in Japan gradually grew beyond the permissible extent of US occupation policy and conflict began to arise. The occupation policy of the GHQ was changed, and the GHQ began to oppress such movements. A letter sent by the SCAP to the Japanese Government, dated 22 July 1948, stated that

> those whose service is devoted to public office, being under unconditional obligation to loyalty toward the public trust that has been bestowed upon them by the very fact of being employed or appropriated, anyone who has a position within the Japanese government or a related organization by employment or appointment must not appeal to strikes or any other delay strategies that might affect efficient government management.[10]

The Ashida Cabinet responded by issuing Government Ordinance no. 201 on 31 July 1947. The ordinance withdrew from all governmental workers the right to bargain collectively as well as the right to strike and provided for criminal punishment in the event of contravention.

The government also issued the Organization Control Ordinance on 4 April 1949 in order to restrict left-wing associations such as the Japan Communist Party. Article 1(1) stated that

> this cabinet order aims to secure public knowledge of the character of political organizations and to prohibit the formation and direction of secret, militaristic, ultra-nationalistic, terroristic and anti-democratic organizations and the activities of such organizations or individuals, except with respect to the purposes and activities specifically mentioned in this cabinet order.[11]

10 Cited in Mori 2001: 175–6.

11 See Itoh and Beer 1978: 24.

A number of left-wing organizations were dissolved.

Finally, in 1950, the 'Red Purge' came into effect. On 6 June 1950, shortly before the Korean War began, General MacArthur ordered the exclusion of all 24 members of the Central Committee of the Japan Communist Party (JCP) from public office. He also ordered 17 members of the editorial staff of *Akahata*, the newspaper of the JCP, to be excluded from public office (Beer 1984: 81).

Denial of Militant Democracy by Miyazawa and Higuchi

Post-war Japanese constitutional theory has thus not borrowed the idea of militant democracy. That is not to say, however, that the idea of militant democracy is unknown in Japan. Quite the contrary is true. It is the arguments of two leading constitutional scholars of post-war Japan that have had a decisive influence over the application of the concept of militant democracy in Japan.

Toshiyoshi Miyazawa, a late professor of the Faculty of Law at the University of Tokyo, examined the idea of militant democracy in the 1960s. Miyazawa described militant democracy as 'the response of Bonn' to 'the lesson from the failure of the Weimar Republic' (Miyazawa 1968: 160, 164). This formulation is very popular within Japanese constitutional theory. The main feature of his argument is that he understood militant democracy as 'the dilemma inherent in democracy'. Thinking that militant democracy was a safeguard of democracy against the enemies of democracy, he asked how a liberal democracy could be intolerant towards illiberal and anti-democratic groups without compromising and relinquishing its claim to liberal democratic legitimacy (Miyazawa 1968: 169–71). He called this dilemma the 'difficulty' of militant democracy.

It seemed to Miyazawa that the adoption of the idea of militant democracy in the post-war German Constitution was perfectly rational against the background of recent German history. He wrote that 'no one could or would deny the choice of the Basic Law as long as he had studied the constitutional history of the Weimar Republic' (Miyazawa 1968: 172). Miyazawa, however, rejected the idea of militant democracy at the level of constitutional philosophy as follows (Miyazawa 1968: 173):

> Since the very essence of democracy is the protection of human rights, and democracy cannot discard this essence without becoming undemocratic, then even in fights against its enemy who uses the mechanisms of democracy as a Trojan horse, democracy should not fight against human rights but fight against its enemy through human rights.

Yoichi Higuchi, a professor of the Faculty of Law at the University of Tokyo, comes to the same conclusion. Higuchi also recognizes that whether we should allow the benefits of constitutional freedom to the enemy of constitution and freedom is a very difficult problem to resolve (Higuchi 1998: 92). Nonetheless, he rejects the siren call from militant democracy. He prefers the classical liberal view that freedom of expression affords ordinary adequate protection of freedom even to the enemy of freedom (Higuchi 1979: 58–60).

It seems to me, however, that Higuchi's argument is more complicated than Miyazawa's, and his rejection of the idea of militant democracy is more interesting. First of all, Miyazawa and Higuchi view militant democracy differently in terms of comparative constitutional law. For Miyazawa, militant democracy still remains the choice of post-war Germany. In contrast to Miyazawa, Higuchi takes militant democracy as involving the transition from modern constitutionalism to contemporary constitutionalism. According to him, 'the concept of allegiance to the constitution' has increasingly become significant as one of the basic features of post-war Western democracy, and the German Constitution is a typical example of this trend. It therefore seems to me more difficult for Higuchi to reject the idea of militant democracy than it does for Miyazawa.

Second, unlike Miyazawa, Higuchi is fully aware of the context of the choice of militant democracy during the Cold War. As relations between the United States and the Soviet Union deteriorated from cooperation to full-fledged cold war, and as West Germany was located at the forefront of the Cold War, the militant democracy of post-war West Germany was extended to the fight against communism, resulting in the German Federal Constitutional Court's upholding of a ban on the German Communist Party in 1958. Higuchi fully understands the meaning of the choice of militant democracy in Germany as a weapon of war against communism. However, he perceives the same kind of militancy in socialist and communist regimes. To him the democracies of socialist and communist countries are also militant democracies. Many communist countries deny the enemy within the benefits of constitutional freedom.

Until the 1970s, Marxists had a powerful voice – at least in the field of legal scholarship – in Japan and Higuchi was an anti-communist and a militant liberal. Higuchi cautioned the people of Western democracies that if the spiritual superiority of Western democracy over communist democracy were to be grounded in the protection of intellectual freedoms in the former, the only legitimate path Western democracies could take must be to grant full recognition and protection of the freedom of thought and speech to all comprehensive political doctrines, however, pernicious (Higuchi 1979: 60–62). Thus, in contrast to the path taken by Germany, he advises the avoidance of the idea of militant democracy, not in spite of, but because of, anti-communism.

Thus understood, the dominance of anti-communism both in Japanese society in general and in legal academic circles in particular helps to explain why post-war Japanese constitutional scholars turned a deaf ear to the call of militant democracy.

Why Denial?

However, I believe things are not so simple. Anti-communism is a double-edged sword which could cut in either direction, toward the adoption of a militant democracy or toward the rejection of one. It depends upon how one perceives constitutional identity.

During the Cold War era, there appears to have been a debate even in the United States as to whether democracy should be more militant against the enemy of freedom. On the one hand, some scholars used the logic of militant democracy to justify the repression of communists. Harry V. Jaffa, a conservative political writer, asked as follows (Jaffa 1970):

> Yet in the field of civil liberties there is profound confusion as to what, in crucial cases, decent, freedom-loving citizens may do. With respect to freedom of speech and the closely related freedoms of assembly, association, and the right of petition, the question continually arises: Can we deny these freedoms or rights to Communists, or their agents or coadjutors, without ourselves ceasing, by that denial and to the extent of the denial, to constitute a free society? … Does a free society prove false to itself if it denies civil liberties to Communists, Nazis, or anyone else who would use these liberties, if he could, as a means of destroying that free society? (Jaffa 1970: 145, 151)

For him, the answer was clearly not:

> Those who think that every denial of civil liberties is equally derogatory of the character of a free society, without reference to the character of the persons being denied make … fundamental error: They confuse means with ends. Free speech is a priceless and indispensable attribute of a free society because it is a necessary means for deliberating upon public policy. But this deliberation does not extend to everything; above all, it does not extend to the question of whether the community shall exchange its freedom for slavery (Jaffa 1970: 151–2).

Carl A. Auerbach, then professor of law at the University of Wisconsin, wrote, in the context of discussing the constitutionality of the Communist Control Act of 1954, that 'no principle of the Constitution or of democracy requires that a political movement be permitted to engage in the struggle for power if its objective is to crush democracy itself' (Auerbach 1956: 186).

On the other hand, we could find the directly opposite answer in the dissenting opinion of Justice Douglas in *Dennis v. United States*.[12] In this decision, the US Supreme Court upheld the convictions of Communist Party leaders who had been convicted of advocating the overthrow of the Government of the United States. In a dissent, Douglas argued that American democracy should tolerate dissent so as

12 341 U.S. 494 (1951).

not to reproduce the evils of communism. He closed his opinion with the statement (341 U.S. 494 (1951) p. 591):

> Vishinsky wrote in 1930 in The Law of the Soviet State, 'In our state, naturally, there is and can be no place for freedom of speech, press, and so on for the foes of socialism'. Our concern should be that we accept no such standard for the United States. Our faith should be that our people will never give support to these advocates of revolution, so long as we remain loyal to the purpose for which our Nation was founded.

In the Cold War, the United States fought against the Communist Bloc in the name of defending liberal democracy. Justice Douglas had a strong desire to articulate a form of constitutionalism that distinguished the United States from the Soviet Union.

Thus understood, both the advocacy of militant democracy by Jaffa and of anti-militant democracy by Douglas could be interpreted as manifestations of anticommunism (Primus 1996). Anti-communism alone cannot explain the difference between the United States and Germany.[13]

We should, therefore, search for other grounds with which to understand the rebuke of militant democracy by post-war Japanese constitutional scholars. Why did post-war Japanese constitutional scholars persist in declining to respond to the siren call from militant democracy?

Liberal constitutional scholars in post-war Japan have been haunted by the fact that the political forces in power in post-war Japan failed to accept the legitimacy of the constitution and fully embrace the concept of constitutionalism. If there was an enemy of democracy and freedom in post-war Japan, it was the ruling party itself. The overcoming of fascism and the fight against the political forces in power forms the particular perspective from which post-war Japanese constitutional scholars have estimated the merits and demerits of adopting a militant democracy in Japan.

The Constitution of Japan of 1946 was imposed on an extremely reluctant conservative Japanese Government by the occupying forces after the Second World War. At the beginning of the occupation, the Japanese Government maintained that despite the surrender, the basic constitutional structure, *kokutai*, was still intact, and there was no need to revise the *Meiji* Constitution. The astonishing fact that this view was shared by leading constitutional scholars suggests how fragile and insecure the future of constitutionalism was. Many leading scholars could not imagine that the basic defects of the *Meiji* Constitution caused the disaster.

---

13 Unlike the aversive constitutionalism of post-war Germany, the aversive constitutionalism of the US contributed to produce a 'militant' procedural democracy. See Scheppele 2003: 312–24.

> The Meiji Constitution was founded both on a Japanese element – an emperor who ruled by his divine authority – and universal elements of Western constitutionalism. In interpreting the Meiji Constitution, there was a fierce debate among constitutional scholars. One school of thought, called 'divine right school', stressed quasi-mystical loyalty to *kokutai*. The Meiji Constitution was conceived under the strong influence of the Prussian Constitution of 1850. The Prussian Constitution adopted a monarchial constitutionalism which favored the community over the individual and permitted the exercise of individual freedoms only in so far as they did not threaten the order within the group. The 'divine right school', took this idea one step further, suggesting that the state was an actual person, the Emperor himself. They preferred a quasi-theocratic form of constitutionalism to the secular form of German constitutionalism.[14]

On the other hand, another school of thought, called the 'constitutionalist school', stressed universal elements. Tatsukichi Minobe, representative of this school, developed a more secularized (therefore more German) theory that the state was a legal person and the Emperor was merely an organ of the state. The aim of this school was democratization of the Japanese governmental system by strengthening the power of Parliament. After a fierce debate with the 'divine right school', Minobe's theory won adherents in academia and gradually became the accepted theory by the bureaucracy.

However, as the Great Depression of 1929 exacerbated domestic political tensions and spurred imperialistic instincts, the military finally gained control of the government. The militaristic forces began to strike back against Minobe's theory. In 1935, although Minobe was not opposed to the emperor system itself, his theory was officially suppressed. He had to resign from the House of Peers and his publications were banned. This was a crucial moment of full retreat of constitutionalism in pre-war Japan (Higuchi 2001: 4–5). After this incident, all political parties were forced to form a grand coalition in support of war efforts and dissent was harshly suppressed.

When the time for the revival of constitutionalism came in Japan with her defeat in the Second World War, Minobe could not recognize the critical defects in the constitutional structure of the *Meiji* Constitution due to the suppression. He was of the opinion that the *Meiji* Constitution was not necessarily an obstacle to the establishment of democracy in Japan; it was not the Constitution itself, but an erroneous interpretation and implementation of it by militaristic forces that had led the nation to war. Even Minobe could not imagine the need for constitutional revision.

Although the *Meiji* Constitution had to be revised to implement fully the terms of surrender set by the Potsdam Declaration, the Japanese Government was extremely reluctant to revise it. Having ended the war with the *kokutai* intact, the government feared that a new constitution would abolish the *kokutai* (Otake 2001: 44).

14 Ford 1996: 7–8.

When General MacArthur suggested the revision of the *Meiji* Constitution, the Japanese Government reluctantly established an unofficial committee to consider constitutional reform. The name of this committee, The Committee to Study Constitutional Problems (usually referred to as the 'Matsumoto Committee') shows how reluctant the Japanese Government was to revise the constitution. The members of the Committee included several prominent constitutional scholars, such as Toshiyoshi Miyazawa of the University of Tokyo and Shiro Kiyomiya of Tohoku University. Even Minobe served on this committee as an adviser. They shared the view that there was no need to revise the *Meiji* Constitution. The chairman, State Minister Joji Matsumoto, explained the nature of this committee in this way: 'Since the main purpose of this committee is to undertake a scholarly study, we are not thinking of preparing a draft even if we reach the conclusion that it is necessary to revise the Constitution.'[15]

At the first meetings of the committee, one of the advisers, Junji Nomura, asked the crucial question of whether in connection with the Potsdam Declaration's statement about 'revising and strengthening democratic tendencies', the committee would also have to touch upon Articles 1 and 4 to complete democratization. He said the United States would certainly mention them. Article 1 of the *Meiji* Constitution provided: 'The Empire of Japan shall be reigned over and governed by a line of Emperors unbroken for age eternal,' and Article 4 provided for imperial sovereignty as follows: 'The Emperor is the head of the Empire, combining in Himself the right of sovereignty, and exercises it, according to the provisions of the present Constitution.' Recognizing that revising these two articles would necessarily change the *kokutai*, Matsumoto responded that

> since the Potsdam Declaration says that this issue shall be determined by the free will of the Japanese people, even America cannot forcefully order it. The general will of the Japanese people is as unmovable as a mountain. Therefore, there is no need to mention articles one and four. It is simply not the case that Japan cannot be democratic without revising articles one and four. Although there are many things that should be revised, I consider this part of the Constitution permanent.

Minobe agreed with Matsumoto.

However, due to both the international and domestic climate of hostility towards the imperial regime, the committee was forced to change its mind and prepare to respond to the demands for constitutional revision. After several months of deliberation, the committee drew up several draft proposals, the content of which was the same as the Meiji Constitution with only minor changes. On the morning of 1 February 1946, the *Mainichi Shinbun* (one of the leading newspapers in Japan) published on its front page the full text of one of the drafts made by

15 *Mainichi Shinbun* (Mainichi Newspaper), 26 October 1945, cited in Koseki 1997: 50.

the committee and the reaction to it was extremely unfavourable. This led the newspaper to comment: 'We think that most people will feel disappointed that it is so conservative and does nothing more than preserve the status quo.'[16]

This shows that 'the Japanese Government never truly understood the implications of the Potsdam Declaration and clung to both the Meiji Constitution and the Meiji system of power' (Hamano 1999: 430), and that there was an ideological gap between the ordinary Japanese people and the elite. Even many leading constitutional scholars still remained imprisoned in the Emperor system of the *Meiji* Constitution.

Accordingly, on 3 February 1946, General MacArthur instructed Courtney Whitney, Chief of the Government Section of SCAP, to prepare a draft constitution incorporating three basic principles: a limited monarchy; the renunciation of war; and the abolition of feudalism. On 13 February, a draft constitution prepared by the GHQ was presented to representatives of the Japanese Government. Whitney said to the Japanese side: 'As the draft of constitutional revision which you have submitted to us is wholly unacceptable, we have prepared a draft' (Koseki 1997: 99).

The Japanese side never imagined that a draft constitution would be presented to them as they had submitted a Matsumoto draft on 8 February and had come to the meeting merely in order to receive the SCAP's response to it. They were, therefore, stunned to be presented with the GHQ draft.

According to the SCAP record, Whitney also said to them (Koseki 1997: 101):

> As you may or may not know, the Supreme Commander has been unyielding in his defense of your Emperor against increasing pressure from the outside to render him subject to a war criminal investigation. He has thus defended the Emperor because he considered that that was the cause of right and justice, and will continue along that course to the extent of his ability. But, gentlemen, the Supreme Commander is not omnipotent. He feels, however, that the acceptance of the provisions of this new constitution would render the Emperor practically unassailable … The Supreme Commander has directed me to offer this constitution to your government and party for your adoption and your presentation to the people with his full backing if you care to do so, yet he does not require this of you. He is determined, however, that the principles therein stated shall be laid before the people – rather by you – but, if not, by himself.

Given the fact that many nations, in particular the Soviet Union and Australia, took a strong stand against the Emperor and were ready to put him on trial before a war tribunal, the Japanese Government did not have any other options to shield the Emperor from prosecution as a war criminal except acceptance of the GHQ draft. After a period of internal turmoil and some resistance, the Japanese Government agreed to accept the draft.

16 *Mainichi Shinbun*, 1 February 1946, cited in Koseki 1997: 61.

After minor adjustments to the GHQ draft, the Japanese Government released an outline of the new constitution to the press on 6 March 1946. On 3 November 1946, the constitution of Japan was finally promulgated into law.

That was the story of the birth of the constitution of Japan of 1946 in brief. It shows that the political elite, including leading constitutional scholars, could not recognize the necessity of constitutional reform even after the nation's defeat in the Second World War. They could not imagine that 'their country might adopt a constitution that was so democratic and so strongly protective of individual liberties' (Hasebe 2003: 225), because they could not recognize the critical defects of the pre-war Japanese constitutional system. In short, they could not imagine that post-war Japanese society should import and borrow the idea of modern constitutionalism. Thus, modern constitutionalism was forcibly imposed upon Japan through the adoption of the 1946 Constitution. The founder of modern constitutionalism was not Japanese, but the Occupation Forces.

The reaction of the Japanese people to the new constitution was overwhelmingly favourable. The same was true among constitutional scholars. After the enactment of the new constitution, many of them were converted into being supporters of it. For example, although Miyazawa was a member of the Matsumoto Committee that recommended against fundamentally amending the constitution, he admitted later that he was filled, upon reading the GHQ draft, with joy and converted into its fervent supporter.[17] Post-war constitutional scholars devoted their energy to defending the Constitution and to realize its potential as the embodiment of modern constitutionalism.

In sharp contrast, the political forces in power began to question the legitimacy of the Constitution after the outbreak of the Korean War. They called it 'MacArthur's Constitution' with evident sarcasm. They argued that the Constitution of Japan was null and void since it had been drafted by Americans and imposed on the Japanese Government and people. They oftentimes were concerned with defending the national identity and traditional values of Japan against the values of liberal democracy. In short, they did not embrace modern constitutionalism at all.

It should also be noted that there is a sharp contrast between post-war Japan and Germany with respect to overcoming the past. In post-war Germany, it was generally accepted that liberal democracy had taken roots in the hearts and minds of citizens only after Auschwitz. The German Government devoted great energy and resources to atoning for Nazi aggression. On the other hand, for decades many Cabinet members made the statement that the colonization of Korea and the invasion of China and Southeast Asia could be justified as safeguarding them against invasion from the West and withdrew these statements only after Korean and Chinese people protested against them. It is well known that Japanese textbooks were 'censored' in order to exclude some descriptions of the atrocities which the Japanese military perpetrated during wartime. The Japanese Government still fails to make settlements and peaceful relationships with neighbouring countries.

17 Hasebe 2003: 225, citing Kobayashi 1977: 18.

The reaction of post-war constitutional scholars to the concept of militant democracy should be examined in terms of these peculiar political circumstances. In short, it is not too much to say that it was the very political forces, that held the reins of power themselves, that were indeed the true 'enemies of freedom and democracy'. Thus understood, it was (or is) both futile and dangerous to incorporate a concept of militant democracy into Japanese constitutional law (Higuchi 1979: 79–80). It was futile, because the 'enemy of freedom and democracy' was the occupant of the ruling position in post-war Japan. It was dangerous, because it was possible to abuse the concept of militant democracy in justification of the restriction of the civil liberties of dissenters.

I believe that is the real reason why liberal scholars still decline to heed the siren call of militant democracy. In other words, 'constitutional patriotism' may take the form of opposing the concept of militant democracy in Japan.

References

Ackerman, Bruce (1997) 'The Rise of World Constitutionalism', *Virginia Law Review* 83(4): 771–97.

Auerbach, Carl A. (1956) 'The Communist Control Act of 1954: A Proposed Legal-Political Theory of Free Speech', *University of Chicago Law Review* 23(2): 173–220.

Beer, Lawrence W. (1984) *Freedom of Expression in Japan: A Study in Comparative Law, Politics, and Society.* Tokyo: Kodansha International.

Beer, Lawrence W. (1990) 'Constitutionalism and Rights in Japan and Korea', in Louis Henkin and Albert Rosenthal (eds) *Constitutionalism and Rights: The Influence of the United States Constitution Abroad.* New York: Columbia University Press, 225–59.

Currie, David P. (1994) *The Constitution of the Federal Republic of Germany.* Chicago: University of Chicago Press.

Doehring, Karl (1988) 'The Special Character of the Constitution of the Federal Republic of Germany as a Free Democratic Basic Order', in Ulrich Karpen (ed.) *The Constitution of the Federal Republic of Germany: Essays on the Basic Rights and Principles of the Basic Law with a Translation of the Basic Law.* Baden-Baden: Nomos, pp. 25–44.

Dworkin, Ronald (1977) *Taking Rights Seriously.* Cambridge: Harvard University Press.

Eberle, Edward J. (1997) 'Human Dignity, Privacy, and Personality in German and American Constitutional Law', *Utah Law Review* (4): 963–1056.

Ford, Christopher A. (1996) 'The Indigenization of Constitutionalism in the Japanese Experience', *Case Western Reserve Journal of International Law* 28(1): 3–62.

Fox, Gregory H. and Nolte, Georg (1995) 'Intolerant Democracies', *Harvard International Law Journal* 36(1): 1–70.

Griffin, Leslie C. (2003) 'Fundamentalism from the Perspective of Liberal Tolerance', *Cardozo Law Review* 24(4): 1631–44.

Hamano, Sylvia Brown (1999) 'Incomplete Revolutions and Not So Alien Transplants: The Japanese Constitution and Human Rights', *University of Pennsylvania Journal of Constitutional Law* 1, 415–91.

Hasebe, Yasuo (2003) 'Constitutional Borrowing and Political Theory', *I-Con – International Journal of Constitutional Law* 1(2): 224–43.

Heyd, David (ed.) (1996) *Toleration: An Elusive Virtue.* Princeton: Princeton University Press.

Higuchi, Yoichi (1979) *Hikaku no naka no Nihonkoku Kenpo* (Japanese Constitution in the Comparative Perspective). Tokyo: Iwanami Shoten.

Higuchi, Yoichi (1998) *Kenpo* (Constitutional Law). Tokyo: Sobunsha.

Higuchi, Yoichi (2001) 'The 1946 Constitution: Its Meaning in the Worldwide Development of Constitutionalism', in Yoichi Higuchi (ed.) *Five Decades of Constitutionalism in Japanese Society.* Tokyo: University of Tokyo Press, pp. 1–8.

Issacharoff, Samuel (2007) 'Fragile Democracies', *Harvard Law Review* 120(6): 1405–67.

Ito, Masami (1995), *Kenpo* (Constitutional Law), 3rd edn. Tokyo: Kobundo.

Itoh, Hiroshi and Beer, Lawrence W. (1978) *The Constitutional Case Law of Japan: Selected Supreme Court Decisions, 1961–70.* Seattle: University of Washington Press.

Jacobs, David A. (1993) 'Recent Development, The Ban of Neo-Nazi Music: Germany Takes on the Neo-Nazis', *Harvard International Law Journal* 34(2): 563–80.

Jaffa, Harry V. (1970) 'On the Nature of Civil and Religious Liberty', in William F. Buckley Jr. and Charles R. Kesler (eds) *Keeping the Tablets: Modern American Conservative Thought.* New York: Harper and Row, pp. 145–58. Originally published in de Toledano, Ralph and Hess, Karl (eds) (1960) *The Conservative Papers.* New York: Doubleday Anchors, 250–68.

Kobayashi, Naoki (1977) 'Miyazawa Kenpo-gaku no Kiseki' (The Trajectory of Miyazawa's Constitutional Theory), *Jurisuto* 634: 10–30.

Kommers, Donald P. (1997) *The Constitutional Jurisprudence of the Federal Republic of Germany*, 2nd edn. Durham: Duke University Press.

Koseki, Shoichi (1997) *The Birth of Japan's Postwar Constitution* (translated by Ray A. Moore). Boulder: Westview Press.

Larmore, Charles (1996) *The Morals of Modernity.* Cambridge: Cambridge University Press.

Loewenstein, Karl (1936) 'Law in the Third Reich', *Yale Law Journal* 45(5): 779–815.

Loewenstein, Karl (1937a) 'Militant Democracy and Fundamental Rights I', *American Political Science Review* 31(3): 417–32.

Loewenstein, Karl (1937b) 'Militant Democracy and Fundamental Rights II', *American Political Science Review* 31(4): 638–58.

Luney Jr., Percy R. (1993) 'The Judiciary: Its Organization and Status in the Parliamentary System', in Percy R. Luney Jr. and Kazuyuki Takahashi (eds) *Japanese Constitutional Law*. Tokyo: University of Tokyo Press, 123–49.

Matsui, Shigenori (2002) *Nihonkoku Kenpo* (Japanese Constitutional Law), 2nd edn. Tokyo: Yuhikaku.

Miyazawa, Toshiyoshi (1968) *Horitsugaku ni okeru Gakusetsu* (Theory of Legal Scholarship). Tokyo: Yuhikaku.

Mori, Hideki (2001) 'Workers' Rights in Japanese Labor Praxis', in Yoichi Higuchi (ed.) *Five Decades of Constitutionalism in Japanese Society*. Tokyo: University of Tokyo Press, 171–93.

Murphy, Walter F. and Tanenhaus, Joseph (eds) (1977) *Comparative Constitutional Law: Cases and Commentaries*. New York: St. Martin's Press.

Nonaka, Toshihiko, Nakamura, Mutsuo, Takahashi, Kazuyuki and Takami Katsutoshi (2006) *Kenpo* (Constitutional Law), *vol. I*, 4th edn. Tokyo: Yuhikaku.

Otake, Hideo (2001) 'Two Contrasting Constitutions in the Postwar World: The Making of the Japanese and the West German Constitutions', in Yoichi Higuchi (ed.) *Five Decades of Constitutionalism in Japanese Society*. Tokyo: University of Tokyo Press, pp. 43–26.

Primus, Richard (1996) 'A Brooding Omnipresence: Totalitarianism in Postwar Constitutional Thought', *Yale Law Journal* 106(2): 423–57.

Rawls, John (1993) *Political Liberalism*. New York: Columbia University Press.

Rawls, John (2001) *Justice as Fairness: A Restatement*. Cambridge: Harvard University Press.

Sajó, András (2004) 'Militant Democracy and Transition towards Democracy', in András Sajó (ed.) *Militant Democracy*. Utrecht: Eleven International Publishing, 209–30.

Sato, Koji (1995) *Kenpo* (Constitutional Law), 3rd edn. Tokyo: Seirin Shoin.

Scheppele, Kim Lane (2003) 'Aspirational and Aversive Constitutionalism: The Case for Studying Cross-Constitutional Influence through Negative Model', *I-Con – International Journal of Constitutional Law* 1(2): 296–324.

Takami, Katsutoshi (2001) 'From Divine Legitimacy to the Myth of Consensus: The Emperor System and Popular Sovereignty', in Yoichi Higuchi (ed.) *Five Decades of Constitutionalism in Japanese Society*. Tokyo: University of Tokyo Press, pp. 9–26.

Tsujimura, Miyoko (2004) *Kenpo* (Constitutional Law), 2nd edn. Tokyo: Nihon Hyoronsha.

Wise, Judith (1998) 'Comment, Dissent and the Militant Democracy: The German Constitution and the Banning of the Free German Workers Party', *University of Chicago Law School Roundtable* 5: 301–44.

Chapter 11
Spain

Carlos Vidal Prado

Introduction

As opposed to the state about which Niccolò Machiavelli and Jean Bodin theorized, the current one is characterized as a democratic and social state governed by the rule of law, internationally integrated and with parties (Torres del Moral 2006: 210 et seq.). Of these features, the one that is today the main one and which gives meaning to the others, is that the state is democratic. But this is not conceivable without the rule of law, and vice versa. There is no greater rule of law than democracy. The current model of a state of parties has contributed towards closely linking these two aspects.

This concept of rule of law – which owes its origin to Robert von Mohl and reached us through the French doctrine of the supremacy of the law as expression of the general will and the English doctrine of the rule of law – is not only descriptive but prescriptive (or, if you wish, regulatory). The true rule of law incorporates the elements of the idea of justice and the limitation and control of the power by the law as a guarantee of the citizens' freedoms and rights. And it is precisely the participation of the citizens in the creation of the legal regulations which undoubtedly guarantees that it incorporates their subjective rights. As such, the rule of law can only be fully achieved in a democracy.

It is in this context that Article 1 of the Spanish Constitution of 1978 must be understood where it states that 'Spain is hereby established as a social and democratic State, subject to the rule of law'. This constitutional formula must be taken into consideration in a unitary manner, and each of its elements is closely linked to the others. As García Pelayo said: 'In the present historic situation none of the terms can be affirmed without interaction with the others' (García Pelayo 1995: 93–4).

The Prescriptive (or Substantial) and Descriptive (Procedural) Concept of Democracy

The democratic state adds to the social state the elements of popular sovereignty, political pluralism and citizen participation in the political, social, cultural and economic life. It also incorporates sufficient citizen rights so that freedom and equality are real and effective. But this democratic and social state cannot go beyond the limits of the rule of law, because otherwise it would stop being legitimately democratic. The established legal procedures and the basic content of the legal regulations, in which prevail certain values and certain basic principles the most palpable manifestation of which is the guarantee of the citizens' rights and freedoms, must be scrupulously respected.

Putting into practice the principles on which the democracy is based is not easy. Giovanni Sartori states that no human company depends as much on the force of the ideas and our ability to use them as democracy (Sani and Sartori 1983; Sartori 1965). As Jean-Jacques Rousseau says, the aim is 'to find a form of association which defends and protects with all common force the people and property of each associate and which, everybody joining together, only obeys itself and remains as free as before' (Rousseau 1762 [1988]: 14).

A fundamental element of democracy is the one defined as self-government of the people or, more graphically, in the words of Abraham Lincoln: Government of the people, for the people, by the people. It has also been said that democracy is the government of public opinion or the regime of popular sovereignty governed by the majority. All of these concepts are descriptive because they focus on the procedures of governance. Their interest lies in the espression of elements of the democratic regime. Those concepts that identify democracy with the elements of control and responsibility of the power, an opposition, and the alternation in the power are also descriptive, as are those that focus on pluralism and on elections.

Together with the descriptive (or procedural) description of the democracy, a 'prescriptive' – some refer to 'substantial' (Revenga Sánchez 2005: 14–19) – description has been prepared which defines the binding values (Torres del Moral 2004a: 282–4). From this perspective, it is affirmed that the democracy, more than a method, is a culture, an ethos, a way of life based on participation and tolerance; a faith in freedom, pluralism and equality. In other words, it professes values and pursues objectives which are ethically positive.

An example of the first conception is that of Hans Kelsen who, in his work 'Essence and value of democracy', defines democracy as a method and even considers it compatible with the accumulation of power and with the annihilation of freedom. It is an axiologically relativist and sceptical concept. On the other hand: those who identify democracy with certain values and their defence are those who, with different overtones, talk of a 'militant democracy'.

In view of the practical realization of democracies, all of these terms presently need to be qualified as between the various concepts there are intermediate positions – democracies which could be placed at either extreme as pointed out by Gregory H. Fox and Georg Nolte (1995: 1 et seq.). These authors apply the variables of 'tolerant' or 'militant' to the two models of democracy, 'substantive' and 'procedural'. And as such, there are tolerant procedural democracies (United Kingdom) and militant procedural democracies (United States); and, equally, there are tolerant substantive democracies (France) and militant substantive democracies (Germany).

Notwithstanding this, even this distinction must be put in quarantine as stated by Revenga Sánchez (2005: 17):

> Is it not the case that the tolerant France can dissolve political associations using simple Decrees from the Cabinet (*Décrets*), while the militant Germany has to instigate complex proceedings before the Constitutional Court? Between 1936 and 2003, France banned no less than 80 political associations. And Germany, on the other hand, seems to have made the procedures to defend Articles 18 (abuse of law as a cause for the individual privation of certain rights) and 21.2 of the constitution (prohibition of parties against the liberal-democratic order) historical curiosities fit for exhibition in the museums as they have not stood up to the test of time.[1]

Notwithstanding what we may actually come across in the democratic countries, the truth is that it is not a democracy if there is no belief in the values and principles of freedom, justice, equality, human dignity and responsibility of the public authorities. Neither can a system be considered a democracy that professes certain values due to the mere majority situation of the citizens (and/or its representatives), but can go the other way due to another – opposite – situation. Under these terms, it would be a 'democracy under suspicion'.

The Democratic Model of the Spanish Constitution

The Spanish Constitution of 1978 has in its favour the longest democratic period in Spanish history. It is a constitution that has transformed Spanish political culture and is quite reiterative concerning the democratic idea. The term 'democracy' (or its derivatives) appears at times, such as when the Preamble talks of democratic coexistence and advanced democratic society, when Article 1(1) defines the political regime as a 'social and democratic State, subject to the rule of law', when all recognized groups and organizations (political parties, unions, associations, companies, professional associations, etc.) are required to have 'democratic internal structure and functioning' and, finally, when the objective of the educational system is required to respect the democratic principle of coexistence.

In other places, the democratic idea is expressed without using the term; for example, when the political pluralism is lifted to a higher plane in the legal regulations, when the constitution recognizes a varied typology of social pluralism

1 Translation by the author. The episode of the (frustrated) prohibition of the German neo-Nazi *Nationaldemokratische Partei Deutschlands* (NPD, National Democratic Party of Germany), resolved definitively with the Judgment of the German Federal Constitutional Court, of 18 March 2003, seems to attest Revenga Sánchez' statement. The data of France are taken from the parliamentary Document, Rapport fait au nom de la Comisión d'Enquête sur les agissements, l'organisation, le fonctionement, les objetifs du groupement de fait dit 'Département Protection Securité'(at http://www.assemblee-nat.fr/dossiers/dps/r1622p03.asp).

or when it affirms the principle of popular sovereignty and its derivate: the right to political participation.

The 'Spanish nation' referred to in Article 1(2) of the constitution is made up of all Spaniards. As such, justice emanates from the people, and the Parliaments represent the Spanish people. Article 9(2) of the constitution contains the double idea of a social and democratic state combining freedom with equality, the individual with the social group and the economic, social and cultural participation with the political participation.

Another example is the synthesis that the constitutional Preamble makes of this complex idea. It speaks of guaranteeing the democratic coexistence and of establishing an advanced democratic society. The advanced democratic society is not a reality or a static concept but rather intrinsically dynamic, always moving towards the future in pursuit of higher degrees of freedom, justice and progress. This expression in the Preamble is the synthesis of the constitution's ethos, which may also be focused on the concept of progress understood in the broad sense which extends the limits of the economy and advances cultural development (Tajadura Tejada 1997). But in pursuing these objectives, the public authorities always come across the impassable limit of the respect for the law and the legal regulations.

Article 1 of the Spanish Constitution continues by saying that the social and democratic State, subject to the rule of law establishes and advocates freedom, equality and political pluralism as higher values of its legal regulations. Against those who believe that a declaration like this has no regulatory value, in my opinion it must be stated that it contains a top class structural principle which is developed throughout the articles, and which also pervades the constitutional text and the rest of the values that it advocates. We are dealing with one of the constitutional rules of the regime established by the constitution.

The Spanish Constitution is prodigious in mentioning values and technical legal principles. As stated by Hernández Gil, the non-ideological adscription of the constitution is not the same as indifference. The constitution is not a chess board where all of the moves are still to be made, rather there are some facts, such as, among others, the proclamation of the higher values of the regulations (Hernández Gil 1982). Article 1 of the constitution openly enunciates such values, it classifies them as superior and precedes them with the verb 'advocate' which means proclaim, encourage and defend. It also talks of the dignity of the person with their inviolable rights as 'foundation of the public order and social peace', Article 10(1). It is not that freedom, justice, equality, political pluralism and dignity are lacking in other legal regulations because they are not mentioned in their constitutions. They may be induced in the constitutional text and the laws. But it is not irrelevant that the supreme law itself is so explicit in this matter. So the values gain credibility and certainty as a point of reference for the legal operators and the citizens.

The language used in the constitution could be classified as 'strong' or blunt, belonging to a 'militant' democracy. We are, however, dealing with the first conceptual problem which it is important to mention before going on to deal with the specific issue of the Spanish democracy. The concept of militant democracy comes, as is well known, from the title of an essay published by Karl Loewenstein in 1937 from his exile in the United States (Loewenstein 1937a, 1937b). It is a concept of combat, conceived to shake the conscience of people faced with the 'legalistic self-complacency' of some naïve democracies, and unable to notice that their rules were being (in Loewenstein's words) the 'Trojan horse in which the enemy invades the city.' The concept is later taken on by the German *Bundesverfassungsgericht* (Federal Constitutional Court) with the expression '*streitbare*' or '*wehrhafte Demokratie*'.[2]

Carl Schmitt, on the other hand, identifies what he believes is the source of the problem (Schmitt 1932): linking the possibilities of defending democracy to the existence of an unbreakable constitutional nucleus resistant to reform. Years later, he believed that his thesis had been confirmed in the post-war unreformability clause of Article 79(3) of the *Grundgesetz* (the German Constitution).[3] This German author does not stand alone in identifying this model of democracy with the correlative existence of an intangible constitutional clause, in other words, prohibiting the modification of certain basic elements of the constitutional system. But there is no similar rule in the Spanish Constitution. Apparently, the reform regulations in the constitution allow for any type of modification of the constitution. The constitution is divided in two parts: one part seems to be easier to reform than the other, but this is only at first sight. Because as regards the rules which are more difficult to reform (the heading, the nuclei of the most important fundamental rights, the regulations relating to the Crown, and the total revision), the requirements are so demanding that, in fact, they appear designed to avoid any reform. Critics have stated that allowing every constitutional provision to be reformed, but establishing a reform procedure for certain elements of the constitution which is so difficult that it is almost better not to even try, is a symptom of 'political schizophrenia' (Revenga Sánchez 2005: 20).

It cannot be denied that, when we talk about 'militant democracy', we are mainly looking at the German model. And, as a result, the idea of a militant democracy is identified with the existence of an intangibility clause. But it is also clear that it would be absurd to find a democracy that lacked instruments to defend its own values.

Classifying a democracy as 'militant', in short, refers to specific forms of protection which act in the opposite direction to a system of freedoms thanks to which it is possible to conceive, express and aspire to see any political project

2 BVerfGE 5, 85 (134, 137). See Lameyer 1978: 22 et seq.; Schmidt 1983: 219 et seq.; see, concerning Spain, Denninger 2001: 445–55.

3 See the 'Introduction', written by Carl Schmitt, to an edition of the book published in 1968, and starting from which was carried out the Spanish version: *Legalidad y Legitimidad* (1971, Madrid: Aguilar) pp. IX–X.

become reality. And these specific forms of protection are identifiable in any democracy, although they are not, as is logical, the same in every case.

In every case, the defence of the democracy continues being an issue which is far from closed. In many cases, the measures adopted initially either were useless or trivial. And this is due to the simple reason that its effectiveness was conditional, in inverse proportion, to the degree of consolidation and support enjoyed by the groups that are the objects of these measures (Capoccia 2001: 431 et seq.).

The Spanish Democratic Model and the Political Parties

Article 6 of the constitution requires the political parties to have a democratic internal structure and functioning. But for many years, this article was not completed with a legal development regulation which sufficiently detailed the minimum requirements that the parties had to fulfil in order to comply with the said constitutional formula. The 'democratic clause' applied to the parties in the constitution was controversial in the debate on the said article, a debate in which various valuations were stated from the interpretation of a similar clause in the German *Grundgesetz* by the *Bundesverfassungsgericht* (Federal Constitutional Court) (Pérez Royo 2005: 659).

Act 54/1978, on Political Parties, provided scarce development, was almost limited to repeating the constitutional formula, and allows the judicial dissolution of parties in two cases: (1) when they incur in events typified as unlawful association in the Criminal Code, and (2) when their organization or activities are against the democratic principles. Faced with the deficiency of the act, the ordinary and constitutional case law had to integrate the will of the legislator in an interpretation of the act in accordance with the constitution and, in particular, with its regulations relating to the fundamental rights.

Between 1978 and 2002, such regulations were never applied. The clearest example is that of *Batasuna* ('Unity' in Basque language), a party which legally existed since 1978 and is linked to the terrorist organization *Euskadi Ta Askatasuna* (ETA). *Batasunas* identification with the objectives and means used by the terrorists has not varied since the beginning of the Spanish democracy. Not only were there no acts against this political party, but also attitudes were tolerated which at the very least could be considered as 'disloyal' to the system, if not direct aggressions against its foundations, in collusion with the violent acts of ETA (Ferreres Comella 2004).

The arguments that justified this attitude were not convincing. The Spanish judges, for example, have said that in a constitution open to the reform of all of its articles there are no prohibited objectives. And under such conditions, the obligation in the constitution cannot be more demanding on the parties than it is, in general, on the citizens and the public authorities, Article 9(1) of the constitution. Thus, the Constitutional Court removed any substantial value from the requirement to swear and promise compliance with the constitution, included in the parliamentary rules, and allowed elected members of *Batasuna* to manipulate the formula at their will.[4] Not to abide by the constitution, or doing so half-heartedly 'due to legal imperative', is in itself a symptom of disloyalty and 'dirty play' which could have been sufficient in order to start up the prohibitive mechanisms under the parties' act. But during many years of tolerant passiveness, nobody wanted to go into more details of what the constitution wanted to say by demanding that the parties act 'democratically'.

The political passiveness, and not the lack of legal and constitutional instruments, is what led us to the situation in which action was avoided against the political parties and the courts were limited to criminal cases against the individual offences of terrorism or supporting it which, in many cases, were committed by the elected representatives (councillors or Members of Parliament) from the said parties (mainly from *Batasuna*). There was no judicial control, whether preventative or subsequent, relating to the political activities of the parties despite the fact that the Security Forces was gathering sufficient material in order to act against them. The result was to protect with all of the constitutional guarantees the behaviour of those who were making political complicity with the killing and terrorist violence of ETA an essential ingredient of their offer to the electors. And such behaviour was also generously financed with public resources for those who were eligible under the Electoral Act, as they obtained elected positions at various elections.

The attitude held towards *Batasuna* perfectly fits in to the diagnosis that, when there is an excessively tolerant attitude to the enemies of democracy, it is because there is little democratic tradition (Duch and Gibson 1992: 237 et seq.). It was thought for almost 25 years that the more tolerance shown, the more the alleged grounds justifying the terrorism would be weakened. In the legal regime governing the parties, this led to the impossibility of extracting any consequence from the lack of loyalty or hostility to the rules of the democratic play.

The New Parties Act, a Decisive Step Towards Militant Democracy

After the *Partido Popular* (Popular Party) came to power in 1996, and particularly following the rupture of the ETA ceasefire a few months later, the judicial and police net tightened around the terrorist organization and *Batasuna*. All of the leaders of *Batasuna* were convicted by the Supreme Court in December 1997 for the offence of collaboration with an armed organization.[5] In a very dubious

4 See Judgments of the Spanish Constitutional Court, STC 101/1983 and STC 119/1990.

5 The facts that gave place to the condemnation of the members of the '*Mesa*' (directive committee) of *Batasuna* consisted on the diffusion of a videotape, during the electoral campaign of 1996, where three terrorists of ETA, covered with hoods, explained the official points of view of the organization regarding the political situation of the Basque country.

judgment, the Constitutional Court quashed the conviction two years later, but not on the grounds that the offence of collaboration was not proven, but because the sentence envisaged in the Criminal Code at the time violated, in the court's opinion, the principle of proportionality, as it could not be applied on a sliding scale depending on the type of collaboration provided.[6] Although the Constitutional Court can, under certain circumstances, act as 'negative legislator', it must not interfere with the legislator's competence, such as for fixing the sentences for certain criminal offences.

The situation changed more clearly after December 2000, when the two main Spanish Parties (PP and PSOE) signed an agreement 'for freedoms and against terrorism', which sought, among other things, to promote legal reforms against the 'attitudes and behaviours which objectively constitute collaboration or incitation of terrorism'. One of the first results of the agreement was the reform of the Criminal Code to better define the offence of exaltation of terrorism. This made it possible to bring criminal charges against those promoting homage for the terrorists, a common practice of *Batasuna*.

Another of the objectives to reform the Criminal Code was to protect the victims of terrorist offences and their families against those acts which can cause them to feel 'discredited, despised or humiliated'.[7] This point of view, which refers to the dignity of certain people, concerns the minimum moral requirements requested from the democratic order of a 'civil society'. In my opinion, we are again dealing with an attempt to justify the limits of the political action in a democracy without directly resorting to the concept of 'militant democracy'. As such, the paradigms that would justify the prohibition of the parties are anti-extremism, negative republicanism and 'civil society' (Niesen 2002).

But the clearest result of the agreement was, without doubt, the new Organic Act 6/2002 on Political Parties.[8] The experience in applying and interpreting the old Parties Act through the case law over almost 25 years led to Organic Act 6/2002, expressly taking into consideration the doctrine of the Constitutional Court Judgment (STC) 56/1995, to which it refers in the Statement of Grounds. The aim is to better set out the minimum requirements for a political party to be considered democratic (as required by Article 6 of the constitution) so that the illegalization of parties, such as *Batasuna*, mere 'mouth piece' of the terrorist organization ETA, can be dealt with. But it is not an act with aspires to completely

6 See Judgment of the Spanish Constitutional Court STC 136/1999. The members of *Batasuna* had been condemned to seven years of imprisonment.

7 Article 578 of the Spanish Criminal Code: 'The exaltation or the justification for any means of public expression, or diffusion of the crimes of terrorism or of those who have participated in their execution, or the realization of acts that involve bad reputation, contempt or the humiliation of victims of the terrorist crimes or of their relatives, will be punished with a prison sentence from one to two years.'

8 For an analysis of this law, and of the prohibition of political parties in general, see Montilla Martos 2004.

regulate the regime of the parties. On this matter, main criticisms are that the act does not deal with the issue of their financing, and that there is not enough detail about the minimum requirements of their internal democratic structures. On the other hand, it is very detailed when it comes to regulating the behaviours which may give rise to a declaration of illegality.[9]

Article 9 of the Parties Act starts by generally acknowledging the parties' freedom in the exercise of their activities – with the only limit that they respect the constitutional values stated in the democratic principles and Human Rights, Article 9(1). Parties can be declared illegal, when their activities represent a threat to the democratic principles, Article 9(2). The illegalization of the party is considered as an instrument for the defence of democracy (Pérez Royo 2005: 661).

The law prohibits the conduct which, in a reiterated and serious manner, shows sympathy with violent or terrorist acts.[10] But it also refers to the ban on conduct that involves 'excluding or persecuting persons due to their ideology, religion or beliefs, nationality, race, sex or sexual orientation'. In a way, the act requires from the political parties a 'democratic commitment' expressed by clearly distancing themselves from terrorism. To do this, it bans them doing certain things and obliges them to do others, for example, to take disciplinary measures against any party member who forms part or collaborates with a terrorist or violent group.

In August 2002, shortly after the act was passed, a new mortal attack by ETA, accompanied by *Batasuna*'s normal reaction (tacit or more or less explicit support), led to the *Congreso de los Diputados* (the lower chamber of the Parliament) exercising the action for illegalization envisaged in the Parties Act before the Supreme Court. At the same time, several criminal cases were brought in the *Audiencia Nacional* (the National Court) against members of *Batasuna* for the offence of collaboration with an armed organization, which led to the preventative suspension of the party and the closure of its offices. This change of attitude was a clear step by the Spanish Constitutional system towards a militant democracy, and responded to a profound change in the general attitude against those who politically support or justify the terrorist violence.

Immediately after the Parties Act was passed, apart from starting the illegalization process of *Batasuna*, the Basque Government presented an appeal for unconstitutionality against the act which was based, among other things, on

9 I remit to the different analyses published about the law; among them, that of Vírgala Foruria 2002, pp. 203 et seq.

10 This way, for example, when one speaks of 'promoting: to justify or to acquit the attacks against the life or the integrity of people'; 'to foment, to propitiate or to legitimate the violence-like method for the attainment of political objectives'; 'to support the action of terrorist organizations politically'; 'to collaborate habitually with entities or groups that act in systematic way of agreement with a terrorist organization'; 'to use ... symbols or messages or elements that represent or they are identified with the terrorism'; to 'give support expressed or tacit politician to the terrorism'; or 'to include regularly in their directive organs or in their lists electoral condemned people for crimes of terrorism'.

denouncing that the regulation was established on a position of militant democracy and was not compatible with the constitution and attributing it with a pejorative content. This use of the term is to be rejected, but even more surprising is that both the Constitutional Court and the Supreme Court referred to it as if it was a valid accusation against which the act had to be defended. As such, both courts deny that the Spanish Constitution or the law in question establishes a militant democracy, because the Spanish Supreme Law allows for the reformation of all of its text. The defence's argument is, in fact, very weak, because it falls back on the said identification between militant democracy and the existence of intangibility clause, and because it is exclusively based on a single model of a 'militant democracy': the German. In Germany, a party must be prohibited even though 'according to common sense, there is no perspective that in the near future the party is going to be able carry out its unconstitutional goal'.[11] With this interpretation, the Constitutional Court clears the doubt: it is not a condition that the party represents a specific danger. If this was not the case, it would be asking too much of the court, insofar as it would not be a judgable issue, but rather politically (Höver 1975: 28). It is true that the Spanish model does not reach this extreme. But this does not mean that it must be absolutely denied that the Spanish model is a militant democracy.

The Spanish Case Law on Political Parties and the Militant Democracy

There is no democracy without political pluralism.[12] In coherence with this and with Article 1 of the Spanish Constitution, the Spanish Constitutional Court has stated that 'the widening of the regulations to all political options that can and want to grow and articulate themselves in the social reality constitutes a value which must be protected and encouraged'.[13] The political parties are the clearest manifestation of political pluralism. This is also established in the Spanish Constitution when it states in its Article 6 that the parties 'express' the said pluralism. The Constitutional Court acknowledged

> the importance given to the political parties within the constitutional system, and the protection of their existence and their functions, not only from the individual dimension of the right to constitute them and actively participate in them, but also in accordance to the existence of the parties system as essential base for the performance of the political pluralism.[14]

---

11 BVerfGE 5, 85 (142, 143). See, in this sense, Meier 1993: 271.

12 Judgment of the European Court of Human Rights *Refah Partisi (the Welfare Party) et al. v. Turkey* [GC] (13 February 2003), nos. 41340/98, 41342/98, 41343/98 and 41344/98, CEDH/ECHR 2003-II.

13 Judgment of the Spanish Constitutional Court of 12 March 2003.

14 Judgments of the Spanish Constitutional Court: STC 85/1986 and STC 15/2000.

But the European Court of Human Rights has also confirmed the essential role of the parties 'in order to maintain the pluralism and proper functioning of the democracy'.[15] As such, the freedom to create parties is proclaimed in the same Article 6 of the constitution.

Accompanying this freedom of parties is another element that is also in the service of the pluralism, which is the freedom of expression of the political groups. The European Court of Human Rights has emphasized that

> protecting opinions and the freedom to express them in the sense of article 10 of the Convention constitutes one of the objectives of the freedom to meet and association enshrined in article 11. This is applied more extensively in the case of political parties in view of their essential role in maintaining pluralism and the proper functioning of the democracy.[16]

But the pre-eminent position of pluralism in the Spanish Constitutional regulations does not mean that pluralism must be absolute and unlimited. There is behaviour and political positions which do not enjoy the cover of the said superior value of the regulations. The pluralism cannot justify, under any circumstances, the violation of other people's rights or the defence of positions which involve infringing certain rights, for example, of the minorities. The pluralism cannot be used precisely to deny the legitimate aspirations of others to exercise their rights, including those deriving from pluralism itself. 'Pluralism and democracy are based on a commitment which requires various concessions by the individuals and groups of individuals which must at times accept some limitation on the freedoms that they enjoy in order to guarantee the greater stability of the country as a whole'.[17]

However, when it comes to justifying the limits of pluralism and, therefore, the possible banning of political groups, the Spanish Courts have at all times avoided basing these limits on any type of militant democracy. The Spanish Constitutional Court held in 2003 that in our constitutional rules

> there is no space for a 'militant democracy' model … meaning a model in which positive adhesion to the regulations and, above all to the Constitution is imposed, which goes beyond respect,

15 Judgments of the European Court of Human Rights, *Socialist Party et al. v. Turkey* (25 May 1998) and *Refah Partisi (the Welfare Party) et al. v. Turkey* [GC] (13 February 2003), nos. 41340/98, 41342/98, 41343/98 and 41344/98, CEDH/ECHR 2003-II.

16 Judgment of the European Court of Human Rights *Refah Partisi (the Welfare Party) et al. v. Turkey*. In another Judgment the European Court says that the freedom of speech, beautiful for all, it is particularly it for the political parties and their active members: see Judgment of the European Court of Human Rights *United Communist Party et al. v. Turkey* (30 January 1998).

17 Decision of the European Court of Human Rights *Petersen v. Germany* (22 November 2001), no. 39793/98, CEDH/ECHR 2001-XII.

because what is lacking is

> the inexcusable supposition of the existence of a regulatory nucleus inaccessible to the constitutional reform procedures which, due to their intangibility, may become autonomous parameters of judicial correction, so that the mere intention to affect it would convert the behaviour in unlawful.[18]

Following this doctrine, the Spanish Supreme Court stated that the Spanish Constitution has not chosen a system of 'militant democracy, but rather an extremely tolerant system, if you want "aggressively" tolerant, in favour of all political postulates'.[19]

Following this thesis, the Supreme Court held that

> in our constitutional system, there is room for all ideas and all political projects even, in the words of the European Court of Human Rights (Judgments of 7th December 1976 and 13th February 2003), those which 'offend, shock or worry'. There is even room, unlike in other codes, for those ideas which are contrary to the constitutional system, seeking to substitute or derogate or advocate formulas for territorial organization other than those chosen in the constitution.

The court bases this opinion on the doctrine of the European Court of Human Rights, according to

> the fact that a group of persons requests autonomy or even secession of part of the territory of the country, and thereby requires constitutional and fundamental territorial changes, does not automatically justify the prohibition of its meetings.[20]

As a result of this thesis, the Supreme Court went on to affirm that the only limit on pluralism is the prohibition of the use of violence and encroachment on the fundamental rights of others.[21] However, the Supreme Court itself recognizes that Organic Act 6/2002 'guarantees the supremacy of the constitution and the democratic principles in relation to the activity of the political parties'. It later appears to mean more than that held by the court, and does not rest with the mere rejection of violence. The Supreme Court denies in this context that one can talk of 'political offences' or 'political criminals' as upheld by some sectors and is still

18 Judgment of the Spanish Constitutional Court of 12 March 2003.

19 Judgment of the Spanish Supreme Court of 27 March 2003 (*Batasuna* case).

20 Judgment of the European Court of Human Rights *Stankov and the United Macedonian Organisation Ilinden v. Bulgaria* (2 October 2001), nos. 29221/95 and 29225/95 (Sect. 1), CEDH/ECHR 2001-IX.

21 Judgment of the Spanish Supreme Court of 3 February 2003.

maintained in Spain. What both courts, in my opinion, are in fact denying is that Spain is a militant democracy like Germany, which we would have to agree with.

The declaration of grounds in Organic Act 6/2002, regulating the Political Parties considers that 'any project or object is understood compatible with the constitution' provided that 'it is not defended by an activity that violates the democratic principles or the fundamental rights of the citizens'. That same declaration later ratifies, giving plentiful reasons which are not, however, superfluous, that 'the aim is clearly not to prohibit the defence of ideas or doctrines, however, far removed from the constitutional framework and even if they question it'. This is another paragraph which, without doubt, goes beyond a mere manifestation of pluralism and its limits. It is acknowledging that the 'democratic principles' and the 'fundamental rights of the citizens' cannot be affected by the activity of the political parties, in other words, they will not be covered by political pluralism and its resulting freedom of parties.

The regulation does not establish grounds for banning parties because they defend certain ideas, but because their activity violates the democratic principles, because that activity seeks to deteriorate or destroy the regime of freedoms or makes it impossible or eliminates the democratic system, and due to the performance of a series of 'conducts', performed in a repeated and serious manner, which the law describes in detail. This distinction between a hypothetically unlimited 'freedom of ideas' and a limited 'freedom of action' is another element that leads some to affirm that there is no 'militant democracy' in Spain because, just like the Constitutional Court, they identify the existence of this principle with that of an 'intangibility clause' in the constitution, which is not the case in the Spanish Constitution.

Both the ordinary and the constitutional case law is based on another line of arguments in order to justify the illegalization of political parties, avoiding resorting to the idea of militant democracy. It is true – they say – and it could not be otherwise, that violence is incompatible with political freedom, and cannot be covered by it. The ECHR stated that

> a political party whose leaders incite resort to violence or who put forward a political project which does not respect one or more of the rules of democracy or which considers its destruction, as well as disdain of the rights and freedoms that it recognises, can not call on the protection of the constitution against the sanctions imposed for these reasons.[22]

The same court has recognized the difficulty in fighting against violent attitudes and terrorism,[23] and stated that 'the victory over terrorism is in the maximum public interest in a democratic society'.

22 Judgment of the European Court of Human Rights *Refah Partisi (the Welfare Party) et al. v. Turkey* (31 Juli 2001), nos. 41340/98, 41342/98, 41343/98 and 41344/98.

23 Judgments of the European Court of Human Rights *Aksoy v. Turkey* (18 December 1996), *United Communist Party et al. v. Turkey* (30 January 1998), *Refah Partisi (the Welfare Party) et al. v. Turkey* (31 Juli 2001).

Invoking violence or its justification therefore not only authorizes the restrictions on the activities of the political parties, but also on their additional freedom of expression. The European Court of Human Rights has also stated that

> an essential factor to take into account is the issue of whether there has been a call to the use of violence, an uprising or any other form of rejection of the democratic principles … when there has been incitation of violence against a person, public agent or sector of the population, the State authorities enjoy the widest margin of appreciation when examining the need to interfere in the freedom of expression.[24]

These attitudes cannot be isolated,[25] but repeated or within a normal context of collaboration with terrorist groups, as is the case of *Batasuna* in Spain, and was recognized by both the Constitutional and the Supreme Court.

In short, the two courts limit themselves to justifying the existence and the application of the new Parties Act in the requirement to reject violent conduct, but deny that the Spanish model is a militant democracy and that the Parties Act is a step towards it, with which they accept the sense that this expression has received, docile and acritically, from one sector of the doctrine. It was perhaps Ignacio de Otto y Pardo who was one of the first to hold that in Spain there is no guarantee that could uphold the viability of this imbalance between legality and legitimacy, that there are no singular instruments which make militant democracy a principle, and as such neither are there guarantees and, therefore, the possibility of extracting from the general drafting of Article 9(1) of the Spanish Constitution a adhesion to said postulates must be categorically denied (De Otto y Pardo 1985: 45). But again I insist, we are talking about a specific model of militant democracy, which is the German model. De Otto y Pardo's thesis was later taken on, to a greater or lesser extent, by Jiménez Campo (1981: 173); Solozábal Echavarria (1985: 158 et seq.); and Aragón Reyes (1990: 49–59), and is summed up in the idea that in Spain it would not be constitutionally lawful to establish limits on the programmes or ideas of the political parties given that in our constitution there are no material limits for its reformation.

Another more recent example is in the interpretation of Rodríguez-Zapata, when he reported some risk that the militant democracy would have:

24 Judgment of the European Court of Human Rights *Stankov and the United Macedonian Organisation Ilinden v. Bulgaria* (2 October 2001), nos. 29221/95 and 29225/95 (Section 1), CEDH/ECHR 2001-IX.

25 Judgments of the European Court of Human Rights *Dicle pour le Parti de la démocratie c. Turquie v. Turkey* (10 December 2002), no. 25141/94 (Sect. 4), *Stankov and the United Macedonian Organisation Ilinden v. Bulgaria* (2 October 2001), nos. 29221/95 and 29225/95 (Section 1), CEDH/ECHR 2001-IX, *Incal v. Turkey* (9 June 1998).

> The greatest risk against which we have to be prepared and from which we have to protect our constitutional model if we wish to keep it healthy, is that a limitation on political parties starts a dynamic of subtraction. What I am trying to say is that the exclusion of the enemies of the democratic order is followed by the exclusion of the opposition and then of the dissenters, until we pervert our system and only allow for the adhesion to certain principles and values. Defending the constitution is to guarantee it against that risk. Guarantee, in short, that it never stops being a framework of coincidences where there is space for all imaginable ideas and values with the only condition that they inexcusably respect the rules of democratic play.

After reporting these risks, according to the author, it falls to the Constitutional Court to save the situation: 'The risk of that perversion has been robustly cleared. In fact, judgment 48/2003 … has underlined that there is no space amongst us for the concept of *militant or combative democracy*' (Rodríguez-Zapata 2003: 124 et seq.). In short, it appears that the concept of militant democracy is a risk to be avoided.

The most traditional conception of militant democracy is thus assumed, and it is attributed with a pejorative nuance which is not correct. It also seeks to show that, given that in the Spanish Constitution everything can be reformed, everything can be defended provided that the means are lawful. The aforementioned author says that

> militant democracy requires that the very constitution imposes material limits on its aggravated reform procedure, declaring unviable the revision projects which affect certain material decisions, values or principles, which thereby become indisputable and nonnegotiable.

But it does not have to be like this. All democracies need instruments of legal defence, and their degree of 'combativity' or 'militancy' may have nuances. And the German model is not the only militant democracy; rather it can be held that there are other types. It is true that the German model would set out some problems. When trying to consider the aims of a party according to its ideological programmatic suitability to that established in the constitution and in the legal code, we are entering delicate ground. As Klaus Stern says about the German experience, there is always the question of whether the practical application of this type of control, in the hands of the Federal Constitutional Court, 'has managed a theoretically satisfactory synthesis between militant democracy and the idea of democratic parliamentary state governed by the rule of law inspired by mutual tolerance' (Stern 1987: 404).

On this matter, it is true that Article 6 does not expressly demand from the political parties a duty to adhere to the ideological postulates contained in the constitution, in the German sense of militant democracy, but this does not mean that there are not other mechanisms for defending democracy which can also be understood as those of a militant democracy (Vírgala Foruria 2004). It has been assumed that the only possible model of militant democracy is the German one; however, in my opinion this is not the case. As opposed to the thesis of the Spanish doctrinal sector, which I have just referred to, there is the other sector that defends the existence of implicit material limits on constitutional reform, deriving from the intrinsic logic of the constitutional state and which would justify the constitutional legitimacy of the control of the ideology of the political parties. Hence, according to Santamaría Pastor, Article 6 of the constitution 'points towards the possibility of configuring the requirement of respect of the constitution as the requirement for a certain degree of adhesion to its basic principles which goes beyond merely formal compliance' (Santamaría Pastor 2001: 100). Along the same lines are Alzaga Villamil (1978: 121), Morodo and Lucas Murillo de la Cueva (2001: 137). More recently, Tajadura Tejada argues that there are implicit material limits on constitutional reform, and from these limits it is deduced that the legislator can impose limits on the political programmes and party ideologies and, of course, on the activity of the parties (Tajadura Tejada 2004: 97 et seq.).

In any event, as our highest courts are aligned with the first doctrinal sector and refuse to accept the possibility that there is a constitutional basis for establishing ideological limits on the parties, they reject any line of argument that in this case – and in other similar cases – would have been decisive. As Revenga Sánchez (2005: 31) has rightly said

> the resistance of the legal arguments to classify as militant a democracy which has decided to commit itself to the fight against terrorism, can only be understood as the tribute that we continue paying to doctrinal constructions from a period which is not our own.

As can be seen from my opinions given above, I believe that the Spanish democracy can be considered as militant, as can any other democracy that wishes, in the sense that it has instruments to defend its own survival. As such the Preamble, Articles 1; 9(2); 10; etc. set up the idea of the constituent as an advanced democracy which promotes certain values; in a single word: the constituent sets up a militant democracy which is based on a series of values that the very constitution promotes; personal dignity and the rights of the person, which promotes a policy of real and effective equality and freedom.

Another weak point in the Constitutional Court's line of arguments is the insistence in emphasizing that the law does not persecute ideas. The critics of the Parties Act (starting with the Basque Government) say that the act was passed to 'persecute ideas', and that 'the ideas do not commit offences'. The court says that this is not the case, but it does not appear that this is an admissible line of arguments. Think, for example, about a party which, within its ideological ideas, considers terrorist violence legitimate against another type of institutional or other type of violence and even defends a constitutional reform which makes violence a legitimate instrument. Would the constitution and the political pluralism proclaimed in it cover this type of idea?

It has been said that advocating political pluralism as a superior value does not mean defending all kinds of political organizations, but rather all types of ideologies. But this disregards that, when it comes to organizing to defend these ideas, the limits of political pluralism must be taken into consideration, given that there is no space for paramilitary or secret organizations, or those created to commit offences, or terrorist organizations or those that are used as their accomplices or as fronts.

The new Parties Act is a step towards militancy as opposed to complicity vis-à-vis terrorism, but it needs judicial decisions in order to be effective. This has led to a complex situation because the *Batasuna* environment, which enjoys considerable popular support (around 10–15 per cent) in the Basque Country and Navarra, tries to rearticulate itself for the elections through new parties and platforms every time elections are called. The act envisaged such contingencies by adding to the Electoral Act a paragraph which prohibits the presentation of lists of candidates to 'electoral groups which *de facto* continue or succeed the activity of a party judicially declared illegal'.[26] This has led to numerous judicial decisions, both from the Supreme Court and from the Constitutional Court.[27] Many of these cases have reached the European Court of Human Rights, which recently resolved already some of them. As expected, this Court has confirmed the Spanish Courts' decisions which are extensively supported by the case law from Strasbourg, particularly that relating to the prohibition of parties in Turkey.[28]

In any event, the Constitutional Court identifies pluralism as the legitimacy of different political and governance options within the constitutional limits. The problem is whether these limits are only procedural or there are other types (for example, material). Some authors have turned to another concept to justify the existence of implied limits: the concept of constitutional loyalty.

With this line of arguments, similar to the Constitutional Court, the legislative reforms and the judicial actions tending to cleanse the political party system are justified, excluding those that do not adjust – due to their means or to their objectives

26 Article 44(4) of the Electoral Act, according to the writing given to the same one by the Additional Disposition 2ª of the Organic Act 6/2002 on Political Parties.

27 See Judgments of the Spanish Constitutional Court STC 48/2003 of 12 March 2003, STC 85/2003, of 8 May 2003 and Judgments of the Spanish Supreme Court of 27 March 2003 and 3 May 2003.

28 Judgments of the European Court of Human Rights *Aksoy v. Turkey* (18 December 1996); *United Communist Party and others v. Turkey* (30 January 1998); *Refah Partisi (the Welfare Party) et al. v. Turkey* (31 July 2001); *Sadak and others v. Turkey* (no. 2) (11 June 2002) nos. 25144/94, 26149/95 to 26154/95, 27100/95 and 27101/95 (Section 4); CEDH/ECHR 2002-IV; *Dicle pour le Parti de la démocratie c. Turquie v. Turkey* (10 December 2002), no. 25141/94 (Section 4); *Socialist Party et al. v. Turkey*, Judgment of 25 May 1998; *Freedom and Democracy Party (ÖZDEP) v. Turkey*, Judgment of 8 December 1999; *Yazar, Karatas, Aksoy and the People's Labour Party (HEP) v. Turkey*, Judgment of 9 April 2002; *Herri Batasuna and Batasuna v. Spain; Etxeberria, Barrena Arza, Nafarroako Autodeterminazio Bilgunea and others v. Spain; Herritarren Zerrenda v. Spain*, Judgments of 30 June 2009.

– to the concept of political party established in Article 6 of the constitution or serve the objectives of political participation which in this rule are set up as their true and ultimate *raison d'être* (Rodríguez-Zapata 2003: 127). But this concept of 'constitutional loyalty' is very close to that of 'militant democracy' in the broad sense that we are defending here.

It has also to be emphasized that, although our constitution does not contain intangibility clauses, there are implicit limits on constitutional reform because there are changes and modifications that break up democracy and devastate the constitution (Torres del Moral 2004a: 175–81, 2004b: 148 et seq.). If the final result of a reform is not democratic, we would stop being able to talk about a constitutional regime or a true constitution. There are therefore some limits. Because it is not *per se* a constitution which in any country is enacted as such, nor is a simple method of adopting decision by majority a democracy.

Democracy must be defended against those who deny freedom, equality and justice for others, and from those who combat the pluralism of others in the name of their own right to pluralism, which, more than a contradiction, is the highest form of political cynicism. Hence there can be no non-militant democracy. That would be a contradictory democracy; a democracy under suspicion; a 'pseudo-democracy'. And the Spanish Constitution is far from being like this.

References

Alzaga Villamil, Oscar (1978) *La Constitución española de 1978.* Madrid: Civitas.

Aragón Reyes, Manuel (1990) *Constitución y Democracia.* Madrid: Tecnos.

Capoccia, Giovanni (2001) 'Defending Democracy: Reactions to Political Extremism in Inter-War Europe', *European Journal of Political Research* 39(4): 431–60.

Denninger, Erhard (2001) 'Democracia militante y defensa de la Constitución', in Ernst Benda, Werner Maihofer, Hans-Jochen Vogel, Konrad Hesse and Wolfgang Heyde (eds) *Manual de Derecho Constitucional.* Madrid: Marcial Pons, 445–58.

Duch, Raymond M. and Gibson, James L. (1992) 'Putting Up With Fascism in Western Europe: A Comparative, Cross-Level Analysis of Political Tolerance', *Western Political Quarterly* 45, 237–73.

Ferreres Comella, Victor (2004) 'The New Regulation of Political Parties in Spain, and the Decision to Outlaw Batasuna', in András Sajó (ed.) *Militant Democracy.* Utrecht: Eleven International Publishing, 133–56.

Fox, Gregory H. and Nolte, Georg (1995) 'Intolerant Democracies', *Harvard International Law Journal* 36(1): 1–70.

García Pelayo, Manuel (1995) *Las transformaciones del estado contemporáneo.* Madrid: Alianza Editorial.

Hernández Gil, Antonio (1982) *El cambio político español y la Constitución.* Barcelona: Planeta.

Höver, Bernd (1975) *Das Parteiverbot und seine rechtlichen Folgen.* Bonn: Rechts- und Staatswissenschaftliche Fakultät.

Jiménez Campo, Javier (1981) 'La intervención estatal del pluralismo (Notas a una sentencia del Tribunal Constitucional', *Revista Española de Derecho Constitucional*) 1981(1): 161–83.

Lameyer, Johannes (1978) *Streitbare Demokratie.* Berlin: Duncker and Humblot.

Loewenstein, Karl (1937a) 'Militant Democracy and Fundamental Rights I', *American Political Science Review* 31(3): 417–32.

Loewenstein, Karl (1937b) 'Militant Democracy and Fundamental Rights II', *American Political Science Review* 31(4): 638–58.

Meier, Horst (1993) *Parteiverbote und demokratische Republik: Zur Interpretation und Kritik von Art. 21 Abs. 2 des Grundgesetzes.* Baden Baden: Nomos.

Montilla Martos, José Antonio (coord.) (2004) *La prohibición de partidos políticos.* Universidad de Almería.

Morodo, Raúl and Lucas Murillo de la Cueva, Pablo (2001) *El ordenamiento constitucional de los partidos políticos.* México: Universidad Nacional Autónoma de México.

Niesen, Peter (2002) 'Anti-Extremism, Negative Republicanism, Civic Society: Three Paradigms for Banning Political Parties – Parts I and II', *German Law Journal*, 3(7) (at http://www.germanlawjournal.com).

De Otto y Pardo, Ignacio (1985) *Defensa de la Constitución y Partidos Políticos.* Madrid: Centro de Estudios Constitucionales.

Pérez Royo, Javier (2005) *Curso de Derecho Constitucional*, 10th edn. Madrid: Marcial Pons.

Revenga Sánchez, Miguel (2005) 'El tránsito hacia (y la lucha por) la democracia militante en España', *Revista de Derecho Político* 62, 11–31.

Rodríguez-Zapata, Jorge (2003) 'Partidos políticos y democracia combativa', *Revista valenciana d'estudis autonomics*, 39–40, 122–135.

Rousseau, Jean-Jacques (1762 [1988]) *Du Contrat Social, Book I* (Spanish edition *El contrato social*). Madrid: Tecnos.

Sani, Giacomo and Sartori, Giovanni (1983) 'Polarisation, Fragmentation and Competition in Western Democracies', in Hans Daalder and Peter Mair (eds) *Western European Party Systems: Continuity and Change.* London: Sage, 307–40; Spanish version in *Revista de derecho político* 1980 (7): 7–37.

Santamaría Pastor, Juan Alfonso (2001) 'Comentario al artículo 6 de la Constitución', in Garrido Falla, Fernando (dir.) *Comentarios a la Constitución*, 3rd edn. Madrid: Civitas.

Sartori, Giovanni (1965) *Democratic Theory.* New York: Praeger.

Schmidt, Thomas (1983) *Die Freiheit verfassungswidriger Parteien und Vereinigungen. Zur Schrankenlehre im Rahmen von Art. 21 Abs. 2 und Abs. 2 GG.* Berlin: Duncker and Humblot.

Schmitt, Carl (1932) *Legalität und Legitimität.* Berlin: Duncker and Humblot.

Solozábal Echavarria, Juan José (1985) 'Sobre la constitucionalización de los partidos políticos en el Derecho Constitucional y en el ordenamiento español', *Revista de Estudios Políticos* 45, 155–64.

Stern, Klaus (1987) *Derecho del Estado de la República Federal Alemana.* Madrid: CEC.

Tajadura Tejada, Javier (1997) *El preámbulo constitucional.* Granada: Comares.

Tajadura Tejada, Javier (2004) *Partidos políticos y constitución.* Madrid: Civitas.

Torres del Moral, Antonio (2004a) *Estado de Derecho y democracia de partidos*, 2nd edn. Madrid: Servicio de Publicaciones de la Universidad Complutense.

Torres del Moral, Antonio (2004b) *Principios de Derecho Constitucional Español*, 5th edn. Madrid: Servicio de Publicaciones de la Universidad Complutense.

Torres del Moral, Antonio (2006) 'Democracia militante', in Manuel Carrasco Durán, Francisco Javier Pérez Royo, Joaquín Urías Martínez and Manuel José Terol Becerra (eds) *Derecho constitucional para el siglo XXI: actas del VIII Congreso Iberoamericano de Derecho Constitucional, vol. I.* Navarra: Thomson-Aranzadi, 209–24.

Vírgala Foruria, Eduardo (2002) 'Los Partidos políticos ilícitos tras la LO 6/2002', *Teoría y Realidad Constitucional* (10–11): 203–62.

Vírgala Foruria, Eduardo (2004) 'Los límites constitucionales a los partidos políticos en la LO 6/2002', in José Antonio Montilla Martos (coord.) *La prohibición de partidos políticos.* Universidad de Almería, 45–98.

Chapter 12
Turkey

Bertil Emrah Oder

Roots of 'Militant Democracy' in Turkey: Modernity, Authoritarianism and Europeanization

'Militant democracy', put as a pressing need for survival of democracy in Turkish constitutional discourse, became widely popular after the dissolution of the *Refah Partisi* (Welfare Party) in 1998. Referring to this concept explicitly before the European Court of Human Rights (ECHR), the government asserted that, when confronted with the risk that political Islam represented for a democratic system based on human rights, the system was entitled to take measures to protect itself from the danger. However, long before its popularity, militant democracy has been co-determinate of the Turkish political paradigm whose germination is driven by radical political changes including Turkish revolution and modernization, authoritarian political culture as well as military coups that broke down constitutional continuity in 1960 and 1980.

Leaving aside political turbulences and historical details, the factors germinating and fostering militant democracy in Turkey are contradictory in their nature. First, modernization values, especially secularism and gender equality, mostly intersect with the liberal democratic values to be protected. Second, in different veils, authoritarian approaches excluding plurality and limiting individual development became decisive for patterns of militant stand. Since this contradiction is deeply embedded in political imagination, studying militant roots of democracy in Turkey inevitably covers almost all ingredients of Turkish Constitutional Law – which means a journey through the constitutional patchwork of the republican era, that is the 1921 Constitution (as amended in 1923) and the 1924, 1961 and 1982 Constitutions.

There is no doubt that the military intervention in 1980 has contributed tendencies of authoritarianism by creating a new form of it that converts modernization values and the unitary state into a Turkish–Islamic genre. The transformation of constitutional law, which was initiated by the 1995 amendments as regards political participation and consolidated by 2001 amendments, is a postponed counter-attack against 1980 authoritarianism. In spite of this, it keeps with the basic structure of the 1982 Constitution. At sub-constitutional level, constitutional liberalization has been implemented through legislative packages after 2001, following the National Programme prepared to comply with political Copenhagen criteria as provided in the Accession Partnership with the European Union.

The following observations attempt to shed light over the complex nature and operation of militant democracy in Turkey. Here this contribution is twofold: first, the current pattern of the Turkish militant stand is the product of a trilogy: Modernity, Authoritarianism and Europeanization. Second, 'militant democracy' is definitely a ubiquitous feature of the Turkish legal system, establishing a defensive network of norms both at constitutional and sub-constitutional level. This leads to specifying Turkey among 'militant substantive democracies' where an 'unalterable core' of the constitution aims to protect the democratic regime from its internal opponents.

Interaction of Constitutional Values and 'Militant Democracy' in the 1982 Constitution

Establishing Constitutional Boundaries for Ideological Pluralism in the Preamble

The 1982 Constitution sets forth the constitutional boundaries for ideological pluralism in its Preamble through both juridical and meta-juridical references. These boundaries do not only clarify legal and political inspirations of the *pouvoir constituant,* but also 'ideas, beliefs and resolutions' which are to be regarded in constitutional interpretation and implementation. The explicit wording of the Preamble, in the first instance, orders that the constitution should be understood to embody legal and political choices in the Preamble. Second, it speaks of respect and absolute loyalty to the letter and spirit of the constitution that is in accordance with 'ideas, beliefs and resolutions' within the Preamble.[1] The constitutional amendment in 1995 provided a less militant wording in the Preamble. The constitutional amendment in 2001, including the Preamble, which represents the major constitutional shift towards a liberal understanding for restriction of fundamental rights and freedoms, is a follow-up of the 1995 attempt. The amendment package in 1995 rewrote some parts of the Preamble and removed references, such as 'sacred Turkish state', 'separatist, destructive and bloody civil war unprecedented in the Republican era', that is the anarchy in 1980, or 'military body' (the National Security Council), and consultative assembly as 'legitimate representatives of the nation'. In 2001, a phrase, which signals the exclusive nature of Turkish constitutional paradigm and reveals non-liberal political choice in case of freedom of expression, has been removed. Before the amendment, paragraph 5 of the Preamble stated:

> no protection shall be afforded to *thoughts and opinions* contrary to Turkish national interests; the principle of the existence of Turkey as an indivisible

1 For elaboration of the Preamble as a reference norm in constitutional review, see Yüzbaşıoğlu 1993: 130–31.

> entity with its state and territory; Turkish historical and moral values; and the nationalism, and principles, reforms and modernism of Atatürk [emphasis added].

Without dealing with the values protected, the 2001 amendment replaced the phrase 'thoughts and opinions' with 'activities'. The first amendment draft prepared by the Inter-Party Committee suggested a term, namely 'conduct', which is regarded as availing a more protective interpretation for the freedom of expression. However, the Constitutional Committee did not follow the first draft and preferred the term 'activities' that inclines to wording in Article 17 of the European Convention of Human Rights (EConvHR) on the abuse of rights.[2] Article 17 of EConvHR prohibits 'any activity or any act' aimed at the destruction of rights or freedoms set forth in the convention or at their limitation to a greater extend than is provided for in the convention. It is also remarkable that the term 'activities' – compared with the term 'conduct' – could easily be understood as cumulative and deliberate 'expressions' against the values and principles set forth in the Preamble. Therefore, an absolute value of the freedom of expression is not the political choice of the amendment.

The constitutional amendment in 2001 does not touch the 'ideas, beliefs and the resolutions' as constitutional values preserved in the Preamble. Some of those values are put into concrete terms in specific constitutional norms; they are non-ideological and available for objective methods of constitutional interpretation. Those can be observed especially in the protection of national sovereignty; an unitary state; the separation of state powers; the rule of law including the supremacy of the constitution; and an emphasis on secularism requiring no interference of religious feelings in state affairs and politics. As regards Atatürk nationalism, there exists, on the one hand, a protection clause in Article 2 of the constitution as one of the irrevocable principles of the Republic. On the other hand, the definition of Turkish citizenship in Article 66 of the constitution as a constitutional bond of a person to the state identifies the non-ethnic, non-racist and non-religious nature of such nationalism. Besides, Atatürk's reforms in form of modernization laws are preserved through a specific clause (Article 174 of the Constitution). The Preamble also contains principles which ascertain a basic concordance of the constitutional order with international law. The implicit reference to the equality of states and a peaceful coexistence of the international community as prescribed in the United Nations Charter could be observed in different paragraphs. Paragraph 2 of the Preamble defines Turkey as a full and honourable member of the 'world family

2 During the discussions in the Constitutional Committee the daily newspapers published a letter of 'sensitivities' which was submitted by the Chief of the General Staff to the Prime Minister. It was argued that the Constitutional Committee did not ignore these 'sensitivities' and took them into consideration in replacing the phrase 'thoughts and opinions', see, for example, 'Reform Paketinde Askerin Istediği Oldu', *Radikal*, 20 September 2001: 10.

of nations'. In paragraph 7, there is a reference to a well-known call of Atatürk: 'Peace at home, peace in the world'.

The most disputable feature of constitutional values set forth in the Preamble is to be found in purely ideological references that reproduce the Turkish–Islamic genre of national conservative thought. In fact, it can be suggested that they also contradict the democratic–liberal interpretation of the Kemalist modernization process and represent an authoritarian approach that regards the individual freedom as less favourable. Here, purely ideological (Turkish–Islamic), defensive and even vague concepts are striking: the Preamble speaks of 'Turkish national interests' and 'national and spiritual values of Turkishness'.[3] A juridical interpretation of those values is impossible as they always interact with political choices and presuppose a political question. To classify such values as 'reference norms' endangers the system's constitutionality, since they push judges to a review of appropriateness which leads to questioning constitutional authority of their judgments. Further challenges of the interpretation of such values become obvious in the first headscarf case (*Headscarf I*).[4] Here, the majority opinion of the Constitutional Court defends the pure interpretation of the secular state to provide 'educational peace' in universities and other higher education institutions without any reference to 'Turkish historical and spiritual values'. However, in his dissenting opinion, Judge *Çınarlı* refers explicitly to the Preamble to reach an opposite conclusion: 'To let headscarf free complies with Turkish historical and spiritual values, since our grandmothers and mothers have worn it for centuries.'[5]

It is also remarkable that in the constitutional jurisdiction the 'Turkish national interest' as a component of the Preamble is one of the decisive references in review of laws as regards foreigners' ownership of real property.[6] In such cases, constitutional values, such as state independence, territorial integrity, state security and reciprocity in international relations are concurring references.

Moreover, through references, such as 'national culture', 'national honour, pride, joy and grief' or 'realization of national life' in paragraphs 6 and 7, the Preamble puts emphasis on collectivity and solidarity. Accordingly, it is the birthright of every Turkish citizen to lead an honourable life and develop his or her material and spiritual resources pursuant to 'national culture', civilization and the rule of law through the exercise of fundamental rights and freedoms, and in conformity with equality and social justice. However, the Turkish citizens as a collective are united in 'national honour and pride, in national joy and grief, in their rights and duties towards their existence as a nation, in blessings and burdens, and in every realization of national life'. Those references were widely criticized

3 For critical review of those references and their meta-juridical nature, see especially Erdoğan 2004: 191–2; Hakyemez 2000: 163–5; Özbudun 2002a: 72; Parla 1993: 218–19; Sabuncu 2004: 17–19; Tanör 1986: 130–34, 1994: 198, 2004: 68–71.

4 E. 1989/1, K. 1989/12, K.t. 7 March 1989, AYMKD 25, 141–158.

5 E. 1989/1, K. 1989/12, K.t. 7 March 1989, AYMKD 25, 159.

6 E. 2003/70, K. 2005/14, K.t. 14 March 2005, AYMKD 41, 405.

because that intellectual, ideological, cultural and even psychological imagination of the individual and society is coded and predetermined. Especially the reference to national culture within the framework of the right to self-development of 'Turkish citizen' cannot be regarded as a legitimate limit in a democratic society. Therefore, the 1982 Constitution is conceived as an attempt to build an authoritarian and global politico-social model or project for the state and the individual.

Disputable references in the 1982 Constitution changed also the meaning of constitutionalism in Turkey established by the 1961 Constitution which emphasized liberal and democratic values in its Preamble.[7] Therefore, especially in early constitutional writings, the descriptions of 'legal authoritarianism' and 'anti-constitution' for evaluation of the 1982 Constitution are remarkable.[8] Ideological reflections in the Preamble are still seen as 'political favouring of the state' which aims at establishing a state mandated society and enhancing sociocultural as well as ideological homogeneity.

Shortly after the 1982 Constitution was put into effect, the Constitutional Court intensively supported the ideological boundaries of the Preamble by regarding the Preamble as an absolute imperative and defining national interests as priorities which overwhelm any other necessity in constitutional framework.[9] In addition to that, the court held that the principles set forth in the Preamble belong to the irrevocable principles of the republic,[10] and interpreted the concrete constitutional values – such as Atatürk's principles and reforms – as an absolute prohibition for abstract political priorities in programmes of political parties.[11] The philosophy and basic pillar of the constitution is found in Atatürk's principles and reforms in order to strengthen the legal reasoning for the dissolution of an anti-laic political party, the *Huzur Partisi*. Such interpretation has been defined as an existence of an 'official ideology' in the 1982 Constitution that presupposes an exclusive political game and, consequently, a 'consolidated system' limiting political plurality.

Irrevocable Constitutional Principles

In general, Article 4 of the 1982 Constitution defines the provisions in Articles 1, 2 and 3 as irrevocable and excluded from future amendments and amendment

7 The Preamble of 1961 emphasizes 'peace and welfare of individual and society' instead of 'self-development of Turkish citizens pursuant to national culture'. Besides, it makes reference to following constitutional values: 'human rights and freedoms; national solidarity; social justice; establishing democratic state based on rule of law with its all legal and social fundamentals'. Here, democratic state based on rule of law is recognized as a pre-requisite for realization of other constitutional values cited.

8 See especially Tanör and Sağlam, cited by Tanör 1986: 154–5, footnote 34.

9 E. 1983/2, K. 1983/2, K.t. 25 October 1983, AYMKD 20, 363; E. 1984/14, K. 1985/7, K.t. 13 June 1985, AYMKD 21, 173.

10 E. 1984/14, K. 1985/7, K.t. 13 June 1985, AYMKD 21, 173; E. 2003/70, K. 2005/14, K.t. 14 March 2005, AYMKD 41, 405.

11 E. 1983/2, K. 1983/2, K.t. 25 October 1983, AYMKD 20, 363.

proposals. These provisions cover the form of state (Article 1); the characteristics of the republic (Article 2); and specific constitutional choices as to state integrity and state symbols (Article 3). The principle of irrevocability, which traces back to the 1961 Constitution, is considered as a legal device for the realization of pluralist democratic order controlling despotic tendencies of the parliamentarian majority. Therefore, the Constitutional Court pointed out in 1975 that the contemporary constitution preferred a more differentiated system compared with classic democracies and protected itself against unwanted amendments.[12] Here, it contemplated the principle of irrevocability as a translation of the term 'national resistance' into terms of a strong legal guarantee for the protection of national sovereignty and the republic.

Republican State Form

The Republican form of state is laid down in the simple constitutional wording of Article 1: 'The Turkish State is a Republic'. However, the very essence of such simplicity has a deeper meaning since the republican state form was proclaimed as a constitutional amendment in 1923. The striking feature of 1921–1924 was the constitutional duality.[13] The National Assembly conducting the War of Independence accepted the 1921 Constitution and provided that the Constitution of the Ottoman Empire (1876) could be applied to the extent that it did not contradict the 1921 Constitution. This impaired an absolute hierarchy of the 1876 Constitution and, of course, the Ottoman constitutional institutions and political elites, even though the 1921 Constitution stipulated in a specific provision its own end in case of 'achievement of the goal'. The goal was not constitutionally defined, but cited in a specific law, namely the *Law on Parliamentary Quorum* (1920); it was the defeat of the Allied Forces invading Anatolia and to seize the Sultanate and Caliphate.[14] However, in 1922, the Ottoman Empire was ended and the Sultanate was abrogated as an institution through parliamentary resolutions (30 September 1922 and 1–2 November 1922). But the constitutional duality vanished only when the 1924 Constitution was put into effect and the annullation of the 1876 Constitution was laid down in a specific provision (Article 104). The

12 E. 1973/19, K. 1975/87, K.t. 15 April 1975, AYMKD 13, 428.

13 See Tanör 1996: 268, 283–5. As clarified by Tanör, in 1919 a congressional government in eastern Anatolia proclaimed independence and republic autonomously by making a democratic constitution. This was a denial of the Ottoman sovereignty and its policies approving invasion of Anatolia after the First World War. It was named *Republic of Southern Eastern Caucasian Government* which represented a role model for future Turkish Republic, see Tanör 1992: 108–14.

14 The 1921 Constitution referred to Law on Parliamentary Quorum in a specific provision. Accordingly, determination of achievement of the goal was a matter of parliamentary decision which meant also renewal of elections. However, a qualified majority of assembly members was required to adopt such a decision. To the non-application of this procedural rule in 1923 elections, see Tanör 1996: 282.

1921 Constitution was a flexible constitution; the proclamation of republican state form was in fact a simple law amending this constitution. However, the title of the amending law claimed that it was an 'explanatory amendment', which assumes that republicanism is an inherent feature of the 1921 Constitution and also the will of dominant political elites in the National Assembly. In constitutional imagination, this assumption leads to the distinction of different meanings of 'republic' (Tanör 1996: 264).[15] First, national sovereignty and the National Assembly as the 'unique and real representative' of the nation as prescribed in the original, not amended version of the 1921 Constitutional is regarded as a 'republic in broader sense'.[16] Second, the explanatory amendment that formally proclaims the republic and prescribes the President of Republic instead of the Ottoman Sultan is defined as 'republic in strict sense'.

Besides those conceptual distinctions, 'republic' has been interpreted as a unique national entity interacting with constitutional order or as an achievement that cannot be defined without a relation to Turkish modernism based on a secular state. Emphasizing the unique nature of the Turkish Republic as an historical entity and fact, the Constitutional Court concludes that different definitions based on numerous views, assumptions, methods, ideologies or forms of republic observed in other countries would not be eligible for the analysing of the Turkish Republic.[17] In this context, the interaction between the protection of constitutional order and 'republic' is confirmed, because the court suggests that the nature of 'Turkish Republic' is to be determined according to the constitutional principles shaping it. It defines 'republic' as an embodiment of constitutional principles including fundamental institutions as well as rights and duties so that the violation of irrevocability would amount to the distortion of constitutional harmony. In *Headscarf I*, the Constitutional Court followed a modernist approach and stated that the secular state is the essence of Turkish revolution and the republic. The court's interpretation is not surprising since it reflects an established paradigm: the reasoning of the 1961 Constitution as to Article 1 has defined 'republic' as a legal formulation of the Turkish revolution.

It is also remarkable that it identifies 'republic' with a democratic state: '(this chapter) explains that the Turkish Republic is a democratic state denying all kinds of monarchy as well as personal or group sovereignty'.[18] Such a substantial analysis equalizing democratic and republican state does not take place in the reasoning of the 1982 Constitution. It prefers clearly the 'republic in strict sense' where the State President is elected by the nation or the National Assembly as the representative of the nation. As mentioned above, such a formal understanding of republic in the reasoning of the 1982 Constitution is not regarded as an obstacle to follow the modernist and substantial interpretation of the 'republic' in *Headscarf I*.

15 For conceptual distinctions, see Gözler 1999: 51.

16 See Articles 1 and 2 of the 1921 Constitution.

17 E. 1973/19, K. 1975/87, K.t. 15 April 1975.

18 For reasoning, see Öztürk 1966: 947.

The question why the 1982 Constitution defined 'republic' in the strict sense could be explained by a Constitutional Court's decision concerning constitutional amendments in the 1970s. The only irrevocable provision in the 1961 Constitution was Article 1 on the republic as a state form, but the specific characteristics of a republic were not protected against amendments by a constitutional clause. In 1970 and 1975, the Constitutional Court annulled laws challenging characteristics of the republic. A 1970 judgment denies interpreting the 'republic' *stricto sensu* and reads as follows:

> it does not comply with … the constitution to consider only the word 'republic' could not be amended while other principles and rules could be. Accordingly, the principle of irrevocability in Article 9 aims at establishing a state system formulated as 'republic' whose nature has been determined by Article 1, 2 and basic principles in the Preamble cited by Article 2. In other words, it is not the word 'republic' that Article 9 puts under the principle of irrevocability, but the republican regime whose characteristics are determined by the constitutional articles cited above.[19]

The judicial activism of the Constitutional Court was tried to be limited in 1971 by a constitutional amendment so that constitutional amendments could be reviewed only as to their compliance to procedural rules ('formal review'). However, in 1975, the court proved that it still had a strong motivation for judicial activism regarding the protection of the republic including its characteristics.[20] It has interpreted a formal view not as a matter of compliance with constitutional quorum and regarded the principle of irrevocability as a procedural rule with substantial elements. The court realized that the prohibition of amendment proposals through the principle of irrevocability is a procedural component that binds the Members of Parliament. Such a prohibition prevents the application or verification of other procedural requirements. In fact, this progressive approach has altered the logic and intent of constitutional amendments in 1971 definitively and provided a material review of constitutional amendments, the compliance with substantial elements of the 'republic'. This judgment has led to a political controversy around judicial activism of the court where constitutional review is repeatedly defined as an obstacle against parliamentarian majority. The court's interpretation is criticized as *ultra vires*.[21]

Characteristics of the Republic and Implementing Legislation

Departing from the 1961 Constitution, the 1982 Constitution put the characteristics of republic under protection of irrevocability. Moreover, in accordance with the

19 E. 1970/1, K. 1970/31, K.t. 16 June 1970, AYMKD 8, 323.

20 E. 1973/19, K. 1975/87, K.t. 15 April 1975, AYMKD 13, 428.

21 For the controversy, see Balcıgil 1982: 133, 141, 174.

shift of constitutional paradigm in 1982, the characteristics of republic were reformulated. Article 3 defines the Republic of Turkey as a democratic, secular and social state governed by the rule of law, bearing in mind the considerations of public peace, national solidarity and justice, respecting human rights, obliged to loyalty to the nationalism of Atatürk and based on the fundamental principles set forth in the Preamble.

Since the 'republic' priciple and its characteristics are protected through laws, their normative character is without any doubt confirmed and strengthened. The following laws are remarkable.

The Turkish Criminal Code protects the 'republic' or the 'characteristics of republic' through criminal norms. Expressions of thought aimed at criticizing and degrading the 'Turkish Republic' are subject to imprisonment from six months to two years, Article 301(1). The Turkish Criminal Code speaks of 'fundamental national interests' in another provision and punishes to get financial profit for conducting activities against them. Here, 'fundamental national interests' are explained as including 'independence, territorial integrity, national security, and characteristics of republic as determined in the constitution', Article 305(4). Attempts to alter the constitutional order, establish a different constitutional order, or prevent application of the constitutional order by using force and violence are also punished (Article 309).

Article 4 of the Law on Radio and Television Broadcasting states that broadcasting activities of televisions and radio institutions in languages traditionally used by Turkish citizens in their daily lives should not contradict with 'characteristics of the republic determined in the constitution'. For radio, television and data broadcasting, 'existence and independence of Turkish Republic as a state, indivisibility of its nation and territory as well as Atatürk's reforms and principles' are among general principles to be observed. Violation of those principles leads to suspension of broadcasting or annulment of relevant licenses, while owners of such institutions, their managers and persons who worked for such broadcasting will be punished according to Turkish Criminal Code (Supplementary Article 2).

In the context of general aims of national education, particular characteristics of republic are cited. Article 2 of the Fundamental Law on National Education speaks of training each Turk to become a citizen loyal and responsible to principles and reforms of Atatürk, his nationalism, the principles set forth in the Preamble as well as the democratic, secular and social state based on the rule of law, and respecting human rights.

The Turkish Civil Code prescribes that foundations violating characteristics of the republic determined by the constitution shall not be established, Article 101(4). Foundations pursuing prohibited aims or carrying out prohibited activities could be dissolved by a court order if there is no possibility to convert the aim (Article 116). However, Turkish Civil Code prohibits establishment of associations pursuing unlawful and immoral aims without any reference to the 'republic' (Article 56). The Law on Associations refers to 'republic' only as regards the use of it in title of an association. A list of words including 'republic', 'Atatürk' or 'Mustafa Kemal',

'Turk', 'Turkey', 'national' are subject to permission of the Ministry for Internal Affairs to be used in the title of an association (Article 28).

The Law on Trade Unions orders that the statutes of trade unions shall not contradict with characteristics of republic determined in the constitution and democratic principles (Article 6). This prohibition is equally valid for their activities (Article 37). Sanctions for unlawful statutes are twofold: suspension of activity or disclosure at request of the governor or the ministries concerned. Among disclosure grounds of trade unions, 'aiming at or pursuing activities to endanger existence of republic' represents a specific ground. Other prohibited activities or aims leading to disclosure are: distorting indivisible integrity of state's territory and nation; destroying fundamental rights and freedoms; providing governance of the state by a person or a group or sovereignty of a class over the other and causing discrimination based on language, race, religion and sect (Article 58).

The Law on Collective Bargaining, Strike and Lockout has various articles that refer to the 'republic' and the integrity of state. First, collective agreements shall not contain provisions against these principles (Article 5). Persons who violate this imperative are to be sentenced to imprisonment from six months to one year (Article 68). Strikes and lockouts against the 'integrity of state with its nation and state', the 'republic' as well as national sovereignty and security are also prohibited (Articles 25–26). Such strikes or lockouts represent a specific category and are to be punished by increased penalties unless they fall within the scope of other criminal norms (Article 74).

The Law on Political Parties refers to 'republic' and its characteristics as well as all irrevocable provisions within the context of protection for democratic state, Article 78(a). Moreover, endangering the existence of the republic and the Turkish state is also prohibited.[22]

Article 1 of the Anti-Terror Law defines terror through its methods, perpetrators and activities conducted by different kinds of aims. Accordingly, terror includes all kinds of criminal activities aiming at altering characteristics of republic determined by the constitution or political, legal, social, secular and economic order; distorting invisible integrity of state with its territory and nation; endangering the existence of the republic; weakening, destroying or seizing state authority; destroying fundamental rights and freedoms; or disturbing state's security, public order and common health.

The Law on Internal Service of Turkish Armed Forces has specific references to the 'republic'. It defines military service as an obligation of learning and exercising an 'art of war' to protect 'Turkish land, independence and (Turkish) republic' (Article 2). Article 35 reads: the 'duty of the Armed Forces is to protect and defend Turkish land and Turkish Republic determined by the constitution'. In respect of

---

22 Destroying legal and political existence of the Turkish Republic falls also under prohibitory provisions protecting nation state. In this respect, state independence and equality in respect of international law are emphasized, see Article 79(a) of the Law on Political Parties.

military oath and duties of a soldier, 'to sacrifice himself for land, republic and duty' or 'loyalty to the republic' are especially remarkable commitments (Articles 37 and 39). Article 35 has played a significant role as a specific reference norm after military intervention in 1980. The military authority has tried to legitimize the intervention by depending on its duty 'to protect the republic' (Tanör 2004: 4). However, such a legitimization attempt fails even on the ground of wording of Article 35, since it does not refer to the republic at all and emphasizes specifically the constitution, which has been, in fact, altered after the military intervention.[23]

The characteristics of the 'republic', as set forth in the 1982 Constitution, are, at first, the democratic, secular and social state governed by the rule of law and the respect of human rights. Those intersect with characteristics determined by the 1961 Constitution, even though the latter spoke of a state 'based on human rights', which is regarded as a strong commitment for limited government and liberal constitutionalism. However, the 1982 Constitution refers also to different characteristics compared with the 1961 Constitution. The former emphasizes considerations of public peace, national solidarity and justice, loyalty to the nationalism of Atatürk and fundamental principles set forth in the Preamble. In a comparison, the following conclusions could be drawn: the trilogy of 'public peace, national solidarity and justice' did not occur explicitly in Article 2 of the 1961 Constitution on characteristics of republic. However, 'public peace' was mentioned in its Preamble and as matter of reference, it was part of characteristics indirectly. That is the reason why the Constitutional Court referred to 'public peace' in 1964 reviewing Article 312 of the previous Turkish Criminal Code, punishing to incite hatred and hostility between the different classes in society, thereby creating discrimination based on membership of a social class, race, religion, sect or region.[24] It considered that such a criminal provision serves to prevent distortions of peace and harmony among the citizens and approved its constitutionality. Explicit reference to public peace in the 1982 Constitution within the context of irrevocable principles clarifies also constitutional justification ground of similar provisions protecting the same value that could be easily observed on the Law on Radio and Television Broadcasting (Article 4[b]) and the Law on Trade Unions (Article 5).

23 After military intervention, National Security Council adopted a law, namely the 'Law on Constitutional Order', which may be regarded as a legal ground of deconstitutionalization process. Provisions of the 1961 Constitution would be applied to the extent that they do not contradict with this law. It altered legislative and executive organs, and provided that laws which will be adopted by the National Security Council could not be regarded as unconstitutional.

24 E. 1963/193, K. 1964/9, K.t. 29 January 1964, AYMKD 2, 48. Article 216(1) of the current Turkish Criminal Code prescribes punishment for the same crime, however, by making reference to clear and present danger for public security. The judicial practice as to application of Article 312 of previous Turkish Criminal Code has been criticized on the ground that 'clear and present danger test' is not respected and this provision created a 'thought crime' which has no place in a democratic society. For critics, see Tanör 1997: 123, 1999: 131.

As proceedings of the Constitutional Convention in 1960 clearly identify, defining 'nationalism' as a characteristic in the constitution was discussed intensively. Civil and military bodies of the Convention – the Assembly of Representatives and the Committee for National Unity – fell apart on the point where a reconciliation committee had the last word. Debates on inclusion of nationalism draws attention, since the 1924 Constitution already had defined nationalism as a characteristic of state among other principles, which simultaneously served as 'six principles' of the Republican People's Party. Nevertheless, in 1960, the Assembly of Representatives rejected the inclusion of 'nationalism' among characteristics mainly on the ground that the description of the 'nation state' in the constitution as an objective concept is satisfactory in contrast with the vague and misleading concept of nationalism. In any case, the representatives against 'nationalism' supported that the Turkish revolution has a notion of 'positive, proportional and peaceful nationalism' which is not racist.[25] Recalling German, Italian and Japanese nationalist experiences and the Second World War, they were afraid of the fact that nationalism would lead to negative and offensive interpretations; a liberal member, also a constitutional lawyer, regarded such interpretations as 'perverse ideologies'.[26] A constitutional safeguard for nationalism is treated as a threat that would impair the unity of Turkish nation.[27] However, the majority voting in the Committee for National Unity supported the introduction of 'nationalism' to the 1961 Constitution, even though some of the members suggested that nationalism is an inherent feature of the constitution, and that an unitary state as a constitutional principle reflects nationalism in fact.[28] Finally, the conflict on 'nationalism' was handed over to the Reconciliation Committee that rejected an inclusion of 'nationalism'. Besides all those controversies, the Preamble of the 1961 Constitution mentions 'Turkish nationalism' as a source of constitutional inspiration (paragraph 3). Therefore, it may be assumed that the 1961 Constitution implicitly recognizes 'Turkish nationalism' as a republican characteristic (Article 2).

The Turkish constitutional experience reveals that even the rule of law would serve for a militant stand, since it is considered as a reflection of state sovereignty. Defining independence of justice within the rule of law, the Constitutional Court refers to the negotiations of the Lausanne Peace Treaty (1924) which historically proclaims the Turkish Republic as an independent state and covers various political issues, such as minority rights, the exchange of Greek–Turkish population, and the state borders.[29] During the negotiations of the Lausanne Treaty and shortly after the establishment of the republic, independence of justice was regarded as a reflection of an independent state. The court recalls this historical point.

---

25 See especially the speech of Muammer Aksoy, Enver Ziya Karal, Tarık Zafer Tunaya and Hıfzı Oğuz Bekata in Öztürk 1966: 1031, 1035, 1054, 1099.

26 See Tarık Zafer Tunaya, in Öztürk 1966: 1054.

27 See Enver Ziya Karal, in Öztürk 1966: 1035.

28 See Emanullah Çelebi, in Öztürk 1966: 1085.

29 E. 1988/32, K. 1989/10, K.t. 28 February 1989, AYMKD 25, 121–122.

However, it is no doubt that nationalism in Atatürk's sense and the secular state are prominent characteristics of the 'republic'. The constitutional norm which clarifies the Atatürk nationalism is Article 66 on Turkish citizenship. It speaks of 'being Turk' in the sense of citizenship without taking into account any racial, ethnic or religious references, and states: 'Everyone bound to the Turkish State through the bond of citizenship is a Turk.'[30] Accordingly, citizenship is defined as a 'constitutional bond' to the state which confers Turkish citizen rights and duties, since in specific constitutional provisions, such as right to form political parties or entry into the public service, only citizens are presumed to be addressees. Taking into account that 'being Turk' constitutionally corresponds to being a citizen, constitutional references like 'Turk' and 'every Turk' does not refer to racial or ethnic identity, but to the 'constitutional bond' of citizenship. Therefore, Atatürk's nationalism is described in constitutional literature also as 'constitutional nationalism' (Tunç and Bilir 1998: 207). On various occasions, the Constitutional Court puts emphasis on non-discriminative, peaceful and neutral nature of Atatürk's nationalism parallel to democratic historical writing that regards Kemalist nationalization as anti-monarchist; anti-cultural; anti-racist; anti-class; anti-Islamist; and anti-xenophobic.[31] In this respect, the court speaks of 'contemporary understanding of nationalism'.[32] It could be suggested that taking into account the citizenship notion of 'being Turk' as a ground for the systematic interpretation of the constitution, even 'Turkishness' is to be comprehended as Turkish nation composed of Turkish citizens with different racial, ethnic or religious origins. However, the famous decision of the High Court of Appeal in 1974 on foundations of non-Muslim Turkish citizens protected by the Lausanne Treaty explicitly contradicts with such peaceful and inclusive understanding of citizenship. The High Court did not hesitate to define the relevant foundations as 'legal personalities established by non-Turks'.[33] In a recent judgment on the interpretation of 'Turkishness', the High Court referred to religious values as a component of Turkish nation. It considered that 'Turkishness' means 'human, religious, historical values, which create Turkish nation, and national and spiritual values composed of national language, national feelings and national customs'.

30 See also Article 54(1) of the 1961 Constitution.

31 E. 1963/73, K. 1965/40, K.t. 26 September 1965; AYMKD 4, 256; E. 1984/9, K. 1985/4, K.t. 18 February 1985; AYMKD 21, 59; E. 1993/3, K.1994/2, K.t. 16 June 1994; AYMKD 30/2, 1019; for humanitarian aspects of Kemalist nationalization, see Tanör 1998: 226–7. As to non-discriminative and secular features, Atatürk's definition of nation clarifies the point: 'People of Turkey establishing the Republic of Turkey are called the Turkish nation.'

32 E. 1996/1, K. 1997/1, K.t. 14 February 1997, AYMKD 34/2, 747.

33 A relevant decision limited real property rights of so-called 'community foundations' extensively. Through amendments, which intend to approximate necessities of the 'European Union Partnership' arising from Copenhagen political criteria, property rights of such foundations are recognized, even though problems as to implementation of new legislation are reported, see Oran 2005: 102.

Atatürk's nationalism and its citizenship notion interact with the unitary state. It is striking that – except for Preamble and Article 2 – the nationalism of Atatürk is not explicitly cited in further constitutional provisions. However, there are various references to 'principles and reforms of Atatürk' as a whole in specific constitutional norms which also cover 'nationalism' as a principle.[34]

As an earlier remark on protection of the secular state, the Constitutional Court has established four pillars through which legitimate interventions as well as boundaries of the secular state become visible.[35] First, religion shall not be decisive or effective in state affairs. Second, religion is under the protection of a constitutional guarantee, while the private and spiritual sphere of the right to religion is secured on the ground of non-discrimination. Third, in cases where religious activities are beyond the private and spiritual sphere of the individual and they affect the social sphere, the state may impose restrictions with the aim of protecting public order, public security and the public interest. It may also prohibit the abuse and exploitation of religion. Fourth, as the protector of public order and rights, the state has the authority to control religious rights and freedoms.

Unitary State, Official Language, Capital and Sovereignty Symbols

A further irrevocable provision is to be found in Article 3 of the constitution, which declares the state as an indivisible entity with its territory and nation where the official language is Turkish. The flag which is composed of a white crescent and a star on a red background and the national anthem named 'Independence March' are also protected by Article 3.[36] Accordingly, Ankara as a capital falls within the scope of irrevocability. In the reasoning of Article 3, flag and national anthem are defined as spiritual values and 'sacred symbols' which gather Turkish State and nation. The religious term 'sacred' is used here for identification instruments of the state. This may be regarded as an attempt to legitimize secular symbols through a spiritual reference. As cited above, in different laws the unitary state as 'indivisible integrity of state with its territory and nation' and the 'republic'

34 See, for example, Article 42(3) on conducting education along the lines of principles and reforms of Atatürk; Article 58 on training and development of youth in line with the principles and reforms of Atatürk; Article 81 on the oath text of Members of Parliament; and Article 134 on the establishment of the 'Atatürk High Institution of Culture, Language and History' for dissemination of information on thought, principles and reforms of Atatürk.

35 See especially E. 1986/11, K. 1986/26, K.t. 4 November 1986, AYMKD 22, 312–313; E. 1990/36, K. 1991/8, K.t. 9 April 1991, AYMKD 27/I, 299–301.

36 The Turkish Criminal Code describes Turkish flag and national anthem as indications of state sovereignty and punishes degrading of them (Article 300). Degrading 'Independence March' publicly is subject to imprisonment from six months to two years, whereas degrading the Turkish flag publicly by 'tearing, burning or similar methods' would lead to imprisonment from one year to three years.

are protected simultaneously. The Law on Duties and Competences of Police allows intelligence activities as measures to protect the indivisible integrity of the state with its territory and nation.[37] Theatre plays, shows, displaying videos or films as well as broadcasting on Internet could be suspended by the highest administrative authority, if police reaches clear evidence that they are harmful for territorial and national integrity.[38] However, the protection of the unitary state is extensively disputed and analysed in the context of political parties since the constitution and the Law on Political Parties prohibit aims and activities altering the unitary state.

Before the constitutional amendments in 2001, the protection of official language had an authoritative character, because a language other than the official one could be prohibited by law. Article 26(3) of the constitution authorized a judge or a competent authority designated by law to seize any written or printed documents, phonograph records, magnetic or video tapes and other means of expression in a language prohibited by law.[39] The act implementing this constitutional prohibition was the Law on Dissemination in Languages Other than Turkish, and it was abrogated by Article 23 of the Anti-Terrorism Law in 1991. After the abrogation, the constitutional prohibition became ineffective, because the legislative act it refers to was not in force. Therefore, the 2001 amendment eliminated the constitutional ground of laws which may be enacted to implement the prohibition in future and secured dissemination of ideas in regional or ethnic languages.[40] Implementing the underlying logic of the constitutional amendments in 2001, the Law on Foreign Language Education and Teaching as well as the Law on Radio and Television Broadcasting provided specific guarantees for broadcasting and private teaching in 'different languages and dialects used traditionally by Turkish citizens in their daily lives'. Nevertheless, such broadcastings should also respect characteristics of Turkish Republic and indivisible integrity of the state with its territory and nation.[41]

Constitutional Duties of the State

The principles which fall into the scope of irrevocability are also mentioned within the context of state aims and duties in Article 5 of the constitution. However, Article

37 See Supplementary Article 7 of Law on Duties and Competencies of Police.

38 See Article 8 of Law on Duties and Competencies of Police.

39 Before the 2001 amendment, Article 28(2) of the constitution has a parallel prohibition which reads as follows: 'Publication shall not be made in any language prohibited by law'. The 2001 constitutional package eliminated this prohibition.

40 However, the Law on Political Parties keeps on making reference to 'languages prohibited by law', even though constitutional ground for such a prohibition does not exist and there is no prohibition in fact, see Article 81(c): '... Statutes and programs of political parties could be translated into foreign languages saved as languages prohibited by law'.

41 See Article 4 of the Law on Radio and Television Broadcasting.

5 does not confine with to restate the content of irrevocability; it also focuses on rights of individual in a social democratic state based on the rule of law. According to Article 5, the state has to pursue the following aims and duties:

> *to safeguard the independence and integrity of the Turkish nation; territorial integrity; republic and democracy;* to ensure the welfare, peace, and the happiness of the individual and; to strive for the removal of political, social and economic obstacles which restrict the fundamental rights and the freedoms of the individual in a manner compatible with the principles of justice and of the social state governed by the rule of law; and to provide the conditions required for the development of the individual's material and spiritual existence [emphasis added].

Without denying the references as to protection of republic and democracy in Article 5, the Constitutional Court considers that the provision puts emphasis on the maximization of individual self-development and, to this end, removal of political, social and economic obstacles restricting fundamental rights and freedoms.[42] Without any hesitation, such an interpretation reads aims and duties of the state not from perspective of defending the state, but from view of protection and enhancement of individual rights.

Presupposed Constitutionality for Modernization Laws of Revolution

As a consolidation clause for republican modernization, Article 174 of the constitution provides presupposed constitutionality of eight specific laws adopted between 1924 and 1934. They cover unification of education system; the wearing of hats; the prohibition of wearing certain garments; the closure of dervish convents and tombs; the abolition of certain titles and appellations; the principle of civil marriage; and the adoption of the Latin alphabet and international numerals. Those provisions are praised as legal instruments of social transformation, this is 'raising Turkish society above the level of contemporary civilization', and as safeguards of a secular republic or 'monuments of revolution'.[43] Therefore, concordance between those laws and specific constitutional norms is established by a rule of interpretation. Accordingly, no provision of the constitution could be construed or interpreted as rendering the modernization laws unconstitutional. The Constitutional Court recognizes the specific status of the modernization laws, compared with ordinary laws. In *Headscarf I*, it interpreted the secular state with extensive references to modernization laws that they determined the constitutionality of the law concerned.[44] However, in 1998, it has astonishingly

42 E. 1990/15, K. 1991/5, K.t. 28 February 1991, AYMKD 27, 171–172.
43 E. 1989/1, K. 1989/12, K.t. 7 March 1989, AYMKD 25, 155–158.
44 E. 1989/1, K. 1989/12, K.t. 7 March 1989, AYMKD 25, 156.

rejected without any detailed reasoning their constitutional effect and involvement as reference norms in constitutional review.[45]

Militant Reflections for Fundamental Rights and Freedoms

Restriction and Misuse of Fundamental Rights

Article 13 of the constitution lays down the principles for restriction of fundamental rights and freedoms:

> Fundamental rights and freedoms may be restricted only by law and in conformity with the reasons mentioned in the relevant articles of the constitution without infringing upon their essence. These restrictions shall not be in conflict with the letter and spirit of the constitution and the requirements of the democratic order of the society and the secular republic and the principle of proportionality.

Before the amendment in 2001, Article 13 was stating general grounds and principles for the restriction of all kinds of rights and freedoms. The general grounds were: 'the indivisible integrity of the state with its territory and nation; national sovereignty; the Republic; national security; public order; general peace; the public interest; public morals; and public health'. Additionally, Article 13(3) reads: 'The general grounds for restriction set forth in this article shall apply for all fundamental rights and freedoms.' The constitutional amendment in 2001 abolished general restriction grounds and reformulated specific restriction grounds in relevant articles on freedoms and rights. This eliminated a cumulative restriction dynamic, this is the restriction through both general and specific grounds, which has been criticized as an illiberal approach.[46] The amendment reintroduces the 'essence of the right' as previously adopted in the 1961 Constitution,[47] and explicitly refers to the 'principle of proportionality' which has been used in constitutional review as an unwritten principle for a long period of time. The reintroduction of the 'essence of the right' as a limit of restriction has political importance revealing liberal sensitivity in the amendment, since the Constitutional Court has considered it as a surviving concept correlating requirements of democratic order. However,

---

45 E. 1997/62, K. 1998/52, K.t. 16 September 1998, AYMKD 36/1, 283.

46 As approved by the Constitutional Court in respect of freedom of expression, general grounds could be applied for rights and freedoms which have also specific restriction grounds. Moreover, provisions on rights and freedoms which did not prescribe any specific restriction grounds could be restricted with reference to general restriction grounds. See E. 1985/8, K. 1986/27, K.t. 26 November 1986, AYMKD 22, 381; E. 1991/18, K. 1992/20, K.t. 31 March 1992, AYMKD 28/1, 295.

47 For a comparative analysis of essence of the right from perspectives of Turkish and German constitutional interpretation, see Sağlam 1982: 141 et seq.

in respect of limits of restriction, 'secular republic' is a totally new criterion to be respected. It is remarkable that an element of the militant democracy (the 'secular republic') has been regarded not as a restriction ground, but as a limit of restriction. The question if the amending majority was aware of such a distinction is not easy to answer. In view of the preparatory works of the amendment, one may also suggest that the emphasis on 'secular republic' only aims at revealing its higher political role as the underlying logic of Turkish modernism and republican reforms.

The prohibitory clause on misuse of fundamental rights and freedoms enhances the militant stance of the constitution. Article 14 of the constitution prohibits exercise of fundamental rights and freedoms in form of 'activities' which aim at destroying the indivisible integrity of the state with its territory and nation, and the democratic and secular republic based on human rights. As a general misuse clause, Article 14 establishes a constitutional ground for militant laws sanctioning 'activities' against unitary, democratic and secular state based on human rights.

Suspension of Fundamental Rights and Freedoms in State of Emergency

In times of war, mobilization, martial law or state of emergency, the exercise of fundamental rights and freedoms can be partially or entirely suspended, or measures may be taken, which derogate the guarantees embodied in the constitution. However, Article 15 of the constitution prescribes limits for measures of suspension or derogation by referring to international law and exigencies of the situation. Moreover, Article 15(2) enshrines specific rights – so-called 'core rights' – which should be untouched even in times of war, mobilization, martial law and state of emergency. It provides that individual's right to life and the integrity of his or her material and spiritual entity shall be inviolable except where death occurs through lawful act of warfare; no one may be compelled to reveal his or her religion, conscience, thought or opinion, nor be accused on account of them. Offences and penalties may not be made retroactive, nor may anyone be held guilty until so proven by a court judgment.

The constitution establishes different categories of emergency regimes with different constitutional grounds and procedure. The state of emergency could be declared either in the event of natural disaster, dangerous epidemic diseases, a serious economic crisis or – as occurred for years in south-eastern Anatolia – in the event of serious indications of widespread acts of violence aimed at the destruction of the free democratic order established by the constitution or of fundamental rights and freedoms, or serious deterioration of public order because of acts of violence. The state of emergency could be declared by the Council of Ministers, meeting under the chairmanship of the President of the Republic. Chairmanship of the President, who chairs the Council of Ministers in ordinary times only if he finds it necessary, is a constitutive element of the declaration act. In an event of violence, the state of emergency could be declared after consultation with the National Security Council. The state of emergency may be declared in one or more regions or throughout the country for a period not exceeding six months. In any case, it should be submitted immediately to the Parliament for approval. If the Parliament is in recess, it should be assembled immediately. It may alter the duration of the state of emergency, extend the period, for a maximum of four months only, each time at the request of the Council of Ministers or may lift the state of emergency.

The declaration of martial law follows a similar procedure. However, it requires more qualified reasons as regards deterioration of public order and existence of the state. Those are: widespread acts of violence which are more dangerous than the cases necessitating a state of emergency, and which are aimed at the destruction of the free democratic order or the fundamental rights and freedoms embodied in the constitution or in the event of war; the emergence of a situation necessitating war, an uprising, or the spread of violent and strong rebellious actions against the motherland and the Republic; or widespread acts of violence of either internal or external origin threatening the indivisibility of the country and the nation. An extension of the period of martial law for a maximum of four months each time requires a decision by the Parliament. However, in the event of state of war, the limit of four months does not apply. Martial law commanders exercise their duties under the authority of the Chief of the General Staff. The declaration of general or partial mobilization and of the state of war is of confusing nature, since they are not clearly regulated in the constitution, but stipulated in a specific law, the Law on Mobilization and State of War, which was prepared under military regime in November 1983 and became immune from judicial review until the 2001 constitutional amendment. Surprisingly, in 2000 the Law on Mobilization and State of War has been amended so that the Council of Ministers and General Staff could exercise their powers before the declaration of mobilization in times of 'tension and crisis' necessitating war. As an excessive pre-emptive measure, this amendment has been criticized that a new category of 'tension and crisis' cannot be established by law since the constitution orders the application of martial law in cases where emergency situation does not necessitate declaration of mobilization or of the state of war.

The state of emergency is primarily based on a specific law, the Law on State of Emergency. Nonetheless, during many years of emergency in Turkey,[48] emergency decrees having the force of law became prominent instruments. Those are issued – without any preliminary authorization act of the Parliament – by the Council of Ministers meeting under the chairmanship of the President of the Republic.[49] The

48 Eastern and south-eastern regions of Turkey were under state of emergency regime between 1984–2002. It has been also pointed out that martial law or the state of emergency has been applied approximately for 40 years in Turkey after establishment of the republic; that makes 52 per cent of the republican history.

49 These decrees are published in the Official Gazette and should be submitted to the Parliament on the same day for approval. They should be discussed and concluded in parliamentary commissions and plenary session in 30 days.

Constitutional Court asserts that emergency decrees can no longer be applied after the state of emergency is lifted. This also means that emergency decrees lose their validity by the end of state of emergency and cannot be automatically put into force in case of future emergency declarations.[50] Moreover, the court does not allow amendments in the Law on State of Emergency through emergency decrees since the former could be applied in any potential emergency situation depending on the declaration of the state of emergency while, the latter is time limited and case specific.[51] However, as a constitutional derogation of the rule of law, emergency decrees are immune from juridical review.[52] Such a disputable feature legitimizes critical observations as regards emergency decrees which have established a regional governor for definite cities of eastern and south-eastern Anatolia and granted him and the security forces under his authority extensive powers without effective judicial control. Those powers ranged from evacuation of villages and compulsory immigration or deportation to the prohibition of strikes.[53] Article 7 of Decree 285 prohibited filing annulment cases against administrative acts of the Regional Governor. As the most striking provision of judicial immunity, Article 8 of Decree no. 430 provided:

> No criminal, financial, or legal responsibility may be claimed against the Minister of Interior, Regional Governor, or provincial governors within a state emergency region in respect of their decisions or acts related to the exercise of powers entrusted to them by this decree, and no application shall be made to any judicial authority to this end.

Both were regarded by the Constitutional Court in 1991 as emergency provisions immune from judicial review, even though the court in fact applied a tripartite test to determine whether a formal emergency decree is of emergency nature in a material sense.[54] In contrast with this, in 2003, it has repealed a former provision prohibiting annulment cases against administrative acts of Regional Governor.[55] Here, the court clearly emphasizes the absolute nature of judicial review of administrative acts as provided in Article 125 of the constitution, and does not

50 E. 1990/25, K. 1991/1, K.t. 10 January 1991, AYMKD 27/1, 101; E. 1991/6, K. 1991/20, K.t. 3 July 1991, AYMKD 27/1, 398–399.

51 C.f. E. 1990/25, K. 1991/1, K.t. 10 January 1991, AYMKD 27/1, 107.

52 See Article 148 of the constitution: '… no action shall be brought before the Constitutional Court alleging the unconstitutionality as to the form and substance of decrees having the force of law issued during a state of emergency, martial law, or in time of war'.

53 See especially Article 4(h) of Decree no. 285 and Articles 1, 2, and 3 of Decree no. 430.

54 See E. 1990/25, K. 1991/1, K.t. 10 January 1991, AYMKD 27/1, 92–102; E. 1991/6, K. 1991/20, K.t. 3 July 1991, AYMKD 27/1, 396–400; for argumentation of unconstitutionality see especially dissenting opinions of judges Özden, Şahin, Tüzün, Sezer and Acargün in E. 1991/6, K. 1991/20, K.t. 3 July 1991, AYMKD 27/1, 415–417.

55 E. 2003/28, K. 2003/42, K.t. 22.5.2003, AYMKD 40/1, 92.

allow any derogations unless they are constitutionally prescribed. In respect of this specific case, not only judicial activism, but also democratic deficit as regards parliamentary control of emergency decrees becomes obvious since the relevant decree was put into force in 1987, but not discussed by Parliament for 15 years. Such a delay was unconstitutional, since Article 128 of Rules of Procedure – as provided in 1996 – orders that emergency decrees should be discussed in commissions and plenary session in 30 days under urgent procedure.[56] The parliamentary discussion is of legal importance because the Parliament could repeal emergency decrees or adopt them, when necessary with amendments, in form of laws. The transformation of emergency decrees to laws could make the constitutional ban of judicial review ineffective and eliminate constitutional and political contestations as regards democratic supervision of emergency regime in Turkey.[57] Taking into account deficits of both parliamentary and judicial control, and allegations of serious human rights violations against Turkey which were in numerous cases upheld by the ECHR, it is to be concluded that emergency applications have gone beyond the limits of militant democracy where constitutional guarantees as regards 'requirements of international obligations' or 'core rights' are in fact ignored.[58]

Militant Democracy as Regards Specific Rights

Freedom of Expression

Article 26 of the constitution, as amended in 2001, recognizes the freedom of expression and the dissemination of thought, and stipulates qualified restriction grounds which shall also be applied for the freedom of press. Everyone has the right to express and disseminate his thoughts and opinion by speech, in writing or in pictures or through other media, individually or collectively. This right includes the freedom to receive and impart information and ideas without interference from official authorities. Reflections of militant democracy could be identified in qualified restriction grounds, since they include:

56 Article 122(3) prescribed that emergency decrees shall be submitted to the Parliament, and the time limit and procedure for their approval by the Parliament shall be indicated in the Rules of Procedure. However, such a clear constitutional obligation, which requires amendment in the Rules of Procedure, has not been fulfilled by the Parliament until 1996.

57 For critics of Social Democratic Popular Party as regards 'by-passing' Parliament in case of emergency decrees, see *Türkiye ve Güneydoğu* (Yeni Yüzyıl Kitaplığı: Türkiye'nin Sorunları Dizisi-3), 30.

58 See ECHR, *Akdıvar et al. v. Turkey*, App. Nr. 21893/93, 16.9.1996; *Ogur v. Turkey*, App. Nr. 21594/93, 20 May 1999.

> protecting national security, public order and public safety, the basic characteristics of the Republic and safeguarding the indivisible integrity of the state with its territory and nation, preventing crime, punishing offenders, withholding information duly classified as a state secret, protecting the reputation and rights and private and family life of others, or protecting professional secrets as prescribed by law, or ensuring the proper functioning of the judiciary.

This provision contrasts with Article 20 of the 1961 Constitution, since the latter did not prescribe any specific restriction grounds for the freedom of thought and expression. This absence of specific grounds was regarded in constitutional literature as an indication for an absolute nature of the free expression where any content regulation is excluded (Tanör 1969: 175).

The criminal responsibility of writers and publishers and specific measures, such as the suspension of distribution or seizure of printed materials, are prescribed in Article 28 of the constitution. Here, the militant nature of the constitutional order becomes definitely visible:

> Anyone who writes or prints any news or articles which threaten the internal or external security of the state or the indivisible integrity of the state with its territory and nation, which tend to incite offence, riot or insurrection, or which refer to classified state secrets and anyone who prints or transmits such news or articles to others for the above purposes, shall be held responsible under the law relevant to these offences. Distribution may be suspended as a preventive measure by the decision of a judge, or in the event delay is deemed prejudicial, by the competent authority designated by law.

Different ways of expression as regards freedom of science and art are constitutionally recognized, this is the right to study and teach freely, explain and disseminate science and arts, and to carry out research.[59] However, in respect of dissemination of science and art, irrevocable principles of the constitution set a boundary: 'The right to disseminate shall not be exercised for the purpose of changing the provisions of Articles 1, 2 and 3 of this constitution.'[60]

The limits of the freedom of expression were discussed by the end of the 1960s and during the 1970s to clarify the 'constitutional openness' to socialism and communism. Articles 141 and 142 of the previous Criminal Code became the centre of constitutional dispute, since they prohibited spreading propaganda as well as establishing associations aiming at the domination of one social class over the others, annihilating a social class, overturning the fundamental social and economic

59 According to explicit wording of Article 27(3) of the constitution, the freedom of art and science does not preclude regulation by law of the entry and distribution of foreign publications in the country.

60 Article 28(3) states that this prohibition should be equally valid for limitations of the freedom of press.

order or the political or legal order of the state. Even though coercion was not an element of such crimes, the Constitutional Court affirmed the constitutionality of the aforementioned articles. It clarified that 'socialist propaganda' and socialist parties are permitted as far as they obey constitutional limits. Consequently, the court's ruling strengthened the position that the constitutional order is open to socialism while it definitely excludes communism (Alacakaptan 1965–1966). This has been strongly criticized on the ground that freedom and openness cannot be determined according to constitutional limits or philosophy, since those limits or philosophy establish not the ceiling, but the minimum standards for free expression (Soysal 1968: 270; Tanör 1979: 15–16). In fact, such critics has favoured the 'clear and present danger test' and challenged 'thought crimes' based on a differentiation between 'thoughts including coercion by definition' (communism) and 'thoughts without any coercion' (socialism). However, Articles 141 and 142 have been intensively applied after the military declaration on 12 March 1970 without any diligence to the delicate balance between expressions and offensive activities. Following illiberal tendencies in criminal writing, the High Court of Appeal did not hesitate to punish the publication of scientific and artistic products, such as poems of Bulgarian poet Milev or Léfebre's book on Karl Marx's life and works (Tanör 1979: 125). Here, a specific observation could be made to demonstrate the legitimizing efforts of the intensive application of Articles 141 and 142 in the 1970s. Even illiberal writing, which has steered criminal case law, used the liberal test of 'clear and present danger' to endorse 'thought crimes' in a manipulated sense that danger could be 'predetermined' for each society and culture distinctively by legislation (Dönmezer 1973; Tanör 1979: 101).

After the abrogation of Articles 141 and 142 in 1991, Article 8 of the Anti-Terror Law has been regarded as a new criminal device. The first version of it, which was valid until its amendment in 1995, prohibited written and spoken propaganda, meetings, assemblies and demonstrations aimed at undermining the territorial integrity of the Republic of Turkey or the indivisible unity of the nation, 'irrespective of the methods used and the intention'. This provision has been criticized as lacking legal certainty and being irreconcilable with the principle of *nullum crimen sine culpa* as well as the right of information.[61] In criminal case law, especially the ignorance regarding 'methods and intention' has led to punishment of journalists and writers even in cases where the incitement of terrorism or the endorsement of terrorist organizations was not clearly established.[62] In 2006, the Anti-Terror Law has been amended, and 'propaganda of terrorist organization' and specific propagandist activities, such as carrying symbols of terrorist organization, have been defined as crimes instead of 'propaganda against indivisible integrity of the state'. However, the 2006 amendments prescribe punishments for owners

61 For the plea of unconstitutionality, see Özek 1999–2000; for critics regarding the absence of coercion in Article 8, see Hafızoğullari 1994: 18.

62 For a different and favourable treatment of scientific and artistic activities, see Tanör 1991: 168–9.

of press and media institutions as well as their responsible editors even if they are not principals or accessories of propaganda crime. This is equally valid for publications regarding possible terror victims and identities of anti-terror officers. Amendments have also provided the temporary suspension of periodicals which incite or praise crimes within the activities of terrorist organizations or include propaganda of terrorist organizations. The constitutionality of those provisions has been challenged by President Ahmet Necdet Sezer on the grounds of personal criminal responsibility, proportionality and specific guarantees for freedom of press before the Constitutional Court, where the case is still pending.

Recent discussions on the freedom of expression, accelerated by the Accession Partnership with the European Union, concentrate on Articles 216 and 301 of the Turkish Criminal Code. The former stipulates 'inciting people to hostile feelings and hatred' as crime, which was also prohibited by Article 312 of the previous Turkish Criminal Code and had a bad reputation under this numerical classification, since it has been used extensively by judiciary. The latter was well known under Article 159 of the previous Turkish Criminal Code, which punishes insult against Turkishness and specific public institutions. Following constitutional amendment in 2001, a process of legislative harmonization has been initiated and the definition of crime on 'inciting people to hostile feelings and hatred' has been reformulated. The harmonized version of Article 312(2), 'endangering public order', became an element of crime by definition. It stated:

> An individual who publicly incites hostile feelings or hatred in people on the basis of differences of social class, race, religion, sect or region in such a way as to endanger public order shall be punished by imprisonment of one to three years.

The new Turkish Criminal Code (2004) rewrites crime on 'inciting people to hostile feelings and hatred' in Article 216. Article 216(1) speaks of 'inciting hostile feelings or hatred in a section of society having different characteristics as regards social class, race, religion, sect or region against other section'. Such an incitement is punishable only in cases where it reveals 'clear and present danger as regards public security'. The conceptual change from 'endangering public order' to 'clear and present danger as regards public security' is remarkable. Such a change explicitly impels to apply the 'clear and present danger test' which does not deal with the content *in abstracto*, but makes a careful analysis of circumstances concerning the impact of the expressions concerned.[63] Additionally, Article 216(2) punishes publicly degrading of a section of society on the basis of 'differences' as regards social class, race, religion, sect, sex or region. In contrast with the harmonized version of the previous Criminal Code, Article 216(2) does not refer to the protection of 'human dignity' any more. In 2004, the High Court of Appeal did not apply the previous Article 312 of Criminal Code to offensive

63 For views on the incorporation of the 'clear and present danger test', see Kalaycıoğlu and Batum 2001.

expressions, for example, 'unbelievers', 'committees of conspiracy and atheism and their supporters', 'impiousness' and 'clean the world from dirt'.[64] However, in 2005, the High Court has applied the previous Article 312 of the Criminal Code to insulting and hostile expressions in a newspaper article regarding a group of society approving the headscarf ban in public institutions, such as 'irreligious and shrew minority', 'dangerous and militant religiously converted Sebatayists' (Semitics of Thessalonica), or 'hostile groups against Islam and Muslims'.[65] The court has identified a potential threatening effect of such offensive expressions in the concrete case and referred to 'violence words' in the article.

Article 301 of the Turkish Criminal Code punishes 'publicly degrading of Turkishness, the republic and Parliament' and of the 'government of the Republic of Turkey, judiciary, military and security forces of the state'. Article 159 of the previous Criminal Code has protected same values and institutions against 'insult and ridicule'. In contrast to the current version, the prosecution of such 'insults and ridicules' could not be carried out without permission of the Ministry of Justice.[66] Article 159 became subject of harmonization laws three times. Harmonization provided that limits of penalties were progressively reduced (2002 and 2003 amendments) and a specific rule of application was, at first, introduced (2002) and then modified (2003). Despite changes in the wording, in the current version of the Turkish Criminal Code holds: 'expressions of thought made with the purpose of criticism shall not constitute crime'. Despite harmonization efforts and reformulation in the new Turkish Criminal Code, this 'degrading' or 'insult norm' is placed in the centre of political discussion, since prosecutions targeted writers and journalists, including Nobel laureate, Orhan Pamuk. Even though inferior courts interpreted the insult of public institutions in favour of freedom of expression or rejected cases of 'Turkishness' on the ground of ripeness, the High Court of Appeal construed 'Turkishness' and 'insult' broadly in a remarkable case.[67] Hrant Dink, a journalist and leading intellectual of Armenian origin, has published eight articles in a newspaper designed mainly for Armenian minority in Turkey, namely *Agos*. He was also general director of the newspaper. In his eighth article, he expressed: 'Clean blood replacing that poisonous blood which will pour out from the Turk exists in noble vein of Armenian that he will establish with Armenia.' The High Court of Appeal, referring to a very disputable definition of 'Turkishness' including 'religion and spiritual values', concluded that the author insulted and ridiculed Turkishness by using 'poisonous blood' for Turks.[68] After

64 Yargıtay Ceza Genel Kurulu, E. 2004/8-130, K. 2004/206, İtirazname: 183264.

65 Yargıtay Ceza Genel Kurulu, E. 2004/8-201, K. 2005/30, T. 15 March 2005, Yargıtay Kararları Dergisi, Cilt 31, Temmuz 2005, Sayı: 7, 1060–1146.

66 See Article 160(2) of the previous Turkish Criminal Code.

67 Yargıtay Ceza Genel Kurulu, E. 2006/9-169, K. 2006/184, İtirazname: 34001.

68 The High Court of Appeal ignored to analyse impact of articles, although *Agos* is a very small sized newspaper with a limited number of readers. For critics, see dissenting opinions in Yargıtay Ceza Genel Kurulu, E. 2006/9-169, K. 2006/184, İtirazname: 34001.

assassination of Hrant Dink in 2006, protests and dispute regarding Article 301 have become heated. In April 2008, Article 301 was amended, and the 'Turkishness' was replaced by 'Turkish nation'.

Freedom of Religion and Elimination of Religious Symbols from Public Sphere

Article 24 of the constitution provides absolute protection for freedom of religious belief and conviction ('private sphere protection'). However, manifestations of religious beliefs (acts of worship, religious services and ceremonies) are free as long as they do not violate the general clause on abuse of rights in Article 14 of the constitution. As a specific abuse clause, Article 24(5) of the constitution reads:

> No one shall be allowed to exploit or abuse religion or religious feelings, or things held sacred by religion, in any manner whatsoever, for *the purpose of personal or political influence*, or for even partially basing the *fundamental, social, economic, political, and legal order* of the state on religious tenets [emphasis added].

The criminal norm for the implementation of this specific constitutional abuse clause, Article 163 of the previous Turkish Criminal Code, which was applied also for fundamentalist propaganda, has been abrogated by the Anti-Terror Law in 1991, even though it is suggested that such an abrogation makes constitutional prohibition ineffective (Kanadoğlu 2006: 187–9; Tanör 2000: 105). However, Article 24(5) has been also treated negatively as a norm excluding religion from social order and politics in constitutional writing (Erdoğan 2002: 130–31).

In respect of freedom of religion, the militant stand of the secular state can be best observed in jurisprudence regarding the headscarf problem. As a landmark case for religious symbols, *Headscarf I* offers an analytical approach to identify constitutional reasons of militant stand for the secular state in respect of freedom of religion. The case dealt with a statutory provision which explicitly allows the veiling of head and neck for higher education students 'on the ground of their religious belief'. Careful reading of the Constitutional Court's judgment reveals that the annulment of the relevant provision rests on two arguments regarding the interpretation of the secular state which are repeatedly observed under different headings of review. First, the secular state prohibits – as a major component of the constitution – all kinds of legal instruments based on religious requirements or beliefs.[69] Consequently, allowing the headscarf in higher education by a public law provision has been considered as an act which deters religious neutrality and non-religious identity of the state ('wall of separation'). Referring to the dominant role of the secular state in the constitution, the court has not attempted to provide interpretative balance between religious symbols and secular needs. Instead, it

69 E. 1989/1, K. 1989/12, K.t. 7 March 1989, AYMKD 25, 148, 152 and 154; cf. Danıştay 8. Dairesi, E. 1988/1173, K. 1989/652, 7 July 1989.

has noticed that the secular state cannot be impaired for the sake of liberties. Second, the court evaluates the effects of headscarf applications on the students who do not veil.[70] Such a 'rights of the others' argument is the *Leitmotiv* of the judgment which is identified not only in respect of equality. The court refers to peaceful religious coexistence in higher education institutions where allowing the headscarf would lead to religious pressure, manipulation, orientation or polarization. Hence, the contested provision is regarded as a threat which may incite religious separatism.[71] This conclusion definitely blurs the militant stand of the secular state regarding religious symbols in the higher education institutions. The specificity of the *Headscarf I* judgment rests on the fact that it deals with a religious symbol attached to majority religion in a society. This point also represents the uniqueness of Turkey regarding the use and judicial elaboration of headscarf practices. The court found the solution by creating a non-religious sphere in higher education where the headscarf could not act as a symbol of religious pressure and, finally, does not disturb the public order. In *Headscarf II*, the Constitutional Court strengthened its position, since it ordered the exclusion of headscarfs from higher education by a rule of interpretation.[72] Here, the court has found a statutory amendment constitutional by an interpretative reservation, because as a neutral norm amendment stipulates 'free attire' in higher education as long as it is in conformity with 'the laws in force'. However, now and then, there is no law in force dealing with the case so that the conformity reference in the amendment was blank. The court concluded that such a provision is constitutional under the reservation of its previous interpretation in *Headscarf I*, which does not allow veiling in higher education institutions.[73] Compared with *Headscarf I*, *Headscarf II* represents a more active stand enhancing a militant approach for the interpretation of laws which seemingly comply with secular requirements. In *Leyla Şahin v. Turkey*, the ECHR first recognized the headscarf ban within the 'margin of appreciation' of Turkey and then upheld the proportionality of the restriction.[74]

The Constitutional Court's approach to the headscarf problem has been approved and implemented for students and public servants in administrative case law constantly.[75] Moreover, the High Administrative Court has not permitted headscarf photographs of female journalists on 'yellow press cards' which are

70 E. 1989/1, K. 1989/12, K.t. 7 March 1989, AYMKD 25, 152–153, 157–158.

71 E. 1989/1, K. 1989/12, K.t. 7 March 1989, AYMKD 25, 153.

72 E. 1990/36, K. 1991/8, K.t. 9 April 1991, AYMKD 27/1, 306.

73 For extensive critics of Headscarf II, see Erdoğan 2002: 119–21.

74 ECHR, *Leyla Şahin v. Turkey*, App. Nr. 44774/98. 10 November 2005; for critics, see Belelieu 2006: 609.

75 For example, Danıştay 8. Dairesi, E. 2004/837, K. 2005/3796, 27 September 2005; E. 2002/17, K. 2003/3161, 26.6.2003; E. 1998/5912, K. 2000/4951, 27 June 2000; for previous case law see Danıştay 8. Dairesi, E. 1983/207, K. 1984/330, 23 February 1984; E. 1986/105, K. 1987/63, 12 February 1987; E. 1987/128, K. 1987/486, 16 November 1987.

granted by the Prime Ministry and give specific privileges in public institutions.[76] Referring to European Commission of Human Rights (ECommHR) decisions concerning headscarf photographs on university diplomas, the court holds that journalists perform 'public service' which should be in conformity with the requirements of the secular state and the principle of equality. Questioning a teacher's headscarf in 2006, the High Administrative Court esteemed the secular state and Atatürk's principles as prescribed among the aims of education in the Fundamental Law on National Education.[77] The plaintiff was appointed as director to a kindergarten;[78] however, she has been recalled through an administrative decision and appointed to a primary school as a teacher for child development. According to the testimonies of witnesses, she occasionally wore a headscarf at her previous school, on the way to the school and while leaving the school. The court also referred to similar attitudes of her in the past which led to disciplinary sanctions and to the fact that she would be a role model for kindergarten children who are not able to draw logical conclusions. As emphasized by the court, her attitudes are to be accepted unlawful even if she wore the headscarf while she was 'arriving and leaving the school'. This demonstrates that – in sensible cases, such as the protection of kindergarten children – necessities of the secular state prevail, and a 'potential threat' could be eliminated.

The headscarf issue was crucial in the dissolution of the *Fazilet Partisi* in 2001, since, at that time, it has been made visible as a strong political symbol by a parliamentarian who entered the General Assembly with her headscarf to take her oath. Here, the Constitutional Court has reiterated a discriminating effect, religious pressure and intolerance attached to the headscarf.[79] Finally, 'veiling' has been also discussed for founding members of a political party. In a warning order in 2002, the Constitutional Court differentiates between the status of founding members and Members of Parliament.[80] It accepts specific attire limitations only for Members of Parliament on the ground that parliamentarian status amounts to public duty in a public sphere.

76 Danıştay 1. Dairesi, E. 1999/98, K. 1999/116, 12 July 1999.

77 Danıştay 2. Dairesi, E. 2004/366, K. 2005/366, 26 October 2005. This judgment was claimed to be the reason of an armed attack to Chamber II of the High Administrative Court on 17 May 2006, when one of the judges was murdered and others were injured.

78 In this specific case, the kindergarten was in a military zone, namely in Gölbaşı garrison. Before entering into the garrison, officials made an identity control and refused plaintiff's identity card including a photo with headscarf. Since she could not submit any other identity card without a headscarf, she was not able to reach her workplace. As soon as the District Directorate for National Education was informed, an investigation was initiated. The Directorate ordered a disciplinary sanction and offered to appoint her as a child development teacher to a primary school.

79 E. 1999/2, K. 2001/2, K.t. 22 June 2001, AYMKD 37/2, 1494.

80 E. 2001/8, K. 2002/9, K.t. 9 January 2002, AYMKD 38/2, 816.

Entry Into Public Service, Security Investigations and Oath for Loyalty to the Constitution

Article 70 of the constitution confers the right to enter the public service only on citizens. It prescribes that no criteria other than the qualifications for the office concerned shall be taken into consideration for recruitment into public service. However, this would not mean that security investigation and archive research procedure for candidates of public service is excluded. According to the Law on Security Investigation (1994) and the implementing act of the Council of Ministers (2000), different categories of persons could be subject to procedure of security investigation and archive research.[81] Those are candidates who will work at Turkish Armed Forces; police and intelligence services; and criminal enforcement institutions and prisons. Persons who work at units and departments of ministries as well as public institutions and entities with secrecy degrees are also subject to security investigation and archive research. Both the law and the implementing act on security investigation and archive research presume that these persons have information and documents which may endanger or violate state security, national and international interests, national existence and integrity, if unauthorized persons would receive them. The implementing act defines secrecy degrees and determines the investigation authorities as General Directorate of Security (Police), local authorities of central administration and National Institution for Intelligence, who could carry out security investigation for different groups of public services. The principles of investigation are laid down in the relevant administrative act implementing the Law on Security Investigation. Security investigation and archive research covers following information: the candidate's identity and its verification, his or her citizenship status and change of it, criminal and intelligence records, records of 'destructive activities and challenges' against the Law on Crimes against Atatürk and principles and reforms of Atatürk, drug, alcohol and gambling addictions and attitudes conflicting with morals and manners which effect the candidate's dignity and performance, reasons and real aspects of the candidate's relations to foreigners, especially to citizens of enemy or presumably enemy states and the candidate's capacity of keeping secrets. Destructive activities are defined in a specific provision as activities aiming at impairing the indivisible integrity of state with its territory and nation, endangering the existence of the state and the republic as well as destroying fundamental rights and freedoms.[82] Regarding the transparency of documents obtained by security investigations and archive

---

81 See the Law on Security Investigation, Restitution of Rights for Public Servants Removed from the Office or Candidates Refused to be Employed and Amendments regarding Martial Law Nr. 1402 (RG Sy: 22100, 3 November 1994); By-Law on Security Investigation and Archive Research (RG Sy. 24018, 12 April 2000).

82 Even though investigation and research cover only destructive activities in Article 11 of the By-Law on Security Investigation and Research, Article 4 on definition of terms explains both 'destructive and separation activities'.

research, the Law on Access to Information (2003) can be regarded as a guarantee. It provides that access to information extends to civil and military intelligence documents, if they are capable of effecting professional honour and work life of the person concerned.[83] In any case, investigation extends to the 'environment' of the candidate concerned. The High Administrative Court interpreted 'environment' as including social relations of the candidate and concluded that the extension of investigation to the 'environment' of the candidate is not in conflict with constitutional guarantees, such as personal criminal responsibility.[84]

Security investigations concerning employees in the private sector or excessive applications, such as reporting of citizens, according to their ideological positions as well as their 'sympathy' to the state were well-known 'dark practices' which are extensively criticized because they violate constitutional guarantees, for example, the right to privacy and the freedom of thought and opinion.[85] In 1988, the insecure nature of security investigation was brought before the High Administrative Court in a striking case where a former high-level soldier, namely General Staff, sued the Prime Ministry for the conduct of security investigation carried by the National Institution for Intelligence. The High Administrative Court ordered compensation because the relevant intelligence report violated personal rights of the former General Staff.

The loyalty of public servants to the constitution as a duty and responsibility arises from the Law on Public Servants.[86] Besides loyalty to the constitution, the public servants' oath also refers to specific values and principles, even though some of those are inherent features of the constitution. Accordingly, loyalty extends to principles and reforms of Atatürk and 'Turkish nationalism' in the constitution. Regarding 'commitments' of public servants, oath taking includes the application of laws in accordance with the principles of neutrality and equality. Impartiality and commitment to the state is particularly stipulated, so that specific prohibitions for public servants are prescribed. Political and ideological expressions and activities as well as discriminative conduct are prescribed as incompatible with impartiality. Public servants are obliged to protect the state's interests in any case and avoid activities which endanger the state's independence and integrity, or contradict the constitution and the laws. Among others, violating the following prohibitions lead to removal from the office absolutely. Being a member of a political party that is disturbing peace and order with ideological and political aims; printing, developing and distributing ideological; political manifestoes, plates; etc., hiding wanted persons listed as perpetrators of ideological and political activities at the work

83 See Article 18 of Law on Access to Information; for critical remarks on 'veil of secrecy' as to previous legislation, see Tanör 1994: 36.

84 Danıştay 1. Dairesi, E. 2003/15, K. 2003/40, 25 March 2003; see also Article 38(6) of the constitution: 'Criminal responsibility shall be personal'.

85 For analysing security investigation as 'legal perversion', see especially Aksoy 1988: 89; Nebiler 1988: 16; for examples of 'dark practices', see also Tanör 1994: 32–8.

86 See especially Article 6 and Article 7 of the Law on Public Servants.

place; disclosure of secret documents with prior authorization; and infringement of the Law on Crimes against Atatürk.[87] Regarding the secular state and the military service, European human rights supervision seems to approve the loyalty approach of Turkey in cases of religious extremism. The ECHR held that the state may decide to impose on its serving or future public servants the duty to refrain from taking part in the Islamic fundamentalist movement, whose goal and plan of action is to bring about the pre-eminence of religious rules. This has been conceived as a part of its role as the neutral and impartial organizer of the exercise of religious beliefs.[88]

Constitutional Bans Regarding Political Rights and Deprivation

Indications of a militant democracy in Turkey could be easily observed in respect of political rights. Prescribing conditions for eligibility of being a Member of Parliament, Article 76 of the constitution, as amended in 2002, states:

> persons … who have been convicted for offences related to disclosure of state secrets, of involvement in terrorist activities and incitement and encouragement of such activities, shall not be elected deputies, even if they have been pardoned.[89]

Among others, the conviction for terrorist activity prevents also a membership of a political party.[90] As an eligibility criterion of the Law on Political Parties, party members who have been convicted of terrorist activity could be objected before the Constitutional Court which may issue a specific precautionary decision, called 'warning'.[91] A succeeding trial of offences which prevent eligibility of being a

87 See Article 125 of the Law on Public Servants.

88 See ECHR, *Kalaç v. Turkey*, App. Nr. 20704/92, 1 July 1997, para. 28; see also ECommHR, 14524/89 Yanaşık, 6 January 1993, DR 74, 14.

89 See also Article 11 of Law on Parliamentary Election. As a result of constitutional ban before the 2002 amendment, the right to be elected could not be exercised in case of conviction of offences as to 'ideological and anarchist activities'. This meant that conviction of a hate crime was an obstacle for candidacy of membership in the Parliament. The amendment enabled the candidacy of Prime Minister, Recep Tayyip Erdoğan, who has been constitutionally banned because of his previous conviction of a hate crime. He has been elected in fact after general elections and after the constitutional amendment, when in a district of south-eastern Anatolia polling was annulled and election was necessarily renewed. The overwhelming majority of Erdoğan's Party proposed and supported the amendment, and Erdoğan became Prime Minister. Bans regarding 'ideological activities' even in cases of pardons were occasionally criticized, see for a proposal Teziç and Yüzbaşıoğlu 2001: 37; for critics concerning the vague and broad nature of term 'ideological activity', see Özbudun and Yazıcı 2004: 27.

90 See Article 11 of the Law on Political Parties.

91 See Article 104 of the Law on Political Parties; see also E. 2001/12, K. 2002/8, K.t. 9 January 2002, AYMKD 38/2, 800; E. 2001/8, K. 2002/9, K.t. 9 January 2002, AYMKD 38/2, 807.

Member of Parliament may also lead to the loss of membership in the Parliament. Article 84(2) of the constitution orders that loss of membership through a final judicial sentence shall take effect after the final court decision in the matter has been communicated to the plenary of the National Assembly. Moreover, the parliamentary status of a Member of Parliament, whose statements and activities are cited in a final judgment by the Constitutional Court as having caused the permanent dissolution of his party, shall terminate on the date when the decision in question and its justifications are published in the Official Gazette.[92]

Among exceptions of parliamentary immunity, the misuse of fundamental rights has been specifically emphasized. Parliamentary immunity, which protects Members of Parliament against arrests, detentions, interrogations and trials, cannot be raised in cases of misuse of fundamental rights as prohibited in Article 14 of the constitution, if an investigation has been initiated before the election.

Neither a specific procedure nor a specific authority is prescribed in the constitution regarding the deprivation of political rights. In fact, the Consultative Assembly of the 1982 Constitution proposed deprivation as a sanction in the case of misuse of rights which could be ordered by the courts.[93] Even though this was rejected during constitution-making process, the deprivation of rights became subject of criminal legislation and the Law on Political Parties. Article 95 provides a kind of 'automatic' deprivation: members of a political party, whose statements and activities have caused the dissolution of the party, are not allowed to be member, founder, executive and controller of any other political party for five years beginning from the publication date of the Constitutional Court's dissolution judgment. Such persons cannot take place in candidate lists of the political parties.[94] The Turkish Criminal Code prescribes deprivation of political rights or status as a legal consequence of premeditated crimes which require imprisonment. In such cases, political rights or status to be deprived are specifically stipulated in Article 53(1a, b and d): public service; membership in the Parliament; all kinds of service and official posts depending on election or appointment that are determined by the state and local administrative units as well as institutions and entities reviewed and supervised by them, the eligibility to elect and to be elected, and the exercise of other political rights, being executive and controller of a political party.[95] The deprivation of rights as a consequence of criminal law ends with the execution of the sentence. In contrast with the previous Turkish Criminal Code, the present code (2004) does not prescribe any judicial procedure on 'restitution of prohibited

92 See Article 84(5) of the constitution.

93 Article 13(1) of the Draft Constitution, Danışma Meclisi, S. Sayısı 166, Türkiye Cumhuriyeti Anayasa Tasarısı (1/463).

94 For problems of proportionality see ECHR, *Kavakçı v. Turkey*, App. Nr. 71907/01, *Sılay v. Turkey*, App. Nr. 8691/02, *Ilıcak v. Turkey*, App. Nr. 15394/02, 5 April 2007.

95 In face of the fact that exercise of political rights is subjected to deprivation generally in Article 53(1b), it is not obvious why Article 53(1a) and (1d) stipulates deprivation of specific political rights.

rights after execution of the sentence' depending on time limits and good manner, since it does not provide that specific rights could be deprived for an indefinite period.[96]

Militant Devices for Political Parties

Drastic and Less Drastic Devices: Dissolution of Political Parties, Warning Order and Deprivation of State Aid

The constitution recognizes in Article 68 that political parties, as 'indispensable elements of democratic political life', can be formed without prior permission, while they are under obligation to pursue their activities in accordance with the provisions set forth in the constitution and the law. Boundaries for statutes and programmes as well as the activities of political parties are clearly identified in Article 68(4). They must not be in conflict with the independence of the state, its indivisible integrity with its territory and nation, human rights, the principles of equality and the rule of law, the sovereignty of the nation, and the principles of democratic and secular republic. Political parties cannot aim to protect or establish class or group dictatorship or dictatorship of any kind, nor are they allowed to incite citizens to crime. The dissolution of political parties is decided finally by the Constitutional Court after the filing of a suit by the office of the Chief Public Prosecutor of the Republic. The permanent dissolution of a political party is to be decided when it is established that the statute and programme of the political party violate the constitutional boundaries regulated in Article 68(4). The decision to dissolve a political party permanently conducting activities violating constitutional boundaries may be rendered only when the Constitutional Court determines that the party in question has become a 'centre for such unconstitutional conducts'.[97] To clarify the limits of party dissolution, the 2001 constitutional amendments have explicitly defined such conducts. 'Unconstitutional conducts' must be committed by party members and supported explicitly or implicitly by the organs or representatives of the party: the general congress, the leader of the party, the main decision-making or administrative organs, or the general assembly or administrative assembly of the parliamentary fraction. In cases where such conducts are committed directly by the above-mentioned party organs deliberately, the party becomes a centre of unconstitutional activities as well. Until the constitutional amendments in

96 The High Board on Elections confirmed in various occasions that 'restitution of prohibited rights' as a legal institution removes constitutional barriers regarding the conditions of eligibility to be elected in cases where specific types of criminal conviction prevent candidacy for membership in the Parliament, see citations for relevant decisions, Bilir 2001: 61 footnote 219.

97 For historical and critical analysis of 'centre', see Hakyemez 2000: 243–7.

2001, the judicial appreciation of the Constitutional Court was decisive for the evaluation of constitutional activities where it could apply judge-made criterion and tests, such as the 'clear and present danger', according to its legal choice. Therefore, it has been assumed that the conditionality of becoming a centre as provided by 2001 amendment would make it difficult to apply the 'clear and present danger test', even though it aims to harden party dissolution through limiting judge's appreciation (Öden 2003: 192). Indeed, conditionality might have a reversed effect since dissolution will be necessary when the conditions are fulfilled. If the court does not integrate the 'clear and present danger test' in its future jurisprudence constantly despite its ignorance in 2001 amendment, this point could be part of a potential amendment (Öden 2003: 193).

The decision of dissolution is to be taken by a three-fifths majority of the regular members of the court. Instead of dissolving a political party, the Constitutional Court may rule the concerned party to be deprived of state aid wholly or in part with respect to 'intensity of the conducts'. The deprivation of state aid has been provided by 2001 amendments as a less drastic measure in order to establish a gradual system combating unconstitutional parties.[98] Depending on the 'intensity of the conducts', the deprivation order should engage careful application of the principle of proportionality to strike the right balance where the 'clear and present danger test' would have a decisive role (Öden 2003: 172). Taking into account terminological inconsistency in the constitution, 'conducts' are to be interpreted as including not only activities, but also statutes and programmes, according to the liberal spirit of the 2001 amendment (Can 2005: 152; Öden 2003: 108 footnote 8).[99] In that case, unconstitutional statutes and programmes would not lead to dissolution automatically. However, the deprivation order could be effective only in cases where a political party is entitled to state aid. Therefore, in cases where the party is not eligible for state aid, a specific order of declaration has been suggested that is not explicitly provided by the constitution (Can 2005: 175). This would be a judge-made order which is merely of declarative and informative nature; it could not prevent a file of dissolution in future. In fact, it could be a proper solution to regulate a gradual approach – warning, deprivation or pecuniary sanctions and dissolution – more explicit.[100] The Venice Commission has proposed, at the first stage, an application of less radical measures to protect the free and democratic order instead of dissolution or prohibition as a particularly far reaching one.[101]

98 See also Article 102(1) and (3) of the Law on Political Parties.

99 See also Article 101(2) of the Law on Political Parties.

100 See Hakyemez 2001; Sağlam 1999: 181. For unconstitutionality of deprivation in cases where the party does not fulfil the requirements of warning order, see E. 2008/5, K. 2009/81, K.t. 11 June 2009, RG Sy. 27281, 7 July 2009.

101 Guidelines on prohibition and dissolution of political parties and analogous measures, CDL-INF (2000) 001, Strasbourg, 10 January 2000.

Besides deficiencies of deprivation, the dissolution of political parties on grounds of their statutes and programmes represents a delicate issue. As regards statutes and programmes, ECHR explicitly stated in *TBKP v. Turkey* and *ÖZDEP v. Turkey* previously:

> a measure as drastic as the immediate and permanent dissolution of the *TBKP*, ordered before its activities had even started and coupled with a ban barring its leaders from discharging any other political responsibility, is disproportionate to the aim pursued and consequently unnecessary in a democratic society.[102]

> ÖZDEP was definitively dissolved with immediate effect, its assets were liquidated and transferred *ipso jure* to the Treasury and its leaders were banned from carrying on certain similar political activities. Such drastic measures may be taken only in the most serious cases.[103]

A party which has been dissolved permanently, cannot be founded under another name. The members, including the founders of a political party whose acts or statements have caused the party to be dissolved permanently cannot be founders, members, directors or supervisors in any other party for a period of five years. This political exclusion begins from the date of publication of the Constitutional Court's final decision which permanently dissolves the party. Neither parliamentarian immunity nor procedures of parliamentarian review, for example, investigation, impedes the dissolution.[104]

Article 104 of the Law on Political Parties provides a warning order in cases where imperative norms other than those leading to dissolution are infringed, for example, in case of the use of forbidden signs or names. The warning order could be issued by the Constitutional Court at request of the Chief Public Prosecutor.

At this stage, observations may be twofold. Even though the constitutional reforms of 1995 and 2001 as well as further amendments to the Law on Political Parties aim at providing a more liberal and accessible approach to the right of political association in Turkey, the complicated and extensive nature of legal limitations are still remarkable. Dissolution grounds are extensively elaborated and applied by the Turkish Constitutional Court on various occasions. Since its pattern of constitutional interpretation was challenged before the ECHR in landmark cases, the Turkish experience with the concept of 'militant democracy' – its approval or disapproval by the ECHR as well – gains specific importance to identify the limits of ideological pluralism in Europe. Except for *Refah Partisi*, the Turkish

102 ECHR, *United Communist Party of Turkey v. Turkey* (TBKP), 133/1996/752/951, 30 January 1998, para. 61.

103 ECHR, *ÖZDEP v. Turkey*, App. Nr. 23885/94, 8 December 1999.

104 See *Refah Partisi*, E. 1997/1, K. 1998/1, K.t. 16 January 1998, AYMKD 34/2, 1019–1020; Öden 2003: 114–15; Sağlam 1999: 141–3.

dissolutions were found contrary to the European Convention of Human Rights.[105] Here, *TBKP v. Turkey* represents an extreme case since it was dissolved not only on a material ground, the unitary state, but also on the purely formal ground that the TBKP had included the word 'communist' in its name, contrary to Article 96 (3) of the Law on Political Parties. The ECHR considered that a political party's choice of name cannot in principle justify a measure as drastic as dissolution, in the absence of other relevant and sufficient circumstances.[106] Filing a dissolution case against the *Turkish Communist Party* in 2003, the Chief Public Prosecutor raised a plea of unconstitutionality in regard of the provision prohibiting the word 'communist' in the title of the party.[107] The plea referred to the constitutional case law in *Socialist Party*.[108] In this revolutionary ruling, the Constitutional Court differentiated 'class sovereignty' and 'class government' and only the former was considered as unconstitutional since it amounts to class dictatorship, excluding a change of government through free and competitive elections.

Dissolution in Constitutional Case Law: Mighty Questions of Balancing

As the utmost applied instrument of militant democracy in Turkey, the dissolution is conceived as an indispensable constitutional institution which is to be respected by the legislator. The Constitutional Court does not only see its application necessary if 'political parties address to destroy basic democratic order', or if 'they address to endanger it considerably', but also limits the appreciation of legislator preventing or hardening dissolution through statutory amendments. Statutory rules should, in any case, avail the court to establish and sustain a delicate balance between prohibitions of political parties, on the one hand, and freedom of expression and association, on the other. It is striking that the court has emphasized the interdependence and interaction between political parties and democratic order, even though the constitution only refers to the indispensable nature of the latter. Accordingly, the main function of political parties in the formation of democracies cannot be denied, but their reason of existence is, in turn, the liberal democratic

105 For a summary of European case law regarding party dissolutions in Turkey, see Koçak and Örücü 2003: 407–18. After *restitutio in integrum* was provided in the 2003 amendments regarding the judgments of the ECHR, some of the parties have made applications before the Constitutional Court. TBKP's application for renewal of the trial before 2003 was refused by the Constitutional Court. The court refused applications after 2003 on merits, see TBKP, E. 2003/6, K. 2008/4, K.t. 8 January 2008, RG Sy. 26824, 22 March 2008; HEP, E. 2003/1, K. 2008/2 and ÖZDEP, E. 2003/2, K. 2008/3, K.t. 8 January 2008, RG Sy. 26895, 3 June 2008; Akartürk 2008: 294.

106 ECHR, *United Communist Party of Turkey v. Turkey* (TBKP), 133/1996/752/951, 30 January 1998, para. 54.

107 See S. Kanadoğlu 2004: 390–93; despite the 2003 amendments, the relevant case is still pending. For the same plea and its rejection as regards warning order, see TKP, E. 2001/11, K. 2002/7, K.t. 9 January 2002, AYMKD 38/2, 795–796.

108 Sosyalist Parti, E. 1988/2, K. 1988/1, 8 December 1998, AYMKD 24.

regime.[109] Regarding the aims of political parties, the court's approach refers to both 'democratic state and democratic society', not only for statutes and programmes, but also – emphatically – for any type of activities and political discourse.[110] 'Danger' as a component of court's adjudication has been occasionally taken into consideration in dissolution cases both for statute and programmes and activities. Regarding the unitary and secular state, judicial sensitivity of danger becomes visible in references to 'incitement to hatred, hostility or prohibited activities' – for example, *Sosyalist Parti*, *Emek Partisi*, *Refah Partisi*, *Fazilet Partisi* and *HADEP* – or anti-laic activities destroying the public order, which create anxiety and threat for the other members of society, for example, *Refah Partisi*.[111] Before the constitutional amendment in 2001, the court has explicitly referred to 'present and visible danger' (*Sosyalist Birlik Partisi*, *Demokrasi ve Değişim Partisi* and *Fazilet Partisi*) or an increasing danger potential under Turkey's specific conditions (*Demokrasi ve Değişim Partisi* and *Fazilet Partisi*).[112] In the *Fazilet Partisi* decision, the support of the party leader and the parliamentarian group for the presence of a Member of Parliament wearing a headscarf is defined as 'qualified violation of the secular state that has a specific place and significance in Turkish Republic experienced in its history theocratic state'.[113] Here, the potential election success of *Fazilet Partisi* was also considered to determine the 'high danger' for secular and democratic order. In the *HADEP* case, the court concentrates on 'solidarity' and the 'strong link' of the party with the *Partiya Karkerên Kurdistan* (PKK), and interprets the dangerous activities of the party in conjunction with intense and constant terrorist activities of PKK, which are a serious, present and great danger.[114] The observance of Turkey's specific circumstances by the Constitutional Court is legitimate, since the Venice Commission admits that the general situation

109 E. 2000/86, K. 2000/50, K.t. 12 December 2000, AYMKD 36/2, 901.

110 *Fazilet Partisi*, E. 1999/2, K. 2001/2, K.t. 22 June 2001, AYMKD 37/2, 1496–1497.

111 *Sosyalist Parti*, E. 1991/1, K. 1992/2, K.t. 10 July 1992, AYMKD 28/2, 794; *Emek Partisi*, E. 1996/1, K. 1997/1, K.t. 14 February 1997, AYMKD 34/2, 760; *Refah Partisi*, E. 1997/1, K. 1998/1, K.t. 16 January 1998, AYMKD 34/2, 1029–1032, 1039, 1041, 1044, 1048; *Fazilet Partisi*, E. 1999/2, K. 2001/2, K.t. 22 June 2001, AYMKD 37/2, 1498; *Halkın Demokrasi Partisi*, E. 1999/1, K. 2003/1, K.t. 13 March 2003, AYMKD 39/2, 1101.

112 *Sosyalist Birlik Partisi*, E. 1993/4, K. 1995/1, K.t. 19 July 1995, AYMKD 33/2, 635–636; *Demokrasi ve Değişim Partisi*, E. 1995/1, K. 1996/1, K.t. 19 March 1996, AYMKD 33/2, 724; *Fazilet Partisi*, E. 1999/2, K. 2001/2, K.t. 22 June 2001, AYMKD 37/2, 1498–1499.

113 *Fazilet Partisi*, E. 1999/2, K. 2001/2, K.t. 22 June 2001, AYMKD 37/2, 1498–1499.

114 *Halkın Demokrasi Partisi*, E. 1999/1, K. 2003/1, K.t. 13 March 2003, AYMKD 39/2, 1101; for earlier comments to the 'normalization' potential of *HADEP*, see Güney 2002: 135.

in a country is an important factor for evaluation.[115] Nevertheless, the court has, on various occasions, concentrated on the 'final or real purpose' of the political party rather than activities, for example, *Sosyalist Parti*, *Halkın Emek Partisi*, *Demokrasi Partisi* and *Fazilet Partisi*.[116] Without any doubt, the 'final or real purpose' criterion is not constitutionally eligible alone. For a proper judicial appreciation, qualitative and quantitative features of activities should overwhelm (Öden 2003: 156).

However, the critical discussion regarding constitutional values relates to their concretization in the Law on Political Parties, which was originally made in 1983 during the military intervention period, and has been exempted from constitutional review until 2001 by a specific constitutional clause, provisionary Article 15(3). The Law on Political Parties – with its exceptional constitutional immunity for 18 years – raises the question whether it implements constitutional values or if it extends constitutional limits (Can 2005: 142–3; Hakyemez 2000: 216; Koçak 2002: 144; Öden 2003: 121–2; Özbudun 2002b: 60–61; Sağlam 1997: 377–80, 1999: 122–6, 172, 2000: 244–8; Tanör 1997: 38–9; Turhan 1996: 418; Uygun 1992: 75–6, 2000: 267–8). Since those values – as dissolution grounds – are limited and cannot be extended or redefined by ordinary legislation,[117] this point is of specific importance for constitutional supremacy. First, as regards the 'indivisible integrity of state with its territory and nation', the Law on Political Parties goes beyond territorial and national integrity and prohibits to suggest or to defend the existence of minorities or to create minorities through promoting their language and culture.[118] Second, in respect of the secular state, political parties are not allowed to challenge the constitutional status of the Department of Religious Affairs (DRA), this is its position in central government, according to Article 89 of the Law on Political Parties.[119] The constitutional interpretation regarding

115 Guidelines on prohibition and dissolution of political parties and analogous measures, CDL-INF (2000) 001, Strasbourg, 10 January 2000.

116 *Sosyalist Parti*, E. 1991/2, K. 1992/1, K.t. 10 July 1992, AYMKD 28/2, 810–811; *Halkın Emek Partisi*, E. 1992/1, K. 1993/1, K.t. 14 July 1993, AYMKD 29/2, 1177–1179.

117 *Demokratik Barış Hareketi*, E. 1996/3, K. 1997/3, K.t. 22 May 1997, AYMKD 36/2, 1023; preliminary question regarding *Türkiye Sosyalist İşçi Partisi*, E. 2003/21, K. 2003/13, K.t. 1 April 2003, AYMKD 39/1, 468.

118 Article 81 of the Law on Political Parties: 'Political parties shall not (a) assert that there exist within the territory of the Turkish Republic any national minorities based on differences relating to national or religious culture, membership of a religious sect, race or language; or (b) aim to destroy national unity by protecting, promoting or disseminating a language or culture other than Turkish, to create minorities on the territory of the Turkish Republic or to engage activities in that way …'. For the abrogation of Article 81, see Üskül 2006: 204–205.

119 The constitution does not allow the establishment of autonomous religious communities endowed with rights and duties. Instead, the DRA is placed in central government (Article 136). It should exercise its duties in accordance with the principles of secularism, removed from all political views and ideas, and aiming at national solidarity and integrity, see Özbudun 2006: 96.

the application of the Law on Political Parties is not clear and stable enough to determine the unconstitutionality of such statutory concretization. Concerning the minority question, the Constitutional Court did not find unconstitutionality pleas for a similar provision of the previous legislation serious to review.[120] Regarding the Department of Religious Affairs, the court in 1997 ignored the relevant provision of the Law on Political Parties and directly applied the constitutional dissolution grounds to reject the dissolution.[121] Astonishingly, in 1999, it did not hesitate to reconsider political challenges against the provision concerned.[122]

In dissolution cases, it is easily discernible that the protection of the unitary state – with an emphasis on minority interpretation – and the secular state plays a central role. Hence, both could be characterized as mainstream features and 'hardcore principles' identifying Turkish dissolution practice. However, the case law on the protection of the secular state seems more solid and in conceptual integrity, compared with the adjudication concerning the unitary state. The prevention of racism and the protection of equality could also be observed as accompanying grounds of dissolutions in case law, despite the hegemony of 'hardcore principles'. Among constitutional values, the unconstitutionality of a party in respect of the rule of law needs further elaboration. Here, a pending case concerning the *Democratic People's Party (DEHAP)* might offer an opportunity for concretization. The case deals with the claims that the party did not obey organizational rules as to eligibility for general elections and made election fraud misleading the High Board of Elections.

Regarding the unitary state, the Constitutional Court approves that national and territorial integrity covers the prohibition of creating minorities as well as regionalism and racism, and the protection of equality.[123] The court defines citizenship as an institution which is a legal bond reflecting a unifying and integrating nationalism without any denial of ethnic origins: 'according to the constitution, not the race, but belonging to national community is politically significant'. Here, the court endeavors to prevent discrimination by challenging the conceptual category or identification as a minority in a multiethnic society, since it regards different ethnicities as parts of majority that build 'Turkish nation' through the bond of citizenship.[124] In the court's view, compared with the

---

120 See *Türkiye İşçi Partisi*, E. 1971/3, K. 1971/3, K.t. 20 July 1971, AYMKD 9, 103–108; *Türkiye Emekçi Partisi*, E. 1979/1, K. 1980/1, K.t. 8 May 1980, AYMKD 18, 25–34; 25-34; HAK-PAR, E. 2002/1, K. 2008/1, K.t. 29 January 2008, RG Sy. 26923, 1 July 2008.

121 *Demokratik Barış Hareketi Partisi*, E. 1996/3, K. 1997/3, K.t. 22 May 1997, AYMKD 36/2, 978–1033.

122 *Demokratik Kitle Partisi*, E. 1997/2, K. 1999/1, K.t. 26 February 1999, AYMKD 37/2, 719–900.

123 *Halkın Demokrasi Partisi*, E. 1999/1, K. 2003/1, K.t. 13 March 2003, AYMKD 39/2, 1100.

124 *Halkın Demokrasi Partisi*, E. 1999/1, K. 2003/1, K.t. 13 March 2003, AYMKD 39/2, 1100; *Sosyalist Parti*, E. 1991/2, K. 1992/1, K.t. 10 July 1992, AYMKD 28/2, 802.

position of the majority, trying to become a minority is a less favourable position which would lead to separatist movements and threaten national cohesion and historical solidarity among 'citizens with Kurdish origin, Turks from different tribes and people of other origins', the constituents of Turkish nation.[125] Therefore, definitions or dichotomies, such as 'Kurdish nation – Turkish nation' are regarded as 'racist divisions' changing citizenship notion.[126] In the *Emek Partisi* case, where the division of 'Turks and Kurds' is regarded as separatism and racism within the unitary state, the court specifically refers to 'incitement, contribution and support to inconvenient activities'.[127] Emphasizing sociological and historical facts, Turkish is defined not only as the official language, but also as the language of culture and education as well as the common instrument of communication.[128] Repeating its tripartite formula – 'uniformity of nation, unitary of state, integrity of territory' – the court does not accept the existence of minorities other than provided in the Lausanne Peace Treaty and in a specific agreement between Turkey and Bulgaria.[129] Since the court's citizenship notion is non-ethnic and non-regional, it definitely rejects 'religious, cultural and ethnic privileges as specific rights other than human rights' for unity.[130]

These assumptions on minority build a rigid part of constitutional case law. However, the interpretation of the expressions concerning the reform of central and local administration represents a more liberal and less dogmatic approach. In the *Demokratik Kitle Partisi* decision, the court seems departing its absolute approach rejecting 'all types of federalism, regional autonomy and administrations of self-government'.[131] Even though the *Demokratik Kitle Partisi* proposed a minimization of central government, the transformation of local assemblies to local Parliaments and a power extension for local administration with reference to Spain and France, the court considers those aims as efforts 'making local authorities more effective',

– For an assessment that the transgression of the cultural into the political is deemed by the court as a threat, see Kogacioglu 2003.

125 *TBKP*, E. 1990/1, K. 1991/1, K.t. 16 July 1991, AYMKD 27/2, 959.

126 For example, *TBKP*, E. 1990/1, K. 1991/1, K.t. 16 July 1991, AYMKD 27/2, 964; *Sosyalist Parti*, E. 1991/2, K. 1992/1, K.t. 10 July 1992, AYMKD 28/2, 816; *Sosyalist Birlik Partisi*, E. 1993/4, K. 1995/1, K.t. 19 July 1995, AYMKD 33/2, 635–636; *Emek Partisi*, E. 1996/1, K. 1997/1, K.t. 14 February 1997, AYMKD 34/2, 752; *Demokratik Kitle Partisi*, E. 1997/2, K. 1999/1, K.t. 26 February 1999, AYMKD 37/2, 896.

127 *Emek Partisi*, E. 1996/1, K. 1997/1, K.t. 14 February 1997, AYMKD 34/2, 760.

128 *Sosyalist Parti*, E. 1991/2, K. 1992/1, K.t. 10 July 1992, AYMKD 28/2, 808.

129 *TBKP*, E. 1990/1, K. 1991/1, K.t. 16 July 1991, AYMKD 27/2, 961.

130 *Sosyalist Parti*, E. 1991/2, K. 1992/1, K.t. 10 July 1992, AYMKD 28/2, 803; *Halkın Emek Partisi*, E. 1992/1, K. 1993/1, K.t. 14 July 1993, AYMKD 29/2, 1163; to the strong connection of unity and democracy in constitutional case law, see Kogacioglu 2004: 453.

131 *Halkın Emek Partisi*, E. 1992/1, K. 1993/1, K.t. 14 July 1993, AYMKD 29/2, 1167; *Emek Partisi*, E. 1996/1, K. 1997/1, K.t. 14 February 1997, AYMKD 34/2, 751.

but not as a challenge against the unitary state.[132] At last, in the *HADEP* decision constitutional obligations of political parties as regards the unitary state have been interpreted both in negative and positive terms. Accordingly, political parties should avoid activities which might deter territorial or national integrity directly or indirectly, and carry out their activities in a manner that would consolidate such integrity.[133]

The interpretation of the unitary state by the Constitutional Court has been found incompatible by the ECHR on various occasions.[134] European case law reveals that 'danger' or threatening facts are not conceived by the Constitutional Court and the ECHR in the same way. In the *ÖZDEP* case, the ECHR demands more eloquent and sufficient proofs of danger regarding the programme of the party, even though the rise of separatist terrorism was a discernible fact in that time.[135] In the *Socialist Party* case, the Turkish Government claimed that the party leader had justified the use of violent and terrorist methods, since he emphasized: 'The Kurdish people are standing up,' and

> the Kurd has proved himself through the fight of impoverished peasants by linking its destiny [to theirs]. By holding meetings with thousands of people in the towns and provinces, the Kurd had proved himself and broken down the barriers of fear.

Accepting that such phrases were addressed to citizens of Kurdish origin and constituted an invitation to them to rally together and assert certain political claims, the ECHR found no trace of any incitement to use violence or infringe the rules of democracy.[136] The *Socialist Party* case has made reference to the right to self-determination of the 'Kurdish nation' and its right to 'secede'. The ECHR reads such references in a broader context compared with the Constitutional Court. Thus, it concluded that the statements using such words do not encourage secession from Turkey 'but seek rather to stress that the proposed federal system could not come about without the Kurds' freely given consent, which should be expressed through a referendum'. The ECHR clarifies the 'norm of conflict':

---

132 *Demokratik Kitle Partisi*, E. 1997/2, K. 1999/1, K.t. 26 February 1999, AYMKD 37/2, 733, 746 and 893.

133 *Halkın Demokrasi Partisi*, E. 1999/1, K. 2003/1, K.t. 13 March 2003, AYMKD 39/2, 1100–1101; see TBKP, E. 1990/1, K. 1991/1, K.t. 16 July 1991, AYMKD 27/2, 954–965; *Halkın Emek Partisi*, E. 1992/1, K. 1993/1, K.t. 14 July 1993, AYMKD 29/2, 1156–1168, 1175; *Demokratik Kitle Partisi*, E. 1997/2, K. 1999/1, K.t. 26 February 1999, AYMKD 37/2, 890–891, 896.

134 For a conviction of Turkish militant democracy, see Çağlar and Çavuşoğlu 1999: 180.

135 ECHR, *ÖZDEP v. Turkey*, App. Nr. 23885/94, 8 November 1999, para. 46.

136 ECHR, *Socialist Party v. Turkey*, 20/1997/804/1007, 25 May 1998, para. 46.

> the fact that such a political program is considered incompatible with the current principles and structures of the Turkish State does not make it incompatible with the rules of democracy. It is of the essence of democracy to allow diverse political programs to be proposed and debated, even those that call into question the way a State is currently organized, *provided that they do not harm democracy itself*[137] [emphasis added].

The dissolution of the *Refah Partisi* represents a landmark case in Turkish constitutional case law not only for consolidation of the secular state, but also regarding the assessment of a call of violence for Islamic transformation. In the *Refah Partisi* decision, the Constitutional Court defined democracy as the antithesis of *Sharia*. The principle of secularism was considered as a sign of civic responsibility and impetus which enabled the Turkish Republic to move on from a Muslim religious community (*ümmet*) to a nation. In absolute conformity with its previous case law, the court elaborated the specific role and value of secularism for Turkish modernization and approved it as a hardcore democratic principle:

> Secularism, which has specificity for Turkey on the ground of historical differences, is a rule prescribed and protected by the constitution … With adherence to the principle of secularism, values based on reason and science replaced dogmatic values … Persons of different beliefs have desired to live together and have trusted in state by virtue of its egalitarian attitude towards them … Turkish revolution became meaningful through secularism … Secularism accelerated civilization by preventing religion from replacing scientific thought in the state's activities. *Secularism can not be limited to separation of state affairs and religion. It creates a vast environment of civilization, freedom and modernity. The philosophy of modernization of Turkey is based on a humanist ideal and living in a more human way.* Under a secular regime religion, which is a specific social institution, can have no authority over the constitution and governance of the state … Conferring on the state the right to supervise and review religious matters cannot be regarded as interference violating the requirements of democratic society … *Secularism, which is also the instrument of the transition to democracy, is Turkey's philosophy of life.* In a secular state, religious feelings cannot be associated with politics, public affairs and legal provisions. Such provisions are made not according to religious requirements and thought, but in the light of scientific data, with consideration for the needs of individuals and societies[138] [emphasis added].

---

137 ECHR, *Socialist Party v. Turkey*, 20/1997/804/1007, 25 May 1998, para. 47; ECHR, *ÖZDEP v. Turkey*, App. Nr. 23885/94, 8 November 1999, para. 41.

138 *Refah Partisi*, E. 1997/1, K. 1998/1, K.t. 16 January 1998, AYMKD 34/2, 1027–1029; see *Fazilet Partisi*, E. 1999/2, K. 2001/2, K.t. 22 June 2001, AYMKD 37/2, 1478–1480.

The Constitutional Court pointed out that the *Refah Partisi* had not reacted to offensive public statements and calls of violence in any way or sought to distance itself from them, or at least not before the commencement of the dissolution proceedings.[139] Affirming the dissolution of *Refah Partisi*, the ECHR, in fact, clarified the interaction between secular and democratic order where Turkish secularism served European understanding of democratic order.[140] Striking unconstitutional statements referring to bloodshed, violence and '*jihad*' ('holy war') for Islamic transformation which were made by the party leader, prominent Members of Parliament and a mayor elaborate that point definitely.[141] Besides, the ECHR held two types of activities as inconsistent with the system of EConvHR: (1) *Refah's* intention to set up a plurality of legal systems, leading to discrimination based on religious beliefs,[142] and (2) *Refah's* intention to apply *Sharia* to the internal or external relations of the Muslim community within the context of plurality of legal systems. The ECHR considered that such a societal model of legal plurality cannot be considered compatible with the Convention system. As regards *Sharia*, it emphatically stated that:

> when read together, the offending statements, which contain explicit references to the introduction of *sharia*, are difficult to reconcile with the fundamental principles of democracy, as conceived in the Convention taken as a whole. It is difficult to declare one's respect for democracy and human rights while at the same time supporting a regime based on *sharia*, which clearly diverges from Convention values, particularly with regard to its criminal law and criminal procedure, its rules on the legal status of women and the way it intervenes in all spheres of private and public life in accordance with religious precepts.[143]

---

139 *Refah Partisi*, E. 1997/1, K. 1998/1, K.t. 16 January 1998, AYMKD 34/2, 1042, 1054.

140 To problems of endorsing militant democracy at European level for hybrid democracies, see Harvey 2004.

141 For example, the statements of Necmettin Erbakan, Şevki Yılmaz, and Şükrü Karatepe: '*Refah* will come to power and a just order will be established. The question we must ask ourselves is whether this change will be violent or peaceful; whether it will entail bloodshed … Today Turkey must take a decision. *Refah Partisi* will establish a just order, this is certain' – 'Jihad is the name given to the quest for power for the advent of justice, for the propagation of justice and for glorification of Allah's Word. Allah did not see that task as an abstract political concept; he made it a requirement for warriors. What does that mean? That jihad must be waged by an army!' – 'This system must change. We have waited; we will wait a little longer. Let us see what the future has in store for us. And let Muslims keep alive the resentment, rancour, and hatred they feel in their hearts'.

142 To the relationship of militant democracy and legal pluralism, see Macklem 2006.

143 ECHR, *Refah v. Turkey*, Third Section (31 July 2001) Grand Chamber (13 February 2003), App. Nr.: 41340/98, 41342/98 and 41344/98, paras. 72 and 123.

In the *Fazilet Partisi* decision, facts against the secular state were concentrated on promotion of a headscarf and compared with *Refah*, they had a less cumulative nature, even though they touched a very sensitive issue shortly after the dissolution of *Refah*.[144] In the *Fazilet* case, disobedience of the prohibition of a headscarf in public sphere, wearing it in the Parliament and applauses by the Members or Parliament, 'incitement of hatred and hostility' against public servants not allowing a headscarf in public institutions and offering the candidacy of *Merve Kavakçı*, who had defended the headscarf actively and made anti-laic statements referring to *jihad* previously, were considered as unconstitutional. Here, the Constitutional Court implicitly refers to resemblances between anti-laic and totalitarian ideologies which are not protected by the EConvHR. The court's imagination has built up a 'democratic society' where a headscarf could be banned for public peace and religious non-discrimination is provided without any kind of incitement of hatred or hostility.[145] Considering the dominance of headscarf discussion in the judgment, the *Fazilet Partisi* case transcends the dissolution compendium and submits a follow-up of constitutional case law in *Headscarf I* and *Headscarf II*.

Recent Developments

In 2008, Turkish militant democracy has been revised by constitutional case-law. In January, the Constitutional Court accepted that statutes and programs of political parties shall be deemed as a reflection of freedom of expression if they do not directly establish a clear and present threat to democratic life (*HAK-PAR*).[146]

In February 2008, the parliamentarian majority accepted constitutional amendments providing 'freedom for headscarf' in higher education institutions. Those were annulled by the Constitutional Court in June 2008 (*Headscarf III*).[147] In fact, the wording of the amendments did not contain any references to religion or religious symbols. Without confining with the wording and objective meaning, the court referred to their general reasoning that explicitly allowed headscarfs in higher education. The court did not limit itself to a formal review of the amendments – as stipulated in the Constitution – and followed its progressive approach established in the 1970s. *Headscarf III* decision emphasizes components of a balance between religion and democratic society as provided in ECHR case-law: Muslim majority in Turkey; dominant and politicized religious symbols; instrumentalization of religion; failure of deliberative democracy on major disputes (e.g., headscarf); and difficulties for the protection of the rights of the others.

---

144 The *Fazilet Partisi* was founded in December 1997 and obtained approximately 24 per cent in the 1999 municipal elections and almost 15.5 per cent in the general election of the same year. It had 111 members in the Parliament when it was dissolved in 1999.

145 *Fazilet Partisi*, E. 1999/2, K. 2001/2, K.t. 22 June 2001, AYMKD 37/2, 1499.

146 *HAK-PAR*, E. 2002/1, K. 2008/1, 29 January 2008, RG Sy. 26923, 1 July 2008.

147 E. 2008/16, K. 2008/116, 5 June 2008, RG Sy. 27032, 22 October 2008.

In July 2008, the Constitutional Court accepted that governing party, *Adalet ve Kalkınma Partisi* ('Justice and Development Party') became a center of anti-laic activities against the Constitution.[148] Here, statements of Prime Minister Erdoğan and prominent politicians of the party as regards headscarf and Islamic legal order were of crucial importance. The court applied deprivation of state aid as a sanction for the first time, since the party in question did not use or incite violence and its parliamentarian majority supported Europeanization policies through various legal amendments. In this case, Europeanization played two different roles for Turkish militant democracy: First, deprivation – which was accepted to comply with European case-law – provided a less drastic solution. Second, the Europeanization policy of a suspected party served as an argument for rejecting dissolution.

Conclusion

The constitutional and sub-constitutional analysis of the Turkish 'militant democracy' reveals that liberal and illiberal tendencies coexist at both conceptual and interpretive level. Illiberal tendencies, which range from meta-juridical references of the Preamble to contradicting judicial interpretations, become especially visible in the construction of vague concepts, such as 'Turkishness', and provisions that are not subject to comprehensive and well-thought amendments, for example, the Law on Political Parties. However, despite illiberal tendencies the Turkish system is able to produce a substantive democratic pattern in which liberal understanding or justification has overwhelmed. Liberal tendencies have been enhanced for a more inclusive democracy after the 1995 and 2001 constitutional amendments at sub-constitutional level. As regards ways and methods of judicial interpretation, case law on political parties proves that the Constitutional Court has moved progressively to a more elaborate approach where 'incitement to hatred, hostility or prohibited activities' and 'present and visible danger' are discernible and peaceful amendment proposals, aimed at the decentralization or the change of the status of the Department of Religious Affairs (DRA), are respected. Without any doubt, the Turkish militant democracy practice is depicted with two major constitutional values, namely the unitary state and the secular state.

References

Akartürk, Ekrem Ali (2008) *Avrupa Hukukuna Uyum Süreci Açısından Türk Hukukunda Siyasi Parti Yasakları*. İstanbul: Yeditepe Üniversitesi.

148 *Adalet ve Kalkınma Partisi*, E. 2008/1, K. 2008/2, 30 July 2008, RG Sy. 27034, 24 October 2008.

Aksoy, Muammer (1988) 'Güvenlik Soruşturması Denilen Hukuksal Sapıklığın MİT Raporlarındaki Korkunç Yanlış ve Yalanlar Işığında Değerlendirilmesi', *Bahri Savcı'ya Armağan*. Ankara: Mülkiyeliler Birliği: 69–164.

Alacakaptan, Uğur (1965–1966) 'Demokratik Anayasa ve Ceza Kanununun 141 ve 142', *Maddeleri* (1–4): 3–20.

Balcıgil, Osman (ed.) (1982) *İki Seminer ve Bir Reform Önerisinde Tartışılan Anayasa*. İstanbul: Birikim Yayınları.

Belelieu, Christopher D. (2006) 'The Headscarf as a Symbolic Enemy of the European Court of Human Rights' Democratic Jurisprudence: Viewing Islam Through a European Legal Prism in the Light of Sahin Judgment', *Columbia Journal of European Law* 12, 573–624.

Bilir, Faruk (2001) *Türkiye'de Milletvekilliği ve Milletvekilliğinin Sona Ermesi*. Ankara: Nobel.

Çağlar, Bakır and Çavuşoğlu, Naz (1999) 'Parti Kapatma Davalarında Mermer-Mozaik İkilemi', *Anayasa Yargısı* (16): 143–87.

Can, Osman (2005) *Demokratikleşme Serüveninde Anayasa ve Siyasi Partilerin Kapatılması*. Ankara: Seçkin.

Dönmezer, Sulhi (1973) *Devletin Ülkesi ve Milleti ile Bütünlüğü ve Bölünmezliği İlkesi, 50. Yıl Armağanı, Cumhuriyet Döneminde Hukuk*. İstanbul: 1973, İÜHF: ayrı bası.

Erdoğan, Mustafa (2002) *Anayasa ve Özgürlük*. Ankara: Yetkin.

Erdoğan, Mustafa (2004) *Anayasa Hukukuna Giriş*. Ankara: Adres.

Gözler, Kemal (1999) 'Hukuk Açısından Cumhuriyet ve Monarşi Kavramlarının Tanımı Sorunu', *Ankara Üniversitesi Siyasal Bilgiler Fakültesi Dergisi* 54(1): 51–62.

Güney, Aylin (2002) 'The People's Democracy Party', *Turkish Studies* 3(1): 122–37.

Hafızoğullari, Zeki (1994) 'Liberal Demokratik Bir Hukuk Düzeninde İfade Hürriyetinin Sınırı', *İHMD, Ekim* 1994, Cilt II, Sayı 2: 10–21.

Hakyemez, Yusuf Şevki (2000) *Militan Demokrasi Anlayışı ve 1982 Anayasası*. Ankara: Seçkin.

Hakyemez, Yusuf Şevki (2001) '2001 Yılında Yapılan Anayasa Değişikliklerinin Siyasal Parti Özgürlüğü Üzerindeki Etkileri', *Anayasa Yargısı* 19, 550–571.

Harvey, Paul (2004) 'Militant Democracy and the European Convention of Human Rights', *European Law Review* 29(3): 407–20.

Kalaycıoğlu, Ersin and Batum, Süheyl (2001) *Türkiye'de Demokratikleşme Perspektifleri ve AB Kopenhag Siyasal Kriterleri – Görüşler ve Öncelikler/no 2: Düşünce Özgürlüğü*. İstanbul: TÜSIAD.

Kanadoğlu, Korkut (2006) *Din İstismarı ve Kötüye Kullanılması*, Prof. Dr. Bülent Tanör Armağanı. İstanbul: Oğlak.

Kanadoğlu, Sabih (2004) *Alaturka Demokrasi*. Ankara: Arkadaş.

Koçak, Mustafa (2002) *Siyasal Partiler ve Türkiye'de Parti Yasakları*. Ankara: Turhan.

Koçak, Mustafa and Örücü, Esin (2003) 'Dissolution of Political Parties in the Name of Democracy: Cases from Turkey and the European Court of Human Rights', *European Public Law* 9(3): 399–424.
Kogacioglu, Dicle (2003) 'Dissolution of Political Parties by the Constitutional Court in Turkey, Judicial Delimitation of the Political Domain', *International Sociology* 18(1): 258–76.
Kogacioglu, Dicle (2004) 'Progress, Unity, and Democracy: Dissolving Political Parties in Turkey', *Law and Society Review* 38(3): 433–62.
Macklem, Patrick (2006), 'Militant Democracy, Legal Pluralism and the Paradox of Self-Determination', *I-CON* 4(3): 488–516.
Nebiler, Halil (1988) *Ben Devletim Fişlerim*. İstanbul: BDS.
Öden, Merih (2003) *Türk Anayasa Hukukunda Siyasi Partilerin Anayasaya Aykırı Eylemleri Nedeniyle Kapatılmaları*. Ankara: Yetkin.
Oran, Baskın (2005) *Türkiye'de Azınlıklar/Kavramlar, Teori, Lozan, İç Mevzuat, İçtihat, Uygulama*. İstanbul: İletişim.
Özbudun, Ergun (2002a) *Türk Anayasa Hukuku*. Ankara: Yetkin.
Özbudun, Ergun (2002b) *2001 Anayasa Değişiklikleri ve Siyasi Reform Önerileri*. İstanbul: TESEV.
Özbudun, Ergun (2006) 'The Nature of the Kemalist Political Regime', in Ali Kazancıgil and Ergun Özbudun (eds) *Atatürk: Founder of a Modern State*. London: Hurst: 79–102.
Özbudun, Ergun and Yazıcı, Serap (2004) *Democratization Reforms in Turkey (1993–2004)*. İstanbul: TESEV.
Özek, Çetin (1999–2000) 'Terörle Mücadele Yasasına İlişkin Bir Anayasaya Aykırılık İddiasi', *MHB, Prof. Dr. Aysel Çelikel'e Armağan*, Yıl 19–20, Sayı (1–2): 713–31.
Öztürk, Kazım (1966) *Türkiye Cumhuriyeti Anayasası, Cilt II, Madde 1–75*. Ankara: Türkiye İş Bankası Kültür Yayınları.
Parla, Taha (1993) *Türkiye'nin Siyasal Rejimi: 1980–1989*. İstanbul: İletişim.
Sabuncu, Yavuz (2004) *Anayasaya Giriş*. Ankara: İmaj.
Sağlam, Fazıl (1982) *Temel Hakların Sınırlanması ve Özü*. Ankara: Ankara Üniversitesi.
Sağlam, Fazıl (1997) 'Anayasa Hukukumuz Açısından Siyasal Parti Kurumunun Güncel Sorunları', *Anayasa Yargısı* (14): 367–83.
Sağlam, Fazıl (1999) *Siyasal Partiler Hukukunun Güncel Sorunları*. İstanbul: Beta.
Sağlam, Fazıl (2000) 'Siyasi Partiler Kanunu'nda Uluslararası Standartlara Uygunluk Sağlamak İçin Yapılması Gereken Değişiklikler', *Anayasa Yargısı* (17): 233–54.
Soysal, Mümtaz (1968) 'Anayasa Hukuku Açısından Kapalılık ve Açıklık Kavramları', *AÜSBFD* (1): 261–74.
Tanör, Bülent (1969) *Siyasi Düşünce Hürriyeti ve 1961 Türk Anayasası*. İstanbul: Öncü.

Tanör, Bülent (1979) *TCK 142. Madde Düşünce Özgürlüğü ve Uygulama, Anayasa Mahkemesinin Son Kararı Üzerine Kısa Bir Not*. İstanbul: Forum.

Tanör, Bülent (1986) *İki Anayasa*. İstanbul: Beta.

Tanör, Bülent (1991) 'Gedanken zum türkischen Gesetz Nr. 3713 ("Antiterrorgesetz"- ATG)', *Zeitschrift für Türkeistudien* (2): 153–74.

Tanör, Bülent (1992) *Türkiye'de Yerel Kongre İktidarları (1918–1920)*. İstanbul: AFA.

Tanör, Bülent (1994) *Türkiye'nin İnsan Hakları Sorunu*. İstanbul: BDS.

Tanör, Bülent (1996) *Osmanlı-Türk Anayasal Gelişmeleri*. İstanbul: YKY.

Tanör, Bülent (1997) *Türkiye'de Demokratikleşme Perspektifleri*. İstanbul: TÜSIAD.

Tanör, Bülent (1998) *Kuruluş Kurtuluş*. İstanbul: Çağdaş.

Tanör, Bülent (1999) *Türkiye'de Demokratik Standartların Yükseltilmesi*. İstanbul: TÜSIAD.

Tanör, Bülent (2000) 'İnanç ve Din Özgürlüğü', *İnsan Hakları*. İstanbul: YKY: 98–105.

Tanör, Bülent (2004) in Tanör, Bülent and Yüzbaşıoğlu, Necmi (eds) (1982) *Anayasasına Göre Türk Anayasa Hukuku*. İstanbul: Beta, 68–71.

Teziç, Erdoğan and Yüzbaşıoğlu, Necmi (2001) *Siyasi Partiler ve Milletvekili Seçimi Kanunlarına İlişkin Görüşler, Türkiye Genç İşadamları Derneği*. İstanbul: TÜGİAD.

Tunç, Hasan and Bilir, Faruk (1998) 'Cumhuriyet Dönemi Anayasalarında Milliyetçilik Anlayışı ve Atatürk Milliyetçiliği', *Gazi Üniversitesi Hukuk Fakültesi Dergisi* (2), Sayı 1-2: 205–11.

Turhan, Mehmet (1996) 'Demokratik Devlet İlkesi Açısından Siyasi Partilerin Kapatılması ile İlgili Hükümlerdeki Uyumsuzluklar', *Yeni Türkiye* 2(10): 416–26.

Üskül, Zafer (2006) *Türk Demokrasisinde 130 Yıl (1876–2006)*. İstanbul: TÜSİAD.

Uygun, Oktay (1992) *1982 Anayasası'nda Temel Hak ve Özgürlüklerin Genel Rejimi*. İstanbul: Kazancı.

Uygun, Oktay (2000) 'Siyasi Partilerin Kapatılması Rejiminin Avrupa İnsan Hakları Sözleşmesi Çerçevesinde Değerlendirilmesi', *Anayasa Yargısı* (17): 256–72.

Yüzbaşıoğlu, Necmi (1993) *Türk Anayasa Yargısında Anayasallık Bloku*. İstanbul: İÜHF.

Chapter 13
United Kingdom

Richard Mullender[1]

> The first public obligation is to avoid extremes of suffering.
>
> Berlin 1998: 14

Introduction

Few British lawyers are acquainted with the term 'militant democracy'. However, bodies of law that address a central concern of militant democracy – the maintenance of constitutional fundamentals – have long been a feature of the legal system in Britain. For this reason, when we examine particular examples, we will encounter laws rooted in pre-democratic history that now speak to the question: 'How to defend a democratic legal order?' This is true, for example, of the offence of treason which has existed, in statutory form, since the fourteenth century.[2] But it is important to emphasize that, while Britain lacks a doctrine of militant democracy, government has used law in more recent times to defend democratic values. Thus, in 1988, Mrs Thatcher's administration placed a broadcasting ban on *Sinn Fein* (an Irish nationalist political party). This was because *Sinn Fein*'s paramilitary wing was proscribed as a terrorist organization. Hence, the Thatcher Government denied a body uncommitted to the democratic process the 'oxygen of publicity' by placing a restriction on the right to free expression (Turpin and Tomkins 2007: 781–2).[3] Moreover, agencies of the state operating in a legal netherworld have sought to defend democratic values. This is true of the Security Service, MI5, during the Cold War. In the years before the legislature placed MI5's operations on a statutory basis, this organization used, *inter alia*, bugging devices to monitor the risks to the integrity of the state posed by Soviet spies. At this time, MI5's personnel were supposed to act in accordance with the 'cardinal principle' that the

---

1 I would like to thank my colleagues John Alder, Colin Murray, Patrick O'Callaghan and Ian Ward for their comments on earlier drafts of this chapter.

2 For a detailed overview of the law relating to treason, see Smith and Hogan 1978: 796–808 (noting, *inter alia*, that 'the Treason Act 1351 … was passed to clarify the uncertainty and arbitrariness of the common law').

3 See also *R v. Secretary of State for the Home Department, ex P Brind* [1991] 1 AC 696 (in which the House of Lords held, *inter alia*, that 'the restriction was justified by the important public interest in combating terrorism', *per* Lord Bridge).

defence of the realm was their sole concern.[4] However, Security Service personnel regularly mounted operations that paid scant regard to this principle. For example, monitoring the activities of left-wing politicians including (in the 1970s) a Labour Prime Minister, Harold Wilson (Turpin and Tomkins 2007: 777 et seq.).

MI5's activities during the Cold War bring into sharp focus an assumption common to those who have employed the various bodies of law we will examine in this discussion. This is an assumption that finds explicit expression in the political philosophy of Carl Schmitt. According to Schmitt, politics in its purest form is a clash between friends and foes (Schmitt 1996: 26 et seq.). In the struggles described by Schmitt, each side seeks to ensure that its agenda determines the basic terms of social life and is ready to crush into submission (or even extirpate) its opponents. Moreover, the examples on which we will concentrate most attention (the state's response to fascism in the 1930s and to radical Islam today) will point up a source of great practical difficulty. The circumstances in which a particular group merits classification as 'the foe' (in the sense of a threat to our most fundamental values) are not always obvious.

Just as the Schmittian understanding of politics informs government's resort to law in the examples we will examine, so too does a commitment to piecemeal intervention in practical life. As used here, 'piecemeal intervention' denotes at least two things. First, it embraces a readiness to respond to the activities of a particular group in ways that speak concretely to the threat it appears to pose. Second, it relates to official reluctance to justify intervention in practical contexts by reference to a grand overarching theory. This piecemeal approach has obvious affinities with the school of philosophy most commonly associated with the British: Empiricism. On an empiricist view, we acquire knowledge through experience (Honderich 1995: 226–9). Jeremy Paxman has summed up this approach to practical questions (which is particularly associated with the English) in the following terms (Paxman 1999: 191):

> The characteristic English approach to a problem is not to reach for an ideology but to snuffle around it, like a truffle hound, and when they have isolated the core, then to seek a solution.

This empirical outlook finds clear expression in the areas of law we will examine. As we will see later, ministers and other officials spent years trying to make sense of fascism in Britain before they acted to address the various problems it posed. This approach lays British law open to a telling criticism: ministers and other public officials show little interest in overarching principle as a means by which to express a commitment to the pursuit of justice. For this reason, we will examine the question as to whether ministers, judges and other public officials could pursue the agenda of militant democracy in a more principled fashion in the United Kingdom.

4 The 'cardinal principle' noted in the text is described in, for example, Wade and Bradley 1985: 564.

But, before doing so, we must examine British law in some detail. We will first consider some of the many ways in which the piecemeal approach to the defence of constitutional fundamentals and, more recently, militant democracy has found expression in Britain. We will then examine a set of circumstances in which the piecemeal approach worked effectively. This was the response to the threat posed by the British Union of Fascists (BUF) in the 1930s. We will, then, examine the threat posed by radical Islamists today. In light of the conclusions drawn from this discussion, we will then consider the arguments for and against the adoption of a more principled approach to militant democracy.

The Piecemeal Approach to Militant Democracy

Before considering particular bodies of law that reveal a commitment to militant democracy (or to the defence of constitutional fundamentals), we must examine the legal context in which they have been fashioned or mobilized. The most fundamental norm in the British constitution is the doctrine of parliamentary sovereignty. This doctrine (which has had foundational status in Britain since – at least – the 'Glorious Revolution' of 1688) specifies that Parliament (the sovereign legislature) may make or unmake any law it chooses (Turpin and Tomkins 2007: 40). Hence, Parliament is able to abrogate even those laws that appear to establish constitutional fundamentals (Turpin and Tomkins 2007: 334). One such law is the European Communities Act 1972 (by operation of which Britain acceded to the European Community in 1973). Another is the Human Rights Act 1998 (which has given rights within the European Convention on Human Rights force on the plane of municipal law). While Parliament is sovereign, judges have enjoyed, for centuries, the power to elaborate legal norms at common law (Postema 1986: Chapters 1 and 2). Thus, substantial bodies of law owe their existence to the judiciary. This is true of, *inter alia*, administrative law, contract law and the law of tort.

Given that Parliament can make or unmake any law and that the judiciary can reconfigure common law norms, we find in the United Kingdom considerable scope for altering the law in the light of circumstances. This is a feature of British law that bespeaks commitment to empiricism (in the sense specified earlier). Practical problems arise, and Parliament or the courts specify or modify law in order to tackle them. Flexibility (in the face of contingency) is thus a prominent feature of British law. This has led some commentators, including John Griffith, to characterize Britain's constitution as 'political' (Griffith 1979: 1). Those who stake out this position see the law as a function of the power wielded by those in a position to shape the basic terms of social life. To this descriptive claim, Griffith adds one that is normative. He argues that, in the context of a political constitution, the law's addressees should relentlessly question those in authority (Poole 1997: 270). On this view, the culture in which the law operates, provides (where it is vibrant) a counterweight to the exercise of power in ways that threaten, *inter alia,* democratic institutions.

Having set the legal scene, we must now turn to those bodies of British law that reveal a commitment to militant democracy (or, in the more distant past, to the defence of constitutional fundamentals).

The French Revolution through British Eyes

In their efforts to preserve constitutional fundamentals, governments in the United Kingdom have on many occasions resorted to the use of emergency powers. The use of these powers has a very long history that predates the emergence of the democratic principle. Prior to the mid-nineteenth century, government sought to counter threats to the existing legal order by passing legislation that suspended the writ of *habeas corpus*. This writ (which originated early in the history of the common law) enjoins those detaining someone to 'have the body brought into court' (Turpin and Tomkins 2007: 7). Moreover, *habeas corpus* has great practical significance since it secures a judicial inquiry into the legality of a person's detention (Turpin and Tomkins 2007: 7).

These points explain why the Pitt administration's decision to suspend *habeas corpus* in the 1790s was deeply controversial in a country with a long-standing commitment to liberty. According to the historian Edward Palmer Thompson, the suspension of *habeas corpus* was the act of a government that was 'scared' that ardour for liberty encouraged by the French Revolution would spread to Britain (Thompson 1968: 158). More specifically, the government was responding to the fact that members of a throng numbering approximately 200,000 had jeered at the King and pelted his carriage in the streets of London (Thompson 1968: 158). With the American Revolution and the collapse of the *ancien régime* in France in mind, Pitt and his colleagues saw in these scenes the danger that the British might embrace the revolutionary agenda of the French Jacobins.

The suspension of *habeas corpus* was only part of a wider counter-revolutionary strategy. Inciting people by speech or writing to hatred of or contempt for the King, the constitution or the government became a treasonable offence (Smith and Hogan 1978: 796–7; Thompson 1968: 158–9). Likewise, it became an offence to hold a meeting of fifty or more persons without notifying a magistrate (Thompson 1968: 159). Moreover, those who defied a magistrate's instructions vis-à-vis meetings were liable to the death penalty. Alongside these measures, Pitt also used spies and watchful magistrates so as to create a climate of fear in which people would be reluctant to challenge the constitutional status quo (Thompson 1968: 161).

In order to grasp the nature of the threat that government saw the French Revolution as posing, we must examine the 'debate on France' (which began in 1790). Edmund Burke triggered this debate when he described the revolutionaries in France as 'the ablest architects of ruin that had hitherto existed in the world' (Philp 1989: 13). Moreover, he characterized the revolution (and the ideals informing it) as a contagion that could infect the British body politic. Thereafter, he sought to point up the attractions of the British constitution in his *Reflections on the Revolution in France*. For example, he argued that the 'cold sluggishness' of British 'national character' found a suitable home in Britain's politico-legal framework (Burke 1968: 181).

But Burke's defence of the status quo produced a response he did not anticipate and that he certainly did not want (Philp 1989: 14). An extra parliamentary movement for political reform grew up. This movement brought the lower orders of society into the political arena. Prominent in this movement were societies for the dissemination of democratic and republican literature (for example, the Society for Constitutional Information). But by far the most prominent and influential proponent of constitutional reform was Thomas Paine (who had earlier played a significant part in the struggle for American independence). Paine's writings stimulated a broad-based popular movement for political reform (Kuklick in Paine 1989: vii–xvii).

The Prime Minister, Pitt, and his ministers saw this upsurge in support for constitutional reform as a significant threat to the existing order (Philp 1989: 16). Consequently, they decided to prosecute Paine on the ground that Part Two of his *The Rights of Man* was a libel on the constitution (Philp 1989: 16). In response to this decision, Paine (prior to trial) described the existing constitution as lacking legitimacy. He also called for a national convention to frame a more adequate order. Subsequently, the Society for Constitutional Information and the London Corresponding Society sought to call just such a convention. This led the government to prosecute the leaders of these societies for treason in 1794. By this time, Paine (who had fled England in 1792) had been found guilty (in his absence) of libelling the constitution. By 1797, opposition politicians, such as Charles James Fox, were denouncing Pitt's 'reign of terror' (Philp 1989: 81–2).

The British response to the French Revolution brings to light a certain awkwardness in employing the term 'militant democracy' in a pre-democratic context. For Paine and other advocates of a new constitutional order regarded themselves as the champions of democracy. Hence, we might see the debate on France and the government's response to the spectre of revolution as yielding a thoroughly undemocratic outcome. But some commentators take a rather different (and perhaps more subtle) view. For example, in his *English Social History*, George Macaulay Trevelyan recognized that Paine was a proponent of democratic reform (Trevelyan 1967: 471). He also recognized that 'during the period of anti-[revolutionary] repression it was "safer to be a felon than a reformer"' (Trevelyan 1967: 471). However, this was not, on Trevelyan's analysis, a period during which governmental repression alone explains the failure of the reform movement. For, according to Trevelyan, 'the democratic movement … was suppressed … quite as much by public opinion as by government action' (Trevelyan 1967: 471). This, Trevelyan argues, was because 'the majority of Englishman were … proud of themselves as being a free people'. If Trevelyan is right on these points, then Burke (while not a militant democrat) nonetheless saw himself as defending a just constitutional order.

The example to which we now turn points up a further source of awkwardness in employing the term 'militant democracy' in the context of British constitutional history.

A Bitter Endgame: Ireland in the Twentieth Century

Before scrutinizing the operations of British law in Ireland in the twentieth century, we must examine some relevant historical background. As long ago as 1169, those wielding power in England regarded Ireland as an object of conquest (Davies 2000: 291). In Tudor times, both Queen Mary and Queen Elizabeth encouraged 'the systematic colonization of Ireland' (Ferguson 2003: 55). Consequently, Ireland became 'the experimental laboratory' of Empire (Ferguson 2003: 57). Since the experiments conducted by the English involved, among other things, the massacre of Catholics, relations with Ireland's indigenous people were highly strained (Schama 2003: 169–70). Moreover, this strain did not disappear when, in 1801, Ireland became a constituent part of the United Kingdom of Great Britain and Ireland (with representation in the Westminster Parliament) (Davies 2000: 552). Indeed, the strain intensified and, in the late-nineteenth century, William Gladstone sought to preserve the Union by conferring Home Rule on Ireland (Gamble 2003: 52). However, he could not persuade Parliament to embrace his reform agenda, and, in the first quarter of the twentieth century, members of Ireland's Catholic majority made plain their wish to leave the Union. Matters came to a head in 1916 with the Easter Rising (in which a small group of revolutionaries sought to proclaim the Irish Republic) (Davies 2000: 757–8; Gamble 2003: 54). By 1919, the British were facing an armed rebellion and, in response, invoked emergency powers and engaged in acts of state terror.[5]

In the twentieth century, the British Government has used a variety of emergency powers to counter the threat posed to the integrity of the state by Irish nationalism. For example, in response to serious disturbances in Ireland in 1919–1921, the Westminster Parliament passed the Restoration of Order in Ireland Act 1920. This Act conferred exceptional powers on the executive including the use of martial law. Under this provision, the executive proclaimed martial law in areas of Ireland. Moreover, the General Officer Commanding the Army declared that any unauthorized person found in possession of arms would be subject to the death penalty (Wade and Bradley 1985: 553).

Resort to martial law in Ireland in the early 1920s spawned an extensive body of case law and two decisions in particular throw light on the issues with which the courts had to grapple. In *R v. Allen*, a Military Law Court had sentenced a

5 See Davies 2000: 759; Gamble 2003: 52 and, discussing, *inter alia*, the 'reprisal raid' at Croke Park, Dublin, in which a British armoured car drove onto the pitch during a Gaelic football match and opened fire on the players.

civilian to death for possession of arms.[6] This was an offence for which the death penalty was not available at common law or by operation of statute. Nonetheless, Molony CJ accepted the Attorney General's submission that the military were under 'guerrilla attacks' from the Irish Republican Army.[7] In light of this point, the Chief Justice stated that the government was 'entitled and indeed bound to repel force by force'.[8] Moreover, he found support in the earlier case of *Marais* for the proposition that, 'while war is raging, this court has no jurisdiction to question any acts done by the military authorities'.[9]

Molony CJ's decision contrasts sharply with that of O'Connor MR in *Egan v. Macready*.[10] *Egan* concerned a *habeas corpus* application. O'Connor MR concluded that the *Marais* case was not relevant to the dispute before him. This was because Parliament, in enacting the Restoration of Order in Ireland Act, had specified a 'mode of action' to address 'the military emergency'. The legislature had not done this when the conflict at stake in *Marais* arose. In light of these points, O'Connor MR concluded that martial law could not operate in circumstances where Parliament had passed law to deal with the same problem. On this point, the Master of the Rolls was emphatic. He described the Act 'as not merely enabling, but prohibitory'.[11]

Governmental use of emergency powers did not, however, cease with the partition of Ireland in the 1920s.[12] In 1967, a Catholic civil rights movement embarked on a campaign of marches and demonstrations in pursuit of reform. The response of the Royal Ulster Constabulary was violent. By August 1969, Catholics, Protestants and the police were engaged in 'pitched battles … in the middle of Belfast'. In response, the British Prime Minister, James Callaghan, sent in the British Army to restore order. Towards the end of 1969, the IRA's Provisional Army Council had embraced violence as a means to the end of political change (Marr 2007: 315–18). As the 1960s gave way to the 1970s, the ferocity of the IRA's violent campaign increased. The Government of Northern Ireland, having consulted with the British Government, decided to use the power of internment (imprisonment without trial) it enjoyed under the Civil Authorities (Special Powers) Act (Northern Ireland) 1922. This power could be used against persons suspected of having acted or being about to act in a manner prejudicial to the preservation of peace or the maintenance of order (Wade and Bradley 1985: 559).

6 [1921] 2 IR 241.

7 [1921] 2 IR 244.

8 [1921] 2 IR 268.

9 [1921] 2 IR 269. In *Marais v. General Officer Commanding* [1902] AC 109, the Privy Council extended the range of circumstances in which martial law could operate by holding that it had force where civil courts continued to sit.

10 [1921] 1 IR 265.

11 [1921] 1 IR 275.

12 The Irish Free State came into existence in 1922 (with six counties of Ulster remaining in the United Kingdom). See Davies 2000: 759–60.

These responses to Irish nationalism (like those made to the threat of revolution in the 1790s) provide rather problematic examples of militant democracy. For they have to do with the preservation of a legal order that was the fruit of an imperialist project that began in pre-democratic times. However, the Home Office made one response to the disorder that erupted in Northern Ireland in the late-1960s that has clear relevance to militant democracy. In 1975, it identified 'subversion' as comprising activities 'which threaten the safety or well-being of the state, and are intended to undermine or overthrow parliamentary democracy by political, industrial or violent means'.[13] Moreover, the British response to the breakdown of order in Northern Ireland brings into sharp focus dilemmas often faced by those who seek to advance the agenda of militant democracy. For example, how to act effectively against those threatening the integrity of the existing legal order while acting in accordance with the requirements of the rule of law, natural justice and relevant human rights? The use of martial law in Ireland in the 1920s was incompatible with the basic rule of natural justice *nemo iudex in causa sua* (no one should be a judge in their own cause) (Campbell 1994: 99–100). This was because the British Army performed the functions of judge and jury (and was often the only 'injured party') (Campbell 1994: 100). The use of internment between 1971 and 1975 is hard to reconcile with a commitment to human rights (most obviously the right to a trial) and the proportionality principle.

We now turn to an episode in British history that provides a more obvious (but nonetheless intensely controversial) example of militant democracy.

Countering 'The Enemy Within': The Miners' Strike (1984–1985)

In order to grasp why the concept of militant democracy is relevant to the miners' strike of 1984–1985, we must examine the political history of Britain in the 1970s. Striking miners succeeded, in 1972 and in 1974, in deflecting Edward Heath's Conservative Government from its policy agenda. The miners' strike in 1972 resulted in a 21 per cent wage increase and undercut the government's efforts to restrain public sector wage increases (Davies and Freedland 1993: 327–8). Moreover, Arthur Scargill, a young miners' leader who had played a prominent role in the strike, drew two broad conclusions when reflecting on the success the miners had enjoyed. He identified the strike as having been intensely political. He stated that 'we were in a class war. We were not playing cricket on the village green, like they did in [the General Strike and subsequent miners' strike in] '26' (Crick 1985: 52). He also found, in the success enjoyed by the miners, 'living proof that the working class had only to flex its muscles and it could bring governments, employers and society to a complete standstill' (Weight 2002: 525).

In 1974, the miners went on strike again and effectively mounted a challenge to a statutory incomes policy inaugurated by the Heath Government in late 1972

13 H.C. Deb., 6 April 1978, col. 618.

(Crick 1985: 65–6; Davies and Freedland 1993: 330–31). In response, Heath called a General Election in which he asked the electorate to answer the question, 'Who governs?' (Weight 2002: 563). He also stated that this election would enable the electorate to make a choice between 'moderation' (in the form of a democratically elected government) and 'extremism' (as instantiated by miners exercising industrial muscle) (Sked and Cook 1993: 285). Unfortunately for Heath, he lost the 1974 election. As a result, the miners gained an 'aura of invincibility' and people came to believe that they had 'the power to topple governments' (Crick 1985: 66).

These were considerations that loomed large in the mind of Heath's successor as leader of the Conservative Party, Margaret Thatcher (Thatcher 1995: 217). When she became Prime Minister, she was determined to ensure that the miners would not triumph over her government as they had over Heath's administration. To this end, she found guidance in a report prepared in the 1970s by a Conservative Member of Parliament, Nicholas Ridley (who would later serve in Thatcher's Cabinet) (Sked and Cook 1993: 446–7). Ridley outlined a plan for dealing with challenges to government from 'communist disrupters' in the coal industry. He suggested that a future Conservative government should build up coal stocks (so as to forestall the danger of power cuts). He also suggested that government should 'cut off the money supply to … strikers' (by denying then welfare benefits) and should mobilize 'a large … squad of police equipped … to uphold the law against violent picketing' (Sked and Cook 1993: 446–7).

Before acting on this advice, Thatcher avoided a confrontation with the miners in 1981, when she abandoned a plan to close 23 uneconomic mines (Sked and Cook 1993: 444). When, however, the leader of the National Union of Mineworkers (NUM), Arthur Scargill, commenced a national strike in 1984, Thatcher was ready to act on Ridley's advice. By this time, coal stocks were at an all-time high, the availability of welfare benefits to strikers had been limited and 140,000 police officers had acquired skills in 'tactical operations' (Sked and Cook 1993: 449–51). Moreover, trade unions reforms directed at secondary picketing, trade union ballots and ending trade union immunity from compensation claims 'were a serious obstacle in the path of any strike' (Jenkins 2006: 95).

The clash that then began 'matched a Marxist revolutionary, Arthur Scargill, against the apostle of market forces, Margaret Thatcher' (Sked and Cook 1993: 444). But the government 'pretend[ed] that the dispute was an ordinary one to which normal procedures applied' (Sked and Cook 1993: 449). This meant that the Chairman of the National Coal Board (NCB), Ian MacGregor, bore responsibility for responding to the industrial action mounted by the NUM. MacGregor proceeded with some subtlety. He might have sought injunctions against the NUM under the applicable (and recently reformed) body of trade union law. But he decided not to do so. His aim was to avoid alienating those miners who had remained at work (Davies and Freedland 1993: 494).

While Margaret Thatcher and her ministers repeatedly described the strike as a dispute between the National Coal Board and the NUM, they strove to ensure that the strike would fail. The security services (including MI5) were mobilized to monitor the activity of the strikers and, on some accounts, to mount a 'Get Scargill' campaign (Milne 2004: 307). During the strike, the activity of the police was coordinated from a national centre (the National Reporting Centre) (Sked and Cook 1993: 450). Moreover, the police, on occasion, adopted a highly confrontational approach to the strikers. This was certainly true in the case of the so-called 'Battle of Orgreave'. The police prevented 10,000 miners from shutting down a coking plant. But, in order to achieve this result, they adopted some highly controversial tactics. Mounted police officers charged the strikers with truncheons drawn and inflicted some serious injuries on individuals (Marr 2007: 415).

Ultimately, Margaret Thatcher prevailed in her struggle against the NUM. The strike was abandoned a year after it began. Thatcher had vanquished a group she characterized (in terms that call Carl Schmitt's conception of politics to mind) as 'the enemy within' (Sked and Cook 1993: 451). Assessments of the strike differ greatly. Some see it as a vindication of the democratic process after a protracted period during which trade unions repeatedly deflected governments from the policy goals they committed themselves to pursue when securing a mandate (Sked and Cook 1993: 444, 451). Others, however, draw a much bleaker conclusion. They find in the conduct of the Thatcher Government evidence of 'class instrumentalism'. By this they mean that government used the instrumentality of the state to advance the interests of capital at the expense of the labour movement (Milne 2004: ix).[14] Even if we find this analysis ultimately unconvincing, the determination of the Thatcher administration to prevail is plain to see. When the strike was over, the government had spent £3 billion denying victory to 'the enemy within'.

In light of the discussion so far, we can draw a broad conclusion. When faced with threats to constitutional fundamentals, governments have responded in a wide variety of ways (for example, suspension of *habeas corpus*, the imposition of martial law and alterations in police practice). Thus we find support for the claim made earlier concerning the piecemeal fashion in which law in the United Kingdom has been applied and/or reconfigured in response to threats to the constitutional order. But we should not assume that there is an absence of commitment in the United Kingdom to fundamental principle (in the sense of a readiness to defend morally appealing values embedded in the constitutional order).[15] To the extent

14 See Collins 1982: 27–30, exploring the theme – developed in the writings of Marx and Engels – that the state is 'an instrument of the ruling class'.

15 In our examination of values that have featured in the British constitutional order over large stretches of time, we must (for reasons given by Quentin Skinner) proceed with caution. For conceptual change takes place constantly. Hence, we should, when seeking to grasp the significance of a concept at a particular point in history, seek to set it in an appropriate historical milieu. This does not, however, mean that we should view concepts as nothing more than a function of context. This is because ideological innovators bend them to new uses for the purpose of politicking: this is, as means by which to secure new power shares within the constitutional order. For a summary of the various points made

that the Thatcher administration did, indeed, defend democracy during the miners' strike it staked out a position that we can characterize as principled. This is because it had to do with defending institutional arrangements (the procedures associated with parliamentary democracy) in which all the law's addressees have an interest. Margaret Thatcher certainly saw herself as having secured a victory over the organizers of a 'politically-motivated' strike (Thatcher 1995: 215). But she viewed this victory as having more to do with the successful pursuit of an 'enterprise revolution' than with the agenda of militant democracy (Thatcher 1995: Chapter 26, especially p. 575).

However, if we are correct in assuming that the Thatcher administration's response to the miners' strike had to do with the defence of principle, then it forms part of a tradition that is centuries old. The example to which we now turn illustrates this to be the case.

Intimations of Principle

The Trial of Charles I

Charles I's father, James I (who became King of England in 1603), was a believer in the Divine Right of Kings.[16] He asserted that 'Kings are justly called Gods … They make and unmake their subjects; they have the power of raising up and casting down; of life and death; judges over all their subjects and in all cases accountable to none but God'.[17] James clearly exerted a powerful influence on his son. For, when Charles became King, he made it plain that sovereign and subject were 'clean different things.' Hence, he failed to grasp that 'when push came to shove it [was] the law that was sovereign, not him' (Colls 2002: 37). This misapprehension resulted in three 'national–civil–religious wars' (Colls 2002: 37).[18] By the time disagreement erupted into conflict, the view that the law (and not the monarch) was sovereign had been put forward in clear terms by, *inter alios*, Sir Edward Coke. Coke regarded the law as 'the hedge of England's ancient

---

here, see Palonen 2003: 5 (on politicking), p. 20 (on appropriate historical *milieux*), p. 38 (on continuous conceptual change), p. 39 (on the undesirability of identifying concepts as a function of context), and p. 52 (on innovating ideologists).

16 The divine right of kings embraces the idea that a sovereign rules by divine ordinance and the notion that a sovereign is him- or herself a divinity. See Scruton 1982: 132.

17 James I, 'The Trew Law of Free Monarchies: Or the Reciprock and Mutuall Duetie Between a Free King and His Naturall Subjects', in McIlwain 1918: 66. See also Macedo 1990: 42.

18 See Schama 2003: 11, where the three wars referred to by Colls are placed in the broader category of 'British wars' – which Schama identifies as embracing the American War of Independence.

liberties' (Davies 2000: 486). Moreover, he viewed Charles I as a legal innovator who posed 'the chief threat to established freedom'.

Charles I emerged from the wars in which he engaged on the losing side and the institution of monarchy gave way to a Commonwealth. The Commonwealth regime (led by Oliver Cromwell) charged Charles 1 with being 'the occasioner, author and continuer' of conflict (Robertson 2006: 5). The prosecutor, John Cooke, also identified Charles as 'a tyrant, traitor, murderer and a public and implacable enemy to the Commonwealth of England'. The decision to put Charles on trial was intensely controversial. Common law authority indicated that the King, as the source of law, could do no wrong and, hence, enjoyed immunity from prosecution.[19] Moreover, just three months before the trial began (in January 1649), the Treaty of Westphalia had identified monarchs as enjoying immunity from prosecution (Robertson 2006: 4).

Nonetheless, the new regime was determined to hold Charles accountable for having sought to establish a 'tyranny' and thus destroy law and liberty (Robertson 2006: 5).[20] Cromwell and his colleagues also wanted to ensure that Charles bore responsibility for a variety of wrongs including the torture of prisoners (Robertson 2006: 5). To this end, the House of Commons passed a law that established the High Court of Justice. In this court, Cooke would seek to drive home the message that 'no chief officer or magistrate may hereafter presume traitorously or maliciously to imagine or continue the enslaving and destroying of the English nation' (Robertson 2006: 4). The new regime sought to ensure that Charles enjoyed adequate representation. They offered him the services of London's leading barrister, Matthew Hale (Robertson 2006: 6). However, Charles declined this offer and argued up to the moment of his death that the court lacked jurisdiction (Schama 2003: 138–9). Consistent with his refusal to recognize the court as having jurisdiction, Charles refused to make a plea. Applying a rule in force at this time, the court treated Charles's refusal as an admission of guilt. As a result, the Court of Justice found Charles guilty and ordered that he be 'put to death, by the severing of his Head from his Body' (Schama 2003: 138). Before his execution, Charles delivered a speech in which he identified himself as the legitimate defender of the people's 'Liberty and Freedom' (Schama 2003: 139). But these were the very values that the Commonwealth regime saw itself as vindicating.

On Charles's analysis, Cromwell and his colleagues were usurpers. They were, however, usurpers who had rejected a constitutional order in which 'the monarch ruled mainly by decree, with no Habeas Corpus Act, no independent judiciary, no free press, no free speech and a weak, and often intimidated House of Commons'

19 *R v. Hampden* [1637] 3 State Trials 825.

20 The association between tyranny and the destruction of law has a long history. It finds expression in Plato, *Eighth Letter* 354e–356e, in *Thirteen Epistles of Plato* (Oxford: Clarendon Press, 1925); and in Plato, *Crito* 51c–52a, in *The Last Days of Socrates* (London: Penguin, 1954), where Socrates describes one who disobeys the law as a 'destroyer of law'.

(Colls 2002: 20; Davies 2000: 483). Moreover, the constitutional changes that the Commonwealth regime wrought led John Milton to sum up 'the whole truth' thus: 'Parliament is the *supreme* council of the nation, constituted and appointed by an absolutely free people'.[21] Thus we might see the regicides as staking out a position that points the way (albeit inchoately) towards militant democracy as we understand it today.

Perhaps the most striking feature of this brief examination of seventeenth-century history is a culture in which values like liberty and freedom are such powerful guides to action. We might harbour the hope that such a culture, more than any body of law, provides a particularly secure basis on which to preserve freedom and to sustain a commitment to democracy. Moreover, prominent judges (most obviously, William Blackstone in the eighteenth century) and legal commentators (for example, A.V. Dicey in the nineteenth and early-twentieth century) have identified culture as the ultimate guarantee of freedom (Simpson 2001: 20 – on Blackstone; and p. 36 – on Dicey). But, as we will now see, British judges have (in recent years) identified the common law as a means by which to sustain and foster the same commitment.

Defamation Law in the Twentieth Century

In the case of *Bognor Regis Urban District Council v. Campion*, the defendant circulated a pamphlet that was sharply critical of the claimant local authority.[22] This led the local authority to mount a libel claim against him. At trial, the judge held that the local authority was entitled to vindicate its 'governing reputation' (this is, its reputation for competence). This decision attracted critical comment. For example, Eric Barendt argued that 'civil actions [for defamation] by public authorities are incompatible with the protection of political speech' (Barendt 1985: 174). Moreover, he argued that there is little difference in this context between a readiness to accept defamation claims and criminal prosecutions for sedition (Barendt 1985: 174).

In the later case of *Derbyshire County Council v. Times Newspapers Ltd*, the House of Lords rejected the position staked out in *Campion*.[23] Lord Keith stated that: 'it is of the *highest public importance* that a democratically elected body ... should be open to uninhibited criticism'.[24] Subsequently, Buckley J extended the scope of the rule in the *Derbyshire County Council* case by holding that political parties cannot maintain claims in defamation.[25] The emphasis placed on freedom of expression by Lord Keith and Buckley J certainly reveals a commitment to

21 Colls 2002: 20, citing J. Milton, *Angli Pro Populo Anglicano Defension* (1651) [emphasis added].

22 [1972] 2 QB 169.

23 [1993] AC 534.

24 [1993] AC 547.

25 *Goldsmith v. Bhoyrul* [1998] QB 459.

the pursuit of principle. For both judges were determined to protect an interest (freedom of expression) that is a necessary condition of democracy (Barendt 1985: 20–23).

The *Derbyshire County Council* case merits examination for a further reason. Lord Keith, who gave the leading speech in the House of Lords, justified his decision exclusively by reference to the common law. He saw no need to find support for his decision in the European Convention on Human Rights (EConvHR) (Steele 2007: 794). At the relevant time, the Convention was not operative on the plane of domestic British law. However, judges had identified the Convention as a source of guidance by reference to which they could resolve uncertainties in the common law. Moreover, when *Derbyshire County Council* was in the Court of Appeal, the judges who heard the case agreed that the Convention was a relevant source of guidance. This has led one commentator to identify the position staked out by Lord Keith as 'grudging' with respect to the EConvHR (Wright 2001: 25). However, British judges now find themselves in a very different context. This is because the Human Rights Act 1998 has given the rights set out in the EConvHR further effect in the municipal legal context. This is a development that seems to have encouraged in some judges a heightened sense of rights consciousness (and, arguably, a more principled approach to their work). But while fundamental rights to, among other things, freedom of expression have become a feature of British law, the Human Rights Act has not given domestic effect to Article 17 of the EConvHR. This is an abuse of rights provision and, as such, provides a means by which to address the threat posed by those who engage in totalitarian conspiracies.[26] The failure of Tony Blair's New Labour administration to give further effect to Article 17 is perhaps surprising. For totalitarian conspiracy is, as we will now see, not unknown in the British context.

The Emergence of 'Gutter Fascism' in Interwar Britain[27]

Sir Oswald Mosley and the British Union of Fascists

Many commentators dismiss the possibility that fascism could have entered the mainstream of British politics in the interwar years. For example, Niall Ferguson has recently argued that 'P.G. Wodehouse's [fictive character] Roderick Spode – resplendent in his black shorts – pretty well summed up the general public's derisive view of… fascism [in the 1930s]' (Ferguson 2006: 309).[28] But, at the time,

26 12 YB (the *Greek* case) 1 at 111–112 (1969). See also Harris, O'Boyle and Warbrick 1995: 510–13.

27 The quotation in the subheading is taken from Colls 2002: 136.

28 See also Roberts 2006: 248, noting that, in 1924, Lawrence Welch observed that 'The [pre-Mosleyite] English Fascist movement is commonly regarded as an object of laughter'.

some saw the threat posed by fascism as significant. This was, for example, true of John Marchbanks, the General Secretary of the National Union of Railwaymen. At a rally in Newcastle upon Tyne in 1934 he accused the British Union of Fascists (BUF) and its leader, Sir Oswald Mosley, of 'assembling in the guise of a military machine with the object of overthrowing by force the constitutional government of this country' (Dorril 2007: 311). Marchbanks was not alone in taking this view. Earlier in 1934, the Prime Minister, Stanley Baldwin, had pursued a broadly similar theme. He stated that, '[i]f the people of this country in great numbers were to become adherents of … fascism … there could only be one end to it. And that one end would be civil war' (Dorril 2007: 292).[29]

Before examining the activity of the BUF and the responses made to it by the authorities and other groups, we must look briefly at Mosley's early life and career as a Member of Parliament. Having enjoyed the benefits of an aristocratic upbringing, he served in the Royal Flying Corps during the Great War (Dorril 2007: Chapters 1 and 2). With the war over just a month, Mosley entered Parliament as a Conservative Unionist MP who believed his nation to be 'an ideal homeland of democracy and social justice' (Dorril 2007: 41). Mosley quickly established a reputation as an orator who could 'absolutely flay the skin off anybody inefficient in debate' (Dorril 2007: 46). Moreover, he gained prominence when he criticized Lloyd George's government for engaging in a 'competition in terrorism' with nationalists in Ireland (Dorril 2007: 58).

At the next General Election (in 1922), Mosley re-entered Parliament as an independent Member of Parliament and, in 1924, joined the Independent Labour Party (ILP) (Dorril 2007: 64, 73). Following Labour's victory in the 1929 General Election, Mosley became a minister and bore responsibility for the problem of unemployment. When his colleagues refused to embrace his proposals for tackling unemployment (for example, deficit financing, as advocated by J.M. Keynes), Mosley resigned from the government (Dorril 2007: 131–6). Thereafter, he formed a new parliamentary grouping, the New Party (which resulted in his expulsion from the Labour Party for 'gross disloyalty') (Dorril 2007: 162–6; Roberts 2006: 248). At this point in Mosley's career, an 'evolution to fascism' began (Dorril 2007: 173). By October 1931, Mosley had established a journal that was calling for the creation of a corporate state. The journal's editor explained that it would be '[a] state in which all will possess their proper function. And in which there will be no division and no conflict of interest' (Dorril 2007: 185). At this point, Mosley took as his model the corporate state fashioned in Italy by Mussolini (Dorril 2007: 192–3).

In the 1931 General Election, Mosley and his New Party colleagues lost their seats in Parliament (Roberts 2006: 248). Following this disastrous performance, Mosley wound up the New Party and, in 1932, formed the British Union of Fascists

29 See also p. 312, where the author notes that Mosley later sued Marchbanks successfully for slander. While Mosley won his case, the jury only awarded him a farthing in compensation and thus expressed contempt for his claim.

(BUF). The goal to which the BUF attached priority appeared on the back of its membership card: 'To win power for Fascism and thereby establish the Corporate State' (Dorril 2007: 217). Mosley argued that the corporate state was necessary since the existing political parties could not halt the 'spineless drift to disaster' (Dorril 2007: 218). Warming to this theme, he described them as 'impotent in front of the problems of the day like a hypnotized rabbit in front of a snake' (Dorril 2007: 218). Moreover, he identified the liberal–democratic system within which they worked as the source of their impotence since, on his analysis, it prevented political leaders from governing in a suitably decisive fashion (Pugh 2006: 129).

The alternative offered by Mosley was avowedly totalitarian. He declared that '[t]here will be no room in Britain for those who do not accept the principle "all for the State and the State for all"' (Dorril 2007: 219). While staking out this position, he equivocated for some time on the question as to whether the BUF was anti-Semitic. In April 1933, the BUF's *Blackshirt* newspaper stated in clear terms that members of the organization could not engage in Jew-baiting (Dorril 2007: 231). Mosley also justified this position by reference to the consideration that, for many centuries, religious and racial tolerance had been part of the British character (Dorril 2007: 244). Thereafter, Mosley drew a distinction between 'good' Jews (who assimilated to the national culture) and 'bad' Jews (who did not) before sliding into anti-Semitism of the sort practised by Germany's National Socialists (Dorril 2007: 254).[30] Hence, when he spoke at the BUF's rally at Olympia in London in 1934, his anti-Jewish rhetoric was 'virulent' (Dorril 2007: 296). Moreover, as Mosley spoke, hecklers met a violent response from his more committed supporters (Dorril 2007: 296–9). The editor of the *News Chronicle*, Gerald Barry, 'saw a man lying on the floor', having been 'mercilessly kicked and horribly handled by a gang of Blackshirts' (Dorril 2007: 297). The response of the political mainstream to the violence of the BUF at Olympia was sharply critical. Stanley Baldwin's Parliamentary Private Secretary, Geoffrey Lloyd, told the *Yorkshire Post* that he was 'appalled by the brutal conduct of the fascists'. He also said that Mosley was 'a political maniac and all decent people must combine to kill his movement' (Dorril 2007: 298). Mosley responded to this criticism by describing Lloyd as 'Mr Baldwin's little private jackal' (Pugh 2006: 160). He also posed the rhetorical question: 'Where are the bodies?' (Dorril 2007: 160). In Parliament, Isaac Foot (a Liberal Member of Parliament) initiated a parliamentary debate on Olympia and accused Mosley of employing 'strange methods that are new to our politics' (Dorril 2007: 162).

Following the Olympia rally, officials made a number of responses that had the effect of reducing the BUF's profile. Sir Joseph Ball (a supporter of the Chancellor, Austen Chamberlain) asked newspaper editors not to give Mosley publicity (Dorril 2007: 312). Ball also persuaded newsreel companies not to report on BUF demonstrations (Dorril 2007: 314). At the same time, the British Broadcasting

30 Mosley identified Oswald Spengler as the source of the distinction he drew between 'good' Jews and 'bad' Jews, see Dorril 2007: 280.

Corporation (BBC) imposed an unofficial ban on extremists (most obviously, the BUF and communists). And, in the wake of the violence at Olympia, Lord Rothermere, whose newspaper, the *Daily Mail*, had given enthusiastic support to the BUF, ceased to back Mosley's cause (Dorril 2007: 309).[31] Rothermere took this decision following complaints made to him about his support for Mosley from Jewish firms including Lyons (Dorril 2007: 309). Mosley's response was to complain that Jewish advertizers had exerted pressure 'at the point of an economic gun' (Dorril 2007: 309).

A *Daily Mail* executive who attended the Olympia rally concluded that it had been 'a display of un-English methods' (Dorril 2007: 299). For the BUF's anti-Semitism was complemented by a cult of violence on the Italian Fascist and German National Socialist models. Mosley's readiness to emulate Mussolini and Hitler in this way was far from surprising. In early 1932, before the formation of the BUF, he and some of his New Party colleagues visited Mussolini in Italy. Fascist Italy made a great impact on Mosley. He returned to England unable to 'keep his mind off shock troops' (Dorril 2007: 193). And, when he launched the BUF, he specified that its members must wear the Blackshirt uniform. As Mosley stood on the cusp of his decision to form the BUF, an old associate from his days in the Conservative Party, Harold Macmillan, had advised him not to put his supporters in uniform. On this subject, Macmillan could not have been plainer. He said to Mosley: 'You must be mad. Whenever the British feel strongly about anything, they wear grey flannel trousers and tweed' (Dorril 2007: 225, 327). But Mosley ignored this advice, put his supporters in black shirts, and established a headquarters that was a 'Fascist Fort' (Dorril 2007: 246). This was the 'Black House' in Chelsea, which operated in paramilitary fashion. In operating in this way, the BUF (described by Mosley as a 'movement' rather than a party) lay far outside the mainstream of British politics.

When commentators seek to convey a sense of the threat posed to Britain's liberal–democratic form of life by Mosley's movement, they often use 'Cable Street' as a form of shorthand. For, in this street, in the East End of London, Mosley's readiness to ape the Continental dictators was plain to see. With the fourth anniversary of the BUF's founding fast approaching, Mosley announced that the movement would celebrate by marching through the East End of London (Dorril 2007: 390). Mosley's reason for choosing this location for the march was the presence in the East End of a large Jewish community. Within 48 hours of Mosley's announcement, 77,000 people had signed a petition calling for a ban on the march (Pugh 2006: 227). However, the Home Secretary and his colleagues in government did not wish to interfere with freedom of expression. Hence, Mosley and his supporters were able to engage in their planned celebration.

On the day of the march, 3,500 Blackshirts found themselves confronted by 100,000 anti-fascist protesters. Since the march was lawful, London's entire complement of mounted policemen and 6,000 officers on foot had the task of maintaining order (Dorril 2007: 390). But, when the police entered Cable Street,

31 See also Hobsbawm 1995: 124.

the anti-fascist protesters beat them back. This prompted a Labour Member of Parliament, Fenner Brockway, to telephone the Home Secretary and ask him to call the march off. The Home Secretary's officials advised him that he could not call off a lawful march. However, the Home Secretary did decide to reroute it (Dorril 2007: 391). Mosley accepted this decision and explained that 'the BU obeys the law and does not fight with the police' (Dorril 2007: 391).

Cable Street 'dented' Mosley's image (Dorril 2007: 392). He had arrived for the march in a new, SS-style uniform. But instead of cutting a dash as a Man of Destiny, the anti-fascist protesters had left him looking ineffectual. Nonetheless, the BU remained very active in the East End. A week after Cable Street, Mosley and his followers once again marched through the same area. Moreover, the march ended in violence against Jews, including a pogrom. This led a visiting American, Felix Frankfurter (who became a Justice of the US Supreme Court three years later) to describe the BU as a form of 'organised gangsterism' (Dorril 2007: 397). A German commentator, Dietrich Aigner, made a more troubling assessment. As Mosley's supporters chalked the legend 'Perish Judah' on the walls of the East End, Aigner concluded that 'anti-Semitism [is] in the air. England [is] becoming "Jew-Conscious"' (Dorril 2007: 397).

Aside from seeking to foment hatred against Jews, Mosley signalled his intention to change British politics and society in fundamental ways. In 1935, he stated that the BUF would, having won two general elections, bring about the 'fascist revolution' (Dorril 2007: 364). But when the Prime Minister, Stanley Baldwin, called a general election in October 1935, Mosley decided not to field any candidates. Instead, he described the election as a 'sham battle'. To this he added the further observation that 'not until fascist candidates enter the field as challengers will any reality be introduced into British politics' (Dorril 2007: 364). However, observers, with claims to expertise on the subject of fascism, were not convinced. Joseph Goebbels concluded that 'fascism is a plant that does not grow in the soil of Britain' (Dorril 2007: 364). Hitler offered a variation on the same theme. He concluded that 'fascism did not lie in the English character, and although Mosley might be a fine person and had grasped the weakness of English politics, he could not seduce a whole nation' (Dorril 2007: 461).

In one particular context, enthusiasm for politics on the model favoured by Mosley, Hitler and Goebbels was growing in Britain. King Edward VIII was a Nazi sympathizer (Pugh 2006: Chapter 13). Moreover, the King's favourable attitude towards Nazism might have had practically significant consequences during the abdication crisis of 1936. When Edward revealed to the Prime Minister, Stanley Baldwin, that he intended to marry the American divorcee, Wallis Simpson, he met with an uncompromising response. Baldwin told the King that he would resign if the marriage went ahead (Dorril 2007: 403). After this meeting, ministers feared that the King might dismiss Baldwin and invite Mosley to form a government. At this time, Mosley (who was in close contact with the King through intermediaries) was contemplating 'governing without Parliament' (Dorril 2007: 404). Baldwin was alarmed by this development. Hence, he ordered officials to undertake 'delicate inquiries' concerning 'the Constitution and ultimate issues of sovereignty' (Dorril 2007: 404). But before the issue of sovereignty became a pressing concern, the King concluded that by 'making a stand' he would have left 'the scars of civil war' on Britain (Dorril 2007: 405). Thereafter, he abdicated and Mosley's hope of leading the country into a fascist future dwindled.[32]

While Baldwin did not have to face the 'civil war' contemplated by the King, he did recognize that his government had to address the problem of BU-related disorder and violence. The government's response came in the form of the Public Order Act 1936. Since 1934, the Commissioner of the Metropolitan Police, Lord Trenchard, had been calling on the Baldwin administration to ban the Blackshirt uniform. Trenchard took the view that BUF members were, when wearing their uniforms, participating in 'unauthorized exercises, movements or evolutions' contrary to the Unlawful Drilling Act 1819 (Dorril 2007: 276). While Home Office officials were uneasy about placing restrictions on liberty, the new legislation spoke to Trenchard's concerns. The Act banned uniforms and criminalized the conduct of those who used displays of physical force in order to promote political objects.

According to the Home Secretary, Sir John Simon, the 1936 Act worked like a 'charm' (Dorril 2007: 408). Certainly, the new legislation meant that Mosley and his followers could not engage in profile-raising paramilitary displays. But we should hesitate before accepting the claim made by Herbert Morrisson that the 1936 'smashed private armies and … commenced the undermining of fascism in [Britain]' (Dorril 2007: 408). The Act forced Mosley to become more 'respectable' in order to attract followers. In this, he enjoyed some success. But Mosley was never able to win mass support. In our efforts to explain his failure, we need to take account of a multiplicity of factors. They include the 1936 Act, the political forces ranged against the BUF and a modest economic recovery in the years leading up to the Second World War (Dorril 2007: 367).

The activities of the BUF were, from the moment of its founding, monitored by the security services. As the Nazis overran Western Europe, prompting an invasion scare in Britain, the government decided to intern Mosley and his leading supporters under Defence Regulation 18B (Pugh 2006: 302).[33] Regulation 18B conferred on the Home Secretary power to detain without trial persons whom he believed to be capable of acts prejudicial to the state. Moreover, officials were not

32 On the abdication crisis, see Pugh 2006: 242–6. Pugh rejects the view that 'a very English obsession with morality and sex' gave rise to the crisis. On his analysis, the Prime Minister used the King's wish to marry Wallis Simpson as a pretext for forcing him to abdicate. Pugh argues that Baldwin acted with 'uncharacteristic speed and determination' because he did not trust Edward to discharge his constitutional duties in a suitably circumspect way. Pugh also notes that Baldwin and his ministers were troubled by the Nazi sympathies that Edward and Wallis Simpson shared.

33 The Emergency Powers (Defence) Act 1939 authorized government (by Order in Council) to put measures, such as Regulation 18B, in place so as to promote public safety, the defence of the realm and public order. See Wade and Bradley 1985: 558.

obliged to give reasons for their decisions to detain individuals (Dorril 2007: 478).[34] Mosley sought unsuccessfully in a number of hearings to have his internment order overturned (Dorril 2007: Chapter 23). The files relating to these hearings (which contain papers from the Cabinet Office; the Home Office; MI5; and the police) throw light on the relationships built up by Mosley with the fascists in Italy and the National Socialists in Germany. These relationships led the government to conclude that Mosley could, if not interned, become a focus for collaboration with the Axis powers (Dorril 2007: 488).[35]

The basis on which the Home Secretary interned Mosley and his supporters troubled Winston Churchill. He recognized that detention without trial by jury was 'in the highest degree odious … [and] the foundation of all totalitarian government whether Nazi or Communist' (Pugh 2006: 302).[36] Churchill thus found himself confronting what Niall Ferguson (drawing on Norman Mailer) has called 'the osmosis of war'. This is the adoption of practices associated with and constitutive in part, at least, of the threat posed by the enemy against whom one is struggling (Ferguson 2006: 505).

Mosley and the Far-Right in Post-War Britain

Following the defeat of the Nazis and their allies in the Second World War, 'British fascism revived remarkably quickly' (Kynaston 2007: 270). In the immediate post-war years, many people believed that Jews were responsible for running the black market. Moreover, the hanging of two captured British troops in Palestine by Zionists intensified anti-Jewish feeling (Kynaston 2007: 270). The upshot was

34 In *Liversidge v. Anderson* [1942] AC 206, the House of Lords scrutinized Defence Regulation 18B. The majority of their Lordships concluded that the Home Secretary was 'answerable to Parliament' and not to the courts for the way he exercised his discretion. Lord Atkin dissented from this view and accused his colleagues of being 'more executive-minded than the executive.'

35 See also pp. 403 and 520 (noting the difficulties encountered by government and associated agencies in identifying funding streams from Italy and Germany to the BUF.) The author also notes that Adolf Hitler took the same view of Mosley as did the Churchill administration. For Hitler stated in early 1940 that 'we shall have friends who will help us in all the enemy countries'. These 'friends' included Mosley. The US Ambassador in Paris took a similar view. On 16 May 1940, he stated, in a telegram to President Roosevelt, that 'You should have in mind the hypothesis that, in order to escape the ultimate consequences of absolute defeat, the British may install a government of Oswald Mosley … which would co-operate fully with Hitler' (Dorril 2007: 496).

36 In November 1943, the Home Secretary, Herbert Morrison, decided to release Mosley from internment. While many people complained to the Home Office about the release of 'Number One Traitor', the Prime Minister regarded Morrison's decision as sound. In a communication to Morrison he stated: '[e]xtraordinary powers assumed by the Executive with the consent of Parliament in emergencies should be yielded up when and as the emergency declines'. See Dorril 2007: 536–8.

a series of anti-Jewish riots in several British cities in 1947. This was a context in which Mosley was able to conclude that there was a place for him in British politics. In 1948, he launched the Union Movement (UM), the purpose of which was to win support for the idea that Europe should become a nation and seek to advance an extreme right-wing political agenda. The Union Mosley had in mind was to be, among other things, 'a white man's club' (Dorril 2007: 624).[37] This explains why he sought to foment hatred against the large number of West Indians and Asians who entered Britain in the 1940s and 1950s (Sandbrook 2006a: Chapter 9).

When white youths mounted race riots in London's Notting Hill district in 1958, Mosley saw an opportunity to win support for his views. He described the rioters as 'fine virile types' and, after the riots, 'began a sustained campaign to build on … support for the UM' (Dorril 2007: 614–15).[38] To this end, he repeatedly made inflammatory statements, for example: 'Every white man in a job knows that he has got a coloured man at his elbow, ready to take his job at a cheaper rate' (Dorril 2007: 618). Statements of this sort did not draw support to Mosley. In 1959, he stood for Parliament in the North Kensington constituency and lost his deposit. This reverse at the polls indicated how far out of the mainstream of British life Mosley and his supporters were. Moreover, the sentences imposed by Salmon J on some of those who had rioted in Notting Hill sent out a denunciatory message. The judge imposed exemplary sentences on the rioters and stated that 'you are a minute and insignificant section of the population but you have brought shame on the district where you live and have filled the nation with horror, indignation and disgust' (Dorril 2007: 615).[39] In the aftermath of the riots, Mosley also found himself ranged against groups who were determined to call his policy agenda into question. Thus the Institute for Race Relations (established after the Notting Hill riots) spearheaded the fight against racism in the late 1950s and 1960s (Sandbrook 2006a: 339).

Mosley, nonetheless, continued to campaign against the 'coloured invasion' (Dorril 2007: Chapter 27). In response to his efforts and those of others to foment hatred against minority groups, Harold Wilson's Labour Government enacted legislation criminalizing incitement to racial hatred. Section 6 of the Race Relations Act 1965 made it an offence to publish written matter or to make a speech in public, which was threatening, abusive or insulting, and likely to stir up

37 See also p. 572 on Mosley's claim that races were the 'First Reality of European Union'.

38 Where the author also notes that the Trade Union Congress condemned Mosley for 'fanning the flames of racial violence'.

39 Exemplary sentences are supposed to 'make an example' of a defendant (and thus advance the agenda of general deterrence). Aggravating features of a defendant's conduct may provide a judge with grounds for imposing such sentences. However, they stand in a relationship of acute tension with the ideal of retributive justice according to which wrongdoers should receive their just deserts. See Walker 1991: 19–20, 72–82.

racial hatred (Barendt 1985: 163). In response to criticisms made in Parliament by, *inter alios*, Peter Thorneycroft MP, the government sought to ensure that the new legislation took adequate account of free expression. For this reason, the new provision specified that those wishing to mount a prosecution could only do so with the permission of the Attorney-General (Barendt 1985: 162). Shortly after Labour's legislative intervention in 1965, Mosley decided that the time had come for him to draw a halt to active campaigning. He remained committed to the right-wing views he had propounded and continued to hope that Britain would one day need the 'Man of Destiny' that he had for so long regarded himself as being (Dorril 2007: Chapter 28).

For a brief moment in 1968, Mosley might have thought that his time had come. In May of that year, Cecil King, the head of the International Publishing Corporation (IPC), met Lord Mountbatten (the last Viceroy of India and a cousin of the Queen). King was no democrat. He believed that the welfare of society depended on great men (among whom he numbered himself) ruthlessly establishing order through the exercise of their will (Sandbrook 2006b: 614). Moreover, he predicted that 'the [Labour] government would disintegrate, [and] there would be bloodshed in the streets, [and] the armed forces would be involved' (Sandbrook 2006b: 617). King's closest associates found in this remark (and others like it) evidence that he was 'well on his way' to megalomania (Sandbrook 2006b: 615). This was a sound assessment. For King, on meeting Mountbatten, urged him to consider seizing control of the country. On hearing this, Mountbatten sought the opinion of Sir Solly Zuckerman (the government's Chief Scientific Adviser) who was also attending the meeting. Zuckerman's view was that the course of action King was contemplating amounted to 'rank treachery' (Sandbrook 2006b: 618). A 'stunned silence' followed these words. But eventually Mountbatten told Zuckerman that he was right and stated that the plan was 'simply not on' (Sandbrook 2006b: 618).

King did not, however, abandon his plan. Two days later, in the *Daily Mirror*, he called for 'a fresh start under a new [national] leader' (Sandbrook 2006b: 619). Moreover, he met Mosley outside Paris and discussed with him the possibility that he might play a part in the 'government of national unity' that King wished to bring into existence (Horrie 2003: 11). However, King's plans came to nothing. Journalists working for the *Daily Mirror*'s rivals roundly abused him for his anti-democratic outpouring (Sandbrook 2006b: 619–20). To the chorus of abuse directed at King, the satirical magazine *Private Eye* added mockery. Its cover featured a picture of Napoleon and a statement from 'Cecil Harmsworth Gnome', parodying King's message to the nation (Sandbrook 2006b: 620). In light of these responses, IPC dismissed King.

This reverse did not, however, prompt King to abandon his anti-democratic ambitions. In 1973, Geoffrey Ripon, the minister who had led the negotiations for Britain's entry to the EEC, remarked to friends: 'We [are] on the same course as the Weimar government with runaway inflation and ultra-high unemployment in the end' (Weight 2002: 537). By the mid-1970s, the National Association for Freedom was contemplating a coup with the aim of establishing a military junta.

It was in this febrile context that the military historian, John Keegan, heard Cecil King deliver a speech at Sandhurst in which he urged senior military personnel to seize control of the country. Keegan later described King's speech as 'a treasonable attempt to suborn the loyalty of the Queen's officers' (Wheen 1998: 25). But there was no coup, and Britain lurched from crisis to crisis until (in 1979) Margaret Thatcher embarked not on a political but, rather, on an economic revolution. The following year, Mosley died. *The Times*' obituary described his 'impatience with the slow processes of democratic government' (Dorril 2007: 644). It also stated that 'some inherent flaw of character' had sent him 'off the rails' and prompted him to embrace fascism (Dorril 2007: 644). But P.G. Wodehouse had captured the spirit of the man over four decades earlier. In 1938, he described his fictive fascist, Sir Roderick Spode, as a 'perfect perisher' (Dorril 2007: 443).

The Far-Right After Mosley

In 1967 (as Mosley's career was drawing to a close), a collection of far-right groups formed the National Front (NF). In the early 1960s, one of the NF's founders, Andrew Fountain, repeatedly attempted to contact the Prime Minister, Harold Macmillan, in order to urge him to deny Asians and West Indians access to the United Kingdom. Macmillan repeatedly rebuffed him. Recounting his exchanges with the Prime Minister on the telephone, Fountain made this revelation: '[Macmillan] would pick up the receiver, and as soon as he'd heard it was me, [he would] pretend he was the butler' (Weight 2002: 542). While Macmillan was thus able to brush Fountain off, his successors could not ignore the NF. By 1977, it was Britain's fourth largest political party. The NF owed its rise to prominence, in large part, to the poor performance of the economy in the late 1960s and 1970s. As Britain's economic performance worsened, the NF's leaders took the opportunity to scapegoat the members of minority groups. A significant increase in the number of those in minority groups who, at this time, suffered physical and/or verbal abuse points up the extent of the NF's impact at this time (Weight 2002: 537).

After the 1979 General Election, support for the NF fell away sharply. One explanation for this decrease in support is Margaret Thatcher's determination, from the moment she assumed leadership of the Conservative Party, to speak to the concerns of those who were troubled by large-scale immigration (Weight 2002: 539). In 1978 (and just over a year before she became Prime Minister), Thatcher stated that she could understand the concerns of those who feared that the country was being 'rather swamped by people with a different culture' (Weight 2002: 538). Moreover, following Thatcher's victory in the 1979 General Election, her Home Secretary, William Whitelaw, said that 'it is time to dispose of the lingering notion that Britain is somehow a haven for all those whose countries we used to rule' (Weight 2002: 538).

With statements such as these, Thatcher effectively drove the National Front out of political business. However, a new political party emerged on the far-right: the British National Party (BNP). The BNP has pursued the same themes as the NF.

And, like the NF, it has become associated with violence against minority groups. Thus, in 2001, it played a part in fomenting hatred and violence in a number of Pennine towns that issued in public disorder.[40] Notwithstanding its association with hate-mongering and violence, the BNP has begun to gain a foothold in local government. Those BNP members who have secured victories in local elections have done so by, among other things, arguing that local authorities treat minority groups more favourably than indigenous groups (Fletcher 2007: 4).

The violence with which the BNP is associated has found more vivid expression in the activities of two associated groups, Combat 18 and Redwatch. Combat 18 gained national prominence when, in the 1990s, its members mounted attacks on immigrants and left-wing opponents. Between 1998 and 2000, operations involving the Metropolitan Police and MI5 resulted in the arrest and prosecution of Combat 18 members for a variety of offences. Just as the police and security services have taken a close interest in Combat 18, so too government has monitored (and has contemplated proscribing) the activities of Redwatch. This is because it publishes the names of and seeks to incite violence against those whom its members regard as political opponents (for example, members of the Anti-Nazi League) (Taylor 2006: 12). Following a review of Redwatch's activities, the government has decided not to remove particular websites from the Internet. Moreover, the minister with responsibility for addressing the problems posed by extremist websites is unable, for 'operational reasons', to describe the strategies employed by the Home Office, the police and other agencies.[41]

Before turning to our examination of radical Islamism in Britain, an essay on British culture written by Arthur Koestler provides a basis on which to gain analytic purchase on the state's response to those on the extreme right. Moreover, it provides grounds for doubting whether the state is well equipped to address the threats posed by radical Islamists.

The Lion and the Ostrich

Drawing on his experience of life in England, Koestler (who was born in Hungary) observed (Koestler 1963: 7):

> The average Englishman … strikes one as a hybrid between a lion and an ostrich. In times of emergency he rises magnificently to the occasion. In between emergencies he buries his head in the sand … [This] attitude guarantees that a new emergency will soon arise.

40 http://news.bbc.co.uk/hi/english/static/in_depth/programmes/2001/bnp_special/roots/; see BBC, *Panorama*, 'BNP: Under the Skin' (2001).

41 Personal communication to the author from Mr Vernon Coaker MP, Parliamentary Under-Secretary of State (at the Home Office), 22 August 2007 (held on file in Newcastle Law School).

So how does this relate to fascism in the 1930s? Well, for years the government and associated agencies did little to address the problems created by the emergence of fascism in the United Kingdom. As a result, Sir Oswald Mosley was able to go about his anti-democratic business with few constraints. He could foster a cult of violence. He could bait Jews. He could build alliances with (and access funds from) Mussolini and Hitler. During the 'Phoney War' (between Britain's declaration of war in September 1939 and the commencement of hostilities in Western Europe), he could campaign for peace. Admittedly, the Public Order Act 1936 reduced his freedom of action somewhat. But to say, as the Home Secretary did, that it worked like a 'charm' is a gross overstatement. For Mosley remained a player in the great game of politics until the spring of 1940. During this period, he was able, among other things, to disseminate anti-war propaganda (Dorril 2007: 475). Only with the Nazis striking westwards into France was he interned. This, if we accept Koestler's claims, was the point at which the ostrich turned into the lion.[42]

But this may be over simple. We might, for example, relate the ostrich-like propensities described by Koestler, to the ideal of tolerance. On this view, we could see in the government's response to Mosley a readiness to endure conduct that its members looked on with disapproval.[43] If this is correct, then the British Government was doing rather more than refusing (in an ostrich-like manner) to face up to an unprepossessing reality. It was treating an ideal (tolerance) widely assumed to be a prominent feature of Britain's form of life as a reason for action (Dorril 2007: 346).[44] The government's attitude towards the BU at the time war broke out supports this claim. The Home Office regarded BU pamphlets as 'mischievous and defeatist' (Pugh 2006: 292). But the Home Secretary, Sir John Anderson, resisted the urge to suppress or ban Mosley's organization.[45]

We might place alongside the governmental commitment to tolerance suggested here an empirical orientation towards practical problems. For we find the Home Office, MI5, MI6 and other agencies gathering more and more information on Mosley and his confederates as the 1930s progress. Plainly, these bodies grasped

---

42 To put the point made in the text another way, we might say that the imminent threat of invasion issued in the process characterized earlier as 'the osmosis of war'.

43 On toleration, see Raz 1986: 402, stating that '[t]oleration … is the curbing of an activity that is likely to be unwelcome to its recipient or of an inclination so to act which is in itself morally valuable and which is based on a dislike or an antagonism towards the person or a feature of his life, reflecting a judgment that these represent limitations or deficiencies in him, in order to let that person have his way or in order for him to gain or keep some advantage'.

44 Noting that 'bemused tolerance' was commonly a feature of official pronouncements concerning the BUF in the pre-War years. On toleration as a feature of English (and more generally, British) culture, see Scruton 2001: 47, drawing on the analyses of Voltaire and Montesquieu.

45 See also Dorril 2007: 475, noting that, in late 1939, Ministers regarded Mosley's anti-war propaganda as harmless and concluded that prosecution of those campaigning for peace would do more harm than good.

that Mosley's movement posed a problem in the context of a liberal democracy. They then spent a protracted period of time trying to get to grips with this problem by, *inter alia*, enacting public order-related legislation. In other words, they proceeded in an empirical and piecemeal manner. Had not Hitler focused their minds by seizing large swathes of Western Europe, they might have spent a good deal longer mulling over the information they had gathered. Moreover, when the government rounded up those BU members it saw as posing a threat to national security in May 1940, the empirical grounds for depriving them of their liberty were, to say the least, shaky. MI5 had not been able 'to come up with evidence of fifth-column activities' on the part of most of those detained (Pugh 2006: 302).

While the concepts of empiricism and tolerance throw light on the response made by government and other agencies to fascism up to May 1940, the approach adopted looks decidedly unsystematic. This is a view that would certainly be supported by those who identified the security services prior to and during the early years of the Second World War as amateurish (Lacey 2004: 100).[46] However, we might see the ostrich-cum-lion stance of government as a means by which to discharge what Isaiah Berlin has called 'the first public obligation' (Berlin 1998). On Berlin's account, this is the obligation to 'avoid extremes of suffering'. To this end, government made only modest inroads into the liberty of Mosley and his supporters while they posed a very limited threat to liberal democracy. But as the Nazi war machine drew near to the United Kingdom, government had to give priority to the imperative of national survival. This analysis finds support in the recollections of Jenifer Hart, the private secretary to Sir Alexander Maxwell, the Home Office Permanent Under-Secretary. Hart describes Maxwell and the Home Secretary as 'the personification of the Home Office tradition that civil liberties should be restricted as little as possible and only then as a result of urgent … necessity' (Dorril 2007: 481).[47] Certainly, when the Home Secretary decided to intern Mosley and other BU members, MI5 had concluded that, without immediate action, 'there would be no democracy, no England, no Empire' (Dorril 2007: 499).[48]

We now turn to radical Islam in the British context and address, *inter alia*, the question as to whether government is equipped to meet the obligation described by Berlin.

---

46 Noting that Herbert Hart, while working for MI5 in the early 1940s, found 'amateurishness and lack of direction' to be features of his working environment.

47 See also Simpson 2001: 20, on the English 'tradition' of 'protecting liberty against the executive', and 23, on the governmental commitment to a 'due balance between the rights of the individual and … the ordered life of a community'.

48 While the point cannot be pursued in detail here, we might see empiricism (and perhaps even tolerance) as linked in significant ways to defence as described in von Clausewitz 2007: 159.

Radical Islamism in Britain

The Rushdie Affair and the Covenant of Security

As we noted earlier, large-scale migration to Britain from the West Indies and the Indian subcontinent took place from the 1950s onwards. Among those who entered Britain at this time were Muslims from Pakistan. Since the 9/11 attacks by *Al-Qaeda*, government and the security services have assumed that a subset of those in this group pose a significant terrorist threat (Gove 2006: 2). Subsequent terrorist activity in Britain (most notably on 7 July 2005) has confirmed the fears of ministers and officials (Gove 2006: 4). Moreover, the views on the Islamic faith expressed by some Muslims resident in Britain seem to be at odds with the democratic institutions and values that lend Britain's form of life its liberal character. For example, in 2006, Anjem Choudray stated that England 'belongs to Allah' and dismissed the suggestion that he should accommodate his beliefs and practices to the norms of a liberal democracy (Gove 2006: 10).[49]

The possibility that liberal values and commitment to the Islamic faith may be at odds with one another became apparent over a decade before the 9/11 attacks. In 1988, Salman Rushdie (a Briton who was born into a Muslim family) published *The Satanic Verses*, a satirical attack on Islam.[50] This satire was a source of offence to Muslims across the world. Given that Rushdie had named the book's prophet-like central character Mahound (which means 'false prophet') and had described him as lecherous and unscrupulous in the exercise of power, this is not surprising (Lee 1990: 73). Ayatollah Khomeini (the head of Iran's theocratic state) responded to *The Satanic Verses* by issuing a *Fatwa*, sentencing Rushdie to death. The Ayatollah's pronouncement forced Rushdie to go into hiding and to live the life of a fugitive. The Khomeini *Fatwa* was also notable as the first occasion on which a religious leader in an Islamic country had issued an edict 'regarding a Muslim living in a non-Muslim country' (Burleigh 2006: 457).

In the wake of Khomeini's *Fatwa*, Muslims in Britain protested against the publication of *The Satanic Verses*. At the same time, a number of prominent British Muslims called for Rushdie's death. For example, Sayed Abdul Quddus, the Secretary of the Bradford Council of Mosques, identified 'hanging' as the appropriate penalty for Rushdie (Phillips 2006: 45–6). The Thatcher administration described this and other statements of the same sort as totally 'unacceptable' (Phillips 2006: 46). But no prosecutions for incitement to murder followed. This less than robust response and others like it have led Melanie Phillips to argue that

49 Choudray plays a leadership role in *al-Ghurabaa* (a British-based Islamist group). The statements noted in the text were made on the BBC's *Newsnight* television programme in February 2006.

50 Six years before the publication of *The Satanic Verses*, Rushdie attacked Islam in *Shame*. See Sim 1998: 353.

Britain's leaders have failed to recognize 'a major and systematic threat to the British state and its values' (Phillips 2006: 47).

The 'threat' identified by Phillips is, in fact, a complex of considerations. Prominent among them is criminality: a readiness to engage in incitement. Also prominent is a lack of respect for the rule of law and 'the cardinal value of free speech' (Phillips 2006: 47). Alongside these considerations, Phillips also lists 'the emergence of British Muslims as a distinct and hostile political entity' and 'the supine response of the British establishment' (Phillips 2006: 47). In some respects, this analysis is overstated. For example, Phillips is too sweeping when she conveys the impression that *all* Muslims in Britain are part of a 'hostile political entity'. But while her analysis is insufficiently refined, it throws light on the context in which government has sought to address the practical problems posed by radical Islam in the wake of the 9/11 attacks.

A prominent feature of this context was a tacit understanding that had grown up in Britain in the years before the attack mounted on the US by *Al-Qaeda*'s suicide-murderers in September 2001. This was the so-called 'covenant of security'. On one account, the 'principle' behind the covenant was 'simple' (Gove 2006: 85). Successive governments allowed proponents of radical Islam to enjoy 'safe haven on one condition: that they did not involve themselves in direct violent action within the UK' (Gove 2006: 85). Thus the ostrich described by Koestler continued to draw breath in the late-twentieth and early-twenty-first centuries. Consequently, a number of prominent radical Islamists were free to act in ways that, in retrospect, have not served the public interest in maintaining the integrity of liberal-democratic values in the United Kingdom.

Among them, we may number Abu Hamza. As long ago as 1997, he celebrated the terrorist murder of 58 European tourists in Egypt. In 1999, he coordinated the kidnap of Western visitors to Yemen. Moreover, he used the mosque in London's Finsbury Park to foment anti-Western hatred and as a terrorist training facility (Gove 2006: 86). Hamza was engaging in just this sort of activity (shielded by the covenant of security) when Mohammed Atta and his associates mounted their successful attack on the United States in September 2001. So too was Omar Bakri Mohammed who established the first branch of *Hizb ut-Tahrir* (the Islamic Liberation Party) in Britain, before forming his own organization, *al-Muhajiroun* (O'Neill and McGrory 2006: 106). Bakri Mohammed had, by this time won a reputation as the 'Tottenham Ayatollah' on account of his readiness to urge, *inter alia*, holy war (*jihad*) (O'Neill and McGrory 2006: 106).[51] As Bakri Mohammed, Hamza, and others enjoyed the benefits of the covenant of security, intelligence chiefs in France, bemused by the ostrich-like behaviour of the British, renamed the British capital 'Londonistan' (O'Neill and McGrory 2006: 106).

51 See also p. 113, noting that Bakri Mohhammed identified John Major (when Britain's Prime Minister) as 'a legitimate target' for attack.

British Responses to 9/11

Following the 9/11 attacks, the government passed the Anti-Terrorism, Crime and Security Act 2001 with 'unseemly haste' (Alder 2007: 539). Under Section 23 of this Act, the Home Secretary could indefinitely detain without trial foreign nationals whom he suspected of participation in terrorist activity (Alder 2007: 539).[52] In December 2001, the Home Secretary, David Blunkett, used this power to detain nine foreign nationals in Belmarsh Prison, London. Moreover, Blunkett did not allow these suspects to see the intelligence evidence that had prompted him to detain them. In light of the Home Secretary's response to the threat he perceived and the fact that detainees spent 22 hours a day in their cells, human rights organizations described Belmarsh as a British Guantanamo.[53]

In the subsequent case of *A v. Secretary of State for the Home Department*, the Belmarsh detainees argued that the Home Secretary's decision to incarcerate them had constituted a breach of their human rights. The House of Lords (when hearing the arguments put forward by the men on appeal) accepted (by a majority of eight to one) that their human rights had been breached.[54] The majority identified indefinite detention as a disproportionate interference with the right to liberty under Article 5 of the EConvHR. They also identified it as a discriminatory measure that breached Article 14 of the Convention (Turpin and Tomkins 2007: 762). However, the most striking feature of the House of Lords' decision in *A*'s case is scepticism towards the national security-related arguments put forward by the government. Baroness Hale, for example, responded to these arguments by observing that '[u]nwarranted declarations of emergency are a familiar tool of tyranny'.[55] Lord Hoffmann took a rather different tack. In an analysis that ranged over many centuries of British history, he pondered the question, 'What is meant by "threatening the life of the nation"'.[56] His answer made uncomfortable reading for the government. For he concluded that '[t]he real threat to the life of the nation, in the sense of people living in accordance with its traditional laws and political values, comes not from terrorism but from laws such as these'.[57] Thus we find his Lordship drawing the conclusion that the government had succumbed, too readily, to the 'osmosis of war' (as described earlier).

52 Anticipating challenges to the adoption of the power noted in the text, the government derogated from Article 5(1) of the European Convention on Human Rights (the right to liberty and security of the person). See Turpin and Tomkins 2007: 7.

53 D. Winterman, 'Belmarsh – Britain's Guantanamo Bay?' 6 October 2004, (at http://news.bbc.co.uk/1/hi/magazine/3714864.stm). Gearty 2007: 116, identifying the Home Secretary's decision as involving 'a *de facto* return to internment'.

54 *A v. Secretary of State for the Home Department* [2005] 2 AC 68.

55 *A v. Secretary of State for the Home Department* [2005] 2 AC 226.

56 *A v. Secretary of State for the Home Department* [2005] 2 AC 91–97.

57 *A v. Secretary of State for the Home Department* [2005] 2 AC 97.

In response to this decision, the government enacted the Prevention of Terrorism Act 2005 (Marr 2007: 583). This Act introduced a system of 'control orders' that, like the practice of indefinite detention, proved 'deeply controversial' from a human rights point of view (Turpin and Tomkins 2007: 278). Control orders place restrictions on, *inter alia*, travel, use of the Internet, and the use of telephones (Alder 2007: 544). However, in circumstances where they do not amount to house arrest, inhuman or degrading treatment, or infringements of privacy, they are compatible with EConvHR rights (Alder 2007: 544). Having introduced these orders, the government imposed them on the men previously detained in Belmarsh Prison. In defence of the government's decision to do this, the Leader of the House of Lords, Baroness Amos, emphasized that, in the relevant circumstances, they were a necessary response to a grave threat.[58]

The exceptional nature of the circumstances facing the government became apparent on 7 July 2005 when four British-born Islamist terrorists detonated explosive devices in London, killing 52 people and wounding 770 others (Gove 2006: 2; Marr 2007: 582). As a result of 7/7, the government decided to legislate again. The Terrorism Act 2006 has increased the period of time during which the police may detain individuals without charge from 7 to 28 days.[59] The 2006 Act has also brought a number of new offences into existence, for example: encouragement of terrorism, including the glorification of terrorist activity (Section 1); preparation for terrorist acts (Section 5); training for terrorism (Section 6); and trespassing on nuclear sites (Section 12) (Turpin and Tomkins 2007: 755).

While the Terrorism Act 2006 extended the powers of the police to combat the threat posed by terrorists, government failed to extend the power to detain suspects without charge for the period originally planned. On 9 November 2005, government introduced an amendment to the Terrorist Bill that would have extended the period of detention without charge to 90 days. This amendment reflected Tony Blair's belief that 'the rules of the game are changing' and that the threat posed by a 'fanatical fringe' of the Muslim community necessitated reduced protection for human rights.[60]

In the weeks before the introduction of the 90-day amendment, senior police officers expressed support publicly for such a measure.[61] But Parliament rejected their views and those of the government and inflicted on the Blair administration its first defeat on the floor of the House of Commons (Turpin and Tomkins 2007: 755). Moreover, some members of Parliament criticized those senior police officers who had called for a 90-day detention period on, *inter alia*, the ground that such

58 'Control Orders "Could Target IRA"', *BBC News 24*, 17 March 2005.

59 Terrorism Act 2006, Section 23.

60 See www.number10.gov.uk/output/Page8041.asp.

61 The Assistant Commissioner of the Metropolitan Police, Andrew Hayman; the Chief Constable of Greater Manchester Police, Michael Todd; and the Chief Constable of the Police Service in Northern Ireland, Sir Michael Orde, were among those officers who supported the 90-day amendment.

conduct threatened to result in the politicization of the police. This matter became intensely controversial. For it later emerged that the Home Secretary, Charles Clarke, had (as he put the point) 'suggested to the Association of Chief Police Officers that chief constables write to MPs' in support of the amendment.[62]

More recently, the judiciary have scrutinized the control order regime. In *Secretary of State for the Home Department v. JJ et al.*, the House of Lords concluded that the power to impose curfews that operate for 18 hours a day is incompatible with Article 5 of the EConvHR.[63] But their Lordships did identify 12-hour curfews as acceptable. The House also examined the question as to whether those subject to control orders should have access to some of the evidence supporting the decision to restrict their liberty. The Law Lords concluded that the government and associated agencies would not have to disclose sensitive intelligence. However, they qualified this point by saying that the power of non-disclosure should not be so sweeping as to deprive suspects of a fair hearing. In response to this decision, the Home Secretary, Jacqui Smith, expressed disappointment that the House of Lords 'found against control orders containing 18-hour curfews' (Ford 2007: 26). She added that she regarded such restrictions on liberty as 'required to protect national security' (Ford 2007: 26).

Just as detention powers have been a source of controversy, so too has been the creation of the glorification of terror offence. For this offence sits uneasily alongside New Labour's commitment to foster a human rights culture in the United Kingdom (as expressed in the White Paper that preceded enactment of the Human Rights Act 1998).[64] In order to explain why this is so, we must focus on the term 'glorification', which poses a threat to freedom of expression as protected by Article 10 of the EConvHR. 'Glorification' is rich in significance: it appears to denote both behaviour and an associated disposition. The behaviour in question seems to be expressive activity that presents terrorism in a very attractive – indeed, noble – light. The associated disposition appears to be a preference for disorder over order or, more specifically, a desire to destroy institutions oriented towards the pursuit of justice (on a pluralist model). Assuming that these points are sound, 'glorification' (as used in this context) has meaning. Nonetheless, we may be uncertain as to when we should apply this term to the conduct of individuals. For example, do those who refer to the Air Marshall who led the Royal Air Force's Bomber Command in the Second World War glorify terrorism when they refer to him (affirmatively) as 'Bomber' Harris?[65] That it is even possible to ponder this

62 'Government Uses Police Opinion Only When it Suits', *The Daily Telegraph*, 12 November 2005 (letters), 25 (letter from the Home Secretary).

63 [2007] UKHL 45; [2007] 3 WLR 643.

64 *Rights Brought Home*: *The Human Rights Bill* (Cm. 3782, 1997), para. 1.18 and para. 1.19).

65 On Bomber Harris (and British and American misgivings concerning the bombing of civilian targets in Germany), see Ferguson 2006: 558–71.

question provides a basis on which to conclude that the offence under discussion will exert a chilling effect on free expression.

This criticism has particular force when viewed in the light of a number of fairness-related principles that inform criminal law in the United Kingdom (Ashworth 2006: 68–77). One such principle concerns maximum certainty. It specifies that lawmakers should set out criminal prohibitions in clear language so as to give potential offenders 'fair warning' of the circumstances in which the law applies (Ashworth 2006: 74–7). Against this concern with fairness, we should, however, set a number of countervailing considerations that inform criminal law in the United Kingdom. Among them, we may number the policy of social defence, according to which the criminal law works to protect individuals from harm and to maintain the integrity of society (Ashworth 2006: 65–6).[66] Likewise, we may include the thin-ice principle which identifies as fit objects of punishment those who seek to exploit uncertainties in the law for the purposes of wrongdoing (Ashworth 2006: 73–4).[67]

The relevance of the thin-ice principle to the activities of radical Islamists becomes immediately apparent when we consider the conduct of Omar Bakri Mohammed and Abu Hamza. While resident in Britain, Bakri Mohammed, among other things, heaped praise on the 9/11 suicide murderers, describing them as 'the Magnificent Nineteen' (Gove 2006: 87). Before the Charity Commission dismissed him from his post, Abu Hamza preached at London's Finsbury Park mosque. The fare Hamza presented to his audiences was rich in content. He sought to incite violence against Jews, gays, lesbians and Muslim women who disobeyed their husbands. He also advocated the pursuit of *jihad* by means of, *inter alia*, suicide bombings (O'Neill and McGrory 2006: Chapter 4).[68]

The British authorities charged Hamza with 15 offences including soliciting murder and inciting racial hatred. Of the 15 offences, the jury found him guilty of 11. In his judgment, Hughes J told Hamza: 'I do not make the mistake that you represent Islamic thinking generally.'[69] The judge, then, spoke at some length on the expressive activity in which Hamza had engaged: 'You are entitled to your views, and in this country you are entitled to express them up to the point where you incite murder or incite racial hatred. That, however, is what you did. You used

66 See also Turpin and Tomkins 2007: 755, noting that'[s]ince the time of Thonas Hobbes, if not before, governments have regarded their first responsibility to be to secure, as best they can, peace and order within the jurisdiction'.

67 The thin-ice principle finds expression in Lord Morris's speech in *Knuller v. DPP* [1973] AC 435.

68 See also pp. 286–7, on the regulatory role of the Charity Commission vis-à-vis charitable organizations such as the Finsbury Park mosque. In 2007, the Government decided (as part of its wider counter-terrorism agenda) to strengthen the Charity Commission's regulatory role. See http://www.hm-treasury.gov.uk/newsroom_and_speeches/press/2007/press_23_07.cfm and http://www.charitycommission.gov.uk/tcc/faithsc.asp, on the Charity Commission's 'Faith and Social Cohesion Unit'.

69 'Timeline: Hamza Trial', *BBC News 24*, 7 February 2006.

your authority to legitimise anger and to encourage your audiences to believe that it gave rise to a duty to murder. You commended suicide bombing, you encouraged them to kill in the cause you set for them' (O'Neill and McGrory 2006: 310). This was certainly true. Among those who heard Hamza preach at Finsbury Park were Mohammed Sidique Khan, Shehzad Tanweer and Jermaine Lindsay, each of whom perpetrated suicide murders on 7 July 2005 (O'Neill and McGrory 2006: 269).

Just as the government has sought to address the practical problems created by terrorism-related expressive activity, so too it has focused attention on hate speech directed at Muslims in Britain. To this end, it has created a new offence: incitement to religious hatred. When Tony Blair's administration first proposed the creation of this offence, the upshot was a sharply critical response. For example, the comedian Rowan Atkinson, argued that free expression would be unduly restricted if incitement to religious hatred became a crime (Demetriou 2004: 18). But the critics did not persuade the government to abandon its plan. Blair and his ministers saw hate speech directed at Muslims as a serious problem. This was, *inter alia*, because racists, using religion as a ground on which to attack minorities, could sidestep the incitement to racial hatred offence (Card 2000: 185).

In criminalizing incitement to religious hatred, the government also wished to demonstrate that it would balance its anti-terrorism legislation with a provision serving the interests of Muslims. This suggests a commitment, on the Blair administration's part, to the ideal of distributive justice. This ideal specifies that public institutions (such as the law) should defensibly accommodate the interests of all society's members. To act in accordance with this ideal is to adopt an approach to practical life that we might categorize as 'principled'. For our aim is to establish basic terms of social life that all relevant persons could rationally endorse.[70] While seeking to pursue distributive justice, Tony Blair emphasized his determination to defend Britain's liberal politico-legal framework. After the 7/7 bombings, he declared that '[o]ur tolerance is part of what makes Britain, Britain. So conform to it; or don't come here. We don't want the hate-mongers' (Marr 2007: 601). In emphasizing conformity to liberal norms, Blair echoed a statement made by the Dutch politician, Pim Fortuyn, shortly before he was murdered. While challenging the orthodoxy of multiculturalism, Fortuyn declared that '[t]his is our country, and if you can't conform, you should get the hell out, back to your own country and culture' (Buruma 2006: 67). These statements share more than a theme. The tone adopted by both Blair and Fortuyn is aggressive and suggests a movement in the direction of politics on the Schmittian model. For Schmitt argues that 'every concrete antagonism becomes that much more political the closer it approaches the extreme point, that of the friend–enemy grouping' (Schmitt 1996: 29).

This movement in the direction of friend-versus-foe politics is at its clearest in New Labour's participation in the US-led incursions into Afghanistan and Iraq as

70 The conception of distributive justice outlined in the text bears similarities to that defended in Rawls 1971: 4 et seq.

part of a policy of 'forward' defence (Gove 2006: 128). Each of these incursions has worked to deny terrorists 'space' in which to train *jihadis* and in which to organize operations, such as the suicide murders perpetrated on 9/11 (Gove 2006: 131). This policy has to do with more than the occupation of space: it also embraces, *inter alia*, the democratic elections that took place in Iraq in 2005 (Gove 2006: 133). To the extent that democracy takes root in Iraq, terrorists based in that country will find themselves in a less accommodating environment.

But even if we accept that the military is implementing a policy of forward defence, we have to recognize that Britain and her allies have acted in maladroit ways. Thus, in southern Iraq, the Foreign and Commonwealth Office has been committed to a policy of constructive engagement with Iran. What this has meant in practical terms is a readiness on Britain's part to appease Iran (Gove 2006: 132). To this end, the military has ceded territory to Iranian backed militias. And, as the military has given up territory, so too it has suffered a loss of authority and prestige. In these circumstances, British forces are able to do little more than pursue the modest goal of self-preservation. Certainly, they are not well placed to pursue the end of a just set of practical arrangements and thus present themselves as the agents of principle. More generally, we have to contemplate the possibility that the incursion into Iraq is 'a recruiting sergeant for Islamic extremism' (Marr 2007: 589).

The leader of the Conservative opposition, David Cameron, has followed his predecessors in supporting the Blair administration's decision to go to war with Iraq (Winnett 2007: 2). However, he has, more recently, expressed doubt concerning the ability of states to 'create utopias' abroad and, thereby, forestall terrorism on their own soil (Winnett 2007: 2). Moreover, he has argued that Britain should put 'national security first' (Winnett 2007: 2). To this end, he has stressed the importance of improving community relations within Britain since 'the people who let off bombs on London's public transport system … were British citizens' (Winnett 2007: 2). A speech delivered in November 2007 by Jonathan Evans, the Director-General of MI5, suggests that there is an urgent need to improve community relations. Evans identified the number of known Islamist terrorist suspects in the United Kingdom as having reached 2,000 (Evans and Webster 2007: 6). But he added that there may, in fact, be 4,000 persons in the United Kingdom ready to emulate the 7/7 bombers. He also described Islamist terrorist groups as 'radicalising, indoctrinating and grooming young, vulnerable people to carry out acts of terrorism' (Evans and Webster 2007: 6).

The need to act decisively against perceived terrorist threats may also produce outcomes that impede the pursuit of improved community relations. Relevant here is the shooting of Jean Charles de Menezes (a Brazilian national) in London on 22 July 2005. Due to poor intelligence and failures of communication, two Metropolitan police officers wrongly believed that de Menezes was a member of a four-man group who had sought to wage *jihad* in London on 21 July by detonating bombs. To counter the imminent threat they saw de Menezes as posing, they shot him dead in Stockwell Tube Station. As a result, the Metropolitan Police have had to pay a fine of £175,000 (due to a breach of health and safety legislation) (O'Neill and Sanderson 2007: 1). The imposition of this fine prompted criticism from London's Mayor, Ken Livingston. He stated that '[m]istakes are always going to happen in wars or situations like this' (Aaronovitch 2007: 19). While this is surely true, the shooting of Jean Charles de Menezes provides Islamist hate-mongers with material that will serve to present the British state in an unappealing light.

'Community relations', and the desirability of improving them, are issues that the New Labour administration has spoken to in its efforts to establish a body of law that adequately accommodates the interests of all the law's addressees. This feature of New Labour's response to Islamist terrorism is normatively appealing insofar as it bespeaks a commitment to principle. But the pursuit of principle is, for the reasons given below, an enterprise that is fraught with difficulty.

Principle and its Discontents

As the earlier critique of the glorification of terror provision shows, one aspect of a principled approach to militant democracy is a strong commitment to the rule of law and associated principles (for example, maximum certainty). But to this commitment we must add others that, as an ensemble, make up a principled approach. One such commitment finds expression in a body of law that adequately protects the interests of all its addressees. This is a commitment to distributive justice. In the context of the United Kingdom, pursuit of this ideal of justice is associated with a liberal political agenda. Moreover, the pursuit of this agenda involves establishing a legal framework within which individuals enjoy broad freedom of action. This freedom is widely assumed to be valuable since it affords individuals the 'space' to live autonomously: this is, to be, in substantial part, the authors of their own lives (Raz 1986: 155–7, 377–8).

A commitment to liberalism (and autonomy) finds expression in New Labour's decision to enact the Human Rights Act 1998 so as to give effect to EConvHR rights on the plane of municipal law.[71] Moreover, this decision has relevance to our present concern (the pursuit of a principled approach to militant democracy) for a further reason. This is because government can only place restrictions on qualified Convention rights where it is able to satisfy the exacting requirements of the proportionality principle. This principle specifies that restrictions on Convention rights are only acceptable where they are authorized by law and necessary in order to protect the interests of others or to secure the public interest (Alder 2007: 402–404). But pursuit of a principled approach to militant democracy may require

71 Convention rights to, *inter alia*, freedom of expression and privacy form part of a distributively just set of practical arrangements since they secure (for all the law's addressees) a range of social primary goods (for example, rights to free expression and privacy) as described in Rawls 1971: 62, identifying social primary goods as 'things that every rational man is presumed to want' in order to pursue a 'rational plan of life'.

more than commitments to autonomy; fundamental rights; the rule of law; and proportionality. It may be necessary to integrate into British law an abuse of rights provision, such as the one that appears in Article 17 of the EConvHR. Article 17 specifies that the rights-based protection afforded by the Convention will not be enjoyed by those who 'engage in any activity' that is 'aimed at the destruction' of others' rights and freedoms (Harris et al. 1995: 510).

The European Court of Human Rights (ECHR) has indicated how judges might apply Article 17 in the British context. For in *Norwood v. United Kingdom* it pointed up the relevance of an abuse of rights provision to the operations of British law.[72] In this case, the prosecution secured a conviction under Section 5 of the Public Order Act 1986 (which criminalizes 'behaviour likely to cause harassment, alarm or distress'). The defendant had placed in his window a picture of the carnage wrought by the 9/11 attack on New York's Twin Towers. This picture had a textual accompaniment. It took the form of the suggestion that all Muslims should leave Britain. Since the defendant's expressive activity was political, the domestic courts addressed the question as to whether his Article 10(1) qualified right could be restricted under Article 10(2). They answered this question in the affirmative: 'The rights of others' were at stake and prosecution under Section 5 was a proportionate response. However, the European Court took a significantly different view. On the ECHR's analysis, the defendant's purpose was to destroy the rights of others. This being so, the ECHR concluded that the Article 10(2) balancing exercise was unnecessary. The obvious objection to this approach is that it denies right-based protection to political expression.[73] But we have to set against this the consideration that the ECHR's response to the defendant's conduct underscores the importance of distributive justice in a society committed to militant democracy. For it gives expression to the view that entitlements enjoyed by individuals are not absolute guarantees. Rather, they are contingent on willingness to act in ways that serve to sustain a legal order in which the fundamental interests of *all* the law's addressees enjoy a significant measure of protection.

Given the range of considerations (autonomy; fundamental rights; the rule of law; and distributive justice) that inform a principled approach to militant democracy, it is an ambitious undertaking. This point is worth pondering. For the extent of the ambition that informs a principled approach provides a basis on which to suggest that it tends in the direction of utopianism: pursuit of an ideal state of affairs.[74] Examination of the proportionality principle as a means by which to mediate individual rights and, *inter alia*, the public interest lends support to this view. This is because judges typically identify themselves as 'balancing' competing interests when they apply the proportionality principle. 'Balancing' is a term that conveys the impression that the competing interests at

---

72 *Norwood v. DPP* [2003] EWHC 1564.

73 For a critical response to the ECHR's decision in *Norwood v. UK*, see Turenne 2007: 881.

74 On utopianism, see Berlin 2003: 211–12.

stake in a particular dispute (for example, free expression and public order) are commensurable: this is, amenable to ranking on a common scale (Adler 1998: 1371–2, 1378–83). However, the assumption that judges are able to make finely calibrated determinations as to the significance that they should attach to competing considerations is highly questionable. This is because the consequences judges consider are typically 'imponderables' and the weights assigned to them are, as a result, 'inescapably subjective' (Posner 2006: 24). Hence, talk of 'balancing' suggests a capacity to achieve an optimal outcome – a step on the road to utopia, we might say – that is likely to be illusory.

In a further respect, the normative appeal of the principled approach to militant democracy may not be quite as great as we might, at first, suppose. The large (perhaps even utopian) ambitions we have detected in this approach suggest a commitment to enterprise association as described in the writings of the political philosopher Michael Oakeshott. By 'enterprise association' Oakeshott meant a social order that works to bring about and/or sustain a particular end-state that gives expression to a shared sense of purpose, for example, the pursuit of distributive justice (Oakeshott 1975: 279–311). On Oakeshott's account, such an association (even where operating to establish a normatively appealing end-state) places significant constraints on individual freedom (Oakeshott 1975: 274–8). This is because those who wield the levers of state power typically downplay the significance of individualism as they pursue the common project that gives society its *raison d'etre*. This feature of enterprise association troubled Oakeshott and led him to defend an alternative model of human association that, on his analysis, better protected the freedom of individuals. This model is 'civil association'. By a 'civil association' Oakeshott meant a modest framework within which individuals are free to pursue the plans that they choose, subject to a limited number of constraints: for example, not harming others (Oakeshott 1975: 124).

While a civil association as described by Oakeshott is an accommodating social context, we can expect some of the law's addressees to regard it as deeply unappealing. This is true of that subset of the Muslim community who wish to establish a theocracy (founded on their faith) in the United Kingdom. Those who take this view are intolerant of otherness. This becomes clear when we consider their attitude towards the society within which they currently live. They wish to supplant the liberal agenda of human rights with *Sharia* law. This would be true, for example, of Anjem Choudray who has argued that Britain 'belongs to Allah'. Moreover, those in this group seem unlikely to accept the argument that a liberal society provides a 'space' within which they are free to practise their faith. An essay by Stanley Fish provides a basis on which to explain why this is so. Fish argues that those who see their faith as a true statement of the way the world is will be dissatisfied if the law does not underwrite the ontological status of their beliefs (Fish 1999: 156 et seq.). On Fish's analysis, they will conclude that the defenders of the liberal *status quo* are determined to reduce their faith to a trivial lifestyle option and, thereby, advance the agenda of 'boutique multiculturalism' (Fish 1999: 56 et seq.).[75]

But the only way to assuage this sort of dissatisfaction is to make a particular set of religious beliefs the basis of social life. And that is precisely what liberal states (committed as they are to the accommodation of diverse beliefs) cannot do (Fish 1999: 138). Thus, a liberal practical agenda and the pursuit of theocracy are uncombinable (Dworkin 2006: 32).[76] For we cannot simultaneously embrace a particular set of religious beliefs and tolerance of diverse beliefs as the basis on which to order our practical affairs. How should we respond to this feature of our practical situation? Some argue that 'the increasingly sharp definition of what is at stake is itself surely part of the solution' (Burleigh 2006: 483). But this may not be true in the case of radical Islam in the context of contemporary Britain. For the fundamentals of the Islamic faith and liberal political philosophy constitute, in each case, exclusionary reasons for action. This is, reasons for excluding other relevant reasons from consideration when contemplating practical questions.[77] These reasons also play a large part in constituting the self-understanding of those who inhabit the normative worlds of liberalism and radical Islam. This being so, the stakes could hardly be higher. Moreover, the upshot may be conflict between the denizens of these two worlds. In this connection, the circumstances in which the Dutch broadcaster Theo Van Gogh was murdered are instructive. Van Gogh identified radical Islam as a threat to Holland's liberal politico-legal order. Thereafter, a radical Islamist, Mohammed Bouyeri, expressed his commitment to his faith by murdering Van Gogh (Buruma 2006: Chapter 1).[78]

In this sequence of events, politics on the Schmittian model confronts us. We find the same incendiary approach to practical life in Britain. It is apparent in statements made by, *inter alios*, Anjem Choudray and Abu Hamza. Likewise, it is apparent in the actions of the 7/7 bombers. Some see in these manifestations of radical Islam, the 'death rattle' of a pre-modern faith (Dalrymple 2005: 295). Others find in the same expressions of commitment to radical Islam support for the conclusion that mass-casualty terrorism will be a threat in the United Kingdom 'to which we can see no end' (Ferguson 2007: 25; Walden 2006: 120). One way to respond to this unappealing prospect would be to forsake the pursuit of principle and proceed in a more piecemeal fashion. Government could, as it has in the past, address practical problems as they arise. But we would not bring the clash between uncombinable exclusionary reasons and the normative worlds that they underpin into sharp focus. In adopting this approach, we would suffer a loss in transparency

75 See also p. 59, where Fish states that 'boutique multiculturalism … honors diversity only in its most superficial aspects because its deeper loyalty is to a universal potential for rational choice'.

76 See also Mullender 2008.

77 See Mullender 2007: 370. On exclusionary reasons more generally, see Raz 1990: 35–48.

78 Describing 'Holy War' in Amsterdam.

in our practical affairs. But the piecemeal approach may work to reduce (or, at least, not intensify) tension. Hence, it may afford a means by which 'to avoid extremes of suffering' and, thereby, discharge the 'first public obligation' (borne both by individuals and government).[79] However, we have to face up to the fact that a subset of the community are ready to embrace suffering (in, for example, the form of martyrdom) and to inflict it on others in pursuit of theocracy.

Conclusions

Britain lacks a doctrine of militant democracy on the model that exists in, for example, Germany. But it has a rich history of legal and political interventions aimed at securing constitutional fundamentals. For centuries, these interventions have been piecemeal. This approach has persisted into the twentieth century (for example, as Britain played its imperial endgame in Ireland). Moreover, this approach to the defence of constitutional fundamentals is, on the analysis offered here, empirical in orientation. Government and associated agencies have sought to gather knowledge of and gain experience concerning the relevant threat before acting in ways intended to counter it. This was the case in, for example, the 1930s as government sought to make sense of, and assess the threat posed by, Mosley's British Union of Fascists.

While piecemeal responses to particular threats have made up the great bulk of the examples we have surveyed, we have also found intimations of a principled approach to the defence of constitutional fundamentals (including democracy). Consider Margaret Thatcher's response to the miners' strike. It looks distinctly piecemeal: a response tailored to the problem of industrial militancy in one sector of the economy. And, yet, the Thatcher administration made this response in order to vindicate parliamentary democracy. This looks principled. Moreover, this commitment to principle has a long history. We were able to trace it back to the English Civil War and its aftermath. In the conduct of Oliver Cromwell and his fellow regicides, we found a determination to defend practical arrangements that adequately accommodated all relevant interests.

This approach (in a suitably egalitarian form) seems attuned to the context of contemporary Britain (where human rights and distributive justice are practical concerns). For this reason, the British should address the question as to whether the pursuit of principle should supplant piecemealism as the approach typically adopted when democracy comes under threat. In pondering this matter, they should address the more specific question as to whether they need an abuse of rights provision (on the models offered by the EConvHR and the German *Grundgesetz*). Such a provision might encourage a less ostrich-like response to the incendiary rhetoric of those who (like Hamza and Bakri Mohammed) yearn to supplant liberalism with a theocratic monoculture.

---

79 The phrases quoted in the text are taken from Berlin 1998.

Rhetoric of this sort merits examination for a further reason. When we scrutinize the response made by government to radical Islam, we find that the issue of hate speech bulks large in the minds of ministers. Governmental concern with hate speech finds expression in the prohibitions on incitement to religious hatred and glorification of terrorism. Given that this type of expressive activity is Schmittian (for it carves the world into friends and foes), governmental concern is entirely understandable. But a preference for politics on the Schmittian model does not adequately capture the extent of the threat posed by hate speech in the context of a liberal democracy. This is because anti-discrimination norms feature prominently in liberal–democratic contexts. For liberal democracies seek to approximate the regulative ideal of the kingdom of ends described by Immanuel Kant. Those who inhabit such a normative universe have the status of ends and thus enjoy (at least formal) equality (Caygill 1995: 273). Hate speech is an assault not just on particular groups who inhabit the frameworks within which we seek to approximate Kant's ideal. It is an assault on the framework itself and thus a central case of subversion.

In light of the egalitarian aspirations informing liberal–democratic frameworks of law, there is much in them to value and applaud. However, we should not assume that these frameworks are an unalloyed good. They are, as we noted earlier, vulnerable to criticism from an Oakeshottian standpoint. For they underwrite the assumption that society is an enterprise association. Such an association is, on Oakeshott's account, itself something of a threat to freedom. For it integrates the individual into the pursuit of an overarching goal or set of goals that invest society with a shared sense of purpose. One way in which to address this difficulty would be to embrace civil association. Given that twentieth-century British history has been closely bound up with enterprise association (during the world wars and while establishing and seeking to sustain a welfare state), this seems an unlikely development. But civil association would provide a context in which the British could retain the piecemeal approach to practical problems (to which they have long been wedded). For piecemealism typically serves to advance some modest end: for example, maintaining order by preserving central features of the existing legal framework.

But whether we talk about 'piecemealism' or 'principle', 'enterprise association' or 'civil association', we assume, on the part of all relevant individuals and groups, a readiness to share the same framework. Making this assumption in contemporary Britain is highly problematic. For a subset of the Muslim community in Britain and beyond is implacably opposed to Western liberal democracy in its British or any other form. Instead, they wish to establish a theocracy in which the writ of *Sharia* law will run. How democrats in Britain should respond to those who take this view is a very large question. On one point, however, we can be clear: when we reach the foundations of liberal democracy and radical Islam, we find exclusionary reasons that preclude commingling with one another. Moreover, each is a prominent feature of practical life and shows no sign of fading from view. This is a state of affairs that calls to mind Michel Foucault's concept of a heterotopia. By 'heterotopia', Foucault means a set of circumstances in which distinct normative universes (or 'worlds') sit side by side (Foucault 1967).[80] But, while those who inhabit these worlds are proximate to those in the world alongside, they do not engage in dialogue. If this is the state of affairs in which we find ourselves, then we do not seem to have democracy's most powerful means of defence, dialogue, at our disposal.

But we do have a problem that (like the sectarian troubles in Northern Ireland in the 1970s) seems to have become a settled feature of Britain's politico-legal landscape (Beckett 2009: 121–2). We brace ourselves for the searing reality of a terrorist attack and wonder what form it will take (possibly Mumbai-style gunmen – only now on the loose in a shopping mall like the Trafford Centre or Bluewater). We are relieved when terrorists botch such an attack (as happened when some inept *Jihadis* struck at Glasgow airport in 2007).[81] But we remain uneasy. This is unsurprising. For 'terrorism looms', in our minds, as 'inherently and unexceptionally unacceptable' (Rosenfeld 2008: 76). We edge towards a state of permanent foreboding (rather than simple fear) to which Montesquieu gave the name '*crainte*' (Shklar 1987: 84). The policy of forward defence (still being prosecuted in Afghanistan) is supposed to be a source of reassurance. But we watch the body count grow and ask ourselves whether successful military operations (for example, *Operation Panther's Claw* in July 2009) offset the loss of prestige suffered by ill-equipped, overstretched fighting units.[82] And as Britain's economy shrinks in the 'credit crunch', we watch the leader of the British National Party crow over the seats his organization has gained in local government and in the European Parliament.[83] Government, meanwhile, seeks to sound lion-like (in Koestler's sense). Thus, Gordon Brown, on becoming Prime Minister in 2007, sought to extend the power to detain terror suspects to 42 days. In this he failed. The House of Lords rejected his initiative by 309 votes to 118, while the Official Opposition accused him of engaging in 'political posturing'.[84] And while the politicians huff and puff, academics and other commentators continue to reflect.

80 Foucault's concept is explained in clear terms in McHale 1987: 44–5. For less bleak variations on Foucault's theme, see Sen 2006: 156 et seq., on the problems of a 'plural monoculture', and Sachs 2007: 23, arguing that '[m]ulticulturalism has led not to integration but to segregation'.

81 'Bomb plot doctor jailed for life', 17 December 2008 (at http://news.bbc.co.uk/1/hi/uk/7786884.stm.

82 'Afghan insurgents are weakened', 3 August 2009 (at http://news.bbc.co.uk/1/hi/uk/8181970.stm); 'Troops "at risk" over helicopters', 16 July 2009 (at http://news.bbc.co.uk/1/hi/uk_politics/8153129.stm).

83 M. Wainwright, 'EU elections: BNP's Nick Griffin wins seat in European Parliament', 8 June 2009 (at http://www.guardian.co.uk/politics/2009/jun/07/european-elections-manchester-liverpool).

84 'Brown Pushes for 42-day detention', 20 January 2008 (at http://news.bbc.co.uk/1/hi/uk_politics/7198837.stm); 'Ministers shelve 42-day detention' , 13 October 2008 (at http://news.bbc.co.uk/1/hi/uk_politics/7668477.stm.

Kenan Malik criticises government for restricting free speech (so as to protect the public from terrorism and to secure the interests of vulnerable Muslims) (Malik 2009: 191). Ian Ward tells us that 'we must ... have courage ... and ... hold to our own deepest convictions' (Ward 2009: 192). He means, among other things, that we should remain tolerant and resist the urge (when it arises) to vilify the Other. But not everyone can exhibit such commendable restraint. Hence, we find Julie Burchill, for example, complaining of 'Islamofascism' (Burchill and Raven 2007: 23). Her ire would, doubtless, extend to the likes of Ward, in whose analysis we might expect her to find the authentic voice of *Guardian*-reading complacency. But she would be wrong. For we catch in Ward's analysis, and that of Malik too, the outlines of Koestler's ostrich. For this reason, their respective contributions are valuable. But we must set Ward's (and likewise Malik's) views alongside those of others who are deeply uneasy, such as George Walden. Walden is ready to contemplate the effects of a dirty bomb or worse in London (Walden 2006: 183–4). He thus forces us to address some grim question: Should the capital of this over-centralised country be devastated, could the British co-ordinate a response that would minimise the inevitable suffering?[85] Could the British sustain a form of life in which attractive political ideals like toleration feature prominently? The answers to these questions are by no means obvious. This surely gives the British reason to follow the lead of others and to think hard about the idea of militant democracy.

References

Aaronovitch, David (2007) 'Who Really Killed de Menezes? It Was this Man', *The Times*, 6 November 2007.

Adler, Matthew (1998) 'Incommensurability and Cost-Benefit Analysis', *University of Pennsylvania Law Review* 146(5): 1371–418.

Alder, John (2007) *Constitutional and Administrative Law*, 6th edn. London: Palgrave Macmillan.

Ashworth, Andrew (2006) *Principles of Criminal Law*. Oxford: Oxford University Press.

Barendt, Eric (1985) *Freedom of Speech*. Oxford: Clarendon Press.

Beckett, Andy (2009) *When the Lights Went Out: Britain in the Seventies*. London: Faber and Faber).

Berlin, Isaiah (1998) *The Proper Study of Mankind: An Anthology of Essays*. London: Pimlico.

Berlin, Isaiah (2003) *The Crooked Timber of Humanity*: *Chapters in the History of Ideas*. London: Pimlico.

85 In circumstances of the sort contemplated by Walden, government could make emergency regulations by Order in Council under the Civil Contingencies Act 2004 (Turpin and Tomkins 2007: 450; Campbell 2009: 513–4).

Burchill, Julie and Raven, Daniel (2007) *From the Grand to the Gutter: Modern Britain as Seen From Beside the Sea*. London: Virgin Books).
Burke, Edmund (1968) *Reflections on the Revolution in France*. London: Penguin Books.
Burleigh, Michael (2006) *Sacred Causes: Religion and Politics From the European Dictators to Al Qaeda*. London: Harper Press.
Buruma, Ian (2006) *Murder in Amsterdam: The Death of Theo Van Gogh and the Limits of Tolerance*. London: Atlantic Books.
Campbell, Colm (1994) *Emergency Law in Ireland, 1918–1925*. Oxford: Oxford University Press.
Campbell, David (2009) 'The Threat of Terror and the Plausibility of Positivism'. *Public Law*, 501 et seq.
Card, Richard (2000) *Public Order Law*. Bristol: Jordans.
Caygill, Howard (1995) *A Kant Dictionary*. Oxford: Blackwell.
Clausewitz, Carl von (2007) *On War*. Oxford: Oxford University Press, translated by M. Howard and P. Paret.
Collins, Hugh (1982) *Marxism and Law*. Oxford: Oxford University Press.
Colls, Robert (2002) *Identity of England*. Oxford: Oxford University Press.
Crick, Michael (1985) *Scargill and the Miners*. Harmondsworth: Penguin Books.
Dalrymple, Theodore (2005) *Our Culture, What's Left of It: The Mandarins and the Masses*. Chicago: Ivan R. Dee.
Davies, Norman (2000) *The Isles: A History*. London: Macmillan.
Davies, Paul and Freedland, Marc (1993) *Labour Legislation and Public Policy: A Contemporary History*. Oxford: Clarendon Press.
Demetriou, Danielle (2004) 'Atkinson Takes Fight with Religious Hatred Bill to Parliament', *The Independent*, 7 December 2004.
Dorril, Stephen (2007) *Blackshirt: Sir Oswald Mosley and British Fascism*. London: Penguin Books.
Dworkin, Ronald (2006) 'Even Bigots and Holocaust Deniers Must Have Their Say', *The Guardian*, 14 February 2006.
Evans, Michael and Webster, Philip (2007) 'Children of 15 Groomed to Carry out Terrorist Acts, MI5 Head Says', *The Times*, 6 November 2007.
Ferguson, Niall (2003) *Empire: How Britain Made the Modern World*. London: Penguin Books.
Ferguson, Niall (2006) *The War of the World: History's Age of Hatred*. London: Allen Lane.
Ferguson, Niall (2007) 'The Merchants of Venice Have All Left … New York Take Note', *The Sunday Telegraph*, 13 May 2007.
Fish, Stanley (1999) *The Trouble With Principle*. London: Harvard University Press.
Fletcher, Martin (2007) 'The British National Party Gains Strength', *The Times*, 19 April 2007.
Ford, Richard (2007) 'Curfews for Terror Suspects Should Not Exceed 12 Hours, Law Lords Rule', *The Times*, 1 November 2007.

Foucault, Michel (1967) *Des Espace Autres*, (available online at http://foucault.info/documents/heteroTopia/foucault.hetero.topia.en.html).

Gamble, Andrew (2003) *Between Europe and America: The Future of British Politics*. London: Palgrave Macmillan.

Gearty, Conor (2007) *Civil Liberties*. Oxford: Oxford University Press.

Gove, Michael (2006) *Celsius 7/7*. London: Weidenfeld and Nicolson.

Griffith, John A.G. (1979) 'The Political Constitution', *Modern Law Review* 42:1, 1–21.

Harris, David J., O'Boyle, Michael and Warbrick, Colin (1995) *Law of the European Convention on Human Rights*. London: Butterworths.

Hobsbawm, Eric J. (1995) *The Age of Extremes: The Short Twentieth Century, 1914–1991*. London: Abacus.

Honderich, Ted (ed.) (1995) *The Oxford Companion to Philosophy*. Oxford: Oxford University Press.

Horrie, Chris (2003) 'Revealed: The Fascist Past of the *Daily Mirror*', *The Independent*, 11 November 2003.

Jenkins, Simon (2006) *Thatcher and Sons: A Revolution in Three Acts*. London: Allen Lane.

Koestler, Arthur (1963) 'The Lion and the Ostrich', in Arthur Koestler (ed.) *Suicide of a Nation: An Enquiry into the State of Britain Today*. London: Hutchinson.

Kynaston, David (2007) *Austerity Britain 1945–1951*. London: Bloomsbury.

Lacey, Nicola (2004) *A Life of H.L.A. Hart: The Nightmare and the Noble Dream*. Oxford: Oxford University Press.

Lee, Simon (1990) *The Cost of Free Speech*. London: Faber and Faber.

Macedo, Stephen (1990) *Liberal Virtues: Citizenship, Virtue, and Community in Liberal Constitutionalism*. Oxford: Clarendon Press.

Malik, Kenan (2009), *From Fatwa to Jihad: The Rushdie Affair and Its Legacy*. London: Atlantic Books.

Marr, Andrew (2007) *A History of Modern Britain*. London: Macmillan.

McHale, Brian (1987) *Postmodernist Fiction*. London: Routledge.

McIlwain, Charles Howard (ed.) (1918) *The Political Works of James I*. Cambridge: Massachussetts.

Milne, Seumas (2004) *The Enemy Within: The Secret War Against the Miners*, 3rd edn. London: Verso.

Mullender, Richard (2007) 'Book Review: Zygmunt Bauman, *Identity: Conversations with Benedetto Vecchi*', *History of Political Thought* 28, 368–70.

Mullender, Richard (2008) 'Liberalism, Radical Islam and Identity', *Political Quarterly* 79(1): 131–3.

Oakeshott, Michael Joseph (1975) *On Human Conduct*. Oxford: Clarendon Press.

O'Neill, Sean and McGrory, Daniel (2006) *The Suicide Factory: Abu Hamza and the Finsbury Park Mosque*. London: HarperCollins.

O'Neill, Sean and Sanderson, David (2007) 'Met Chief Urged to Quit Over Shooting', *The Times*, 1 November 2007.

Paine, Thomas (1989) *Political Writings* (ed. by Bruce Kuklick). Cambridge: Cambridge University Press.

Palonen, Kari (2003) *Quentin Skinner: History, Politics, Rhetoric.* Cambridge: Polity Press.

Paxman, Jeremy (1999) *The English: A Portrait of a People.* London: Penguin Books.

Phillips, Melanie (2006) *Londonistan: How Britain is Creating a Terror State Within.* London: Gibson Square.

Philp, Mark (1989) *Paine.* Oxford: Oxford University Press.

Poole, Thomas M. (1997) 'Tilting at Windmills? Truth and Illusion in "the Political Constitution"', *Modern Law Review* 70(2): 250–77.

Posner, Richard A. (2006) *Not A Suicide Pact: The Constitution in a Time of Emergency.* New York: Oxford University Press.

Postema, Gerald J. (1986) *Bentham and the Common Law Tradition.* Oxford: Clarendon Press.

Pugh, Martin (2006) *'Hurrah for the Blackshirts!' Fascists and Fascism in Britain Between the Wars.* London: Pimlico.

Rawls, John (1971) *A Theory of Justice.* Oxford: Oxford University Press.

Raz, Joseph (1986) *The Morality of Freedom.* Oxford: Clarendon Press.

Raz, Joseph (1990) *Practical Reason and Norms*, 2nd edn. Princeton, New Jersey: Princeton.

Roberts, Andrew (2006) *A History of the English-Speaking Peoples Since 1900.* London: Weidenfeld and Nicolson.

Robertson, Geoffrey (2006) *Crimes Against Humanity: The Struggle for Global Justice*, 3rd edn. London: Penguin Books.

Rosenfeld, Michel (2008), 'Derrida's Ethical Turn: The Case of Terrorism', in Peter Goodrich, Florian Hoffmann, Michel Rosenfeld and Cornelia Vismann (eds), *Derrida and Legal Philosophy.* Basingstoke: Palgrave Macmillan, 71–98.

Sachs, Jonathan (2007) 'Wanted: A National Culture', *The Times*, 20 October 2007.

Sandbrook, Dominic (2006a) *Never Had It So Good: A History of Britain From Suez to The Beatles.* London: Abacus.

Sandbrook, Dominic (2006b) *White Heat: A History of Britain in the Swinging Sixties.* London: Little Brown.

Schama, Simon (2003) *A History of Britain, vol. II: The British Wars 1603–1776.* London: BBC Worldwide.

Schmitt, Carl (1996) *The Concept of the Political.* London: University of Chicago Press.

Scruton, Roger (1982) *A Dictionary of Political Thought.* London: Macmillan Press.

Scruton, Roger (2001) *England: An Elegy.* London: Pimlico.

Sen, Amartya (2006) *Identity and Violence: The Illusion of Destiny.* London: Penguin Books.

Shklar, Judith N. (1987), *Montesquieu.* Oxford: Oxford University Press.

Sim, Stuart (ed.) (1998) *The Icon Critical Dictionary of Postmodern Thought.* London: Icon Books.

Simpson, Brian A.W. (2001) *Human Rights and the End of Empire: Britain and the Genesis of the European Convention.* Oxford: Oxford University Press.

Sked, Alan and Cook, Chris (1993) *Post-War Britain: A Political History*, 4th edn. London: Penguin Books.

Smith, John C. and Hogan, Brian (1978) *Criminal Law*, 4th edn. London: Butterworths.

Steele, Jenny (2007) *Tort Law: Text, Cases, and Materials.* Oxford: Oxford University Press.

Taylor, Matthew (2006) 'Web of Hate', *The Guardian*, 4 October 2006.

Thatcher, Margaret (1995) *The Path to Power.* London: Harper Collins.

Thompson, Edward P. (1968) *The Making of the English Working Class.* London: Penguin Books.

Trevelyan, George M. (1967) *English Social History: A Survey of Six Centuries, Chaucer to Queen Victoria.* London: Penguin Books.

Turenne, Sophie (2007) 'The Compatibility of Criminal Liability with Freedom of Expression', *Criminal Law Review* 2007, 866–81.

Turpin, Colin and Tomkins, Adam (2007) *British Government and the Constitution*, 6th edn. Cambridge: Cambridge University Press.

Wade, E.C.S. and Bradley, Anthony W. (1985) *Constitutional and Administrative Law*, 10th edn. Harlow: Longman.

Walden, George (2006) *Time to Emigrate?* London: Gibson Square.

Walker, Nigel (1991) *Why Punish?* Oxford: Oxford University Press.

Ward, Ian (2009), *Law, Text, Terror.* Cambridge: Cambridge University Press.

Weight, Richard (2002) *Patriots: National Identity in Britain 1940–2000.* London: Macmillan.

Wheen, Francis (1998) 'The Stagnant Years', *The Modern Review*, March 1998.

Winnett, Robert (2007) 'Cameron Questions Iraq War Rationale', *The Daily Telegraph*, 26 October 2007.

Wright, Jane (2001) *Tort Law and Human Rights: The Impact of the ECHR on English Law.* Oxford: Hart Publishing.

Chapter 14
United States of America

Mark V. Tushnet

Introduction

The term 'militant democracy' is absent from constitutional discourse in the United States of America. Only one court has ever used the phrase. In 1938, a federal trial court was faced with a constitutional challenge to a policy adopted by the political machine controlling Jersey City, New Jersey. The policy prohibited union organizers from expressing their opinions in the city, allegedly because doing so would promote 'riot, disturbance and disorderly assemblage'. The trial judge asserted that the case 'seeks the solution of the problem inevitable and inherent in a democratic form of government'. The judge then set forth a series of propositions, among which was that repressing thought was 'dangerous'. In support of this, the judge cited Aristotle, Baruch Spinoza and John Locke. Those citations were followed by the signal 'But see contra', followed by a quotation from Karl Loewenstein's article setting out the concept of militant democracy. The judge held the city's policy unconstitutional, and the United States Supreme Court affirmed.[1]

For purposes of this chapter, 'militant democracy' refers to restrictions on freedom of expression to ensure that democratic processes are not used to destroy democracy. The typical target of 'militant democracy' regulations are extremist groups, but the concept does not have any necessary connection to extremism. Threats to the democratic process from the exercise of constitutional rights closely associated with democracy can emanate from a variety of sources.

The United States' constitutional law on this topic reflects the fundamental individualism of legal culture in the country. The relevant law takes individual misconduct subject to criminal sanction as the central problem case. If someone *acts* to subvert the political order, he or she is potentially subject to criminal punishment. But speech alone, and even strong advocacy of subversion, is insufficient for criminal punishment. Nor is mere membership in an organization whose leaders might be committed to organizing subversive actions; a member of such an organization can be punished only if the member actually engages in prohibitable conduct. In the 1950s, the United States briefly flirted with the idea that some political organizations might be so threatening to the political order that

1 *Committee for Industrial Organization v. Hague*, 25 F. Supp. 127 (D.C. N.J.), aff'd 307 U.S. 496 (1939).

they might be outlawed. The United States Supreme Court endorsed that idea in principle, but then blocked every effort to impose sanctions on the Communist Party, the only organization against which the government had taken action.

The focus on individuals' actions characterizes other doctrinal areas treated elsewhere under the heading of militant democracy. Mere membership in a suspect organization cannot be the reason for denying a person a public job, nor for denying the person an opportunity to work even in such a sensitive field as national defence. Public employees can be required to take an oath to uphold the US Constitution, but permissible oaths cannot go much beyond that, and the Supreme Court has indicated that 'upholding the constitution' means only a guarantee that the person will use lawful means to change the law. Hate speech can be restricted only in narrow circumstances, where the speech is reasonably understood to pose a real threat of imminent harm to a particular person who is its target.

There may be today only two areas of US constitutional law where some resonance of the idea of militant democracy can be found. The first arises from recent efforts to combat terrorism. US law makes it a crime to provide 'material support' for terrorism. The government has taken the position that a person can provide such support not merely by supplying money or goods, but also by supplying his or her own effort. Taken to its logical conclusion, this definition of 'material support' could lead to making membership in terrorist organizations a crime even without a showing that the person took action to advance the group's prohibited goals. Although the Supreme Court has not addressed the question, lower courts have generally required the prosecution to show that the accused did in fact take some action to promote the group's goals beyond mere membership. A more important area in which there are echoes of militant democracy are campaign finance rules, where restrictions on expression have been upheld not because the content of the expression, but because the sources and amounts of campaign advertising pose threats to democracy as a whole.

This chapter begins with an examination of the law of subversive advocacy (section 'subversive advocacy and the requirement of personal responsibility for illegal action'). That examination brings out the law's focus on individual action closely connected to illegal conduct by others. The next section on 'illegal political organizations' describes the Supreme Court's treatment of efforts to make political organizations illegal, and the section on 'loyalty oaths and related regulations of employment opportunities' deals with the restrictions the Supreme Court has allowed – quite limited ones – on public employment because of the employee's political beliefs. Hate speech regulation is the subject of the section on 'regulation of hate speech and verbal attacks on public officials', and the chapter concludes with a brief discussion of the areas in which something like militant democracy characterizes contemporary US constitutional law (section on 'campaign finance regulation').

A preliminary word on the general structure of US constitutional law is necessary. The constitutional law of militant democracy rests on the application and interpretation of the constitution's protection of freedom of expression. That protection is provided against national legislation by the free speech clause of the First Amendment to the constitution and against state legislation by the due process clause of the Fourteenth Amendment. The Supreme Court has held that these two provisions provide the same substantive protections, and this chapter refers generically to 'free speech' protections – and sometimes to the First Amendment – without distinguishing between national and state legislation. In addition, the United States is a federal system, and its sub-national units ('states') have substantial law-making authority of their own, even in areas where the national government also has law-making power. Where law-making power overlaps, the national government may displace state law. In the present context, the Supreme Court held that the national government's statute banning attempts to overthrow the national government pre-empted state laws on the same topic.[2] Most observers believe that the decision, which overturned a 20-year sentence for advocating sedition, was motivated at least as much by free speech concerns as by concerns about the proper allocation of law-making authority between the states and the nation.

Subversive Advocacy and the Requirement of Personal Responsibility for Illegal Action

The fundamental principles of US constitutional law dealing with restrictions on political advocacy, including extremist advocacy, derive from principles of criminal law. This has two major consequences: (1) the focus is always on individual responsibility. The criminal law focus gives great rhetorical power to arguments against 'guilt by association', leading to strong suspicion of imposing liability or other sanctions for a person's 'mere' membership in an extremist or subversive organization (for a recent discussion, see Issacharoff 2007); and (2) there are no sanctions, such as ineligibility for government jobs or presence on the ballot, independent of criminal sanctions. Put another way, satisfying the standards for criminal liability is a predicate for the imposition of any other sanction or disability.

The applicable law began with the criminal law focus, but it took decades for the law to become as restrictive of government power to sanction extremist speech as it is today (a good recent overview is Stone 2004). The Supreme Court's first important decisions arose out of US participation in the First World War and its subsequent intervention in revolutionary Russia. The cases involved prosecutions for conspiracy to obstruct the military draft and interfere with war production.[3] The 'conspiracies' consisted of distribution of pamphlets and speeches criticizing

2 *Pennsylvania v. Nelson*, 350 U.S. 497 (1956).

3 *Schenck v. United States*, 249 U.S. 47 (1919) (prosecution for conspiracy to obstruct the draft); *Abrams v. United States*, 250 U.S. 616 (1919) (prosecution for conspiracy to 'urge curtailment of production of war materials').

the nation's wartime policies. The Supreme Court upheld the convictions. Justice Oliver Wendell Holmes wrote the first important opinion. He drew upon his experience as a state judge in applying ordinary criminal rules to inchoate crimes – attempts and conspiracies. '[T]he character of every act depends on the circumstances in which it is done … The question in every case is whether the words used are used in such circumstances and are of such a nature as to create a clear and present danger that they will bring about the substantive evils that Congress has a right to prevent. It is a question of proximity and degree.' If a properly instructed jury found that the words used were sufficient 'close' to the harm and might cause it, the First Amendment was not violated. As Holmes put it in a later case, 'by the same reasoning that would justify punishing persuasion to murder, the United States constitutionally may punish speech that produces or is intended to produce a clear and imminent danger that it will bring about forthwith certain substantive evils'.[4]

The court adhered to the 'clear and present danger' formulation for several decades, but Justice Holmes and his liberal colleague Louis Brandeis soon became uncomfortable with the way the test was applied. Their concern was that juries – and their colleagues on the Supreme Court – were too ready to find that words alone posed an imminent danger of lawbreaking. As they saw it, people who made essentially political speeches were being found liable to criminal punishment under circumstances so remote from actual harm that no one would ever have thought of finding that a person who made similar statements was guilty of conspiracy to commit murder. The connection between ordinary criminal law theory and the law of subversive advocacy had become broken, in their view. The difficulty, though, was to devise some better doctrinal formulation that would compensate for the susceptibility of juries and judges to the passions of the moments when people feared that extremists were likely to take power. In one of Justice Brandeis's most powerful phrases, 'men feared witches and burned women', and contemporary prosecutions for subversive advocacy were equally overwrought.[5]

Justice Brandeis's comment came in a case that presented an important variant on the earlier prosecutions. Those prosecutions were for speeches that, the prosecution contended, were causally connected to illegal activity. In that context, the 'clear and present danger' test might exercise some constraining force. What, though, of prosecutions for subversive advocacy as such – that is, for words that the legislature identified as extremist? Justices Holmes and Brandeis continued to argue that such prosecutions were constitutionally permissible only if the prosecution showed that the words were used in circumstances that posed a clear and present danger. Their colleagues believed, in contrast, that the 'clear and present danger' test was not well suited for prosecutions for subversive advocacy. In those prosecutions, the conditions for liability under the statutes were satisfied simply by showing that the defendants uttered the words the legislature had identified as extremist. Perhaps

4 *Abrams v. United States*, 250 U.S. at 627 (Holmes J., dissenting).

5 *Whitney v. California*, 274 U.S. 357, 376 (1927) (Brandeis J., concurring).

the legislature made a categorical judgment that uttering those words would often or generally pose a clear and present danger. Then the question would be: was that judgment constitutionally permissible? Obviously the 'clear and present danger' test could not itself answer that question. Rather, the courts had to decide whether the legislature's identification of words that, in general, were sufficiently closely related to 'substantive evils' was a constitutionally permissible one.

During the 1920s, the Supreme Court began to reformulate the law of subversive advocacy in a way that ultimately turned out to be quite helpful. During that decade the cases arose out of prosecutions for 'criminal anarchy' or 'criminal syndicalism', offences that were defined as the advocacy of 'the duty, necessity or propriety' of overthrowing the government 'by force or violence or by assassination'.[6] The defendants were typically associated with the left-wing of the Socialist Party or with the newly organized Communist Party. Upholding convictions for criminal anarchy, the court pointed out that the statutes at issue did not 'penalize the utterance or publication of abstract "doctrine" or academic discussion having no quality of incitement to any concrete action', and were not 'aimed against mere historical or philosophical essays'. Nor did they 'restrain the advocacy of changes in the form of government by constitutional and lawful means'. Rather, they prohibited words advocating governmental overthrow by unlawful means, which 'impl[ied] urging to action'.[7]

The court's next major confrontation with subversive speech came during the Cold War, in a series of prosecutions of leading figures in the Communist Party for violating the national Smith Act, which made it a crime to conspire to 'knowingly or willfully advocate, abet, advise or teach the duty, necessity, desirability or propriety of overthrowing or destroying any government in the United States by force or violence'. The earlier prosecutions had involved political organizations that were of little domestic importance. Especially in the early years of the Cold War, the Communist Party seemed different. It had some influence in domestic affairs, mostly through its effects on various labour and cultural organizations. More important, though, the US Communist Party was seen as the domestic arm of the external enemy, the Soviet Union, associated not simply with political advocacy but with espionage and (it was feared) sabotage.

The court had available two distinct lines of analysis. The 'clear and present danger' test remained central in discussions of free speech theory. The cases of the 1920s supplemented that test with an important distinction between constitutionally protected 'abstract doctrine' and advocacy of major changes in the government's form by lawful means, on the one hand, and, on the other, 'incitement' or 'urging' to action. The Supreme Court first refrained from choosing between the two approaches and then, as Cold War pressures diminished, began to focus on the second, initially as a matter of statutory interpretation and then as a matter of constitutional law.

6 *Gitlow v. New York*, 268 U.S. 652 (1925); *Whitney v. California*, 274 U.S. 357 (927).

7 *Gitlow v. New York*, 268 U.S. at 664–665.

Dennis v. United States (1951) upheld the convictions of the Communist Party's major leaders.[8] Chief Justice Frederick M. Vinson's opinion, which had the support of only three other justices and therefore did not state the views of a controlling majority of the court, relied on a reformulated version of the 'clear and present danger' test. Adopting the tort-like rule articulated by the noted appeals court judge Billings Learned Hand, Vinson said that the test required juries to consider whether 'the gravity of the "evil", discounted by its improbability, justifies such invasion of free speech as is necessary to avoid the danger'. The jury's evaluation was to be checked by a similar judicial assessment. The Hand formulation was particularly useful for prosecutors in the circumstances of the 1950s, when few believed that a Communist takeover was near at hand – the evil was quite improbable – but such a takeover, if it occurred, would be enormously harmful. The test allowed the government to punish people who posed an extremely small risk of very great harm.

The additional votes needed to uphold the convictions were supplied by Justices Felix Frankfurter and Robert H. Jackson. Frankfurter stated that punishment for speech alone was permissible only if, on balance, the harm averted by the punishment was more substantial than the harm to free expression by the punishment itself. But, in applying this balancing test, Frankfurter insisted that the courts had to defer to the legislative judgment that advocacy of violent overthrow of the government presented an extremely serious risk. Referring to his experience as the chief prosecutor at the major war crimes trials at Nuremburg, Justice Jackson reverted to the approach suggested at the outset of the court's treatment of the problem of subversive advocacy. The problem as he saw it was one of ordinary conspiracy law, in which a person's words could demonstrate his participation in the conspiracy.

With the convictions of the first line leaders of the Communist Party in hand, the government turned to prosecutions of secondary leaders. Here, though, it ran into resistance from the Supreme Court. In 1957, reviewing the convictions of some of these second line leaders, the court held that the Smith Act did not prohibit 'mere advocacy' of the 'abstract doctrine' that forcible overthrow of the government is desirable.[9] Instead, it prohibited only 'advocacy directed at promoting unlawful action'. The distinction, according to the court, was that 'those to whom the advocacy is addressed must be urged to *do* something, now or in the future, rather than merely to *believe* in something'.

The distinction between advocacy of belief and advocacy of (future) action was extremely difficult to administer: why could not the government rely on the sensible assumption that a person who came to believe that forcible overthrow of the government was a good idea would take action to effectuate that belief when appropriate circumstances presented themselves? And, in fact, the distinction proved fatal to prosecutions under the Smith Act. Four years later,

8 341 U.S. 494 (1951).

9 *Yates v. United States*, 354 U.S. 298 (1957).

the Supreme Court reviewed convictions the government had obtained after retrials of the second line leaders. According to the court, the Smith Act made it a crime to be a member of a subversive organization only if the government demonstrated that the defendant's membership was 'active and purposive … as to the organization's criminal ends'.[10] Carefully examining the evidence presented at trial, the court vacated the convictions of several defendants and upheld only one conviction. Notably, the convictions of most of the second line party leaders – state party organizers, publicists and the like – could not survive this scrutiny. If the government could not successfully prosecute even second line leaders, its prospects for convictions of ordinary members were non-existent, and the effort to pursue criminal convictions of Communists ended.

The court's interpretation of the Smith Act in these cases was strongly influenced by its judgment that interpreting the Act to allow convictions for advocacy of abstract doctrine would render the statute unconstitutional. The court's rethinking of the law of subversive advocacy culminated in *Brandenburg v. Ohio* (1969).[11] The Smith Act prosecutions had involved the Communist Party, which during the Cold War might have seemed to pose a real threat to the United States. *Brandenburg*, in contrast, was a prosecution of a 'leader' of a small Ku Klux Klan group in Ohio; the trial testimony showed that Brandenburg spoke to about a dozen supporters. The organization had no connection whatever to anything reasonably understood to be a threat to the political order. Yet, the decision was handed down at a time when protests against the war in Vietnam, sometimes violent, were a matter of some concern, and the decision seems aimed at discouraging prosecutors from attempting to penalize war protestors for their speech.

Charles Brandenburg was convicted of violating Ohio's 'criminal syndicalism' statute for making a speech in which the strongest of his statements was: 'We're not a revengent organization, but if our President, our Congress, our Supreme Court continues to suppress the white, Caucasian race, it's possible that there might have to be some revengence taken.' The court seemingly tightened the prior 'clear and present danger' test, although many commentators continue to refer to that test as if it survived *Brandenburg* unmodified. According to the *Brandenburg* decision, the First Amendment is violated by convictions for words advocating violence unless the government demonstrates that the 'advocacy is directed to inciting or producing imminent lawless action and is likely to incite or produce such action'. This test has several components. The most important is probably the requirement that lawless action be imminent. The 'revengence' Brandenburg may have threatened would occur in the indefinite future, and so was not imminent. Demonstrating how stringent the imminence requirement is, in a subsequent case

10 *Scales v. United States*, 367 U.S. 203 (1961); *Noto v. United States*, 367 U.S. 290 (1961).

11 395 U.S. 444 (1969). – The decision was issued *per curiam*, that is, without identifying its author. It was written by Justice Abe Fortas, who resigned from the Supreme Court before the opinion was released.

the court overturned the conviction of a person at a riotous street 'demonstration' who, it was shown, had told others to leave in the face of a police response but continued: 'We'll take the fucking street later.'[12] There violence was ongoing, but the conviction was for urging renewed violence, and under *Brandenburg* could not be sustained.

In addition, *Brandenburg* requires that the defendant *intend* that lawless action occur. And, perhaps only slightly less important than the imminence requirement is the requirement that the speech constitute 'incitement' to lawless action. That requirement is important for two reasons. First, as a matter of free speech theory, it allows convictions not when the speaker persuades others to act once they have considered the reasons the speaker offers, but only when the speaker's words are so powerful as to bypass a listener's rational or deliberative capacities.[13] Second, at least as a general matter, it is easier for a reviewing court to examine a speaker's words to determine whether they constituted 'incitements' than it is to asses whether, in the circumstances, the speech was on balance likely to produce lawless action. Focusing on incitement, that is, reduces the difficulties Justice Frankfurter thought were associated with direct balancing of speech interests against the social interest in order.

Prosecutions for subversive advocacy have been extremely rare since *Brandenburg*. Increasing concern about terrorism has revived interest in criminalizing extremist speech. The national government obtained a criminal conviction based on speech that incited violence in a case against a religious leader who counselled his followers in ways that led them to place a bomb at the World Trade Center in 1993, although it should be noted that the defendant was convicted of substantive conspiracy offences as well.[14] The court of appeals that reviewed the conviction observed that the defendant's words that 'instruct[ed], solicit[ed] or persuade[d] others to commit crimes of violence ... violate[d] the law' even though they were said 'in public, or in administering the duties of a religious ministry'.

The cases from the Cold War era and later all involved prosecutions for words alone. The fight against terrorism revived earlier forms of prosecution, where free speech objections were raised against prosecutions for substantive crimes. The legislature made it a crime to provide 'material assistance' to terrorist organizations. The core of the crime, of course, involved providing supplies or financing to such organizations. The government took the position that a person could violate the statute by enhancing the organization's effectiveness by joining it: a person provided material assistance to a terrorist organization by supplying it with 'human capital', so to speak. That position was in obvious tension with the cases holding that mere membership in a subversive organization was protected by the First Amendment. The few courts that have considered the

12 *Hess v. Indiana*, 414 U.S. 105 (1973).

13 For a discussion of the 'persuasion' principle, see Strauss 1991.

14 *United States v. Rahman*, 189 F. 3d 88 (2nd Cir. 1999).

government's position have required the prosecution to show the same degree of knowing assistance to the organization's illegal ends as was required by the Cold War era cases.[15]

Illegal Political Organizations

Governments in the United States, whether on the national or state levels, have rarely sought to outlaw political organizations as such. Instead, they have focused on the activities of the organizations' members. For example, the revival of the Ku Klux Klan, a violent racist group, in the 1920s led many states to adopt laws banning public parades by people wearing masks, a characteristic of the Klan's operations. Early decisions upheld the constitutionality of these statutes, but the modern trend is to find them unconstitutional unless the prosecution establishes that the parade occurred with the intent to intimidate specific targets (see also the section on 'regulation of hate speech and verbal attacks on public officials' below). This trend is consistent with the themes noted in the section on 'subversive advocacy and the requirement of personal responsibility for illegal action' above of insisting that individuals themselves engage in improper activities and of avoiding the imposition of liability simply because of membership in an organization many members of which might engage in such activities.

The one substantial effort to outlaw a political party occurred in the 1950s. The Internal Security Act of 1950, known also as the McCarran Act after its chief sponsor, created the Subversive Activities Control Board (SACB), an administrative agency charged with determining whether organizations were Communist-action, Communist-front, or Communist-infiltrated. If the SACB made such a finding, the organization would have to register with the SACB, and members of registered organizations would be denied various rights – the opportunity to work in federal jobs or in federal defence-related industries and the right to a passport, for example. The SACBs first action, naturally, was against the Communist Party itself. Ordered to register, the Communist Party refused, mounting a broad-scale challenge to the Internal Security Act. Extensive litigation followed, taking more than 11 years. At its conclusion, a sharply divided Supreme Court in 1961 upheld the registration order, but deferred consideration of the constitutionality of the Act's sanctions until they were applied.[16]

Over the course of the next decade, the court invalidated every sanction it dealt with. The ban on passports for party members was held to violate a constitutionally protected right to travel because it failed to take account of the different degrees of

15 See, for example, *United States v. Assi*, 414 F. Supp. 2d 707 (E.D. Mich. 2006) (holding that the statute would not be violated if a person merely became a member of a terrorist organization, associated with its members, espoused its views or advocated on behalf of its goals).

16 *Communist Party v. Subversive Activities Control Board*, 367 U.S. 1 (1961).

involvement party members had in the party's activities,[17] a requirement that party members themselves register was held to violate the constitutional ban on self-incrimination because identifying oneself as a Communist exposed a registrant to a variety of criminal penalties,[18] and the ban on working at defence facilities was held to violate the free speech clause because it denied a person – who might have been a mere passive party member – a job without requiring any showing that the person posed any real threat to national security.[19] By the end of the 1960s, the SACB had essentially nothing to do. With its efforts to suppress the Communist Party thwarted, the SACB had no chance of suppressing other organizations. In the early 1970s, the Nixon administration decided not to seek funding for the SACBs operation, and it went out of existence.

The early 2000s saw some renewed efforts to suppress organizations, but not – at least nominally – for the views they held. The George W. Bush administration successfully froze the assets of several purportedly charitable organizations which had, the administration contended and courts agreed, provided 'material support' to terrorist organizations overseas by sending them money raised in the United States. The organizations contended that they had a constitutional right to raise funds for charitable activities overseas. The courts' response was to observe that money was 'fungible', in that funds from the United States used to maintain hospitals and the like, allowed the foreign terrorist organizations to use money raised elsewhere to support their terrorist activities.

Finally, the Supreme Court has upheld a variety of efforts by governments to regulate access to the ballot, that is, whether a party's name and candidates can appear on the ballot. None of the permissible regulations, though, examine the content of a party's platform or programme. Access to the ballot can be restricted, the court has held, if the government shows that the party does not have some minimal degree of support in the community, and that allowing ballot access to too many parties would unnecessarily confuse voters without providing a substantial benefit to democratic self-government.[20]

Loyalty Oaths and Related Regulations of Employment Opportunities

In 1892, a widely noted decision by Oliver Wendell Holmes Jr., while he was a state court judge, stated a general rule that would have allowed governments complete discretion as employers to hire or fire based on the employee's political views. In Holmes's words, '[t]he petitioner may have a constitutional right to talk politics, but he has no constitutional right to be a policeman … The servant cannot

17 *Aptheker v. Secretary of State*, 378 U.S. 500 (1964).

18 *Albertson v. Subversive Activities Control Board*, 382 U.S. 70 (1963).

19 *United States v. Robel*, 382 U.S. 70 (1965).

20 For a summary of the cases, see Stone et al. 2005: 802–804.

complain, as he takes the employment on the terms which are offered him'.[21] This theory had implications far beyond the employment context. It would seem to eliminate the possibility of finding unconstitutional any conditions the government chose to place on its grant of any discretionary position, including licensing of businesses. With the expansion of government regulatory power in the twentieth century, Holmes's theory gradually went into decline, although it continued to exert some influence in the background of the doctrines the court developed.

Yet, if the constitution did not allow governments to place whatever conditions they chose on public employment, did it allow them to place specific conditions? Could a government deny employment to a person who, outside of work, expressed racist views? Over the course of the second half of the twentieth century the Supreme Court gradually imposed more and more limits on the conditions a government could place on its employees' non-work-related speech.

An early confrontation with the problem of political conditions on employment came in the aftermath of the Civil War. Federal and state statutes required that lawyers and other professionals, including members of the clergy, take an oath that they supported the national government and had not supported the South's unsuccessful attempt to secede from the Union. The Supreme Court invalidated these oaths as impermissible *ex post facto* laws, imposing new disabilities on people who had engaged in actions lawful at the time, and as bills of attainder, imposing punishment by means of legislation rather than adjudication.[22]

The court next dealt with the problem during the Cold War.[23] New York adopted a statute denying positions as public school teachers to anyone who was a member of an organization that advocated the violent overthrow of the government, with knowledge of the organization's advocacy. The Supreme Court upheld the statute against what later came to be understood as a 'facial' challenge, that is, a claim that there were no circumstances under which the statute could be applied without violating the constitution.[24] The court observed that teaching was a 'sensitive' activity, dealing with how 'the attitudes of young minds' are shaped. Although the school authorities should be concerned only with the teacher's fitness, the teacher's associations had some bearing on determining whether the teacher was fit. Over the next decade, this holding eroded as the court invalidated employment restrictions on a variety of grounds. The capstone was another case from New York, in which the court revisited the statute it had upheld in 1952. This time it struck down the state's restriction on public employment of members of 'seditious' organizations because the term was so vague that no one could reasonably be expected to know

---

21 *McAuliffe v. Mayor of New Bedford*, 155 Mass. 236 (1892).

22 *Cummings v. Missouri*, 71 U.S. 277 (1867); Ex parte Garland, 71 U.S. 333 (1867).

23 For discussions of the history of test oaths and their use during the Cold War, see Brown 1958; Hyman 1959.

24 *Adler v. Board of Education*, 342 U.S. 485 (1952).

whether he or she was a member of such an organization.[25] Considered solely as involving questions about what ordinary people would think prohibited, the court's analysis was rather strained. It asked, for example, whether a teacher 'who carried a copy of the Communist Manifesto on a public street' could be said to 'advocate' criminal anarchy, or whether a teacher who 'informs his class about the precepts of Marxism and the Declaration of Independence' violated the state's ban on 'advising' the 'doctrine' of violent overthrow of the government. These hypotheticals indicate that the court was more concerned with the restriction on free expression than with any real vagueness in the statute.

The Civil War era cases invalidated retrospective oaths. Forward-looking oaths remained on the books, but once again the court chipped away at them during the 1960s. In 1966 the court struck down an oath required of public employees, in which they had to swear that they were not 'knowingly' members of the Communist Party or of any other organization having as one of its purposes the overthrow of the state's government.[26] The Smith Act cases had held that a person could not be convicted of violating *that* statute without a showing that he or she was an 'active' member of the group with a specific intent to bringing out the organization's unlawful ends. The court applied this rule to the oath requirement as well. It was unconstitutional because '[t]hose who join an organization but do not share its unlawful purposes and who do not participate in its unlawful activities surely pose no threat, either as citizens or as public employees'.

What remained were simple oaths to uphold the constitution. In *Cole v. Richardson* (1972), the court addressed a challenge to the following oath: 'I do solemnly swear (or affirm) that I will uphold and defend the constitution of the United States of America and the constitution of the Commonwealth of Massachusetts and that I will oppose the overthrow of the government of the United States of America or of this Commonwealth by force, violence, or by any illegal or unconstitutional method.' Before dealing with the specific oath, the court summarized its prior decisions on oaths:

> We have made clear that neither federal nor state government may condition employment on taking oaths that impinge on rights guaranteed by the First and Fourteenth Amendments respectively, as for example those relating to political beliefs. Nor may employment be conditioned on an oath that one has not engaged, or will not engage, in protected speech activities such as the following: criticizing institutions of government; discussing political doctrine that approves the overthrow of certain forms of government; and supporting candidates for political office. Employment may not be conditioned on an oath denying past, or abjuring future, associational activities within constitutional protection; such protected activities include membership in organizations having illegal purposes unless one knows of the purpose and shares a specific intent to promote the

25 *Keyishian v. Board of Regents*, 385 U.S. 589 (1967).

26 *Elfbrandt v. Russell*, 384 U.S. 11 (1966).

> illegal purpose. Thus, … the Court sustained inquiry into a bar applicant's associational activities only because it was narrowly confined to organizations that the individual had known to have the purpose of violent overthrow of the government and whose purpose the individual shared. And, finally, an oath may not be so vague that 'men of common intelligence must necessarily guess at its meaning and differ as to its application, [because such an oath] violates the first essential of due process of law.' Concern for vagueness in the oath cases has been especially great because uncertainty as to an oath's meaning may deter individuals from engaging in constitutionally protected activity conceivably within the scope of the oath.

The first part of the oath involved in *Cole* was entirely conventional, tracking the oath required by the constitution of the president and other major public officials. And – the court held – the second part, dealing with opposing the overthrow of the government by illegal or unconstitutional methods, basically restated the first part. The holding and the summary of prior decisions make clear how innocuous are the constitutionally permitted oaths one must take to hold a public job.

The Supreme Court has reinforced the separation of ordinary civil service positions from politics by holding it unconstitutional for public employers to consider the political affiliations or views of ordinary civil servants in making decisions about hiring, promotion or firing.[27] The court recognized one exception to this rule for employees who had a close and confidential relation to a policymaker. So, for example, a police department might be able to dismiss the department's spokesperson if he or she supported a mayoral candidate who promised to dismiss the city's chief of police.

This exception deals with political activity generally, not with extremist or democracy threatening activity specifically. The lower courts have regularly dealt with cases in which low-level civil servants, including ordinary police officers, are dismissed or disciplined because of their endorsement of extremist views outside the context of their work. A typical case involves a police officer who takes part in an extremist political rally on his non-work time. Most of the litigated cases appear to uphold dismissals under such circumstances. The courts adopt various theories: the public notoriety of the officer's action is sometimes said to impair the officer's ability to perform his ordinary duties; public knowledge of the officer's activity is sometimes said to run a risk that the public will mistakenly conclude that the employer itself endorses the officer's extremist views. Yet, although the dismissals are often upheld, the courts are visibly uncomfortable in doing so. They recognize the tension between imposing a job-related sanction on a person for their non-work-related political activity, even extremist activity, and the assumptions underlying the Supreme Court's suspicion of political criteria for civil service employment. What seems to matter is a combination of the egregiousness of the

27 See, for example, *Elrod v. Burns*, 427 U.S. 347 (1976); *Branti v. Finkel*, 445 U.S. 507 (1980).

employee's activity and the degree to which the employee actually comes into contact with members of the public who would be dismayed to know that they had to deal with an extremist civil servant.

By the beginning of the twenty-first century, US constitutional law tolerated essentially no categorical prohibitions on public employment for members of extremist groups, even in quite sensitive positions, such as the police or teaching. Particular individuals could be dismissed, but only if their political activities had some discernible impact on their ability to perform their public functions, a condition that courts found satisfied only in relatively extreme cases.

Regulation of Hate Speech and Verbal Attacks on Public Officials

The US political discourse has always been characterized by slashing attacks on political opponents and their supporters. As Chief Justice William Rehnquist once observed, 'Despite their sometimes caustic nature, from the early cartoon portraying George Washington as an ass down to the present day, graphic depictions and satirical cartoons have played a prominent role in public and political debate.'[28] After the Second World War concern grew about the civic consequences of such rhetoric. In 1952, the Supreme Court decided *Beauharnais v. Illinois*, a prosecution for violating a state law making it a crime to distribute material 'that portrays depravity, criminality, unchastity, or lack of virtue of a class of citizens, or any race, color, creed or religion, which ... exposes [such] citizens ... to contempt, derision or obloquy'.[29] Joseph Beauharnais was the president of the White Circle League, an organization devoted to stopping 'the further encroachment, harassment and invasion of white people, their property, neighborhoods and persons, by the Negro'. One of their leaflets referred to 'the aggressions ... rapes, robberies, knives, guns and marijuana of the negro'. Justice Felix Frankfurter's opinion for the court referred not only to 'the tragic experience of the past three decades', but to more recent experiences in Illinois of racial violence provoked by 'willful purveyors of falsehoods'. Analogizing the statute to unquestioned law allowing individuals to recover for injuries to their reputations as a result of the dissemination of false statements about them, the court asserted that the state legislature could reasonably believe that a person's reputation might be just as much harmed by libels about the groups of which he or she was a member as by libelous statements focused on the individual. The court deferred to the legislature's judgment that prohibiting group libel might limit its adverse impact on public discourse.

Beauharnais was decided shortly after the court had begun to develop its modern framework for analysing restrictions on free expression. That framework distinguished between what has come to be known as 'high value' speech, such as political discourse and 'low value' speech. In 1942, *Chaplinsky v. New Hampshire*

28 *Hustler Magazine v. Falwell*, 485 U.S. 46, 54 (1988).

29 *Beauharnais v. Illinois*, 343 U.S. 250 (1952).

upheld the conviction of a Jehovah's Witness who had confronted a police officer attempting to remove him from a public sidewalk with the words 'You are a God damned racketeer!'[30] This violated a state law making it an offence to 'address any offensive, derisive or annoying word to any other person' in a public place. The court's theory was that Walter Chaplinsky's words fell within one of the 'well defined and narrowly limited classes of speech, the prevention and punishment of which have never been thought to raise any Constitutional problem'. Those classes included 'the lewd and obscene, the profane, the libelous and the insulting or "fighting" words'. Such utterances, the court said, 'are no essential part of any exposition of ideas, and are of such slight social value as a step to the truth that any benefit derived from them is clearly outweighed by the social interest in order and morality'. As the court saw things in 1952 *Beauharnais*, a criminal libel case, did not involve a statute that violated the constitution because civil libel law did not.

Over the next decades, the court discovered serious difficulties in this two tier account of free speech law. Cases arose in the areas of libel and obscenity in which liability was imposed on statements that, to the justices, did seem to have enough social value to be protected against punishment. The turning point came in the 1964 case of *New York Times v. Sullivan*.[31] The *New York Times* published an advertisement describing events in Montgomery, Alabama, during the civil rights movement. The advertisement contained some minor misstatements of facts about what police officers had done. Sullivan, who was in effect the chief of police, sued for libel, claiming that these false statements seriously damaged his reputation; a jury, plainly influenced by its dislike for the civil rights movement and 'outsiders', such as the *New York Times*, awarded damages of $500,000, far larger than any reasonable estimate of the damage to Sullivan's reputation. The Supreme Court vacated the judgment and ordered the case dismissed.

The *Sullivan* decision held that the constitution allowed public figures – a class that included everyone who held a public office – could recover damages for injury to their reputations only under quite restrictive conditions. They had the burden of showing that damage to reputation had occurred and they could recover only actual, not presumed, damages. Most important, though, public figures could recover only if they showed that the publisher had disseminated false statements with 'actual malice', which the court defined as knowledge of the statements' falsity or reckless disregard of the statements' truth or falsity. And, later cases held, public officials cannot recover for disparaging statements of opinion, because, as the court put it, 'under the First Amendment there is no such thing as a false idea' and statements of opinion are ideas.[32]

The *Sullivan* rule opens public officials to highly disparaging comments. It was applied beyond the context of libel to the tort of intentional infliction of emotional

30 *Chaplinsky v. New Hampshire*, 315 U.S. 568 (1942).

31 376 U.S. 254 (1964).

32 *Gertz v. Robert Welch, Inc.*, 418 U.S. 323, 339 (1974).

distress in *Hustler Magazine v. Falwell*.[33] A pornographic magazine had published a 'parody' advertisement asserting that Jerry Falwell, a politically prominent preacher, had had his first sexual experience with his mother in an outhouse toilet. The court held that Falwell could not recover under the *Sullivan* rule.

The 'actual malice' rule was an attempt to define the boundaries of the categories of low value speech with great care, but the effort often seemed unavailing. The constitutional law of libel grew increasingly complex, although the basic requirement that public officials could recover damages for libelous statements only if they showed that the speaker had acted in a quite egregious manner remained in place. By the time a political movement gained enough power to generate real support for regulation of hate speech, the categories of low value speech were far more narrow than they had been in 1952, and it is doubtful that *Beauharnais* would be decided today as it had been a half century ago. These developments made it effectively impossible for legislatures to regulate hate speech.

In the terms used in US constitutional law, most forms of hate speech unquestionably fall into the category of high value speech. Holocaust denial, for example, is a proposition about history with implications for contemporary policy. Political platforms that assert the responsibility of non-citizens for crime and disease make factual assertions in support of policy programmes. Standard doctrine in the United States holds that the proper response to such assertions, when they are made in contexts where the speech falls generally within the category of high value speech, is to combat the false assertions with true ones.

Those who sought to regulate hate speech had three options: (1) they could seek to persuade the courts to abandon the two tier approach in favour of a more generalized balancing approach, akin to proportionality analyses used elsewhere in constitutional discourse. So, for example, the mere fact that a political candidate uttered hate speech in the course of seeking election would not in itself preclude regulation even if no imminent harm seemed likely. Instead, the courts could balance the value of the candidate's speech against the social harm it caused and, presumably, could sometimes find the speech subject to regulation; (2) they could attempt to persuade the courts that hate speech should be added to the list of low value speech; and (3) they could attempt to shoehorn hate speech regulation into the established categories of low value speech.

Neither the first nor the second course was likely to succeed. The extensive history of free speech jurisprudence in the United States had made the two tier structure quite attractive. Judges believed that such a structure provided adequate protection to speech without licensing judges to override sensible legislative determinations about the regulation of forms of speech that did cause real harm. By the 1990s, the court's experience with low value speech made it reluctant to expand the list. In theory, the court might have created a new category as it had identified the old ones – by balancing the harm caused by the entire category of

33 485 U.S. 46 (1988).

prohibited speech against the social benefits of allowing its dissemination. The court's general discomfort with balancing approaches in First Amendment law and elsewhere, because of the discretion they gave courts, suggested that it was unlikely to create a new category of low value speech.

Advocates of hate speech regulation therefore argued that hate speech should be considered 'fighting words'. The court's doctrine on fighting words, though, was not at all favourable here either. As *Chaplinsky* had said, fighting words were 'those which by their very utterance inflict injury or tend to incite an immediate breach of the peace'. The image here is of a process in which injury occurs without substantial cognitive processing by the person who hears the fighting words: hearing, the person is automatically injured or automatically seeks to fight, that is, to attack the speaker. Hate speech does not operate in that way. It injures because its targets engage in cognitive processes that lead them to believe themselves to be outsiders to the community and potential targets of violence.

The Supreme Court invalidated a local hate speech ordinance in *R.A.V. v. City of St. Paul*.[34] A teenage boy burned a cross on the lawn of a black family's home. He was prosecuted for violating a city ordinance that, as construed by the state courts, prohibited racial or religious 'fighting words' (but not fighting words relating to other categories). In a confusing opinion, the Supreme Court held that, although fighting words were of low value, they were not 'invisible' to the First Amendment. The city ordinance ran afoul of the basic First Amendment rule that distinctions drawn among expressions on the basis of the viewpoints they expressed could rarely be justified. The court said: 'Selectivity of this sort creates the possibility that the city is seeking to handicap the expression of particular ideas.' The difficulty here is that the ordinance was confined to a subset of fighting words, a class that, the court had already held, was 'no essential part of any exposition of ideas'. It is therefore difficult to understand how selectivity could handicap the expression of any ideas. *R.A.V.* is better understood as an attempt by the court to signal its discomfort with the then proliferating hate speech codes adopted by US colleges and universities than as creating a coherent doctrine about hate speech.

Some forms of hate speech, of course, can be direct threats of planned harm. *R.A.V.*'s action in burning a cross is a classic example: cross burning has historically been associated with the Ku Klux Klan and terroristic threats to African Americans. Sometimes, though, cross burning can be a statement of a political viewpoint without any necessary connection to an immediate threat. A decade after the *R.A.V.* decision, the Supreme Court addressed a different and arguably narrower ban on hate speech.[35] Virginia made it a crime to burn a cross 'with the intent of intimidating any person or group of persons'. The Supreme Court considered two cases brought under this statute. In one several young white men attempted to burn a cross in an African American neighbour's yard, apparently to 'get back' at the neighbour for complaining about shots the neighbours had heard. The other case

34 505 U.S. 377 (1992).

35 *Virginia v. Black*, 538 U.S. 343 (2003).

arose out of a small 25 person rally of the Ku Klux Klan, at which the defendant made a speech about what the Klan believed in and then ignited a cross.

The Supreme Court started from the premise that true threats, no matter how expressed, were not protected by the First Amendment. But, it held, the Virginia statute had been construed in a way that required juries to infer from the fact that a cross was burned that the defendants intended to intimidate. Requiring that inference was impermissible. Doing so converted the statute, which seems to bar only threats, into a flat ban on cross burning. Yet, as the Klan rally showed, sometimes a person might burn a cross in a setting where no real threat was intended. In contrast, the cross burning in the neighbour's yard might well have been intended to intimidate, but a jury had to be given the chance to draw that inference from the case's particular facts.

Finally, it should be noted that international law plays no role in US hate speech law. The US ratification of the International Covenant on Civil and Political Rights (ICCPR) contained an explicit reservation: 'Article 20 [requiring prohibition of war propaganda and other forms of hate speech] does not authorize or require legislation or other action by the United States that would restrict the right of free speech and association protected by the Constitution and laws of the United States.' Scholars of international law in the United States generally hold that this reservation is a valid one because it is of sufficiently narrow scope, relative to the entire range of rights protected by the ICCPR, that it does not undermine the treaty's object and purpose. A different question might arise were the United States to ratify a narrow purpose treaty targeted specifically at hate speech and include a similar reservation. Such a reservation, in a treaty with a limited scope, might be inconsistent with the treaty's object and purpose. Because the United States generally adheres to the dualist view of international law, requiring that international obligations be adopted as domestic law (with narrow exceptions), hate speech regulation under the hypothesized treaty would still be unconstitutional, although the failure to adopt it would place the United States in breach of its international obligations. Of course, this scenario would never arise, because the United States would simply refrain from ratifying the treaty in the first place.

The US constitutional law of hate speech regulation seems to limit sharply the circumstances under which people can be punished for hate speech. It may be worth noting, though, that the *R.A.V.* decision did not slow the pace at which colleges and universities adopted hate speech codes, sometimes as part of their disciplinary rules and sometimes as part of suggestions about proper conduct. These codes are rarely enforced through disciplinary proceedings, presumably because of constitutional concerns, but they do have substantial social support behind them and may be effective in guiding conduct even in the absence of coercive enforcement.

Campaign Finance Regulation

The most politically salient area in which there is contemporary controversy about restricting constitutional rights to protect democracy against itself is the law dealing with the financing of political campaigns. Although a small portion of campaign activity in the United States is financed by public taxation, by far the larger portion is financed by private contributions. For over a century, corporations and labour unions have been prohibited from contributing directly to political campaigns. But individuals can do so, and can communicate their interests to the candidates they support financially. In addition, corporations and labour unions can use many lawful devices to evade the prohibition on direct financial support of campaigns.

The private financing of political campaigns has persistently raised public suspicion that wealthy contributors or those who, such as corporations and labour unions, can aggregate smaller contributions from individuals, are unduly influencing the development of public policy. This concern is typically described as a concern about corruption, but scholars and courts acknowledge that the problem is not that contributors buy favours from politicians that the politicians would not otherwise support – typically described as '*quid pro quo*' corruption – but rather that contributors finance candidates who support positions the contributors favour, and that disparities in the ability to provide financing produce policies that do not, in some important sense, reflect the true preferences of politicians' constituents. Typical regulations limit the amount an individual can contribute to a political campaign or, far more controversially, the amount an individual can spend independently – that is, without coordinating with an intended beneficiary candidate – to support a candidate.

The US constitutional law of campaign finance regulation is highly specialized and, to a non-specialist, almost unbearably arcane. It begins from the perception that regulating campaign finance is equivalent to regulating speech, because political candidates need money from somewhere to assist them in getting their messages across. And the speech that these regulations affect is political or high value speech. On some views, that fact alone is sufficient to cast serious doubt on any substantial efforts to regulate campaign finance on corruption-related grounds. The reason is that regulations of high value political speech can be justified only by a strong showing that they address a serious problem. Opponents of campaign finance regulation agree that combating *quid pro quo* corruption would be a sufficient basis for regulation, but deny that the regulations in place are aimed at doing so – and proponents of regulation appear to agree that the purpose is not that.

Proponents of campaign finance regulation argue, though, that such regulations fit into a category known as 'content-neutral' regulations, which are generally permissible. That is, they argue that the limitations are imposed on everyone, no matter what position they seek to support or which candidate they hope to assist. The difficulty with this position is that proponents of campaign finance regulation are generally aware of, and indeed celebrate, the fact that they hope their efforts will change the shape of debate by limiting the effects the wealthy have on public discourse.

The US Supreme Court has been mildly receptive to legislative efforts to control campaign finance excesses. To that extent, something like an idea of militant democracy – or at least moderately assertive democracy – is part of US constitutional law. The difficulty, though, is that if private financing of political campaigns threatens democracy, it can be met effectively only through truly militant measures, of a sort the Supreme Court appears to be unwilling to support. The first major effort at campaign finance reform occurred in 1976, the second in 2002. The Supreme Court upheld major portions of both statutes.[36] Yet, the court's moderate doctrine made it easy for creative lawyers to develop and exploit 'loopholes' in the statutes, and some of those loopholes might be required by the First Amendment. If campaign finance regulation is the locus of militant democracy in the United States, its democracy is not all that militant.

Conclusion

This chapter began with the observation that the term 'militant democracy' was not part of US constitutional discourse. Perhaps even more striking is that, with the exception of the 1950s, the mechanisms used elsewhere to protect democracy against its own abuses – restrictions on political parties because of their programmes, for example – are also not part of US constitutional law. One indication of these absences is the fact that, with the exception of hate speech regulation, there has been no sustained scholarly attention over the past few decades to questions of exclusions of political parties or to political tests for ordinary civil service positions. What accounts for these differences between US constitutional law and constitutional law elsewhere?

Some of the reasons have been suggested above. In connection with hate speech, the absence of constitutional provisions specifically protecting human dignity or cognate ideas means that the only constitutional interest at play is the interest in free expression, and balancing a constitutional interest against non-constitutional ones systematically produces rules protective of speech. On a deeper level, US constitutional law is committed to principles of individualism and individual responsibility, as can be seen in the suspicion in constitutional doctrine of affirmative action programmes, which allocate resources to people based not on their individual characteristics but on their membership in groups. When the government claims that a political party or group threatens democracy, the individualistic tendency in US constitutional law almost instinctively shifts from the group to its individual members, allowing regulation when an identified individual has engaged in threatening action, but not simply on the basis of the individual's affiliation with an extremist group.

---

36 *Buckley v. Valeo*, 424 U.S. 1 (1976); *McConnell v. Federal Election Commission*, 540 U.S. 93 (2003).

That mechanisms associated with militant democracy were adopted and generally approved in the 1950s is also suggestive. Aside from the present, that period was the only one in the modern era when political elites believed that the nation was at serious risk from *internal* threats. In the absence of such perceptions, there is also no perceived need to defend democracy against those who would subvert it. There have always been internal extremists in the United States, but – the Cold War era aside – political elites always believed that the threat of extremism could be met within the bounds of ordinary politics. Neither communist nor fascist candidates, for example, ever received more than trivial success in politics. When democracy is not seen as under internal threat, the mechanisms of militant democracy will not be as seen necessary.

References

Brown, Ralph S. (1958) *Loyalty and Security: Employment Tests in the United States.* New Haven: Yale University Press.

Hyman, Harold M. (1959) *To Try Men's Souls: Loyalty Tests in American History.* Berkeley: University of California Press.

Issacharoff, Samuel (2007) 'Fragile Democracies', *Harvard Law Review* 120(6): 1405–467.

Stone, Geoffrey (2004) *Perilous Time: Free Speech in Wartime from the Sedition Act of 1789 to The War on Terrorism.* New York: W.W. Norton and Co.

Stone, Geoffrey, Seidman, Louis M., Sunstein, Cass R. and Tushnet, Mark V. (2005) *Constitutional Law*, 5th edn. New York: Aspen Law and Business.

Strauss, David A. (1991) 'Persuasion, Autonomy, and Freedom of Expression', *Columbia Law Review* 91, 334–71.

Chapter 15
Comparative Aspects

Markus Thiel

Introduction

Democracy is a fragile gem. And there is a good enough reason to fear for its integrity. Not only internal and external threats and endangerments[1] by violent enemies of the democratic system and its fundamental principles and values give cause for concern. The democratic idea suffers from intrinsic problems as well. The citizens' disenchantment with politics, for example, leads to a dramatically decreased turnout of voters and to a lingering erosion and devaluation of the electoral processes; this development could be a gateway for anti-democratic parties and organizations which – more or less covertly – aim at the abolishment of the democratic system. The relatively stable condition of most Western democracies must not mislead us: there are still serious threats. The modern 'civil society'[2] with its culture of democratic discourse and conflict resolution has mitigated them, but the 'civic type' of democracy is dependent on a minimum of moral standard among the citizen (Preuß 2002: 116 et seq.). This minimum seems to be frequently absent; as long as there are political parties and other organizations that deny 'the civil acceptance one owes in a democracy even to opponents' (Frankenberg 2004: 131),[3] the democratic system must at least make sure that the rights of minorities are adequately protected. Where the 'others' are not regarded as equal, the democratic community is out of balance (Preuß 2002: 117).[4]

Therefore, the discourse on the 'militant democracy' has by no means become obsolete with the political achievements of the last two decades. The country reports of this volume impressively prove that the question of a democracy's self-defence is still vivid even after the end of the Cold War and the decline of the Eastern communism. With regards to threats and dangers posed to democratic systems and to the fundamental principles and values of democracy, 'every generation got its own disease'. In a historical retrospective, the problem of the self-defending democracy, in general, 'can be traced back to the very beginning of democratic theory itself' (Pfersmann 2004: 47); the 'state's most natural characteristic' is self-

1 See, for example, Klamt 2007: 153; Thiel, Chaper 6.

2 See Frankenberg 2004: 130 et seq.

3 To the remaining potential threats to democracy by political extremism, see Capoccia 2001: 452 et seq.; Papier and Durner 2003: 341 et seq.

4 On this 'minimum' degree of protection, see Chapter 6.

defence (Sajó 2004b: 213). And the community of states is, unfortunately, far away from being able to bid farewell to the 'self-defence' issues as relicts of the past.

One of the most eminent examples is the fact that several democratic countries face and have to deal with international terrorism at present[5] – challenges hitherto unknown and unimaginable to this extent. As have often been the case in connection with security issues, society and scientific community divide into two camps regarding their attitude towards the so-called 'war against terrorism'. As Mark Tushnet (2005: 1) states:

> Most recent public discussion on the U.S. Constitution and war – both the war on terrorism and the war with Iraq – has been dominated by two voices: alarmists who see in every action taken by the Bush administration a portent of gross restrictions on the civil liberties of all Americans, and administration shills who see in those actions entirely reasonable, perhaps even too moderate, accommodations of civil liberties to the new realities of national security.

This statement on the current debate in the United States of America sounds like a timeless description of the eternal clash of the advocates of absolutely indefeasible fundamental rights and freedoms,[6] and the supporters of a flexible security policy that has to be adapted to the changing risk potential and that can therefore lead to more restrictive legal provisions.[7] This 'doves and hawks' dichotomy can be discovered in any democratic country that has to answer the question of self-defence.

The idea of a 'militant democracy' deals with internal threats. Therefore, the problems associated with the international terrorism are not completely congruent with the 'militancy' issue. Nevertheless, it can be regarded as being in close connection with this issue; in particular with regard to provisions decreed and measures taken to defend against terror attacks conducted on home soil. Precautionary instruments necessarily play an important role here. Nevertheless, 'anti-terrorism laws could be constructed and defended without reference to the problematic idea of militant democracy, namely the idea that democracies are justified in denying freedom associated with democracy to those who reject democracy' (Roach 2004: 171). The 'war on terrorism' and the 'militant democracy' feature at least a considerable intersection, even more so because both topics belong to the overarching issue of internal security.

International terrorism is not the only 'plague in the time of feast' (Bobbitt 2008: 3). Many countries have to deal with specific burdens of the past that cause

---

5 See Bobbitt 2008; Luban 2005; Mouffe 2004: 75 et seq.; Posner 2006; Roach 2004; Tushnet 2005.

6 As regards to the freedom of expression and 'free speech', see the detailed and instructive book by Geoffrey R. Stone (Stone 2004).

7 Roach 2004: 176 et seq. provides an instructive survey on anti-terror legislation related to 'militant democracy' issues 'in the West' (especially in Canada and the United Kingdom) and (Roach 2004: 189 et seq.) 'in the East' (Indonesia and Hong Kong).

enduring or recurrent security problems, for example, extremist political parties, other violence-prone organizations or separatist terrorists.[8] The question arises if, in a democratic system, fire should be 'fought with fire' (Klamt 2007: 133). As we have seen in the precedent country reports, this question is far away from being answered unanimously.[9] John Rawls (1971: 218) has clearly advocated a 'defensive' notion of democracy and rejected the idea of a 'suicidal' aloofment:

> justice does not require that men must stand idly by while others destroy the basis of their existence … the only question, then, is whether the tolerant have the right to curb the intolerant when they are of no immediate danger to the equal liberties of others.

On the other hand, an extension of restrictive legal provisions in order to fight, for example, international terrorism entails grave risks. As Miguel Revenga Sánchez (2003: 20) has stated:

> Our responsibity, as citizens committed to our way of life, is to be alert in order to prevent the struggle against terrorism becoming a 'carte blanche', which can be lethal for the rule of law.

The self-defence of democracy carries the poison of misuse within itself.[10]

This fundamental gap between two elementarily different concepts is mirrored in the opposition between a 'libertarian' and a 'protectionist' democracy. Günter Frankenberg (2004: 119) describes these antipodes as follows:

> The relevant literature can easily be divided into two camps, differing in matters of principle due to their contrary views as to the legal admissibility of regulations concerning political freedom, in particular the formation and organization of political parties. Accordingly, we need to differentiate between two legal regimes: the libertarian regime based on the principle of 'non-interference' (*Nichteinmischung*), which is critical of the 'militancy,' and the protectionist regime, which raises no principled objections against such 'militancy.'

The political and constitutional reality teaches that there hardly are 'full-fledged' libertarian or protectionist democratic systems; most democracies only show a tendency or combine elements of both types. Of course, a country, such as Germany, can be qualified as a ('restrained') protectionist democracy (Frankenberg 2004: 121), but most other countries resist a classification that facile.

---

8 See, for example, Neuberger, Chapter 8 and Vidal Prado, Chapter 11; on current 'right-wing populism', see Mouffe 2004: 71 et seq.

9 See, euphemistically, Klamt (2007: 136): 'the concept of Militant Democracy and especially its legal manifestation is not acknowledged everywhere'.

10 See, for example, Klamt 2007: 153.

As pointed out by Thiel (Chapter 1), a comparative legal analysis especially in the field of constitutional law has to overcome several obstacles.[11] Besides the particular problems of legal comparison (Thiel, Chapter 6), the 'militant democracy' issue is found at the intersection of legal, political and social sciences, making it difficult to establish unambiguous methodical and substantive criteria for evaluation. In addition to that, criticism is often characterized by indefinite, mistakable or emotional thoughts and arguments.

In this chapter on comparative aspects of the 'militant democracy' idea, I will first clarify the variety of arrangements in the different countries and second, treat the customary models for the classification of democratic countries with regard to the 'militance issue'. On the basis and by using the example of Karl Loewenstein's books on 'militant democracy', I will try to group the (legal) provisions and measures of self-defence into seven 'clusters', composed of similar regulations. In addition to that, I will deal with the questions if international or European law constitutes a duty to establish a certain degree of 'militancy', at which level of legal provisions elements of 'militancy' should be located, and if those elements can be regarded as successful and effective. Finally, the problem of possible alternatives to legal provisions of democratic self-defence will be discussed.

A Diversity of Arrangements

It is not very surprising that the countries analysed in the preceding country reports show a wide diversity of arrangements regarding the problem of democratic self-defence. They each look back on a quite different history of democratic probation. Several of the countries chosen for this comparative study have experienced more or less extensive periods of dictatorship, some before and during, some after the Second World War. During the formation of their constitutions, it was – as with transitional democracies in general[12] – an important task 'to rid societies of unjust and oppressive forms of political rule' (Offe 2000: 3). Because stability for such societies 'result from their effective demarcation from past regimes' (Niesen 2007: 11), democratic systems have to draw up 'an antithetical relationship toward the old "bad" regime with its perpetrators, victims and resistance fighters, its atrocities and failures, and to entrench this antithesis in the collective consciousness of the population', so that people 'know about the kind of setbacks to beware of and about the better principles to be held up' (Offe 2000: 5). This 'separation from the past' procures a democratic identity closely connected to the idea of a 'constitutional patriotism'[13] and is a very important feature of 'militancy', especially because – apart from the threats posed by international terrorism and its aims abolish the 'Western' democratic structures – 'there is very little contemporary competition

11 See Tushnet 1999: 1225 et seq.

12 See, in general, Sajó 2004b: 209 et seq.

13 See this chapter, p. 417 et seq.

between systems' today (Niesen 2007: 11).[14] In Germany, for example, the implementation of Article 21 Section 2 of the Basic Law, which allows bans of unconstitutional political parties by the Federal Constitutional Court, is widely regarded as a 'coming to terms with the past' (*Vergangenheitsbewältigung*).[15] This 'mechanisms for defending democracy that refer back to and repudiate *particular* national pasts' (Müller 2007: 112) are called 'negative republicanism' (Frankenberg 2004: 127 et seq.; Niesen 2003: 81 et seq.). As Peter Niesen (2003: 83) has defined:

> Negative republicanism carries in indexical reference to a society's past and expresses the concrete negation of historical wrongs in the name of democracy.

But the 'militant democracy' issue is not confined to questions of bans and dissolutions of extremist political parties and organizations. In a broader sense, 'militant democracy' can be considered a 'constitutional risk aversion' (Sajó 2004b: 213). Although not all elements of 'militancy' are stipulated at the constitutional level, this statement is true; therefore, the adjective 'militant' may be mistakable. It creates the impression that a democratic system is aiming at a dissemination of its own democratic model. It would be more appropriate to use the term 'self-defendant democracy' (as, for example, in Italy: *democrazia difendersi*) or 'democracy prepared to defend itself'; this accentuates the *reactive* or *responsive* (or preventive) character of – as far as can be seen – all elements of the 'militant democracy'. Pre-emptive strikes are unknown to the 'militant democracy' conception. Therefore, the 'militant democracy' term is imprecise and – because it actually is a *political* term – not perfectly suitable for a legal study. However, in recognition of Karl Loewenstein's work and the fact that the term 'militant democracy' is one of the most common, we will cling to this denomination.

We have seen that the idea of 'militant democracy' is of German origin or at least roots in the German experiences with the downfall of the Weimar republic and with National Socialism. The initial point of this chapter has been the question if the German conception of a 'militant democracy' as an overarching constitutional principle can be found in other democratic systems, or maybe can be regarded as a viable model for other countries. The country reports have shown that the German conception of 'militancy' is, apart from the Israeli case, an exceptional one. It is neither possible nor desirable to transfer the German model of a 'militant democracy' on other countries as it stands. Karl Llewellyn has warned Stefan A. Riesenfeld:

14 On the other hand, the triumphal course of 'democracy' in the last decades can be regarded as predominantly 'verbal'. Since the downfall of the fascist 'empires', there is merely any political current that does not pretend to be democratic (Pelinka 1974: 20). The label of 'democracy' should not appease us too much.

15 See Niesen 2007: 11, with further references.

> [He] told me never to reveal when I relied on an idea coming from continental Europe, because that would be 'the kiss of death'.[16]

This warning sounds exaggerated today, in a climate of friendly and cooperative comparison of legal and political systems. But it contains a grain of truth: because every country has made its own experiences with extremism and other forms of threats to their democratic systems and fundamental constitutional principles and values, every country has to cut its own path concerning self-defensive issues; and as we have seen, they did. The differences in the modalities of implementing elements of 'militancy' in their legal orders (especially on the level of constitutional law) is, in addition to that, 'closely related to the development of national legal cultures' (Klamt 2007: 154).

Models of Classification

The variety of arrangements brings about the question how we can comprehend the problem of 'militancy' in a comparative way. If we aim at detecting similarities and differences, comparison groups have to be formed, and criteria have to be established. Most of the scholars dealing with the 'militant democracy' issue from a comparative point of view have aimed to develop a model of classification or typification of democratic countries. After a presentation of the most common theories of classification, I will try to draft an own model based on the findings of the preceding country reports.

'Militant Democracy': 'On' or 'Off'? A Coarse Binary Approach

The most simplistic possible classification would indubitable be the discovery if a certain democracy is a 'militant' one or not.[17] This distinction is obviously useless. Although there are countries where the idea of a 'militant democracy' is unknown or disapproved in political and constitutional discourse,[18] and others that accept it as a genuine part of their constitutional reality, it is barely conceivable that a country does not have (and never has) taken legal defensive measures to fight, for example, against political extremists or terrorist threats.[19] Especially when we include a historical retrospective in the survey, we can hardly detect a country that has been untroubled by such menaces or that did not respond to them. The 'militant democracy' idea did not appear from nowhere, such as a *deus ex machina*

16 Riesenfeld 1994: 14.

17 See Buis, Chapter 5.

18 See, for example, Ceccanti and Clementi, Chapter 9, Irving, Chapter 2 and Tushnet, Chapter 14.

19 See, again, Ceccanti and Clementi, Chapter 9, Irving, Chapter 2 and Tushnet, Chapter 14.

in the 1930s, and it has not been completely new in 1937, when Karl Loewenstein set out his cogitations. He did not invent the conception, but at least coined the term. He 'provided ample evidence for the observation that the legislation of many European democracies had already introduced measures to meet the new threats posed by totalitarian movements' (Rensmann 2003: 1118). As shown in the preceding country reports, many countries look back on briefer or longer periods of increased vigilance or a more restrictive treatment of 'enemies' of the democratic system, the state or fundamental values of the particular constitution. Namely, in most countries following a 'non-militant' policy now, there has been considerable legislation against communist parties and communist individuals.[20]

This leads to two consequences: first, a comparative review on the 'militant democracy' principle must not be a 'snapshot' of the current situation, but has to comprise historical experiences, especially with periods of fascism, totalitarianism or of remarkable endangerment by extremists. And second: from a coarse qualification of a democratic system as 'militant' or not, we will obtain no benefit.

Procedural or Substantive, Tolerant or Militant? Four Categories of Militancy

A more common classification is based upon the distinction between two fundamentally different comprehensions of 'democracy' in general and approaches to the dilemma of a self-defendant democracy in particular: the 'procedural democracy', on the one hand, and the 'substantive democracy', on the other hand – the 'broad camps' of democratic theory (Fox and Nolte 1995: 14). Usually, a 'procedural democracy' is, in several variants, described as a system providing at least basic procedures and institutions to secure a democratic formation and realization of opinions.[21] A democracy, from this point of view, is 'the institutional arrangement for arriving at political decisions in which individuals acquire the power to decide by means of a competitive struggle for the people's vote' (Schumpeter 1947: 269). Some features are essential, for example, free and fair elections, the separation of the legislature from the executive, free press, free speech and the freedom of assembly, and the existence of some form of civil society. It is obvious that these elements guarantee only a 'framework' to enable the citizens to take part in the democratic processes. The 'procedural' conception focuses on the *form* and the *process* of governance. With the accentuation of the principles of participation, political equity and majority rule, it alludes to the 'how' of political decision-making.

A decided exponent of the 'procedural' view is Brian Barry (1979: 155 et seq.). He follows

20 See, for example, Tushnet, Chapter 14. Countries with a more 'militant' orientation show such legal provisions as well, see, for example, Sakaguchi, Chapter 10 and Thiel, Chapter 6.

21 See, for example, Baynes 1996; Dahl 1979.

> those who insist that 'democracy' is to be understood in procedural terms. That is to say, I reject the notion that one should build into 'democracy' any constraints on the content of outcomes produced, such as substantive equality, respect for human rights, concern for the general welfare, personal liberty and the rule of law.

Because of its restriction to procedural, institutional or 'systemic' elements, the 'procedural democracy' is often considered as a 'minimum standard' and a solid foundation of democracy, or even as imperfect or insufficient, because a pure procedural point of view would qualify a completely and unscrupulously corrupt, but orderly elected government as democratic. This objection is justified to a certain degree, but it is important to bear in mind that a large number of democracies is not able to provide a system of direct participatory democracy without representatives or other intermediates. In an indirect, representative democracy, the procedural aspects gain a great importance. In addition to that, the establishment of a 'procedural democracy' is regarded as an important first step in consolidating an emerging or transitional political system, and in the development from an authoritarian regime towards a functioning democracy. Nevertheless, a 'procedural democracy' is explicitly dedicated to tolerance and pluralism, so the 'enemies of democracy will be among the likely participants' and the electoral process is opened to its critics (Fox and Nolte 1995: 15).

The 'substantive democracy' model, in contrast, concentrates on the content of policy and decision-making. While the 'procedural' view emphasizes that the democracy has to keep neutrality towards the content of the decisions made, refraining from prescribing substantive guidelines or drawing contentwise boundaries and serving only as a mechanism for regulating different interests, a 'substantive' or 'normative democracy' asks for the specific democratic ideals behind each decision. A 'substantive democracy' secures the people's participation in policymaking as regards contents.

The 'substantive' model raises the problem of disagreement on the objectives and ideals the legal and political system should pursuit and observe, and the question how this disagreement is to be solved. Anyway, in a 'substantive democracy' the citizens take part in this solution. As Fox and Nolte (1995: 16) have clarified:[22]

22 Fox and Nolte refer to the examples of John Rawls and Carl Schmitt. Rawls (1971: 214 et seq.) emphasized that the principles of liberty (that he has hypothetically assumed to exist in a fictional 'original position') are 'not derived from practical necessities or reasons of state' and carry their own imperative. Schmitt (1932 [2005]) accentuated an 'unalterable core' of substantive principles that were the result of a decision by the people (the *pouvoir constituent*) and, therefore, are not subject to changes by the elected *pouvoir constitué*; see, in general, Schmitt 1931 [1996], on the question of the 'guardian of the constitution' in the Weimar republic.

> The substantive view begins from the proposition that majorities are fluid. In order for citizens to move in and out of the majority as issues change, they must at all times enjoy a core of political right that ensures effective participation. In this view, democratic procedure is not an end in itself but a means of creating a society in which citizens enjoy certain essential rights, primary among them the right to vote for their leaders.

It would be too short-sighted to define the 'substantive democracy' as a system with – in comparison to a 'procedural democracy' – an extended supply of democratic elements in favour of the citizens. The difference is not a quantitative, but a qualitative one. Anyhow, 'substantive democracies' today represent a minority (Revenga Sánchez 2003: 5).[23]

At first glance, the differentiation between a 'procedural' and a 'substantive democracy' does not have a clear reference to the 'militancy' issue. But it is obvious that a purely 'procedural democracy' is not reliant on specific substantial values written down, for example, in the constitution or articulated by Constitutional Courts. A democracy of that type is, with this 'disinterest' in substantive principles, not likely to provide defensive measures to protect these principles and values from attacks or the intention to change them. Certainly, even a 'procedural' democracy owns characteristics worth protecting and possibly endangered by 'enemies' of the democratic system, for example, the freedom of elections.[24]

In their influential essay on 'Intolerant Democracies' (Fox and Nolte 1995), Gregory H. Fox and Georg Nolte apply the distinction between 'procedural' and 'substantive' democracies on a number of countries and add the categories of 'tolerant' and 'militant' democracies.[25] They declare it one 'clear line of demarcation' between these categories 'whether the constitution can be amended to alter or eliminate democratic institutions' (Fox and Nolte: 1995: 24). In this article, Fox and Nolte (1995: 6) describe the phenomenon of 'intolerant democracies':

> Such an issue arises when a democratic country takes restrictive measures to prevent the change of its own democratic character by the election of anti-democratic parties. This is a particularly troublesome aspect of the right to democratic government which has become evident as issues of state governance move from the exclusive realm of national constitutional law to the purview of international human rights law.

---

23 Revenga Sánchez qualifies 14 countries belonging to the European Council as 'substantive': Armenia, Azerbaijan, Bosnia and Herzegovina, Cyprus, France, Germany, Greece, Italy, Moldova, Norway, Portugal, Romania, Turkey and Ukraine. 'The others allow reforms in every section of the Constitution, although following more or less complex procedures' (Revenga Sánchez 2003: 5).

24 Therefore there are, according to the classification by Fox and Nolte, 'militant procedural' democracies.

25 In addition to that, see Fox and Nolte 2000.

From these categories, four combinations result: tolerant procedural democracies; militant procedural democracies; tolerant substantive democracies; and militant substantive democracies (Fox and Nolte 1995: 22 et seq.).[26]

If we apply this categorization to the countries covered in the preceding chapters, some of them can be classified clearly; Fox and Nolte have offered a subsumption for some of these countries in their essay before. Beginning with the most intensive occurrence of 'militancy', Germany can be qualified as a 'militant substantive democracy' (Fox and Nolte 1995: 32 et seq.) without doubt. The German Basic Law (and many other sub-constitutional legal acts) contain and provide measures to fight against attacks on the 'free democratic basic order' which consists of a couple of substantive values that have to be safeguarded (Klamt 2007: 136 et seq.; Thiel, Chapter 6), so that there is an extensive armoury against the democracy's enemies, not only to save the democracy in its procedural functions, but also with its fundamental contents. Günter Frankenberg has stated that the German instruments of 'militant democracy' 'have protectionism written on their foreheads' (Frankenberg 2004: 122). This explicit 'militancy' is a reaction on the experiences with the fascist past and the raising of communism in the East, which 'fostered a strongly anti-totalitarian mindset in the framers of the *Grundgesetz*' (Fox and Nolte 1995: 32). The 'militant democracy' in Germany is regarded as an overarching constitutional principle with a legal relevance on its own (Thiel, Chapter 6).

The situation in Germany is comparable to that in Israel. Here, the topic of a self-defending democracy arose especially in connection with threats by Arab nationalists and by right-wing Jewish nationalist extremists. By fighting these movements, a more tolerant approach has been predominant in the young state of Israel, but – by degrees – a more restrictive approach came to the fore, beginning in the 1960s with the verdicts against *El-Ard* and the Socialist list. The High Court rendered a couple of decisions decidedly following a 'militant democracy' conception. It is important to remark that these judgments were led by High Court justices of German–Jewish origin who had doubtlessly been influenced by the 'Weimar effect' and the German concept of 'militant democracy'. Here, we face the interesting case of a form of 'constitutional import', not by a rather abstract influence of foreign legal and constitutional systems on a newly formed constitution in the course of the constitution-making process,[27] but by an individually transferred legal opinion. Therefore, the Israeli democracy can be classified as a 'militant substantive' democracy (Fox and Nolte 1995: 34 et seq.).

Fox and Nolte number Austria among the group of 'militant substantive democracies', because the country 'makes it a criminal offense to found an

26 Günter Frankenberg provides another system of categories with his differentiation between 'restrained' and 'unrestrained' democracy; and, 'libertarian' and 'protectionist' democracy; Frankenberg 2004: 116 et seq.

27 Which is a very common phenomenon in connection with state formation or 'nation building'.

association dedicated to endangering national independence or the constitutionally mandated form of government' (Fox and Nolte 1995: 36). This statement does not correspond with the country report by Andreas Auprich;[28] although he highlights that the Austrian democratic system 'is inspired by the strong spirit of freedom and political neutrality' (which would rather suggest a classification as 'procedural'[29]), he concurrently demonstrates that Austria only provides 'singular militant aspects to protect the democratic and republican system', for example, 'the prevention of a reinstallation of a monarchy and a pronounced prohibition of any resurgence inspired by Nazi ideologies' (Auprich, Chapter 3). Andreas Auprich follows the opinion that Austria is a 'mixed constitutional order', 'combining neutrality against political movements in principle with a number of material policy prohibitions', and that 'the Austrian democracy is not a militant one in the sense of Karl Loewenstein's pleadings, because there are no legal provisions to hinder an abolishment of the democratic system with legal and democratic ways and means' (Auprich, Chapter 3). The Austrian constitution 'lacks apparently any material constraints on a potential abolition of the democratic form of government' (Klamt 2007: 142).[30] This setting complicates a classification of Austria according to the four categories developed by Fox and Nolte (and proves once more the impreciseness of the 'militancy' term). Perhaps we have the strange situation here that a democracy is 'substantive' because it is deeply committed to political neutrality and provides legal measures to safeguard this neutrality. Or Austria could be qualified as 'substantive' and 'militant' because the country unmistakably fights 'National Socialist movements and their legal heritage' (Klamt 2007: 142).[31] Both arguments are not convincing. Why should an decided aversion against a single political tendency manifested in legal regulations and measures qualify a democracy as 'substantive' and 'militant', although it does not feature, apart from that, any provisions to protect democracy or other substantial elements at all? Here, we can detect a first disadvantage of Fox and Nolte's model of categories. While the demarcation of a substantive democracy from a procedural democracy raises difficulties, but is possible in the end due to passably serviceable criteria, the differentiation between 'tolerant' and 'militant' throws us back to the inoperative 'binary' model of 'militant or not'.[32] The criterion of demarcation Fox and Nolte have provided, the question if a given democratic system prevents the use of democratic rights to abolish the democracy, may be distinct and suits for a first rough classification, but does not give consideration to the 'militancy' issue's high degree of complexity. According to Fox and Nolte's differentiation, a country that

28 And the insights of Klamt 2007: 141 et seq., who calls the Austrian form of government 'apparently unprotected'.

29 See Klamt 2007: 142: In Austria, high procedural obstacles contribute to the constitution's defensive qualities.

30 See Boventer 1985: 199.

31 Klamt 2007: 142 describes this as a 'special feature' of 'militant democracy'.

32 See Chapter 14.

features any common provisions of 'militancy', for example, the possibility to ban political parties; the forfeiture of fundamental rights; the curtailment of the freedom of expression with regard to hate speech or incitement to violence; strong duties of allegiance of public servants; loyalty oaths enforced by penalty – and thus is armed to the teeth would have to be qualified as 'tolerant' because it allows the use of democratic rights and freedom to overcome the democratic system as a whole. This bizarre consequence in mind, Fox and Nolte do not consequently carry out this distinction and classify several countries against the background of a more 'gradual' view of 'militancy'.[33] At last, Austria may be considered as a 'border case' between tolerance and militancy, which makes this couple of terms scarcely useful and requires a more 'gradual' perception of 'militancy'.[34]

France has often been taken as an example for a 'tolerant substantive democracy' (Fox and Nolte 1995: 27); the constitution of 1958 provides that the republican form of government shall not be subject to amendment (Article 89). Article 4 of the constitution orders that all political parties 'must respect the principles of national sovereignty and democracy'. These – controversial (Fox and Nolte 1995: 29) – provisions identify France as a substantive democratic system. With regards to the categories of 'tolerant' or 'militant', Claire-Lise Buis points out that France represents a halfway case between liberal '*laissez-faire*' and a militant democracy in the German conception (Buis, Chapter 5). Therefore, France may, as Austria, be considered as a 'border case' between tolerance and militancy. Fox and Nolte accentuate that '(e)vidently, a comparatively tolerant political culture since 1958 has made the elaboration of a more militant form of democracy unnecessary' (Fox and Nolte 1995: 29). Their classification of France as 'tolerant' is doubtable. As the Spanish scholar, Miguel Revenga Sánchez, has stated:

> Is it not paradoxical that the *tolerant* France can dissolve political associations by the means of a Counsel of Ministers' Decree (*Décrets*), while in *militant* Germany it is necessary, as a result of the so called '*Privilegienpartei*',[35] to initiate a complex procedure before the Constitutional Court? What is more, while France had banned no less than 80 political associations between 1936 and 2003, in Germany the defence mechanism from political parties (Art. 21.2 of the Constitution) which has not been applied since 1956, now shows symptoms of withering away.

The United Kingdom can be classified as a 'tolerant procedural' democracy (Fox and Nolte 1995: 22), especially because of its traditional lack of written substantive principles and values and the important (procedural) role of the Parliament. The Parliament can enact legal provisions to defend the democratic system in case of

33 See, for example, their classification of the United States of America; see Chapter 14.

34 See Chapter 14.

35 *Sic*, the proper term would be '*Parteienprivileg*'.

necessity; it exercised that option in a couple of cases, for example, in connection with Irish nationalism; defamation law; fascist movements; and the threats of radical Islamism (Mullender, Chapter 13). For this reason, the United Kingdom's approach to the 'militancy' issue and its treatment of enemies of the democratic system are regarded as 'piecemeal' (Mullender, Chapter 13). In addition to that, the regulations have been regarded as 'fairly benign' in 'the scheme of possible restrictions on political actors' (Fox and Nolte 1995: 23). Nevertheless, Richard Mullender discovers some traces of a more 'principled' approach to the question of a self-defendant democracy in the recent past, for example, strong commitments to the rule of law; to distributive justice; and to liberalism and the autonomy of the individual (Mullender, Chapter 13). Hence, the 'tolerant procedural' character of the British democratic system is modified towards a kind of 'substantive charging', with – as Richard Mullender points out – problematical consequences. This may be due to the fact that many European countries have experienced an impact by the regulations of the European Union.[36]

A similar democracy model can be found in Japan, which has as well been qualified as a 'tolerant procedural' democracy (Fox and Nolte 1995: 24). Shojiro Sakaguchi proves this classification in his country report (Sakaguchi, Chapter 10) and emphasizes that the absolutely prevailing opinion among legal and political scholars vehemently refused the German model of a 'militant democracy' and concluded that the Japanese democracy takes a completely different position (Sakaguchi, Chapter 10). The implementation of the 'militant democracy' idea into Japanese constitutional law has been and is regarded as futile, on the one hand, and dangerous, on the other hand (Sakaguchi, Chapter 10). Like other countries, Japan relies on the self-regulative powers of politics and on an attitude of 'constitutional patriotism'[37] among the citizens. Nevertheless, Japan has experienced a period of increased 'militancy' practised by the Occupation Forces that conducted extensive purges from public office and dissolutions of political organizations, targeting members of the Communist Party, its sympathizers, and, more general, left-wing followers (Sakaguchi, Chapter 10).

The United States of America pursues a 'risk-taking' policy towards enemies of democracy (Sakaguchi, Chapter 10) and therefore can be qualified as a 'procedural' democratic system. Although the term 'militant democracy' is absent from constitutional discourse in the United States (Tushnet, Chapter 14), Fox and Nolte classify this country as representing the 'militant' variant of a 'procedural democracy', *inter alia* because it has 'enacted qualitatively more restrictive anti-subversion legislation than has the United Kingdom' (Fox and Nolte 1995: 25).[38]

36 See Chapter 13.

37 See Müller 2007 and Chapter 10.

38 They name the 'Smith Act' of 1940 (18 U.S.C. § 2385 [1982]), the 'Internal Security Act' of 1950 (50 U.S.C. §§ 781–836 [1991]) and the 'Communist Control Act' of 1964 (50 U.S.C. §§ 841–844 [1991]). See Tushnet, Chapter 14. Pfersmann names the influence of Montesquieu's thoughts on the 'Founding Fathers' of the United States Constitution as one

This diagnosis is correct; as Mark Tushnet clarifies, there have been several legal provisions regulating, for example, the treatment of subversive action; illegal political organizations; hate speech; restrictions of campaign finance; or the loyalty oaths in public service. The United States provides a system of defensive measures without recognizing any substantive principles and values that have to be protected absolutely. The United States Supreme Court mainly has fortified the procedural aspects of the constitution.[39] Mark Tushnet emphasizes that only in the 1950s 'mechanisms associated with militant democracy were adopted and generally approved'; at present, 'political elites' do not believe 'that the nation was at serious risk from *internal* threats' (Tushnet, Chapter 14). But it is obvious that the United States would not tolerate offences against their democratic system. Of course one may say that the United States never was afraid of internal threats, but after the 9/11 terrorist attacks, the differentiation between internal and external threats cannot be carried out consistently.[40] The United States provided an extensive arsenal of measures against the terrorist menace.

The other countries treated in the precedent country reports have not been explicitly classified by Fox and Nolte. In the following, a classification according to the four categories is attempted.

In Australia, the idea of 'militant democracy' is quite unfamiliar, and the 'tendency of both Australian law and culture has been liberal rather than repressive' (Irving, Chapter 2).[41] Nevertheless, Australia had to deal with threats of different provenance, especially in the recent decades. In addition to that, the country was confronted – like many others – with the 'problem' of communist parties, beginning with the 1950s.[42] The 'genuine commitment to the institutions of democracy' (Irving, Chapter 2) and the lack of a Bill of Rights argue for a classification of the country as a 'procedural democracy'. The decision if Australia is 'tolerant' or 'militant' is faced with similar problems as with regards to other countries. A qualification as 'tolerant' seems more likely.

In Chile, Section 8 of the constitution of 1980 has implemented the idea of a 'militant' or 'combative' democracy, following the German example (Aldunate Lizana, Chapter 4). This norm prohibited and penalized the propagation of 'doctrines against family, or which advocate violence or a concept of society, the State or the legal order, of a totalitarian character or based on class warfare'. It has been repealed in 1989 and was replaced by a regulation in Section 19 of the

---

of the reasons why 'certain forms of traditional militancy can be found' in this constitution (Pfersmann 2004: 47).

39 See Fox and Nolte 1995: 24 et seq.

40 See Klamt 2007: 155: 'A concept of Militant Democracy, which is relevant in the real world of today, also pays attention to threats from outside domestic polities. Anti-terrorism legislation in several states … also has to pass the critical test of the concept: not at the risk and cost of violating fundamental principles'.

41 See Dyzenhaus 2004: 19 et seq.

42 See the 'Communist Party Dissolution Act' of 1950 (Irving, Chapter 2).

constitution (Aldunate Lizana, Chapter 4), containing less restrictive provisions and measures and declaring: 'The political constitution guaranties political pluralism.' The new provision declares parties and organizations unconstitutional that 'do not respect the basic principles of a democratic and constitutional regime, pursue the establishment of a totalitarian system, as well as those using, promoting or inciting violence as a means of political action'. This allows the assumption that Chile now can be classified as a 'procedural' democracy with but few elements of 'militancy'.

By contrast, Hungary has encountered extremist right-wing violence in the recent past (Uitz, Chapter 7), a threat to the democratic system that must be taken seriously. The Hungarian legal system provides an armoury of provisions and measures associated with the idea of a 'militant democracy' and applicable to fight against menaces, such as the anti-democratic ambitions of political extremists. Renáta Uitz emphasizes that Hungary is 'a transitional democracy which has all the tools in its lawbooks to defend itself from anti-democratic forces', but has, nevertheless, 'repeatedly failed to put them in operation even in cases where the stakes are visibly high' (Uitz, Chapter 7). One reason for this failure in recent years could be the fact that the elements of militancy have been introduced to the Hungarian legal system 'in the very beginning of transition to democracy, at a time of fear, distrust and uncertainty' (Uitz, Chapter 7) – maybe, the country does not need these elements any more. Hungary has to be regarded as a 'militant procedural' democracy, although the failure of the legal provisions discloses a further problem of 'militancy': are the elements of a 'militant democracy' really functional or can they only serve as 'scarecrows', deterring enemies of the democracy and the fundamental democratic principles and values from active and aggressive attempts to abolish the democratic system?[43]

Italy has not provided large-scale 'militant' features. As Stefano Ceccanti and Francesco Clementi (Chapter 9) point out, the Italian democracy primarily widely relied and still relies on the political self-regulative powers and the integration and implementation of extremist parties or, more general, parties at the boundaries of the political scope. Nevertheless, even a country such devoted to the political and electoral processes has sporadically stipulated legal provisions to confine the influence of extremist parties (Ceccanti and Clementi, Chapter 9),[44] and the Italian constitution guarantees a 'protected core' – the republican principle – in Article 139 (Klamt 2007: 143). In addition to that, Article 54 of the constitution obliges every citizen to be loyal and to respect the constitution and the law.[45] Article 139 and 54 of the constitution are a sign of a 'substantive' character of the Italian democratic system,[46] especially because the unalterable republican principle spreads its protection on several other values and principles, for example, the fundamental

43 See Chapter 7.

44 See Klamt 2007: 143 et seq.

45 Klamt 2007: 143; Boventer 1985: 184.

46 For a classification of Italy as 'substantive', see Revenga Sánchez 2003: 5.

rights (which are, therefore, indirectly protected by Article 139 of the Italian constitution; Klamt 2007: 143). Moreover, Italy can be qualified as a 'tolerant' democracy with 'punctual militant exceptions'. As Austria, Italy eludes a simple assignment, if one does not want to take singular (sometimes only triggered by the respective historical circumstances and repealed after their change) 'militancy' features *pars pro toto* as a sufficient requirement for a 'militant democracy'. The intrinsic problem of the classification conception established by Fox and Nolte comes to the fore here once more.

Spain's exceptional political and constitutional history, comprising decades of military dictatorship after the Second World War, bred a special legal treatment of the 'militancy' issues. With a relatively short democratic 'tradition' (Klamt 2007: 145), Spain had to deal, in addition to that, with numerous terrorist attacks by Basque separatists (Vidal Prado, Chapter 11). Nevertheless, the Spanish constitutional framework does not contain substantive restrictions (Boventer 1985: 199; Klamt 2007: 145)[47] and predominantly relies on formal regulations, for example, relatively high hurdles for constitutional revision,[48] and on the obligation of citizens and public authorities to the constitution by Article 9 Section 1 of the constitution. Therefore, Spain can be classified as a 'procedural' democracy, while the assignment to the 'tolerant' or the 'militant' version is problematic again. Carlos Vidal Prado leans towards the assumption that Spain is 'militant'. The Spanish concept of 'constitutional loyalty' is very close to that of 'militant democracy' (Vidal Prado, Chapter 11), and although the Spanish constitution 'does not contain intangibility clauses, there are implicit limits on constitutional reform because there are changes and modifications that break up democracy and devastate the constitution' (Vidal Prado, Chapter 11). Carlos Vidal Prado holds the view that there 'can be no non-militant democracy', a thesis congruent with the doubts that have arisen about the benefits of a sharp cut differentiation between 'tolerant' and 'militant' democracies.[49]

Turkey can be considered as a 'substantive' democracy (Revenga Sánchez 2003: 5). The 1982 constitution, amended in 1995, 'sets forth the constitutional boundaries for ideological pluralism' (Oder, Chapter 12). Especially the Preamble contains several references to substantive principles and values apparently associated with Kemal Atatürk's conception of a Turkish nation and state (Oder, Chapter 12). Some constitutional principles are declared 'irrevocable' in Article 4 of the 1982 constitution, for example, the republican principle (including the conception of a 'secular state') and the 'unity' of the state (Oder, Chapter 12). The Turkish constitution therefore features a decided substantive orientation. As regards the distinction 'tolerant' and 'militant', the practice of the prohibition of political parties in Turkey is, *inter alia*, a prominent example for an increased level

47 The German model has been considered and discussed in the process of constitution-making, but in the end has been rejected; see Klamt 2007: 145; furthermore, see Tardi 2004: 95 et seq.

48 See, in detail, Klamt 2007: 146.

49 See Chapter 11.

of 'militancy' that even kept the European Court of Human Rights busy.[50] This allows the conclusion that Turkey is a 'militant substantive' democracy.

The attempt to classify the countries covered in the preceding essays shows a significant weakness of the 'four categories' conception established by Fox and Nolte. Hence, it is not surprising that this conception met with criticism soon after its publication. Martti Koskenniemi objects the 'initial pairing of the notions of democratic government/undemocratic opposition' and points out that 'political passions in the modern age are not enlisted as struggles for or against "democracy"' (Koskenniemi 1996: 231).[51] The definitions of 'procedural' and 'substantive' democracy that both 'capture democracy mainly as having to do with the realization of individual rights within a political realm' is criticized as curtate (Koskenniemi 1996: 233). Miguel Revenga Sánchez (2003: 4) states:

> Fox and Nolte's work about 'Intolerant Democracies' is a good example of applying models that only exist on paper ... The defining criterion lies precisely as defined in Carl Schmitt's work: the possibility (or lack of it) to reform any precept of the Constitution ... Reaching this point, one may ask whether finger-pointing at constitutional reform is really the key to the question or not. Constitutional reform is simply an instrument to consolidate the supremacy of the Constitution ... But in practice, it is dubious that reform could be a valid criterion to qualify Democracy. As a matter of fact, it is quite difficult to find instances where constitutional reform has had any effective influence upon the process of destruction of the Constitution.

The distinction of 'tolerant' and 'militant' democracies is burdened with a further disadvantage. The choice of terms casts a damning light on those countries that have decided for a 'militant' democracy – 'tolerant' sounds so much better. This dilutes the important cognition that the classification as 'tolerant' or 'militant' is not connected with any value judgement at all. Finally, the most convincing objection against the classification of Fox and Nolte presumably is the fact that – as we have seen before[52] – a clear distinction between 'tolerant' and 'militant' is impossible.

---

50 See Chapter 12; Klamt 2007: 154 with further references; Tardi 2004: 100 et seq.

51 This brings Carl Schmitt's 'friend or foe' differentiation into mind; see, for example, Schmitt 1927/1932 [2002]. On Schmitt, see Dyzenhaus 2004: 15 et seq. – Chantal Mouffe emphasizes that the 'strategy of the neo-conservatives who are behind George Bush's "war against terrorism" is not – as is assumed here and there – influenced by Schmitt's view of politics', because Schmitt 'always stressed' that the friend/enemy discrimination 'should be drawn in a properly political way, not on the basis of economics or ethics' (Mouffe 2004: 75). Schmitt 'would certainly not have condoned Bush's use of moral categories of "good" and "evil" to designate his enemies and he would have rejected Bush's messianic discourse about the American duty to bring freedom and democracy to the world' (Mouffe 2004: 75). On the question of the 'just war' and the conception's 'renaissance', see Schulze 2005.

52 See Chapter 6.

A Linear Point of View. The Gradual Scale of 'Militancy'

The disadvantages of Fox's and Nolte's conception have brought a number of scholars to develop alternative modes of classification. An eminent example is Otto Pfersmann, who favours a 'linear' point of view. His core thesis is that 'democracies are always *more or less* militant' (Pfersmann 2004: 53):

> militant democracy – as a legal structure – is on a scale of degree with other forms of democracy, in other words, that democracies are always more or less militant. At the same time, making democracy more militant increasingly modifies the structure from which it starts, so that a continuous extension of the domain of protection may amount to a decrease of the liberal heritage of constitutional democracy.

Pfersmann describes the 'open democracy' as the one end of the scale. This form of democracy is defined as

> a legal system in which the addressees participate in the production of the general norms by majoritarian decisions, directly or through the election of representatives in charge of enacting such general rules. In this 'pure' setting, we do not include any other requirement but participation in the production of general norms, i.e., those obligations, prohibitions, or permissions that affect all individuals falling under the jurisdiction of the legal system in consideration … Let us, furthermore, set aside the question of how these laws will be applied to particular cases and enforced against those who may violate their exigencies. Democracy may remain 'pure' as long as these constitutive features, and only these, are given.[53]

Pfersmann clearly names the risks of 'open democracies' (Pfersmann 2004: 54):

> the competence of the open democratic legislator is unrestricted. This means that any possible human behavior can be the target of such normative provisions, including the abolition of the open democratic procedures and their replacement by more oligarchic decision-making or even dictatorship. In such a structure, democracy is legally contingent on the democratic stances of the majority of direct or higher-order voters. If they are in favor of maintaining the system as it goes, it will be maintained; if, for whatever reason, discontent becomes majoritarian, open democracy will openly and democratically disappear.

Pfersmann alludes to the so-called 'democratic paradoxon' here. Although the danger of 'self-abolishment' without any impact of, for example, violent or threatening organizations is rather low, such a 'pure' open democracy is precarious.

53 Pfersmann 2004: 53.

It is not only the 'big change', the subversion of the whole democratic system that is alarming, but the arbitrariness of decision-making without any absolute limits. By means of the democratic process, acquisitions of centuries could be disposed. For example, would the abolishment of women's suffrage by majority decision really be 'democratic'?

Emanating from this model of a 'pure open democracy', Otto Pfersmann then develops a 'scale of stability', beginning with the introduction of obstacles to structural change which necessarily 'restricts pure democracy' (Pfersmann 2004: 55 et seq.). At first glance, this gradual scale seems more appropriate than the statical conception of Fox and Nolte, especially because many democracies have responded to the new threats imposed by Islamic fundamentalists by installing further defensive legal measures. This means that a democratic system may oscillate between different grades of militancy, which brings forth a more general aspect of the 'militant democracy'. The core intention of any democracies dealing with questions of defence is to balance the two most important objects of legal protection, freedom and security. And it is a political question whether a democracy favours freedom or security in any given situation. To complicate this duty of balancing, one is, according to Richard A. Posner (2006: 31 et seq.),

> not to ask whether liberty is more or less important than safety. One is to ask whether a particular security measure harms liberty more or less than it promotes safety.[54]

As regards the important role of civil liberties and Human Rights in a democracy, one may claim a natural primacy of freedom. But as any democratic country has a vital interest in defending itself and its fundamental principles even if the use and the protection of Human Rights have to be limited for this purpose, it may decide in favour of security and 'militancy'.

On closer examination, the 'linear' or 'gradual' conception of Pfersmann does not differ that much from the classification categories provided by Fox and Nolte. In fact, the statement that all democracies are 'more or less' militant throws us back to the challenging differentiation between 'tolerant' and 'militant'. Without solving the problems that are caused by the dichotomy of 'procedural' and 'substantive' democratic system, the gradual or linear conception actually removes the advantages of the four categories of Fox and Nolte. Therefore, the suitability of the – correct – insight that all democracies are more or less militant for a comparative study is marginal. As Martin Klamt has added, it 'has to be examined whether and to what extent different constitutional orders have installed a Militant Democracy' (Klamt 2007: 136). Claire-Lise Buis, in addition to that,

54 Posner emphasizes the role of the judiciary in the balancing of security and freedom and points out that this balancing is 'inescapably subjective' due to the judge's preconception (Posner 2006: 24). In addition to that, he criticizes 'knowledge deficits' of the judiciary 'regarding issues of national security' (Posner 2006: 36).

shows that the 'linear' model provided namely by Otto Pfersmann refers primarily on the *legal* framework of democracy (Buis, Chapter 5). She prefers a 'third way, turning toward a multidimensional approach to militancy' and adding a 'dimension of discourse' that 'enables the articulation of the relation between norms, political culture and the identification of the "enemies" of democracy' (Buis, Chapter 5).

Clusters

We have seen that, in terms of 'militancy', no two countries are 'like peas in a pod'.[55] Every society 'opts for the form of democracy it considers correct, fitting or tolerable' (Frankenberg 2004: 117). Therefore, the classification provided by Fox and Nolte is useful only to a certain extent. The 'linear' conception of Otto Pfersmann may serve as a starting point for further examinations. But the 'grade' of militancy of a given country can only be determined by an analysis of the existing legal provisions (and concurring political options) to secure a certain level of self-defence. It is quite obvious that most countries were guided by their own individual historical experiences when drafting their constitutions and legal framework. This applies to countries with an autocratic or fascist past as well as to countries that did not encounter dictatorship. Nevertheless, the question if a country is more or less 'militant' is only to be answered based on the current regulations and measures.

To alleviate a comparison of democratic countries with regard to the 'militancy' issue and to offer a model of classification, we will develop a model of 'clusters' below. We can hearken back here to the comparative work of Karl Loewenstein.

Loewenstein's Legacy

Karl Loewenstein's relevant articles on 'militant democracy' contain a survey of regulations and measures taken by several countries to fight fascist movements and extremist efforts in general. They provide, after some 'illustrations' of militant democracy,[56] a 'more systematic account of anti-fascist legislation in Europe'.[57]

Loewenstein starts with the statement that:

---

55 See Klamt 2007: 150 et seq., who recapitulates that 'not every country in the first group [*Austria*, *Germany* and *Italy*, the editor] with a similar historical experience of autocratic regimes protects democracy in the same way. … The second group of countries [*Greece*, *Portugal* and *Spain*, the editor] consists of countries that experienced (fascist) military dictatorships, which came into power by violent means. Neither of these countries followed the same method of protecting their democratic core.'

56 Loewenstein deals with Austria, Czechoslovakia, Estonia and Finland, see Loewenstein 1937a and 1937b, cited from the reprint in Sajó 2004a (Loewenstein 2004: 245 et seq.).

57 Loewenstein 2004: 245.

> democracy in self-defense against extremism has by no means remained inactive. At last, the terrifying spell of fascism's basilisk glance has been broken; European democracy has overstepped democratic fundamentalism and risen to militancy. The fascist technique has been discerned and is being met by effective counteraction. Fire is fought with fire. Much has been done; still more remains to be done. Not even the maximum of defense measures in democracies is equal to the minimum of self-protection which the most lenient authoritarian state deems indispensible.[58]

When tracing the provisions different countries have made to protect their own democratic system, Loewenstein is completely aware of the limited suitability of legal regulations for the protection of democracy:

> To over-estimate the ultimate efficiency of legislative provisions against fascist emotional technique would be a dangerous self-deception. The statute-book is only a subsidiary expedient of the militant will for self-preservation. The most perfectly drafted and devised statutes are not worth the paper on which they are written unless supported by indomitable will to survive.[59]

He even clear-sightedly recognizes the conflicts a 'militant' conception of democracy would bring about in a country with a strong liberal tradition as, for example, the United States of America. The question is

> whether legislative measures against incipient fascism are perhaps required in the United States … If, however, the question be answered in the affirmative, a second problem becomes that of devising federal or state anti-extremist legislation in conformity with the elaborate fundamentalism of constitutional rights enshrined in the American constitution.[60]

Besides these general statements and an examination of the current legal provisions in several countries, Karl Loewenstein presents a 'Summary of Anti-Fascist Legislation'[61] where he groups the various legislative measures in 14 sections which can be summed up as follows:[62]

---

58 Loewenstein 2004: 261 (in Sajó 2004a).

59 Loewenstein 2004: 261 (in Sajó 2004a).

60 Loewenstein 2004: 262 (in Sajó 2004a).

61 Loewenstein 2004: 250 et seq. (in Sajó 2004a).

62 Loewenstein includes the legislation in: Belgium, Czechoslovakia, Denmark, England, Finland, France, the Irish Free State, Lithuania, the Netherlands, Norway, Sweden and Switzerland.

1. Provisions in the countries' criminal codes against acts bordering on or falling in the category of high treason or rebellion and additional regulations regarding martial law and the conferment of extraordinary powers for the state of siege.
2. Provisions allowing for the prohibition of 'subversive movements', especially the ban or dissolution (extremist) political parties.
3. Legislation against the formation of private paramilitary armies, the wearing of political uniforms or parts thereof, and other symbols which serve to denote the political opinion of the person in public.
4. Provisions against the constitution of intolerable competitors of the state's own armed forces, serving as stewards, assault troops or as bodyguards.
5. Legislation against illicit manufacture, transport, wearing, possession and use of firearms or of other offensive weapons or any kind.
6. Provisions against the abuse of parliamentary institutions by political extremism (for example, regulations permitting the exclusion of adherents of subversive parties from representation in political bodies).
7. Provisions against the incitement to violence, agitation or hatred against other sections of the population and against violent campaigning.
8. Provisions to curb the tactics of disturbances in or wrecking meetings by militarized parties.
9. Provisions to curtail the freedoms of speech, expression, public opinion and press in order to prevent revolutionary and subversive propaganda, for example, vilifying, defaming, slandering and ridiculing the democratic state itself, its institutions or leading personalities of the existing régime.
10. Provisions against the practice of morally aiding and abetting political criminals and the 'symbolism of martyrs and heroes'.
11. Provisions regarding the political activities of members of the armed forces and the police.
12. Provisions regarding the special role of public servants (for example, the duty of allegiance, loyalty oaths or the curtailment of certain fundamental rights).
13. Provisions on special authorities to discover, repress, supervise and control anti-democratic and anti-constitutional activities and movements (administrative protection of the constitution).
14. Provisions against political activities of foreigners or alien emissaries on the national territory, the importation of anti-democratic foreign newspapers, the wearing of fascist symbols by foreign visitors or residents and the activities of foreign party organizations within the border.

Karl Loewenstein has rendered pioneer work in the typification of provisions and measures connected with the idea of a 'militant democracy'. The grouping of those regulations depending on their *substantial* content and purpose allows for a more differentiated classification of the democratic countries regarding the 'militancy' issue. Nevertheless, Loewenstein's 14 categories are only loosely sorted. It would be reasonable to combine them to a smaller number of groups topically interconnected. In addition to that, Loewenstein's account naturally is dated and roots in a historical situation completely different from the present. Nevertheless, the idea to group factually connected legal provisions and measures in a number of 'regulatory combinations' is convincing. These combinations we will call 'clusters' in the following.

As a first 'cluster of militancy', we could name the (constitutional) protection of an inviolable and unalienable 'democratic core'.[63] The second 'cluster' comprises the treatment of extremist political parties and other organizations,[64] and of their members, holding, for example, an office in public service or being members of Parliament (or of other representative institutions elected by the people). The third 'cluster' is formed by provisions and measures takes against organizations and persons misusing their fundamental rights and freedoms to abolish the democratic system or its core values and principles.[65] In a fourth 'cluster', we could merge all regulations and measures taken against institutions of the 'state', especially the government and the judiciary, which are preparing or conducting a 'coup d'état' by the extirpation of the prevailing democratic structures or which are obviously and considerably violating fundamental constitutional law. The fifth 'cluster' comprises the regulations on the administrative protection of the constitution, the sixth 'cluster' the legal provisions regarding a 'state of emergency', a 'state of siege' or the 'state of war'. In the seventh 'cluster', we will file all regulations and provisions that cannot be classified as belonging to the other clusters or form an own cluster, or that actually have no direct connection to the 'militancy' issue, but contribute to the protection of the democratic system and the constitution. It is important to remark that the following sections do not completely display all corresponding legal provisions and measures in the countries comprised in this book; the following considerations are confined to a exemplary overview and present a more detailed treatise only if necessary to clarify regulation variants.

(Constitutional) Protection of an Inviolable and Unalienable 'Democratic Core'

The first cluster consists of regulations that protect an inviolable and unalienable 'democratic core'. All 'substantive' democracies feature such regulations by definition. We can differentiate between countries that protect a 'democratic core' on the level of constitutional and countries that hold sub-constitutional law provisions.

In Germany, the 'Clause of Eternity' in Article 79 Section 3 of the Basic Law contains the absolute guarantee of a number of inviolable constitutional values and principles (Thiel, Chapter 6). Article 79 Section 3 of the Basic Law reads:

---

63 See Klamt 2007: 135.

64 See Klamt 2007: 135.

65 See Klamt 2007: 135.

> Amendments to this Basic Law affecting the division of the Federation into Länder, their participation on principle in the legislative process, or the principles laid down in Articles 1 and 20 shall be inadmissible.

A prime example of 'substantive militancy', this norm was made to prevent a 'legal revolution' (Klamt 2007: 137).

The Italian constitution of 1948 protects the republican form of government with a similar 'Clause of Eternity' in Article 139:

> The republican form of the state may not be changed by way of constitutional amendment.

Indirectly, the republican principle as an 'unalterable core' protects a number of other principles and values enumerated in Articles 1–12 of the Italian constitution. Article 2 reads, for example:

> The republic recognizes and guarantees the inviolable human rights, be it as an individual or in social groups expressing their personality, and it ensures the performance of the unalterable duty to political, economic, and social solidarity.

In Turkey, Article 4 of the constitution of 1982 contains a rule regarding 'irrevocable provisions':

> The provision of Article 1 of the Constitution establishing the form of the state as a Republic, the provisions in Article 2 on the characteristics of the Republic, and the provision of Article 3 shall not be amended, nor shall their amendment be proposed.[66]

Article 89 Section 5 of the French constitution of 1958 provides that the republican form of government shall not be the object of any amendment. Article 1 of the constitution declares:

> France shall be an indivisible, secular, democratic and social Republic.

66 Article 2: 'The Republic of Turkey is a democratic, secular and social state governed by the rule of law; bearing in mind the concepts of public peace, national solidarity and justice; respecting human rights; loyal to the nationalism of Atatürk, and based on the fundamental tenets set forth in the Preamble.'; Article 3: 'The Turkish state, with its territory and nation, is an indivisible entity. Its language is Turkish. Its flag, the form of which is prescribed by the relevant law, is composed of a white crescent and star on a red background. Its national anthem is the "Independence March". Its capital is Ankara.' – The reference to the Preamble in Article 2 of the constitution incorporates the provisions regulated there into the protection of Article 4. See Oder, Chapter 12.

Extremist Political Parties and other Organizations

'Militant democracy' today is 'most commonly understood as the fight against radical movements, especially parties and their activities' (Sajó 2004b: 210). The ban or dissolution of political parties and other organizations therefore can be regarded as a 'core element' of militancy. Many countries provide the possibility to ban or dissolve parties and organizations if they behave anti-democratically or violate other important rule, principles and values. On closer, comparative examination, these provisions are quite heterogeneous and we can introduce a couple of differentiations.

Regarding the treatment of extremist groups, there are countries where a difference is made between political parties and other organizations. In Germany, political parties play an eminent role in political decision-making in the formation of the people's will and enjoy a special protection provided by Article 21 Section 1 of the Basic Law. While organizations that cannot be qualified as 'political parties' can be dissolved by a decree of the Minister of the Interior (Thiel, Chapter 6) if they violate the values and principles in Article 9 Section 2 of the Basic Law, the hurdle to ban political parties is noticeably higher: the *Parteienprivileg* requires a banning decision by the Federal Constitutional Court (Thiel, Chapter 6). Section 19 of the Chilean constitution does not differentiate between political parties and other organizations and movements, and provides in Subsection 15 paragraph 6 that:

> Parties, movements and other organizational forms whose objectives, acts or behaviours do not respect the basic principles of a democratic and constitutional regime, pursue the establishment of a totalitarian system, as well as those using, promoting or inciting violence as a means of political action, are unconstitutional.

According to Article 9(2) of the State Treaty of 1955, Austria undertakes to dissolve all fascist-type organizations existing on its territory, political, military and paramilitary, and likewise any other organizations carrying on activities hostile to the United Nations or which intend to deprive the people of their democratic rights (Auprich, Chapter 3). Therefore, Austria does not differentiate between fascist political parties and other fascist organizations. In Australia, 'organizations' defined as 'terrorist' can be banned by the executive in Australia. Following the *Criminal Code Amendment (Terrorist Organisations) Act* 2004 (Cth), the Attorney General is empowered to proscribe such organizations by regulation (Irving, Chapter 2).

A further differentiation concerns the location of the provisions. Some countries have regulated enforcing measures against political parties on the level of constitutional law (with further specifications in special sub-constitutional legal acts), others only on the level of sub-constitutional law. In Germany, Article 21 Section 2 of the Basic Law declares political parties unconstitutional that seek to undermine or abolish the free democratic basic order or to endanger the existence of the Federal Republic of Germany (Thiel, Chapter 6). In Spain, the 'creation and the exercise' of the activities of political parties are 'free insofar as they respect the constitution and the law' (Article 6 of the constitution). Because the Spanish constitution does not contain any further regulations, the prohibition of political parties 'has only legal validity at the sub-constitutional level' (Klamt 2007: 147);[67] especially in Article 9 of the Parties Act (Vidal Prado, Chapter 11). In Australia, there have been sub-constitutional acts to prohibit the *Communist Party* in the 1950s, but this act was defeated before the High Court (Irving, Chapter 2). According to Article 68 Section 4 of the Turkish constitution, the

> statutes and programmes, as well as the activities of political parties shall not be in conflict with the independence of the state, its indivisible integrity with its territory and nation, human rights, the principles of equality and rule of law, sovereignty of the nation, the principles of the democratic and secular republic; they shall not aim to protect or establish class or group dictatorship or dictatorship of any kind, nor shall they incite citizens to crime.

Article 69 Section 1 adds:

> The decision to dissolve a political party permanently owing to activities violating the provisions of the fourth paragraph of Article 68 may be rendered only when the Constitutional Court determines that the party in question has become a centre for the execution of such activities.

And according to Article 69 Sections 5 and 6 of the Turkish constitution:

> The dissolution of political parties shall be decided finally by the Constitutional Court after the filing of a suit by the office of the Chief Public Prosecutor of the Republic.
>
> The permanent dissolution of a political party shall be decided when it is established that the statute and programme of the political party violate the provisions of the fourth paragraph of Article 68.

Another differentiation regards the question of legal competence. In Germany, only the Federal Constitutional Court can declare the unconstitutionality of a political party. Article 69 Sections 1, 5 and 6 of the Turkish constitution declare the competence of the Constitutional Court.[68] According to Section 19 Subsection 15 of the Chilean Constitution, the Constitutional Court has the jurisdiction to declare the unconstitutionality of parties, movements, or other organizational forms that 'do

67 See Tardi 2004: 95 et seq.

68 See Chapter 12.

not respect the basic principles of a democratic and constitutional regime, pursue the establishment of a totalitarian system, as well as those using, promoting or inciting violence as a means of political action' (see Aldunate Lizana, Chapter 4).

The countries comprised by this study differ in the modalities of a party ban or dissolution. In Germany, an anti-democratic party *is* unconstitutional by decree of the Basic Law. But this unconstitutionality has to be declared by the Federal Constitutional Court to carry legal consequences. Regarding this legal consequences, we have to make a first conceptual distinction between the ban and the dissolution of a political party. A ban prevents a party, for example, from taking part in elections and other political processes, while the organization itself may continue to be. The party is only deprived of their rights of participation in politics and in the formation of the political opinion and will of the people, but not completely abolished. The dissolution abolishes the very existence of the political party. Most countries do not clearly distinguish between these two alternatives, but most provisions content themselves with the declaration of unconstitutionality. This declaration – mostly declarative, not constitutive – has further consequences.

A second question deals with the coverage of the ban, concerning the banned party and successor organizations, for example, newly founded political parties with identical structures and membership – the banned party just with a replaced 'door plate'. These successor organizations have to be banned separately, but the cognitions of preceding banning procedures, especially of investigations of the facts, can be drawn on.

We can further differentiate between countries where (constitutional or sub-constitutional) law prohibits a certain political ideology and such countries where all anti-democratic extremist parties are prohibited or declared unconstitutional. In many countries, the treatment of extremist political parties can be qualified as a 'disposal of the past' (Frankenberg 2004: 124);[69] one would suspect that several countries only provide the ban or dissolution of parties and organizations of the extreme right or left, depending on the historical experiences. Nonwithstanding, most democratic systems do not distinguish between the political currents if a political party is conducting anti-democratic activities. In Germany, for example, political parties of the right and of the left have been banned by the Federal Constitutional Court on the basis of Article 21 Section 2 of the Basic Law (Thiel, Chapter 6).[70] On the contrary, in Austria only National Socialist Parties and organizations can be dissolved. According to the prevailing opinion (and judicial practice), Article 9 Section 2 of the State Treaty only applies to fascist organizations (Auprich, Chapter 3).

The ban of political parties, 'militant democracy's flagship provision', is 'facing a crisis today' (Niesen 2007: 1). Besides other objectives, the 'irregularity'

69 For Germany, see Dubiel and Frankenberg, *Die Zeit*, 18 March 1983:12.

70 Klamt 2007: 151 et seq., names Greece among the countries that do not prohibit a certain ideology; see Klamt 2007: 148 et seq. on the 'militant' features of the Greek legal system.

of a party ban can be seen in the fact that a part of the electorate is deprived of the possibility to be equally represented in Parliament and in the political public (Preuß 2002: 106). In a representative democracy, the political parties play an eminent role in the realization of the political opinion and will of the citizens; a party ban or dissolution locks parts of the voters out. Although they are not hindered to exercise their vote, the limitation of the scope of eligible parties violates their right to *free* suffrage. It would be too narrow-minded to argue that the vote is confined to the existing parties anyway, so that the voters have to decide for the party with which they agree the most. If the foundation of political parties is largely free, the ban of an existing party curtails the scope for electoral decision-making.

A party ban does not target at a specific political idea, but at their possible impact on the democratic system; it is not an 'interdiction of thought', but an 'interdiction of organization' (Preuß 2002: 113). Therefore, it would be starry-eyed to expect that a dissolution could eliminate anti-democratic thought among the dissolved parties' followers. But their political influence and their access to the voters are weakened (Preuß 2002: 114). The dissolution inhibits the peril that an anti-Democratic Party could be able to transform its ideas into 'destructive social energies', that – without the party – would 'float around directionless and vegetate diffusely, inarticulately and as private resentment on the edge of society'.[71]

Although political parties are entitled to participate in politics, this right features an intrinsic limitation. As Gregory Tardi (2004: 111) has stated:

> It is a characteristic of democratic regimes that in order to participate in the system of governance, political parties must, at the key junctures, accept the most fundamental rule, that of pluralism and of the concomitant alternation of parties in government.

A party that disregards this duty has to face the consequences.

Nevertheless, there are 'practical' disadvantages of measures taken against political parties. A successful ban or dissolution may produce political 'martyrs' who possibly become more popular among other extremists or even people wavering afore. And a failing banning procedure may cause triumphant victory celebrations or, perhaps worse, a subtle assumption that, for example, a court decision repudiating the banning motion attests the constitutionality and democratic innocuousness of the named party (Preuß 2002: 104). The court responsible for the party ban must not be blamed for the consequences of a negative dissolution decision – even if a ban is highly desirable among politicians and in public opinion (as it has been in Germany with the NPD), the court must not be convinced of the political necessity of a ban. The court should rather be inured to political pressure; the German Federal Constitutional Court is conceived as an institution with a high degree of political neutrality.[72]

---

71 Preuß 2002: 114, translation from German by the editor.

72 See, for example, Preuß 2002: 105.

Misuse of Fundamental Rights and Freedoms

Constitutional and sub-constitutional law of the countries comprised by this study contains a variety of provisions prohibiting or punishing the 'misuse' of political rights and freedoms. The regulation of a 'forfeiture' of certain fundamental rights in Article 18 of the German Basic Law (Thiel, Chapter 6) may be an exceptional provision here. But this 'cluster' comprises the quite varied treatment of 'hate speech', incitement to sedition or violence, and other restrictions of fundamental rights and freedoms that are used to attack the democratic system and its fundamental principles and values.

While the problem of party bans and dissolutions play an important role in explicitly 'militant' and substantive democratic systems, the handling of 'hate speech' and other abuse of fundamental rights, especially the freedom of expression, seems to be the problematical counterpart in procedural democracies. In the United States of America, for example, 'hate speech' can be restricted in narrow circumstances (Tushnet, Chapter 14). The United States criminal law prohibits subversive advocacy on the level of sub-constitutional law, although prosecutions for subversive advocacy have been extremely rare recently (Tushnet, Chapter 14). In Australia, there are several regulations restricting the freedom of speech in case of sedition (Irving, Chapter 2).[73]

Regulations and Measures Taken Against Institutions of the 'State'

This 'cluster' comprises regulations and measures taken against institutions of the 'state', including provisions regarding the role of public servants. Prominent examples are the duty of allegiance of public servants as provided, for example, in Germany (Thiel, Chapter 6), Chile (Aldunate Lizana, Chapter 4), and, with modifications, in France (Buis, Chapter 5), and the so-called 'loyalty oaths', for example, in the United States of America (Tushnet, Chapter 14).

In Germany, there are further regulations belonging to this group, for example, the 'right to resist' in Article 20 Section 4 of the German Basic Law (Thiel, Chapter 6), or the possibility to file a motion of impeachment ('*Präsidentenanklage*') against the *Bundespräsident* (the Federal President, Article 61 of the Basic Law), in the case of a deliberate infringement of the constitution.

Administrative Protection of the Constitution

The administrative protection of the constitution includes legal provisions regarding the activities of special authorities, for example, the German *Bundesamt für Verfassungsschutz* and its equivalents in the *Länder* or, in general, intelligence services in charge of the protection of the constitution against internal threats.

73 On hate speech issues in the United Kingdom, see Mullender, Chapter 13.

States of Emergency

Several countries provide special regulations for the so-called 'state of emergency'.[74] These provisions may be regarded as a marginal area of 'militancy', but they secure the functionality and pertinence of the democratic system even in a situation of extraordinary pressure and strain. In general, the legal norms applying in a 'state of emergency' confine the options of legal protection and simplify or abbreviate legal procedures, for example, the process of legislation. In Germany, there are elaborated constitutional provisions for the so-called '*Notstandsfall*' (Thiel, Chapter 6). Article 36 of the French constitution outlines the declaration of the 'state of emergency', and Article 16 endows the President with an immense authority, often called 'exceptional power', and allows him to take 'the measures required by the circumstances' according to two conditions: 'where the institutions of the Republic, the independence of the nation, the integrity of its territory or the fulfillment of its international commitments are under serious and immediate threat', and 'where the proper functioning of the constitutional public authorities is interrupted' (Buis, Chapter 5). In Turkey, fundamental rights can be restrained in times of war, mobilization, martial law or state of emergency, although there are certain rights that cannot be suspended even in the named cases according to Article 15 Section 2 of the constitution (Oder, Chapter 12). The Turkish constitution contains detailed provisions on the state of emergency (Oder, Chapter 12). Even in the United Kingdom, the government regularly resorted to special emergency powers (Mullender, Chapter 13).

Miscellaneous Provisions and Measures

In this 'cluster' we can finally file all those regulations and provisions that cannot be classified as belonging to the other clusters or form an own cluster, or that actually have no direct connection to the 'militancy' issue but contribute to the protection of the democratic system and the constitution. For example, particular requirements for the majority in Parliament to amend the constitution establish a hurdle that impedes arbitrary changes on the level of constitutional law – in Germany, a law changing the Basic Law requires a majority of two-thirds in the *Bundestag* as well as in the *Bundesrat* (Article 79 Section 3 of the Basic Law). Other 'indirect' provisions to protect the democratic system comprise, for example, regulations in education law that enumerate the acceptance of the constitutional order as an educational objective. The range of possible regulations is very broad here.

74 On the 'state of emergency' in international law, see Fox and Nolte 1995: 54 et seq.

A Duty of Providing 'Militant Elements'?

We have seen that several countries have decided to implement elements of 'militancy' in their democratic systems. This leaves the question if there are binding directives in European or international law that demand a certain level of 'militancy' and, therefore, establish a duty of providing 'militant elements' for those countries that are subject to the particular legal regime.

European Law

For the member states of the European Union and the countries subject to the judicature of the European Court of Human Rights,[75] the further development of 'militancy' and defensive legal measures will be decisively influenced by the European legal framework.[76] On 13 February 2003, the Grand Chamber of the European Court of Human Rights delivered a judgment approving the ban of the 'Welfare Party' in Turkey (see Oder, Chapter 12; Rensmann 2003: 1135; Tardi 2004: 103 et seq.).[77] The applicants alleged that the dissolution of *Refah Partisi* (the Welfare Party) and the temporary prohibition barring its leaders from holding similar office in any other political party had infringed their right to freedom of association, guaranteed by Article 11 of the Convention. As in an earlier decision,[78] the court emphasized that 'European countries have a common heritage of political tradition, ideals, freedom and the rule of law'. In the *Refah Partisi* decision (§ 99), the court recognized the dangers a democratic system is exposed to and declared:

> that it is not at all improbable that totalitarian movements, organised in the form of political parties, might do away with democracy, after prospering under the democratic regime, there being examples of this in modern European history.

The court considered (§ 98)

> that a political party may promote a change in the law or the legal and constitutional structures of the State on two conditions: firstly, the means used to that end must be legal and democratic; secondly, the change proposed must itself be compatible with fundamental democratic principles. It necessarily

75 The contracting parties (all 47 member states of the Council of Europe) of the 'Convention for the Protection of Human Rights and Fundamental Freedoms' of 4 November 1950. The court has been installed as a permanent institution with effect from 1 November 1998 by Protocol no. 11, an amendment to the Convention.

76 See Rensmann 2003: 1135; for a general overview, see Koch 2002: 1388.

77 *Refah Partisi (the Welfare Party) and others v. Turkey* (Applications nos. 41340/98, 41342/98, 41343/98 and 41344/98).

78 *United Communist Party of Turkey and others v. Turkey* (judgment of 30 January 1998), Reports of Judgments and Decisions 1998-I, pp. 21–22, § 45.

> follows that a political party whose leaders incite to violence or put forward a policy which fails to respect democracy or which is aimed at the destruction of democracy and the flouting of the rights and freedoms recognised in a democracy cannot lay claim to the Convention's protection against penalties imposed on those grounds.

This consideration partly resembles the basic idea of a forfeiture of fundamental rights in Article 18 of the German Basic Law. The legal provisions of rights and freedoms in favour of the citizens become inapplicable and do not give cover against the state's sanctions when these rights and freedoms are misused, for example, by making use of the freedom of expression to propose a change in law, legal or constitutional structures not compatible with the fundamental democratic principles. In summary, the European Court of Human Rights endorsed the possibility of a political party's ban stipulated in constitutional law or sub-constitutional legal regulations. Moreover, and this may be regarded as the core statement with respect to the 'militant democracy' issue, the court allowed the state the provision of a defensive system. It conceded (§ 102)

> that a State cannot be required to wait, before intervening, until a political party has seized power and begun to take concrete steps to implement a policy incompatible with the standards of the Convention and democracy, even though the danger of that policy for democracy is sufficiently established and imminent.

Although several measures demonstrating the idea of 'militancy' are criticized, deemed unconstitutional, or deplored as contradiction with the regulations of the European law, the *Refah Partisi* decision gives reason for hope that the European Court of Human Rights will appreciate the member states' vital interest of self-defence in the future and resort to a policy of self-restraint regarding the question of legal defensive measures.

On its path to a written constitution on its own, it was due that Europe would come up on the question of militancy. Article 6 Section 1 of the 'Treaty on European Union' of 7 February 1992 rules:

> The Union is founded on the principles of liberty, democracy, respect for human rights and fundamental freedoms, and the rule of law, principles which are common to the Member States.

Section 2 adds:

> The Union shall respect fundamental rights, as guaranteed by the European Convention for the Protection of Human Rights and Fundamental Freedoms signed in Rome on 4 November 1950 and as they result from the constitutional traditions common to the Member States, as general principles of Community law.

Article 7 of the Treaty provides a monitoring and sanctions procedure against member states where a 'serious and persistent breach … of principles mentioned in Article 6(1)' is determined.[79] Article 7 Section 2 of the Treaty allows:

> Where such a determination has been made, the Council, acting by a qualified majority, may decide to suspend certain of the rights deriving from the application of this Treaty to the Member State in question, including the voting rights of the representative of the government of that Member State in the Council. In doing so, the Council shall take into account the possible consequences of such a suspension on the rights and obligations of natural and legal persons.

These regulations show that the European Union is aware of possible threats to fundamental principles and rights and therefore arranges for sanctions. But it is important to remark that these sanctions do not hit the enemies of the named principles and rights, but the member state tolerating 'serious and persistent breaches'. The Treaty contains a kind of a 'deficiency guarantee' for dormant member states that may be forced to take measures against the causers of the determined breach by the suspension of membership rights. The Council fulfills the task of a superintendent and thus indirectly obliges the member states to provide legal defensive measures on their own. In addition to that, Article 130u Section 2 of the Treaty of Maastricht orders that 'community policy' in the 'sphere of development cooperation'

> shall contribute to the general objective of developing and consolidating democracy and the rule of law, and to that of respecting human rights and fundamental freedoms.

Article 17 of the European 'Convention for the Protection of Human Rights and Fundamental Freedoms' of 4 November 1950 contains a prohibition of the abuse of rights:

> Nothing in this Convention may be interpreted as implying for any State, group or person any right to engage in any activity or perform any act aimed at the destruction of any of the rights and freedoms set forth herein or at their limitation to a greater extent than is provided for in the Convention.

The European Union's legal system comprises substantial specifications for its member states.[80] The 'dense institutional framework of European integration and human rights tradition obliges European states to base their government systems on common democratic values' (Auprich, Chapter 3). Even if such a state does not provide defensive legal provisions, the Treaty serves as a 'safety net'. This

79 See Rensmann 2003: 1135.

80 See Auprich, Chapter 3.

may be regarded as an unrequested intervention by the community law and raises difficult questions on sovereignty, the assignment of sovereign powers and the relationship between the member states' constitutional law and the Treaty. The latter issue will further gain in importance when the attempts to engineer a Pan-European constitution will finally succeed.

International Law

It is rewarding to take a closer look at international law. Fox and Nolte (1995: 38 et seq.) and Andreas Auprich (Chapter 3) have examined the regulations concerning 'militancy', especially on the treatment of anti-democratic political parties. Several treaties of international law provide rules of a decided 'substantive' character, for example, the 'International Covenant on Civil and Political Rights' of 19 December 1966.[81] Andreas Auprich emphasizes the 'strong commitment of the international community to promote democratic standards' (Auprich, Chapter 3), and Fox and Nolte (1995: 60 et seq.) derive a 'duty not to abolish democratic rule' from the Covenant. They stress that 'the drafters of the Political Covenant evidently believed that the "suicide" of a democracy is of concern not only to its own citizens but to the international community as well' (Fox and Nolte 1995: 63). Regarding the question if the duty not to abolish democratic rule implicates a complementary 'duty to adopt self-protective measures', Fox and Nolte refer to the criteria of 'necessity' used in Article 2 Section 2 of the Covenant (Fox and Nolte 1995: 64):

> In states which face, or may face, real threats from anti-democratic groups, self-protective legislation may be necessary. In others, with few such threats either in their history or in their contemporary political landscape, self-protective legislation may not be needed … These principles suggest that the question of whether self-protective legislation is required in a particular state will be an extremely difficult and fact-intensive inquiry.

Fox and Nolte 'have prepared the way towards a globalization of the project they call "Intolerant Democracy" by insisting on two factors', one of which is the assumption that there 'is a near-universal rough consensus at a general level on the need for some form of self-protection' (Niesen 2007: 6).

We arrive at the conclusion that international law does not contain a 'sufficiently identifiable democratic obligation', leading to a 'legal duty for a democracy to be militant', but installs a couple of binding democratic minimum standards (Auprich, Chapter 3). Therefore, international law can be regarded as comprising noticeable 'substantive' elements.

The assumptions of Fox and Nolte regarding the international law's tendency towards a certain notion of 'democracy' (and its substantive elements) have been

81 Entered into force on 23 March 1976.

vehemently criticized, especially by Martti Koskenniemi (1996) and Brad R. Roth (1996). The strongest point of criticism Koskenniemi objects is that Fox and Nolte – as other 'liberal internationalists' – act on the assumption of a ubiquitous, universally applying idea of 'democracy' that 'we' ('international lawyers, Western liberals') have to put on 'them' ('Others') (Koskenniemi 1996: 232 et seq.). This is an objection that does not only hit Fox's and Nolte's conception, but clarifies a sometimes forgotten relativeness of the notion of democracy.[82] The idea of a 'militant democracy' is admittedly not affected by this conclusion: a 'militant democracy' is no 'export goods' of democratic thought and the militancy conception does not feature any 'missionary zeal' beyond the country's frontiers and the area of application of its constitution. Therefore, it does not 'extravertedly' aim to install its own democratic model in another country. But a 'militant democracy' safeguards the particular, 'relative' democratic system in the country providing defensive legal provisions and measures. Brad R. Roth points to the ideological character of the term 'democracy'; he warns against the transfer of the problem of democratic governance 'from the realm of rhetoric to the realm of legality' (Roth 1996: 236) and the resulting formation of an 'ideological legitimism', taking possession of international law, which primarily serves 'as an overlapping consensus among societies that otherwise radically differ on fundamental matters' (Roth 1996: 236). A 'benevolent' ideological legitimism would deprive international law of this role, while a 'less benevolent ... will make international law the plaything of interventionist powers' (Roth 1996: 236). Regarding the example of Algeria that Fox and Nolte have mentioned, Roth declares that a 'truly substantive view would transform the democratic entitlement into precisely the ideological battleground' he fears (Roth 1996: 237). Fox and Nolte (1996: 238 et seq.) refuse the allegations of being committed to 'a comprehensive international blueprint of democratic legitimism' or 'viewing national political struggles through a "distorting" external lens'.

Neither the European not the international law force the particular member states to provide a certain level of 'militancy', although both legal regimes contain decided substantive elements in favour of fundamental principles and values of democratic systems.

The 'Double Layer' of Protection. Regarding Individual Rights and Freedoms

The idea of a 'militant democracy' has often been criticized as an undissolvable discrepancy in respect of liberal democratic theory. But it is important to remark

82 Here, we can follow the critical attitude of Carl Schmitt towards a 'liberal universalism with its pretension of offering the only true and legitimate political system', see Mouffe 2004: 75 et seq. Schmitt 'was adamant that any attempt to impose one single model worldwide would have dire consequences'.

that we must not regard the 'militant democracy' issues as problems exclusively associated with the self-defence of the democratic system in force. Persons and organizations aiming at abolishing the democracy and its fundamental values and principles are potentially violent not only against the state and its institutions; their activities necessarily will affect fundamental rights and freedoms of the citizens. This becomes obvious with regard to Islamic terrorists who plan to replace the liberal democratic order by, for example, a theocratic system with dramatically impaired or suppressed personal rights and freedoms. In addition to that, 'enemies of the constitution' or of the democracy in general will conduct their sinister plans regardless of the life; the physical integrity; the health; or the personal freedom of the people getting in their way. The 'militant democracy' does not only protect itself, but – and this may be regarded is its main justification – the fundamental values and principles, especially the liberal rights. Even a 'procedural' democracy will safeguard at least indirectly a bundle of features indispensable for the 'democratic life'. Therefore, the idea of a 'militant democracy' comprises a 'protection goal' in favour of the legally protected rights and freedoms of the people.

Peter Niesen stresses that point using the example of the German National Democratic Party ('*Nationaldemokratische Partei Deutschlands*') (2007: 15):

> If we look at the harms and dangers emanating from a party like the NPD in this way, it allows us to conceive of party bans as a means to 'defending democracy', but under a richer, and possibly more controversial understanding of what democracy entails. It would have to include the claim that, for an order to be fully democratic, everybody would have to be able to speak out and participate in political activity without fear. The legitimacy of restricting the political activity of NS-affine organisations then would follow from the fact that such activity does not allow everybody's enjoyment of equal political liberty.

If fundamental rights are threatened or violated, consequences have to be drawn. As Otto Pfersmann has pointed out (Pfersmann 2004: 62):

> Such norms [*fundamental rights*, the editor] are deprived of legal meaning if their violation cannot be quashed (or amended in order to be in conformity with the constitutional requirements) by a qualified organ. Rights that lack these properties are not 'fundamental' in the meaning here retained.

This does not only apply to violations of fundamental rights by legal acts, but has to be considered in connection with activities against the democratic system (including fundamental rights and freedoms) by parties, other organizations or individuals. In a more general view, Justice Robert Jackson[83] may be right when he states:

83 In his dissenting opinion in *Terminiello v. City of Chicago* (337 U.S. 1 [1949]). He added that there 'is danger that, if the court does not temper its doctrinaire logic with a little practical wisdom, it will convert the constitutional Bill of Rights into a suicide pact'.

> The choice is not between order and liberty. It is between liberty with order and anarchy without either.

Besides tangible violations of fundamental rights and freedoms, parties and organizations affine to National Socialism are characterized by 'the display of their capacity for organized violence' (Rühl 1995: 564); they are able to create a 'climate of fear' (Niesen 2007: 14). Because such 'intimidation best succeeds on the background of past experience of violence' (Rühl 1995: 564), severe infringements of valuable individual interests could be detected in many activities of extremist parties and organizations, not only in Germany, and not only by right-extremist groupings. It is demanding to precisely classify these infringements and interests with regards to *legally* protected values, a mere 'feeling of intimidation' may not overstep the barrier to activate an assumable 'duty of care' of the state. Some scholars have qualified threats, intimidation and aggressively displayed preparedness to violence as human rights violations (Fox and Nolte 1995: 60).[84] The display of power and preparedness to violence can intimidate bystanders to that extent that they become not free in the process of the formation or in the expression of their own political opinion and preferences (Pace 1988: 365). Peter Niesen (2007: 15) has stated:

> Where people withdraw from public political activity out of fear of pressure and sanctions, a democratic basic order, whatever else this notion entails, cannot be said to be comprehensively upheld.

This aspect relates to the idea of a 'procedural' democracy[85] and, therefore, is applying to 'procedural' as well as to 'substantive' democracies. As we have seen, there is no absolute duty to install elements of 'militancy' in every country's constitutional or sub-constitutional framework established by European or international law, but the individual 'direction of protection' of the 'militant democracy', as described above, justifies such elements anyway.[86] This is one of the core statements of the European Court of Human Rights in its *Refah Partisi* decision: the court

> finds that the acts and speeches of Refah's members and leaders cited by the Constitutional Court were imputable to the whole of the party, that those acts and speeches revealed Refah's long-term policy of setting up a regime based on sharia within the framework of a plurality of legal systems and that Refah did not exclude recourse to force in order to implement its policy and keep the system it envisaged in place. In view of the fact that these plans were incompatible with

84 See Niesen 2007: 15.

85 See this chapter, p. 385 et seq.

86 Müller has denied that there is an 'obvious place for an affirmation of militant democracy at the EU level' (Müller 2007: 119).

> the concept of a 'democratic society' and that the real opportunities Refah had to put them into practice made the danger to democracy more tangible and more immediate, the penalty imposed on the applicants by the Constitutional Court, even in the context of the restricted margin of appreciation left to Contracting States, may reasonably be considered to have met a 'pressing social need'.

If such a 'pressing social need' can be detected, a party dissolution does not infringe Article 11 of the Convention. Although the European Court of Human Rights basically refers to the specific (historical) situation in Turkey, the criteria of 'pressing social need' can be generalized. As Peter Niesen has accentuated, the problem of intimidation and threat by, for example, National Socialist parties and organizations, can evoke such a 'pressing social need', justifying a dissolution (Niesen 2007: 15).

Remaining Questions

Even if the implementation of elements of 'militancy' is justified to a certain degree, some questions remain.

The 'Domicile' of 'Militancy'. Questions of Consistency

A first question concerns the 'location' of legal provisions and measures regulating elements of 'militancy'. Should they be implemented on the level of constitutional or sub-constitutional law? Otto Pfersmann accentuates that the relation between legal provisions that contain, for example, measures aimed at protecting majoritarian decision-making, and the constitution turns out 'to be extremely problematic' (Pfersmann 2004: 63). Norms like newly introduced provisions against international terrorism might contradict to fundamental elements of the constitution (Pfersmann 2004: 64). This leads to the question *where* elements of a 'militant democracy' should be located. Pfersmann regards it as 'the only way to overcome this difficulty' to introduce these direct measures 'into the constitution itself' (Pfersmann 2004: 64). Several constitutions admittedly do not contain such specific regulations; Germany is one exception here again (and therefore has often been qualified as an 'anomaly'[87]); most of the 'militancy' elements in Germany are to be found in the Basic Law. But there are several other countries where the written constitution comprises such provisions, for example, the Turkish or the French constitution.

The question of the 'domicile of militancy' cannot be answered in general. The answer depends on the particular legal system. If there is no written constitution, 'militancy' elements will be enacted in the common process of legislation; the statutory framework of the 'militant democracy' will be established on a sub-

87 See, for example, Morlok 2001: 2932 et seq.

constitutional level. In countries with a strong tradition of constitutional charters, it is reasonable to put 'militancy' elements into force on the level of constitutional law to assure their priority over sub-constitutional statutes.

Does it Work? Questions of Functionality

At the same time the dispute emerged if the 'militant democracy' is 'good or bad', it was discussed 'how it works politically and legally' (Pfersmann 2004: 47). Frequently, it has been doubted if a 'militant democracy' works at all.

We can distinguish two cases here. If an element of 'militancy' has been enacted in reaction to a concrete threat, the appraisal has to be carried out according to the criteria of common legal impact assessment. As with most other issues of security, the legislator in charge of regulating provisions and measures connected with the idea of a 'militant democracy' has to learn by trial and error; at least, they can refer to historical experiences in their own country and insights gained by a closer look at the situation in other countries. And if an element of 'militancy' primarily serves as a determent, the fact that it has not been applied yet is a reliable proof of its functionality. After all, the 'militant democracy' definitely works.[88]

Good-Bye to 'Militancy'? Questions of Alternatives

The idea of a 'militant' democracy has been, as we have seen in the preceding country reports, vehemently criticized since its establishment. Several scholars have proposed alternatives; to deal with all of them would go beyond the scope of this book, especially because they often allude to the specific situation in a single country.

At least a common 'alternative' deserves a closer look, because it mirrors the dichotomy of 'tolerant' and 'militant' democracies depicted above.[89] It has been proposed that democracy should refrain from providing legal regulations and measures of a 'militant' provenance and (mainly or solely) rely on the self-regulative powers of the electoral und political processes. This point of view is based on a quite optimistic idea of man: it assumes that every citizen is able and willing to develop a notion of 'constitutional patriotism' and to align themselves with the insights gained from this rational and objective attitude. It is a nice dictum of Justice Louis D. Brandeis, that 'those who won our independence believed liberty to be the secret of happiness and courage to be the secret of liberty',[90] but it is doubtable if a courage to defend the democracy can be ask for today, even if the enemies of the democratic system and its fundamental principles and values are extraordinarily violence-prone.

---

88 See Uitz, Chapter 7 on the specific problems with the application of legal provisions and measures in Hungary.

89 See this Chapter.

90 *Whitney v. California*, 274 U.S. 357 (1927).

On the other hand, Jan-Werner Müller has doubted the aptitude of politicians and judges to reasonably design the 'tool kit' of 'militant democracy' (Müller 2007: 115):

> Politicians ... would often be suspected of hypocrisy – that is, of promoting their own popularity or the national interest of their country behind the veil of moral concern. Judges, on the other hand, react more slowly, and, of course, *should* react more slowly, and be constrained by procedural logic. Thus, politicians might be not political enough in the case of anti-democratic challenges. These potential problems are not specific to the European level, but they might be exacerbated once one shifted beyond the framework of a particular nation-state.

Richard A. Posner has similarly criticized the skills of the judiciary regarding questions of national security (Posner 2006: 36):

> Cases involving national security are only a tiny part of their docket. They cannot afford to devote much time to them ... The resulting knowledge deficit may incline judges confronting national security cases, depending on the judges' ideology, temperament, and intuition about relative risks, either to defer to the executive branch, where the relevant expertise largely resides, or to take an adversary stance ... National security work tends, moreover, to select for people who place less weight on civil liberties than judges do ... In this clash of perspectives, it is unclear why a judicial perspective should rule.

Müller (2007: 115) comes to the conclusion that:

> The defense of democracy – and the protective and, in particular, the promotional aspects of constitutional patriotism – might, then, in many cases be left to civil society and civic associations within the polity and in other polities, rather than the state as such.

He recognizes the problem that:

> Leaving militancy to civil societies carries the danger of charging highly vocal but potentially unrepresentative militant minorities with the defense of democracy.

The idea of a civil society able and willing to defend the democratic system and its fundamental principles and values even against, for example, an influential and inimical political organization or a mob of violent enemies of the constitution is intriguing. But this idea and the belief in an electorate that self-confidently proves in elections that such organizations are beyond the pale maybe are just wishful thinking. With the experiences of the past in mind, the reliance on the self-regulating powers of the electoral and political processes is at least a little bit 'venturesome'. It harbours the risk that just those groups of people are exceptionally present in general public or in public political discourse that try to abolish the democratic system. Perhaps their leaders are engaging and charismatic; perhaps their political objectives are convincing; perhaps a lack of alternatives and a general disenchantment with politics cause an electoral decision deviating from the rational insights of 'constitutional patriotism'.

That people are seducible by intriguing, though anti-democratic or otherwise unconstitutional perception is taught by history's lessons. Therefore, when a democratic system decides to arrange for self-defence, 'constitutional patriotism' cannot serve as an adequate substitute for legal provisions and measures of the 'militant democracy'. It is undoubtedly desirable that the citizens in democratic countries develop a positive attitude towards their constitution and its fundamental values and principles, and constitutional patriotism is 'a crucial part of a conception of critical citizenship' (Müller 2007: 146). Therefore, it would be purposeful to intensify political education in schools and for adults, and to increase the democratic sense of responsibility and the awareness of the rights and duties of citizenship.[91] But as the historical experience has shown, the constitutional patriotism of the people and their positive attitude towards their own democratic system is not all too reliable. Furthermore, the grade of constitutional patriotism is not commensurable, so that its ability to reject anti-democratic activities, supported by a deep rootage in the people's consciousness and their willingness to actively fight anti-democratic activities (which cannot, due to the problem of intimidation,[92] be taken for granted) is not guaranteed at any time. The idea of 'constitutional patriotism' is a term with nice connotations (although the 'patriotism' component reminds of a 'national state' conception which has been widely superseded today), but it may be criticized as 'constitutional folklore' without any concrete effect on the political landscape. On the other hand, most 'tolerant' democracies explicitly rely on the self-regulative and self-purification powers of the electoral and political procedures and, as we can diagnose, this model is successful as well as the 'militant' democracies. Any proposal to reduce or to increase the number of 'militant' elements in any given country is, therefore, coercive by no means.

The decision whether a democratic system should be more or less militant, is, after all, exclusively conferred on the democratically legitimated (constitutional) legislator. Even in Germany, where the 'Clause of Eternity' in Article 79 Section 3 of the Basic Law inhibits the change of some intangible constitutional values and principles (Thiel, Chapter 6; Zacharias 2003), it would be possible to establish a completely new constitution that does not contain a provision, such as Article 79 Section 3 of the Basic Law, anymore; a *complete* revision of the constitution is feasible. If some elements of a 'militant democracy' should be provided in the constitution and such gain a special legal rank and relevance, has to be decided by

91 See, for example, Thiel 2000: 113 et seq., on the education in public state-run schools, and, more general, Tillmanns 2003: 44 et seq.

92 See this chapter, p. 415 et seq.

the constituent power (or, if constitutional law is chiefly shaped by judicature, by the law courts in charge). And 'militant' elements on the level of sub-constitutional law can be enacted by the legislature. Of course, all these provisions have to respect limits set by constitutional law (and, if applicable, by international or European law). The legislator represents the 'learning sovereign' here (Frankenberg 2004: 113):[93] the history of 'militancy' appears to be a history of 'trial and error' and of legislators 'reacting' on the particular recent developments. But according to the democratic principles and rules of allocation of competences and responsibility, this has to be accepted.

Some scholars recommend a version of 'militancy' that similarly relies on the self-regulative powers of the 'civil society', but at least provides regulations and measures to protect the '*minima moralia et legalia*' of democracy (Frankenberg 2004: 131). This point of view does not see the democratic system as a whole in danger (or accepts this danger), but secures the rights of people in a minority situation. As Günter Frankenberg (2004: 132) has stated:

> A self-declared democracy must develop an increased sensitivity toward outbreaks of violence, hate, rascism, and anti-Semitism. When and to what extent an intervention is adequate is outlined by a script that is well-defined by the principle of subsidiarity, rules of graduated tolerance, and reciprocal recognition. First come discussion and enlightenment, self-healing and self-help, like the somewhat pathetically named 'uprising of the decent' … democratic self-control, and soft social-educational interventions … However, where genuine civil relief is not available or simply insufficient, the civil society paradigm proposes an individual or even collective liability for organizations in the form of criminal sanctions, specifically regarding serious violations of the democratic way of life. If the democratic argument is ineffective and the daily contempt, persecution, and violations are organized and carried out under the cover of legality, more extensive constitutional sanctions in the form of organization or party bans cannot be ruled out.

This perception has realized the fact that democracies which can be classified as 'tolerant procedural' democracies according to the four categories model by Fox and Nolte, tend to be less stable than militant substantive democracies. Such a tolerant democracy may transit to an 'intolerant' system. A democratic system that does not want to bear this risk has to resort to the armoury of the 'militant democracy'. Here the circle closes: the knot of the 'democratic dilemma' cannot be untangled. It just can be cut like the Gordian knot by enduring the dangers a tolerant democracy is exposed to, on the one hand, or by providing a certain amount of 'militancy' elements, on the other hand.

Because the decision for the implementation of 'militancy' elements is conferred to the legislator, its effect ends at the frontiers. Regardless of all efforts

---

93 Instructive on the question of sovereignty Haltern 2007.

regarding the internationalization and harmonization of legal systems even in the field of internal security, the question of 'militancy or not' is one of the last residual domain of the national legislator. Martin Klamt has rightly stated that although the 'international dimension of threats requires responses at the same level', proper 'instruments beyond the domestic level may not yet be available and therefore have to be developed first' (Klamt 2007: 153).

Conclusion

The country reports and the comparative analysis have shown that there is no ubiquitous, universally applicable idea of a 'militant democracy' of constitutional rank. In addition to that, there is no consensus on the question if a democracy should provide a certain number or self-defensive regulations and measures on constitutional or sub-constitutional law. The countries comprised by this study feature a wide range of different legal arrangements – therefore, a classification on the basis of the categories of 'procedural' or 'substantive' and 'tolerant' and 'militant', as proposed by Fox and Nolte (1995), appears to be a generalization that may have benefits for a first typification, but has the disadvantage of a blurry distinction between 'tolerant' and 'militant' – 'pure' occurrences do not exist. The linear or gradual models of classification, for example, by Otto Pfersmann (2004), share the problem of discrimination. Therefore, a classification according to terminology-based categories or alongside a 'scope of militancy' is not sufficient to comprehend the complex issue of self-defensive democracies. A classification orientated on the actual provisions and measures, combined to 'groups' or 'clusters', seems to be more appropriate. The elements of 'militancy' existing in the legal systems of the countries comprised by this study can be classified in seven 'clusters'.

Although there is no duty to implement elements of 'militancy' into the legal order, those elements can be justified by the fact that they do not only protect the very existence of the current form of state, but, in addition to that, important principles and values, such as the fundamental rights and freedoms. The questions whether, to which extent, and on which level of the legal system elements of 'militancy' should be provided, cannot be answered universally – the answers to this questions are to be given by the particular democratically legitimated legislator and based upon the customary procedures of political discourse. As Günter Frankenberg has stated: every society 'opts for the form of democracy it considers correct, fitting or tolerable' (Frankenberg 2004: 117).

References

Barry, Brian (1979) 'Is Democracy Special?', in Peter Laslett and James Fishkin (ed.) *Philosophy, Politics, and Society.* Oxford: Blackwell, 155–96.

Baynes, Kenneth (1996) *Procedural Democracy and the Limits of Liberalism*, CSST Working Paper #118. Ann Arbor: The University of Michigan.

Bobbitt, Philip (2008) *Terror and Consent. The Wars for the Twenty-First Century*. New York: Alfred A. Knopf.

Boventer, Gregor Paul (1985) *Grenzen politischer Freiheit im demokratischen Staat: das Konzept der streitbaren Demokratie in einem internationalen Vergleich*. Berlin: Duncker and Humblot.

Capoccia, Giovanni (2001) *Defending Democracy: Reactions to Extremism in Interwar Europe*. Baltimore: The John Hopkins University Press.

Dahl, Robert (1979) 'Procedural Democracy', in Peter Laslett and James Fishkin (eds) *Philosophy, Politics, and Society*. New Haven: Yale University Press, 97–133.

Dyzenhaus, David (2004) 'Constituting the Enemy: A Response to Carl Schmitt', in Sajó András (ed.) *Militant Democracy*. Utrecht: Eleven International Publishing, 15–45.

Fox, Gregory H. and Nolte, Georg (1995) 'Intolerant Democracies', *Harvard International Law Journal* 36(1): 1–70.

Fox, Gregory H. and Nolte, Georg (1996) 'Fox and Nolte Response', *Harvard International Law Journal* 37(1): 238–42.

Fox, Gregory H. and Nolte, Georg (2000) 'A defense of the "intolerant democracies" thesis', in Gregory H. Fox and Brad R. Roth (eds) *Democratic Governance and International Law*. Cambridge: Cambridge University Press, 445 et seq.

Frankenberg, Günter (2004) 'The Learning Sovereign', in András Sajó (ed.) *Militant Democracy*. Utrecht: Eleven International Publishing, 113–32.

Haltern, Ulrich (2007) *Was bedeutet Souveränität?* Tübingen: Mohr Siebeck.

Klamt, Martin (2007) 'Militant Democracy and the Democratic Dilemma: Different Ways of Protecting Democratic Constitutions', in Fred Bruinsma and David Nelken (eds) *Explorations in Legal Cultures (Recht der Werkelijkheid 28:3)*. Den Haag: Elsevier, 133–59.

Koch, Thorsten (2002) 'Parteiverbote, Verhältnismäßigkeitsprinzip und EMRK', *Deutsches Verwaltungsblatt* 117(20): 1388–93.

Koskenniemi, Martti (1996) '"Intolerant Democracies": A Reaction', *Harvard International Law Journal* 37(1): 231–5.

Loewenstein, Karl (1937a) 'Militant Democracy and Fundamental Rights', part I, *American Political Science Review* 31(3): 417–32.

Loewenstein, Karl (1937b) 'Militant Democracy and Fundamental Rights', part II, *American Political Science Review* 31(4): 638–58.

Loewenstein, Karl (2004) 'Militant Democracy and Fundamental Rights' (reprint of parts I and II), in András Sajó (ed.) *Militant Democracy*. Utrecht: Eleven International Publishing, 231–62.

Luban, David (2005) 'The War on Terrorism and the End of Human Rights', in Mark Tushnet (ed.) *The Constitution in Wartime: Beyond Alarmism and Complacency*. Durham and London: Duke University Press, 219–31.

Morlok, Martin (2001) 'Parteiverbot als Verfassungsschutz – Ein unauflösbarer Widerspruch?', *Neue Juristische Wochenschrift* 40(54): 2931–42.

Mouffe, Chantal (2004) 'The Limits of Liberal Pluralism: Towards an Agonistic Multipolar World Order', in András Sajó (ed.) *Militant Democracy.* Utrecht: Eleven International Publishing, 69–79.

Müller, Jan-Werner (2007) *Constitutional Patriotism.* Princeton and Oxford: Princeton University Press.

Niesen, Peter (2003) 'Anti-Extremism, Negative Republicanism, Civic Society: Three Paradigms for Banning Political Parties', in Russell A. Miller and Peer Zumbansen (eds) *Annual of German and European Law.* New York and Oxford: Berghahn Books, 81–112.

Niesen, Peter (2007) *Banning Parties in Germany: Lessons from Europe?* Working Paper no. 9, Institut für Politikwissenschaft, Technische Universität Darmstadt.

Offe, Claus (2000) 'Democracy and Trust', *Theoria* 96, 1–13.

Pace, Alessandro (1988) *Problematica della Libertà Costituzionale.* Padua.

Papier, Hans-Jürgen and Durner, Wolfgang (2003) 'Streitbare Demokratie', *Archiv des öffentlichen Rechts* 128(3): 340–71.

Pelinka, Anton (1974) *Dynamische Demokratie. Zur konkreten Utopie gesellschaftlicher Gleichheit.* Stuttgart: Verlag W. Kohlhammer.

Pfersmann, Otto (2004) 'Shaping Militant Democracy: Legal Limits to Democratic Stability', in András Sajó (ed.) *Militant Democracy.* Utrecht: Eleven International Publishing, 47–68.

Posner, Richard A. (2006) *Not a Suicide Pact: The Constitution in a Time of National Emergency.* Oxford and New York: Oxford University Press.

Preuß, Ulrich K. (2002) 'Die empfindsame Demokratie', in Carl Leggewie and Horst Meier (ed.) *Verbot der NPD oder Mit Rechtsradikalen Leben?* Frankfurt a.M.: Suhrkamp, 104–19.

Rawls, John (1971) *A Theory of Justice.* Cambridge: Harvard University Press.

Rensmann, Thilo (2003) 'Procedural Fairness in a Militant Democracy: The "Uprising of the Decent" Fails Before the Federal Constitutional Court', *German Law Journal* 4(11): 1117–36.

Revenga Sánchez, Miguel (2003) *The Move Towards a (and the Struggle for) Militant Democracy in Spain*, Paper for the ECPR Conference, Marburg, 18–21 September 2003.

Riesenfeld, Stefan A. (1994) 'Reminiscences of Karl Llewellyn', in Ulrich Drobnig and Manfred Rehbinder (eds) *Rechtsrealismus, multikulturelle Gesellschaft und Handelsrecht. Karl N. Llewellyn und seine Bedeutung heute.* Berlin: Duncker and Humblot, 11 et seq.

Roach, Kent (2004) 'Anti-Terrorism and Militant Democracy: Some Western and Eastern Responses', in András Sajó (ed.) *Militant Democracy.* Utrecht: Eleven International Publishing, 171–207.

Roth, Brad R. (1996) 'Democratic Intolerance: Observations on Fox and Nolte', *Harvard International Law Journal* 37(1): 235–8.

Rühl, Ulli F.H. (1995) 'Versammlungsrechtliche Maßnahmen gegen rechtsradikale Demonstrationen und Aufzüge', *Neue Juristische Wochenschrift* 48: 561–4.

Sajó, András (ed.) (2004a) *Militant Democracy.* Utrecht: Eleven International Publishing.

Sajó, András (2004b) 'Militant Democracy and Transition towards Democracy', in András Sajó (ed.) *Militant Democracy.* Utrecht: Eleven International Publishing, 209–30.

Schmitt, Carl (1927/1932 [2002]) *Der Begriff des Politischen*, 7th edn. Berlin: Duncker and Humblot.

Schmitt, Carl (1931 [1996]) *Der Hüter der Verfassung*, 4th edn. Berlin: Duncker and Humblot.

Schmitt, Carl (1932 [2005]) *Legalität und Legitimität*, 7th edn. Berlin: Duncker and Humblot.

Schulze, Jan-Andres (2005) *Der Irak-Krieg 2003 im Lichte der Wiederkehr des gerechten Krieges.* Berlin: Duncker and Humblot.

Schumpeter, Joseph Alois (1947) *Capitalism, Socialism and Democracy*, 2nd edn. New York and London: Harper and Brothers.

Stone, Geoffrey R. (2004) *Perilous Times. Free Speech in Wartime. From the Sedition Act of 1798 to the War on Terrorism.* New York and London: W.W. Norton and Co.

Tardi, Gregory (2004) 'Political Parties' Right to Engage in Politics: Variations on a Theme of Democracy', in András Sajó, (ed.) (2004) *Militant Democracy.* Utrecht: Eleven International Publishing, 81–111.

Thiel, Markus (2000) *Der Erziehungsauftrag des Staates in der Schule. Grundlagen und Grenzen staatlicher Erziehungstätigkeit im öffentlichen Schulwesen.* Berlin: Duncker and Humblot.

Tillmanns, Reiner (2003) 'Wehrhaftigkeit durch Werthaftigkeit – der ethische Grundkonsens als Existenzvoraussetzung des freiheitlichen Staates', in Markus Thiel (ed.) *Wehrhafte Demokratie. Beiträge über die Regelungen zum Schutze der freiheitlichen demokratischen Grundordnung.* Tübingen: Mohr Siebeck, 25–56.

Tushnet, Mark (1999) 'The Possibilities of Comparative Constitutional Law', *Yale Law Journal* 108, 1225–309.

Tushnet, Mark (2005) 'Introduction', in Mark Tushnet (ed.) *The Constitution in Wartime. Beyond Alarmism and Complacency.* Durham and London: Duke University Press, 1–7.

Zacharias, Diana (2003) 'Die sog. Ewigkeitsgarantie des Art. 79 Abs. 3 GG', in Markus Thiel (ed.) *Wehrhafte Demokratie. Beiträge über die Regelungen zum Schutze der freiheitlichen demokratischen Grundordnung.* Tübingen: Mohr Siebeck, 57–97.

Index